ORDINANCE
LAW
ANNOTATIONS

———

A COMPREHENSIVE DIGEST OF AMERICAN CASES THAT INTERPRET OR APPLY CITY AND COUNTY ORDINANCES

———

By The Publisher's Editorial Staff

WESLEY H. WINBORNE
Editor in Chief

J. F. CORCORAN
Managing Editor

JOHN W. KENNEDY
Contributing Editor

———

VOLUME 4B

SEWERS

TO

SUNDAY LAWS

———

SHEPARD'S/McGRAW-HILL
P. O. Box 1235, Colorado Springs, CO 80901

———————————————————————

McGraw-Hill Book Company
*New York ★ St. Louis ★ San Francisco ★ Colorado Springs ★
Auckland ★ Bogota ★ Düsseldorf ★ Johannesburg ★ London ★
Madrid ★ Mexico ★ Montreal ★ New Delhi ★ Panama ★ Paris ★
São Paulo ★ Singapore ★ Sydney ★ Tokyo ★ Toronto*

ISBN 0-07-056710-7

CONTENTS

VOLUME 1A

VOLUME 1B

VOLUME 2

VOLUME 3A

Planned Unit Development
Pleading and Proof of Ordinances
Plumbing; Heating; Air Conditioning
Police Officers
Pool Halls; Billiard Parlors
Prostitution
Railroads
Recall
Recreation
Redevelopment and Public Housing
Religion
Rent Control
Repeal of Ordinances
Restaurants
Schools and Colleges
Secondhand Stores

VOLUME 4B

VOLUME 5A

Taxation
Taxicabs
Telephones; Telegraph; Alarm Systems
Television; Radio
Theft; Lost Property
Time Zones
Topsoil
Trading Stamps
Traffic
Trespass
Vagrancy
Validity of Ordinances
Vending Machines; Juke Boxes; Amusement Devices

Veterans
Warehouses
Water Pollution

VOLUME 5B

Water Systems; Water Supply
Waterways and Waterfronts; Harbors; Facilities
Weapons
Weed Abatement
Weights and Measures
Welfare
Zoning

VOLUME 6

ABBREVIATIONS

A—Atlantic Reporter
A2d—Atlantic Reporter 2d Series
Abs—Ohio Law Abstract
AD—Appellate Decisions, New York
ADC—Appeal Cases, District of Columbia Reports
AD2d—Appellate Decisions 2d Series, New York
Adv—Advertising
Affd—Affirmed
Ala—Alabama Reports
AlaAp—Alabama Appellate
Alas—Alaska Reports
Alas F—Alaska Federal Reports
ALR—American Law Reports
ALR2d—American Law Reports 2d Series
ALR3d—American Law Reports 3rd Series
Amer—America, American
Ann—Annual
Apart—Apartment
Ariz—Arizona Reports
ArizApp—Arizona Appeals Reports
Ark—Arkansas Reports
AS—Massachusetts Advance Sheets
ASA—Massachusetts Appellate Court Advance Sheets
Assn—Associates, Association
At—Atlantic
Auth—Authority
Bd—Board
Bev—Beverage
Bk—Bank
Bros—Brothers
C2d—California Supreme Court Reports 2d Series
C3d—California Supreme Court Reports 3rd Series
CA—California Appellate Reports
CA2d—California Appellate Reports 2d Series
CA3d—California Appellate Reports 3rd Series
Cal—California Supreme Court Reports
Cal LR—California Law Review
CaR—California Reporter
CaU—California Unreported
CC—Ohio Circuit Court Reports
CCns—Ohio Circuit Court Reports, New Series
CD—Ohio Circuit Decisions

Cent—Central
Chi LR—University of Chicago Law Review
Co—Company
Colo—Colorado Supreme Court Reports
ColoAp—Colorado Appellate Reports
ColumLR—Columbia Law Review
Com—Commercial
Comm—Commission (er)
Conn—Connecticut Reports
Conn CC—Connecticut Circuit Court
Conn Supp—Connecticut Supplement
Constr—Construction
Cont—Contractors
CornLQ—Cornell Law Quarterly
Corn LR—Cornell Law Review
Corp—Corporation
Ct—Court
DC—District of Columbia
DCh—Delaware Court of Chancery
Del—Delaware Reports
Devel—Development
Dist—District
DRep—Ohio Decisions Reprint
Educ—Education
Elec—Electric
Est—Estate(s)
F.—Federal Reporter
F2d—Federal Reporter 2d Series
Fla—Florida Reports
Fla Supp—Florida Supplement Reports
FRD—Federal Rules Decisions
F Supp—Federal Supplement
Ga—Georgia Reports
GaApp—Georgia Appeals Reports
Gen—General
Harv LR—Harvard Law Review
Haw—Hawaii Reports
Hun—Hun's Supreme Court Reports
Ida—Idaho Reports
Ill—Illinois Reports
IllAp—Illinois Appellate Court Reports
IllAp2d—Illinois Appellate Court Reports 2d Series
IllAp3d—Illinois Appellate Court Reports 3rd Series
IllD—Illinois Decisions

Ill2d—Illinois Reports 2d Series
Ind—Indiana Reports
IndAp—Indiana Appellate Court Reports
Ins—Insurance
Inv—Investment, Investor
Iowa—Iowa Reports
IT—Indian Territory Reports
Kan—Kansas Reports
KanAp2d—Kansas Appellate Court 2d Series
KLR—Kentucky Law Reporter
Ky—Kentucky Reports
La—Louisiana Reports
La Ann—Louisiana Annual Reports
LaApp—Louisiana Court of Appeals Reports
L&CP—Law and Contemporary Problems
LEd—Lawyers' Edition, U. S. Supreme Court Reports
LEd2d—Lawyers' Edition 2d Series
Mass—Massachusetts Reports
MassAp—Massachusetts Appellate Reports
Md—Maryland Supreme Court Reports
MdApp—Maryland Appellate Reports
Me—Maine Reports
Mich—Michigan Reports
Mich Ap—Michigan Court of Appeals Reports
Mich LR—Michigan Law Review
Minn—Minnesota Reports
Minn LR—Minnesota Law Review
Misc—Miscellaneous Reports, New York
Misc2d—Miscellaneous Reports 2d Series, New York
Miss—Mississippi Reports
Mo—Missouri Reports
MoApp—Missouri Appeal Reports
Mont—Montana Reports
Nat—National
NC—North Carolina Supreme Court Reports
NCApp—North Carolina Appellate Reports
ND—North Dakota Reports
NE—Northeastern Reporter
NE2d—Northeastern Reporter 2d Series
Neb—Nebraska Reports
Nev—Nevada Reports
NH—New Hampshire Reports
NJ—New Jersey Reports

NJEq—New Jersey Equity Reports
NJLaw—New Jersey Law Reports
NJM—New Jersey Miscellaneous Reports
NJS—New Jersey Superior Court Reports
NM—New Mexico Reports
NP—Ohio Nisi Prius Reports
NPns—Ohio Nisi Prius Reports, New Series
NW—Northwestern Reporter
NW2d—Northwestern Reporter 2d Series
NW LR—Northwestern Law Review
NY—New York Reports
NYCr—New York Criminal Reports
NY2d—New York Reports 2d Series
NYS—New York Supplement Court Reports
NYS2d—New York Supplement Court Reports 2d Series
NYU LR—New York University Law Review
OA—Ohio Appellate Reports
OA2d—Ohio Appellate Reports 2d Series
OCA—Ohio Courts of Appeals Reports
OD—Ohio Decisions
OFD—Ohio Federal Decisions
Ohio—Ohio Reports
Okla—Oklahoma Reports
Okla Cr—Oklahoma Criminal Reports
OLR—Ohio Law Reporter
OM—Ohio Miscellaneous
Op—Ohio Opinions
Op2d—Ohio Opinions 2d Series
Ore—Oregon Supreme Court Reports
OreAp—Oregon Appellate Reports
Ore Tax Ct—Oregon Tax Court
OS—Ohio State Reports
OS2d—Ohio State Reports 2d Series
OSu—Ohio Supplement Court Reports
OSU—Ohio Supreme Court Decisions, Unreported Cases
P—Pacific Reporter
P2d—Pacific Reporter 2d Series
Pa—Pennsylvania Reports
Pac—Pacific
PaCmwlth—Pennsylvania Commonwealth Court
Pa LR—University of Pennsylvania Law Review
PaS—Pennsylvania Superior Court Reports
Pollack—Ohio Unreported Judicial Decisions

Prod—Products
Pub—Public
RI—Rhode Island Reports
Rlty—Realtor, Realty
RR—Railroad
Ry—Railway
Sav—Savings
SC—South Carolina Reports
Sch—School
SCt—United States Supreme Court Reports
SD—South Dakota Reports
SE—Southeastern Reporter
SE2d—Southeastern Reporter 2d Series
So—Southern Reporter
So2d—Southern Reporter 2d Series
Stan LR—Stanford Law Review
Sup—Superior
Supp—Supplement
SW—Southwestern Reporter
SW2d—Southwestern Reporter 2d Series
Sys—System
Tel—Telegraph
Tel—Telephone
Tenn—Tennessee Reports
TennApp—Tennessee Appeals Reports
Tex—Texas Reports
TexCr—Texas Criminal Reports
Tex LR—Texas Law Review
Tr—Trust
Urban—Urban Lawyer
US—United States Supreme Court Reports
Utah—Utah Reports
Utah2d—Utah Reports 2d Series
Va—Virginia Reports
Va LR—Virginia Law Review
Vt—Vermont Reports
Wash—Washington Supreme Court Reports
WashAp—Washington Appellate Reports
Wash2d—Washington Supreme Court Reports 2d Series
Wis—Wisconsin Reports
Wis2d—Wisconsin Reports 2d Series
W Va—West Virginia Reports
Wyo—Wyoming Reports
Yale LJ—Yale Law Journal

SEWERS

EDITORIAL COMMENT. The disposal of sewage is a public utility type of operation that is nearly always conducted by cities or local districts. It is so vital to the public health that cities are given very broad powers in the field, although these powers are usually defined and limited by state statutes.

Much of the material is similar to that classified under other publicly owned or operated utilities, and especially to that found in STREETS; SIDEWALKS; BRIDGES. Thus, the cases hereunder are largely concerned with such things as land acquisition and condemnation (§§ 60, 61) financing (§§ 44-58) and special assessments (§§ 27-43), and construction contracts (§§ 62-70). One aspect that is unique to sewers is the power of the municipality to compel landowners to connect with sewers (§§ 73-77).

I. MUNICIPAL POWERS, DUTIES, AND LIABILITIES

A. Generally

§1. Municipal Discretion

A city which envelops county land and holds a monopoly on disposal of sewerage may not block development of the surrounded territory by denying sewer hook-ups.

Cal Barbaccia v Santa Clara County (1978) 451 F Supp 260.

Ordinances authorizing a municipality to lease a waterworks and sewage plant are not invalid for failure to specify the rental. Contract provisions authorizing rental on a formula based on an appraisal of the property are valid.

Md Bowie v Area Development Corp (1971) 261 Md 446, 276 A2d 90.

Inverse condemnation is not involved in the city entering into the water and sewage treatment services previously operated by a private individual. The incorporation of the town and subsequent providing of services with a prohibition against septic tanks if a sewer line is within 200 feet, which provision has not been enforced, does not deprive the private service company of any protected rights.

Tex   Brown v Corinth (1974) 515 SW2d 722.

Where a statute authorizes sewer construction the plan or method of improvement, as well as the necessity therefor, is solely within the discretion of the legislative body and is beyond review by the courts, in the absence of a showing of fraud or corruption.

Ky   Baker v Princeton (1928) 226 Ky 409, 11 SW2d 94.
Bayes v Paintsville (1915) 166 Ky 679, 179 SW 623.
NY   Campbell v Nassau County (1948) 192 Misc 821, 82 NYS2d 179.

An ordinance providing for the drainage of sewage into Lake Michigan is not void as against public policy. Whether the lands of a city shall be drained, and how and when it shall be done, are matters within the legislative discretion of the council.

Ill   Rich v Chicago (1894) 152 Ill 18, 38 NE 255.

The objection to an ordinance for construction of sewer system, that the village has no water supply, and therefore should provide for water before undertaking to construct the sewer system, is not tenable, since such matter is within the legislative discretion of the council.

Ill   Millstadt v Bereitschaft (1931) 344 Ill 550, 176 NE 746.

An ordinance establishing a public highway may not be impeached on the ground of fraud, on evidence that the real purpose of the extension of the street was to provide routes or ways for sewers for a joint sewer district, since the city has authority to develop a general scheme for improvements in any section of the city, including streets and sewers.

Mo   St Louis v Semple (1917) 199 SW 967.

A charter authorizing the city council to erect bridges in the streets for sewerage and drainage, and conferring power to grade, improve, or extend streets does not imply nor expressly authorize power to construct bridges over railroads.

Mich   Phelps v Detroit (1899) 120 Mich 447, 79 NW 640.

Whether the location and character of an intercepting sewer is useful or desirable for municipal purposes is a legislative matter for determination by the city council, subject to judicial review only for abuse of power.

Ill Chicago v Sanitary Dist (1916) 272 Ill 37, 111 NE 491.

In order for a city to pass an ordinance for the construction of a new sewer system to handle an overflow of effluent from the old system, it is not necessary that the city acquire ownership of the old system, under the statutory authorization of municipalities to construct sewers wherever and whenever needed and to issue revenue bonds for their construction payable by income from the new system.

Ark Freeman v Jones (1934) 189 Ark 815, 75 SW2d 226.

An ordinance setting forth the minimum wages for laborers on city work is subordinate to a legislative act specifically empowering the sewerage commission to insert in the specifications for its contract work, conditions as to hours of labor, wages, and character of workmen to be employed by the contractor.

Wis State v Niven (1923) 180 Wis 583, 194 NW 30.

An ordinance establishing a sewer district and providing for construction of a sewer will not be held invalid on the ground that the sewer was constructed in greater dimensions than necessary, so that it would carry off the waters of a stream draining an area outside as well as within the district, in the absence of proof of fraud, that it is manifestly arbitrary or unreasonable, or that the assessment is palpably unjust and oppressive.

Mo Jennings Heights Land & Improvement v St Louis (1914) 257 Mo 291, 165 SW 741.

An ordinance providing for the installation of sewers as a condition precedent for the city commission's approval of a plat is valid.

Mich Allen v Stockwell (1920) 210 Mich 488, 178 NW 27.

A sewer system ordinance requiring payment of $500 per house before a building permit will be issued for certain unsubdivided land is valid as applying equally among persons of the same class since it sets a reasonable imposition of a financial obligation on that class which is most likely to cause a necessity for enlargement and increase of the sewerage system.

NY Stanco v Suozzi (1958) 11 Misc2d 784, 171 NYS2d 997.

§2. Power to Construct

A city, through exercise of the police power, may make all regulations necessary to secure the general health of its inhabitants, and by ordinance to authorize construction of sewers since a sewer system is a public necessity.

> **Cal** Longridge Est v Los Angeles (1960) 183 CA2d 533, 6 CaR 900.
> Sullivan v Los Angeles (1953) 116 CA2d 807, 254 P2d 590.
> **Ga** Barr v Augusta (1950) 206 Ga 750, 58 SE2d 820.
> **Ky** Princeton v Pool (1916) 171 Ky 638, 188 SW 758.
> **Tenn** Warren v Bradley (1955) 39 TennApp 451, 284 SW2d 698.
> **W Va** WV Water Service v Cunningham (1957) 143 W Va 1, 98 SE2d 891.

A grant of authority by a state to municipalities to zone also defines the boundaries of its exercise. Therefore, since sewer construction is not one of the uses a municipality is authorized to regulate with respect to a state operated institution, unless some contrary statutory grant exists the zoning authority cannot obstruct the implementation of state purpose and authority. Therefore, although a statute subjects a residential treatment facility operated by the state to landscaping standards of a town zoning authority, that zoning authority does not extend to sewer construction in connection with the treatment facility and issuance of a permit for landscaping cannot be conditioned on procuring a sewer construction permit from the town.

> **Vt** Morse v Vt Division of State Buildings (1978) 388 A2d 371.

Providing for treatment facilities aimed at the ultimate disposal of sewage, including "sludge," is an appropriate utility use as legislatively defined and as limited by the zoning ordinance and therefore a grant of special exception to the water district to construct and operate such a facility is proper.

> **Me** Pride's Corner v West Brook Bd of Zoning (1979) 398 A2d 415.

The levy of taxes for city purposes is a municipal affair; the collection, treatment and disposal of city sewage and the making of contracts therefore are likewise municipal affairs. Neither is circumscribed except as expressly limited by the city's charter.

> **Cal** Cramer v San Diego (1958) 164 CA2d 168, 330 P2d 235.
> Grass Valley v Walkinshaw (1949) 34 C2d 595, 212 P2d 894.

The power of a city to construct sewers and drains is incidental to the power to construct and maintain streets.

> **Cal** Harter v Barkley (1910) 158 Cal 742, 112 P 556.

An enabling act authorizing municipalities to make local improvements warrants the enactment of an ordinance authorizing the construction of a sanitary sewer.

> **Wyo** Henning v Consolidated Building & Loan (1936) 50 Wyo 315, 62 P2d 540.

An ordinance establishing a contract between the city and a private company for the construction of a sewage disposal ditch, to be maintained by the company over a 99-year period, is within the city's charter power to establish and regulate sewers.

Tex   San Antonio v San Antonio Irrigation (1929) 118 Tex 154, 12 SW2d 546.

Where the legislature has delegated to a city council authority to construct sewers, the city has no power to delegate this power to others, and an ordinance that either creates new officers or appoints agents to perform the functions thus delegated to the council is void.

Ky   Lowery v Lexington (1903) 25 KLR 1882, 79 SW 202.

Where a charter empowers the county to regulate water and sewage utilities, an ordinance establishing a county sewer board for regulating such service does not conflict with the constitutional provision vesting such authority in the legislature, for such an interpretation would mean that only the legislature could make any rule relating to public utilities.

Fla   Carol City Utilities v Dade County (1966) 183 So2d 227.

Ordinances providing for a sewerage system, issue of bonds in payment, and the operation of the system by a private corporation in case of default are in violation of the state constitution which specifically deprives the state of the power to delegate the management of municipal property to a private corporation, since the city is the governmental agent of the state and is subject to the same prohibition.

Pa   Lighton v Abington (1939) 336 Pa 345, 9 A2d 609.

§3. Private Sewers

Lease of a waste processing system, and use of the lease to guarantee bonds of the private corporation, do not constitute a loan of the municipality's credit to a private corporation. The city is directly benefited, with only incidental benefits to the private corporation.

Neb   Cosentino v Omaha (1971) 186 Neb 407, 183 NW2d 475.

A system for sewage disposal may not be denied on the premise that the land on which the system is proposed is set aside for open space use. While the building permit may be denied on lack of right to use the property, approval of the system itself depends on it meeting ordinance specifications.

Fla   Metropolitan Dade County v Centex Homes Corp (1974) 291 So2d 231.

A conditional-use permit may be denied for construction of a single-family dwelling when the proposed sewage disposal system fails to meet the zoning ordinance requirement that a septic tank be placed downslope a specified distance from domestic water supply.

> **Minn**   Dedering v Johnson (1976) 307 Minn 313, 239 NW2d 913.

The county board of commissioners' determination that an environmental impact statement was not necessary before a plat for a mobile home park could be approved was clearly erroneous where evidence indicated that the land had potential septic tank problems by virtue of its soil composition and that state requirements would shortly be more stringent than those currently expressed by county ordinances.

> **Wash**   Newaukum Hill Protective Assn v Lewis County (1978) 19 WashAp 162, 574 P2d 1195.

A grant of power to a city to regulate privies and cesspools, where regulation is the only practical means of control, does not militate against its power to prohibit them as nuisances when a less hazardous method of sewage disposal becomes available.

> **Ill**   Nokomis v Sullivan (1958) 14 Ill2d 417, 153 NE2d 48.

A municipal administrative code provision giving the health department power to abate public nuisances at the expense of property owners applies to vacant land as well as improved property and extends to a nuisance created by a private sewer.

> **NY**   Barkin, Application of (1947) 189 Misc 358, 71 NYS2d 267.

An ordinance requiring that treated sewage waste from private septic tanks of a trailer court be discharged into a "continuously flowing stream" is an unreasonable and unconstitutional exercise of police power.

> **Ill**   Krol v Will County (1968) 38 Ill2d 587, 233 NE2d 417.

An ordinance requiring that any privy vault that abuts on a public sewer be emptied and then filled with fresh earth by the owner after notice given by city officers is not invalid as conferring arbitrary power on such officers merely because the ordinance might not be impartially enforced, since the ordinance makes it the duty of the officers named to give all persons having privy vaults abutting on a public sewer the notice required.

> **Ky**   Treasy v Louisville (1910) 137 Ky 289, 125 SW 706.

Where a city by resolution authorizes an excavation permit for construction of private sewer, it may not thereafter, without condemnation and payment therefor, appropriate the sewer for public use through connection with a city sewer line, and such appropriation and use will be enjoined though the injury to the city exceeds the benefits to which the claimant may be entitled.

> **Mo** Gunn v Versailles (1959) 330 SW2d 257.

Where an ordinance makes it unlawful to build or install a septic tank without a permit from the health officer, any distinction that may be drawn between the words "build" and "install" constitutes a mere play on words, and an indictment charging defendant with failure to get a permit to build or install a septic tank, and with failure to have the same inspected, did not charge an offense in the alternative.

> **NC** State v Jones (1955) 242 NC 563, 89 SE2d 129.

An ordinance providing that the sanitary board shall administer and enforce the rules and regulations of the state department of health regulating individual sewerage systems, and to construe as mandatory certain other regulations, is not unconstitutional as being so vague and indefinite as to prevent a defendant from determining what is prohibited.

> **Pa** Commonwealth v Collins (1964) 203 PaS 125, 199 A2d 470.

An ordinance, requiring one who desires to connect with a private sewer to obtain the written consent of the owner, and to obtain a city permit, and another ordinance requiring one about to erect a building to make a connection with a public sewer if one is in the street, are enacted under the police power, and may not be circumvented on a claim of property rights.

> **Mo** Van Trump v Kansas City (1915) 187 MoApp 190, 173 SW 32.

Purchasers of a residence, the plumbing system of which empties into a cesspool or septic tank which was not discovered at the time the property was inspected because the rear yard was heavily overgrown, who are required by ordinance to make the connection to the parish sewerage system, are entitled to reimbursement of the expense of connection from the vendor.

> **La** Deshotel v Higgins (1959) 109 So2d 805.

ANNOTATION

Right of private sewerage system owner to enjoin tortious acts or unauthorized use of facilities, 76 ALR2d 1329.

§4. Nuisance and Damage Liability

The general rule is that a municipal corporation that by ordinance assumes the control and management of a sewer system constructed by it and under its supervision is bound to use reasonable care, and is liable for negligence or creation of a nuisance to a property owner who is damaged after reasonable notice to the city of the clogged condition of the sewer.

> **Ga** Brannan v Brunswick (1934) 49 GaApp 62, 174 SE 186.
> Augusta v Cleveland (1919) 148 Ga 734, 98 SE 345.
> **Iowa** Hines v Nevada (1911) 150 Iowa 620, 130 NW 181.
> **Okla** Holdenville v Moore (1956) 293 P2d 363, 59 ALR2d 276.

A city which creates a municipal sanitation district, and transfers the existing sewerage system to it, is liable for injuries caused by pre-existing conditions. The district is not obligated to examine each pipe within the municipality to determine whether it is part of the sewer system and needs repair or replacement.

> **Ky** Louisville & Jefferson County Metropolitan Sewer Dist v Louisville (1970) 451 SW2d 172.

Where a city by ordinance enters into a contract with property owners for an easement across their land for extension of a sewer, but uses the land for a temporary outlet beyond and outside of said land, and sewage accumulates, giving off offensive, intense and noxious odors, such use may be enjoined as a permanent nuisance and damages assessed accordingly.

> **Mo** McCleery v Marshall (1933) 65 SW2d 1042.

Where a city constructs a sewer and it becomes a nuisance owing to the acts of individual lot owners, who make connections therewith, and where such acts are in violation of an ordinance, the city is not absolved from liability, since it possesses the power to abate any nuisance created, or, if it does not possess such power, it can acquire it by the exercise of the power of eminent domain.

> **Iowa** Hines v Nevada (1911) 150 Iowa 620, 130 NW 181.

An ordinance forbidding the drainage into the sewers of effluent, such as from a canning factory, does not exempt the municipality from liability where it does not enforce the ordinance. The ordinance merely enables the city to protect itself from liability by preventing the pollution of streams which carry away its sewage.

> **Minn** Huber v Blue Earth (1942) 213 Minn 319, 6 NW2d 471.

An ordinance constituting a contract between a city and nonresidents, made voluntarily and with legislative sanction, and establishing a sewer rate structure for nonresidents may relieve a city from liability for negligent breach of a contractual obligation, such as allowing the backing of sewerage into serviced homes.

> **NC** Smith v Winston-Salem (1957) 247 NC 349, 100 SE2d 835.

A city, in reconstructing part of an existing sewer system, acts in a governmental capacity, so that an ordinance letting a contract for the work cannot become ground for a suit for damages allegedly caused by the contractor's negligence in allowing sewage to escape.

> **Ark**   Fort Smith v Anderson (1967) 241 Ark 824, 410 SW2d 597.

Where private individuals through violating an ordinance requiring sewer connections create a nuisance, the city is not liable for injuries resulting from the nuisance, on the theory that it failed to enforce the ordinance.

> **Ky**   Talbert v Winchester (1939) 277 Ky 164, 125 SW2d 1002.

Where a city, though not under obligation to do so, undertakes by ordinance to permit the use of a sink hole by private sewers, and, being notified that the sink hole is insufficient to carry away the sewage and the surface water, fails to remedy the situation, its conduct is negligence, and for damages therefrom the city is liable.

> **Mo**   Kinlough v Maplewood (1918) 201 SW 625.

Where an ordinance authorizes the construction and maintenance of public sewers, and a private sewer is, without municipal authority, connected thereto, the city is not liable for stoppage in the private sewer resulting from acts of the city in maintaining the public sewer.

> **Mo**   Van Trump v Kansas City (1915) 187 MoApp 190, 173 SW 32.

Residents of a city who are compelled by ordinance to connect to the sewer system are not thereby rendered proper parties to a suit for damage from the discharge of the sewer system onto the property of other residents.

> **Ark**   Carmichael v Texarkana (1889) 94 F 561.

Where, within a city's sanitary sewer district created by ordinance, a sewer is laid as a permanent structure the length of a lot but without acquisition of rights of the landowner by deed or condemnation, any cause of action resulting to the landowner for damages for violation of a right of property did not pass to a subsequent purchaser by a conveyance of the land.

> **Okla**   Long v Tulsa (1947) 199 Okla 217, 184 P2d 800.

A municipal administrative code provision requiring one to remove or otherwise protect and replace sewer mains and fixtures so that the city may construct and lay water mains and pipes comprising a part of its waterworks system does not subject the city to liability for the expenses incurred in such removal and relocation.

> **NY**   Jamaica Water Supply v New York City (1952) 280 AD 834, 114 NYS2d 79.

ANNOTATIONS

Drains or sewers, municipality's liability for damage resulting from obstruction or clogging, 59 ALR2d 281.

Municipality's liability arising from negligence or other wrongful act in carrying out construction or repair of sewers and drains, 61 ALR2d 874.

Sewage disposal plant as nuisance, 40 ALR2d 1177.

Maintenance of a municipal sewerage disposal plant as governmental or proprietary function, 57 ALR2d 1336.

Pollution of water by operation of sewage disposal plant, 40 ALR2d 1212.

§4.1. Prohibition of Building Because of Inadequate Facilities

A zoning order completely prohibiting multi-family dwellings because of inadequate sewerage treatment facilities is invalid. It is a taking of property of one person for the benefit of the public without compensation. Though limited restriction or a moratorium on building permits is not objectionable, a blanket prohibition is.

> **NY** Westwood Forest Est v South Nyack (1969) 23 NY2d 424, 297 NYS2d 129, 244 NE2d 700.

A moratorium on new subdivisions and new construction because of sewage problems, which have been a problem for years without any action by the city, constitutes an invalid and unlawful attempt to prevent low cost housing.

> **NY** Kennedy Park Homes Assn v Lackawanna (1970) 318 F Supp 669.

While a municipality may properly limit lot sizes, a limitation to three- and four-acre tracts is unreasonable. The claim that sewage disposal facilities are inadequate may not be used as a basis for excessive lot size to prevent construction of homes for people who desire to move into the area.

> **Pa** Kit-Mar Builders, Appeal of (1970) 439 Pa 466, 268 A2d 765.

A preliminary injunction will not be issued to enjoin the enforcement of a moratorium resolution suspending the construction of high density apartment dwellings pending a sewage system survey. The courts will not enjoin the passage of any ordinance regardless of its constitutionality, or interfere with the legitimate research of a problem by the municipality.

> **Ky** Real Estate Devel Co v Florence (1971) 327 F Supp 513.

Rezoning from multiple dwelling to single-family residential on the basis of insufficient sewer service is invalid. Rezoning which singles out a particular developer in a situation which is uniform within the town amounts to confiscation without compensation.

> **NY** Nattin Rlty v Ludewig (1972) 40 AD2d 535, 334 NYS2d 483; affirming (1971) 67 Misc2d 828, 324 NYS2d 668.

A resolution to deny sewer and water services to projects not in accordance with the comprehensive zoning plan may not be given retroactive application. Denial of sewer service to an apartment complex commenced under valid zoning may not be denied on amendment of the zoning for residential only.

> **Md** Dist Land Corp v Washington Suburban Sanitary Comm (1972) 266 Md 301, 292 A2d 695.

A variance may be denied on testimony of the sewage authority that the additional sewage could not be handled. The variance for medium size apartments would be inappropriate to the public safety, health, morals, or general welfare.

> **Pa** Marple Gardens v Bd of Zoning Adjustment of Marple Township (1973) 8 PaCmwlth 436, 303 A2d 239.

An ordinance requirement for sanitary sewers before construction of apartments near a lake may not be nullified by the health board's approval of the site plan using a septic system. Approval of the plan without an on-site examination when violation of the county ordinance is also involved is a nullity and the action is arbitrary and capricious in approving the site plan without considering the pollution possibilities.

> **NY** Walsh v Spadaccia (1973) 73 Misc2d 866, 343 NYS2d 45.

A variance to construct an office building and stores is not justified on a showing that an on site sewer system might not be approved. The prior approval for a group of stores on one of the two lots which indicates the possibility of sewer problems is insufficient to show that the physical characteristics of the property preclude its use as zoned.

> **Pa** J Richard Fretz v Hilltown Township Zoning Hearing Bd (1975) 18 PaCmwlth 471, 336 A2d 464.

The existence of an overwhelming health problem due to an antiquated sewer and water supply system justifies rezoning from six-story apartment buildings to single-family and two-story garden apartments.

> **NY** Pacific Blvd Assn v Long Beach (1975) 48 AD2d 857, 368 NYS2d 867.

A county ordinance may not overrule contractual obligations and prefer builders in one area of the county over those in another. An authorization for an interconnection between two sewage treatment facilities, one operating at capacity and the other below capacity, which brings the facility operating below capacity to its capacity and allows buildings in the area of the facility operating at capacity to secure occupancy permits may not be the basis to deny building permits to a party who has a commitment from the treatment facilities which would have had capacity to handle his buildings.

> **Fla**   Heinzman v US Home of Fla (1975) 317 So2d 838.

ANNOTATION

Exclusionary zoning, 48 ALR3d 1210.

B. EXERCISE OF POWERS BY OFFICIALS

§5. Officers; Appointees; Legislative Officials

Violation of their preelection promises by members of the city council, in voting for an ordinance authorizing construction of sewers at the expense of abutting owners, has no bearing on the validity of the ordinance.

> **Ky**   Hodge v Princeton (1929) 227 Ky 481, 13 SW2d 491.

An ordinance for a sewer bond election is invalid when passed by the incumbent officers of a town after it was raised to a second class city and new city officials had taken office.

> **Ark**   Lewis v Tate (1946) 210 Ark 326, 195 SW2d 640.

Where members of a city council sign a petition for construction of a sewer improvement in a district designated by ordinance, the ordinance is not void because the same members of the city council vote for its passage, since they are acting in legislative capacity and their personal interests do not disqualify them.

> **Ark**   Lewis v Forrest City (1923) 156 Ark 356, 246 SW 867.

An ordinance authorizing sewer construction and assessing the cost against abutting owners is not rendered invalid by being favorably voted on by a council member, a dealer in sewer pipe, who possesses merely a remote possibility of selling sewer construction materials to an unknown successful bidder.

> **Ky**   Hodge v Princeton (1929) 227 Ky 481, 13 SW2d 491.

A municipal corporation and its officers are not liable in damages to contractors who make bids based on excessive estimates made by the city engineer for the construction of sewers when the contractors are thereby precluded from payment for work done because of the unenforceability of the ordinance levying assessments for construction costs.

Okla Reed v Bartlesville (1925) 108 Okla 62, 234 P 642.

Where an ordinance authorizes construction of a district sewer, tax bills issued for work completed thereunder are not invalid on the ground that the ordinance was not approved and signed by the mayor, as required, where it was approved and signed by the acting mayor, since in the absence of a showing to the contrary it will be presumed that the acting mayor acted rightly.

Mo Deming v Springfield (1920) 224 SW 1004.

An ordinance making the mayor the manager of the city waterworks and sewer system, with a salary for both functions is not a mere increase in salary to the mayor. It is void because the offices are incompatible since they may require the mayor, as an officer of the municipality, to make a contract with himself acting as manager of the sewer system or waterworks.

Ark Davis v Doyle (1959) 230 Ark 421, 323 SW2d 202.

The mayor may not make an appointment for the operation of sewage works, where an ordinance provides that the construction, acquisition, improvement, equipment, operation, and maintenance of sewage works shall be under the supervision and control of the board of public works.

Ind Princeton v Woodruff (1952) 230 Ind 536, 104 NE2d 748.

An ordinance authorizing a firm to prepare specifications and plans for a sewer system is not a direction for the payment of money under the statutory limitation on cities that every bill that contemplates payment of money shall be referred to the treasurer for his endorsement that a sufficient sum stands to the credit of the city, unappropriated, in the fund covered by such ordinance.

Mo Benham v Marceline (1923) 213 MoApp 653, 251 SW 748.

§6. Engineering Officials

Where a city engineer, in preparing a preliminary estimate of the cost of sewer improvements, knowingly increased it 25 per cent to cover a probable discount of that amount of the par value of warrants to be issued to the contractor, the ordinance levying assessments was nevertheless valid, but the assessments were to be equitably adjusted downward.

Okla Bartlesville v Keeler (1924) 107 Okla 14, 229 P 450.

An ordinance assessing property for sewer improvements will not be voided by reason of excessive estimates of the city engineer.

Okla　Bartlesville v Riggs (1926) 114 Okla 181, 245 P 603.

Where a city having no engineer adopts an ordinance for the construction of district sewers, and designates the mayor as the proper officer "to procure, approve and present" plans, specifications and estimates of costs, and the mayor, not an engineer, employs an engineer of wide experience to prepare such estimate, which the mayor carefully studies, signs and presents to the board of aldermen, the procedure is valid.

Mo　Tabb v Burt (1927) 296 SW 820.

An ordinance directing that the city engineer fix the grade of a sewer is not a delegation by the council of its legislative function, since the fixing of the grade of the sewer is more executive than legislative.

Ky　Rich v Woods (1904) 118 Ky 865, 82 SW 578.

Tax bills issued for construction of a sewer are invalid, where an ordinance provides that all work relating to public improvements shall be done under the supervision and direction of the city engineer who shall personally inspect the work as it progresses, where an inspector is appointed by the city engineer to carry out such supervision responsibilities, and where the city engineer makes no personal investigation to determine whether or not the report of the inspector is correct as to measurements and charges for rock excavation.

Mo　Ernst v Springfield (1910) 145 MoApp 89, 130 SW 419.

An ordinance establishing a sewer system, and providing for construction of 63 manholes and 176 catch basins, to be located as directed by the superintendent of public works, is not invalid as indefinite, since it is necessary in the construction of public works that supervisory powers over such details be vested somewhere.

Ill　Rich v Chicago (1894) 152 Ill 18, 38 NE 255.

C. INTERCITY COOPERATION

§7. Operation and Financing

A loan or grant of money to a sewer authority by the city can be by motion. The subsequent ordinance authorizing the money as a grant is equally valid, since the municipality has the power to make both loans and grants.

Pa　Laux v Harvey's Lake (1971) 2 PaCmwlth 297, 276 A2d 366.

Under an ordinance authorizing a contract for sewage disposal, in which the only financial obligation the city incurs is to pay for the benefits received by it in using another city's sewage disposal facilities, the nonowning city does not thereby become a stockholder, or lend its credit to the other city, where the latter issues and sells its own revenue bonds for the facilities.

Ky   Russell v Flatwoods (1965) 394 SW2d 900.

An ordinance authorizing a contract by one city to pay another city a monthly sum to be determined by the amount of sewage does not create an indebtedness in violation of constitutional limitations.

Ky   Russell v Flatwoods (1965) 394 SW2d 900.

Where an ordinance authorizes an agreement with another city for construction of a cooperative sewer system to be financed by a bond issue, the authorized agreement is not ultra vires, since the contingent passage of a bond issue would impose no indebtedness on the city.

Mo   Kansas City v Raytown (1967) 421 SW2d 504.

Under an ordinance proposing the construction of a sewage disposal plant, the operation and management of which will be assigned to another municipality, the city has the right to make such a transfer when authorized to do so by the legislature.

Ky   Johnson v Louisville (1953) 261 SW2d 429.

Where in the solution of their respective municipal sewer problems it becomes necessary for several contiguous cities to contribute to the conduct of a joint survey of the entire area affected, the expenditure of funds of each such city in this manner is a proper municipal expenditure.

Cal   Oakland v Williams (1940) 15 C2d 542, 103 P2d 168.

§8. Electoral Approval

An ordinance authorizing the lease of a portion of sewage treatment facilities is subject to referendum.

NJ   McLaughlin v Millville (1970) 110 NJS 200, 264 A2d 762.

Where an ordinance is adopted authorizing execution of an agreement with another city for a cooperative sewer system, and at two subsequent elections bond issues for financing the agreement are turned down by the electorate, an ordinance authorizing a third election for consideration of such bonds is construed to have been called on the question of a cooperative and not of a go-it-alone system, previous conduct on the part of some of the aldermen to the contrary notwithstanding.

> **Mo**   Kansas City v Raytown (1967) 421 SW2d 504.

There is no constitutional prohibition against a municipality participating with another municipality in a function it is permitted or required to perform by itself and by which its inhabitants will reap a commensurate benefit; and with the approval of the voters a city may by ordinance authorize the construction of a sewage disposal plant to be financed by a bond issue, and to be managed and controlled by another municipality.

> **Ky**   Johnson v Louisville (1953) 261 SW2d 429.

D. EXTRATERRITORIAL FACILITIES AND SERVICES

§9. Municipal Authority and Duties

An ordinance authorizing the extension of sanitary sewers outside the corporate limits on petition of a majority of the property owners is not rendered void by a subsequent agreement to allow tap-ins by the grantors of easements. Nor is the appropriation invalid where it simply provides for sewer extension. It is not necessary to specify the various costs involved.

> **Ill**   Continental Ill Nat Bk & Tr Co of Chicago v Park Forest (1972)
> 4 IllAp3d 811, 282 NE2d 167.

A requirement that the city may not dispose of any utility without a vote of the people is overruled by state statute. The statutory authorization for boroughs with extraterritorial jurisdiction authorizes them to take over the sewer system and operate it for the entire area.

> **Alas**   Jefferson v State (1974) 527 P2d 37.

A home rule city's health regulations may not be applied to a regional sewage treatment plant. The sewer district is not obligated to follow the health requirements nor secure a permit when it has fulfilled the statutory requirements. Since the district is composed of several home rule cities the "reluctant host" of the treatment plant is attempting to impose its local governing authority on a matter of area-wide concern.

> **Ill**   Metropolitan Sanitary Dist of Greater Chicago v Des Plaines (1976) 63 Ill2d
> 256, 347 NE2d 716.

Where an ordinance is enacted authorizing a bond issue for the extension of water and sewer service into an area to be annexed, the expenditure of funds for those purposes outside the corporate limits, pursuant to legislative authority, is for a public purpose and is not violative of the Fourteenth Amendment.

> **Ky** Williams v Barbourville (1952) 246 SW2d 591.
> **NC** Thomasson v Smith (1958) 249 NC 84, 105 SE2d 416.

Municipalities have legislative permission to extend their sewer and water lines beyond corporate limits. Such extensions may be made either because necessary to effective operation of the improvement within the city or to provide for profit beyond the corporate limits. Bonds for the latter purpose may be issued only when the electorate has expressly so authorized.

> **NC** Eakley v Raleigh (1960) 252 NC 683, 114 SE2d 777.

An ordinance to construct a sewer system to be financed by a municipal bond issue is within the city's implied powers, though the system will also benefit inhabitants outside the city's boundaries.

> **Ky** Johnson v Louisville (1953) 261 SW2d 429.

A city has power to incur a bonded indebtedness for the purpose of providing funds for construction of a sewage disposal plant after approval by the voters, where legal title to the sewer system will remain in the city, though the disposal plant will be operated by a metropolitan sewer district and will also serve property beyond the city's boundaries.

> **Ky** Johnson v Louisville (1953) 261 SW2d 429.

A taxpayer cannot rely on objections to special contracts whereby townships outside the municipality were permitted to use portions of the municipality's sewerage system, to invalidate an ordinance that does not impose a charge for that service.

> **Pa** Gericke v Philadelphia (1945) 353 Pa 60, 44 A2d 233.

An ordinance assessing property outside the city limits for sewer construction is invalid to that extent. However, on annexation of that property to the city the owner may be required to pay a pro rata share of the cost for the privilege of connecting with the sewer.

> **Okla** Tulsa v Bell (1929) 137 Okla 159, 278 P 642.

An ordinance assessing the cost of sewer construction on abutting owners is not invalid merely because it failed to assess abutting property lying outside the city, since the city has no authority to assess property outside its boundaries.

> **Ky** Gesser v McLane (1914) 156 Ky 743, 161 SW 1118.

Although a municipal corporation has authority to extend mains to obtain an adequate water supply, or to continue sewer lines to obtain an outlet, beyond the corporate limits, a city cannot pass an ordinance extending its water and sewer lines beyond the corporate limits to provide service to a proposed federal youth administration facility and applying revenues derived from one system to the other to pay the cost of construction.

Ark   Mathers v Moss (1941) 202 Ark 554, 151 SW2d 660.

An ordinance providing that the city shall not be liable for the maintenance of water mains or service pipes lying outside the corporate limits does not prevent the city from entering into a valid contract to operate sewer and water mains outside of the city, if the transaction does not create an indebtedness.

Okla   Wewoka v Billingsley (1958) 331 P2d 949.

§10. Charges to Users

A municipality may by contract provide for the collection and disposal of sewage originating outside of its corporate limits. A contract provision whereby the city promised to provide a system at a price equal to the rate charged city residents, plus 50 per cent and a flat fifty cent per month sewer maintenance charge, in exchange for a lien in the city's name on property for any unpaid charges or fees provides sufficient consideration by both parties to be valid.

Ill   Cabak v St Charles (1978) 61 IllAp3d 57, 377 NE2d 548.

An ordinance levying a charge on persons outside the corporate limits for use of the city's sewer system is valid, where the system was paid for by direct levy of taxation on property owners of the city. Nonresidents cannot, by injunctive relief, prevent the city from disconnecting its line from their line at the city limits and plugging the city line.

Miss   Wells v Jackson (1955) 223 Miss 228, 77 So2d 925.

An ordinance providing that the owners of property outside the city limits must pay a sewer connection fee in order to tie up with the city sewer system is not invalid as levying a tax on such property. The rates and fees that may be charged for connecting with the city sewer system are matters to be determined within the city's sound discretion.

NC   Atl Constr v Raleigh (1949) 230 NC 365, 53 SE2d 165.

Where the board of supervisors of a sanitary district adjoining a city has knowledge of ordinances offering to enter into contracts with nonresidents for the use of its sewers, and where the supervisors do not enter into an express contract with the city for this service, the board is bound by implied contracts to pay for such services at the rate fixed by the ordinance.

> **Va**   Henrico County v Richmond (1934) 162 Va 14, 173 SE 356.

Under an ordinance providing for treatment of the raw sewage of another city, the sewage system must be considered as a whole for the purpose of determining the reasonableness of the rate to be charged.

> **Mich**   Detroit v Highland Park (1949) 326 Mich 78, 39 NW2d 325.

An ordinance imposing a service charge for sewer connections to dwellings outside the city is not discriminatory though no similar charge is made to city residents, where the city owns the system and those outside the city can acquire the right to use the system only by contract with the city.

> **Cal**   Hobby v Sonora (1956) 142 CA2d 457, 298 P2d 578.

Though sewage services furnished by one municipality to another are effectuated by ordinance, they are on a contractual basis, and the acceptance of services implies a promise to pay therefor at the established rates.

> **Mich**   Detroit v Highland Park (1949) 326 Mich 78, 39 NW2d 325.

An ordinance of one city authorizing its officials to discontinue sewer service by disconnecting sewer lines to another city in order to compel acceptance of a rate ordinance which provides rates in excess of those specified in the original contract is not a reasonable notice of termination of that contract.

> **Ohio**   Grandview Heights v Columbus (1963) 174 OS 473, 23 Op2d 117, 190 NE2d 453.

That nonresident users of a city sewer system have spent substantial sums on sewer connections creates no right to a continuance of the privileges in the absence of a contract or of estoppel. Such nonresident users assume the risk that the city might be unable to continue the service or might find it expedient to increase its charges.

> **Ky**   Davisworth v Lexington (1949) 311 Ky 606, 224 SW2d 649.

Courts do not inquire into the motives of a municipal council in the enactment of an ordinance. Thus, plaintiffs have no right to equitable relief in a suit to determine the validity of an ordinance providing that an assessment should be made for the privilege of connecting or continuing connections with a sewer system of the city outside the city's corporate limits, where the plaintiff alleged that the ordinance was enacted through malice or spite.

> **Ga**   Barr v Augusta (1950) 206 Ga 750, 58 SE2d 820.

§ 11. Justifying Annexation

The duty of a city to furnish water and sewer facilities may be conditioned on annexation. Where the original grant of water and sewer service was made for national defense purposes, and no contract was executed for continuation of the service on termination of the national defense construction, the city may terminate service if the owners of the property resist annexation.

ND   Satrom v Grand Forks (1968) 163 NW2d 522.

A city may properly refuse to furnish water and sewer services to an area outside the city limits that opposes annexation where no contract agreement has been made with the property owners. The furnishing of water and sewer services before enactment of the annexation ordinance does not impose an implied contract.

ND   Williams Bros Pipeline Co v Grand Forks (1968) 163 NW2d 517.

The wish of a municipal corporation to install a sanitary sewerage system in territory to be added at the same time such system is being installed within the present corporate limits is not sufficient ground for extending the city boundaries.

Miss   Extension of Boundaries of Indianola, In re (1956) 226 Miss 760, 85 So2d 212.

E. Acquiring Existing Facilities

§ 12. Generally

Evidence of sewage overflow and inadequate filtering do not justify a town's recording of a deed held in escrow by a town under an agreement allowing the town to record the deed to the sewage disposal facilities if the owner failed to provide adequate service after 20 days' notice of default given pursuant to town resolution, when there is no showing of any actual or imminent health danger which will result from the deteriorated condition of the facilities.

NY   Nick Guttman Inc v Vines (1978) 63 AD2d 998, 406 NYS2d 130.

A resolution for condemnation of all private water and sewer companies to be included in one county operated system may be conditioned on dropping the proceedings if it is not financially feasible. The county may terminate the eminent domain proceedings by failing to deposit any award into the court.

Fla   Dade County v Gen Water Works Corp (1972) 267 So2d 633.

An ordinance seeking to condition the town's consent to a sanitation district's construction of a sewer line within the town's boundary on the vesting of the right, title and interest in the sewer in the town is void, as authorizing confiscation of private property without due process of law.

Colo   Sheridan v Valley Sanitation Dist (1958) 137 Colo 315, 324 P2d 1038.

An easement dedicated for storm sewer purposes on a subdivision plat may, under a general dedication ordinance, be used for sanitary sewer purposes.

NC   Sampson v Greensboro (1978) 240 SE2d 502.

Where city ordinances were in effect at the time advising those outside the city who were permitted to connect with the city water and sewer mains that whenever the territory in which they were located should be incorporated within the city limits, the water and sewer lines and fixtures, equipment, easements, rights and privileges pertaining thereto should become the property of the city, plaintiff's subdivision having been laid out within one mile of the corporate limits of the city, knowledge of such ordinances was presumed.

NC   Spaugh v Winston-Salem (1952) 234 NC 708, 68 SE2d 838.

A municipality is entitled to specific performance where it exercises its option, reserved in an ordinance granting a franchise to the plaintiff's predecessors, to take over at cost the sewer system constructed under such franchise ordinance.

Md   Camden Sewer v Salisbury (1932) 162 Md 45, 160 A 4.

II. DISTRICTS

§13. Creation and Control

A referendum election may not be held in order to repeal an ordinance creating a sewage treatment association. The statutory scheme for enactment and dissolution of the sewage treatment districts must be followed, and a mere repeal of the ordinance would not affect the continuation of the district.

Pa   Deer Creek Drainage Basin Auth v Bd of Elections of Allegheny County (1977) 475 Pa 491, 381 A2d 103.

Where the affected parties are satisfied with the existing system and it adequately serves its purpose the creation of a new sewer improvement district is unjustified.

Ill   Glencoe v Jackson (1969) 102 IllAp2d 65, 243 NE2d 865.

When a municipal utility authority has been created it has the exclusive means of providing the sewage facilities. An extension of existing service may not be assessed as a local improvement by the city.

NJ   Darrah v Evesham Township (1970) 111 NJS 62, 267 A2d 70.

On failure to publish notice of the formation of a sewer district and require protest within 15 days the city has not acquired the power to cause the improvements to be made, to contract for them, or to levy the assessments.

Okla   Lance v Sulphur (1972) 503 P2d 867.

In an ordinance for sewer construction, the city has power to divide itself into sewer districts, especially where there is a substantial difference in the topography of the various sections of the city.

Ky   Jackson v Riffle (1927) 219 Ky 689, 294 SW 142.

An ordinance creating a special storm and sanitary sewer district within a city, and providing for the issuance of bonds to defray the cost, is a valid enactment under the Municipal Improvement Bond Act.

Nev   Western Rlty v Reno (1946) 63 Nev 330, 172 P2d 158

An ordinance creating a sewer district is presumptively valid, and in a challenge of its validity the existence of the facts essential to validity will be presumed.

Kan   Schulenberg v Reading (1966) 196 Kan 43, 410 P2d 324.

Although a city has statutory authority to establish and levy assessments for a sewer outlet situated outside an improvement district, where a petition to create a sewer improvement district calls for connection of the same into a system of septic tanks, but the ordinance creating the district provides for conducting the effluent to a river beyond the district, the ordinance is void because of variance from the petition and the added cost of acquiring rights of way and laying mains, which could not reasonably have been anticipated by the property owners in the district.

Ark   Kraft v Smothers (1912) 103 Ark 269, 146 SW 505.

A sewer district created by an ordinance is not destroyed on annexation of the city to another city, and tax bills issued for construction of the sewer are validly assessed against benefited property.

Mo   Parker-Washington Co v Field (1919) 202 MoApp 159, 214 SW 402.

Where by charter a city is authorized to construct one section of a sewer at a time, and is also authorized, when the cost of an entire project would be of such magnitude as to exceed the amount of money in the treasury, to adopt an ordinance for the whole work and contract for its construction in sections, an ordinance may authorize construction of a joint district sewer as part of a sewer system without authorizing the whole project.

Mo   Heman Constr v Lyon (1919) 277 Mo 628, 211 SW 68.

An ordinance authorizing municipal bonds for the purpose of constructing adequate sanitary sewage treatment and disposal facilities consisting of a complete sewage disposal plant does not provide for construction of the sewer system in a local improvement district in a portion of the city where the resolution creating the improvement district assesses cost of its sewer system against property in the improvement district, according to benefits.

    Ida   Russell v Boise (1950) 70 Ida 199, 214 P2d 472.

Where a city's charter provides that sewer districts may be changed before but not after installation, an ordinance authorizing construction of part of a sewer, the cost to be assessed against the entire district, is valid. Property owners not immediately benefited have a vested right in completion of the sewer in due course.

    Mo   McGhee v Walsh (1913) 249 Mo 266, 155 SW 445.

A first class city has no statutory jurisdiction or authority to levy special assessments on property in one sewer district for portions of a sewer constructed or reconstructed within another sewer district.

    Neb   Besack v Beatrice (1951) 154 Neb 142, 47 NW2d 356.

The addition of a village to a sanitary district system will not preclude its enactment of an ordinance for construction of a system of relief sewers, where nothing has been done by the sanitary district with respect to the village except to locate the proposed route of its main channel in proximity to the village.

    Ill   Gage v Wilmette (1907) 230 Ill 428, 82 NE 656.

Where by authority of Constitution and statute a city may create one or more sewerage districts within its limits and enlarge or consolidate them it has the authority, after it has extended the corporate limits, to enlarge the sewer system and consolidate one or more districts to serve the new territory if the redistricting does not result in an overlap.

    La   Nanney v Leesville (1941) 198 La 773, 4 So2d 825.

Where an ordinance divides an area into sewer districts and a later ordinance authorizes construction of a main or trunk sewer the cost of which is to be assessed against several sewer districts, construction of the trunk sewer may not be enjoined on the ground that some of the property assessed will receive no direct benefit therefrom, since such districts are within the drainage area to be served by the trunk sewer on completion of the system and the assessed properties therefore receive a present benefit in the increased value of the land affected thereby.

    Mo   Whitsett v Carthage (1917) 270 Mo 269, 193 SW 21.

Where a sewer district has been established and a sewer constructed, the district cannot be enlarged by ordinance and another district sewer constructed in the territory added, with the cost assessed against the property in the enlarged district, including that in the old district as well as that in the new.

> **Okla**   Stone v Sapulpa (1911) 28 Okla 864, 115 P 1113.

§ 14. Joint Districts

Where several ordinances create separate joint sewer districts, as authorized by charter, the court will not question the reasonableness of the procedure on the ground that the drainage could have been accomplished through formation of a single district, or that they could have been built together at less cost, since discretion in the matter resting with the common council will not be interfered with by the courts in the absence of a showing that the improvements were unnecessary, fraudulent, arbitrary, or oppressive.

> **Mo**   Sills v Mo Securities (1928) 319 Mo 178, 5 SW2d 389.

Where an ordinance authorizes extension of a sanitary sewer system by the creation of separate joint sewer districts and the construction of separate joint district sewers, servient areas not benefited by a joint district sewer constructed on upper levels should be omitted from the joint sewer districts successively created.

> **Mo**   Sills v Mo Securities (1928) 319 Mo 178, 5 SW2d 389.

Under a city's constitutional charter authority to classify sewers as public, district, joint district and private, an ordinance establishing a joint district sewer is not an unconstitutional classification, where the costs thereof are assessed against benefited property rather than paid for out of public revenue, since all subjects of the class are affected equally and uniformly in like circumstances.

> **Mo**   Haeussler Inv v Bates (1924) 306 Mo 392, 267 SW 632.

An ordinance establishing a joint sewer district will not be held invalid on the ground that it is a public sewer which should be paid for out of revenue of the city, where all or nearly all of the land in the district lies along and is contained in the same natural drainage area.

> **Mo**   Kirkwood v Hillcrest Rlty (1921) 234 SW 1023.

A city having statutory authority to establish general and joint sewer systems may, by ordinance, establish either without first establishing the district sewer, and tax bills issued in payment therefore are valid.

> **Mo**   Harris v Cameron (1924) 218 MoApp 605, 265 SW 862.

III. PRELIMINARY PROCEEDINGS

A. GENERALLY

§15. Notice and Hearing

A court cannot permanently enjoin a city from carrying out any action authorized by a sewage disposal resolution passed at a city council meeting which is invalid due to defective notice where the defect can be cured by the council in a subsequent meeting which complies with all statutory requirements.

Neb Pokorny v Schuyler (1979) 202 Neb 334, 275 NW2d 281.

Where it appears that a sewer improvement ordinance is for the benefit of the entire sewer system, it constitutes a public rather than a local improvement. No question of special assessment is involved, and hence there is no requirement for public hearings.

Ill Wolcott v Lombard (1944) 387 Ill 621, 57 NE2d 351.

§16. Review

An action challenging the validity of a resolution adopted by a board of county commissioners incorporating a sewer district cannot be maintained by a private individual, since actions questioning the validity of proceedings creating a municipal corporation may be prosecuted only in a direct proceeding by the state, acting through its proper officers.

Kan Bishop v Shawnee & Mission Townships (1959) 184 Kan 376, 336 P2d 815.

The right of a party to judicial review of an ordinance in a proper case cannot be denied simply because of the nature of the agency or instrumentality to whom the legislature has delegated the rate making function.

Ind State v Grant Circuit Ct (1959) 239 Ind 315, 517 NE2d 188.

Where a county is empowered by statute to adopt an ordinance for appropriate police measures to promote health and suppress disease and to regulate the disposal of sewage, the courts will consider whether such an ordinance has a definite and substantial relation to a recognized police-power purpose, though they will not inquire into the wisdom of an ordinance enacted under such authority.

Ill Krol v Will County (1968) 38 Ill2d 587, 233 NE2d 417.

B. ORDINANCES AND RESOLUTIONS

§17. As Condition Precedent

A town board has no power to proceed with sewer improvements or to levy assessments in connection therewith, without a valid ordinance adopted in accordance with statute.

> **Okla**　Bonney v Britton (1950) 202 Okla 399, 214 P2d 249.

The authority of municipalities to make local improvements by special assessments is statutory, and an improvement ordinance must strictly follow the statute, in order to establish a valid assessment. Thus assessments cannot be enforced unless a valid ordinance authorizing the improvement has been passed.

> **Ill**　Chicago v Jerome (1922) 301 Ill 587, 134 NE 92.
> **Okla**　Jones v Whitaker (1912) 33 Okla 13, 124 P 312.

All local improvements must originate with the board of local improvements which, by resolution, recites the general nature, extent and cost of improvements as a prerequisite to subsequent action by the city council, which supplements the resolution by its ordinance, specifying a precise and complete description thereof; and the enactment of a local improvement ordinance without such prior originating resolution of the board is a nullity.

> **Ill**　Walker v Chicago (1903) 202 Ill 531, 67 NE 369.

When a mayor and two city commissioners sit together as a legislative body, with the mayor having no veto power, the traditional distinctions between an ordinance and a resolution lose their force, and a resolution by this body, granting a contractor permission to lay a private sewer line to subdivisions of the city, is valid in spite of the statutory rule that no use of streets may be granted except by ordinance.

> **Ark**　Fort Smith v Taylor (1958) 228 Ark 722, 310 SW2d 13.

Where an ordinance providing for construction and regulation of sewers is invalid because the oral vote of the council is not recorded, it does not affect the special assessment since a statute provides in detail a method of procedure to be followed and an ordinance is not necessary.

> **Iowa**　Hardwick v Independence (1907) 136 Iowa 481, 114 NW 14.

The formality of enactment and publication of an ordinance is not necessary in order to validate the award of a contract by a city to construct a sewer system, since the execution of the contract could be authorized and effectuated by a resolution or other proper means.

> **Kan**　Botts v Valley Center (1927) 124 Kan 9, 257 P 226.

The passage and publication of an ordinance of necessity for the establishment of a sewer district and the construction of sewers, with the cost apportioned against abutting property and to be assessed by ordinance, confers jurisdiction to proceed.

Okla Barnett v Waynoka (1930) 148 Okla 24, 296 P 972.
Hancock v Muskogee (1917) 66 Okla 195, 168 P 445.

The general rule is that an ordinance of necessity for establishing sewer districts is final, and cannot be reviewed by the courts, in the absence of circumstances indicating fraud or oppression.

Okla Crawford v Cassity (1920) 78 Okla 261, 190 P 412.

Proper notice was not given to an interested property owner, where a municipality did not adopt an ordinance providing for improvement in sewage disposal facilities before advertising for bids for construction of the project.

Ind Wilcox v North Liberty (1967) 250 Ind 180, 230 NE2d 423.

§18. Procedural Requirements

An ordinance authorizing a storm drainage system may only be repealed through an ordinance passed under the same proceedings as the original ordinance. A reconsideration vote alone is not sufficient to repeal the ordinance and prevent a referendum vote.

Ohio Reiff v City Council of Hamilton (1972) 32 OA2d 224, 289 NE2d 358.

The enactment of a resolution of necessity by a municipal corporation to make a sewer improvement, to be paid for in whole or in part by special assessments, requires the affirmative vote of three-fourths of the members elected to the legislative authority of the municipality.

Ohio Davis v Willoughby (1962) 173 OS 338, 19 Op2d 270, 182 NE2d 552.

Under a statute providing that no ordinance is passed unless on its final passage a majority of the members elected to the council shall vote therefor, and that the ayes and nays shall be entered on the journal, an ordinance assessing the cost of sewers in a sewer district, which the records showed was passed by a vote of the 12 members of the council present, but of which the ayes and nays were not recorded, is invalid. However, it may be validated by a nunc pro tunc order on presentation of proper evidence to show and record what the vote actually was, not as a change in the record but as an expansion of the same.

Mo Independence v Hare (1962) 359 SW2d 33.

A resolution of a village council for the extension of water and sewer lines and enlargement of certain existing lines and authorizing payment therefor from existing water and sewer fund surpluses, prescribes a permanent rule of conduct, is not of an ephemeral or temporary nature, and is in substance an ordinance rather than a resolution.

Ohio   Shoemaker v Granville (1958) 79 Abs 573, 156 NE2d 757.

§19. Contents; Specificity

A special assessment, to be valid, must have as its foundation a legal and sufficient ordinance prescribing the nature, character, locality and description of the improvement.

Ill   Bloomington v Davis (1923) 309 Ill 20, 140 NE 4.
Chicago v Jerome (1922) 301 Ill 587, 134 NE 92.

The legislative purpose in requiring a preliminary resolution declaring the necessity for and describing the property to be included in a sewer improvement district is to give the property owner notice of the intention of the city to make the improvement and assess his property so that he might take action to protect his rights. A resolution that fails to set out any description, even in general terms, of the property to be subjected to the sewer construction costs is invalid.

Ky   Newport v Klatch (1920) 189 Ky 300, 224 SW 844.

An ordinance levying an assessment on certain land to construct a sewer is valid, though it does not specify that the location is in the city, since the general rule of presumptions is that the council has not intended to exceed its territorial jurisdiction and legislative functions.

Ill   Stanton v Chicago (1894) 154 Ill 23, 39 NE 987.

Where a charter authorizing a city to construct or reconstruct district sewers by proceedings begun by the adoption of a resolution stating the nature of the improvement and requiring notice to owners interested therein, a resolution in accordance therewith is required only to state the nature of the improvement, its character, location and course, without details incident to construction.

Mo   Badger Lumber v Mullins (1925) 310 Mo 602, 275 SW 957.

Where resolutions declaring the necessity for the construction of sewers within described zones do not name the streets on which the sewers are to be constructed they are fatally defective, since it is not possible for a property owner to ascertain from the resolutions whether or not his property would have to bear its proportion of the cost, and he is thus deprived of opportunity to be heard with respect to assessments against his property.

Ky   Katterjohn v King (1924) 202 Ky 69, 258 SW 960.

Where a resolution declaring the necessity for sewer construction refers to a map filed with the commissioner of public works on which the location of sewers is indicated, this is not a sufficient compliance with the statutory requirement that the resolution reasonably describe the property.

> **Ky**   Katterjohn v King (1924) 202 Ky 69, 258 SW 960.

Where an ordinance apportioning the cost of sewer construction gives the name of the street, the number of front feet and the amount of the assessment, under a statute prescribing that when the work is done and accepted no error of the proceedings shall exempt any property from the lien of an assessment, the description of the property is sufficient.

> **Ky**   Lyons v Sanders (1924) 205 Ky 695, 226 SW 373.

An ordinance of intention to establish a main trunk sewer district, the boundaries of which are identical with those of the incorporated village, and declaring that the improvement district shall contain all the real property within the corporate limits of the village, sufficiently complies with the statutory requirement that the ordinance include a clear description of the property to be benefited.

> **Ida**   Caldwell v Mountain Home (1916) 29 Ida 13, 156 P 909.

A statutory requirement that a resolution determining the necessity for sewer improvement describe in general terms the properties subject to assessment for the cost is mandatory and jurisdictional and its omission renders the assessment invalid.

> **Ky**   Mulligan v McGregor (1915) 165 Ky 222, 176 SW 1129.

The statutory provision that ordinances shall contain no subject not clearly expressed in the title is intended to prevent the practice of joining, in the same ordinance, incongruous subjects, having no relation or connection with each other and foreign to the subject embraced in the title. Matters germane to the general subject expressed in the title may be united. The title need not be an index to the act; nor need it state a catalog of all the powers intended to be bestowed. An abstract of the law is not required in the title; nor need the title state the mode in which the subject is treated, nor the means by which the ends sought by the enactment are to be reached (ordinance appropriating certain property for sewers, watermains, streets, and boulevards).

> **Neb**   Webber v Scottsbluff (1951) 155 Neb 48, 50 NW2d 533.

Under a contract for the construction of a sewer, as described in an ordinance, an assessment for the purpose of paying for a block of sewer not described in the ordinance was invalid.

> **Iowa**   Bennett v Emmetsburg (1908) 138 Iowa 67, 115 NW 582.

An ordinance authorizing the establishment and construction of a sewer district, and providing that before advertising for bids the city engineer shall make detailed plans and specifications for the work, complies with the charter requirement that a sewer must be of such dimension, material and character "as shall be prescribed by ordinance", where the general plans were on file outlining the proposed work, though they did not include some details afterwards embodied in the contract.

Mo　Waddell Inv v Hall (1914) 255 Mo 675, 164 SW 541.

An ordinance for a sewer improvement, providing that catch basin walls shall be 8 inches thick, and shall rest on a solid bottom of two-inch oak plank, spiked to cross planks, is not invalid for insufficiency for not stating dimension of the cross planks or the kind of wood, or the material in which they are to be imbedded, since only a reasonable degree of specificity is required.

Ill　Smythe v Chicago (1902) 197 Ill 311, 64 NE 361.

An ordinance providing for the construction of a sewer system, which specifies the streets to be improved, and gives the internal dimensions of the improvement, the grade of sewer on each street, the material to be used, and the character of the work in detail, is valid, as containing a sufficient description of the improvement.

Ill　Walker v People (1897) 170 Ill 410, 48 NE 1010.

In an ordinance providing for the construction of a sewer, failure to specify the height of manholes does not invalidate the ordinance, where the height of the sewer throughout its length is shown, since the height of the manholes can be determined by the difference between the sewer and the surface of the ground.

Ill　Bickerdike v Chicago (1900) 185 Ill 280, 56 NE 1096.

An ordinance providing for the construction of a sewer which fails to provide for necessary connections for outflow is void for uncertainty as to how connections are to be made.

Ill　Gage v Chicago (1901) 191 Ill 210, 60 NE 896.

A local improvement ordinance, providing for the construction of a sewer, which does not specify the depth to which the sewer pipes are to be laid, is invalid as lacking a necessary element of description.

Ill　Lawrenceville v Hennessey (1910) 244 Ill 464, 91 NE 670.

An ordinance providing for a local improvement will be deemed of sufficient specificity where the grade of the sewer or street is shown by reference to the city's datum.

Ill　Hillsboro v Grassel (1911) 249 Ill 190, 94 NE 48.

An ordinance providing that a sewer shall be constructed of vitrified tile pipe, a certain number of inches in diameter, is not invalid for failure to designate the thickness of the pipe, since it is well known that manufacturers of that type of tile pipe have established a standard size.

Ill   Hynes v Chicago (1898) 175 Ill 56, 51 NE 705.

An ordinance for the construction of a sewage treatment plant, which provides that it "shall consist of a septic tank of the following form, dimensions and specifications, or its equal in efficiency", is void as insufficient, since the provision for substitution destroys the certainty that the plant will be constructed in the manner and of the materials prescribed by the ordinance.

Ill   Lena v Kable (1927) 327 Ill 246, 158 NE 409.

Though a public sewer improvement ordinance must describe the proposed improvement and its component parts with certainty, it is unnecessary to describe in minute detail every particular of the improvement and every circumstance of the work, since some discretion must necessarily be left to the board of local improvements.

Ill   Lena v Kable (1927) 327 Ill 246, 158 NE 409.

§20. Recitals

Where a recital in a sewer construction ordinance indicates that the outlet is in a natural stream with sufficient capacity to carry off all sewer drainage, and there is no question of the city's right to drain into the stream, an objection to the ordinance that it fails to specifically provide an outlet is untenable.

Ill   North Chicago v Cummings (1915) 266 Ill 575, 107 NE 776.

Where the title of an ordinance is "An ordinance creating and establishing sewer improvement district number, and defining the boundaries of same," and one provision states "that the sewer improvement district is so created for all purposes of local improvement within the boundaries thereof," the title may be used for arriving at the legislative intention that the ordinance relates only to sewer purposes since no other improvement is mentioned.

ND   McKenzie v Mandan (1914) 27 ND 546, 147 NW 808.

An invalid provision in an ordinance providing for construction of a sewer improvement is severable from the remainder, and the improvement may be made.

ND   McKenzie v Mandan (1914) 27 ND 546, 147 NW 808.

Where a local improvement ordinance providing for construction of a sewer drain specifies that the drain shall fall uniformly at a specified grade from a designated point, the term "fall" will be construed to mean "rise", where it is apparent from other sections of ordinance and from the plan and profile of the improvement that use of "fall" was a clerical mistake, inserted in error for "rise", and a literal construction would lead to an absurd consequence.

Ark   Webster v Ferguson (1910) 95 Ark 575, 130 SW 513.
Ill   Chicago v Municipal Eng & Constr (1918) 283 Ill 160, 119 NE 40.
          Steele v River Forest (1892) 141 Ill 302, 30 NE 1034.
ND   McKenzie v Mandan (1914) 27 ND 546, 147 NW 808.

A general sewer ordinance provision that uses the "front-foot" rule as a continuing definition of adjacent property is not superseded by a legislative act providing for an assessment in proportion to benefits.

Iowa   Dunker v Des Moines (1913) 160 Iowa 567, 142 NW 207.

§21. Incorporation of Specifications

A resolution or ordinance providing for construction of a sewer may validly refer to plans and specifications on file in the proper municipal office and thereby satisfy specification notice requirements.

Cal   Haughawout v Raymond (1905) 148 Cal 311, 83 P 53.
Ida   Dement v Caldwell (1912) 22 Ida 62, 125 P 200.
          Williams v Caldwell (1911) 19 Ida 514, 114 P 519.
Mo   Waddell Inv v Hall (1914) 255 Mo 675, 164 SW 541.
          Youmans v Everett (1913) 173 MoApp 671, 160 SW 274.

Where a resolution is adopted expressing the necessity for establishing of a sewer district for sanitary and drainage purposes, and ordinances are adopted establishing the district and authorizing construction of a sanitary and drainage sewer to be built according to plans and specifications on file in the city clerk's office which plans are for a sanitary sewer only and where such plans and specifications are made a part of the ordinance, tax bills authorized for construction of the sanitary sewer are valid, and are not defeated by the variance between the resolution and ordinances on the one hand, and the plans and specifications on the other.

Mo   Myers v Wood (1913) 173 MoApp 564, 158 SW 909.

Where its charter authorizes a city to construct district sewers of such dimensions, material, and character "as shall be prescribed by ordinance", and an ordinance is adopted for construction of a sewer by reference to specifications not then in existence, the ordinance is invalid.

Mo   Mullins v Everett (1913) 172 MoApp 186, 157 SW 823.

An ordinance authorizing construction of a district sewer must prescribe on its face the dimensions, material, and character of the sewer, or the omitted provisions must appear in specifications on file in a designated place at the time of enactment of the ordinance to which reference is made in the ordinance. If no such specifications are outlined in the ordinance, or on file, tax bills issued thereunder will be canceled by a court of equity.

Mo Richardson v Walsh (1910) 142 MoApp 328, 126 SW 763.

Where an ordinance authorizing construction of a sewer and the published notice for bids refers for plans and specifications to a different ordinance, which in turn refers to plans and specifications on file in the office of the city clerk, the reference to the different ordinance does not invalidate the proceedings.

Mo Kirksville v Harrington (1930) 225 MoApp 309, 35 SW2d 614.

§22. Multiple Improvements

An ordinance providing for the construction of a new sewer to connect up with one presently in the street, and providing for an assessment for house drain connections every 45 feet is valid where the assessment is for the entire line of the new and old sewers and not merely for one sewer independent of the other, and the installation and connection constitute only one improvement.

Ill River Forest v Chicago & O P Elevated RR (1910) 244 Ill 480, 91 NE 682.

Provision in one ordinance for three sewers having no actual connection with each other is not objectionable and will not invalidate the ordinance as constituting a "double improvement."

Ill Hinsdale v Shannon (1899) 182 Ill 312, 55 NE 327.

A city, in providing for a sewer system, is not restricted in each ordinance to providing for one street alone, but may include in one ordinance provisions for an entire sewer system, without having the ordinance declared invalid as a double improvement.

Ill Walker v People (1898) 170 Ill 410, 48 NE 1010.

That the storm water drains provided for in a sewer construction ordinance may also be used for house connections will not render the ordinance invalid as a double improvement, since they are part of the main improvement.

Ill Ownby v Mattoon (1923) 306 Ill 552, 138 NE 110.

An ordinance providing for the construction of sidewalks in a certain street and the construction of a sewer for the purpose of draining such sidewalks is not invalid as a double improvement.

> **Ill**　Staunton v Bond (1917) 281 Ill 568, 118 NE 47.

An ordinance authorizing construction of a main sewer with branches is not invalid as providing for more than one improvement, since the branch sewers are merely integral parts of a single sewer system.

> **Ill**　Payne v South Springfield (1896) 161 Ill 285, 44 NE 105.

Ordinances combining the city's sewerage system and its waterworks system are not invalid on the ground that there is no necessary connection between the two systems, since each is complementary to the other in the interest of providing the city with pure, health-giving water and removing the same after contaminating it through use.

> **Mo**　Maryville v Cushman (1952) 363 Mo 87, 249 SW2d 347.

An ordinance passed to finance completion of a sewer outlet, hindered in construction by quicksand, is void, where a prior ordinance, declaring the whole of the city to be a sewer improvement district, undertook construction of the same outlet as the final step in building a sewer system, because the two ordinances contemplate but a single improvement exceeding 20 per cent of the value of the real property within the district.

> **Ark**　Rogers v Semmes (1916) 123 Ark 467, 185 SW 479.

The ordering by one resolution of a system of sewers covering about two-thirds of the city and involving two different sanitary boards, was not violative of the Constitution or charter.

> **Fla**　State v Miami (1946) 157 Fla 742, 27 So2d 112.

Where one ordinance prolongs an original sewer improvement district for the purpose of maintenance, and a second ordinance assesses the value of benefits to be received to owners of land within an annexation to the original district, both ordinances are void for failure to meet the statutory requirement that two ordinances—one to prolong the life and a second to assess the value of maintenance—be passed to prolong any single improvement district.

> **Ark**　Ragsdale v Cunningham (1941) 201 Ark 848, 147 SW2d 20.

C. Elections

§23. Necessity

While an ordinance authorizes a study in the feasibility of waste water disposal marks the beginning of a legislative history it is not necessary that a referendum petition be filed against it. A subsequent ordinance establishing the water treatment plant is subject to the referendum requirements as the actual operating ordinance for the waste water treatment system.

> **Ohio**   State ex rel Stanley v Avon (1974) 39 OS2d 150, 68 Op2d 96, 314 NE2d 167.

Ordinances that authorize the issuance and sale of revenue bonds for construction of a sewer system, sewage treatment and water system expansion, without a vote of the people, are valid, reasonable and nondiscriminatory exercises of the police power, within the provisions of state and federal Constitutions.

> **Ky**   Davis v Water-Sewer & Sanitation Comm (1963) 223 F Supp 902.

An ordinance authorizing issuance of certificates of indebtedness to improve and extend the city sewerage system is void where it is not submitted to the voters as required by the state Constitution, and its passage without a vote cannot be justified as a permitted emergency measure since no emergency exists.

> **Md**   Baltimore v Hofrichter (1940) 178 Md 91, 11 A2d 375.

That a sewer improvement ordinance is rejected by referendum will not bar reenactment of a substantially identical ordinance, in absence of any statutory bar to such repassage, since municipal residents have an immediate remedy to expunge the new ordinance, by way of petition or protest, and an ultimate remedy through exercise of voting rights at municipal elections.

> **NJ**   Cornell v Watchung (1967) 49 NJS 235, 229 A2d 630.

While a city's charter does not in express terms confer power on a city council to submit to voters the question of a bond issue for sewer construction such power is implied from the constitutional provision requiring the assent of voters to incur an indebtedness in any one year exceeding the income and revenue provided for such year.

> **Ky**   Kimbley v Owensboro (1917) 176 Ky 532, 195 SW 1087.
> Bain v Lexington (1909) 121 SW 620.

An ordinance establishing rates for use of a municipally owned sewage system, such service heretofore furnished without charge, is not subject to constitutional referendum though it proposes to use the money for payment of the cost of operation, maintenance, repair and management, since it does not propose the acquiring or construction of a utility, but merely provides for enlarging and improving an existing utility.

> **Ohio**   Fostoria v King (1950) 154 OS 213, 43 Op 1, 94 NE2d 697.

Where an ordinance authorizes a sewer agreement with another city for construction of a cooperative sewer system, a refusal by the electorate at two subsequent elections to provide for bonds for financing the agreement, does not constitute rejection by the voters of the agreement.

> **Mo**   Kansas City v Raytown (1967) 421 SW2d 504.

An ordinance that increases sewer charges is not subject to referendum, because the provisions for referendum do not apply to executive or administrative matters of the kind covered by the ordinance.

> **Fla**   State v St Petersburg (1952) 61 So2d 416.

Where the Constitution and a statute authorize creation of sewerage districts smaller than the territory of the municipality, a city may create sewerage districts composed of units smaller than its total corporate limits and may issue bonds for constructing, acquiring, extending and improving the sewer system if the action is approved by the electorate.

> **La**   Nanney v Leesville (1941) 198 La 773, 4 So2d 825.

§24. Procedural Requirements

Ordinances authorizing bond issues for sewer improvements are not invalid merely because the bond question was not submitted to the voters at the next regular election after the passage of a statute authorizing the issuance of bonds for such purposes, since the words "at the next regular city election" do not mean just any election but mean any regular city election at which city officers are chosen.

> **Ky**   Ahrens v Louisville (1920) 186 Ky 579, 217 SW 907.

Where an ordinance is adopted authorizing execution of an agreement with another city for a cooperative sewer system, and at two subsequent elections bond issues for financing the agreement are turned down by the electorate, an ordinance authorizing a third election for consideration of such bonds is construed to have been called on the question of a cooperative and not of a go-it-alone system, previous conduct on the part of some of the aldermen to the contrary notwithstanding.

> **Mo**   Kansas City v Raytown (1967) 421 SW2d 504.

Where an ordinance authorizes a sewer agreement with another city for construction of a cooperative sewer system, a refusal by the electorate at two subsequent elections to provide for bonds for financing the agreement does not constitute rejection by the voters of the agreement.

> **Mo**   Kansas City v Raytown (1967) 421 SW2d 504.

Under an ordinance submitting to voters the question whether a bonded indebtedness to finance sewer construction should be incurred, the requisite majority vote is based on the number of votes cast on the question of incurring the indebtedness, not on the number of qualified voters in the city or voting at a simultaneous election of city officers.

> **Ky** Fowler v Oakdale (1914) 158 Ky 603, 166 SW 195.

§25. Necessary Voter Information

Where the notice of election and the question on the ballot submitted to the voters for approval of a bond issue to partly finance a sewer system fail to state the sum to be raised annually by taxation, there is no substantial compliance with mandatory statutory provisions and the election is void.

> **Ky** Milton v Lawrenceburg (1939) 278 Ky 741, 129 SW2d 583.

An election approving a bond issue for a municipal sewer system is not invalidated on the ground that certain sewers shown on the only prospectus and plan available to the voters prior to the election are to be eliminated because of engineering difficulties, where the prospectus and plan were prepared in good faith on the strength of information obtained prior to election and the facts disclose that the elimination is made to restrict prohibitive costs, and does not result in abandonment of the service promised the public.

> **Va** Ennis v Herndon (1937) 168 Va 539, 191 SE 685.

An ordinance containing several propositions sought to be submitted to the electors of the city, including a bond issue for the construction and maintenance of a sewer system and a waterworks extension, substantially complies with the empowering statute that authorizes any city or town to provide for as many of the necessary improvements as the council may deem advisable, where at the time of voting the propositions are so clearly and distinctly submitted to the electors that they can intelligently and positively express their wishes with regard to each, or any, or all of the propositions so submitted.

> **Ida** Platt v Payette (1911) 19 Ida 470, 114 P 25.

Where the resolution providing for issuance of bonds for improving the city's sewerage system provides for retirement of such bonds over a 25-year maximum period, but the ballot submitted to the electors provides a maximum retirement period of 30 years, and the issuance of such bonds is approved by vote of the people, such misstatement in the ballot is not such a departure from the statute as could mislead, deceive or confuse the electorate.

> **Ohio** State ex rel Spitler v Beidleman (1953) 96 OA 210, 54 Op 260, 121 NE2d 561.

The validity of an ordinance submitting to voters a bond issue to construct a sewerage system is not affected merely because it provides that any remaining proceeds of the bond issue after the sewers are built shall be used for macadamizing streets, since the exact cost of the sewer system cannot be determined in advance, and the improvement of a city's streets is as essential to the prosperity of the city as are sewers.

   Ky   Ky Light v Williams & Co (1910) 124 SW 840.

§26. Preelection Publicity

A complaint that promoters of a sewer construction ordinance misled voters by false newspaper advertising concerning the way in which proceeds of the bond issue would be spent is not jurisdictional, and therefore cannot be the basis of a collateral attack on the ordinance.

   Ark   Boswell v Russellville (1954) 223 Ark 284, 265 SW2d 533.

IV. SPECIAL ASSESSMENTS

A.   PROPERTY OWNERS' DUTIES AND REMEDIES

§27. Notice and Hearing Requirements

A city council is not required to give notice to property owners of approval of preliminary plans, specifications and plats for construction in a sewer district where a petition for the improvement, signed by the owners of more than one-half of the proposed district, has been filed with the assessing authority and the city council has adopted a resolution finding the petition sufficient.

   Okla   Horton v Oklahoma City (1977) 566 P2d 431.

An ordinance creating a special service area and providing for its financing is not invalid for insufficient notice where the enabling statute provides that the notice be mailed "to the person or persons in whose name the general taxes for the last preceding year were paid on each lot within the special service area," that is, the owners of record, despite fact that the county sent some notices to mortgagees and did not send notice to all of the owners of record subsequently computed.

   Ill   Andrews v Madison County (1977) 54 IllAp3d 343, 369 NE2d 532.

A hearing on a special assessment is not a mandatory requirement when the assessment is based on a straight cost per front foot basis.

   Del   Paul Scotton Contracting Co v Mayor & Council of Dover (1972) 301 A2d 321.

A resolution ordering the city to construct a sanitary sewer system that complies with the publication of notice statute and provides ample opportunity for objections does not violate state or federal constitutional provisions for due process, and it is not necessary to give personal notice to owners of real estate whose property might become subject to assessment.

> **Neb**   Jones v Farnam (1963) 174 Neb 704, 119 NW2d 157.

Where an ordinance approved by the voters authorizes issuance of general obligation bonds for acquiring rights-of-way, and constructing, extending and improving the sanitary sewerage system of the city, and provides that the city in due course shall levy on benefited property by special assessments which the city shall use to reimburse itself for the amount paid or to be paid on the general obligation bonds, the bonds, in a statutory procedure for approval thereof, will not be declared invalid at the instance of assessed property owners. Notice to affected property owners and opportunity to be heard are not required.

> **Mo**   Raytown v Kemp (1961) 349 SW2d 363.

An ordinance authorized by charter and dividing a city into sewer districts, where no notice is given of proposed construction of relief sewers or of levying taxes exceeding the mill limit, is not invalid for want of due process.

> **Minn**   Delinquent Polk County Real Est Taxes, In re (1920) 147 Minn 344, 180 NW 240.

A municipal administrative code provision that a sewer assessment shall not be vacated or set aside for any omission to advertise, or for irregularity in advertising any resolution or notice is to prevent the setting aside of assessments because of technical irregularities or defects, but cannot be construed so as to dispense with constitutional requirements necessary to authorize an assessment.

> **NY**   Emigrant Industrial Sav Bk v New York City (1946) 62 NYS2d 87.

Where real property owners sue to recover money paid by them under protest as assessments levied for construction of a sewer, no recovery is authorized where no fraud is claimed since an administrative code section provides that no assessment for a local improvement shall be vacated or set aside by reason of any omission to advertise or for irregularity in advertising any notice or other proceeding relative to the improvement except in cases in which fraud is shown.

> **NY**   Emigrant Industrial Sav Bk v New York City (1946) 62 NYS2d 87.

Where a city by its constitutional charter is authorized to establish sewer districts and to construct sewers therein, an ordinance so adopted and assessing costs against benefited property is enacted under delegated legislative authority from the Constitution itself, and not being inconsistent with any general law enacted by the legislature, does not require notice and hearing to property owners on the question whether property would be benefited by establishment of the district.

> **Mo**   Haeussler Inv v Bates (1924) 306 Mo 392, 267 SW 632.

Where statutes authorize any municipal corporation having a population not less than 1,000 to establish a general sewer system and to cause district sewers to be constructed within districts having limits prescribed by ordinance, the cost to be apportioned against all lots and pieces of ground in proportion to area, no hearing is necessary to determine how assessments will be apportioned by an ordinance.

> **Okla**   Hancock v Muskogee (1919) 250 US 454, 63 LEd 1081, 39 SCt 528.

Under an ordinance apportioning sewer costs and assessing abutting owners' property, if the property owner is given an opportunity to be heard at some time during the assessment proceedings, before liability attaches, the constitutional requirement of due process is satisfied.

> **Ky**   Shaw v Mayfield (1924) 204 Ky 618, 265 SW 13.

An ordinance providing for an assessment with no opportunity for hearing until completion of construction, contrary to an express provision of a statute, is void.

> **Colo**   Ellis v La Salle (1922) 72 Colo 244, 211 P 104.

ANNOTATION

Inclusion or exclusion of first and last days in computing time for giving notice of drain or drainage district hearing which must be given a certain number of days before a known future date, 98 ALR2d 1396.

§28. Ordinance Publication Requirements

An ordinance levying an assessment for sewer construction, though defective in some details, is valid where it is published according to statute, and where the ordinance creating the sewer district and authorizing construction is in accordance with statute, is sufficient to give property owners notice, is duly published, and no objection or protest is filed.

> **Okla**   Bartlesville v Keeler (1924) 107 Okla 14, 229 P 450.

It is essential for its validity that a special assessment ordinance with an estimated cost of improvement construction exceeding $100,000, comply with the local improvement act requiring publication.

> **Ill**   Waukegan v Lyon (1912) 253 Ill 452, 97 NE 848.

An ordinance establishing a sewer district to be financed by sewer warrants must be published or posted unless it is an emergency ordinance.

> **Okla**   Bonney v Smith (1944) 194 Okla 106, 147 P2d 771.

§29. Laches and Time Limitations for Protest

A charter requirement that notice of intention to contest special sewer assessments be given within 30 days after confirmation of the special assessment roll, and that suit be commenced within 60 days after such confirmation is invalid, being in conflict with the state statute of limitations.

> **Mich**   Wells v Southfield (1968) 14 Mich Ap 393, 165 NW2d 606.

Where an ordinance purports to create a sewer district and to authorize the construction of sewers at the cost of property owners, and property owners sit by and allow the improvements to be made without taking legal steps to prevent it, they are guilty of laches and cannot thereafter attack irregularities in the proceedings.

> **Okla**   Coalgate v Gentilini (1915) 51 Okla 552, 152 P 95.

Where a city acquires jurisdiction to construct a sewer at the expense of the abutting property owners by enactment and publication of appropriate ordinances, an owner who stands by and sees the sewer constructed with knowledge that he is to be assessed therefor is guilty of laches and barred from enjoining the collection of special assessments.

> **Okla**   Muskogee v Rambo (1914) 40 Okla 672, 138 P 567.

Where an ordinance levying assessments for lateral sewers is void as to a particular assessment, an action to enjoin collection of the void assessment is not barred by limitations or laches. The 60-day statute of limitation applies to suits involving procedural irregularities, but does not apply to jurisdictional defects that render the proceedings void.

> **Okla**   Amer-First Nat Bk v Peterson (1934) 169 Okla 588, 38 P2d 957.
> Woodward v Tulsa (1921) 81 Okla 58, 196 P 683.

Where an ordinance or resolution declaring the necessity for sewer improvements has been properly adopted and published, an action to set aside or enjoin the collection of assessments is barred if not instituted within 15 days after publication of the assessment ordinance.

> **Okla**   Burbank v Sheel (1928) 131 Okla 292, 268 P 1106.

Where a sewer district has been properly created, an action to set aside the property assessments or bonds issued pursuant thereto is barred unless instituted within 60 days from the date of enactment of the assessment ordinance.

> **Okla**   Woodward v Tulsa (1921) 81 Okla 58, 196 P 683.

§ 30. Estoppel

Where adequate legal notice is given an assessment may not be contested after completion of the improvement if the opponents did not appear at the public hearing and file protest or legal action.

> **Fla**   Whitman v North Miami (1969) 223 So2d 105.

Under an ordinance assessing abutting property owners for the cost of the construction of a sewer, an abutting owner is not estopped by silence to question the validity of the assessment unless he knew that the improvement was being made, he had knowledge that the public authorities intended and were making the improvement on the faith that the cost was to be paid by the abutting owners, he knew of the infirmity or defect in the proceedings, and some special benefit accrued to the owner's property, distinct from the benefits enjoyed by the citizens generally.

> **Alas**   Ketchikan Delinquent Tax Roll, In re (1922) 6 Alas 653.

Where property owners know a sewer improvement is being made pursuant to an ordinance and do not raise any objection during the progress of the work, they are not estopped to question the validity of the proceedings after the work has been completed where the defect is jurisdictional. A property owner need not take notice of an improvement made without statutory authority.

> **Ky**   Mulligan v McGregor (1915) 165 Ky 122, 176 SW 1129.

An ordinance assessing costs of a sewer against abutting property, as specified by a panel of viewers prior to construction, is valid though not all benefited property is assessed, where the assessed owners had constructive notice of the assessment and made no objection until completion of the sewer.

> **Ore**   Houck v Roseburg (1910) 56 Ore 238, 108 P 186.

Where a property owner stands by and allows construction work on sewers to proceed to completion, he may not avoid the assessment by contending that the city engineer exercised legislative authority under the ordinance, since by statute no error in the proceedings will exempt the property from payment after the work has been done as required by either the ordinance or the contract.

Ky Noland v Mildenberger (1906) 123 Ky 660, 97 SW 24.

A property owner cannot have an ordinance authorizing construction of a sewer and assessment of the cost against benefited property declared unconstitutional as a deprivation of property without due process, on the claim that he was not accorded a hearing on the assessment of benefits, and that certain benefited tracts were not included, where he availed himself of the benefits by connecting his premises with the completed sewer.

Mo St Louis Malleable Casting v Prendergast Const Co (1922) 260 US 496, 67 LE2d 351, 43 SCt-178.

Where proceedings to construct a sewer are undertaken by a resolution of the city council naming a date for a hearing, and landowners do not appear at the hearing or seek to be heard, an ordinance thereafter adopted for construction of the sewer, and for assessment of the costs will not be held invalid on a claim that the amounts assessed exceed the value of the property assessed, in the absence of a showing of fraud.

Mo Giers Improvement Co v Inv Service (1950) 361 Mo 504, 235 SW2d 355.

Where an ordinance of necessity for the establishment of a sewer district and for the construction of sewers is regularly passed and published, no protests are filed, and the sewer is constructed without objection by the property owners, an injunction will not lie to restrain the authorities from issuing tax warrants against the property, though the advertisement for sealed bids for construction of the sewer may have been defective.

Okla Barnett v Waynoka (1930) 148 Okla 24, 296 P 972.

Where an ordinance creating a sewer district was passed and published, the sewer improvements were made and accepted and a property assessment ordinance enacted, and certificates of indebtedness were issued, an injunction will not lie to review irregularities in the proceedings.

Okla Orr v Cushing (1917) 66 Okla 153, 168 P 223.

§31. Refunding Assessments

Where an ordinance authorizes construction of a sewer and assessment of costs against benefited property, and a subsequent ordinance adopted by popular vote authorizes payment for the sewer by a bond issue increasing the city's indebtedness, and at the same time authorizes refunds of assessments theretofore paid or to be paid, a later ordinance authorizing such reimbursement to be made to any person who has paid such tax bills does not authorize a refund to a present owner who purchased the property after the tax bill had been paid.

> **Mo**   State v Kimball (1926) 313 Mo 460, 282 SW 30.

An ordinance over-assessing abutting properties for sewer improvements is not void for that reason. The excess amounts received should be held for distribution ratably to those who paid them, and those who elected to pay over a 20-year period should have their payments adjusted.

> **RI**   Garcia v Falkenholm (1964) 97 RI 450, 198 A2d 660.

Where statutes fix the interest and penalties to be charged on delinquent special assessments for improvements of districts established before the adoption of the home rule charter, and the charter also fixes the interest and penalties, a city may not, without a grant of special power, accept payment of assessments without accrued interest and penalties by adopting an ordinance to that effect, since to hold otherwise would be to read into the charter an alternative not within the intent of the electors adopting the charter, or within the spirit of the law.

> **Neb**   Falldorf v Grand Island (1940) 138 Neb 212, 292 NW 598.

§32. Installment Payments

The legislature can grant authority to a municipality to compel a property owner to pay a sewer assessment levied under an ordinance in installments, and an ordinance is likewise valid where it requires the assessment to be paid in a lump sum, for the manner of payment is for the legislature to determine.

> **Ky**   Krumpelman v Louisville & Jefferson County (1958) 314 SW2d 557.

Where an ordinance assessing the cost of a sewer construction, expressly providing for payment in installments by the abutting property owners and fixing the time when installments are due is authorized by statute, a property owner has a prima facie right to connect with and use the sewer before full payment is made where he is not in default in his installment payments.

> **Pa**   Bick & Co v George (1933) 313 Pa 77, 169 A 224.

An ordinance making a sewer assessment a lien unless the board of trustees by resolution determines that it may be paid in installments in future years, in which case there is a separate lien for each installment only as it becomes due, does not disclose any intention or attempt by the village to meet the requirements of the statute for installment assessments and the adoption of a

15-year maturity period for the bond issue itself would not necessarily suspend the fixation of the full lien.

> **NY** Ackley v Lawyers Title Ins (1958) 16 Misc2d 402, 182 NYS2d 76.

An ordinance provision authorizing a special sewer improvement and the issue of warrants, that in the event any installment or interest is not paid when due the whole amount of the special tax then unpaid shall become due and payable as to that particular property, is enforceable by mandamus so as to require the sale of the property to collect the entire amount due.

> **Utah** Stinson v Godbe (1916) 48 Utah 444, 160 P 280.

B. Municipal Authority and Duties

§33. Power to Levy Special Assessments

When a municipal ordinance which imposes a charge for sewer use is specifically governed by a state statute permitting cities to assess, without prior notice or hearing, users of sewers a charge for such use, the sewer charge is not a tax which can be attacked as being levied without satisfying state statutory conditions.

> **RI** Costello v Ricci (1979) 401 A2d 38.

A special assessment for preliminary costs in a sewer improvement project may be assessed against the property owners. There is a special benefit conferred on the property in the knowledge that sewer and waste water treatment plants will be or should be constructed and the estimated costs and methods of construction.

> **Ohio** Arvidson v Bd of County Comm (1971) 27 OM 93, 269 NE2d 432.

A sewer assessment against the public school district may be collected when the city's charter authorizes the levy of special assessments against all political subdivisions except the United States and the state.

> **Fla** Titusville v Bd of Public Instructions of Brevard County (1970) 258 So2d 836.

A charter provision that enumerates powers and further provides that they are not exclusive but that other powers implied or appropriate to the exercise are included gives the city the right to make an assessment for sewer and water installation.

> **Del** Paul Scotton Contracting Co v Mayor & Council of Dover (1972) 301 A2d 321.

A local improvement assessment to separate storm sewers and sanitary sewers with repaving and the installation of curbs and gutters is a local improvement.

The fact that separation of the two systems is required by the Environmental Protection Act does not nullify the local benefit in the affected area and thus require that a general assessment be attached.

Ill Hinsdale v Lowenstine (1974) 23 IllAp3d 357, 319 NE2d 83.

A front footage assessment based on one-half of the cost of the sewer construction, adjusted to benefit, is a valid method of collecting for sewer construction. Since a completely equitable manner of financing is not available, a method which reasonably compensates the town for the cost based on the benefit to the property owners is valid in the absence of bad faith.

NH Yencing Rlty Co v Concord (1976) 116 NH 580, 364 A2d 875.

Since municipal corporations have no inherent power to levy special assessments, such authority must originate either in provisions of the organic law, or in some statute conferring it, either expressly or by necessary implication so clear as necessarily to reveal a purpose to grant the power.

Neb Falldorf v Grand Island (1940) 138 Neb 212, 292 NW 598.

That the city formerly built all sewers from taxes or from proceeds of general obligation bonds, and that as a consequence a taxpayer, paying the cost of such bonds and now being required to pay the costs of special assessments for sewer construction, is suffering an inequality in the tax burden in violation of a constitutional provision is not a valid argument. Although a local assessment imposes an involuntary burden on the property improved, it is not strictly speaking a tax within the purview of the constitutional provision.

Ky Krumpelman v Louisville & Jefferson County (1958) 314 SW2d 557.

The legislative power delegated to a city to construct local improvements and levy assessments therefor is to be strictly construed, and every reasonable doubt about the extent or limitation of such power is resolved against the city and in favor of the taxpayer.

Neb Besack v Beatrice (1951) 154 Neb 142, 47 NW2d 356.

Power of a city to make public improvements does not of itself confer power to enact an ordinance levying and collecting special taxes or assessments therefor.

Neb Besack v Beatrice (1951) 154 Neb 142, 47 NW2d 356.

Where a city has charter authority to construct sewers and assess the costs against benefited properties through establishment of sewer districts, an ordinance establishing a sewer district entirely within the city limits is not invalid though by statute the city is authorized to provide for the establishment of sanitary districts for sewers over areas lying partly within and partly without the corporate limits, since the authorization is optional and not mandatory. Accordingly, tax bills issued against benefited property will not be declared invalid where the owner of an assessed tract also owns adjoining property outside the city limits which might well have been included in the project.

Mo Jennings Heights Land & Improvement v St Louis (1914) 257 Mo 291, 165 SW 741.

ANNOTATION

Tax sale as freeing property from possibility of further assessments for benefits to land, 11 ALR2d 1133.

§34. Procedural Requirements

An ordinance establishing a municipal service taxing unit for the acquisition of sewer and water treatment systems and issuance of general obligation bonds is valid. The fact that the ordinance was passed as an emergency is a debatable matter and will not be overruled in the absence of the decision being arbitrary.

Fla Speer v Olson (1978) 367 So2d 207.

Where the county council has power to levy unpaid sewer service charges as an assessment upon property, the levy is invalid when the county council attempts to enact it by resolution rather than by ordinance.

Del Wilmington Tr Co v Caratello (1978) 385 A2d 1131.

The requirement that the determination of a special sewer assessment be included in the initial ordinance does not require a specific dollar and cents determination. Since costs would be unknown at the time of passing the improvement ordinance, an individual's assessment would be a rough guess at best.

Ore Gilbert v Eugene (1970) 255 Ore 289, 465 P2d 880.

A combination of two improvements commenced in different years is invalid. They must be related by the time at which they are instituted, not when they are completed.

Minn Quality Homes v New Brighton (1971) 289 Minn 274, 183 NW2d 555.

The fact that the assessment per square foot is higher than estimated at the first hearing on an improvement district for sewer and water does not make the assessment invalid nor require a second hearing. A mistake in estimating the amount of property subject to the assessment rather than the cost of the project being the cause of the initial lower estimate does not make the hearing a sham.

Minn Hartle v Glencoe (1975) 303 Minn 262, 226 NW2d 914.

The detailed procedure set forth in a statute for the levying of an assessment for the construction of a sewer is mandatory and jurisdictional; and an ordinance passed by the council without following that procedure is invalid. Moreover, the defects can not be validated by an attempted ratification of a subsequently elected council.

Alas Ashley v Anchorage (1951) 13 Alas 168, 95 F Supp 189.

Failure to follow charter directives to estimate the cost of a street improvement, to set up an assessment district, and give notice to persons interested before imposing the assessment or contracting for the improvement violates due process and invalidates an ordinance and sewer improvement assessment for lack of jurisdiction.

NY Schenectady Sewer Assessment, In re (1929) 134 Misc 810, 236 NYS 455.

Where a special assessment for sewer construction is levied without compliance with jurisdictional requirements, it is void and may be assailed collaterally.

Neb Besack v Beatrice (1951) 154 Neb 142, 47 NW2d 356.

Methods prescribed by statutes granting to first class cities authority to levy special assessments for construction of sewers or drains is fundamentally mandatory and jurisdictional, and any assessments otherwise imposed are void and the doctrine of estoppel has no application.

Neb Besack v Beatrice (1951) 154 Neb 142, 47 NW2d 356.

The levying of an assessment for construction of a sewer before the acquisition of the land needed will not affect the validity of the assessment ordinance.

Ill Maywood v Maywood (1892) 140 Ill 216, 29 NE 704.

A tax provided for in an ordinance for the construction of a main artery of a sewer system of a particular district, may not be levied and collected in advance of its completion.

Iowa Sanborn v Mason City (1901) 114 Iowa 189, 86 NW 286.

An ordinance assessing benefits in a prolonged sewer improvement district "according to the assessment list . . . in the office of the city clerk . . . as may be annually readjusted by the board of assessors" is void for failure of the board of assessors to make a direct assessment in accordance with statute.

> **Ark**   Ragsdale v Cunningham (1941) 201 Ark 848, 147 SW2d 20.

Property owners attacking the validity of a sewer assessment ordinance have the burden to show that the assessments are illegal by reason of lack of authority, of defects of substance in the proceedings, or of discriminatory and arbitrary fixing of the portions of the cost to be borne by owners without regard to benefits.

> **NY**   Improvement of Constr of 12 Inch Lateral Sewer, In re (1959) 24 Misc2d 618, 194 NYS2d 279.

§35. Discretion in Determining Property Benefited and Necessity for Improvement

A determination that benefits will accrue to property divided into lots with a depth of 135 feet is reasonable despite the fact that an adjoining subdivision has lots with a depth of only 94 feet. When the legislative determination of benefit is reasonable, it must be upheld despite a decision by the trial judge that his determination of benefits is more reasonable.

> **Ariz**   Peoria v Hensley (1976) 26 ArizApp 30, 545 P2d 992.

A determination that property will be benefited by a contract for sewer treatment by an adjoining town is within the council's authority. It is unnecessary that plans for the project be included since it involves the use of existing facilities.

> **Cal**   Dawson v Los Altos Hills (1976) 16 CA3d 676, 547 P2d 1377, 129 CaR 97.

The determination of benefit to substantiate an assessment on a square foot basis does not necessarily reflect an advance or increase in market value resulting from the improvement, but embraces actual increase in money value and potential as well as added use and enjoyment of the property. A finding of benefit is presumably correct and can only be overcome by strong, direct, clear, and positive proof.

> **Fla**   Meyer v Oakland Park (1969) 219 So2d 417.

The council's determination that property has benefited by a sewer improvement is conclusive unless its action was palpably arbitrary and abusive.

> **Ore**   Gilbert v Eugene (1970) 255 Ore 289, 465 P2d 880.

"Benefits," referring to sewage assessments, is not referable to the general definition, but denotes a special or particular advantage to a special or particular tract of land. A general benefit to the general health and welfare of the city does not require the city to pay a portion of the assessment, where the benefit to the particular tract of land equals the costs.

Ind Indiano v Indianapolis (1971) 148 IndAp 637, 269 NE2d 552.

It is a fact question whether property that is zoned rural reaps rural benefits from a sewer installation.

Ariz Hensley v Peoria (1971) 14 ArizAp 581, 485 P2d 570.

An ordinance providing for a sewer line and levying an assessment therefor is conclusive of the necessity for the improvement, and in applying rules of special assessments for the construction and maintenance to an individual property owner the courts are permitted to interfere only in rare and extreme cases when it is clear that the principle of equality has been entirely ignored and gross injustice done.

NC Raleigh v Mercer (1967) 271 NC 114, 155 SE2d 551.

The question of the necessity for a local improvement being legislative in nature, it is only where the evidence is clear that the action of the municipal authority was taken without reasonable grounds and is oppressive that the courts will interfere to declare such an ordinance unreasonable.

Ill Millstadt v Bereitschaft (1931) 344 Ill 550, 176 NE 746.

A sewer line abuts a tract of land when it crosses a private road which is a part and parcel of the land and is in the control of the owner. The land is therefore subject to assessment on a showing of special benefit.

Ill Chicago Ridge, In re Assessment (1975) 27 IllAp3d 1027, 327 NE2d 422.

Under a statute authorizing sewer assessments a city is given absolute power, in its discretion, to install sewers and apportion the cost by levying special assessments on the property specially benefited; and one who acquires an interest in the land takes it subject to the right not only of the proper governmental authorities to levy general taxes on it but also of a city to impose the burden of paying the expenses of necessary public improvements that confer on the property a special benefit.

Ky Krumpelman v Louisville & Jefferson County (1958) 314 SW2d 557.
Allen v Woods (1898) 20 KLR 59, 45 SW 106.
Mo Giers Improvement Corp v Inv Service (1950) 361 Mo 504, 235 SW2d 355.
Kirksville v Harrington (1930) 225 MoApp 309, 35 SW2d 614.
Ore Beckett v Portland (1909) 53 Ore 169, 99 P 659.

An ordinance authorizing construction of a joint sewer in a joint sewer district will not be held invalid on the ground that the sewer was constructed in greater dimensions than necessary, in order to carry off waters draining an area outside the district, since the action of the city in authorizing the sewer is a final determination of the necessity therefor, in the absence of proof of fraud or that the establishment of the district was arbitrary or unreasonable, or that assessments were palpably unjust and oppressive.

Mo   Kirkwood v Hillcrest Rlty (1921) 234 SW 1023.

Whether to divide a city into drainage areas and then treat the entire system as one unit for the purpose of assessing costs of sewer construction rests in the sound discretion of the city council.

Ky   Lawson v Greenup (1929) 227 Ky 414, 13 SW2d 281.

A petition by a majority of the resident property holders is not a prerequisite to enactment of an ordinance of necessity for establishment of a sewer district and construction of sewers, with the cost to be assessed against abutting property. The city council and mayor are authorized to take such action without the filing of a petition, but are required to take such action on the filing of a petition.

Okla   Perry v Davis & Younger (1907) 18 Okla 427, 90 P 865.

Due process does not require notice or opportunity to be heard regarding a city council's determination that sewers in a specified area are necessary as a health measure, though such determination may result in foreclosing interested landowners from an opportunity to protest. However, where an assessment is imposed, a property owner must be notified of the proposed improvement and given an opportunity to object to the assessment against his property.

Cal   Hoffman v Red Bluff (1965) 63 C2d 584, 47 CaR 553, 407 P2d 857.

A complaint alleging that an ordinance establishing a storm sewer district and providing for the construction of a storm sewer is arbitrary, capricious, and illegal, that the question of benefits to property owners is disregarded, that property holders are deprived of property without due process of law, and that property owners will not be benefited by the sewer suffices to entitle the property owners to an injunction against construction of the sewer.

Colo   Cook v Denver (1954) 128 Colo 578, 265 P2d 700.

Where the city charter authorizes establishment of "necessary" sewers only, and the city council has no charter authority to establish a sewer and assess part of the expense against abutting landowners without a finding of necessity, the court need not consider the effect of an ordinance which provides that whenever the public health and convenience require the laying and establishing of a sewer it shall be done in accordance with the provisions of the charter, since such ordinance operates merely as a restriction upon the exercise of a power conferred by charter.

> **Vt**   Fisher v St Albans (1914) 87 Vt 524, 90 A 582.

A special assessment ordinance enacted for sewer construction, which recites that the assessed area is drained by the sewer, sufficiently complies with a charter requirement that property assessed be "directly benefited".

> **Ore**   Rogers v Salem (1912) 61 Ore 321, 122 P 308.

An ordinance assessing costs of a sewer against benefited property is enforceable against a parcel not abutting on the sewer and not described in the initiatory proceedings under a charter provision not requiring the exact fixing of property to be benefited by an improvement until late in the proceedings.

> **Ore**   Giles v Roseburg (1920) 96 Ore 453, 189 P 401.

Whether an ordinance for the establishment of a sewer system to be financed by special assessment is reasonable is determined from a consideration of the situation and condition of the whole territory embraced within the system, not merely by that of the property of persons objecting.

> **Ill**   Millstadt v Bereitschaft (1931) 344 Ill 550, 176 NE 746.
> Washburn v Chicago (1902) 198 Ill 506, 64 NE 1064.
> **Iowa**   Chicago M & S P Ry v Phillips (1900) 111 Iowa 377, 82 NW 787.
> **Ore**   Masters v Portland (1893) 24 Ore 161, 33 P 540.

An ordinance levying an assessment on the property of a railroad to pay for the construction of a sewer in a sewer district, based on valuations made by the executive council of the state, the relevant statutes providing no means for a separate valuation of the real and personal property of a railroad, is void, as being in part a tax on personal property for the construction of a sewer.

> **Iowa**   Chicago M & S P Ry v Phillips (1900) 111 Iowa 377, 82 NW 787.

An owner challenging the validity of assessments, under an ordinance for sewer improvements, has the burden of showing that a wrong basis of apportionment was followed and that under a proper method he would be required to pay less.

> **Ky**   Bayes v Paintsville (1915) 166 Ky 679, 179 SW 623.

An ordinance establishing a sewer district may not be declared void as discriminatory merely because it embraces certain territory and excludes other, where it appears that for financial or economic reasons not all the territory in the city is included in the district.

> **Ky**   Francis v Bowling Green (1935) 259 Ky 525, 82 SW2d 804.

§36. Necessity of Benefit

Municipal sewer assessments are void if an assessment substantially and materially exceeds the special benefits conferred.

Cal Los Angeles v Offner (1961) 55 C2d 103, 10 CaR 470, 358 P2d 926.
Ky Maysville v Coughlin (1966) 399 SW2d 297.
Krumpelman v Louisville & Jefferson County (1958) 314 SW2d 557.
Mont Power v Helena (1911) 43 Mont 336, 116 P 415.
NY Improvement of Constr of 12 Inch Lateral Sewer, In re (1959) 24 Misc2d 618, 194 NYS2d 279.
Ohio Kangesser Foundation v Euclid (1959) 159 NE2d 919.

An assessment basing cost on zoning and optimum land use is arbitrary and disproportionate. A building used for offices which is permitted in an area for multiple residential buildings does not have the need nor receive the benefits that the optimum use permits.

Fla 7800 Building v South Miami (1974) 305 So2d 860.

Property which is zoned open space and open space-urban development must be excused from future assessments for sewer assessment. The property does not have access to the sewer lines constructed and the reclassification would require that property owners pay for a service for which they have no benefit and would constitute inverse condemnation.

Cal Furey v Sacramento (1978) 81 CA3d 483, 146 CaR 485, reh (1978) 85 CA3d 464, 149 CaR 541.

An assessment may not include the cost of a lift station where a statute specifically excludes such costs, and requires the municipality to pay them, as a benefit to the public in general.

Fla Whitman v North Miami (1969) 223 So2d 105.

Property that has been previously assessed for a sewer trunk line may not be reassessed for a new trunk line from which it received no benefit. Only that portion of the total property that received special benefits from the new sewer line may be assessed.

Minn Independent Sch Dist No 709 v Duluth (1970) 177 NW2d 812.

Two or more improvements that benefit a community may be combined and the average cost assessed against each lot owner. A combination of sewer and water improvements that are not directly connected benefits all the lots in the various projects equally, and the improvements taken as a whole confer special benefits equal to or in excess of the assessment.

Minn Quality Homes v New Brighton (1970) 289 Minn 274, 183 NW2d 555.

The levy, by a municipality, of a special assessment on the owner of private property for the cost of a public sewer improvement in substantial excess of the special benefits accruing to him is, to the extent of such excess, a taking of private property for public use without compensation.

    Mont   Power v Helena (1911) 43 Mont 336, 116 P 415.

Where under an ordinance levying assessments for sewer construction against abutting owners some of the lots assessed are unimproved or are of such a grade that the sewer is of no present use to them, the assessments are not invalid as conferring no benefits since not only is the sewer available to be used when the lots are improved, thereby bringing them new value, but also the health and welfare of the whole city and particularly of the neighborhood is enhanced.

    Ky   Congleton Co v Turner (1934) 256 Ky 788, 77 SW2d 23.
           Baker v Princeton (1928) 226 Ky 409, 11 SW2d 94.
    NM Chapman v Albuquerque (1959) 65 NM 228, 335 P2d 558.

An ordinance imposing special assessments for "the privilege of using" the sewers is unconstitutional where the Constitution grants the right to assess abutting landowners for the "use of sewers" since the constitutional meaning of "use" is "use in fact" or "actual use" not merely the privilege.

    Va   Southern Ry v Richmond (1940) 175 Va 308, 8 SE2d 271, 127 ALR2d 1368.

Where an ordinance and statute provide that assessments shall be made in proportion to special benefits, a lot derives special benefit from a sewer constructed so connection can be made since the opportunity for individual use determines special benefit.

    Iowa Bennett v Emmetsburg (1908) 138 Iowa 67, 115 NW 582.

A charge provided for by an ordinance requiring payment to be made, not only by those availing themselves of the right to connect with a sewer, but also by those to whom it is made available merely by its presence, and imposed without regard to the extent or value of the use made of the facilities, is in legal effect a tax, and the obligation to pay it can be created only by the municipality's exercise of its general taxing power. As a tax it violates a state constitutional provision requiring uniformity.

    Pa   Philadelphia, Petition of (1940) 340 Pa 17, 16 A2d 32.

An ordinance assessing the cost of sewer construction is invalid as to a parcel of land that is not and cannot be drained by the sewer.

    Ore Duniway v Cellars-Murton (1919) 92 Ore 113, 179 P 561.

An ordinance assessing sewer costs to property not abutting the sewer line, but found by the city council to benefit therefrom, is valid where some benefit accrues to the assessed nonabutting property, though the property could be more economically drained in another direction.

Ore Beckett v Portland (1909) 53 Ore 169, 99 P 659.

An assessment for sewer construction is invalid as to nonabutting owners where the ordinance does not specifically state that benefited, nonabutting property shall be assessed.

Ore Kirkpatrick v Dallas (1911) 58 Ore 511, 115 P 424.

An ordinance authorizing construction of a joint district sewer and assessing costs against property in the district is not invalid merely because some of the assessed property is not adjacent to the sewer, in the absence of an affirmative showing that the city acted arbitrarily, fraudulently or oppressively.

Mo Heman Constr v Lyon (1919) 277 Mo 628, 211 SW 68.

While a municipality, under an enabling statute, may provide for and impose a special assessment for establishment of a sewer system, it may not impose charges for construction of a sewer system at some future time to serve undetermined people.

Ill Norwick v Winfield (1967) 81 IllAp2d 197, 225 NE2d 30.

An ordinance providing for a sewer along a street, the half of which is not provided with water mains, is not unreasonable, where a court has power under the Local Improvement Act to modify the assessment roll so that no lot shall be assessed more than it is benefited.

Ill Rochelle v McConaughy (1921) 296 Ill 309, 129 NE 740.

§37. Benefited Lands Exempted

A special assessment for a trunk sewer line, which is applied only to abutting owners, is invalid. The municipality, by excluding assessment against parties who will subsequently be attached to the line, creates an unusually heavy burden on some without considering the benefit to others.

Minn Quality Homes v New Brighton (1971) 289 Minn 274, 183 NW2d 555.

The requirement that "all other pertinent facts relating to the loan, including the method of payment," does not include a requirement that the length of term of water and sewer improvement bonds and the amount of annual tax to be levied must be included. The resolution and published notice which provided that repayment shall be by full faith and credit of the city and which specified the amount of money to be borrowed and the manner in which the money is to be spent constitutes sufficient compliance. Specifying the length of time for maturity and the amount of taxes to be levied is an impractical restriction on a city attempting to enter the bond sale market.

Del   Kirby v Milford (1975) 350 A2d 760.

Where an ordinance authorizes organization of a sewer district and execution of a contract for the construction thereof and the issuance of special tax bills against the real estate within the district, and the district includes a lot in the process of being condemned by the city for use as a public parkway, the city is not liable for payment of tax bills against said lot, since such charge against the city is forbidden by its charter. The hardship imposed on the contractor was a contemplated and calculated risk based on the possibility that the special tax bills might be invalid.

Mo   Municipal Securities v Kansas City (1915) 265 Mo 252, 177 SW 856.

An ordinance authorizing payment by the city of an installment of assessment for a county interceptor sewer against benefited property annexed after completion of the sewer is not in conflict with a statute providing that funds collected from a sewer rental charge shall not be used for extension of a sewer system to unsewered areas since the subject portion of the sewer is an "extension" of the city sewerage system within the city and is not an "unsewered" area.

Ohio   Mead-Richer v Toledo (1961) 114 OA 369, 19 Op2d 389, 182 NE2d 846.

Where an ordinance authorizes construction of a sewer and assessment of costs against benefited property, and one piece of property so assessed is in the process of being condemned under an ordinance authorizing construction of a public parkway but the sewer is completed and assessments thereon are made prior to completion of the condemnation proceedings, the city after taking over the condemned property, which was subject to the sewer assessment, is not liable for the assessment under the terms of the ordinance.

Mo   Municipal Securities v Kansas City (1918) 246 US 63, 62 LEd 79, 38 SCt 224.

Where a turnpike road is within a taxing district designated by an ordinance for sewer improvements, a city, having authority to control streets or highways within the limits fixed by law, has power to construct sewers along such road and to assess the cost against abutting owners.

Ky   Lewis v Schmidt (1897) 19 KLR 1315, 43 SW 433.

That a city will be liable for the costs of sewer construction in front of county property does not invalidate an ordinance relating to said sewer construction unless the debt thus created exceeds the income of the city for that year, in violation of constitutional debt limitations.

> **Ky**   Lawson v Greenup (1929) 227 Ky 414, 13 SW2d 281.

The exemption of public property from "taxation" as provided in the state constitution does not carry an exemption from special assessments for public sewer improvements. Consequently, a city may levy a special assessment for public improvements on real property owned by the State Highway Commission.

> **Kan**   State Highway Comm v Topeka (1964) 193 Kan 335, 393 P2d 1008.

Under an ordinance assessing abutting owners' property for costs of sewer construction, fabricated sale of a portion of a lot abutting the improvement, with intent to avoid an assessment, will not operate to exempt any part of the property.

> **Ky**   Bayes v Paintsville (1915) 166 Ky 679, 179 SW 623.

Where an ordinance authorizes establishment of a sewer district and construction of a sewer, costs assessed against benefited property may include land owned by a cemetery association which holds the fee title to an entire tract, including occupied burial lots for the use of which purchasers hold only an easement.

> **Mo**   Mt St Mary's Cemetery Assn v Mullins (1919) 248 US 501, 63 LEd 383, 39 SCt 173.

An ordinance assessing a parcel of land for the cost of a sewer which reaches such parcel by trespass across an adjoining parcel is unenforceable while the city is attempting to acquire a right-of-way across the trespassed land.

> **Ore**   Duniway v Cellars-Murton (1919) 92 Ore 113, 179 P 561.

Vacant real estate owned by a state university, but not actually used for any governmental purposes in connection with its affairs, can be subjected to an ordinance levying a special assessment for local improvements.

> **Mich**   Auditor Gen, In re (1917) 199 Mich 489, 165 NW 771.

§38. Rules for Apportioning Assessments

In determining the benefits to be received by property from an extension of a sewer line in an area presently served by a private system the cost of the private system may not be deducted from the present value of the land. A determination that the assessment only exceeded the benefits in a small amount makes the assessment invalid, and the determination to deduct the cost of the private system is an unreasonable reduction of the present cash value of the property.

Minn   Carlson-Lang Rlty Co v Windom (1976) 307 Minn 368, 240 NW2d 517.

A sewer assessment ordinance providing for front footage assessment, but an equitable formula for corner property and odd shape property, requires that property used as one unit by the owner at a corner be given the corner assessment. The property may not be divided into two lots though it was originally separate, and may subsequently be subdivided, when it is used as one unit at the time of assessment.

Pa   Detweiler v Derry Township Municipal Auth (1977) 29 PaCmwlth 277, 370 A2d 810.

The provision for special street assessments requiring assessment against property located up to 160 feet from the street will be read as 160 feet from a sewer line, where the provisions are applicable to sewer assessments.

Ore   Gilbert v Eugene (1970) 255 Ore 289, 465 P2d 880.

A storm sewer assessment, though the complainant is above the average elevation, is not invalid, since a benefit is conferred.

Fla   Carson v Ft Lauderdale (1971) 244 So2d 485.

A sewer assessment based on square footage, without regard to type of occupancy, is not invalid where there is no showing that the apportionment was improper or the assessment exceeded the benefits.

Fla   Carson v Ft Lauderdale (1971) 244 So2d 485.

The authorization for a sewer assessment based on front footage may not be subsequently changed by resolution to a square foot assessment. An ordinance may only be changed by another ordinance.

Fla   7800 Building v South Miami (1974) 305 So2d 860.

Where a statute authorizes a municipality to provide for the extension or construction of lateral sewers and to apportion the cost "according to the actual cost of labor and material expended in constructing such lateral along the lot assessed", the court will enjoin the enforcement of an ordinance assessing the costs equally against the various lot owners.

Okla   Jones v Holzapfel (1902) 11 Okla 405, 68 P 511.

Where an ordinance provides that the cost of sewer construction shall be assessed against abutting estates, "estate" means a tract or parcel of land serving a single integrated use, whether it consists of one platted lot or a consolidation of several such lots. An assessment against each of 3 platted lots, comprising one piece of residential property used as a unit for living purposes, therefore is invalid.

> **RI**   Knuth v East Providence (1960) 91 RI 164, 162 A2d 278.

A charter provision directing that the costs and expenses of sewerage improvements are to be charged to the parcels benefited on the basis of running foot frontage on the improved street is mandatory, and prohibits a deviation that excludes some parcels based solely on the opinion of the assessors that they were not benefited.

> **NY**   Day v Dunkirk (1914) 86 Misc 266, 148 NYS 299.

An ordinance imposing a special assessment for sewer purposes, and subdividing land into lots 25 feet wide for the purpose of assessment, is invalid, since property must be specially assessed under its known legal description, and an owner has the right to subdivide his land in any way he sees fit.

> **Ill**   People v Cook (1899) 180 Ill 341, 54 NE 173.

The apportioning of the cost against the entire frontage of a lot under a sewer assessment ordinance is improper where the sewer is only constructed in front of a portion of the lot.

> **Ky**   Paintsville v Wells (1934) 255 Ky 189, 73 SW2d 20.

An ordinance providing that sewer assessments shall be made on the owners of land within a defined territory by fixed uniform rates, based on the estimated average cost of sewers in the territory does not provide for an assessment in excess of special benefits.

> **Mass**   Hester v Thompson (1914) 217 Mass 422, 105 NE 631.

Ordinances imposing an assessment on a square foot basis, in addition to a tax fee, for connections with sewer and water service are not taxes in violation of the state Constitution, as being charges made in excess of actual costs and thus devices to raise general revenue.

> **Colo**   Western Heights Land Corp v Fort Collins (1961) 146 Colo 464, 362 P2d 155.

A city council has power to divide a sewer district into zones, to assess construction costs that do not exceed a fixed amount per abutting foot, and to provide that if the cost does exceed that amount it shall be assessed by the square foot on all the property in the zone.

> **Ky**   Katterjohn v King (1924) 202 Ky 64, 258 SW 960.

A method of assessment, under a sewer assessment ordinance, which applies to all corner lots similarly situated whereby they pay as all other lots do according to frontage, and in proportion to benefits received, is fair and reasonable and is not discriminatory.

> **Ky**   Jackson v Riffle (1927) 219 Ky 689, 294 SW 142.

Where a resolution provides that if any property is situated at an intersection or adjoining more than one street, road, alley or other public highway where sewer lines are constructed which pass in front of, or are contiguous to more than one side of such property, the owner shall be assessed for full frontage of one full side and for only such part of all other sides which exceed 100 feet, property located on a road that arcs at a 90 degree angle so that it fronts on both sides of the arc, should be assessed as provided for properties located at the intersection of two streets.

> **Pa**   Whitemarsh Township v Poorman (1963) 200 PaS 245, 188 A2d 853.

Computation of the assessment imposed under a sewer improvement ordinance on corner parcels serviced by existing sewer lines on intersecting streets may be based on a reduced area that is less than the entire depth of such lots, since the benefit is less than that of encompassed parcels.

> **NY**   Leonhardt v Yonkers (1921) 195 AD 234, 187 NYS 27.

A corner lot may be assessed for sewer construction on each street on which it abuts. The lot owner must bear in part the burdens necessary for the welfare of the whole, since his lot fronts on two or more streets each of which needs to be improved as a whole.

> **Ky**   Rich v Woods (1904) 118 Ky 865, 82 SW 578.

An ordinance assessing sewer costs against abutting owners is not invalid where it imposes two assessments for the improvement of corner or other lots fronting and abutting on more than one street, for an owner may be required to pay for sewer improvements made on each of two streets.

> **Ky**   Ruby v Madisonville (1923) 197 Ky 526, 247 SW 354.

An ordinance assessing the owner of a corner lot for sewer construction on an abutting street is not invalid merely because he was previously assessed for sewer construction on the other abutting street. While it is a hardship, it is a hardship growing out of the disadvantage of owning a corner lot.

> **Ky**   Gesser v McLane (1914) 156 Ky 743, 161 SW 118.

An ordinance authorizing construction of a district sewer and assessing the costs by sewer tax bills against each lot in the district is not invalid as grossly unequal special taxation contrary to the Fourteenth Amendment, where the lots on one side of the street are twice as deep as those on the other side, and no injustice is necessarily done to any of the property owners.

Mo   Landsdown v Kierns (1924) 303 Mo 75, 260 SW 88.

That four-fifths of the cost of a sewer improvement authorized by ordinance is assessed against two-fifths of the area benefited does not deny equal protection of the laws to a landowner who receives notice of the assessment, appears and objects at the hearing, and has a right of appeal guaranteed by the charter.

NY   Adam Schumann Assn v New York City (1930) 40 F2d 216.

Though the maintenance of a sewage system is imposed by law on a city by a decree of court and the essential service is, in a broad sense, for the benefit of the entire city, it cannot follow that each parcel of land in the city furnished with and connected to a new local sewer can be specially assessed for some share of the whole outfall and treatment operation, in addition to its share of the cost of the local improvement. To hold otherwise would permit the city to divert special assessment funds to general taxation purposes.

Cal   Los Angeles v Offner (1961) 55 C2d 103, 10 CaR 470, 358 P2d 926.

A municipality may authorize a number of sewers to be constructed in the same manner under a single ordinance, where the cost of all the improvements is apportioned according to frontage of abutting property.

Ky   Little v Southgate (1927) 221 Ky 604, 299 SW 587.

A council or board of works cannot localize a part of a main intercepting sewer and assess abutting property owners for a part of construction costs where the sewer was constructed past the owners' property two years before and by authority of an ordinance and a board of works resolution it was paid for out of general funds from the sale of city bonds, since there is no statutory authority, either general or specific, that would permit such delayed action and use of two methods to complete the work.

Ind   Huntington v Sonken (1929) 89 IndAp 645, 165 NE 449.

An ordinance of intention to organize a sewer district and issue bonds for the construction of a sewer system is sufficient to confer jurisdiction on the city council where it provides that the sewerage district shall not include for assessment property occupied by the cross streets and alleys, though it omits a statement, required by statute, that such property within the district will not be assessed. Though the ordinance failed to contain such a statement, the statute will intervene and prohibit any assessment being laid on the streets.

Ida   Williams v Caldwell (1911) 19 Ida 514, 114 P 519.

A city has power, by ordinance, to pay or require abutting property owners to pay the cost of constructing sewers at street intersections and crossings; and a statute that relates to assessing the costs of constructing or reconstructing street intersections does not apply to or require the cost of sewers at street intersections to be paid by the city.

    Ky   Lawson v Greenup (1929) 227 Ky 414, 13 SW2d 281.

An ordinance assessing costs of sewer construction against abutting property owners is not invalid merely because the costs are not apportioned on a fair valuation of the property sought to be subjected to the improvements, since the requirement of uniformity in taxation applies only to taxes and has no application to assessments for public improvements, which are for local benefits.

    Ky   Shaw v Mayfield (1924) 204 Ky 618, 265 SW 13.

Ordinances establishing a sewer district and authorizing construction of a district sewer and assessment of costs against lots on an area basis will not be held invalid on the ground: (1) that an original proprietor of some of the property had constructed a sewer in the street, where such sewer was not laid deep enough to drain basements of houses on the street, (2) that the construction contract was not conformed with where part of the sewer was laid on private property, where the city at its own expense relaid that part of the sewer in the street, (3) that required manholes were not properly constructed because secondhand ordinary brick was used and not well cemented, where it appears that the contract in this respect was substantially performed, or (4) that lots on both sides of the improvement were assessed on an area basis, the lots on one side being twice as deep as those on the other, where there is no showing that the more heavily assessed lots did not enjoy greater benefits.

    Mo   Landsdown v Kierns (1924) 303 Mo 75, 260 SW 88.

§39. Reassessment Rules

An ordinance ratifying and confirming all prior proceedings relating to construction of a sewer and providing for a reassessment of its cost on abutting property is enforceable where a statute authorizes reassessment when a special tax or assessment is invalid or its validity is questioned since the statute is not limited in its operation to void or irregular assessments made before its passage.

    Iowa   Gill v Patton (1902) 118 Iowa 88, 91 NW 904.

Ordinances exacting a reassessment against real property for sewers, disposal works and cement walks are void, where the assessment under the original ordinance was not sufficient to pay principal and interest on bonds or the costs of the improvements, and the reassessments were levied after the federal government purchased the land making it property of the United States, exempt from local taxation.

> **Ida**   US v Mullen Benevolent (1933) 63 F2d 48.

§40. Assessments for Maintenance and Repairs

An ordinance to prolong a sewer improvement district and assess maintenance costs against real property owners within the district is within the statutory authority given cities by the legislature.

> **Ark**   Ragsdale v Cunningham (1941) 201 Ark 848, 147 SW2d 20.

An ordinance imposing a special assessment, to cover the cost of maintaining public sewers, on property owners who make use of them and who already have been assessed for the cost of construction, does not deprive them of property without due process of law, since they receive special benefits from the construction of the sewers and the privilege of discharging their private sewers into public sewers.

> **Mass**   Carson v Brockton (1901) 182 US 398, 45 LEd 1151, 21 SCt 860.

An Administrative Code provision authorizing imposition of sewer rent charges on property owners for new works and reconstruction does not authorize assessments for maintenance, operation and repair of the sewer system.

> **NY**   Riverview Est v New York City (1964) 20 AD2d 890, 248 NYS2d 937.

Ordinances authorizing sewer revenue bonds and providing for sewer assessment fees for expansion of the sewer system to other areas do not discriminate against the established sections of the city by instituting assessments against those sections. Though it is contended that no special benefits accrue from the extension of the system and that the assessment is an unfair collection of taxes, the ordinances are valid because the municipality is authorized by statute to levy annual maintenance or service charges and special assessments to defray the expense of maintaining, enlarging, extending, constructing, operating and keeping in repair sewers and sewage disposal plants, and to pay interest and principal on sewer revenue bonds.

> **NM**   Clovis v Crain (1960) 68 NM 10, 357 P2d 667.

§41. Tax Bills

Under an ordinance establishing a sewer district and authorizing construction of a sewer, costs to be charged against property in the district evidenced by tax bills, the city is not liable in contract for tax bills assessed against property to which the city took title in condemnation proceedings by relation back to a judgment dated prior to issuance of the tax bills, where final judgment and payment of the money in the condemnation suit occurred thereafter.

Mo   Municipal Securities v Kansas City (1915) 265 Mo 252, 177 SW 856.

Where sewer districts are authorized, constructed and accepted by the city, tax bills issued on assessments for payment thereof, in the absence of evidence to the contrary, are presumptively valid.

Mo   Harris v Cameron (1924) 218 MoApp 605, 265 SW 862.

Where ordinances authorize establishment of a sewer district, construction of a sewer, and assessment of costs against benefited property by tax bills, with credits to benefited properties for parts of the sewer previously completed, such credits are adequately established by presentation in evidence of the municipal ordinances and records involved, without oral testimony, if the prima facie case made thereby is not refuted.

Mo   Maplewood v Meryl Rlty & Inv (1930) 27 SW2d 433.

Where an ordinance authorizes construction of a sewer and issuance of tax bills to be paid for by assessments against benefited properties, recovery may not be had in a suit on a tax bill where the petition nowhere describes the property against which the bill was issued.

Mo   Barrie v Ranson (1932) 226 MoApp 554, 46 SW2d 186.

Where an ordinance levying assessments against properties for sewer construction is declared void, and the city fails to enact a reassessment ordinance, the holder of tax warrants issued by the city may compel the city by mandamus to enact a reassessment ordinance, but cannot recover damages from the city.

Okla   Guarantee Title & Tr v Sapulpa (1933) 164 Okla 271, 23 P2d 629.

Where an ordinance for construction of sewers provides for payment by special tax bills against land in the sewer district, and that in no event and in no manner whatever shall the city be liable, and the tax bills are later declared illegal, the city is not liable for work done under the contract, since both parties contracted in good faith on the possibility that the special tax bills might be invalid.

Mo   Cotter v Kansas City (1913) 251 Mo 224, 158 SW 52.

Tax bills issued in payment for completed work, under an ordinance establishing a sewer district and providing for construction of sewers, will not be annulled on the ground of irregularities in adoption of the ordinance in that votes of the city council were improperly recorded on the journal, where a nunc pro tunc order can be made to correctly reflect in detail what the record shows in abbreviated form.

Mo   Cunningham v Butler (1953) 256 SW2d 767.

Special tax bills issued for construction of a joint district sewer, authenticated by a party designated by the board of public service, as authorized by the city's charter, are not invalid where not authenticated in the names of the city comptroller and the president of the board of public service, as required by an ordinance. The provisions of the charter with respect to authentication are full, complete, and self-enforcing, and require no ordinance to supplement them.

Mo   Bates v Comstock Rlty (1924) 306 Mo 312, 267 SW 641.

Tax warrants issued by officials of a town in connection with an invalid ordinance providing for the creation of a sewer district are void, and create no liability on the part of the town.

Okla   Bonney v Britton (1950) 202 Okla 399, 214 P2d 249.

§42. Debt Limit

Where the costs of sewer construction are apportioned and assessed against abutting owners, a constitutional debt limitation has no application.

Ky   Shaw v Mayfield (1924) 204 Ky 618, 265 SW 13.

§43. Liens

The legislature may create a lien for general taxes or for local assessments paramount to all other liens regardless of the priority of the latter as to time, and under an ordinance assessing property owners for sewer construction the statutory lien has priority over a mortgage, though the statute creating the lien was enacted after creation of the mortgage debt.

Ky   Krumpelman v Louisville & Jefferson County (1958) 314 SW2d 557.

Where a statute makes a special assessment for sewer construction under a city ordinance a lien on property, but is silent on priority, a lien so created may be given priority over any and all other liens, whether prior or subsequent to the assessment.

Ky   Krumpelman v Louisville & Jefferson County (1958) 314 SW2d 557.

Under an ordinance apportioning the cost of sewer construction against property owners, an apportionment warrant must be recorded within 10 days of its issuance to create a lien; but this provision applies only to a bona fide purchaser for value who bought the property after enactment of the ordinance. It does not apply to a mortgage.

Ky　Krumpelman v Louisville & Jefferson County (1958) 314 SW2d 557.

An ordinance making all sewage and waste fees, due and payable on and after a certain date, a special assessment lien equal in rank to liens for ad valorem taxes and superior to all other liens will not be given retroactive effect. Hence, waste fees due before that date are inferior to an existing mortgage.

Fla　Gleason v Dade County (1965) 174 So2d 466.

An ordinance of intention for the construction of a proposed sewage disposal works, proposing to assess the real property within the district, is valid, under general authority given to cities and villages to construct sewers as well as other public improvements. The issuance of bonds pursuant to the assessments creates a valid and subsisting lien on the assessed property.

Ida　Veatch v Gibson (1916) 29 Ida 609, 160 P 1112.

Where an ordinance provides that a sewer assessment is due on issuance of a permit to tap the sewer, a lien attaches from the date of the levy of the assessment and constitutes an encumbrance on the land, which is recoverable from the grantor for breach of a covenant against encumbrances.

Ohio　G Andrews Espy Rlty v Burton-Rodgers (1952) 94 OA 417, 52 Op 129, 116 NE2d 14.

ANNOTATION

Superiority of special or local assessment lien for drains over earlier private lien or mortgage, where statute creating such special lien is silent as to superiority, 75 ALR2d 1121.

V. NONASSESSMENT FINANCING

A. TAXATION AND APPROPRIATION

§44. Generally

A resolution and referendum authorizing a 10 per cent public utility tax does not create a binding contract between the city and the taxpayers. The city may still make assessments against the adjoining owners for the cost of a general improvement consisting of a storm and sanitary sewer system.

Fla　Carson v Ft Lauderdale (1971) 244 So2d 485.

Where a property tax is levied to secure bonds issued for sewerage, water and drainage improvements and the ordinance reserves the right and declares the intention to cease the levy whenever the surplus net proceeds of another tax suffice to pay the interest on the bonds, there is no contract between the city and property owners that requires the city to cease levying the tax if the stated conditions occur.

La   Rlty Owners v New Orleans (1927) 165 La 159, 115 So 444.

Where after the passage of an ordinance authorizing sewer construction and the assessing of costs against abutting owners the city acquires surplus funds from the sale of a light and water plant, it is authorized by statute to apply these funds to pay all or any part of the unpaid costs of the sewer construction.

Ky   Dowdy v Mayfield (1926) 213 Ky 460, 281 SW 485.

Where an ordinance assesses the cost of sewer construction against abutting owners, the entire cost of the sewer exceeds the maximum amount per foot permitted by statute, and the assessment levied against abutting owners does not exceed that sum, the city is not required to assess all of the property in the sewer district that may be benefited, since the statute gives the city express authority to pay excess costs out of the general fund.

Ky   Gesser v McLane (1914) 156 Ky 743, 161 SW 1118.

An ordinance appropriating money for the construction of sanitary sewers is a proper exercise of municipal authority, under an enabling act.

NJ   Csaki v Woodbridge (1961) 69 NJS 327, 174 A2d 271.

An ordinance authorizing improvement of sanitary conditions in the city and appropriating in payment thereof specified bonds by serial numbers is valid.

Mo   Jennings v Kinsey (1925) 308 Mo 265, 271 SW 786.

Where the cost of sewer construction exceeds the amount per front foot fixed by statute, the city has authority to assess against the abutting owners the maximum so fixed, and to charge the remaining costs against the general funds of the city.

Ky   Johnson v McKenna (1916) 171 Ky 389, 188 SW 480.

Where, before completion of a sewer, the city passed an ordinance directing that the probable cost of the entire improvement be estimated and a tax levied for the payment thereof, plaintiffs were entitled to enjoin the enforcement of the assessment on the ground that such a tax is prohibited by a mandatory statute providing that when an improvement is completed it is the duty of the council to ascertain the cost and assess the same against the property benefited.

Iowa Sanborn v Mason City (1901) 114 Iowa 189, 86 NW 286.

Where statute changed the basis for handling the costs of maintaining and improving sewers by substituting a charge for rent based on water consumption, with due regard to equitable considerations, for the previous practice of financing sewer upkeep largely from property taxes and of paying for improvements with special assessments, a city board of estimates resolution assessing property owners contrary to such statute is void.

NY Riverview Est v New York City (1963) 38 Misc2d 607, 238 NYS2d 762.

B. BONDS

§45. Constitutional and Statutory Powers

Though there is no specific grant of authority for a city to issue negotiable bonds, there is a specific grant of power to do everything that is ordinarily done in the issuing of bonds, and as a necessary incident of such power a city may issue, by ordinance, negotiable bonds for sewer improvements without conflicting with the enabling act.

Ky Hunter v Louisville (1925) 208 Ky 326, 270 SW 841.

An ordinance providing for the combining of a city water-works and a sewerage system, for improvements, and for issuance of revenue certificates is valid as authorized by the municipal charter, since provisions of the state revenue certificate law and the Constitution concerning revenue certificates became a part of the charter of every municipality when adopted.

Ga Reed v Smyrna (1946) 201 Ga 228, 39 SE2d 668.

Where a statute authorizes the issuance and sale of revenue bonds for improving and extending the city's combined waterworks and sewerage system it is not invalid merely because not specifically authorized by the Constitution, since the Constitution is a limitation on the power of the general assembly and not a grant thereof, and the city acts under delegated legislative authority.

Mo Maryville v Cushman (1952) 363 Mo 87, 249 SW2d 347.

An ordinance providing for water and sewer bonds and authorizing a future issue of revenue bonds to enjoy complete parity of lien with bonds of the first issue is not invalid merely because a statute provides that bonds of a subsequent issue shall have inferior rights of claim on revenue.

Ida Schmidt v Kimberly (1953) 74 Ida 48, 256 P2d 515.

An ordinance placing a statutory mortgage lien on new additions to a city water and sewer system does not violate the statutory prohibition against liens on debt free municipal utilities.

> **Ark**   Harrison v Braswell (1946) 209 Ark 1094, 194 SW2d 12, 165 ALR 845.

§46. Procedural Requirements

Ordinances providing for the issuance of sewer and waterworks bonds are invalid where the legal proceedings to raise the community to a city of the second class are declared void, when a census list for the community is not on file for 30 days with the state board of municipal corporations and the population of the community is less than that required by statute.

> **Ark**   Bush v Echols (1928) 178 Ark 507, 10 SW2d 906.

Ordinances authorizing the issuance of bonds for sewer construction are not ordinances for raising revenue, but are ordinances for creating a debt, and they therefore are not invalid merely because they do not originate in the board of councilmen, as is required by statute for revenue measures.

> **Ky**   Central Constr v Lexington (1915) 162 Ky 286, 172 SW 648.

An ordinance authorizing a bond issue for sewer improvements is not invalidated by an incorrect statement of the date of passage of the act authorizing the issue. Mere verbal inaccuracies or clerical errors, in the use of words, or in grammar or spelling, will be corrected by the court whenever necessary to carry out the plain intention of the legislative body.

> **Ky**   Ahrens v Louisville (1920) 186 Ky 579, 217 SW 907.

An ordinance authorizing a bond issue for sewer improvements is not invalid merely because it is silent on the question of what shall become of the proceeds of the bonds or in what depositories they shall be placed, and as to the terms of the interest or the manner of withdrawal, where the enabling act is specific as to these things.

> **Ky**   Hunter v Louisville (1925) 208 Ky 326, 270 SW 841.

Where an ordinance authorizing a bond issue to extend a sewer system directs the giving of public notice of the bond election, and also provides that the ordinance shall be published, failure to comply does not invalidate the bond issue, since the provisions are directory and not mandatory; and where it appears that the public is adequately informed in advance this suffices.

> **Ky**   Gollar v Louisville (1920) 187 Ky 448, 219 SW 421.

Where a statute delegates discretion to a board of councilmen, either to publish a notice under an ordinance proposing a bond issue to finance sewer construction, or to post such notice, the council has the right to make the publication in either manner.

Ky   Fowler v Oakdale (1914) 158 Ky 603, 166 SW 195.

A contention that holders of municipal sewer revenue bonds were not authorized to receive delivery because by resolution the town board authorized delivery of the entire issue to a contractor is untenable. The necessary valid delivery of such bonds to holders in due course may be shown, and a valid delivery by the maker may be conclusively presumed.

Ky   Erlanger v Berkemeyer (1953) 207 F2d 832.

Where pursuant to an ordinance municipal sewer bonds were never delivered to the purchaser but were canceled and destroyed, and the town received nothing, the bonds were never "issued", within the meaning of the statute.

Okla   McMasters v Byars (1950) 203 Okla 498, 223 P2d 545.

An ordinance providing for the refunding of outstanding special assessment bonds, where the assessments already constitute a lien against abutting property for sewer construction is void.

Ky   Paducah v Jones (1938) 274 Ky 460, 118 SW2d 753.

§47. Payment Provisions

An ordinance providing for a bond issue for the construction of a sewerage disposal plant, the first installment of which falls due five years after the earliest possible date of maturity, is constitutional, if the ordinance provides for annual levy and collection of taxes sufficient to pay the interest on the bonds and for their final redemption at maturity.

Ohio   Columbus v Ketterer (1934) 127 OS 483, 189 NE 252.

An ordinance authorizing the issuance of bonds to pay for combining the city's sewerage system and its waterworks system, and for improvements and extensions, is not invalid for requiring the city to maintain six separate accounts, all of which are in accordance with good business practices and sound business policy in the public interest.

Mo   Maryville v Cushman (1952) 363 Mo 87, 249 SW2d 347.

An ordinance authorizing the sale of sewer bonds and covenanting with purchasers that sewer rates will not be reduced until amounts required by the ordinance to be deposited in certain depreciation reserve accounts shall have reached certain maximums, or while there is any default in payment of principal or interest on the bonds, and requiring proper connections to the sewerage system where service is available, is valid, and is not an illegal attempt to control the future action of the city or future city councils.

Mo Sikeston v Sisson (1952) 363 Mo 104, 249 SW2d 345.

An ordinance providing for the issuance of water and sewer bonds to pay the cost of extending a water system and water treatment plant and for a sewage collection system and sewage treatment plant is not unconstitutional where it authorizes the appointment of a receiver for the system on default in payment of principal or interest, since it does not deprive a municipality of its property without due process of law.

Ida Schmidt v Kimberly (1953) 74 Ida 48, 256 P2d 515.

An ordinance submitting to the voters a proposal to issue sewer and waterworks bonds, and, for the purpose of paying interest and creating a sinking fund, levying a continuing annual tax sufficient to pay the bonds at maturity, is valid.

Okla State v Millar (1908) 21 Okla 448, 96 P 747.

An ordinance authorizing a bond issue for sewerage extension to be paid from the speculative profits of future operation of a city water and light plant will be annulled where it is shown that the revenues of the plant are not reasonably certain of collection, that there are no excess revenues from any other source and that a present deficit exists in the city's finances.

La Miller v Minden (1935) 181 La 99, 158 So 634.

An ordinance authorizing issuance of general obligation bonds for payment of only a portion of a sewage disposal system, the balance to be paid from proceeds of an issue of sewer revenue bonds, is enforceable where such issue is authorized by statute and the bonds are a valid city obligation.

Fla State v Miami (1953) 62 So2d 405.

A resolution providing for the refunding of outstanding water, sewer and revenue bonds, at a lower rate of interest, is not invalid merely because the actions are not framed within an ordinance, where municipalities are authorized by state law to issue and sell such bonds by either ordinance or resolution, without a vote of the electors.

Ida Adams v Pritchard (1965) 88 Ida 325, 399 P2d 252.

An ordinance fixing the maximum interest rate to be paid on bonds issued for sewer construction may provide that any coupon interest rate not exceeding the rate fixed in the ordinance may be accepted and later fixed by ordinance, since a sale of bonds by competitive bidding on the interest rate is consistent with economy and sound business financing.

> **Ky**　Funk v Strathmoor Village (1939) 278 Ky 627, 129 SW2d 151.

Where a city passed an ordinance to issue water and sewer bonds for a city owned sewer system serving some customers in an unincorporated area of the county, and the county commissioners ratified the ordinance by resolution, stating that they would do nothing to impair the repayment of the bonds or interfere with rates charged by the city, the commissioners are estopped to order the city to remove a surcharge in the unincorporated area.

> **Fla**　Dade County v Greenlee (1968) 213 So2d 485.

Under an ordinance authorizing a bond issue to finance sewer construction costs the first tax to provide money to pay interest on the bonds and to create a sinking fund is not required to be levied at the time other city taxes are levied.

> **Ky**　Fowler v Oakdale (1914) 158 Ky 603, 166 SW 195.

A municipality is authorized to incur obligations for the purpose of defraying preliminary expenses of sewer projects, provided repayment of such obligations is to be made solely from the proceeds of revenue bonds issued pursuant to an ordinance, and not in any way from tax levies.

> **W Va**　US v Charleston (1957) 149 F Supp 866.

A defect in an ordinance initiating a bond issue to finance sewer construction, in failing to provide for raising annually by taxation an amount necessary to pay the interest on the bonds and to provide a sinking fund, may be cured by an ordinance providing for the levy of such tax before issuance of the bonds.

> **Ky**　Iglehart v Dawson Springs (1911) 143 Ky 140, 136 SW 210.

Municipal bonds that are payable only from revenue derived from the operation of a sewer system do not qualify as negotiable instruments. However, irrespective of a conditional promise to pay, the legislature may make the bonds negotiable.

> **Ky**　Erlanger v Berkemeyer (1953) 207 F2d 832.

§48. Elections

An authorization for additional revenue bonds at parity and equality of liens is not violated by the new bonds having a higher interest rate. Having been approved by the electorate, the revenue bonds meet the requirements of the previous resolution.

> **Cal**　Santa Clara v Von Raesfeld (1970) 3 C3d 239, 474 P2d 976, 90 CaR 8.

A sewer bond election setting interest rates at six per cent, duly approved by the council and 2/3 of the voters, may be amended to raise the interest rate to seven per cent by a like approval of the council and a 2/3 vote of the electorate.

Cal King City v Thommarson (1970) 8 CA3d 651, 87 CaR 757.

A notice of election to approve city water and sewer bonds, published pursuant to an ordinance authorizing the bonds, though it characterizes the bonds, is not ineffective. The error is surplusage, and is a misrepresentation of law only.

Utah State v Salt Lake City (1908) 35 Utah 25, 99 P 255.

Where a city by its electorate approves issuance of bonds for constructing, repairing and improving sewers and drains, and some of the bonds are not issued for 18 years, an ordinance authorizing issuance of those bonds is valid as against the contention that the city's authority to issue them terminated with the adoption of a plan for a metropolitan sewer district, and that there had been unreasonable delay.

Mo St Louis, Petition of (1963) 363 SW2d 612.

An ordinance providing for the issuance of bonds to cover the cost of improving and extending the city's combined waterworks and sewerage system, to be repaid from their revenue, and containing a provision that such bonds may be redeemed prior to maturity on payment of a specified premium, are not invalid for failure to require submission of the premium payment to the voters at a special election, since the call of any bonds prior to maturity is a contingency that may never arise, and such details as to bond maturities are by statute left to the city's governing body.

Mo Maryville v Cushman (1952) 363 Mo 87, 249 SW2d 347.

Ordinances calling for a special election and the issuance of bonds to establish a sewer system and a waterworks system may not be attacked for invalidity on the ground that the mayor had not subscribed to his oath of office provided by statute, and that the mayor and aldermen were delinquent in payment of their taxes at the time they were purportedly elected, since the acts of such public officers de facto, though their titles may be bad, are valid insofar as they concern the public or the rights of third persons affected by their official acts, and their official acts cannot be impeached collaterally.

Mo Clarence v Drain (1934) 335 Mo 741, 73 SW2d 804.

An ordinance authorizing a bond issue for the purpose of constructing a sewer system under an agreement previously entered into with another city is not invalid for uncertainty on the ground that the contract was not incorporated by the ordinance into the election procedure.

    Mo   Kansas City v Raytown (1967) 421 SW2d 504.

§49. Debt Limitations

An ordinance authorizing bonds for sewer construction, financed from sewer revenues or assessments, is not subject to constitutional debt limitations.

    Ill   Edwardsville v Jenkins (1941) 376 Ill 327, 33 NE2d 598, 134 ALR 891.
    Ky   Francis v Bowling Green (1935) 259 Ky 525, 82 SW2d 804.
             Little v Southgate (1928) 223 Ky 692, 4 SW2d 711.
    Mo   Maryville v Cushman (1952) 363 Mo 87, 249 SW2d 347.
    NC   Lamb v Randleman (1934) 206 NC 837, 175 SE 293.
    Wyo   Laverents v Cheyenne (1950) 67 Wyo 187, 217 P2d 877.

Where an ordinance authorizes a bond issue to finance sewer construction on an installment plan basis, and where a statute prescribes that the bonds shall be payable out of assessments against abutting owners to be collected by the city and placed in a street improvement fund, the bonds are obligations of the city and create a personal indebtedness against it where no limitation of city liability is written into the ordinance, notwithstanding that the street improvement fund is set apart for their payment. Consequently the ordinance is invalid where this indebtedness makes aggregate debt of the city exceed permissible constitutional debt limits.

    Ky   Little v Southgate (1927) 221 Ky 604, 299 SW 587.

An ordinance providing for the issuance and sale of city bonds for the purpose of providing funds for storm and sanitary trunk sewer improvements is not valid as an emergency measure considered as a governmental duty, so as to authorize the city to exceed its constitutional debt limit, where the condition necessitating the bond issue did not suddenly appear, but had been a recurring topic of discussion for a long time.

    Wash   Robb v Tacoma (1933) 175 Wash 580, 28 P2d 327, 91 ALR 1010.

An ordinance authorizing the issuance of revenue bonds for the purpose of extending a sewerage system that had been originally financed by other revenue bonds, some of which are still outstanding, is not invalid as against the contention that if the revenues of the whole system are pledged, instead of the revenues derived from the extension alone, it becomes a constitutionally impermissible general obligation of the city, since the issuance of municipal bonds payable solely out of revenue do not constitute general obligations, within the constitutional limitation.

    Wyo   Snyder v Cheyenne (1959) 79 Wyo 405, 334 P2d 750.

A city's covenant to impose charges for sewer services adequate to cover bond payments and expenses of the sewer system does not amount to a guaranty that the system will be successful. The covenant does not create a financial liability measurable in terms of the city's annual income and, therefore, is not contrary to constitutional debt limitations.

Cal   Oxnard v Dale (1955) 45 C2d 729, 290 P2d 859.

Where by ordinance a new sewerage district is created by consolidating two existing districts, in order to serve newly annexed territory, if a bond election to finance improvements complies with statutory directives and the ordinance authorizing issue of the bonds does not impinge on or exceed the constitutional limitation of 10 per cent of assessed valuation of property within the sewerage district when added to outstanding indebtedness, the ordinance and bond issue are valid.

La   Nanney v Leesville (1941) 198 La 773, 4 So2d 825.

C. RENTAL AND RATES

§50. Legal Character; Power to Impose

City regulation of water and sewer rates is effectively repealed by passage of a statute making their regulation of public interest and an exercise of the state's police power. It is not necessary that the ordinance be repealed or a resolution adopting the state regulation be passed.

Fla   Orange City Water Co v Orange City (1971) 255 So2d 257.

An application for sewage service which provides that the applicant will pay all reasonable charges is not limited to charges in effect at the particular time. Service to a subsequently constructed building in the same site may be at an increased rate.

Va   Amer Trading & Production Corp v Fairfax County Bd of Supervisors (1973) 214 Va 382, 200 SE2d 529.

A city being required to operate a sewage treatment plant may require the users to pay the operating expenses directly or indirectly. A chicken processing plant which runs its waste water through a flume to an adjoining dog food processing plant is liable for the charges. Since the dog food plant only removes the solid offal from the waste water for its processing it is not purchasing the water or using it in any manner prior to its entry into the sewer system, and rather than creating waste water is improving the quality of it. The chicken processing plant is therefore liable for payment of the sewer bill based on indirectly disposing of it in the city sewer system.

Ga   Cagle's v Atlanta (1973) 231 Ga 426, 202 SE2d 82.

A properly adopted ordinance establishing a sewerage service charge is not in the nature of a tax for the use of sewer facilities. It is a charge for the use of the municipal sewer facilities in the disposal of polluted water and sewerage which drains into the municipal disposal system.

NC　Covington v Rockingham (1966) 266 NC 507, 146 SE2d 420.

An ordinance imposing a sewer rent charge is for the special benefit conferred on those who use the sewer system and hence is not a tax, and is not to be considered in relation to the constitutional limit.

NY　L X Corp v New York City (1952) 201 Misc 400, 115 NYS2d 120.

Sewer rents imposed by a city pursuant to a resolution are neither taxes nor assessments for local benefit but, like water rates, are charges made for a service rendered—charges which the consumer, by accepting the service, impliedly agrees to pay.

NH　Opinion of Justices (1944) 93 NH 478, 39 A2d 765.

The construction, operation, and maintenance of a sewer system by a municipality is a proprietary function; and as such the municipality is entitled to enact an ordinance requiring payment for the service rendered.

Pa　North East v Piece of Land (1960) 191 PaS 532, 159 A2d 528.

Payments made pursuant to an ordinance requiring the payment of fees for use of a sewer system are not taxes, but rather are charges in the nature of a special assessment, since the sewer enhances the value of the property.

Ky　Francis v Bowling Green (1935) 259 Ky 525, 82 SW2d 804.

An ordinance establishing rates for water and sewerage services is not invalid for a provision that such services shall be deemed to be furnished to both occupant and owner of the premises receiving them, and that both are liable. The owner's obligation is personal on an implied contract from the fact that his real estate benefits from the water and sewerage facilities of the city.

Mo　Maryville v Cushman (1952) 363 Mo 87, 249 SW2d 347.

Where a corporation constructing a large housing project installs a sewerage system, contracts with the county for permanent maintenance of the system, and agrees to pay stipulated inspection and maintenance fees in excess of the standard fees prescribed by ordinance, no conflict exists between the contract and the ordinance which would prevent the county from recovering on the contract.

Va　South Hampton Apart v Elizabeth City County (1946) 185 Va 67, 37 SE2d 841.

Where an ordinance provides that sewer rental charges shall remain in effect so long as the principal and interest of any bonds issued in connection with sewer construction remain outstanding, that provision overrides any implication that the charges would remain in effect for a longer period of time, and precludes the city from attempting to collect such charges after the bonds are retired.

> **Ky**   Maysville v Coughlin (1966) 399 SW2d 297.

The validity of an ordinance that levies a "sanitary tax" is not affected by the limitation on the powers delegated to municipalities to levy and collect ad valorem taxes, since the term "sanitary tax" is used in the ordinance to designate the remuneratory charge imposed on those permitted to maintain sanitary toilets on their premises, the evident purpose being to impose an inspection or service charge on the designated class for the service rendered and privilege permitted.

> **SC**   Marion v Baxley (1939) 192 SC 112, 5 SE2d 573.

An ordinance requiring sewer service charges does not impose a tax, assessment or special assessment, but merely a rental especially authorized by statute to maintain and operate a sewerage system.

> **Ohio**   Grim v Lewisville (1935) 54 OA 270, 20 Abs 295, 4 Op 514, 6 NE2d 998.

An ordinance creating a sewer system at public expense is a valid exercise of police power to promote the public health, and reasonable rental charges may be made for use thereof and an appropriate collection procedure enforced.

> **Ariz**   State v Bartos (1967) 102 Ariz 15, 423 P2d 713.

The power to make a reasonable charge for connection to and use of sewers is a proper incident of a city's police power to provide sewers.

> **Cal**   Longridge Est v Los Angeles (1960) 183 CA2d 533, 6 CaR 900.

An ordinance imposing a sewer service charge on users of premises connected with the city sewer system does not create an ad valorem tax, within the constitutional provision limiting the total tax levy for all public purposes to five cents on each dollar of assessed valuation.

> **Nev**   Harris v Reno (1965) 81 Nev 256, 401 P2d 678.

Though a city entering into a valid contract to permit connection to its sewage system in consideration of a right-of-way may not, by ordinance, impair the contract, it may, by ordinance, levy a charge for sewer service.

> **Cal**   Tronslin v Sonora (1956) 144 CA2d 735, 301 P2d 891.

A public sewer system is a public utility. A municipality may, by ordinance, fix and collect reasonable service charges for the use thereof on a proper basis; and in doing so it relates to a matter of statewide concern.

Neb   Metropolitan Utility Dist v Omaha (1961) 171 Neb 609, 107 NW2d 397.

An ordinance providing for sewer service charges, the validity of which is questionable, may be validated by a curative statute, and when this is done, the subsequent legislative sanction is the equivalent of original authority.

Nev   Harris v Reno (1965) 81 Nev 256, 401 P2d 678.

§51. Enforcement; Penalties; Imprisonment

On failure to pay the garbage collection fee the city may properly discontinue water services to the premises. By operating garbage collection, water and sewer systems as city owned utilities the city may properly suspend service on all for nonpayment of one.

Tex   Breckenridge v Cozart (1972) 478 SW2d 162.

An ordinance authorizing a city to disconnect the water or sewerage connection of a delinquent user is regulatory, not penal, in nature.

Tex   Bexar County v San Antonio (1962) 352 SW2d 905.

In a prosecution for violation of an ordinance punishing the owner of a dwelling who refuses to pay the sanitary closet tax, a charge to the jury that the person would be liable if he failed and refused to pay the tax is erroneous, and a showing of failure but not refusal to pay will not sustain a conviction.

Tex   Christman v State (1915) 76 TexCr 261, 174 SW 342.

A regulation adopted by the director of public service that the water supply be shut off to residents delinquent in payment of water and sewer charges is valid and not unreasonable where a sewer rental ordinance authorizes the director to "make and enforce such bylaws and regulations" necessary for efficient management of the sewerage system.

Ohio   Gatton v Mansfield (1940) 67 OA 210, 32 Abs 662, 21 Op 195, 36 NE2d 306.

Where sewerage rental charges incurred by previous owners and levied on property acquired by complainant are certified pursuant to ordinance, and entered on the general tax duplicate as a lien, the charges are a valid lien in the nature of a tax or assessment which, if paid by complainant, cannot be recovered.

Ohio   Union Properties v Cleveland (1943) 38 Abs 246, 49 NE2d 571.

A regulation promulgated by municipal ordinance which provides that the water supply shall be shut off to residents who are delinquent in payment of sewer charges is valid, and not an unreasonable or arbitrary regulation.

> **Neb** Metropolitan Utility Dist v Omaha (1961) 171 Neb 609, 107 NW2d 397.

An ordinance providing that the water supply be shut off to residents delinquent in paying water and sewer charges is not unreasonable since it is permitted under statute and the sewer rental is based on the amount of water used.

> **Neb** Michelson v Grand Island (1951) 154 Neb 654, 48 NW2d 769.

An ordinance providing that the water supply may be cut off to a premises for nonpayment of the sewage system use charges is valid where the two services are so interlocked that neither can be effective without the other.

> **Fla** State v Miami (1946) 157 Fla 726, 27 So2d 118.
> **Tenn** Patterson v Chattanooga (1951) 192 Tenn 267, 241 SW2d 291.

An ordinance fixing charges for the use of the city sewer system, and providing for removal of the connection made by a property owner in the event of his nonpayment of the charges, is reasonable, and is not in conflict with the penal ordinance requiring the owner to make such a connection.

> **Tex** Wichita Falls v Landers (1927) 291 SW 696.

An ordinance levying a "sanitary tax", and providing for a penalty of fine or imprisonment for violation, does not violate constitutional inhibition against imprisonment for debt.

> **SC** Marion v Baxley (1939) 192 SC 112, 5 SE2d 573.

An ordinance making nonpayment of sewer rental charges a crime punishable by imprisonment is unconstitutional, since such charges are for use of the sewer, and as such constitute a debt, within the constitutional guaranty against imprisonment for debt.

> **Ariz** State v Bartos (1967) 102 Ariz 15, 423 P2d 713.

ANNOTATION

Right to cut off water supply because of failure to pay sewer service charge, 26 ALR2d 1359.

§ 52. Uses of Rentals

A municipal administrative code provision for the imposition of a sewer rental charge, with surplus sewer rental receipts, after payment of current maintenance and annual debt service, to be used only for the construction of sewage disposal and treatment plants and intercepting sewers, does not deprive one of due process in violation of the constitution.

NY Tursellino v Paduano (1951) 202 Misc 74, 107 NYS2d 839.

A charter amendment and conforming ordinance authorizing the city council to establish charges for sewer services, permitting the billing and collection of these charges with water as one item and directing the sewer service charges to be paid into a fund used only for sewer purposes are reasonable and valid.

Cal Cramer v San Diego (1958) 164 CA2d 168, 330 P2d 235.

An ordinance providing that "the operation of sewerage disposal plants shall be treated and construed as being part of the operation of water purification," is not enforceable since its ultimate result is to take moneys from water funds and expend them for purposes other than expressly limited by statute which precludes the transfer of revenues of a non-tax supported public utility to any other purpose.

Ohio Hartwig Rlty v Cleveland (1934) 128 OS 583, 1 Op 233, 192 NE 880.

Since the construction and operation of a sewage disposal system is a governmental function, an ordinance imposing charges on users of the system for the purpose of raising money for construction is valid as a revenue measure in furtherance of a proper municipal function.

Fla Buchanan v Miami (1950) 49 So2d 336.

A 6th class city with power to construct and maintain sewers does not have authority to construct and maintain sewers to raise revenue for general purposes by a toll or tax for the privilege or right to use the sewer. Such means of raising revenue cannot be implied.

Cal Madera v Black (1919) 181 Cal 306, 184 P 397.

Ordinances authorizing the combining of a city's sewerage system with its waterworks system, the improvement and extension thereof, and the issuance of bonds to cover the cost, payable out of revenue from the combined systems, is not invalid from the fact that the sewerage system in the past has been furnished to inhabitants without charge, since a city is not bound to refrain forever from making a charge for its sewerage facilities.

Mo Maryville v Cushman (1952) 363 Mo 87, 249 SW2d 347.

§53. Review

The right to judicial review of an ordinance establishing rates for a city sewage disposal system does not depend on the legislature, but is guaranteed by the due process of law clauses of the federal and state Constitutions.

Ind   State v Grant Circuit Ct (1959) 239 Ind 315, 157 NE2d 188.

In determining the validity and application of an ordinance establishing a sewerage system and prescribing rates, the court's jurisdiction extends only to considering whether it is unreasonable, arbitrary or capricious, and it has no power to establish a new rate, that being exclusively a legislative function vested in the town council.

Wash   Port Orchard v Kitsap County (1943) 19 Wash2d 59, 141 P2d 150.

An ordinance imposing rental fee for use of a public sewer, where the use is optional with the taxpayer, who is not required to pay unless he uses it, does not deprive him of property without due process of law, though it was passed without giving him notice or opportunity for hearing.

Mass   Carson v Brockton (1901) 182 US 398, 45 LEd 1151, 21 SCt 860.

A city's declaratory judgment action to determine the validity of a sewer charge ordinance does not become moot by reason of repeal of the ordinance, since the repeal does not operate to destroy or impair any rights that may have vested under the ordinance before its repeal.

Tex   Eason v Waco (1953) 262 SW2d 760.

§54. Rate Differentials

A differential in rates between single-family residential and apartments and the furnishing of free sewage service to the city's departments are all reasonable classifications. An apartment constitutes an easier and cheaper billing unit and the city is not required to bill itself for its own services.

NH   McGrath v Manchester (1979) 398 A2d 842.

Unless there is a showing that an annual sewer charge of twenty-five dollars per dwelling unit bears no reasonable relationship to the rendered sewage services, a municipal ordinance imposing a sewer charge will not be invalidated on the ground that it is unfair and discriminatory in that dwelling units are charged a flat annual sum whereas manufacturers and industrial users are charged on a flowage basis.

RI   Costello v Ricci (1979) 401 A2d 38.

A change in the manner of assessing sewer use charges which places multiple unit dwellings and mobile home parks in the same category as single-family residential property is reasonable. The fact that the multiple dwellings with one meter have a substantial increase in the rates charged since the rates are based on water consumption does not render the rate structure unreasonable or arbitrary. Likewise the provision for an adjustment subject to reasonable evidence before the board of trustees when one unit has a substantially higher consumption of water does not give the board unreasonable and unrestrained discretion.

> Ill   McDonald Mobile Homes v Swansea (1977) 56 IllAp3d 759, 371 NE2d 1155.

A surcharge may be imposed for excessive industrial waste discharge. The greater the amount of waste the more wear and tear on the treatment facilities.

> Ill   Chicago Allis Manufacturing v Metropolitan Sanitary Dist of Greater Chicago
> (1972) 52 Ill2d 320, 288 NE2d 436.

A city ordinance which imposes a sewer service charge on apartment houses consisting of five or more dwelling units served by a single water meter but not on structures having four or less units or having individual water meters for each unit is not a denial of equal protection. The classification used by the city is the same as that used by the department of water and power for billing collection.

> Cal   Apart Assn of Los Angeles County v Los Angeles (1977) 75 CA3d 13, 141 CaR
> 794.

Sewer rates may properly be based on a minimum charge plus a unit charge for commercial, trailer parks and other commercial enterprises. It is not necessary that the sewer charge be equal for all types of users since many uses do not generate sewage, and the rates may be based-on a reasonable classification.

> Cal   Boynton v Lakeport Municipal Sewer Dist #1 (1972) 28 CA3d 91, 104 CaR 409.

Water and sewer rates may be classified differently for trailer parks than for motels and hotels. However, the department may not differentiate in charges between apartment owners and trailer courts or between trailer courts. The ordinance must be applied uniformly to all in the same class.

> Neb   Reimer v O'Neill (1972) 189 Neb 151, 201 NW2d 706.

A sewage rate for each apartment which is the same as that charged smaller multiple-family dwellings and single-family dwellings is not unreasonable. It is not necessary that a rate of flow be determined for the various types of living accommodations.

> NJ   Piscataway Apart Assn v Piscataway Township (1974) 131 NJS 83, 328 A2d
> 631; affd (1974) 66 NJ 106, 328 A2d 608.

The classification for water, sewage, and garbage collection placing hotels, motels, apartments, and mobile home parks in a different classification from other commercial users is reasonable except as to hotels and motels. The transit nature of the hotel and motel guest lends to a commercial classification.

    Okla   Oklahoma City Hotel & MHA v Oklahoma City (1974) 531 P2d 316.

Where a city's sewer rates are fixed on the basis of amount of water used, that the ordinance prescribes a flat rate in some cases, while others pay by meter, does not render the ordinance per se arbitrary or discriminatory.

    Wyo   Antlers Hotel v Newcastle (1959) 80 Wyo 294, 341 P2d 951.

The rates for sewer services may be properly based on a flat rate for single-family residences and all other uses on a per month per gallon of water used, and a minimum charge. This may be applied to duplexes, apartments, and all other multiple-type dwellings. The rate may properly be set at the end of the meeting called for its consideration, and it is not necessary to approve the ordinance at a subsequent meeting.

    Fla   State v Miami Springs (1971) 245 So2d 80.

An ordinance establishing a schedule of rates for water and sewer services is not invalid as discriminatory on the ground that the charges are not the same in each district, it appearing that the cost of providing services varies in the various districts. Absolute uniformity in public service rates is not required.

    Fla   State v Dade County (1961) 127 So2d 881.

An ordinance providing for a sewer rental system based on flat water rents will not be set aside, provided the flat water rate classifications are reasonable.

    Pa   Hickory v Brockway (1963) 201 PaS 260, 192 A2d 231.

A city has complete liberty to permit or deny the use of its sewer system, as well as the right to impose a reasonable differential in rates, on those outside its borders.

    Ohio   State ex rel Stoeckle v Jones (1953) 96 OA 382, 54 Op 373, 121 NE2d 922, affd (1954) 161 OS 391, 53 Op 303, 119 NE2d 834.

A court is not justified in sanctioning a city council's passage of an ordinance imposing an annual sewer rental charge not apportioned equitably among property owners according to their use of the sewers, merely because of the urgency of the municipality's sewerage disposal problem.

    Pa   Philadelphia, Petition of (1941) 343 Pa 47, 21 A2d 876.

An ordinance fixing the sewer rental at 20 per cent of the water charge is arbitrary, improper, inequitable and unlawful where the city accepts back only five per cent of water furnished a manufacturer because the remainder is polluted, and charges the same price as charged other industries doing the same type work but it accepts back all their waste water.

> **Pa**   North East v A Piece of Land (1960) 191 PaS 532, 159 A2d 528.

An ordinance providing for a sewer rental system and classifying users as commercial or residential is prima facie reasonable.

> **Pa**   Hickory v Brockway (1963) 201 PaS 260, 192 A2d 231.

Though an ordinance setting up a sewer rental system unduly favors some water consumers by fixing uniform rentals for each residence and imposing a fixed charge for each receptacle on the premises of motels, the motel owners are not entitled to a reduction in rates.

> **Pa**   Hickory v Brockway (1963) 201 PaS 260, 192 A2d 231.

An ordinance imposing an annual sewerage charge based on water consumption of the properties served, as measured by water charges for the current year, cannot be struck down in its entirety merely because it provides special rates for charitable institutions and private schools.

> **Pa**   Gericke v Philadelphia (1945) 353 Pa 60, 44 A2d 233.

A sewer charge ordinance, founding its rates principally on the total of individual residents living in dwelling units in the city, is valid where it does not create an arbitrary and discriminatory classification of persons required to pay the quarterly "minimum fee," contrary to the equal protection clauses of the Michigan Constitution and the Fourteenth Amendment to the federal Constitution.

> **Mich**   Land v Grandville (1966) 2 Mich Ap 681, 141 NW2d 370.

An ordinance providing for sewage service to residents and requiring a meter in each apartment, or payment of the flat quarterly fee for each apartment, is not arbitrary, unreasonable or discriminatory since it is normal procedure in municipalities to bill each dwelling unit for sewer services and by their nature, size and additional kitchen facilities as opposed to normal one-room hotel and rooming house accommodations, apartments should be treated like other dwelling units.

> **Pa**   Greenville v Guerrini (1966) 208 PaS 42, 220 A2d 366.

An ordinance imposing annual sewer charges apportioned between users paying by meter and non-metered users paying appliance rates is not an unjust discrimination, but is an equitable apportionment, since the diversity of use, of circumstances, and of quantities used by members of a class cannot be measured with mathematical exactness. An unmetered property owner may install a meter at any time and pass into the other class.

Pa   Gericke v Philadelphia (1945) 353 Pa 60, 44 A2d 233.

An ordinance establishing sewer rates in an addition to the original sewer district cannot be declared invalid if it is shown that residents in the original sewer district are not charged less than residents in the addition. This is evidence that the city council did not act arbitrarily in passing the ordinance.

Ark   Lawrence v Jones (1958) 228 Ark 1136, 313 SW2d 228.

In determining the reasonableness of a sewer or water rate ordinance prescribing different rates for different types of users, the court will adhere to the doctrine that not every discrimination is condemned, but only discrimination that is arbitrary, since it is impossible to measure the justness of a rate on a mathematical basis.

Wyo   Antlers Hotel v Newcastle (1959) 80 Wyo 294, 341 P2d 951.

The rendition of sewerage and water service by a municipal rather than a privately owned utility does not change the rule prohibiting unreasonable discrimination in rates charged, and the municipal plant is subject to the rules applicable to a privately owned utility.

Ill   Conner v Elmhurst (1963) 28 Ill2d 221, 190 NE2d 760.

ANNOTATIONS

Validity and construction of regulation by municipal corporations fixing sewer-use rates, 61 ALR3d 1236.

Discrimination between property within and that outside municipality or other governmental district as to rates for use of drains or sewers, 4 ALR2d 610.

§55. Computation of Amount

A classification under which a village's charge for sewer service to multifamily structures with individual meters for each unit was a monthly charge multiplied by the number of units but the charge for service to structures with one meter would be 75 per cent of the water bill for the entire structure if greater than the monthly charge multiplied by the number of units did not deny equal protection, since the rational basis for classification could be provided by the fact that it may have been counter-cost effective to determine for individually metered apartments whether 75 per cent of the water bill exceeded the monthly charge but it may have been cost effective to make the determination for large apartment complexes with a single meter.

> **Ill**   Highcrest Management v Woodridge Village (1978) 60 IllAp3d 763, 377 NE2d 315.

A charter provision prohibiting a public utility from enacting emergency legislation does not apply to a rate increase for a municipal sewer district.

> **Ohio**   Columbus ex rel Willits v Cremean (1971) 27 OA2d 137, 57 Op2d 201, 276 NE2d 271.

An ordinance establishing sewer rates may make allowance for depreciation of the existing plant. Rates which cover actual operating expense and only a portion of depreciation are not unreasonable or excessive.

> **NJ**   Crowe v Sparta (1969) 106 NJS 204, 254 A2d 801.

While the rates for a public utility may be determined on the prudent investment theory or original cost basis there must be a determination that the rates are not confiscatory or deprive the utility of its right to a fair return. The exclusion of contributed services, such as lines layed by subdividers, may be deducted; however, their life expectancy and replacement cost must be considered.

> **Fla**   Westwood Lake v Dade County (1972) 264 So2d 7.

An initiative measure may not be used to effect a tax levy or appropriation for current expenses. Therefore, an initiative measure to change the method of determining sewer rates is ineffective, as an attempt to change tax levies.

> **Cal**   Dare v Lakeport (1970) 12 CA3d 864, 91 CaR 124.

A utility regulation ordinance providing for rates to be established on the actual legitimate cost of the property does not allow the hearing board to substitute purchase price. The original cost minus depreciation can be reconstructed by engineer's estimates and must include contributions made to determine replacement value.

> **Fla**   Fla Crown Utility Services v Utility Regulatory Bd of Jacksonville (1973) 274 So2d 597.

An increase in the water and sewer rates is not a tax and therefore is within the rights of the city though the increase produces more revenue than necessary for operation and debt retirement. The excess may properly be transferred to the general funds under the authority to supplement the budget for items not contemplated; however, the resolution requiring approval by the Attorney

General and the Department of Finance and Administration is binding on the city.

NM   Apodaca v Wilson (1974) 86 NM 516, 525 P2d 876.

An ordinance imposing a sewer fee for the use of a public sewer, basing the amount on the amount of water used and making the person purchasing the water liable for the sewer fee, is valid.

Okla   Sharp v Hall (1947) 198 Okla 678, 181 P2d 972.

An ordinance imposing a sewer service charge on the users of the city sewage disposal facilities, basing the amount on the amount of water used, and making the person purchasing the water liable therefor does not impair the obligation of contract.

Okla   Chastain v Oklahoma City (1953) 208 Okla 604, 258 P2d 635.

A flat rate sewer charge is not arbitrary. The town is authorized to collect the cost of sewer installation and construction and may base residential property on a flat rate and commercial on a water use rate.

Pa   Glen Riddle Park v Middletown Township (1974) 11 PaCmwlth 574, 314 A2d 524.

An ordinance imposing a sewer rental rate based on the assessed valuation of property served is not authorized by the dependence of the cost of sewage disposal on the type and quantity of sewage, since the value of the property has no relation to type of sewage.

Pa   Philadelphia, Petition of (1941) 343 Pa 47, 21 A2d 876.

It is not necessary that an ordinance providing for sewer rentals base the rates on water cost or water consumption.

Pa   Hickory v Brockway (1963) 201 PaS 260, 192 A2d 231.

A sewer ordinance imposing an annual charge based on water consumption measured by charges for the water supplied for the current calendar year is not invalid on the ground that utility charges cannot be founded on a base rate fluctuating by the year, where the rate remains the same though the total revenue may not be the same every year.

Pa   Gericke v Philadelphia (1945) 353 Pa 60, 44 A2d 233.

An Administrative Code provision basing a sewer charge for industrial firms on the average concentration of excess pollutants in a user's sewage, multiplied by its estimated volume, with the product of these factors multiplied by the unit cost of treatment in the city's sewage treatment plant, is constitutional as applied to sweetgoods wholesale bakers.

> **NY**   Larsen Baking v New York City (1968) 30 AD2d 400, 292 NYS2d 145, affd (1969) 24 NY2d 1036, 303 NYS2d 80, 250 NE2d 356.

A contract with a dairy establishing sewer rates approved by resolution of the board of trustees is void. The authority to establish sewage rates is contingent on their being set by ordinance or local law, and a resolution does not satisfy this requirement.

> **NY**   Canastota v Queensboro Farm Products (1974) 44 AD2d 276, 354 NYS2d 451.

An ordinance imposing a sewer rental is valid though a large portion of the sewer usage consists in draining off storm water and the individual who uses the sewers for his sanitary and industrial sewage must pay for it rather than the taxpayers as a whole, since only 25 per cent of the sewer construction cost is allotted to storm water collection and the direct benefit to the property warrants its inclusion in the charge.

> **Pa**   Gericke v Philadelphia (1945) 353 Pa 60, 44 A2d 233.

An ordinance establishing sewer rates based on the construction of new facilities by a municipal authority with a lease back to the municipality is valid. The fact that previous quarterly rentals paid to the adjoining town were substantially less does not make the fee unreasonable.

> **Pa**   Brandywine Homes v Caln Township Municipal Auth (1975) 19 Pa Cmwlth 193, 339 A2d 145.

In a sparsely populated area in which a high percentage of the population lives in apartment complexes and mobile home courts, a sewer construction charge may be determined on a per unit rather than front footage basis.

> **Wash**   Silver Shores Mobile Home Park v Everett (1976) 87 Wash2d 618, 555 P2d 993.

§56. Charge without Use

A sewer rental charge may properly be assessed to a user even though his refuse is not presently being disposed of in the waste water treatment center. The collection of the fee for previously established sewer systems is proper since the city has only one system regardless of the disposal of the sewage.

> **NH**   McGrath v Manchester (1979) 398 A2d 842.

The assessment of full sewer service charges on the owners of a condominium apartment building under an ordinance providing that sewer service charges begin on the date the user is connected to the sewer main, is not an unconstitutional deprivation of property rights even though a significant number of the condominium apartment units are unoccupied. Sewage charges which are reasonably related to the value received from the service rendered either as actually consumed or as readily available for use are not within the constitutional proscription against deprivation of property rights.

Fla Redington Shores v Redington Towers (1978) 354 So2d 942.

A sewer use charge per family unit in a duplex and apartment building or residence regardless of occupancy, but exempting residence during the period they are vacant, discriminates against apartment owners.

Mo Blue Inv Co v Raytown (1972) 478 SW2d 361.

A charge for sewer usage against persons not connected to the city sewage system is invalid.

Kan Jennings v Walsh (1974) 214 Kan 398, 521 P2d 311.

A charge imposed by ordinance for sewer service must be based on actual use and must be reasonably proportional to the value of service rendered, not in excess of it.

NY Rock Hill Sewerage v Thompson (1966) 27 AD2d 626, 276 NYS2d 188.
Pa North East v A Piece of Land (1960) 191 PaS 532, 159 A2d 528.
    Philadelphia, Petition of (1941) 343 Pa 47, 21 A2d 876.

Where a sewerage service for which money is collected by a municipality as provided by an ordinance is abandoned, the city must make restitution.

Minn Knutson Hotel v Moorhead (1957) 250 Minn 392, 84 NW2d 626.

An ordinance permitting sewer rental charges by a sewerage disposal corporation only when the facilities are connected and used by property owners is not unconstitutional on the ground that it deprives the corporation of property without due process of law, where the only alleged rights of the corporation accrue as the result of an illegal and void ordinance. The corporation may not recover charges levied under an unlawful agreement stemming from a void resolution.

NY Rock Hill Sewerage v Thompson (1966) 27 AD2d 626, 276 NYS2d 188.

A charge for use of a sewer is not a tax or special assessment. It is a charge for a service rendered, and is based on contract. Thus, land located 200 feet from a sewer but not using the sewer cannot be charged for its use, as the non-use means there is no acceptance of the city's offer of the service and thus no contract.

> **Ore**   Stanfield v Burnett (1960) 222 Ore 427, 353 P2d 242.

§57. Charge for Future Use

A storm sewer fee may not be collected from each home site when the facilities have not been provided. The fee is neither a tax nor assessment, and since no storm sewer construction has been commenced during the eight years of collection the fee is invalid.

> **Colo**   Aurora v Bogue (1971) 176 Colo 198, 489 P2d 1295.

An ordinance imposing an annual sewer rental that increases on an annual basis for a five-year construction period is reasonable and the charges are equitably apportioned since it is assumed that the council intended to legislate constitutionally and did not intend to charge a property owner for the use of a system before it is available.

> **Pa**   Gericke v Philadelphia (1945) 353 Pa 60, 44 A2d 233.

§58. Exempt and Nonexempt Users

A contract whereby the city agrees to furnish all services without charge to a public housing authority that are furnished to the citizens of the town makes the authority liable for sewerage charges when applied to residents. A sewerage rate charge against the residents to cover revenue bonds is also applicable to the housing authority.

> **Pa**   Scranton Housing Auth v Scranton (1971) 2 PaCmwlth 489, 284 A2d 148.

A municipal housing commission created by statute for the purpose of clearing slums and developing low cost housing projects may be required to pay sewer service charges to the city under an ordinance imposing "a sewer service charge in the nature of a toll or rental upon every person who purchases water from the city", notwithstanding an agreement with the city that certain enumerated public services and facilities would be furnished without cost or charge.

> **Ky**   Danville Municipal Housing v Danville (1958) 319 SW2d 460.

An ordinance fixing sewer usage rates applies to outlets discharging sewerage from federal lands, in spite of an agreement between the city and the federal government waiving sewer charges in lieu of federal contributions to the cost of building the city sewer system, because a city cannot contract away its delegated legislative authority to provide for the safety and health of its residents.

Ark Lamar Bath House v Hot Springs (1958) 229 Ark 214, 315 SW2d 884.

A sewer rental ordinance is valid though the city does not collect from itself an annual charge for the use of the sewers, since the situation is not within the rule that a public utility corporation may not render free service to a patron and there is no legal reason why the city, which owns and operates the system, should take money from its taxpayers to pay itself for the use of its own sewers.

Pa Gericke v Philadelphia (1945) 353 Pa 60, 44 A2d 233.

Under an ordinance imposing an annual sewer rental on the city as the trustee and owner of certain leased premises, the sewer rental is within the meaning of the term "city and school taxes and any other taxes or charges of like nature" that may be imposed, in a present lease for adjustment of rental, either as an increase or decrease in taxes occurs.

Pa Philadelphia v Snellenburg (1949) 163 PaS 507, 63 A2d 480.

Sewer rents are not restricted to private consumers, but extend unquestionably to the state, where the officials who accept the service have the power to act in the matter.

NH Justices, Opinion of (1944) 93 NH 478, 39 A2d 765.

§58.1. Referendum

Referendum proceedings may not be instituted against an ordinance raising the rates for water and sewer fees.

Mich Yurek v Sterling Heights (1971) 37 Mich Ap 386, 194 NW2d 474.

VI. LOCATION OF FACILITIES; LAND ACQUISITION

A. ZONING

§59. Generally

When a state planning enabling act does not give counties the authority to use zoning to control the location of sewage facilities, a later statutory provision expressly granting cities and towns full jurisdiction and authority to regulate and control sewage treatment facilities is controlling. A municipality's eminent domain power under such a statutory scheme is superior to a county's zoning regulations so as to allow the placement of a sewage treatment plant in a county general use zone without the necessity of obtaining an unclassified use permit or a substantial development permit normally required under local regulations.

> **Wash**   South Hill Sewer Dist v Pierce County (1979) 22 WashAp 738, 591 P2d 877.

A sanitary district with the power of eminent domain is not subject to zoning ordinances within a host city.

> **Ill**   Des Plaines v Metropolitan Sanitary Dist of Greater Chicago (1971) 48 Ill2d 11, 268 NE2d 428.
> People ex rel Scott v Northshore Sanitary Dist (1971) 132 IllAp2d 854, 270 NE2d 133.

An 1891 ordinance providing for the construction of a sewer but not specifically describing the location of the sewer was not notice to the landowner of the sewer's existence or notice of the adverse claim or use by the city for the purpose of establishing in the city an easement by prescription.

> **Ill**   Seefeldt v Lincoln (1978) 373 NE2d 85.

Construction of a sewerage treatment plant is a governmental function for the continued well-being and health of the community, as well as of those in nearby sections. Where the state has enacted considerable legislation on water pollution, the municipality acts as an arm of the state government and is not restricted by zoning ordinances. Thus, a treatment plant may be constructed in a residential area without regard to a restriction on government buildings.

> **Vt**   Kedroff v Springfield (1969) 127 Vt 624, 256 A2d 457.

Operation of a sewage disposal plant is a governmental function, and therefore is not subject to the city's zoning ordinances.

> **Fla**   A1A Mobile Home Park v Brevard County (1971) 246 So2d 126.

A variance may be granted on showing special reasons and a negative showing that the public good would not be affected. It is not necessary that the particular property be useless for the permitted use or that other hardships exist. A variance for a tertiary sewage treatment plant may be permitted when the existing septic tank system is unsatisfactory.

> **NJ**   Wickatunk Village v Marlboro (1972) 118 NJS 445, 288 A2d 308.

An ordinance enacted by a county, under authority of its constitutional home rule charter, zoning land in a district exclusively for residential use, and excluding such land from use for construction and operation of a sewage treatment plant and related facilities, is enacted as a governmental function to promote the public health, and statutory authority vested in cities to construct sewage treatment plants may not be exercised to the contrary.

    Mo St Louis County v Manchester (1962) 360 SW2d 638.

A sewerage lift station constructed above ground as part of a vital and necessary private sewer system, not yet dedicated for municipal use and located in a residential district, is not subject to the setback and yard requirements established for the district by the zoning ordinance, and though the lift station is not permitted in the district the penalties for unauthorized use may not be imposed where the city has acquiesced in and suffers the existence of a considerable number of other lift stations without attempting to enforce the setback restrictions.

    NY Howell v Liebowitz (1952) 116 NYS2d 537.

A zoning ordinance restricting an area to single family dwellings allows the operation and maintenance of a sewage treatment and disposal plant as a municipal use, where it furnishes a sewage disposal system for 309 families in the township.

    Pa Lees v Sampson Land Co (1952) 372 Pa 126, 92 A2d 692.

Treatment lagoons for the waste product from an apple and peach canning plant are an accessory use to the plant. A variance or reclassification to permit their location in a residential zone is improper when the areas have made provisions for industrial uses. The treatment plant is not a separate operation but is a use accessory to the principal use of fruit processing and packing.

    Pa Red Cheek v Supervisor of Ruscombmanor Township (1976) 26 PaCmwlth 530, 364 A2d 542.

A variance to permit an enlargement of a sewage facility's sludge drying beds was warranted where it appeared that a denial would produce undue hardship approaching confiscation of its property, that such hardship is not shared generally by other properties in the district, and that granting the variance would not adversely affect the health, safety or general welfare of the neighborhood.

    Va Tidewater Utility v Norfolk (1968) 208 Va 705, 160 SE2d 799.

B. Land Acquisition; Eminent Domain

§60. For Construction

The disposal of sewage is a governmental function, and the use of land for a sewage disposal plant is a public use, for which a city may, by ordinance, condemn property.

> **Wash**   Church v Superior Ct (1952) 40 Wash2d 90, 240 P2d 1208.

The discretionary power vested in a city council to determine what property shall be taken for a sewer line is not subject to judicial control, except where the municipal authorities act fraudulently.

> **Ky**   First Nat Bk of Paducah v Paducah (1924) 202 Ky 48, 258 SW 938.
> Jackson v Riffle (1927) 219 Ky 689, 294 SW 142.

A city operating under the general law has no power to own and operate a sewage disposal plant within the limits of a home rule city, without the latter's consent and may not condemn land so situated for that purpose.

> **Tex**   Plano v Allen (1965) 395 SW2d 927.

An ordinance directing the construction of a sewer on certain streets is an acknowledgment by the city that they are public ways and is sufficient to constitute their acceptance. The ordinance is not invalid merely because the streets were not previously accepted as public ways.

> **Ky**   Mulligan v McGregor (1915) 165 Ky 122, 176 SW 1129.

ANNOTATION

Construction or maintenance of sewers, water pipes, or the like by public authorities in roadway, street, or alley as indicating dedication, 52 ALR2d 263.

§61. Procedural Requirements

A resolution for condemnation to extend sewer and water mains is invalid when it does not contain a finding of necessity. The proposed extension and requirement that the adjoining owners connect to the system is not sufficiently complied with when the owner of one of the properties would be adjacent to the lateral and the area in which the extension is contemplated is not a block as normally described.

Wis Vandervelde v Green Lake (1976) 240 NW2d 399.

A description of real estate is sufficient for purposes of condemnation for a sewage disposal plant, if the land can be identified by one skilled in such matters, such as a surveyor or an engineer. The office of the description is not necessarily fully to identify, but to furnish the means by which the land may be identified with certainty.

Ind Hagemann v Mt Vernon (1958) 238 Ind 613, 154 NE2d 33.

Where land is taken by eminent domain under an ordinance appropriating the land for sewers, the owner is entitled to receive the full market value as of the date of appropriation.

Neb Stuhr v Grand Island (1933) 124 Neb 285, 246 NW 461.

While the invasion of private property by public authorities and its subjection to public use for sewer purposes is a taking of property within the meaning of constitutional provisions requiring just compensation a claim for such compensation cannot be made a setoff or counterclaim in a suit to enforce the lien for the work done in the construction of the sewer, where the contractor asserting it does the work in accordance with the plans and ordinances of the municipality.

Ky Fischer v James A Diskin Co (1933) 247 Ky 694, 57 SW2d 538.

Notwithstanding that the language used in an ordinance appropriating certain property for city use, and setting forth the time and place for assessors to meet and fix the amount of damages of each of the landowners could have more clearly stated the same, it was at most an irregularity and was waived by not raising it when appeal was taken to the district court.

Neb Webber v Scottsbluff (1951) 155 Neb 48, 50 NW2d 533.

An ordinance condemning certain property in order to construct an impounding lagoon for treatment of waste, and providing that the municipality might refuse to accept the property or to pay the award of the assessors if the amount, manner of payment, and terms should not be satisfactory, is invalid as an exercise of the power of eminent domain when the city has not complied with the requirements to exercise it.

Ga Thomas v Cairo (1950) 206 Ga 336, 57 SE2d 192.

Under an ordinance levying assessments for sewer construction, where the authority of the city to build a sewer to follow the natural drainage and over private property wherever it could acquire a right-of-way is not disputed, and where a property owner stands by and acquiesces in the construction of the sewer through his property until long after the work is completed, the city is deemed to have acquired a right-of-way over such property.

Ky Fischer v James A Diskin Co (1933) 247 Ky 694, 57 SW2d 538.

Where, within a city's sewer district created by ordinance, a sewer is laid as a permanent structure the length of a lot, but without acquisition of the right from the landowner by deed or condemnation, any cause of action resulting to the landowner for damages for violation of a property right does not pass to a subsequent purchaser by a conveyance of the land.

Okla Long v Tulsa (1947) 199 Okla 217, 184 P2d 800.

A provision in an ordinance for the construction of a sewer to be built through a private alley that the improvement was to be paid for by special assessment constituted an assertion on the part of the city that it would exercise its power to procure the property, and assessed property owners may not object that the property was not yet procured at the time of the assessment.

Ill People v Sass (1898) 171 Ill 357, 49 NE 501.

VII. CONTRACTS; CONSTRUCTION OF FACILITIES

A. Bids

§62. Necessity; Effect on Contract

Where a city has authority to construct a sewer at a cost not exceeding the city engineer's estimate with no statutory command as to the manner of letting the contract, though an ordinance is enacted requiring the work to be let to the lowest and best bidder, a contract let without requiring such bids and without the execution of a written contract and a performance bond is invalid; tax bills issued under such unwarranted procedure are void; and one purchasing property against which such a tax bill has been issued may not, on payment thereof, recover from the former owner on a claim that the tax bill was a cloud on the title.

Mo Lemon v Shepherd (1914) 180 MoApp 332, 167 SW 1145.

Where an ordinance as amended eliminates an unconstitutional bond issue and the installment improvement plan to the assessment of liens against abutting owners for sewer construction costs, a readvertisement of the bidding and reletting of the contract is not required since the contractor is the lowest and best bidder where his bid is in terms of dollars, and since he need not be paid in bonds, as contended, there is no change in the bidding specifications set forth in the original ordinance.

Ky   Little v Southgate (1928) 223 Ky 692, 4 SW2d 711.

An ordinance authorizing construction of a joint district sewer will not be held invalid for delay in execution of the contract, where all bids on two successive occasions were turned down as excessive and the contract was finally let after the third publication.

Mo   Heman Constr v Lyon (1919) 277 Mo 628, 211 SW 68.

An ordinance providing for the construction of a sewer and the letting of a contract therefor, requiring the city clerk to advertise for bids, and requiring each bidder to furnish a certified check guaranteeing execution of the contract and reserving to the city the right to reject any and all bids is not an offer of a contract, but an offer to receive proposals for a contract.

Mo   Washington v Mueller (1926) 220 MoApp 564, 287 SW 856.

§63. Notice to Bidders

Where a city has statutory authority to construct sewers but is not required to award construction contracts on competitive bidding pursuant to publication of notice thereof, an ordinance directing the city clerk to cause an advertisement for bids to be published, but not providing that the contract shall be let to the lowest bidder, has served its purpose when such publication has been made; and when all bids received in response thereto are rejected, the board is free to negotiate for construction of the project without repealing or amending the ordinance.

Mo   Gast v Langston (1929) 15 SW2d 353.

An ordinance requiring publication of advertisements for bids for construction of a sewer in a local newspaper "for not less than one week" is not complied with where the notice is published for the first time in a local newspaper at 5 PM on December 20, stating that bids will not be received after 9 AM on December 27.

Mo   Williams v Ettenson (1914) 178 MoApp 178, 170 SW 370.

Where an ordinance authorizes construction of a sewer by reference to specifications distributed to bidders and there is no showing that any bidder was actually misled or deterred from bidding or that property owners within the joint sewer district were in fact injured, the ordinance is valid.

> **Mo**   Badger Lumber v Mullins (1925) 310 Mo 602, 275 SW 957.

Where an ordinance authorizes construction of sewers, and provides for advertising for bids in appropriate newspapers by at least two insertions published at least 15 days before the opening of the bids, two publications in one newspaper, the last appearing 12 days before the date of opening of bids, is not sufficient compliance, and tax bills issued thereunder are void.

> **Mo**   Webster Groves v Reber (1919) 212 SW 38.

Where a city by ordinances establishes a sewer district and authorizes construction of a district sewer according to plans and specifications made by the city engineer, and requires the letting of the contract to the lowest and best bidder, a contract let without advertising for bids is not legally authorized, and tax bills issued against benefited property are void.

> **Mo**   Thrasher v Kirksville (1918) 204 SW 804.

Under an ordinance assessing sewer costs against abutting owners, where the deadline date for submission of bids is extended and no notice is given by publication of the extension of time, the assessments are invalid.

> **Ky**   Preston Land v Paintsville (1921) 192 Ky 738, 234 SW 445.

Tax bills assessed for a joint district sewer will not be held invalid on the ground that the ordinance contains no requirement for advertising for bids for the work, where such advertising was nevertheless done in accordance with charter requirements.

> **Mo**   Heman Constr v Lyon (1919) 277 Mo 628, 211 SW 68.

B. Contracts

§64. Generally

A city has not violated an ordinance contract providing for sewage water for irrigation purposes when the transportation of the water through an open canal is prohibited by an injunction. Under the ordinance-contract terms the recipients of the irrigation water do not have a vested right nor a right to compensation if the city is required to change its method of sewage treatment. There is no obligation on the part of the city to construct a covered canal for transportation of the water in order to continue the terms of the original agreement.

> **Tex** Wagner v San Antonio (1977) 559 SW2d 672.

Operation of a treatment plant for packing house waste on a lease-purchase agreement with the city does not require a franchise.

> **Neb** Cosentino v Omaha (1971) 186 Neb 407, 183 NW2d 475.

Formality of enactment and publication of an ordinance is not necessary in order to validate the award of a contract by a city to construct a sewer system, since the execution of the contract could be authorized and effectuated by a resolution or other proper means.

> **Kan** Botts v Valley Center (1927) 124 Kan 9, 257 P 226.
> **Mo** Haskins v DeSoto (1931) 35 SW2d 964.

An ordinance authorizing a contract for sewage disposal is validly enacted without the mayor's signature, when he does not return it to the city clerk with his written objections within the time prescribed by statute.

> **Ky** Russell v Flatwoods (1965) 394 SW2d 900.

An ordinance declared to be an emergency measure for the immediate preservation of the city's peace, health and safety, and authorizing the chairman of the city commission to execute a contract for engineering services on a proposed sewerage system, complies with a statute requiring a political subdivision desiring to make such a survey to adopt a resolution declaring the purpose and necessity therefor.

> **Ohio** Jones v Middletown (1948) 59 Abs 329, 96 NE2d 799.

Under an ordinance and a resolution apportioning the costs of sewer construction on abutting owners, where a member of the city council is directly or indirectly interested or acts as surety on a contract for doing the work, such contract is void and no recovery may be had for the cost of the work, either on the contract or to collect the assessments.

> **Ky** Wilson v Smith (1926) 215 Ky 504, 284 SW 1102.

C. CONTRACTORS

§65. Bonds

In an ordinance regulating installation of a sewage disposal system, a provision requiring the installer of such system to furnish maintenance bond is invalid as beyond the scope of enabling act which contains no provision for a bond.

NJ   Itzen & Robertson v Oakland (1965) 89 NJS 374, 215 A2d 60.

Sewer work in a city and the making of contracts therefor by the city are municipal affairs, and a bond given pursuant to state law in connection with sewer work in a city with a freeholders' charter is without consideration and void.

Cal   Loop Lumb v Van Loben Sels (1916) 173 Cal 228, 159 P 600.

Where an ordinance authorizing construction of a sewer includes plans and specifications on which bids are to be submitted and a requirement that after the bid is accepted the contractor will make a required bond within 20 days from the date of award, and that on his failure to furnish such bond his accompanying certified check for $1,000 shall be forfeited to the city as confessed liquidated damages, a contractor failing to execute the bond as required thereby forfeits his check for liquidated damages and may not ground his failure to execute the bond on the fact that the sewer system as laid out by the city was platted across private property on which easements for right-of-way had not been obtained by the city, where it had not represented that it had obtained such easements.

Mo   Coonan v Cape Girardeau (1910) 149 MoApp 609, 129 SW 745.

§66. Rights and Liabilities

Where an ordinance authorizes a firm to prepare plans, specifications and estimates of cost for a complete sanitary sewer and disposal system, to be paid therefor five per cent of the complete cost of the contract, of which amount three per cent of the estimated cost is to be paid on presentation of final detailed plans and specifications for "such portion of the work which the city council should deem advisable to construct," the firm is entitled to payment thereunder when the city by resolution approves the plans and adopts ordinance for construction of a part thereof, though all bids submitted for the work are rejected.

Mo   Benham v Marceline (1923) 213 MoApp 653, 251 SW 748.

Where a city council orders sewering without the power of a valid ordinance or resolution, a contract between the city and a contractor is invalid and is not binding on the municipality.

Iowa   Citizens' Bk v Spencer (1904) 126 Iowa 101, 101 NW 643.

Where a resolution authorizes the supervising engineer of a sewer construction to take charge of the work and complete it when the contractor abandons the project, the engineer may bring action to recover for his services though he may not perform some duties required of him by his prior contract.

Va Newport News v Potter (1903) 122 F 321.

A municipal corporation and its officers are not liable in damages to contractors who make bids based on excessive estimates made by the city engineer for the construction of sewers when the contractors are thereby precluded from payment for work done because of the unenforceability of the ordinance levying assessments for construction costs.

Okla Reed v Bartlesville (1925) 108 Okla 62, 234 P 642.

Under an ordinance authorizing a tunnel sewer, to be constructed in accordance with plans and specifications prepared by the city engineer and within his estimate, a subsequent restriction imposed by the city prohibiting blasting between the hours of 11 PM and 6 AM does not violate the contract or authorize a recovery of damages by the contractor, where such restriction was acquiesced in by him, was not rigidly enforced, and was reasonably imposed for the peace and safety of nearby citizens.

Mo United Constr v St Louis (1934) 334 Mo 1006, 69 SW2d 639.

Where an ordinance authorizing construction of a sewer does not specify a completion date, but the contract entered into does contain such a date, and an ordinance is enacted ratifying and confirming the contract, completion must be within a reasonable time.

Mo Koch v Shepherd (1917) 193 SW 601.

§67. Necessary Parties to Suit

Where an ordinance authorizes construction of a sewer, the cost of construction to be paid by a sewer tax levied on all real estate, the contractors to do the work are not necessary parties where a taxpayer brings action to enjoin collection of the assessment, contending it is unlawful when applied to him.

Iowa Chicago M & S P Ry v Phillips (1900) 111 Iowa 377, 82 NW 787.

D. CONSTRUCTION REQUIREMENTS

§68. Estimates

Where a city's statutory authority to construct sewers is conditioned on an estimate of the cost being made by the city engineer and submitted to the board

117

of aldermen, and where an ordinance is adopted and a contract awarded without such estimate, tax bills issued to cover the cost of construction will be canceled, in a suit brought by property owners charged therewith.

Mo   Williams v Hybskmann (1925) 311 Mo 332, 278 SW 377.

Under a statutory requirement that before the awarding of any sewer contract by the board of aldermen an estimate of the cost shall be made by the city engineer and submitted to the board, an ordinance awarding the contract, and tax bills issued on assessments to cover the costs thereof, are valid, where the requirement of the estimate has been substantially complied with by filing it on the day after adoption of the ordinance.

Mo   Ferguson v Steffen (1928) 300 SW 1039.

§69. Alterations; Variances from Original Plans

Tax bills issued under an ordinance authorizing construction of a joint district sewer will not be declared invalid on the ground that actual costs exceeded estimated costs, where the ordinance does not require the project to be completed within the estimate.

Mo   Heman Constr v Lyon (1919) 277 Mo 628, 211 SW 68.

Where an ordinance providing for construction of a sewer requires that the city council contract with the lowest bidder, the council may not after acceptance of the low bid alter the specifications under which the bid was submitted and include the added cost of the alteration in the contract, and a special assessment levied under such circumstances is void.

Ore   Smith v Portland (1894) 25 Ore 297, 35 P 665.

Tax bills assessed against benefited property, under an ordinance for construction of a joint district sewer, will not be canceled on the ground that authorized work was not completed at the time the bills were issued, where work was terminated by the board of public service by reason of flood conditions and the contractor was not paid for contracted work which was not done, though use of the completed sewer under the circumstances was denied to property owners beyond the contracted date for completion.

Mo   Haeussler Inv v Bates (1924) 306 Mo 392, 267 SW 632.

§70. Includable Costs

An ordinance providing for construction of a sewer, which was valid when enacted, including an item for the cost of making and collecting assessments, is not rendered void by a subsequent statute requiring that such item be omitted, since the amendment only affected so much of the ordinance as related to the cost of making and collecting assessments, and did not affect the remainder.

Ill Gage v People (1904) 207 Ill 377, 69 NE 840.

In making special assessments for sewers, the assessment can be levied only for the actual cost of the improvement; and the local authorities cannot include the expense of any work that is not necessary to complete the particular improvement in a reasonable and fair mode.

Cal Los Angeles v Offner (1961) 55 C2d 103, 10 CaR 470, 358 P2d 926.

Under an ordinance assessing the cost of construction of sewers against abutting property owners, expenses for engineers' fees or legal fees, advertisements, and so forth are properly included, since they are necessary and incidental to the work and are part of the necessary costs of securing the improvement.

Ky Shaw v Mayfield (1924) 204 Ky 618, 265 SW 13.

An assessment ordinance providing for improving a street by grading, setting cement curb, paving, and constructing the necessary drains, inlets and retaining walls and laying a 6 inch water main does not authorize construction of a sanitary sewer since the word "drain" is not broad enough to include a "sewer".

Ohio Lichtenwalter v Akron (1927) 25 OA 108, 158 NE 651.
Roebling v Cincinnati (1921) 102 OS 460, 132 NE 60.

An objection to an ordinance providing for construction of a sewer, that it lacks any provision for restoration of pavements of the streets involved and thus it is unreasonable, will not be sustained since the tearing up and restoration of pavements is a mere incident to the sewer construction and is included in the estimate of overall cost.

Ill Chicago v Sullivan Machinery (1915) 269 Ill 58, 109 NE 696.

Where an ordinance and contract authorize construction of a 6,000 foot tunnel sewer to be constructed in accordance with plans and specifications prepared by the city engineer at a price within the engineer's estimate, and the work is completed and accepted by the city, an extra charge will not be allowed for additional concrete filling required through the encountering of shale in layers and seams resulting in much extra loose rock to be removed and replaced by concrete, where information concerning rock formations at different depths was available to the contractor on a chart of borings at the city engineer's office and the city in letting the contract had not warranted formations to be as solid rock.

> **Mo**   United Constr v St Louis (1934) 334 Mo 1006, 69 SW2d 639.

E. ANCILLARY FACILITIES

§ 71. Construction and Financing Authority

An ordinance providing for the construction of a sewage treatment plant is valid as within the scope of a statute authorizing county boards to control and regulate the disposal of sewage, to construct certain facilities including sewers, holding basins, and pumping stations, and any other works and improvements deemed necessary to maintain departments of public works.

> **Ill**   People v Smith (1961) 21 Ill2d 572, 173 NE2d 485.

An ordinance providing for the construction of a sewer and assessment of its costs against benefited property, enacted under charter authority to construct sewers "with all necessary manholes, lamp holes, catch-basins and branches", is not invalid as embracing features other than those authorized, though the major portion of the work provided for by the ordinance consists of constructing a pumping plant and wall behind it.

> **Ore**   Pioneer Real Estate v Portland (1926) 119 Ore 1, 247 P 319.

A charter provision authorizing a city to make street improvements does not warrant an ordinance levying a special assessment for a storm sewer underneath the street.

> **Tex**   Dallas Consolidated Elec St Ry v Dallas (1924) 260 SW 1034.

A provision in an ordinance authorizing the construction of a sewer system which calls for the installation of aseptic tanks is valid under the city's clearly implied power to install such tanks as part of the public sewer system.

> **Mo**   Schueler v Kirkwood (1915) 191 MoApp 575, 177 SW 760.

The term "sewer" as used in a statute exempting construction or alteration of sewer mains from a resolution of necessity required for public improvements, includes both storm and sanitary sewers.

> **ND**   Kirkham v Minot (1963) 122 NW2d 862.

Since the control of the use of public sewers is a matter affecting the public health and safety of a community, and is subject to reasonable and equitable regulation, a municipality may provide for the construction of a combination storm water and sanitary sewer and assess the property owners benefited thereby for the cost.

Ill La Salle Nat Bk v Riverdale (1959) 16 Ill2d 151, 157 NE2d 7.

Though the maintenance of a sewage system is imposed by law on a city by a decree of court and the essential service is, in a broad sense, for the benefit of the entire city, it cannot follow that each parcel of land in the city furnished with and connected to a new local sewer can be specially assessed for some share of the whole outfall and treatment operation, in addition to its share of the cost of the local improvement. To hold otherwise would permit the city to divert special assessment funds to general taxation purposes.

Cal Los Angeles v Offner (1961) 55 C2d 103, 10 CaR 470, 358 P2d 926.

Where an ordinance establishing a sewage disposal system contained a plan or system for the construction of the facility and a program of financing, as required by statute, a subsequent amendatory ordinance changing the site of the proposed sewage treatment plant, but containing no system or plan of construction and no program or method of financing, is invalid.

Wash Close v Meehan (1956) 49 Wash2d 426, 302 P2d 194.

§72. Drainage

A village may lawfully enact an ordinance to extend its sewers beyond its limits for the purpose of securing a suitable outlet, since the improvement is within the limits, and the extension and outlet only serve the purpose of giving practical effect to the system.

Ill Maywood v Maywood (1892) 140 Ill 216, 29 NE 704.

An ordinance providing for installation of outfall pipe extending into the ocean for purpose of disposition of sewage, is valid, as an exercise of the police power under municipality's imperative duty to safeguard public health, and particularly so, where municipality has initiated eminent domain proceedings to acquire the land necessary for construction of such pipe.

NJ Faulks v Allenhurst (1939) 122 NJLaw 225, 4 A2d 518.

Although a city has statutory authority to establish and levy assessments for a sewer outlet situated outside an improvement district, where a petition to create a sewer improvement district calls for connection of the same into a system of septic tanks, but the ordinance creating the district provides for conducting the effluent to a river beyond the district, the ordinance is void because of variance from the petition and the added cost of acquiring rights-of-way and laying mains, which could not reasonably have been anticipated by the property owners in the district.

> **Ark**　Kraft v Smothers (1912) 103 Ark 269, 146 SW 505.

The objection to an ordinance for sewer construction, that the disposal plant would drain into a generally dry, small creek, is not tenable, since that is a matter within the scope of the village council's discretion.

> **Ill**　Millstadt v Bereitschaft (1931) 344 Ill 550, 176 NE 746.

In an ordinance providing for the construction of a sewer, an objection that the outlet provided will be insufficient to dispose of the flow is immaterial. The nature or sufficiency of an outlet does not affect the validity of the ordinance or the right to levy an assessment for the improvement.

> **Ill**　Bickerdike v Chicago (1900) 185 Ill 280, 56 NE 1096.

F. CONNECTIONS

§73. Power to Compel

A private sewage disposal ordinance providing that all property must connect to a public sewer line when available which is applied to subdivisions, cities, villages and new construction applies to a sewer line built by private funds but accepted by the city sewer system. A fact that the existing house has an adequate septic system does not relieve the owner from liability to connect to the system which becomes public on acceptance.

> **Ill**　Houpt v Stephenson County (1978) 380 NE2d 1060.

An ordinance which declares that every water-closet or privy not disposing of sewage by means of the village sewer system is a nuisance, provides that the ordinance is inapplicable to premises where connection with the sewage system is not feasible, and declares that such connection is feasible as to any premises serviced by a stub opening into the village lateral sewage lines is not an unconstitutional denial of due process because the terms "feasible" and "water-closet or privy" are vague and indefinite. A person of ordinary intelligence would have fair notice whether the ordinance applied to him or her.

> **Ill**　Riverwoods v Untermyer (1977) 54 IllAp3d 816, 369 NE2d 1385.

An ordinance requiring that any property "emanating sanitary sewage" must connect to existing sewage disposal lines is constitutional. There is no requirement of a finding of inadequacy of the septic system or requirement for payment of compensation.

Mich   Bedford Township v Bates (1975) 62 Mich Ap 715, 233 NW2d 706.

Compelling connection to the public sewer system within one year from the time it is available is authorized, under health department regulations. It is not necessary that a finding be made that the party's private septic system is inadequate.

Mich   Butcher v Grosse Ile (1970) 24 Mich Ap 389, 180 NW2d 367.

A sewer connection ordinance which indiscriminately uses the terms public sewer, Idaho City sewer, and proper sewer is void for vagueness. The lack of a definition of the terms understandably is confusing. The ordinance further provides that an owner must hook up to the proper sewer now located or which may in the future be located within 100 feet of his property line. Failure to allege that a sewer was located within 100 feet of the defendant's property makes the complaint void. It is further void for requiring hook up to a sewer which may be built in the future. The ambiguous provision is impossible of enforcement.

Ida   State v Thomas (1972) 94 Ida 592, 494 P2d 1036.

Zoning for specified commercial use providing that no use is permitted unless sewage disposal is connected to the municipal sanitary sewer system is a valid exercise of public health considerations. The ordinance may not in any degree relax any standards laid down by the state; however, where commercial development would create a health problem if septic tanks were involved they may require connection to the sewer system.

Mass   Decoulos v Peabody (1971) 360 Mass 428, 274 NE2d 816.

A city may properly require connection to a sewer line and disconnect water services on failure to make the necessary connection. The action does not deprive the homeowner of property without due process when it is applied equally to all residents and adequate notice and time for appeal is given.

Tenn   Hodge v Stout (1974) 377 F Supp 131.

A municipal ordinance requiring sewer hookup may not be enforced against the state public school building authority.

Pa   Hummelstown v Lower Dauphin Sch Dist (1976) 24 PaCmwlth 486, 357 A2d 727.

An ordinance requiring that multiple dwellings be connected to the village sewage system is unconstitutional as applied to a landowner who is informed by department of environmental conservation that he cannot connect into the village sewage system until the village corrects its deficiencies, but the village unreasonably delays the correction of those deficiencies.

  NY   Charles v Diamond (1977) 41 NY2d 318, 392 NYS2d 594, 360 NE2d 1295.

An ordinance requiring property owners to connect with sewers is not invalid as imposing too great an expense, since it is an incident of ownership for the owner to bear a fair proportion of government expense and contribute to the maintenance of the health and good order of the community.

  Ark   High v Bailey (1942) 203 Ark 461, 157 SW2d 203.
  Fla   Peoples Water Service v Adkinson (1966) 184 So2d 707.
  Ill   People v Smith (1961) 21 Ill2d 572, 173 NE2d 485.
  La   Fristoe v Crowley (1917) 142 La 393, 76 So 812.
  NY   People v Butcher (1960) 28 Misc2d 24, 209 NYS2d 723.
            Buffalo v Stevenson (1911) 145 AD 117, 129 NYS 125.
  SC   Columbia v Shaw (1925) 131 SC 464, 127 SE 722.

A city may by ordinance condemn and abolish all private structures and facilities used for waste disposal, and may require that all sewage be drained into the municipal sewerage system or into sanitary septic tanks.

  Ill   Nokomis v Sullivan (1958) 14 Ill2d 417, 153 NE2d 48.
  Ky   Nourse v Russellville (1935) 257 Ky 525, 78 SW2d 761.
  Mo   St Louis v Hoevel Real Estate & Bldg (1933) 59 SW2d 617.
            St Louis v Nash (1924) 260 SW 985.

An ordinance requiring connection with a public sewer and providing that on failure to so connect a property owner may be charged with city expense in making the connection is a valid, reasonable exercise of municipal authority.

  Ind   Indianapolis v College Park Land (1918) 187 Ind 541, 118 NE 356.
            Angola v Croxton (1916) 185 Ind 250, 112 NE 385.
  La   Fristoe v Crowley (1917) 142 La 393, 76 So 812.

A county sewer district ordinance, purportedly drawn as a voluntary revenue bond financing program, but which requires householders in the district to connect to the sewer and imposes liens on their properties, without the property owners being given reasonable notice and opportunity to be heard, is in violation of due process.

  Utah Bigler v Greenwood (1953) 123 Utah 60, 254 P2d 843.

An ordinance requiring one who desires to connect with a private sewer to obtain the written consent of the owner, and to obtain a city permit, and another ordinance requiring one about to erect a building to make connection with a public sewer if one is in the street, are enacted under the police power, and may not be circumvented on a claim of property rights.

> **Mo**   Van Trump v Kansas City (1915) 187 MoApp 190, 173 SW 32.

A property owner who was notified as required by an ordinance that required owners of premises on the line of the city sanitary sewers to connect thereto was not deprived of his property without due process of law, merely because there was no provision for a hearing by the board of health.

> **SC**   Columbia v Shaw (1925) 131 SC 464, 127 SE 722.

An ordinance imposing a fine for refusal to connect with the city sewer system after two weeks' written notice is inapplicable, in the absence of an administrative determination that a landowner's existing sanitary installations are below city standards and that public health will be jeopardized by them.

> **Ark**   Mountain Home v Ray (1954) 223 Ark 553, 267 SW2d 503.

A city, in regulating sewerage and compelling property owners to connect with the city system, is not required to gamble against public health risks, and to protect the public health it may adopt the most conservative course which science and engineering offer.

> **Ill**   Nokomis v Sullivan (1958) 14 Ill2d 417, 153 NE2d 48.

§74. Requirement Based on Structure, Location or Character of Property

A provision that every building intended for human occupancy be connected with a sewer and, if possible, by a separate connection makes the determination of a separate sewer connection discretionary. "If possible" does not mean as opposed to physically impossible, but whether it is practical and feasible. Mandamus to require a third party to secure a separate sewer connection when he is not a party to the action will not lie, due both to the discretionary nature of the ordinance and to the fact that the third party is not able to protect his interest.

> **Iowa**   Headid v Rodman (1970) 179 NW2d 767.

A sewer connection charge based on a determination of the type of use from the various classifications and requiring that the money be deposited in the sewer use fund is not a tax with a varying burden on the parties. The city has the power to levy a connection charge reasonably commensurate to the burden imposed or reasonably anticipated.

> **Ore**   Hayes v Albany (1971) 7 OreAp 277, 490 P2d 1018.

An ordinance providing for the issuance of water and sewer bonds to pay the cost of extending the water system and water treatment plant and for a sewage collection system and sewage treatment plant is constitutional though it requires the owner of land in the village within 150 feet of a sewer line to connect buildings with the sewer system and cease the use of any other method of sewage disposal. It is a reasonable exercise of the police power in the interest of public health.

> **Ida**   Schmidt v Kimberly (1953) 74 Ida 48, 256 P2d 515.

A county ordinance requiring each householder whose property is within 200 feet of a newly constructed sewer to connect therewith is enforceable.

> **Utah**   Bigler v Greenwood (1953) 123 Utah 60, 254 P2d 843.

An ordinance prohibiting septic tanks on land within 300 feet of the nearest point of a house is valid as a reasonable exercise of the police power in the interest of the public health, though the owner has obtained a building permit, where his land is only two feet lower than, and 152 feet from, the sewer connection.

> **Iowa**   State v Iowa Falls (1956) 247 Iowa 558, 74 NW2d 594.

An ordinance prohibiting construction of buildings not connected with city sewers is a violation of the statutory proscription against a municipal board of health ordering property owners to construct sewer connections over a distance greater than 300 feet, because it is generally known that there are outlying lots suitable for residence more than 300 feet from any sewer connection in several municipalities of the state. A residence without such a connection is not a nuisance per se, and cannot be enjoined unless clearly dangerous to the public health and safety.

> **Ark**   Bennett v Hope (1942) 204 Ark 147, 161 SW2d 186.

An ordinance requiring all owners of buildings within a sewer district to make connections with the city sewer may not be enlarged by construction to compel an owner to make a connection with the service line of an individual property owner leading to the city sewer system.

> **Kan**   Robbins v Hannen (1965) 194 Kan 596, 400 P2d 733.

Under an ordinance requiring a separate sewer connection for each residence or place of business, the refusal of the city clerk to issue permits for a single sewer connection with houses on several lots was within the purview of the ordinance and a valid exercise of the police power by the city. Sound reasons may be discovered why houses on different lots should have separate connections with the sewer including the fact that the provision may be more effective and that stoppage of one connection will not affect other premises.

Ark   Branch v Gerlach (1910) 94 Ark 378, 127 SW 451.

The reasonableness of ordinances requiring persons to connect their premises with the city sewer system depends largely on the local terrain and the means deemed essential to protect the health and morals of the city.

Fla   State v Daytona Beach (1948) 169 Fla 204, 34 So2d 309.

An ordinance establishing a sewer system is not unreasonable, in requiring each corner lot to have two house slants for connection with the sewers, one on each street, since buildings may be constructed fronting on either street, and connections with the sewer in both may be necessary and desirable.

Ill   Duane v Chicago (1902) 198 Ill 471, 64 NE 1033.

An ordinance requiring the owners of premises on the line of the city sanitary sewers to make connection therewith does not mean that the houses to be connected must face on or immediately abut the street on which the sewer main is. It includes houses on the rear of premises.

SC   Columbia v Shaw (1925) 131 SC 464, 127 SE 722.

§75. Connection Charges

The fee for a sewage and water hookup has been paid and the service connected may not be raised by a subsequent ordinance establishing a different payment level. A letter indicating that the original service and fees were temporary and as a deposit does not constitute a contract though the owner signed the copy of the letter indicating a future revision in the fee schedule.

SC   Spartanburg v Spartan Villa (1978) 253 So2d 501.

Whether the benefits method or foot frontage method of assessment is utilized, such assessment must always be related to the benefits conferred on the property owner. Thus, when owners of a lot fronting on two streets connect their dwelling to a sewer line in one street after sewer lines had been laid in both streets, any benefit given to the lot by the second sewer line to which the dwelling is not connected is speculative and a township municipal sewer authority cannot assess the owners for the portion of the project involving construction of such line.

Pa   Palmer Township Municipal Sewer Auth v Witty (1978) 479 Pa 240, 388 A2d 306.

A city ordinance which provides that tap-on charges shall be collected at the time of issuance of building permits or occupancy permits is not unconstitutional as retroactively applied to property which is physically connected to the city's sewer lines before the ordinance is passed, where the occupancy permit is issued after the ordinance's effective date. The city has the authority to make the sewer charge payable at the time of occupancy because this effectuates the intent of the legislature in passing the enabling statute, whose purpose is to allow municipalities to recover their capital expenditures for sewer systems.

Ill   Pontiac v Mason (1977) 50 IllAp3d 102, 365 NE2d 145.

A city ordinance which provides for the collection of tap-on fees for connection to the city water and sewer lines is valid even though the original cost of construction of the lines has been recovered. The city is not limited to collecting past costs where the ordinance does not specifically provide such a limitation.

Ill   Heinrich v Moline (1978) 59 IllAp3d 278, 375 NE2d 572.

Prior to statutory authorization, a sanitary district may not charge connection fees to a builder connecting to the city's sewer system, which in turn connects to the sanitary district.

Ill   Aurora Sanitary Dist v Randwest Corp (1970) 123 IllAp2d 444, 258 NE2d 817.

An ordinance imposing a tap fee on connections made before or after the enactment is invalid as retroactive legislation affecting a vested right. Those who paid the tap fee prior to the ordinance under the provisions of a prior invalid ordinance are entitled to a refund.

Mich   Metro Homes v Warren (1969) 19 Mich Ap 664, 173 NW2d 230.

A water and sewer capital charge is not discriminatory, where it applies to all new connections, and where it allows special privileges only for previously connected parties.

Mich   R & C Robertson v Avon (1970) 184 NW2d 261.

A tap-in fee for structures constructed and occupied after the effective date of the ordinance in order to pay for the operation of the sewage system is invalid. The installation of sewer lines for which all property was assessed on a front footage basis makes the new ordinance which exempts by implication structures presently existing constitutes unequal treatment.

Mich   Starline Construction Co v Swartz Creek (1974) 224 NW2d 53.

A sewer connection fee ordinance passed after the act of connecting may prescribe a rate chargeable to the users. In the absence of evidence of an excessive or unreasonable charge the property owner is not discriminated against. The charge must approximate the special benefits assessment from a sewer assessment district.

> **Mich** Edward Rose Sales Co v Kalamazoo Township (1971) 33 Mich Ap 481, 190 NW2d 565.

A so-called "sewer connection charge" based on a dollar per front foot basis is not properly charged against a tenant from year to year.

> **Fla** Pizza Palace of Miami v Hialeah (1970) 242 So2d 203.

A contract whereby the state highway department advances funds for the construction of sewer lines is not a third party contract for the benefit of adjoining property owners. They are still subject to the normal charges for sewer connections.

> **Utah** Mason v Tooele City (1971) 26 Utah2d 6, 484 P2d 153.

A $100 sewer connection fee which is deposited in a special fund for improvement and enlargement of the system is valid. It is not an illegal revenue measure since the money is specifically earmarked for improvement of the system.

> **Utah** Home Builders Assn of Greater Salt Lake v Provo City (1972) 28 Utah2d 402, 503 P2d 451.

A difference in connecting fees between houses built by a developer in a new subdivision and those built by an individual on his separately owned property is invalid. A reasonable classification may be made to insure that the newer additions to the sewer system pay a fair proportion of the cost; however, basing the difference on whether built by developer who is required to install his own laterals without reimbursement or by an individual is unreasonable.

> **NJ** S S & O Corp v Bernards Township (1973) 62 NJ 369, 301 A2d 738.

A sewer connection charge for a school based on the cost of the system and the number of users which breaks down to a lower per person charge for the school than for residential rates is not unreasonable and arbitrary.

> **Kan** West Elk Unified Sch Dist v Grenola (1973) 211 Kan 301, 507 P2d 335.

A water pollution control charge established for persons connecting to the city sewer system after a fixed date is reasonable. The fact that parties who have connected prior to the date are not subject to the charge does not make the class suspect and the tax is not discriminatory when based on all parties after the established date.

> **Fla** Ivy Steel & Wire Co v Jacksonville (1975) 401 F Supp 701.

A special connection charge may be established against new subscribers to a water and sewer system to pay the cost of expansion of the system. When connection charges are less than the actual anticipated cost there is no attempt at taxation. The existing ordinance, which made no provisions for handling of the money or restrictions on its subsequent expenditure is invalid, but may be rewritten to regulate proper expenditure of the funds collected.

Fla   Contractors & Builders Assn of Pinellas County v Dunedin (1976) 329 So2d 314.

An ordinance requiring landowners to abandon functional septic tanks and to connect to a public sewer system, for which fees are charged, is not a taking without compensation. The vested rights theory, under which continued use of septic tanks would be permitted as a nonconforming use, is inapplicable to a regulatory ordinance concerning public health, safety and welfare.

Mich   Renne v Waterford (1977) 73 Mich Ap 685, 252 NW2d 842.

A sanitary district's ordinance which classifies uses as "dwelling unit" and "non-dwelling building" for the purpose of fixing connection fees is not an arbitrary classification without basis in reason where the builder of a multiple dwelling building pays the same fee for each dwelling unit as would the owner of a single-family residence. Classification is not required to be scientific if it is reasonably adapted to the purpose for which it is intended and is not purely arbitrary.

Ill   Marriott v Springfield Sanitary Dist (1976) 43 IllAp3d 869, 357 NE2d 666.

An ordinance which authorizes charging only nonresidents a tap-in fee for connecting into the sewer system is not unconstitutionally discriminatory where the funds collected are used to amortize the revenue bonds which permitted the sewer system to be expanded beyond the city's corporate limits. It is proper to charge nonresidents a fee for the purpose of defraying the costs of extending the sewer system which primarily benefits them.

Ill   Knollwood Horizons v Freeport (1976) 43 IllAp3d 901, 357 NE2d 713.

Although municipal sewage connection charges are not limited to the recovery of reasonable costs of inspection and the actual work of connection, charges under an ordinance are invalid where they do not bear any reasonable relationship to the actual cost of new services and facilities.

Ind   Common Council of Crown Point v High Meadows (1977) 362 NE2d 1166.

A city's power to maintain public sewers carries with it the power to provide reasonable regulations and charges for the tapping of and connection to such sewers.

Cal   Harter v Barkley (1910) 158 Cal 742, 112 P 556.
NY   Buffalo v Stevenson (1913) 207 NY 258, 100 NE 798.
Ohio Englewood Hills v Englewood (1967) 14 OA2d 195, 237 NE2d 621.
          State ex rel Stoeckle v Jones (1953) 96 OA 382, 54 Op 373, 121 NE2d 922.

A $100 charge for connecting private users with the sewer main is within the sound discretion of the city officials, under an ordinance providing that the city could do any and all things necessary or proper to furnish, supply, regulate, and control water supply, sewage disposal, sanitation, and sanitary control on the terms and conditions determined by the city council.

    Mich   North Muskegon v Bolema Constr (1953) 335 Mich 520, 56 NW2d 371.

Where an ordinance grants the right of connecting with city mains to a person constructing sewers in a residential subdivision for personal profit, and the point of connection is within a sewer improvement district over which a board of commissioners has not surrendered control to the city, the tie-in cannot be made without payment of a reasonable sum to the district.

    Ark   Peay v Kinsworthy (1916) 126 Ark 323, 190 SW 565.

An ordinance requiring a charge for connecting to a sewage system and requiring residents in certain areas to abandon their present systems and connect to the new one is not objectionable as being discriminatory, on the ground that those making connections in the new area to the new portion of the system are paying more than those the city is charging for connections to the old system, because the basis for the difference is that the original cost of the older system was less and therefore charges for its use would naturally be less.

    Ind   Brandel v Lawrenceburg (1967) 249 Ind 47, 230 NE2d 778.

A trailer park owner was properly charged a hook-up charge of $100 per trailer unit, under an ordinance requiring a hook-up charge of $100 for all parcels of land connected to a sewer in addition to the cost of any extensions or laterals. In platting the trailer park into mobile home sites and renting them to individual families, the owner divided the land into separate parcels subject under the ordinance to the charge for each parcel.

    Mich   Mobile Home Parks v Paris (1968) 9 Mich Ap 8, 155 NW2d 694.

Ordinances imposing a charge for sewer connections measured by the use to which the property, and consequently the city's sewer system, will be put, including number and type of plumbing fixtures to be installed, does not constitute an assessment on the value of the property, but rather is in the nature of an excise tax imposed on all persons applying for building permits for the privilege of connection to the sewer system, and is reasonably commensurate with the burden to be imposed on the system.

    Cal   Associated Home Builders v Livermore (1961) 56 C2d 847, 17 CaR 5, 366 P2d 448.

Where an ordinance grants the right of connecting with city mains to a person constructing sewers in a residential subdivision for personal profit, and the point of connection is within a sewer improvement district over which a board of commissioners has not surrendered control to the city, the tie-in cannot be made without payment of a reasonable sum to the district.

> **Ark**　Peay v Kinsworthy (1916) 126 Ark 323, 190 SW 565.

In the absence of a constitutional inhibition, and under a legislative grant of power, a municipality may by ordinance impose on an owner of improved property the cost of connecting his premises with the public sewerage system and impose a lien on the property to secure payment. Even if the legislature does not provide a special remedy for enforcement of the lien, it does not follow that the statute creating it is without effect and when no special remedy is provided the municipality may resort to ordinary process.

> **La**　Fristoe v Crowley (1917) 142 La 393, 76 So 812.

An ordinance levying special assessments on a tax duplicate evaluation basis to pay for the sewer system is valid where it requires a connection permit fee of $300 on a property owner, though another ordinance required only a $5 fee, since after the first assessment the property was improved. Also, the ordinance is not a second assessment, but merely a charge for permission to connect with the sewer, since the assessment at the established rate would be $435.84.

> **Ohio**　State ex rel Stoeckle v Jones (1954) 161 OS 391, 53 Op 303, 119 NE2d 834.

An ordinance regulating connections with the sewer system and requiring a permit fee of $5 may be repealed, amended, or supplemented by the village since it has made no contract to maintain the status quo, and providing that its actions are within constitutional limits.

> **Ohio**　State ex rel Stoeckle v Jones (1953) 96 OA 382, 54 Op 373, 121 NE2d 922.
> **Tex**　Highland Park v Guthrie (1925) 269 SW 193.

An ordinance imposing a fee for connecting residences in only one section of the city with the city water or sewage system is invalid as in conflict with the statute providing that the rates charged for such services shall be equal and uniform.

> **Colo**　Cernich v Littleton (1951) 124 Colo 522, 239 P2d 306.

If a charge imposed on trunk sewer users be considered a use charge, it is discriminatory in the case of a sewer trunk line constructed in a tract for connection to the line by homeowners with a charge made for the connection, where a similar charge is not elicited from others using similar facilities in the town.

> **Colo**　Cernich v Littleton (1951) 124 Colo 522, 239 P2d 306.

Ordinances attempting to recover construction costs for water and sewer lines not realized out of the proceeds of a tax forfeiture of certain land to the state, by imposing on a new landowner the obligation of paying the amount as the condition of using the facilities violates the expressed will of the legislature in a statute and city charter.

Minn   Fortman v Minneapolis (1942) 212 Minn 340, 4 NW2d 349.

A city is authorized to construct, repair and regulate sewer connections; but it is not authorized to finance such construction by making connection charges in excess of the normal and nominal inspection fee and using the excess to finance the initial construction.

Iowa   Clarke v Bettendorf (1968) 158 NW2d 125.

Where a land developer at his own expense installs all public improvements (water mains, storm and sanitary sewers, sewerage disposal plant, grading, paving and the like), an ordinance preventing connections to a sanitary sewer unless a "tap-in charge" of $350 per connection is paid is void, since the city did not expend any of its funds for the improvements, the cost of operating and maintaining the sewers is provided for by a tax levy, and the charge for the tap-in is not to be used for the cost of supervising the tap-in construction but is to be appropriated for other sewer improvements of the city.

Ohio   Zehman Constr v Eastlake (1962) 92 Abs 364, 28 Op2d 350, 195 NE2d 361.

An ordinance and a resolution requiring all new buildings to pay a sewer tap fee and excepting all existing structures from the same rates where they were not connected to the sewage facilities at the time of adoption create an arbitrary and discriminatory classification of persons required to pay the fee, contrary to the equal protection clauses of the state and federal Constitutions.

Mich   Beauty Built Constr v Warren (1965) 375 Mich 220, 134 NW2d 214.

Though a city may pass an ordinance fixing charges for connecting to its sewage system prior to the installation of the system, no charge can be collected before connection is made. And a charge may not be made to provide water and sewer service to vacant land.

Ohio   Giesel v Broadview Heights (1968) 14 OM 70, 236 NE2d 222.

Where an ordinance contains a charge for connecting to a newly constructed sewage system and requires that residents in certain areas abandon their present systems and connect to a new one, the tax imposed by the ordinance is not a benefit tax because not all the property owners in the area under the ordinance are required to pay the fee. The tax applies only to property requiring sewage disposal.

Ind   Brandel v Lawrenceburg (1967) 249 Ind 47, 230 NE2d 778.

Where a sewer was laid with the stipulation that the connection of consumers with sewer mains to be laid under the contract should be in accordance with the laws, ordinances, rules, and regulations of the city, such stipulation did not place any limitation on the power of the city to enact an ordinance requiring a sewer connection fee.

>   **NC**　Atl Constr v Raleigh (1949) 230 NC 365, 53 SE2d 165.

Requiring a subdivider to pay an outlet sewer charge required by city ordinance, before recording the final subdivision map, is not inconsistent with the statute.

>   **Cal**　Longridge Est v Los Angeles (1960) 183 CA2d 533, 6 CaR 900.

§ 76. Owner's Right to Connect

A county resolution prohibiting further sewer connections when a certain average daily sewage flow is reached will not bar connection of an apartment complex until construction of a pumping station which is a condition precedent to the moratorium against grantees.

>   **Ala**　Custred v Jefferson County (1978) 360 So2d 285.

A municipality may not properly withhold utility services from a subsequent purchaser. While the utilities may be disconnected and remain off until payment of delinquent charges, these may only be collected from the person to whom the utilities were furnished. A purchaser at foreclosure sale may properly pay the delinquent charges under protest, and sue to collect them back.

>   **NM**　Vettini v Las Cruces (1971) 82 NM 633, 485 P2d 967.

An ordinance providing for sewer construction need not specifically provide that abutting landowners shall have a right to attach to the sewer. Such right is inherent in property owners assessed.

>   **Ore**　Rogers v Salem (1912) 61 Ore 321, 122 P 308.

An ordinance providing that before a connection to a sewer system is made by a property owner a permit to connect in the abutting or adjoining street, alley, or other public highway shall be obtained and a signed contract issued only on application to the utilities office is regulatory only and is not irreconcilable with an ordinance requiring owners of improved property to connect within three months after notice and prescribing a fine for failure to comply.

>   **Pa**　Schuylkill Haven v Bolton (1959) 190 PaS 157, 153 A2d 504.

A city may waive ordinance requirements as to form of sewer permits, either expressly or by a course of conduct indicating an intention to do so, and it may be estopped to object to the form of a permit and thus may not require a change in connection from a previously allowed connection with a lateral sewer.

Mich Hack v Detroit (1948) 322 Mich 558, 34 NW2d 66.

Where temporary sewer connection permits have been issued for more than 20 years without approval of a three fourths vote of all the aldermen elect, the city is estopped to object to the validity of such permits, though it passes an ordinance requiring recommendation of the board of public works and adoption by a three fourths vote before connection will be permitted outside the city.

Mich Hack v Detroit (1948) 322 Mich 558, 34 NW2d 66.

Where a distillery acting pursuant to an ordinance obtains a permit and builds a private sewer line to connect its property with the city sewer, the city may be restrained from disconnecting its line from the distillery's, preserving to the city, however, the right to regulate the character of sewage that runs into the public sewer.

Ky Henderson v Peerless Distilling (1914) 161 Ky 1, 170 SW 210.

An ordinance authorizing certain persons to construct and maintain a sewer along a designated portion of their street of residence and providing that any person desiring to connect with the sewer should be permitted to do so on paying to the grantees his proportionate part of the cost is valid since it does not confer to the grantees the power to levy and collect assessments and does not obligate anyone to use the sewer.

Minn Lee v Scriver (1919) 143 Minn 17, 172 NW 802.

An ordinance establishing a sewer system, and providing that all lots and unsubdivided lands within the drainage area shall be entitled to the benefit of the sewer, is not discriminatory because only one house slant is provided for each lot or tract, so that a large parcel will have no more connection than a small lot.

Ill Gage v Chicago (1902) 195 Ill 490, 63 NE 184.

Where a city had constructed a small sewer system and permitted sewer connections by certain owners on payment of a fee, such owners acquired no vested rights preventing the city from interfering or taking away the privilege of using such sewer by levying assessments for construction of a new sewer system, for the protection of the public health.

Ky Baker v Princeton (1928) 226 Ky 409, 11 SW2d 94.

An ordinance requiring property owners to pay a proportionate cost of street improvements made at city expense before an application to tap the sewer main is granted is not unreasonable or void, though the city has been unable to collect the assessment due to defects in procedure or failure to obtain an assessment lien, since it establishes a rule of uniform operation requiring all who would use the sewer connections to bear an equal burden borne by other users.

Ohio   Gundersen v South Euclid (1955) 72 Abs 137, 124 NE2d 460.

Under a city ordinance requiring that all plumbing work "be connected with the public sewer, when such sewer is accessible", a building owner who tenders the necessary fee is entitled to have his property connected with the sewer though he declines to sign an agreement "to pay such rates annually for the sewer as may be fixed", the requirement of fixed charges being essentially a tax which cannot be delegated to a municipality which itself has no subordinate legislative power.

Haw   McCandless v Campbell (1911) 20 Haw 411.

Where a sewer and water main assessment is declared void for failure to file notice of assessment and the city is enjoined from collection, an ordinance providing that no permit for any sewer or water service connection shall be issued unless the improvement assessment is paid is an indirect attempt to collect the void water main assessment, and the ordinance itself is void.

Ohio   State ex rel F B Co v Beachwood (1942) 29 Abs 216, 15 Op 80, 1 OSU 17, aff 37 Abs 366, 46 NE2d 808.

An ordinance prohibiting city officials from issuing a sewer connection permit unless delinquent assessments are paid for the property to be served does not apply to property of a board of education.

Utah   State v McGonagle (1910) 38 Utah 277, 112 P 401.

A formal resolution accepting a proposal to connect certain lots with the city sewer system is sufficient to make a contract. An ordinance is not necessary.

Pa   Gilfillan v Haven (1947) 161 PaS 114, 53 A2d 901.

§77. Legal Proceedings

An ordinance requiring property owners to connect with sewers at their own expense does not authorize the filing of a lien against an owner who fails to connect, under a township code provision giving a lien for failure to pay sewer service charges.

Pa   Jannetta v Recklitis (1969) 214 PaS 171, 251 A2d 713.

A class action may not be brought against the denial of a sewer connection permit. A determination to issue sewer permits for an area on a first come, first serve basis is a matter of individual complaint not taxpayer's action.

> **Ohio** Columbus ex rel Willits v Cremean (1971) 27 OA2d 137, 57 Op2d 201, 276 NE2d 271.

Courts do not inquire into the motives of a municipal council in the enactment of an ordinance. Thus, the contention that an ordinance assessing a charge for the use of city sewers by non-residents was enacted through malice or spite, affords the plaintiffs no right to equitable relief.

> **Ga** Barr v Augusta (1950) 206 Ga 750, 58 SE2d 820.

Where the evidence shows that, in the area affected by an ordinance requiring a charge for connecting to a newly constructed sewage system and requiring that residents of certain areas abandon their present sewage systems and connect to a new one, septic tanks are creating a health hazard and that there is considerable overflow and seepage therefrom, such evidence is sufficient to support the trial court's refusal to grant a temporary injunction in a class action to restrain enforcement of the ordinance, though there is no showing that particular plaintiffs were creating or maintaining a nuisance in the use of their septic tanks.

> **Ind** Brandel v Lawrenceburg (1967) 299 Ind 47, 230 NE2d 778.

An ordinance requiring owners of improved property to connect with the sewer system does not deny the owners of equal protection of the law where the municipality brings action to recover a penalty for noncompliance, since the action is instituted as a test case, the municipality does not relinquish its rights against the noncooperating property owners and there is no showing that the action differs in any way from the remedy in the ordinance.

> **Pa** Schuylkill Haven v Bolton (1959) 190 PaS 157, 153 A2d 504.

VIII. REGULATION

§78. Excessive Industrial Waste

The authority to operate and maintain a sewer system includes by implication the authority to hold hearings and issue cease and desist orders against excessive waste discharge which is detrimental to the system. Industrial waste may be classified as to the amount of particles which are harmful to sewage treatment.

> **Ill** Rauland Division, Zenith Radio Corp v Metropolitan Sanitary Dist of Chicago (1971) 2 IllAp3d 35, 275 NE2d 756.

An ordinance authorizing a charge for excessive industrial waste-water disposal and requiring monthly reports of the excess is a reasonable implied power in the sewage district's right to collect charges. A penalty for failure to file the monthly statements and pay the accrued excessive charge is reasonable as an attempt to enforce compliance with the payment schedules.

> **Ill** Metropolitan Sanitary District of Greater Chicago v On-cor Frozen Foods (1976) 36 IllAp3d 239, 343 NE2d 577.

§79. State Pre-emption

On passage of a solid waste management act by the state a city is precluded from regulating or licensing the disposal of sludge from such operations. All phases of sewage operation are controlled by the state.

> **Pa** Greater Greensburg Sewage Auth v Hempfield Township (1972) 5 PaCmwlth 495, 291 A2d 318.

SHOPPING CENTERS

EDITORIAL COMMENT. The shopping center, either neighborhood or regional, is familiar to everyone. The mushrooming growth of these commercial developments, and their wide variations in size and appearance, have been accompanied by a variety of legal problems. The court decisions are numerous enough to call for a separate treatment of the subject.

Most of the cases deal with zoning; but other important problems arise. These include parking, street use, building restrictions, taxation, and even private police. The cases used in the ensuing paragraphs are all modern, the earliest being 1969.

I. IN GENERAL

§1. Parking

The enforcement of a ban against parking on private property without the owner's permission is not vested solely in the police. A shopping center tenant may on posting "no parking" signs have the offending vehicle towed away without imposing liability on himself or the towing service. A shopping center may properly designate areas for no parking for the safety and convenience of its patrons.

> **Ariz**   Fendler v Texaco Oil Co (1972) 17 ArizApp 565, 499 P2d 179.

The parking requirements for a shopping center are applicable to a four acre tract zoned for a shopping center though being used as a supermarket. Since the ordinance specifically refers to shopping center it applies rather than the general requirements for a supermarket.

> **Pa**   Foodarama Supermarkets, Application of (1971) 3 PaCmwlth 11, 280 A2d 483.

The authority to control traffic in parking yards and to regulate traffic in fire areas includes the right to enact an ordinance prohibiting parking in a fire zone in a shopping center.

> **NJ**   State v Dorman (1973) 124 NJS 160, 305 A2d 445.

An increase in the number of parking places required for an expansion or construction of shopping center or retail installation applies only to new construction. An excess of parking places from the old ordinance applied to a shopping center may not however be used for the new building. The shopping center has a nonconforming use, but would not qualify under the new ordinance and may not devote part of its existing excess from the original ordinance to a new building.

> **Pa**   Manoa Shopping Center v Zoning Hearing Bd of Haverford Township (1974) 11 PaCmwlth 569, 314 A2d 516.

The required parking spaces for a convenience center may not be located on land zoned for PUD and subsequently rezoned for residential. A building permit issued by mistake concerning the parking requirements may be withdrawn by the city.

> **Mont**   State ex rel Center v Missoula (1975) 166 Mont 385, 533 P2d 1087.

In determining the parking lot area in a shopping center to fulfill the ordinance requirements, the planning board may consider property subject to condemnation for highway widening and on which the developer has granted an option to the state. It is not necessary that the developer pave the area for parking in order to fulfill the requirements.

> **NY**   Conway v Kerr (1976) 51 AD2d 758, 380 NYS2d 44.

A parking restriction for stores and shopping centers which exempts stores of under 1,000 square feet is reasonable. The 1,000 foot store corresponds to neighborhood shops which are normally unable to secure offstreet parking. A denial of a variance for the parking for a shopping center is reasonable when

the evidence shows a high volume of traffic on the adjoining streets and a need
to provide parking and a means of a continual traffic flow.

NY   Northtown Rlty Co v Siegel (1976) 86 Misc2d 393, 383 NYS2d 302.

§2. Private Police

Under the ordinance provisions that a member of the police department is held
always to be on duty and subject to orders from proper authorities or to call by
citizens, a police officer working as a security guard at a shopping center is on
official duty when investigating an accident in the parking lot. His activities in
investigating the accident and issuing a summons to a witness are official
police activities rather than acts as an agent for the shopping center.

Md   Leach v Penn-Mar Merchant's Assn (1973) 18 MdApp 603, 308 A2d 446.

A requirement that shopping centers having a parking lot area of over two
hundred thousand square feet must provide police protection under the
direction and supervision of the superintendent of police is invalid. While the
requirement is a reasonable regulation under police powers, it is a matter of
statewide concern and therefore outside the grant of county authority.

Mo   Flower Valley Shopping Center v St Louis County (1975) 528 SW2d 749.

§3. Building Standards

A ramp between the front entrance of a shopping center and its parking lot is
not within the building code protection which sets standards for occupants of
buildings.

Miss   Gowan v Batson (1974) 288 So2d 468.

An environmental protection commission established by ordinance does not
have authority to require changes in a shopping center construction plans nor
attach conditions to the issuance of a building permit. The EPC was
established as an advisory board.

NM   Hyder v Albuquerque (1975) 87 NM 215, 531 P2d 949.

§4. Accessory Buildings

A separate special exception to permit the construction of an additional 500
seat theater does not violate the intent of the ordinance. The theaters with
separate entrances on separate streets and staggered showings with adequate

waiting space are justified under the betterment of the area and the improved financial condition of the district.

> **NY**   New York Life Ins Co v Galvin (1974) 35 NY2d 52, 315 NE2d 778, 358 NYS2d 724.

II. STREETS

§5. Vacating

While a city may take land for streets by eminent domain it must be for a public purpose, and evidence must be presented that the street to be taken and vacated is for the public benefit rather than the private gain of the developers of a shopping center proposed in the area.

> **Pa**   Bruce Ave, Matter of condemnation (1970) 438 Pa 498, 266 A2d 96.

A street easement may be vacated on showing of no harm to the general public and the need for the same for a shopping center. Contest of the closing by a party who does not have a direct interest in the street is invalid.

> **Ark**   Freeze v Jones (1976) 260 Ark 193, 539 SW2d 425.

A decision to vacate a street in order to permit construction of a shopping center must be supported by findings of the fact and conclusions. Since the determination affects a small group of people rather than the general welfare of the public it is an administrative decision rather than legislative. A subsequent resolution that the street has been vacated and relocated is likewise improper where the relocation is not a completed fact but is contingent on construction of the new street.

> **Cal**   Rancho Palos Verdes v Rolling Hills Est (1976) 59 CA3d 869, 129 CaR 173.

§6. Maintenance

A building permit for a shopping center may not be revoked by a change in responsibility for an adjoining road. The center's permit which was approved at the time that the county controlled the access road may not be revoked by a village subsequently incorporated and to which the road has been unilaterally transferred. Both parties are in the same position and neither can force the other to construct or reconstruct the road as originally desired.

> **NY**   Bd of Trustees of Lansing v Pyramid Co (1976) 51 AD2d 414, 381 NYS2d 898.

§7. Restricting Use

A large shopping center with interior streets in a mall is not dedicated to the public and a ban on distributing handbills inside the confines may be enforced.

The mall is only open to public to do business at the shops therein and is not similar to a community business district.

Ore Lloyd v Tanner (1972) 407 US 551, 33 LEd2d 131, 92 SCt 2219.

A shopping center with basically a community sidewalk fronting a variety of stores located on a privately constructed street and parking lots may not ban picketing or distribution of handbills which directly affect one of the merchants in the center. Picketing and handbills against the sale of nonunion lettuce by a grocery store within the center does not constitute a trespass. While picketing with display signs near the entrance on public property may be visible to the 90 per cent of the people who enter the center the distribution of handbills would not be practical since cars are not required to stop and they would only be available to the 10 per cent who walk to the center.

Colo Handen v People of Colorado Springs (1974) 186 Colo 284, 526 P2d 1310.

§8. Sidewalks

While the ordinance sections pertaining to sidewalks constructed in conjunction with street repairs are subject to remonstrances the city still may order construction of sidewalks under a separate section. The separate section providing for construction and maintenance of sidewalk adjoining any street does not authorize remonstrance and is a valid means to order sidewalk construction in a shopping center.

Ore Woodburn v DeKabi (1975) 20 OreAp 426, 531 P2d 913.

III. TAXATION

§9. Sales Tax

A tax based on the gross sale of a merchant or the gross receipts from any service in connection with sales does not apply to sales from a portion of a store located in an adjoining city. Furnishing parking facilities within the taxing district is not such a service as authorizes collection of the tax from the neighboring facilities. Taxes are collectable on the portions of the store located within the taxing district, and on a proportionate share of the sales where departments are located within two adjoining towns, based on the amount of square footage in each area.

Mo May Department Stores Co v University City (1970) 458 SW2d 260.

IV. ZONING

§ 10. Comprehensive Zoning

A comprehensive zoning plan that has been resubmitted for consideration may still form the basis for rezoning portions of the town. When both the plan and the particular area have been subject to consideration for several years there is no indication of haste or insufficient consideration of the change. Accordingly, a new classification for regional shopping centers enacted in an area rezoned for this use does not indicate lack of consideration. However, conditions imposed in a second amendment on the tract of land are invalid as not being made pursuant to public notice.

> **NY**   Albright v Manlius (1970) 34 AD2d 419, 312 NYS2d 13.

A master plan, which has not been adopted by the city, is not entitled to evidentiary weight in considering a zoning change. The hopes of the city in zoning an area for a shopping center, which has not materialized, on a master plan which has not been formally adopted, results in an unreasonable restriction on the property.

> **Mich**   Biske v Troy (1969) 381 Mich 611, 166 NW2d 453.

Prior denial of a special variance and rezoning does not invalidate a subsequent comprehensive rezoning for the town. A change in use to business activities, permitting supermarkets and shopping centers, may be approved on showing the use is not antagonistic to the comprehensive zoning plan.

> **NY**   Blumberg v Yonkers (1973) 41 AD2d 300, 341 NYS2d 977.

An ordinance establishing a regional shopping center does not need to be readvertised when the amendments made at the hearing are minor. The original summary published is sufficient when it provides for the establishing of classification of regional shopping center-planned commercial development as a permitted use and provides for designed criteria.

> **Pa**   Graack v Bd of Supervisors of Lower Nazareth Township (1975) 17 PaCmwlth 112, 330 A2d 578.

An amendment to bring any comprehensive zoning ordinance in line with the comprehensive map and avoid strip zoning by rezoning an area of residential to provide for a shopping center is reasonable. The determination based on deteriorating conditions in the area and the need for shopping facilities by residents within the town rather than in adjoining communities plus the elimination of a potential school overcrowding and highway problems caused by mine entrances, which would be reduced to two, justifies the change.

> **Ore**   Tierney v Duris (1975) 21 OreAp 613, 536 P2d 435.

§11. Public Health, Welfare, and Safety

The rezoning of farm land to allow construction of a shopping center is arbitrary and capricious where the action would have serious detrimental effects on areas outside the city's jurisdiction and would fail to serve the community as a whole.

> **Wash** Save a Valuable Environment (SAVE) v Bothell (1978) 89 Wash2d 862, 576 P2d 401.

Rezoning land, a portion of which was commercial, to residential and prohibiting the construction of a supermarket and offstreet parking is invalid when the use does not adversely affect the public health, welfare, and safety. The unique condition of the land together with commercial development across the street and the property being bounded by two heavily traveled streets makes commercial zoning a matter of right.

> **Ill** LaSalle Nat Bk v Harwood Heights (1971) 2 IllAp3d 1040, 278 NE2d 114.

Denial of a permit for a mini-shopping center based on a reference to the public health, welfare, and safety is invalid. The city would be required to record legally sufficient basis for this determination when the structure meets all the other requirements.

> **Minn** Main Rlty v Pagel (1973) 296 Minn 362, 208 NW2d 758.

§12. Rezoning

The owner of property on which a commercial mall is planned obtains no vested rights in the general commercial classification of the property because of dedication of valuable rights-of-way and substantial expenditure of money in connection with its plan; the land may be properly downzoned before construction begins.

> **Md** Washington Suburban Sanitary Comm v TKU Assn (1977) 281 Md 1, 376 A2d 505.

A city ordinance rezoning property for use as a "dry" shopping center is valid despite the fact that the city council decides that the shopping center will be "dry" without public notice and hearing, where the rezoning of the shopping center development district is supported by adequate notice. The wet or dry status of a development district is a minor matter.

> **Tex** Midway Protective League v Dallas (1977) 552 SW2d 170.

An ordinance rezoning a tract from a commercial classification, which would permit use for a shopping center, to a service commercial classification, which would not permit this use, has a rational basis and is not arbitrary or discriminatory where all undeveloped property along the road is rezoned from commercial to service commercial and where the rezoning is in accord with other official actions intended to promote the orderly growth and development of the community in the manner recommended by the general plan. The city is not estopped from adopting the rezoning ordinances by its promise, made six years earlier when it annexed the property, that the tract would be zoned commmercial, because no representations were made as to the length of time that the commercial zoning would continue, the property owner could be presumed to know that the city had a right to modify its zoning, and the rezoning is in conformance with the general plan.

> **Cal**   Carty v Ojai (1978) 77 CA3d 329, 143 CaR 506.

Rezoning from residential to shopping center is valid when the area was feasible for classification as shopping center at the time of the original annexation and the growth of the area indicates such a need. The construction of a school, sewer and water lines and a temporary highway bypass justifies the classification.

> **NC**   Allgood v Tarboro (1972) 281 NC 430, 189 SE2d 255.

The city may not arbitrarily impede the development of a commercially designated area. A 22-acre triangle at the intersection of two major thoroughfares is properly zoned commercial rather than residential, and is a proper setting for a shopping center. A bill of assurance given by the applicant may be included in the conditions for rezoning.

> **Ark**   Metropolitan Tr Co v North Little Rock (1972) 252 Ark 1140, 482 SW2d 613.

The granting of a shopping center classification is not an assurance that it will continue forever. A change in the public attitude and the fact that a school has been constructed across the street which would create a substantial traffic problem along with the residential character of the balance of the neighborhood does not make the rezoning to residential arbitrary and unreasonable.

> **Del**   Shellburne v Conner (1974) 315 A2d 620; affd (1975) 336 A2d 568.

Rezoning from high density apartment to a service center with a self-service gas station is invalid despite a heavy traffic count. The property having residential uses on two sides and mixed on the other is usable in its present classification.

> **Ark**   Lindsey v Fayetteville (1974) 256 Ark 352, 507 SW2d 101.

A zoning request for shopping center classification may be granted to less than all of the tract in the application. When two owners file a single application and one owner is precluded by the 24-month rule on previous applications the council may approve only that portion not under the 24-month restriction.

Tex Simons Land Co v Dallas (1974) 507 SW2d 828.

Rezoning for a community shopping center is proper at the intersection of two 4-lane highways. The location of a public school adjacent to the property is not detrimental when it is separated by a parking lot, six-foot fence and 30 feet of planting. The isolation of the tract from the nearby residential area by a creek sufficiently protects the neighboring residential area from diminishment of value.

Ill First Nat Bank of Springfield v Springfield (1974) 22 IllAp3d 22, 316 NE2d 648.

Rezoning to permit the construction of a shopping center by a particular individual is invalid. Zoning applies to the use of property rather than inuring to the benefit of a particular individual. While conditions on the type and style of construction may be imposed they may not be limited to a particular applicant.

NY Dexter v Town Bd of Gates (1975) 36 NY2d 102, 324 NE2d 870, 365 NYS2d 506.

A requirement to dedicate a street right-of-way in order to secure rezoning of a portion of a tract is invalid when there is no showing that the rezoning will generate more traffic. The tract which is presently used for a shopping center will not cause a substantial change in the traffic pattern by rezoning a small portion in order to change the location of the center.

Ariz Transamerica Title Ins Co v Tucson (1975) 23 ArizApp 385, 533 P2d 693.

A change to shopping center passed on a three to two vote from a seven-member board is invalid. The requirements for passage by a majority of the members is not met although the vote is by a majority of those present.

NM Dale J Bellamah Corp v Sante Fe (1975) 88 NM 288, 540 P2d 218.

§13. Denial of Rezoning

Rezoning for a shopping center contrary to the comprehensive land use plan will not be approved when there is no evidence to support the change. Since the comprehensive plan contains shopping center sites which have not been developed, and there is no change in the circumstances or surrounding community, there is no justification for rezoning.

Ky Fallon v Baker (1970) 455 SW2d 572.

An intensification of industrial use at a busy intersection does not constitute such a material change in the area as to justify rezoning. The increased population used as a basis for requesting a shopping center classification is insufficient to support the change.

Md   Heller v Segner (1971) 260 Md 393, 272 A2d 374.

To secure rezoning from residential to shopping center there must be a finding of substantial change in the character of the neighborhood, or mistake in the comprehensive plan, and then a finding of need. Increase in population in an area by itself is insufficient.

Md   Hardesty v Dunphy (1970) 259 Md 718, 271 A2d 152.
Chapman v Montgomery County (1971) 259 Md 641, 271 A2d 156.

Change from residential to shopping center is not justified when there is no finding that the immediate neighborhood is the subject of substantial change since comprehensive zoning. The availability of sewer and water, the planned widening and extension of roads, and the increased traffic do not indicate a change in the character of a neighborhood. Its urbanization and increased density is a natural result of the residential zoning, not a change in condition.

Md   Clayman v Prince George's County (1972) 266 Md 409, 292 A2d 689.

Residential use will not be changed to retail business when there is no other commercial development in the area other than a nonconforming neighborhood grocery. An attempted contract zoning across the highway from the proposed land does not affect the classification since the contract has restrictive covenants attached.

Ill   Shibata v Naperville (1971) 1 IllAp3d 402, 273 NE2d 690.

Rezoning for a shopping center is invalid when there is no showing of unreasonableness of the prior zoning or a material change in circumstances. A rezoning not within the public interest and contrary to the comprehensive development plan is invalid.

Mich   Schilling v Midland (1972) 38 Mich Ap 568, 196 NW2d 846.

A nonconforming commercial use on residential property does not justify rezoning to commercial for a service shopping center. The presumed validity of the residential zoning must be overcome by the applicant to justify the change, and a showing that the property is usable for single family residential development and that the nearby area is residential supports the classification.

Ill   Zenith Radio Corp v Mount Prospect (1973) 15 IllAp3d 587, 304 NE2d 754.

The mixed single family and multiple residential characteristics of a neighborhood with a trend towards planned unit development does not justify a change at the intersection to convenience center and gas station. The use of the area is still primarily residential, and the annexation and subsequent commercial zoning across the intersection is not a sufficient commercial development to warrant the change.

Ill Buhrmaster v DuPage County (1973) 16 IllAp3d 212, 305 NE2d 722.

Denial of a shopping center classification for property due to the nearby location of a high school and the undeveloped amount of commercial land in the area is unreasonable. The property which is not suitable for residential development due to congested streets, its barren topography as opposed to nearby wooded residential areas, and the location of a cemetery in the center of the tract makes the residential classification unreasonable. The shopping center with different hours of traffic use than the school or residential and apartment development is appropriate.

Ga Barrett v Hamby (1975) 235 Ga 262, 219 SE2d 399.

A zoning change to permit expansion of a shopping center may properly be denied on evidence of no public need. In the absence of a comprehensive plan it is necessary to show that a change would be in compliance with generally accepted land use standards, and a determination that the buffer zone was necessary and that the public need and welfare would not be served due to the increased traffic hazard amply supports the denial.

Ore Braidwood v Portland (1976) 24 OreAp 477, 546 P2d 777.

Denial of rezoning from residential to shopping center is proper when the residential classification fits the general plan for the city. The fact that the council desires shopping center construction on a different area presently zoned for such, does not constitute economic or competitive restrictions. Denial on the basis of insufficient population basis for the shopping center and detriment to the future residential development of the area constitutes sufficient reason to justify the denial.

Cal Ensign Bickford Rlty Corp v City Council of Livermore (1977) 68 CA3d 467, 137 CaR 304.

§14. Commercial Zoning

The fact that a shopping mall is a permitted use in a designed business development zone does not mean that a town zoning commission must grant an application for site plan approval where the traffic would have an adverse effect on the area and the site plan fails to establish safeguards to protect the neighborhood from detrimental effects on its residential character.

Conn Goldberg v Zoning Comm of Simsbury (1977) 173 Conn 23, 376 A2d 385.

Residential zoning at an intersection of two highways controlled by a stop light is unreasonable. The business and shopping center classification across the highway plus the subsequent rezoning of the third corner for a service station eliminates any use of the highway as a buffer zone and makes it unsuitable as residential property.

> **Ill**   Moist v DuPage County (1973) 10 IllAp3d 473, 294 NE2d 316.

Residential zoning for eight lots, two of which are presently used for parking and the other six are boarded up rental property, across the street from a shopping center and fronting on a major thoroughfare is unreasonable. The property is subject to commercial zoning where all the area with the exception of two houses is commercial.

> **Okla**   Lakewood Devel Co v Oklahoma City (1975) 534 P2d 23.

§15. Reasonableness

A proposed zoning plan, if reasonable, may be a factor in determining the central question of whether or not a property owner's proposed use is an appropriate use of the subject premises. Where property owner's proposed expansion of a commercial shopping center on adjacent property not yet zoned, the court may properly consider evidence put forth by the village of the reasonableness of multi-family dwelling zoning classification for the property in question.

> **Ill**   Pillman v Northbrook (1978) 65 IllAp3d 40, 382 NE2d 399.

When denial of rezoning for a neighborhood shopping center and automobile service constitutes a substantial disadvantage to the property owner and a small benefit to the public by retaining the classification it will be held unreasonable and void.

> **Ill**   Beaver v Bolingbrook (1973) 12 IllAp3d 923, 298 NE2d 761.

Denial of a commercial classification for expansion of a shopping center is arbitrary and unreasonable when based on a lack of need for further commercial development in the area. The subsequent action of a council in approving commercial zoning for a nearby tract is admissible in evidence to confirm the arbitrary nature of the council's action. Lack of need for further commercial development has no bearing on the required criteria of public health, welfare, and changing conditions.

> **Md**   Aspen Hill Venture v Montgomery County Council (1972) 265 Md 303, 289 A2d 303.

Denial of two of the four phases of a zoning change is not necessarily unreasonable. Since the changes primarily involve construction of apartments and a shopping center, a board finding that the area could not sustain the impact in population is reasonable.

Md Wier v Witney Land Co (1970) 257 Md 600, 263 A2d 833.

The change of a major size tract from green-belt buffer zone to an appropriate use as a shopping center with job opportunities and an additional tax base when supported by reasons of necessity and lack of harm to the general welfare is valid. The fact that the change does not conform to the original development plan does not nullify the change since the plan is advisory only.

Conn Lathrop v Planning & Zoning Comm of Trumbull (1973) 164 Conn 215, 319 A2d 376.

When a request for rezoning for a regional shopping center fails because of a tie-vote the court may consider the record in determining the validity of a change. The inability of the council to reach a decision may not be the basis to deny a person valuable property rights. Rezoning approved by the court which was based on research authorized by the city and on unanimous approval by the planning commission is valid.

Nev Bd of Comm of Las Vegas v Dayton Devel Co (1975) 91 Nev 71, 530 P2d 1187.

A planned unit development which contains provisions for a shopping center at the intersection of two major highways may not be denied on the basis that no convenience center locations are provided. It is unreasonable to require a convenience center in the center of the community where it will adversely affect residential development when a major shopping center is within the proposal.

Ill LaSalle Nat Bk v Lake County (1975) 27 IllAp3d 10, 325 NE2d 105.

A shopping center classification directly across a highway from a similarly classified area is unreasonable when the comprehensive plan calls for four convenience centers with the major business and commercial development in the downtown area. It is necessary that a determination be made as to the suitability of the initially classified property or the comprehensive plan be amended to authorize separate constructions and less restrictive commercial development.

Ore Duddles v Council of West Linn (1975) 21 OreAp 310, 535 P2d 583.

A three-step procedure for changing a commercial shopping center district, limited to single-family dwelling and various public, religious and agricultural uses to permit planned shopping center development is valid and does not deny due process. The initial approval of a tentative plan which must be referred to the planning commission for approval and back to the town council for final action is a legislative decision and is only subject to review on reasonableness. The action in ultimately denying the change based on traffic problems, soil and water pollution difficulties and public opposition, is reasonable.

> **NY** Todd Mart v Town Bd of Webster (1975) 49 AD2d 12, 370 NYS2d 683.

§16. Spot Zoning

A rezoning from residential to commercial for an all weather shopping area, where the question could have been decided either way is clearly for the council. The court will not substitute its opinion since the scope of judicial review applies to changes justifying reclassification.

> **Miss** Currie v Ryan (1970) 243 So2d 48.

When the town council has provided adequate conditions to prevent flooding, and determined that a shopping center is not detrimental to neighboring areas, the court may not substitute its opinion unless the council's action was arbitrary.

> **Conn** Stiles v West Hartford (1970) 159 Conn 212, 268 A2d 395.

Rezoning of part of a residential area for a commercial shopping center is not spot zoning since it is for the convenience and benefit of the residents. This is particularly true where the area adjacent to the rezoned parcel has been commercial for a considerable time, and there is other commercial activity in the general vicinity.

> **Iowa** Anderson v Cedar Rapids (1969) 168 NW2d 739.

Rezoning a residential tract at the corner of two four-lane streets controlled by stop lights, though constituting spot zoning, is not necessarily illegal. The underdevelopment of the area and the indication that the entire area will be commercial, plus the apparent need for a neighborhood shopping center, overcomes a presumption of illegal spot zoning.

> **Iowa** Jaffe v Davenport (1970) 179 NW2d 554.

Commercial zoning of a tract at a major intersection containing a shopping center across the road but residential zoning on the applicant's side does not constitute spot zoning. The comprehensive plan which indicates a commercial zoning for the entire highway frontage constitutes a reasonable future development of the area.

> **Pa** Clawson v Harbor Creek Township Zoning Hearing Bd (1973) 9 PaCmwlth 124, 304 A2d 184.

Rezoning a tract for a shopping center constitutes spot zoning when there is no change in circumstances justifying the change. The widening of a street, installation of commercial type street lights, and development of the area is not such a change as to justify the reclassification and consequential spot zoning.

Tex Thompson v Palestine (1974) 510 SW2d 579.

Rezoning from residential estate to shopping center based on public hearing, filing of briefs by the parties, and examination of the site by the commissioners does not constitute arbitrary or unreasonable action. The rezoning does not constitute spot zoning since it involves a classification consistent with land use patterns of the area and has a substantial relationship to public health, safety, morals, and general welfare.

Ala Grund v Jefferson County (1973) 291 Ala 29, 277 So2d 334.

§17. Variances

A variance rezoning a portion of a tract to commercial for a shopping center is not arbitrary and unreasonable in the absence of adverse affect on the surrounding property. The undeveloped nature of the area together with the surrounding commercial zoning and a showing of no damage to existing private homes may justify the change and substantiate the claim of unnecessary hardship under the existing classification.

Okla Hamilton v Barber (1970) 474 P2d 399.

Denial of a variance for a convenience center is unreasonable when the area has been changed by previous variances into a heavily commercialized area. Requiring residential zoning constitutes taking property without compensation.

Ind Metropolitan Bd of Zoning Appeals of Marion County v Sheehan Construction (1974) 160 IndAp 520, 313 NE2d 78.

Denial of a shopping center classification for a half acre lot adjoining two streets, a filling station, and residential property is reasonable. The unnecessary hardship necessary for a variance of the residential requirements and the buffer zone requirements must be shown by substantial proof.

Pa Levinson v Zoning Hearing Bd of Bristol Township (1975) 18 PaCmwlth 612, 336 A2d 899.

§18. Conditional Uses

Zoning permitting retail stores and indicating an intention to have retail development in certain areas with shopping centers as a conditional use places a very small burden of proof on the applicant for a shopping center. There is no differential in the ordinance between a neighborhood, residential, or community shopping center, and the special use permit may not be denied on a negative finding of traffic volume, but must be on the fact that some standard of the zoning ordinance is not met by the plan.

> **Minn**   Inland Const Co v Bloomington (1972) 292 Minn 374, 195 NW2d 558.

While the term "designated shopping center" has not been defined in the ordinance a collection of stores grouped together in an integrated center which is encouraged is not such a designated shopping center. With the exception of a supermarket which is a retail store not otherwise classified in the ordinance a special exception use permit is not necessary. A special exception which was granted to the supermarket on condition of constructing a road, subsequently disapproved by the state department of transportation, may be changed by the city council without resubmitting the application to the zoning board which has to initially consider such special exceptions.

> **NY**   Carriage House Rlty v Yonkers (1975) 80 Misc2d 586, 363 NYS2d 456.

§19. Vested Rights

A planned shopping center, not requiring approval under the subdivision control law, is protected from changes in zoning when the building permit has been issued before notice of hearing is given on a zoning change.

> **Mass**   Nyquist v Acton (1971) 359 Mass 462, 269 NE2d 654.

Expenditures for site plans for a shopping center and the loss in value to the landowners by a change in the shopping center classification are not sufficient expenditures to require a building permit after a zoning change. The amendment to the ordinance during pendency of a mandamus action is valid when no substantial expenditures or liabilities were incurred.

> **NH**   Gosselin v Nashua (1974) 114 NH 447, 321 A2d 593.

When the "perimeter plan" for a shopping center has been approved, a change in zoning prohibiting shopping centers may not be arbitrarily applied. The city may properly require that the plans meet building, health and sanitary conditions, but may not deny a special use permit strictly on the zoning change prohibiting shopping centers.

> **Mass**   Cape Ann Land Devel Co v Gloucester (1976) 353 NE2d 645.

§20. Citywide Restrictions

A town which has a shopping center as a nonconforming use supplying its immediate needs and being adjacent to a large metropolitan district may properly restrict the entire town to residential and associated home occupancy businesses.

Conn Cadoux v Planning & Zoning Comm of Weston (1972) 162 Conn 425, 294 A2d 582.

§21. Special Protection of Business

A zoning change may not be denied strictly to protect existing businesses, but a finding of possible disruption of the economic health of an established and existing business center may be supported by sufficient evidence to justify denial. Other factors than protection of existing businesses may be considered.

Conn Second Norwalk Corp v Westport (1969) 28 Conn Supp 426, 265 A2d 332.

An ordinance reducing the scope of previously authorized commercial use of a parcel for the avowed purpose of preserving the existing retail sales area of the downtown core business district is valid. Retail sales in outlying areas may be restricted to revitalize and rebuild the core area where there are many uses to which the outlying properties can be devoted, though the central area gains a virtual monopoly over retail business. That other owners in close proximity to established businesses may continue to sell at retail does not make the ordinance discriminatory or arbitrary where the established businesses are not great in number.

NJ Forte v Tenafly (1969) 106 NJS 346, 255 A2d 804.

§22. Floating Zones

An ordinance creating a shopping center district classification without any specific location, and shortly thereafter anchoring the district by rezoning an area, does not create a floating zone.

Pa Marino v Zoning Hearing Bd of Harrison Township (1971) 1 PaCmwlth 116, 274 A2d 221.

A party may not object to the enactment of a floating zone for shopping centers which is not attached to any specific property. Until such time as a hearing is had on attaching the zoning to a particular piece of property there is no party aggrieved by the enactment of the ordinance.

Conn Schwartz v Planning & Zoning Comm of Hamden (1975) 168 Conn 20, 357 A2d 495.

§23. Buffer Zones

A sideyard is not required when two tracts of land are used as a unit in the construction of a commercial building. The fact that the property will ultimately be owned by two different persons does not make mandatory a sideyard between the two store buildings which will be constructed as one structure with a common dividing wall.

Md   Feinberg v Southland Corp (1973) 301 A2d 6.

A buffer zone requirement for construction of a shopping center is applicable even though the property abuts an adjoining township. The municipality's failure to specify that it includes adjoining townships does not restrict its operation to residents of the municipality, and it will be interpreted with the requirement that municipal officers must often look beyond their own lines in discharge of their zoning responsibilities.

NY   Albright v Manlius (1970) 34 AD2d 419, 312 NYS2d 13.

Setback and buffer zone requirements which were not made pursuant to public notice establishing a shopping center zone are invalid.

NJ   Quinton v Edison Park Devel Corp (1971) 59 NJ 571, 285 A2d 5.

A change in proposed zoning for a shopping center is not so substantial as to require resubmission to the planning commission when it only requires a buffer zone around the outside of the perimeter of the tract. The amendment is a benefit to the opponents of the rezoning rather than a detriment and is a minor change rather than a revision of the proposed ordinance.

Tenn   Wilgus v Murfreesboro (1975) 532 SW2d 50.

§24. Minimum Size

Rezoning from residential to shopping center with a minimum requirement of five acres is unreasonable. It would require that the property remain residential or that numerous owners combine to form the minimum acreage requirements.

Ohio   Scharnhorst v Zoning Bd of Appeals (1971) 28 OM 37, 237 NE2d 915.

§25. Relief

Changing a shopping center classification to residential is not a statutory duty, and, therefore, may be restrained by injunction. When the court has previously affirmed an ordinance for the shopping center, and directed the clerk to post the ordinance, an attempted reclassification is an illegal attempt by the city to frustrate the order of the court and may be enjoined.

NY   110 Manno Rlty Corp v Huntington (1970) 61 Misc2d 702, 306 NYS2d 746.

§26. Split Zone Lots

A provision that when singularly owned property is in two zoning classifications the least restrictive applied is valid; however, the further provision that approval of use must be by the board of zoning appeals is invalid since there are no standards or guildelines provided.

Me Stucki v Plavin (1972) 291 A2d 508.

ANNOTATION

Validity and construction of zoning regulation respecting permissible use as affected by division of lot or parcel by zone boundary line, 58 ALR3d 1241.

§27. Inverse Condemnation

Rezoning a parcel of land at a busy intersection from shopping center commercial to single-family residential does not constitute inverse condemnation. Rezoning is a legislative act which provides immunity from injury caused by adoption or failure to adopt an enactment.

Cal HFH, Ltd v Superior Ct of Los Angeles County (1975) 15 C3d 508, 542 P2d 237, 125 CaR 365.

§28. Traffic Regulation

Approval of a shopping site plan may not be conditioned on recommendations in a department of transportation letter referring to a previous proposal which has been withdrawn. The city may not condition approval on traffic studies and traffic flows which are the requirement of the state department of transportation.

Pa Bethel Park Minimall v Bethel Park (1974) 16 PaCmwlth 97, 326 A2d 670.

§29. Administrative Remedies

Rezoning of property from residential to a classification for a shopping center is a legislative determination. And as such, the action is not subject to review under the Administrative Procedure Act.

Wyo McGann v City Council of Laramie (1978) 581 P2d 1104.

In determining volume of traffic in front of a proposed shopping center, the council may consider the tentative approval received from the highway commission for relocating and widening access roads.

Conn   Stiles v West Hartford (1970) 159 Conn 212, 268 A2d 395.

A construction by the building officer that a proposed shopping center is a neighborhood convenience center may not be directly attacked by court action. The use which is permitted in the area requires that administrative remedies be followed. The contestant must also have a special interest different than the general public in order to have standing. An increase in traffic and the remote possibility of overflow parking on the contestant's property does not substantially differ from the general public and is not a sufficient basis to confer standing.

Fla   Skaggs-Albertson's Properties v Michels Belleair Bluffs Pharmacy (1976) 332 So2d 113.

SLAUGHTERHOUSES; RENDERING PLANTS; TANNERIES

EDITORIAL COMMENT. Every law student is familiar with the slaughter-house cases, and there is no need for much comment here. The cases reaffirm the rights of municipalities to regulate, license, or prohibit such enterprises. They appear to be a little rougher on slaughterhouses than on some other types of activity that may be almost as noisome.

The cases herein are limited to places engaged in the actual slaughter of animals, and the allied activities of rendering and tanning. The regulation of butchershops and meat markets is covered in FOOD BUSINESSES. And the raising of animals intended for eventual slaughter is treated in ANIMALS, DOMESTIC.

I. MUNICIPAL AUTHORITY TO REGULATE

§1. Delegation by State Constitution

A constitutional provision authorizing the city in the exercise of the police power inherent in the sovereign to regulate the whole subject of slaughtering animals within the city is not an unconstitutional grant of power so as to invalidate ordinances regulating and limiting slaughterhouses.

> **La**   Darcantel v People's Slaughterhouse (1892) 44 LaAnn 632, 11 So 239.

§2. Extent of Power

Where a city has statutory authority to "regulate, suppress and abate slaughterhouses", an ordinance prohibiting slaughterhouses is invalid, since the words "regulate, suppress and abate" refer to something in existence, and do not authorize prevention of its coming into existence.

> **Mo**   State v Kasten (1964) 382 SW2d 714.

A city by ordinance may regulate and restrain all noxious and injurious callings within its limits, may prevent animals from being slaughtered in designated localities within the city, and may designate a particular quarter of the city within which the business may be conducted and prohibit it in others.

> **Cal**   Heilbron, Ex parte (1884) 65 Cal 609, 4 P 648.
> **La**   Darcantel v People's Slaughter House (1892) 44 LaAnn 632, 11 So 239.
> **Me**   State v Starkey (1914) 112 Me 8, 90 A 431.
> **Md**   Mount Airy v Sappington (1950) 195 Md 259, 73 A2d 449.
> **Mo**   State v Steinbach (1955) 274 SW2d 588.

§3. Ordinance Stricter than Statute

Cities, villages and towns may impose stricter regulations on rendering plants than state licensing laws, while cities and villages may prohibit rendering plants entirely within their limits, but towns may not do so.

Wis   Boerschinger v Elkay Enterprises (1965) 26 Wis2d 102, 133 NW2d 333.

§4. Extraterritorial Regulation

Under a statute authorizing municipalities to regulate packing houses within their limits and within one mile outside their limits, the licensing of a packing house located within one mile of the city limits by an adjoining small town will not prevent the city from also licensing and regulating it.

Ill   Chicago Packing & Provision v Chicago (1878) 88 Ill 221.

An ordinance of a second class city giving the mayor jurisdiction over all places and territory within the city limits and within five miles thereof to enforce the rules, regulations and ordinances of the board of health does not give validity to a regulation which attempts to make it criminal to maintain a slaughterhouse outside the city.

Neb   State v Temple (1916) 99 Neb 505, 156 NW 1063.

II. LICENSING

§5. Franchise Distinguished from Monopoly

An ordinance granting the right to operate a slaughterhouse to private individuals, subject to restrictions, inspection and bond, does not violate constitutional restrictions prohibiting granting of a monopoly or exclusive privilege and since additional similar franchises may be granted to others the business is not restricted to the lands and houses of only one individual or corporation and the grants are subject to approval of the board of health.

La   Darcantel v People's Slaughterhouse (1892) 44 LaAnn 632, 11 So 239.

§6. Discretionary Issuance of Permit

Where, because of a statute, towns cannot entirely prohibit rendering plants within their limits, a town zoning ordinance that requires written approval by the board of zoning appeals for construction of a rendering plant and sets forth standards for board approval does not wholly exclude a rendering plant and is thus not invalid.

> **Wis**　Boerschinger v Elkay Enterprises (1965) 26 Wis2d 102, 133 NW2d 333.

Where an ordinance prohibits the slaughter of animals within a certain area, without permission of the common council, the court will not interfere with the exercise of discretion by the council nor will it formulate standards to be used in the exercise of such discretion. Interference is justified only when it is clearly shown that a refusal is unreasonable or is based solely on grounds which, as a matter of law, do not sustain or control the exercise of discretion.

> **NY**　Albany v Newhof (1930) 230 AD 687, 246 NYS 100.

§7. Permission Granted by Resolution

Under an ordinance prohibiting the erection of slaughterhouses without permission of the common council, granting of permission is an administrative rather than a legislative act, and permission can be granted by resolution.

> **NY**　Russell Sage College v Troy (1960) 24 Misc2d 344, 198 NYS2d 391.

§8. Standards when Issued by Board of Health

An ordinance prohibiting the slaughtering of poultry without obtaining a permit from the board of health is not invalid for failure to establish standards for issuance of a permit, where such board is governed not only by the ordinance but also rules and regulations of state sanitary code.

> **NJ**　Kurinsky v Lakewood (1942) 128 NJLaw 185, 24 A2d 803.

§9. License Ownership and Location Transfer

An ordinance restricting the number of poultry slaughterhouse licenses, and authorizing renewals and transfers of ownership, but containing no provision with respect to transfers of license from place to place, will be deemed not to prohibit such transfers.

> **NJ**　Cutaio v Elizabeth (1955) 36 NJS 565, 116 A2d 646.

§10. Extraterritorial Licensing

Under a statute authorizing municipalities to regulate packing houses within their limits and within one mile outside their limits, the licensing of a packing house located within one mile of the city limits by an adjoining small town will not prevent the city from also licensing and regulating it.

> **Ill** Chicago Packing & Provision v Chicago (1878) 88 Ill 221.

§11. Repeal of Licensing Ordinance

Where an ordinance grants a right to establish and maintain a slaughterhouse to an individual, who does so in reliance thereon, a subsequent repealing ordinance is not an unconstitutional impairment of contract obligation. The city may not bargain away its duty to exercise the police power, and it is empowered to adopt, if necessary, a subsequent ordinance declaring slaughterhouses a nuisance.

> **Ore** Portland v Cook (1906) 48 Ore 550, 87 P 772.

Where the operation of a slaughterhouse was excepted from an ordinance as an existing use, an attempted limitation requiring discontinuance of the operation in five years on the granting of permission to make alterations required by the state agricultural department was unauthorized and of no effect.

> **Cal** Ricciardi v Los Angeles County (1953) 115 CA2d 569, 252 P2d 773.

A city does not, by enactment of an ordinance granting the right to operate a rendering plant for 50 years, divest itself of the right thereafter, in the exercise of the police power, to repeal the ordinance and enact a different one.

> **Wis** La Crosse Rendering Works v La Crosse (1939) 231 Wis 438, 285 NW 393.

§12. Proscribing Future Permits

An ordinance providing that no tannery shall be established thereafter without permission from the city council, but permitting tanneries already in existence to continue operation, does not transgress the federal constitutional provision that no person shall be denied the equal protection of the law.

> **Minn** State v Taubert (1914) 126 Minn 371, 148 NW 281.

An ordinance proscribing slaughterhouses, enacted nine months after construction of a slaughterhouse within the city, is valid under a charter provision empowering the city to license, tax, control, and regulate slaughterhouses, or to provide for their exclusion. The provision is intended not only to prevent the future erection but also the present maintenance of slaughterhouses, is a valid exercise of the police power, and violates no constitutional right of the affected slaughterhouse owner.

> **Ore**   Portland v Meyer (1898) 32 Ore 368, 52 P 21.

III. ZONING

A. REGULATION

§ 13. Reasonableness of Location Restrictions

Provisions of a zoning ordinance prohibiting the erection of a building for use as a place for the slaughter and dressing of poultry, except in a heavy industrial zone, are reasonable.

> **NJ**   Greenstein v Bigelow (1927) 5 NJM 124, 135 A 661.

A zoning ordinance prohibiting the slaughtering of cattle and other livestock in the commercial zone of the city is not unreasonable or in violation of any statutory law.

> **Kan**   Kilcoyne v Coffeyville (1954) 176 Kan 159, 269 P2d 418.

An ordinance forbidding the erection or use of a building in a residential district for the storage, cleaning, or renovation of uncured animal hair or the byproducts thereof is not unreasonable or arbitrary, but is a valid exercise of the police power.

> **Ohio**   Ohio Hair Products v Rendigs (1918) 98 OS 251, 120 NE 836.

ANNOTATION

Animal rendering or bone boiling plant or business as nuisance, 17 ALR2d 1269.

§ 14. —Amendment

An amendatory zoning ordinance authorizing construction of a rendering plant in one of four districts previously zoned for industrial use excepting rendering plants is invalid as a denial of equal protection of the law. No distinctions exist which make the operation of the rendering plant in the affected district any less objectionable than its operation in any of the remaining three districts would be.

> **Wis**   Boerschinger v Elkay Enterprises (1966) 32 Wis2d 168, 145 NW2d 108.

§15. Extent of Nonconforming Use Change

Zoning in which the property owner joins by filing a restrictive covenant prohibiting use of the property for slaughterhouse purposes is valid and enforceable. Where the owner then attempts to use it as a slaughterhouse, adjoining owners may file an injunctive suit for trespass from sewerage backup and to enforce the covenant. A previous nonconforming use for processing slaughtered beef is permissible, but operation of a general slaughterhouse will be prohibited until the zoning is changed.

Okla Harrison v Perry (1969) 456 P2d 512.

Under an ordinance providing that the maximum to which a nonconforming use may be extended is 10 per cent of the area of the building or structure being enlarged, "area" means ground area, not floor space, and therefore the owner of a slaughterhouse in a residence district is not entitled to eliminate the second floor square footage of his building and use the surrendered square footage for new construction on the ground floor.

Ohio A Dicillo & Sons v Chester (1951) 103 NE2d 44.

§16. Application to Retail Poultry Trade

A zoning ordinance prohibiting "stockyards, slaughtering of animals," does not prohibit the killing of chickens as carried on in the retail poultry business, because the term "animal" means a quadruped, not a bird or a fowl.

Ohio Del Monte v Woodmansee (1946) 47 Abs 513, 72 NE2d 789.

B. ENFORCEMENT

§17. Injunction for Violation

When ordinance prohibits tallow or rendering factories within a specified area, but such business is conducted in violation of the ordinance, it may be enjoined and declared a nuisance per se even if the odors which are the ligitimate and natural cause of the nuisance are not injurious to health and are not unbearable, but are a source of great discomfort and impair the property owner's enjoyment of his home.

La Perrin v Crescent City Stockyard (1907) 119 La 83, 43 So 938.

§18. Prosecution when Violated Ordinance Repealed

Where an ordinance proscribes slaughterhouses within the city, but a subsequent ordinance authorizes operation by one company of a slaughterhouse, the company may not be prosecuted by the city under the penalty provision of the earlier ordinance, without repeal of the subsequent ordinance. Nor may the city itself question the validity of the subsequent ordinance.

> **Ore**   Zimmerman v Gritzmacher (1909) 53 Ore 206, 98 P 875.

An ordinance licensing a corporation to operate a slaughterhouse does not relieve the corporation of its violations of an earlier ordinance providing penalties for the operation of a slaughterhouse.

> **Ore**   Portland v Cook (1906) 48 Ore 550, 87 P 772.

§19. Permit Revoked by Sanitation Inspector

Where a tannery is operated under a permit in an area zoned for that purpose, a building inspector is without power to revoke the permit on the ground that the tannery violates the city sanitary code. That code has no precedence over zoning provisions, because each occupies a different field and neither is in conflict with the other.

> **Wis**   Great Lakes Tanning v Milwaukee (1947) 250 Wis 74, 26 NW2d 152.

§20. Failure to Appeal Administrative Decision

Where a person fails to appeal from a board of adjustment's denial of his application for an extension permit to operate a slaughterhouse, under a licensing ordinance, he may not, on conviction for violation of such ordinance, collaterally raise by certiorari upon appeal from such conviction, a question as to validity of such ordinance.

> **NJ**   Iannella v Johnson (1948) 136 NJLaw 514, 56 A2d 894.

IV. NUISANCE CONTROL

§21. Abatement of Slaughterhouses

An ordinance declaring a slaughterhouse to be a nuisance is a valid exercise of express delegated power. Federal regulation of slaughterhouses will not affect the validity of the ordinance.

> **Ill**   Streator v Davenport Packing (1952) 347 IllAp 492, 107 NE2d 270.

While a city by statute has authority to prevent nuisances an ordinance that declares a slaughterhouse a nuisance is invalid, since it is not such per se.

Ill   Harmison v Lewistown (1894) 153 Ill 313, 38 NE 628.
       Harmison v Lewistown (1891) 46 IllAp 164.
La   Perrin v Crescent City Stockyard (1907) 119 La 83, 43 So 938.
Md Mount Airy v Sappington (1950) 195 Md 259, 73 A2d 449.
Mo State v Steinbach (1955) 274 SW2d 588.

§22. Affected by Neighboring Nuisances

A finding that the operation of tallow or rendering factories prohibited by ordinance is a nuisance is not affected by the fact that other nuisances presently exist in the same locality and produce similar results, where the nuisance complained of adds to that already existing to such an extent that the injury complained of is measurably traceable thereto. It is not necessary that all of the injury result from the nuisance charged, if it be of such a character and produce such results that standing alone it would be a nuisance. The fact that it is the principal, though not the sole injury-producing agent is sufficient.

La   Perrin v Crescent City Stockyard (1907) 119 La 83, 43 So 938.

V. ODOR CONTROL

§23. Authority to Restrict

An ordinance providing that no person owning or operating a rendering plant shall operate such plant, or permit it to be operated, so as to cause noxious or offensive odors was validly enacted under a statute that provided that the board of selectmen should have power to license, prohibit, or permit, under suitable rules, the carrying on of any kind of trade, manufacture or business prejudicial to the public health.

Conn State v Woolley (1914) 88 Conn 715, 92 A 662.

An instruction to the jury that any employee of a rendering plant could be held for permitting the plant to emanate noxious odors was prejudicial error, since this would permit prosecution of employees who had nothing to do with the actual plant operation.

Conn State v Woolley (1914) 88 Conn 715, 92 A 662.

§24. Conviction of Owner and Operator

Under an ordinance providing that no person owning or operating any rendering plant shall operate such plant or permit it to be operated so as to cause noxious or offensive odors, not only the owner of the plant but also the operator may be liable to the penalties prescribed for violation.

Conn   State v Woolley (1914) 88 Conn 715, 92 A 662.

§25. —Proof of Intent

A conviction of violating an ordinance requiring the destruction or condensation of all offensive odors resulting from meat processing may be sustained though there is no proof of intention to violate the ordinance. Occurrence of a breakdown in the odor control system, allowing the escape of odors before it could be repaired, is not a valid defense.

NY   Depart of Health v Sulzberger (1912) 78 Misc 134, 137 NYS 998.

VI. RENDERING PLANTS

§26. Classification

Where a city has express authority to enact an ordinance regulating or prohibiting rendering within the city, the only question arising with respect to its validity is whether the classification between different types of rendering businesses is valid.

Wis   Maercker v Milwaukee (1912) 151 Wis 324, 139 NW 199.

§27. Abatement

An application to eliminate rendering works from an industrial zoning and its subsequent denial does not give right to an injunction suit without completing administrative remedies. Administrative remedies must be exhausted unless the constitutionality of the ordinance is contested; however, a suit to enjoin construction as a nuisance may be maintained though the use is legal under the zoning.

Colo   Acosta v Jansen (1972) 499 P2d 631.

An ordinance prohibiting the rendering of lard, oil, fat, and grease from animals or animal matter within the city limits, and setting forth a penalty for violation, is invalid where the business is being conducted without interference with the public health, safety, morals, comfort or happiness and is not a nuisance per se.

La   New Orleans v New Orleans Butchers' Co-Op Abattoir (1923) 153 La 536, 96 So 113.

§28. Materials Collected off Rendering Site

An ordinance distinguishing, in the extent of its regulation of rendering offal and shop fats, as between plants where material is rendered from animals slaughtered on the premises and those where the material is collected from butcher shops and other plants, is valid as based on a substantial difference, in that the operation involved in collecting such offensive material throughout the city necessitates stricter regulation than where the entire rendering process is consummated within one building.

Wis   Maercker v Milwaukee (1912) 151 Wis 324, 139 NW 199.

VII. MUNICIPAL ABATTOIRS

§29. Sale of Bonds

Where an ordinance provides for the sale of bonds for the purpose of buying a site and erecting an abattoir for the benefit of the city, the abattoir being intended as a protection against diseased meats, it is a necessary expense for which the city may issue bonds without popular vote.

NC   Moore v Greensboro (1926) 191 NC 592, 132 SE 565.

§30. Use Fees

Fees charged for operation of an abattoir are invalid if the charges attempt to raise revenue, but if the ordinance was passed for the purpose of regulation, from which an incidental profit is derived, it is valid. Thus, an ordinance to raise the use fee charged by a city slaughterhouse to meet current operating costs is valid as within the second category, where no profit is derived from operation of the slaughterhouse and nonresident meat packers are not required to pay the fee.

Ark   Fort Smith v Roberts (1928) 177 Ark 821, 9 SW2d 75.

STREETCARS AND BUSES

EDITORIAL COMMENT. Streetcar and bus operations within cities used to be of strictly local concern. However, the problems have so multiplied, and have become so complicated, that mass transit is now a major concern of the United States Department of Transportation. It nevertheless remains the primary responsibility of cities, under enabling and regulatory state legislation.

Some transit systems are municipally owned and operated, but many are privately owned. The latter are subject to franchise and licensing requirements, and to all sorts of regulations—even to specifying color and temperature. And of course some of the cases hereunder deal with racial segregation. The right of a city to regulate fares is also treated, as are the duties of a transit system with respect to the maintenance and repair of streets and roadbeds.

In addition to the type of transit that is usually thought of in connection with this topic, included below are regulations of jitney buses and sightseeing buses. But excluded are RAILROADS and TAXIS. Certain specific regulations relating to the movement of streetcars and buses are covered below, but the main traffic laws and regulations are covered in TRAFFIC.

I. MUNICIPALLY OWNED TRANSIT SYSTEMS

§1. In General

A charter service operated by the city in conjunction with a mass transit system is incidental to and an accepted part of the general service operation.

    Cal   Ruane v San Diego (1968) 267 CA2d 548, 73 CaR 316.

Operating motor buses outside its limits is a valid exercise of the authority of a municipality where the city purchased the bus line. It is not subject to control by the railroad commission, though the former franchise holder operated under railroad commission authority.

    Tex   Corpus Christi v Continental Bus Systems (1969) 445 SW2d 12.

Under the Constitution and home rule law, municipalities are empowered to acquire, own and operate transit facilities. The power is properly exercised only through valid ordinances.

    NY   Andrello v Dulan (1966) 49 Misc2d 17, 266 NYS2d 738.

Ordinances authorizing municipal operation of bus lines are invalid where the enabling act withholds the power to carry on the business of common carriers.

Expenditures authorized by the ordinances may be enjoined at the suit of a taxpayer.

> **NY**   Browne v New York City (1925) 241 NY 96, 149 NE 211.

An experimental mass transit system operated by the city and known as "dial-a-ride" is not subject to the city's taxicab ordinance. The ordinance applying to persons precludes its application to the city, and the existing taxicab licensees have no basis to prevent the city from operating a mass transit authority.

> **Mich**   Kon v Ann Arbor (1972) 41 MichAp 307, 199 NW2d 874.

Construction of street railway tracks by a city for lease for revenue to a street railway company constitutes work of internal improvement, prohibited to cities under the state Constitution.

> **Mich**   Bird v Detroit (1907) 148 Mich 71, 111 NW 860.

A charter requirement that the city consider offers for the sale of existing public utilities before constructing a new one does not afford a basis of relief to a railroad seeking to prevent construction of a municipal street railway with tracks on two sides of its double track, where a general solicitation of offers for sale to the city of an existing street railway was sent to the railroad.

> **Cal**   United RR v San Francisco (1918) 249 US 517, 63 LEd 739, 39 SCt 361.

ANNOTATION

Right of public utility to discontinue line or branch on ground that it is unprofitable, 10 ALR2d 1121.

LAW REVIEW

Valuing an Unprofitable Business Taken for Continuing Public Use, 68 Colum LR 977.

§2. Enactment of Ordinance or Resolution

The motives of the city officials and of the electors in enacting an ordinance for the construction of a municipal street railroad are not proper subjects of judicial inquiry, as long as the means adopted for submission of the question to the people conform to the requirements of the law.

> **Mich**   Detroit United Ry v Detroit (1921) 255 US 171, 65 LEd 570, 41 SCt 285.

Failure to comply with internal rule of council requiring two weeks' notice to members prior to legislation affecting franchises does not invalidate an ordinance authorizing purchase of a bus line transit franchise, since the ordinance does not operate to change or amend a franchise.

> **NY**　Andrello v Dulan (1966) 49 Misc2d 17, 266 NYS2d 738.

A city has the right to waive conditions pertaining to financing arrangements specified in ordinances and inserted for the city's protection and benefit in a contract to purchase bus line transit facilities, if the city is not prejudiced and is unable or unwilling to perform in that respect.

> **NY**　Andrello v Dulan (1966) 49 Misc2d 17, 266 NYS2d 738.

An ordinance providing that "it is hereby determined and specifically declared that the public interest and necessity demand a construction of street railways over and along certain streets . . . " sufficiently expresses a determination of the public interest and necessity for the construction by the city and county for whom the legislative body acted, though the ordinance omitted reference to a construction "by the city and county."

> **Cal**　Platt v San Francisco (1910) 158 Cal 74, 110 P 304.

A charter amendment establishing a city transit commission carries with it the authority to provide, by ordinance, for the method or combination of methods of transportation by various means to be utilized in the system.

> **Wash**　Dahl v Braman (1967) 71 Wash2d 720, 430 P2d 951.

ANNOTATION

Right of public utility to discontinue line or branch on ground that it is unprofitable, 10 ALR2d 1121.

§3. Obtaining Funds to Construct or Purchase System

An ordinance authorizing the city to operate a mass transportation company and to levy a special tax for its acquisition and operation does not require a three-fifths vote. Since the equipment is being leased and the rental payments are not subject to acceleration on default this is not an obligation in excess of the amount authorized, and a grant from the federal government on the basis of projected improvements of the system is not a commitment to a long-term debt.

> **Cal**　Ruane v San Diego (1968) 267 CA2d 548, 73 CaR 316.

A resolution authorizing joining with a metropolitan rapid transit authority in the collection of the authorized sales tax does not constitute a delegation of legislative authority. The sales tax authorized is a general tax within the political subdivisions belonging to the authority and does not violate a constitutional requirement of uniform taxation.

Ga Camp v Metropolitan Atlanta Rapid Transit Auth (1972) 229 Ga 35, 189 SE2d 56.

Municipalities have the power to acquire, construct, own, lease and operate any public utility, the product or service of which is supplied to the municipality or its inhabitants, and to contract with others for any such product or service; and the issuance of bonds pursuant to ordinance for the purchase of a street railway for the carriage of passengers is within the power.

Ohio Kittel v Cincinnati (1946) 78 OA 251, 47 Abs 81, 33 Op 567, 69 NE2d 771.

Under a home rule charter empowering a county to provide and operate public transportation systems, it has the power to purchase and operate a unified county-wide transportation system, to set machinery in motion and to provide necessary personnel, and may issue revenue bonds to implement the purchase of a transit system.

Fla State v Dade County (1962) 142 So2d 79.

A transit authority is subject to the same restrictions as any municipality. Bonds to be paid by revenue from operations of the system, with any shortage made up from the general revenues, are general obligation, not revenue bonds, and are subject to a vote of the electorate.

Ariz Tucson Transit Auth v Nelson (1971) 107 Ariz 246, 485 P2d 816.

An ordinance authorizing issuance of bonds for reconstruction and rehabilitation of a municipally owned and operated streetcar system is not invalid for uncertainty on the ground that repayment of the bonds as scheduled in the ordinance at a certain amount per year for a given number of years would exceed the total amount of the authorized issue, or on the ground that a specific interest rate is not prescribed per annum.

Ariz Luhrs v Phoenix (1928) 33 Ariz 156, 262 P 1002.

A city has power, by ordinance, to purchase or otherwise acquire and operate, within or without its limits, a street railway system, and to provide for payment therefor by utility revenue bonds; but if a general indebtedness is to be incurred, the ordinance must be submitted to a referendum.

Wash Harlin v Superior Ct (1926) 139 Wash 282, 247 P 4.

An ordinance submitting to the electors a proposition for the issuance of bonds to purchase an existing street railway, or, in the alternative, for the construction of parallel lines, in the discretion of the city, is not invalid as combining several distinct and unrelated objects in one ordinance, since the alternative objects state two related parts of the single purpose of acquiring a street railway.

Wash Tulloch v Seattle (1912) 69 Wash 178, 124 P 481.

In a unified transit system ordinance containing provisions for the city's acquisition of the transit company's property, a provision for cancellation of securities of the company does not constitute a "donation", within the prohibition of the state Constitution, since by cancellation of the securities the city acquires a new, valuable contract right—to purchase valuable property at a correspondingly reduced price. This is not a donation, but an exchange of one thing of value for another.

Ill People v Chicago (1932) 349 Ill 304, 182 NE 419.

§4. Approval of Municipal Ownership by State

The state public service commission is not required to approve the transfer of a public utility bus franchise prior to execution of the contract of sale, and a city purchasing such facility, though required to obtain permission, may not be prematurely required to do so.

NY Andrello v Dulan (1966) 49 Misc2d 17, 266 NYS2d 738.

§5. Operation of System Concurrent with Private System

A prohibition against the establishment of a bus line, competitive with the city's transit over a given route on a fixed schedule unless a certificate is issued to the competing carrier that its line is necessary for the public's convenience gives the transit a legally protectable status.

DC Capitol Transit v Safeway Trails (1953) 201 F2d 708.

An ordinance providing for the grant to a street railway company of the right to operate jointly a subway or street railway owned by the city with a system of street railways already owned and operated by the company, and providing that the gross proceeds shall be used for the payment of existing and hereafter issued securities of the company, is a pledging of the city's credit for the private debts of the street railway company, in violation of the Constitution.

Ohio Campbell v Cincinnati St Ry (1918) 97 OS 283, 119 NE 735.

§6. Construction of Subways

A resolution authorizing condemnation of the fee of a street for subway purposes and imposing an assessment on abutting property for street improvement purposes is void as a taking without due process, since the abutting owners obtain no benefit from the subway, and the city, already having absolute control of the street, does not obtain any greater interest for street purposes.

NY Montague St, In re (1914) 87 Misc 120, 150 NYS 382.

A resolution of necessity which provides for the "construction of subways", rather than for the "construction of a subway", properly expresses a single and not a multiple purpose.

Ohio State ex rel Speeth v Carney (1955) 163 OS 159, 56 Op 194, 126 NE2d 449.

Under its delegated power, a city has authority to enact an ordinance for the construction of subways beneath the surface of its streets, and to regulate their use and the travel therein, since there is no reason why city's right to regulate the surface of its streets should not apply to the subsurface.

Ill Peoples Gas Light & Coke v Chicago (1953) 413 Ill 457, 109 NE2d 777.

An ordinance that requires barriers around floor openings within buildings during the course of construction does not apply to the construction of a subway station. Floor openings are required to be protected only during construction of public, residence and business buildings.

NY Garety v Charles Meads (1936) 247 AD 3, 286 NYS 297.

An ordinance granting a traction company an exclusive franchise to use city subways is not invalid as unreasonable or monopolistic, where the right is limited to the use of tracks in the subway that are under lease to the traction company.

Ill Barsaloux v Chicago (1910) 245 Ill 598, 92 NE 525.

An ordinance granting a metropolitan transit authority the right to use subways is not invalid as creating a monopoly beyond the powers of the municipality, since a city has power to decide whether the operation of a street railway in the city shall be competitive or monopolistic.

Ill People v Chicago Transit Auth (1945) 392 Ill 77, 64 NE2d 4.

ANNOTATION

Rights of the city and abutting owners when the city constructs a rapid transit subway beneath the street, 11 ALR2d 189.

§7. Fares

A general increase of street railway fares on municipally owned streetcars and buses was properly enjoined, though the board of supervisors under the city charter had jurisdiction to consider such increases, where the decision to increase was made before the giving of notice and before consenting to timely intervention by a presidentially-designated agency in compliance with the requirement of the federal stabilization act that the federal agency have an opportunity to be heard.

Cal Bowles v San Francisco (1946) 64 F Supp 609.

§8. Claims against System

Although a city may be granted the same immunity against a claim for damages for acts done in its governmental capacity as is enjoyed by the state, it may not, by ordinance, immunize itself from liability for acts done in its proprietary capacity. Accordingly, it cannot exempt itself from the negligence of its employees in the operation of a street railway system.

Tex Green v Amarillo (1922) 244 SW 241.

Where a municipality acquires a street railway, the obligations assumed by the purchase contract justify the council in authorizing by ordinance payment of a sum to partially meet and be within the rate of pay fixed by the arbitrators as a potential contractual liability and as the justifiable payment of a valid moral claim.

Ohio Sweeny v Stapleton (1942) 38 Abs 213, 49 NE2d 707.

II. PRIVATELY OWNED TRANSIT SYSTEMS

A. FRANCHISE, PERMIT OR LICENSE

§9. Authority of Municipality Generally

A regulation forbidding the operation of unfranchised buses is violated by operating a 12-passenger limousine picking up persons from their homes in a housing development and transporting them to various areas in the city for a fixed charge.

NY People v Schuster (1975) 83 Misc2d 871, 374 NYS2d 951.

Although the streets of a city are available for use by the public, the city has a right to discriminate against those who use them in transporting passengers for hire.

Fla Coral Gables v Miami (1939) 138 Fla 881, 190 So 427.

Where a franchise ordinance provides for and regulates limousine service within designated areas, it is contractual and not penal in nature. Ordinances of a city are of a dual nature. They may be in effect local laws, or they may constitute contracts.

NC Harrelson v Fayetteville (1967) 271 NC 87, 155 SE2d 749.

An ordinance is not invalid as violating an applicant's right of privacy by a provision forbidding a person to drive any motor vehicle used to transport persons for hire on the streets without a permit from the mayor and the city council, and requiring the applicant to furnish a photograph of himself.

Ga Walton v Atlanta (1949) 89 F Supp 309.

An ordinance requiring a license to operate a motor vehicle for conveyance of passengers is valid. It is a lawful subject for regulation by ordinance.

Mass Burgess v Brockton (1920) 235 Mass 95, 126 NE 456.

An ordinance licensing and regulating the business of carrying passengers for hire by motor vehicles in the city limits does not conflict with a statute taxing and licensing or registering motor vehicles.

Minn Jefferson Highway Transport v St Cloud (1923) 155 Minn 463, 193 NW 960.

An ordinance regulating motor bus transportation of passengers for hire from points without the city to points within, and vice versa, and requiring a license therefor, is not nullified by a statute imposing a tax on motor vehicles and prohibiting the imposition of a tax or fee by a city, since the ordinance requires a license.

Minn State v Palmer (1942) 212 Minn 388, 3 NW2d 666.

In enacting ordinances granting franchises for the use of streets by public service corporations, a city is not ordinarily acting in a private or proprietary capacity, or for pecuniary profit, but as an agent for the state, and its franchises represent grants from the state.

Iowa State v Des Moines City Ry (1913) 159 Iowa 259, 140 NW 437.

A city may entirely prohibit those engaged in the carriage of passengers or property for hire from using its streets for a stand for transacting business, or stopping to let off or take on passengers, or any use by which the streets are occupied or appropriated to the exclusion of the public, or any use which causes excessive wear of them, but may not prohibit street use by common carriers strictly as thoroughfares.

> **Ore** Dent v Oregon City (1923) 106 Ore 122, 211 P 909.

An ordinance licensing motor buses and requiring their operators to secure a certificate from the commissioner of public utilities before application for the bus license is not invalid as vesting the commissioner with unreasonable and arbitrary power, if an appeal procedure is provided to guard against unjust action of the commissioner.

> **Ore** Thielke v Albee (1915) 79 Ore 48, 153 P 793.

An ordinance requiring a permit from the city council for use of the streets by motor vehicles carrying passengers for hire, which the council is empowered to refuse if in its judgment the public necessity and convenience does not require its issuance, is valid, where applied to intercity buses.

> **Tex** Winters v Murphey (1927) 297 SW 479.

An ordinance requiring a certificate for the operation of any vehicle used for transporting passengers for hire but excluding vehicles operating on rails or tracks is not discriminatory, since it is based on a reasonable classification of vehicles.

> **Tex** Fletcher v Bordelon (1933) 56 SW2d 313.

The right to use the streets of a city as a common carrier for hire is a privilege and not an inherent right, and may be granted or refused by the city, in the exercise of its police power, at its pleasure, and the city may by ordinance delegate the investigation of the character and qualifications of applicants for permits and licenses to operate motor buses on its streets to the superintendent of police, without violating constitutional guaranties.

> **Va** Taylor v Smith (1924) 140 Va 217, 124 SE 259.

An ordinance licensing motor carriers for hire that operate within the city is not invalid as inconsistent with the statute providing for regulation of motor carriers for hire throughout the state, where the ordinance is merely an extension of the state's regulatory power, since the statute conveys no implication of any intent to deprive municipalities of power to regulate the use of their streets by such carriers.

> **Tenn** Chattanooga v Jackson (1938) 172 Tenn 264, 111 SW2d 1026.

A city may grant a franchise to a motor carrier to operate within the city and its environs despite a lack of express authority in its charter, since a statute conferring on municipalities the exclusive power to regulate local transportation systems beyond their corporate limits became, by implication, a part of the charter of every municipality affected by it.

> **Tenn** City Transportation v Pharr (1948) 186 Tenn 217, 209 SW2d 15.

An ordinance providing for the licensing of buses operating in the city is valid as applied to buses between the city and an adjoining military camp under a contract with the camp commander not constituting a federal franchise, where there is no overriding interest of the United States in the operation of or jurisdiction over the bus operations.

> **Fla** Marshall, Ex parte (1918) 75 Fla 97, 77 So 869.

An ordinance requiring motor bus chauffeurs to obtain a city license to operate within the city does not require a state license; and if an operator secures a state license it does not relieve him of the necessity of securing a city license.

> **Ohio** Klein v Cincinnati (1929) 33 OA 137, 168 NE 549.

An ordinance prohibiting a bus from carrying passengers on routes occupied by a traction service company and requiring a permit from the city council to transport passengers for hire is a valid enactment.

> **Ohio** Sylvania Busses v Toledo (1928) 118 OS 187, 160 NE 674.

The term "franchise" is one of broad connotation, and the right to grant a bus franchise includes the right to grant a terminable permit.

> **NY** Loos v New York City (1939) 170 Misc 14, 9 NYS2d 760.

Operation of buses on city streets without a franchise is a trespass that may be enjoined at the suit of a taxpayer.

> **NY** Blanshard v New York City (1933) 262 NY 5, 186 NE 29.

An agreement between an applicant for a bus franchise and another franchise holder that for a consideration the holder would withdraw opposition to the applicant's request for a certificate of convenience and necessity is void, where by charter provision the city board of estimate controls the streets and has exclusive power to grant franchises or rights or make contracts involving the occupation or use of any streets, including determinations of the money value of franchises and all provisions for rates, fares and charges.

> **NY** New York City Transit Auth v Jamaica Buses (1959) 20 Misc2d 659, 192 NYS2d 72.

An ordinance providing that motor and other vehicles used for transportation of passengers for hire within township shall not be operated by any person not a citizen of United States, is a legitimate exercise of the police power, since the right to pursue the occupation in question is not an inalienable right that belongs to human beings, such as the right to labor for a living, but is rather, a privilege, subject to the control of the township.

>   **NJ**   Morin v Nunan (1918) 91 NJLaw 506, 103 A 378.

An ordinance requiring the owner or driver of a stage used in the transportation of passengers to obtain a license is valid.

>   **NJ**   Belmar v Barkalow (1902) 67 NJLaw 504, 52 A 157.

An ordinance prohibiting the use of any wagon or other vehicle in the transportation of persons or property on the streets without a license is applicable to a vehicle carrying persons for pleasure, as within the term "in use for carrying load", in the enabling statute.

>   **Ill**   Harder v Chicago (1908) 235 Ill 294, 85 NE 255.

An ordinance that lodges discretion in an official to grant or withhold a license for transportation of persons between railroad terminals in a city does not entitle a person to complain, until a license is arbitrarily or unlawfully withheld from him.

>   **Ill**   Atchison T & S F Ry v Chicago (1956) 136 F Supp 476, rev on other grnds (1958) 357 US 77, 2 LEd2d 1174, 78 SCt 1063.

An ordinance prohibiting a person having a livery vehicle license from being associated with anyone sending or receiving calls by radio for taxicab service is not invalid, as restricting the use a radio station licensee may make of his license, which is within the exclusive domain of the Federal Communications Commission. A radio licensee is not amenable to the ordinance and a livery vehicle licensee is not amenable to any regulation of the Commission.

>   **Ill**   Jones v Chicago (1952) 348 IllAp 310, 108 NE2d 802.

The statute authorizing cities to license hackmen, draymen, omnibus drivers and others pursuing like occupations will warrant enactment of an ordinance licensing the operation of street railways, whose carriages are of a like nature as omnibuses.

>   **Ill**   Allerton v Chicago (1880) 6 F 555.

A city is not limited to a simple denial or grant of a privilege or franchise for the operation of a street railway, but may prescribe terms on which the privilege shall be conditioned, if conferred, and by accepting a franchise ordinance burdened with such conditions, the railway company becomes bound to comply therewith.

>   **Ill**   Byrne v Chicago Gen Ry (1896) 63 IllAp 438.

An ordinance authorizing a permit to operate buses on a city street, conditioned on construction work involving widening of the street at the expense of the company, is not ultra vires where the charter authorizes franchises for the use of streets. A grant of use may be conditioned as the city sees fit where not forbidden by law.

La Boyle v New Orleans Pub Service (1964) 163 So2d 145.

Evidence that one interstate carrier is granted the right by a city to use certain streets is not sufficient to establish the right of another interstate carrier, operating under a like interstate authority, to use the same streets.

Neb Council Bluffs Transit v Omaha (1951) 154 Neb 717, 49 NW2d 453.

Since the power of a council, under a statute authorizing it to grant a franchise to a street railroad for the use of streets, is legislative in nature, the court does not have jurisdiction to enjoin the council from enacting an ordinance granting such use of streets.

Wis State v Superior Ct (1900) 105 Wis 651, 81 NW 1046.

Although the provisions of an ordinance granting a street railway franchise, when taken by themselves, indicate an estate in perpetuity, the grant must be deemed to be one for years where the municipal charter especially declares that all franchises shall be limited to a specified number of years.

NC Boyce v Gastonia (1947) 227 NC 139, 41 SE2d 355.

An ordinance requiring a license to operate buses for hire within the city applies to business originating and concluding within the city limits.

Colo Canon City v Kauffman (1932) 91 Colo 138, 12 P2d 1114.

An agreement between rival applicants for a street railway franchise to combine in order to prevent competition between themselves or by others in procuring the franchise, and to avoid the imposition of conditions by the municipal authorities, is void as against public policy. Equity will not compel one party to share the illegal gains with the other.

Va Hyer v Richmond Traction (1897) 80 F 839.

ANNOTATION

Abandonment of part of line of street railway, because unprofitable on condition that bus service be substituted, 10 ALR2d 1159.

§10. Limitations on Authority

An ordinance licensing and regulating interurban auto buses and defining an interurban auto bus as any motor vehicle engaged in the transportation of passengers for hire between points within the boundaries of the city and to or from points or places outside the city, regardless of locality, is void as invading the field of control of motor vehicle carriers already undertaken by the legislature.

Mich   North Star Line v Grand Rapids (1932) 259 Mich 654, 244 NW 192.

Although an ordinance granting a privilege to a company to construct a street railway may be construed as a contract, it is still subject to a constitutional provision thereafter adopted, declaring that no irrevocable grant of special privileges or immunities shall be made, and that all privileges granted by the legislature or created under its authority shall be subject to its control.

Tex   San Antonio Traction v Altgelt (1906) 200 US 304, 50 LEd 491, 26 SCt 261.

An ordinance declaring the right to use the public streets for the purpose of carrying passengers for hire to be a privilege and unlawful unless a certificate of public necessity and convenience has been granted by the city council is in effect a prohibition of the use of the streets for the carrying of passengers for hire, and is outside the city's power to enact.

Tex   Fort Worth v Lillard (1927) 116 Tex 509, 294 SW 831.

In granting a street railway franchise, a city is a state agency; and where the ordinance containing the grant and the general laws of the state conflict, state law governs.

Cal   Los Angeles Ry v Los Angeles (1907) 152 Cal 242, 92 P 490.

A city may not by ordinance grant an exclusive franchise to operate a street railway within the city without express power from the legislature to do so.

Ore   Parkhurst v Salem (1893) 23 Ore 471, 32 P 304.

A city has no power to grant exclusive rights to street railways, except upon authority from the legislature, given explicitly and clearly expressed.

Mich   Detroit Citizens' St Ry v Detroit (1896) 110 Mich 384, 68 NW 304.

An ordinance prohibiting travel on the city streets by interurban common carriers unless authorized by a franchise ordinance is invalid for being in conflict with the statutory powers of the public service commission.

Ore   Dent v Oregon City (1923) 106 Ore 122, 211 P 909.

An ordinance that provides for the licensing of all motor vehicles carrying passengers for hire and contains regulations relative to the use of such vehicles constitutes more than a mere licensing ordinance, and as such is void as being in conflict with the statute that prohibits cities from regulating motor vehicles.

Conn State v Scheidler (1916) 91 Conn 234, 99 A 492.

An ordinance licensing a motor carrier that transports interstate railroad passengers between the city's rail terminals, and imposing various conditions on the issuance of the license, is invalid as imposing an undue burden on interstate commerce, and as an unconstitutional attempt to regulate in an area pre-empted by the Interstate Commerce Act.

Ill Railroad Transfer Service v Chicago (1967) 386 US 351, 18 LEd2d 143, 87 SCt 1095.

An ordinance licensing and regulating a company transporting interstate passengers between railroad terminals within the city is invalid as in conflict with the paramount Interstate Commerce Act which pre-empts that field.

Ill Chicago v Atchison T & S F Ry (1958) 357 US 77, 2 LEd2d 1174, 78 SCt 1063.

Where a municipal corporation was required by statute to provide for the operation of buses by general ordinance, under which public officials retained control and administration, the city had no power by special ordinance to grant a franchise to a bus company for operation of a motor or trolley bus on city streets as a common carrier.

Alas O'Harra Bus Line, In re (1948) 12 Alas 129.

An ordinance relating to the operation of vehicles for hire and the granting of permits, being in conflict with a statute, is null and void.

W Va State ex rel Wells v Charleston (1922) 92 W Va 611, 115 SE 576.

An ordinance regulating bus transportation of passengers for hire from points without a municipality to points within it, and vice versa, and requiring a license therefor, is an invalid exercise of the police power.

Minn State v Palmer (1942) 212 Minn 388, 3 NW2d 666.

An ordinance granting a street railway company the exclusive right to occupy the streets with its railway for a term of years is void as outside the scope of the city's delegated power.

Kan Jackson County Horse RR v Interstate Rapid Transit Ry (1885) 24 F 306.

The common council cannot alienate its exclusive power over city streets by a grant to a street railway company in perpetuity of the right to build and operate railroads through such streets as it may elect. If such a grant were valid, it would amount to a mere offer that could be withdrawn by a repealing ordinance.

> **Ind**   Logansport Ry v Logansport (1902) 114 F 688.

§11. Jitney Buses

"Jitney", as used in an ordinance prohibiting its operation on the streets of a city, means a self-propelled vehicle, other than a streetcar, traversing the public streets between certain definite points or terminals, as a common carrier conveying passengers at a small fare.

> **Tex**   Luna, Ex parte (1924) 98 TexCr 458, 266 SW 415.

An ordinance prohibiting the operation on the streets of a motor bus or jitney, but exempting taxicabs and other motor vehicles carrying passengers for hire, is not invalid, since it is based on a reasonable classification growing out of a substantial difference.

> **Tex**   Luna, Ex parte (1924) 98 TexCr 458, 266 SW 415.

A license to operate jitneys on the city streets, which may be revoked for cause, is not a contract that vests a right, but is merely the grant of a privilege, and consequently such a license is not protected by the constitutional prohibition of impairment of the obligation of contract.

> **Tex**   Peters v San Antonio (1917) 195 SW 989.

An ordinance prohibiting the operation of jitney buses on certain streets without a license is not discriminatory in favor of operators of other vehicles, since the classification is based on a substantial difference in the operation of the two classes of vehicles.

> **Tex**   Polite, Ex parte (1924) 97 TexCr 320, 260 SW 1048.

An ordinance prohibiting the operation in the jitney service of any motor vehicle with a seating capacity of less than 15 persons does not constitute an unreasonable or discriminatory classification, but is based on a substantial difference between the operation of jitneys and other vehicles carrying passengers for hire.

> **Tex**   Davis v Houston (1924) 264 SW 625.

That one ordinance licensing the operation of jitneys restricts them to particular routes, and another ordinance regulating the operation of other motor vehicles for hire does not so limit their operation, does not render either ordinance invalid as constituting an improper or arbitrary classification.

> **Tex** Parr, Ex parte (1918) 82 TexCr 525, 200 SW 404.

The operator of a jitney that comes within the minimum fee class of an ordinance prescribing license fees for the operation of jitneys, graduated according to seating capacity, has no standing in court to challenge the validity of provisions imposing higher license fees.

> **Tex** Bogle, Ex parte (1915) 78 TexCr 1, 179 SW 1193.

In an ordinance licensing the operation of motor vehicles carrying passengers for hire, a provision exacting a higher license fee for jitneys than for taxicabs and other vehicles, and requiring the giving of a bond for jitney operation, not required of other vehicles, is not invalid as discriminatory, since a "jitney" is a class within itself, separate and distinct from other vehicles carrying passengers for hire.

> **Tex** Bogle, Ex parte (1915) 78 TexCr 1, 179 SW 1193.

An ordinance regulating the operation of jitneys, and requiring their operators to furnish a bond for the protection of the public, is not violative of due process by reason of a provision that the license may be forfeited for certain ordinance violations.

> **Tex** Greene v San Antonio (1915) 178 SW 6.

A license fee imposed on jitneys using the streets for the carrying of passengers will not be construed as an occupation tax, which would render it constitutionally impermissible.

> **Tex** Greene v San Antonio (1915) 178 SW 6.

An ordinance licensing jitney buses, and exempting railroad cars, streetcars, sightseeing cars, hotel buses, and taxicabs, is not invalid as discriminatory.

> **Ore** Thielke v Albee (1915) 79 Ore 48, 153 P 793.

An ordinance requiring a franchise for the operation of jitney cars within the city, the purpose being to prohibit their operation until further ordinances are passed to license and regulate them, is valid, since the city has power to prohibit their use on its streets.

> **Ore** Cummins v Jones (1916) 79 Ore 276, 155 P 171.

Since a statute withdraws from local authorities the power to enact or enforce any ordinance imposing a pecuniary charge in the nature of a tax, license, or permit for the use of public highways by motor vehicles registered in accordance with state law, an ordinance imposing an occupation tax on persons engaged in the operation of jitney buses is an attempt to exact a tax for revenue purposes, and is invalid.

> **Okla**   Muskogee v Wilkins (1918) 73 Okla 192, 175 P 497.

A jitney operator not exercising his right to obtain a franchise has only an annual license to operate buses, where the ordinance authorizing grants of franchises has been repealed.

> **Ind**   Schisler v Merchants Tr of Muncie (1950) 228 Ind 594, 94 NE2d 665.

Rights of a licensee may be cut off by revocation without notice or hearing, where they are wholly dependent on the terms of an ordinance authorizing the licensing of transportation of passengers for hire by jitney buses, but not requiring notice or hearing, since his rights can rise no higher than the terms of the ordinance. A jitney bus operator has no absolute rights to conduct his business although he may have made investments in reliance on licenses issued; and he is entitled to no superior standing such as would prohibit revocation of his license.

> **Mass**   Burgess v Brockton (1920) 235 Mass 95, 126 NE 456.

An insurance policy issued pursuant to an ordinance, making it unlawful to drive or operate a jitney bus without a contract of indemnity against loss to persons or property from its negligent operation, covered an accident that occurred while the driver was on his way home to rest in preparation for a night run, since the bus was being operated within the general and incidental service of the jitney bus business.

> **Cal**   Smith v Cal Highway Indemn Exchange (1933) 218 Cal 325, 23 P2d 274.

An ordinance requiring operators of jitney buses to secure a license and post bond to secure any judgments rendered against them for liability due to the carriage of passengers is within the statutory grant of power to cities and is not discriminatory class legislation in restraint of trade where the operators appeared to the city council to be so irresponsible as to make necessary the bond security.

> **Ark**   Willis v Fort Smith (1916) 121 Ark 606, 182 SW 275.

An ordinance prohibiting the operation on city streets of jitneys not doing a local business is invalid, as in conflict with the state statute regulating such vehicles.

> **Mich**   Detroit W & T Transit v Detroit (1932) 260 Mich 124, 244 NW 424.

A municipality may by ordinance regulate or even prohibit the operation of jitney buses on its streets, since such a use is not an ordinary and customary street use, but a special one.

Ohio Murphy v Toledo (1923) 108 OS 342, 140 NE 626.

A city's power under its charter to license, control, tax and regulate traffic, including jitney buses and other vehicles, does not confer authority to prohibit jitney buses, nor does the general welfare clause authorize prohibition when such vehicles are not shown to be inherently dangerous to traffic or the public.

Fla Quigg v State (1922) 84 Fla 164, 93 So 139.

Since jitney buses are common carriers for hire, their use is permitted as a mere privilege, not as a matter of inherent right, and consequently cities may, by ordinance, prohibit their use altogether.

Mich Red Star Motor Drivers Assn v Detroit (1926) 234 Mich 398, 208 NW 602.

§ 12. Sightseeing Buses

A municipal code provision for the licensing of sightseeing buses and other vehicles operating for hire from a fixed point in the city to places of amusement is construed to refer to places of amusement within the city only, and does not refer to a bus under contract to transport a party from the city to a point outside the city.

NY People v Cent Greyhound Lines (1939) 173 Misc 487, 17 NYS2d 463.

A municipal administrative code provision relating to the licensing of sightseeing buses is a valid exercise of the police power of the city, and does not contravene the statute forbidding the requirement of licenses or permits for the use of public highways by local ordinance.

NY People v Oestriecher (1940) 173 Misc 147, 17 NYS2d 468, rev on other grnds (1940) 175 Misc 151, 22 NYS2d 899.

A municipal administrative code provision for a license fee for each sight-seeing bus is a regulatory rather than a tax measure, and is designed substantially to cover the cost to the municipality of inspectional and regulatory service, and is therefore valid.

NY People v Oestriecher (1940) 173 Misc 147, 17 NYS2d 468, rev on other grnds (1940) 175 Misc 151, 22 NYS2d 899.

A municipal administrative code provision requiring a sightseeing bus to secure a license before operating for hire under private contract for special trips contemplates that the hiring must be of such a character that the general public may, on payment of the tariff, board the bus and be transported to some point of destination.

NY   People v Oestriecher (1940) 175 Misc 151, 22 NYS2d 899.

A resolution by a city council granting an exclusive limousine franchise is valid, on a showing that there is not enough business for the service to be maintained on a competitive basis.

Ark   Bridges v Yellow Cab (1966) 241 Ark 204, 406 SW2d 879.

An Administrative Code provision permitting solicitation of hotel or passenger patronage in enumerated public places over which the city has jurisdiction, with a city license, does not authorize one to sell sightseeing tickets on the buses of a public carrier without a license from the carrier.

NY   Third Ave Transit, In re (1956) 233 F2d 310.

§ 13. Enactment of Ordinance or Resolution

The term "bylaws of a general or permanent nature," in the statute requiring publication of such bylaws, and providing that they shall take effect and be enforced at the expiration of five days after they have been published, includes a city ordinance granting a street railway franchise.

Iowa   State v Omaha & C B Ry & Bridge (1901) 113 Iowa 30, 84 NW 983.

A municipal ordinance vacating part of a street, giving a street railway the right to use the part vacated for right-of-way, and granting the fee to the state is not invalid as containing two subjects.

Iowa   Tomlin v Cedar Rapids & Iowa City Ry & Light (1909) 141 Iowa 599, 120 NW 93.

Street railway had mere license from city until enactment of statute empowering city to grant franchise.

Iowa   State v Des Moines City Ry (1913) 159 Iowa 259, 140 NW 437.

A charter provision requiring inquiry by the council into the money value and adequacy of compensation the city will receive for a franchise or grant of a right does not require a determination of the dollar value of the franchise or that its money value be fixed or determined with mathematical exactitude. The inquiry is a legislative function that involves varied and flexible considerations and benefits, and courts will not fix any rules for guidance in granting a bus franchise.

NY   Greenberg v New York City (1934) 152 Misc 488, 274 NYS 4.

Failure to comply with charter directives to hold a public hearing, determine the value of the rights to be granted, and investigate the adequacy of the compensation invalidates a franchise.

NY   Blanshard v New York City (1933) 262 NY 5, 186 NE 29.

A provision of an ordinance authorizing the sale at auction of a group of bus route franchises requiring the successful bidder to operate all routes approved by the public service commission, though some may be rejected, compels the purchaser to accept franchises he does not in fact buy, in violation of the statutory requirement for sale at public auction of each individual franchise to the highest bidder. It also violates the statutory requirement that, for public bidding, the description of the article sold be definite, certain and not subject to change after acceptance of bids.

NY   Yonkers RR v Yonkers (1926) 218 AD 97, 218 NYS 103.

Consent to operate an omnibus is not invalid merely because the trustees fail to comply with an ordinance providing that certain details of the proposed operation should be stated in the application and that the application should be published in a daily newspaper, where a notice of hearing is published in the official newspapers in the village in accordance with a resolution of the trustees and in compliance with the prerequisites fixed by statute to the giving of consent.

NY   DeMatteis v Peekskill (1940) 282 NY 98, 25 NE2d 383.

Where the title of an ordinance providing for the adjustment of controversies existing between a city and a street railway is sufficiently broad to embrace every detail of the provisions contained in the body of the ordinance, it is sufficient.

Ky   Scott v Cincinnati N & C Ry (1937) 268 Ky 383, 105 SW2d 169.

The granting of a franchise to operate a streetcar line, without advertisement or call for bids, renders the grant void.

Ky   Monarch v Owensboro City Ry (1905) 119 Ky 939, 85 SW 193.

An ordinance granting a right to operate buses on city streets from year to year on the operator's compliance with prescribed conditions and payment of a nominal annual fee, grants a franchise, within constitutional limitations requiring that a franchise be granted only on advertisement for bids; and the operation of such buses may be enjoined until the company obtains a franchise right in the manner prescribed by the Constitution.

Ky   Peoples Transit v Louisville Ry (1927) 220 Ky 728, 295 SW 1055.

An ordinance granting an indeterminate permit to operate buses and widen a city street in conformance with a "major street plan" was not a hasty, arbitrary or capricious action of the council, where it was studied by all interested city departments, a public hearing was held and city agencies and the planning commission appeared and voiced their approval.

La Boyle v New Orleans Pub Service (1964) 163 So2d 145.

Where a statute requires that the sale of a street railway franchise under authority of an ordinance is to be made to the "highest bidder," it means the highest bidder in money, and the sale of the franchise is invalid when the specifications call for and the adjudication is made to a highest bidder in "square yards of gravel pavement".

La Hart v Buckner (1892) 54 F 925.

§14. Submission of Grant to Public Vote

An ordinance granting to a street railway company the right to construct and operate a street railway is invalid without the consent of the qualified taxpaying electors.

Colo Baker v Denver Tramway (1922) 72 Colo 233, 210 P 845, 29 ALR 1453.

Under a statute vesting authority in the mayor and council to grant street railway franchises, without any requirement of submitting the matter to referendum, a subsequent amendment to the city charter requiring that an ordinance granting a street railway franchise be submitted to referendum is void.

Wash Benton v Seattle Elec (1908) 50 Wash 156, 96 P 1033.

The initial ordinance granting a franchise for the operation of buses on city streets is legislative in character and therefore subject to referendum; but where a statute requires the city to grant a new franchise before expiration of the old, the ordinance providing for the sale of the new franchise is not subject to either initiative or referendum.

Ky Seaton v Lackey (1944) 298 Ky 188, 182 SW2d 336.

Where a city council passes a resolution submitting to voters a proposed ordinance granting a franchise to a street railway company, but the proposed ordinance is not published as required by statute, the election is invalid.

Ky Newport v Glazier (1917) 175 Ky 608, 194 SW 771.

The constitutional provision that no city shall grant, extend, or renew a franchise without approval of the voters applies to an ordinance granting an original franchise, or to a renewal or extension of the period of time of the original franchise, but does not apply to an ordinance merely extending or enlarging the facilities to be employed in performance of the franchise.

> **Okla**   Overholser v Okla Interurban Traction (1911) 29 Okla 571, 119 P 127.

An ordinance authorizing submission to the electorate of the power to determine whether bond issues, preferentials, subsidies or obligations of public transportation carriers to render public services should be modified is invalid, where the power to readjust or alter such contracts is by statute conferred on a transit commission that can act only with the consent of the local legislative authority.

> **NY**   McCabe v Voorhis (1926) 243 NY 401, 153 NE 849.

§15. Challenge of Grant by Taxpayer

A citizen taxpayer may bring suit directly against a street railway company to enjoin the operation of an ordinance and franchise which it is alleged donates valuable franchise rights in excess of the powers of the council, and it is not necessary to join the city as a party.

> **La**   State v Judge of Div A (1900) 52 LaAnn 1065, 27 So 580.

An ordinance granting a utility franchise holder a permit to operate buses on a street, requiring street construction by the utility company in conformity with a "major street plan", and providing that the work should be done by the transit company at its own expense was a contract between the city and the company that was not illegal or ultra vires. There was no delegation of authority over the streets to the utility company, and the ordinance spelled out in detail the construction work authorized to be done by the company under the supervision of the city.

> **La**   Boyle v New Orleans Pub Service (1964) 163 So2d 145.

A street railway company is a necessary party to a suit to enjoin the enforcement of an ordinance granting it the right to use the streets of the city.

> **Tex**   Dallas v Couchman (1923) 249 SW 234.

An ordinance authorizing sale at auction of a group of bus route franchises, and requiring submission of one bid for all the routes, or only those approved by the public service commission, tends to suppress competition and decrease bids, and the court will enjoin the sale on suit of a taxpayer. Provision of the ordinance reserving to the city the right to require the addition of new routes on the same terms exceeds the statutory power to grant extensions to existing franchises. A grant of additional future franchises does not comply with the statutory requirement for separate public auctions.

> **NY**   Yonkers RR v Yonkers (1925) 214 AD 479, 212 NYS 339.

A clear distinction must be recognized between the right of a citizen and taxpayer to maintain an action to restrain the valid exercise by a city council of its legislative functions and an action in which an injunction is sought to restrain such officers from acting or proceeding illegally. A court of equity may at the suit of a taxpayer restrain the illegal action of public officers, and a taxpayer may maintain a suit for an injunction to restrain enforcement of an ordinance granting a franchise to a street railway, based on an alleged exercise of legislative power.

Iowa   Van Horn v Des Moines (1922) 195 Iowa 840, 191 NW 144.

A railroad that has laid its tracks across a street, pursuant to authority from the city, has no standing in equity to attack the validity of an ordinance granting a franchise for a street railway along that street, since it lacks sufficient interest in the subject matter.

Ill   Atchison T & S F Ry v Gen Elec Ry (1902) 112 F 689.

§16. Acceptance of Grant by Transit System

A written acceptance of an ordinance granting a franchise to a street railway company, signed in the name of the company by its president and secretary and accompanied by its seal is prima facie an acceptance by the company.

Mich   Niles v Benton Harbor-St Joe Ry & Light (1908) 154 Mich 378, 117 NW 937.

An ordinance granting a 50-year franchise to operate a mass transportation system over city streets may be accepted by conduct of the franchise holder, though the ordinance specifies that an acceptance must be filed within a specified time or the ordinance is to become void.

Utah   Salt Lake City Lines v Salt Lake City (1957) 6 Utah2d 428, 315 P2d 859.

No formal resolution accepting an ordinance granting a street railway franchise is necessary if the facts show an actual practical acceptance by the railway company, or action by it that is only explicable on the theory of an acceptance.

Ind   City Ry v Citizens St Ry (1897) 166 US 557, 41 LEd 1114, 17 SCt 653.

An ordinance consenting to the use of the streets by buses creates a contract between the utility and the city if it is accepted by the utility and acted on in conformity with the requirements of the grant. It is not necessary to file a formal acceptance with any city official unless the franchise requires it, nor to actually commence operations, if funds are expended for that purpose.

NY   Colonial Motor Coach v Oswego (1926) 126 Misc 289, 215 NYS 159.

An ordinance consenting to the use of the streets by buses, conditioned on issue of an operating certificate by the state public service commission, is accepted and acted on where the utility hires attorneys, appears at commission hearings, and purchases a bus route that would offer limited competition.

NY Colonial Motor Coach v Oswego (1926) 126 Misc 289, 215 NYS 159.

§17. Nature of Right Obtained by Grant

Ordinances granting to a corporation the right to build and operate street railway lines in the city, upon acceptance by the corporation and expenditure of large sums of money constitute a contract protected by the federal Constitution prohibiting any law impairing the obligation of contract.

Ind Citizens St Ry v City Ry (1893) 56 F 746.

Track laying rights in the city streets, acquired by a street railway company through an ordinance, although subject to the city's police power, are protected by the contract clause of the federal Constitution from destruction by repeal of the ordinance.

Ind Grand Truck Western Ry v South Bend (1912) 227 US 544, 57 LEd 633, 33 SCt 303.

An ordinance granting a street railway franchise for a fixed period with a provision that the city shall not, during that time, confer on any other party any privilege that will impair rights and privileges granted the railroad constitutes a contract.

Ind City Ry v Citizen's St Ry (1897) 166 US 557, 41 LEd 1114, 17 SCt 653.

A franchise to operate buses over city streets for a definite period, which makes no provision for its revocation, grants an absolute right that an acceptance or performance is property that may not be taken without due process of law and just compensation, and an ordinance withdrawing the consent after performance by the grantee is void.

NY Colonial Motor Coach v Oswego (1926) 126 Misc 289, 215 NYS 159.

A franchise ordinance granting permission to operate a bus line over certain streets is a vested property right which the municipality cannot revoke after acceptance and is assignable, taxable, alienable, an asset of credit value, subject to levy and sale under execution and to condemnation under the exercise of eminent domain.

NY Bohl v Schenectady (1927) 128 Misc 863, 220 NYS 349.

The grant of a bus franchise by ordinance creates a vested right, provided the granting authority complies with charter requirements, and that a certificate of convenience and necessity must be obtained by a utility to exercise franchise rights does not degrade the grant to a mere license or diminish its completeness.

NY Greenberg v New York City (1934) 152 Misc 488, 274 NYS 4.

An ordinance granting a street railroad the right to use the streets to lay tracks is not a grant of the land described in the franchise. The consent to such use by the city vests for the life of the charter unless a forfeiture occurs.

NY New York City v N Y Cent RR (1922) 234 NY 113, 136 NE 311.

An ordinance granting a street railway company exclusive authority at its option to construct street railways on all streets within the city, as may be fixed by the common council, is, in effect, an exclusive franchise.

Mich Detroit Citizens' St Ry v Detroit (1896) 110 Mich 384, 68 NW 304.

A franchise granted by a municipality to a street railroad company and accepted by it constitutes a contract mutually binding on both parties, which is terminated by the limitations therein expressed.

Mich Detroit v Detroit United Ry (1912) 172 Mich 136, 137 NW 645.

The conditions contained in a license or franchise granted by ordinance to a street railway company, under a statute authorizing a street railway to construct its road along the streets and highways of a township on such terms and conditions as may be agreed on by the company and the township board, are as binding as though imposed in the statute, and mandamus lies to compel compliance.

Mich Grosse Pointe v Detroit & L S C Ry (1902) 130 Mich 363, 90 NW 42.

An ordinance granting a street railway a franchise for a stated time, and obligating the company during the life of the franchise to charge certain fares and no more, accepted by the railway, constitutes a binding contract which cannot be terminated, in the absence of a showing that the contract is impossible of performance or that, taking the whole term together, the contract will be necessarily unprofitable.

Ohio Columbus Ry Power & Light v Columbus (1919) 249 US 399, 63 LEd 669, 39 SCt 349.

A street railway acquires no interest or estate in the soil by laying its rails on the streets under an ordinance permitting it; and no title to such property vests in the railway company so as to subject it to taxation.

Ill People v Chicago Rys (1938) 369 Ill 128, 15 NE2d 705.

An ordinance granting a franchise to a street railway, to occupy and use the streets for its operations, constitutes a contract, the obligation of which may not be impaired. The railway's property right in the streets is in the nature of real estate, of which the railway may not be deprived without due process of law.

Ill   Chicago City Ry v Chicago (1926) 323 Ill 246, 154 NE 112.

An ordinance whereby a city grants a street railway a franchise to operate its cars on the city streets for a prescribed period of time may constitute a "contract", within the constitutional prohibition against impairing the obligation of contracts.

Wash   Puget Sound Traction Light & Power v Reynolds (1915) 223 F 371.

A municipal ordinance granting a franchise to a streetcar company, and the company's acceptance, constitute a contract.

Wash   Markham v Seattle & R V Ry (1924)) 1 F2d 605.

Where an ordinance grants a street railway an operating franchise providing for a 5-cent fare, its acceptance constitutes a contract protected by constitutional guaranty against impairment of the obligation of contract.

Wis   Duluth St Ry v RR Comm (1915) 161 Wis 245, 152 NW 887.

An ordinance granting a street railway franchise to a private company is not for the benefit of the grantee, but for the benefit of the people of the city, and its acceptance by the company creates an obligation on it to operate continuously during the life of the franchise, with all lines constructed and put into operation under the terms thereof.

Kan   Salina v Salina St Ry (1923) 114 Kan 734, 220 P 203.

A street railroad company operating under a franchise imposing certain conditions as to rates and transfers assumes contractual obligation with respect to such regulations.

Va   Va Passenger & Power v Commonwealth (1905) 103 Va 644, 49 SE 995.

The holder of a mass transportation franchise granted by ordinance cannot denounce the validity of the ordinance, even on constitutional grounds.

Utah   Salt Lake City Lines v Salt Lake City (1957) 6 Utah2d 428, 315 P2d 859.

An ordinance granting a right to construct a street railway line over certain streets does not grant a mere license, but grants a property right protected by the Constitution from arbitrary revocation or destruction, which may not be taken except by due process of law.

> **NC**   Boyce v Gastonia (1947) 227 NC 139, 41 SE2d 355.

An ordinance granting a contractor a franchise to construct and operate a streetcar line does not give the contractor an exclusive privilege to prevent use of the city streets by another street railway company if construction and operation are not begun under the original franchise.

> **Ark**   Citizens St Ry v Jones (1888) 34 F 579.

Acceptance by a street railway company of an ordinance granting it a franchise creates a contractual relation between the municipality and the company.

> **Iowa**   Van Horn v Des Moines (1922) 195 Iowa 840, 191 NW 144.

A bus line franchise in the form of an ordinance may be a contract, and is thus within the federal constitutional prohibition against impairment of the obligation of contracts.

> **Colo**   Pudlik v Pub Service Co of Colo (1958) 166 F Supp 921.

An ordinance that grants a franchise to operate a street railway creates a valid contract.

> **SC**   Spartanburg v S C Gas & Elec (1924) 130 SC 125, 125 SE 295.

Municipalities may enter into agreements with carriers, by way of ordinance or franchise, which shall have the same binding force and effect as though between individuals, and such contracts may not be lawfully changed by one party without consent of the other.

> **Wis**   Superior v Duluth St Ry (1918) 166 Wis 487, 165 NW 1081.

An ordinance granting to a street railway a renewal for 25 years of the right to maintain and operate a street railroad, and fixing terms and conditions, when accepted in writing becomes a binding contract between the city and the company.

> **Ohio**   Cincinnati v Cincinnati St Ry (1933) 45 OA 511, 15 Abs 347, 187 NE 312.

An ordinance granting the right to use the streets for constructing and operating a street railway confers privileges that are exclusive against all persons to whom similar rights have not been granted.

> **Okla**   Tulsa v SW Bell Tel (1934) 5 F Supp 822, affd (1935) 75 F2d 343.
> Tulsa St Ry v Okla Union Traction (1910) 27 Okla 339, 113 P 180.

Right to enjoin business competitor, including motor carriers, from un-licensed or otherwise illegal acts or practices, 90 ALR2d 35.

§18. Construction of Facilities

The grant by a city to a company, organized under the train railway act, of the right to construct and operate a street railway with all necessary tracks and connections, all tracks to be constructed under the supervision and with the approval of the common council, does not authorize the company to make a connection in the streets of the city with the tracks of a company organized and operating under the general railroad laws, and having no franchise from the city, though in the ordinances granting franchises to such train railway company, and to another company organized under the general railroad laws, a connection between them, and transfers from the one to the other, were required.

> **Mich** Monroe v Detroit M & T Short Line RR (1906) 143 Mich 315, 106 NW 704.

Under an ordinance authorizing a street railway company to construct and maintain a single-track railway along certain streets, with the right to construct, use, and operate all necessary and convenient tracks for turnouts, sidetracks, curves, and switches, the same to be constructed and in operation within one year from the date of passage of the ordinance, the company is authorized to construct such turnouts, after the road is constructed, as are made necessary by the increase of travel, without further legislative action on the part of the city.

> **Mich** Detroit Citizens' St Ry v Detroit (1901) 126 Mich 554, 85 NW 1072.

Under an ordinance granting a train railway company the right to construct and operate a street railway and providing that "no wires carrying an electric current shall be placed in said street except the trolley wire," the company may not, without further authority, place in the street an additional feed wire not a trolley wire.

> **Mich** Monroe v Detroit M & T Short Line RR (1906) 143 Mich 315, 106 NW 704.

Where an ordinance granting a franchise to a street railway company requires the company to allow an interurban railroad to use its tracks, and the interurban railroad agrees to comply with the franchise conditions, the latter has the right to construct a spur track without obtaining permission from the city, under a statute allowing interurban railroads to condemn city land.

> **Iowa** Interurban Ry v Des Moines (1924) 197 Iowa 1398, 199 NW 355.

A city acts within the scope of its administrative and police power in authorizing by ordinance the laying of a third rail in connection with the rearrangement of street railroad tracks in connection with street paving, and the question whether it is advisable to lay the rail so that the paving will not have to be broken up at a later date is a matter of legislative discretion, though the right of the company actually laying the rail to make use of it is then involved in litigation contesting the ordinance granting a license to the second user.

> **La**   State v King (1901) 104 La 735, 29 So 359.

Where an ordinance grants a franchise to a street railroad company which provides that no extension of tracks may be made, that no tracks may be laid in or over any street except those then occupied, and that no double tracks, except turnouts and switches, may be laid without permission by ordinance or resolution, construction of a track at nearly right angles to its main track extending about 350 feet, running through one alley and intersecting another to reach the power plant of the railroad, is not authorized, by virtue of the franchise, as an incident to the operation of a railway system, or as a right accruing from the act of the street railway company's predecessor in constructing the power plant at a point not accessible to its existing tracks, since the track is not a switch or turnout.

> **Ind**   Ind Ry & Light v Kokomo (1915) 183 Ind 543, 108 NE 771.

A grant of the right to construct and operate an electric street railway authorizes the company to erect poles for trolley lines; and where the company's operation is not dangerous or in obstruction of city streets it is lawful and will not be enjoined.

> **Ky**   Louisville Bagging Mfg v Cent Passenger Ry (1893) 95 Ky 50, 23 SW 592.

A street railway company may be permitted to change its lines on certain streets, in return for which the city may acquire a portion of land belonging to the railway necessary for the widening of a street, and an ordinance permitting this does not constitute the granting of a franchise inhibited by any constitutional provisions.

> **Ky**   Woodall v South Covington & C St Ry (1910) 137 Ky 512, 124 SW 843.

Under an ordinance granting a franchise for a street railway the franchise holders do not bind themselves to construct the railway in all events where the ordinance only prescribes that they are required to construct it on such streets as would enable it to serve the public properly and make a reasonable profit.

> **Ky**   Scott Admrs v Mayfield (1913) 153 Ky 278, 155 SW 376.

§19. Municipal Aid to Private System

Where it was held, in a taxpayer's proceeding to enjoin a city from fulfilling an agreement by ordinance to lay at its own expense a concrete foundation for a street railway company, that the ordinance was ultra vires, and where, in a later action by the city against the railway company the railway set up a counterclaim for work done in concreting, the decision that the ordinance was ultra vires was not res judicata, the company not having been a party to the former action.

Mich Detroit v Detroit Ry (1903) 134 Mich 11, 95 NW 992.

Neither a charter authorizing a city to establish, pave and improve its streets, nor a statute requiring the city to keep its streets safe and convenient for public travel, will authorize the city to construct streetcar tracks for lease to a private street railway for hire.

Mich Bird v Detroit (1907) 148 Mich 71, 111 NW 860.

An authorization to expend moneys by the city to pay claims which are otherwise illegal or invalid if the public interest will be best served thereby, does not authorize payment of a cash subsidy to aid a transit authority.

NY New York City v N Y Transit Auth (1967) 53 Misc2d 627, 279 NYS2d 278.

An ordinance providing for the sale of bonds to renew, replace, repair or reconstruct the rails, ties, roadbeds, or tracks of a street railway company violates the constitutional provision prohibiting the city from raising money for any company, and is invalid.

Ohio Cincinnati v Harth (1920) 101 OS 344, 128 NE 263.

§20. Rights of Abutting Property Owners Relative to Construction

Where a street is vacated by an ordinance and a right-of-way over the vacated street is given to a street railway company, the company may operate its road without compensating an abutting owner.

Iowa Tomlin v Cedar Rapids & Iowa City Ry & Light (1909) 141 Iowa 599, 120 NW 93.

There is a distinction between street railways and railways. The latter are employed in general freight and passenger traffic (commercial), while the characteristic of a street railway is that it is built on and passes along streets for the convenience of those moving from place to place within the city. Consequently, a municipality may grant a franchise to an interurban railway to lay tracks and use city streets without compensating abutting owners, but if

201

the city grants such a right to a commercial railway the abutting owners must be compensated.

Iowa Anhalt v Waterloo C F & N Ry (1914) 166 Iowa 479, 147 NW 928.

Where a street railway company is granted permission to construct a right-of-way by the city council's establishing of the street grade for this improvement, neither the railway procuring the construction nor the city passing the ordinance will be liable in damages to the owner of abutting property for change of grade, if the railway acts pursuant to the authority granted by the ordinance and the city has not previously adopted formally the natural street surface as the grade line.

Ark Red v Little Rock Ry & Elec (1915) 121 Ark 71, 180 SW 220.

Abutting property owners may require that a street railway be built in the center of the street, if possible, as required by the ordinance granting the company permission to lay its tracks on the street.

Mich Kennedy v Detroit Ry (1896) 108 Mich 390, 66 NW 495.

A city which grants by ordinance a franchise to a street railroad company under authority from the state is not liable for damages to an abutting owner resulting from acts of negligence by the company while erecting its plant.

Mich Tatman v Benton Harbor (1898) 115 Mich 695, 74 NW 187.

An ordinance granting a permit to a street railway company to lay and maintain a spur track in front of private property does not authorize the company to destroy the use of abutting property by its owner, since a municipality may not authorize the creation or maintenance of a nuisance or a deprivation of access to property by abutting owners, and such unauthorized use may be restrained by injunction.

Mo Zimmerman v Metro St Ry (1911) 154 MoApp 296, 134 SW 40.

The rights of owners of lots abutting a public street are property rights, the invasion of which, without authority of the owners, by an electric railway allegedly exercising authority under a franchise ordinance to tear up and excavate the street, may be prevented by injunction.

La Hart v Buckner (1892) 54 F 925.

An ordinance granting a franchise to construct streetcar lines and erect poles for trolley wires is not invalid for failure to provide compensation to abutting property owners on the theory that the poles and wires are an additional burden on the fee, where it does not appear that they will interfere with use of or access to abutting property.

Wis Linden Land v Milwaukee Elec Ry & Light (1900) 107 Wis 493, 83 NW 851.

§21. Interpretation and Constructions of Terms of Grant

A street railway company's interpretation of the ordinance granting it a franchise, for many years acquiesced in by the public, is entitled to consideration in interpreting the franchise.

Iowa   State v Ottumwa Ry & Light (1916) 178 Iowa 961, 160 NW 336.

The conditions existing when a franchise ordinance is enacted can properly be considered in interpreting the franchise.

Iowa   State v Ottumwa Ry & Light (1916) 178 Iowa 961, 160 NW 336.

In view of the rule that an ordinance granting a franchise to a street railroad company must be construed strictly against the company, such an ordinance, though authorizing construction of necessary sidetracks, turnouts, etc., does not allow the company to construct a "loop".

Iowa   Dubuque v Dubuque Elec (1920) 188 Iowa 1192, 177 NW 700.

The meaning of an ordinance granting a franchise to a street railway is to be determined by a fair and reasonable construction of the whole instrument, regard being had to the true intent of the parties as expressed.

Iowa   Dubuque v Dubuque Elec (1920) 188 Iowa 1192, 177 NW 700.

Where doubt exists about the construction to be given an ordinance granting the use of city streets by street railroads, subject to reasonable rules and regulations, it will be construed as a regulatory measure rather than a contract.

Wis   State v Milwaukee Elec Ry & Light (1914) 157 Wis 121, 147 NW 232.

Where, since the inception of a franchise for interurban passenger service, the parties considered transportation of freight in less than carload lots to be part of the authorized service, such practical construction of the franchise by the parties for 22 years establishes the intention to permit carriage of freight on cars used primarily, but not exclusively, for passenger service.

Wis   Milwaukee v Milwaukee Elec Ry & Light (1931) 205 Wis 453, 237 NW 64.

Because of the vital differences between the structures of surface and elevated railroads, the construction of an ordinance granting powers to elevated railroads must be more strict than of an ordinance granting powers to surface railroads, and different principles apply.

Ill   Northwestern Elevated Ry v Chicago (1904) 1 Ill CC 480.

A "street", within the meaning of an ordinance granting a street railway a franchise to operate trains on elevated platforms, includes not only the portion of land between the sidewalks, but also the sidewalks.

Ill   Northwestern Elevated Ry v Chicago (1904) 1 Ill CC 480.

In construing an ordinance that embodies a franchise contract between the city and a street railway, the court should look to the language of the enactment itself, considered in light of the situation obtaining between city and railway at the time of enactment, and should refuse to consider the opinions of council members on the meaning of the ordinance.

Ill   People v Chicago Rys (1915) 270 Ill 87, 110 NE 386.

Operating a bus line does not comply with franchise to operate street railway.

SC   Spartanburg v S C Gas & Elec (1924) 130 SC 125, 125 SE 295.

Ordinances creating street railway franchises are strictly construed, and that construction should be adopted which works the least harm to the public.

SC   Broad River Power v State (1930) 281 US 537, 74 LEd 1023, 50 SCt 401.

Grants under a franchise ordinance are strictly construed in favor of the public and against the grantee. Thus whatever is not unequivocally granted in the ordinance is taken to have been withheld.

Minn   Minneapolis St Ry v Minneapolis (1949) 229 Minn 502, 40 NW2d 353, (1952) 236 Minn 109, 52 NW2d 120.

The operation of one street railway over the tracks of another, pursuant to an ordinance, is evidence that both companies construe the ordinance as authorizing such use, and the city by full acquiescence manifests a like interpretation of the ordinance. Such evidence is entitled to great weight in the event one railway desires to discontinue service.

Va   Va Ry & Power v Richmond (1921) 129 Va 592, 106 SE 529.

An ordinance granting a franchise to a street railway company with the right to use the streets, except certain main streets, and their extensions to the city limits, grants to the railway company the use of all the streets of the city, and extensions, thereafter brought within the city by annexation, except those streets specifically named in the excepting clause of the ordinance, and their extensions.

Okla   Tulsa St Ry v Okla Union Traction (1910) 27 Okla 339, 113 P 180.

Where the charter of a street railway company granted by the state only authorizes it to operate by animal power, an ordinance enacted by the city granting the power to operate by electricity is an anticipatory grant, and is construed to take effect only when the legislature also confers the power.

Ky   Louisville & N RR v Bowling Green Ry (1901) 110 Ky 788, 63 SW 4.

§22. Rights and Duties of Assignee or Successor of Grantee

The obligation of the original grantee under a franchise ordinance to operate a street railroad is assumed by the purchaser of the road, when it is sold "as a going concern" at judicial sale.

Ohio   Gress v Fort Laramie (1919) 100 OS 35, 125 NE 112.

A street railway company purchasing the property of another street railway company, under a statute authorizing any such company to acquire the real and personal property and the rights, privileges, and franchises of any street railway in any village or township, takes the road subject to all the obligations of its grantor, and mandamus will lie to compel it to discharge such obligations.

Mich   Grosse Pointe v Detroit & L S C Ry (1902) 130 Mich 363, 90 NW 42.

An ordinance renewing the consent of a city to the construction and operation of a street railway is not invalid merely because it extends the city's term of consent to a period beyond the corporate life of the railway company.

Mich   Detroit v Detroit Citizens St Ry (1901) 184 US 368, 46 LEd 368, 22 SCt 410.

Where a franchise to operate a street railway is sold at public auction the speculative risk attending the value of the franchise is one which the city and the purchasers bear alike, and if the venture turns out to be more profitable than anticipated the city cannot recover any excess profits nor if it fails can the purchasers recover of the city the purchase price of the franchise.

Ky   Scott Admrs v Mayfield (1913) 153 Ky 278, 155 SW 376.

Where an ordinance grants a franchise to construct a street railway to a named person as grantee and such other persons as he may associate with himself, such grantee's subsequent formation of a corporation with two other persons operates to place ownership of the franchise in such corporation, and it no longer remains in the original grantee.

Ore   Budd v Multnomah St Ry (1887) 15 Ore 404, 15 P 654.

If a grant by ordinance of a franchise to a street railway corporation is to successors or assigns, it does not terminate with the life of the corporation to which it is granted, but may be for a term beyond the corporate life of the original grantee.

> **Iowa**   State v Des Moines City Ry (1913) 159 Iowa 259, 140 NW 437.

An ordinance granting a franchise to a street railway company is not invalid merely because the term of the franchise may extend beyond the corporate life of the company.

> **Minn**   Minneapolis v Minneapolis St Ry (1910) 215 US 417, 54 LEd 259, 30 SCt 118.

Under an ordinance granting a 20-year franchise to a utility for furnishing street railway service, and providing that in case of any removal of trackage on streets or crossings the company shall leave the same in as good condition as before such removal, one who on foreclosure sale purchases the rolling stock and rails may not be held liable for disturbing the condition of the streets.

> **Mo**   Crebs v Lebanon (1898) 98 F 549.

Where a street railway company under its franchise operates cars on tracks within a city, and an interurban company operates a line between that city and another city, and an ordinance authorizes an agreement between the two companies by which the railway company within the city takes over and operates interurban cars within the city, employees of the interurban company for that purpose become employees of the street railway company, and a passenger who pays a fare for city transportation is traveling under the care and control of employees of the street railway company; and for an assault occurring at such time he may not recover from the interurban company.

> **Mo**   Wilcox v Kansas City West Ry (1919) 201 MoApp 510, 213 SW 156.

B. LOSS, AMENDMENT OR EXPIRATION OF FRANCHISE, PERMIT OR LICENSE

§23. Revocation or Forfeiture

A municipality has power to terminate a franchise granted by its own ordinance to an interurban railroad company, without the consent of the state public service commission.

> **Md**   R E Duvall Co v Washington B & A Elec Ry (1932) 60 F2d 315.

A resolution granting a bus company a certificate of public convenience and necessity for operation of a bus system will be construed as the issuance of a license or permit, rather than a franchise, and such a license is not for a definite period but may be altered, suspended or revoked for good cause.

> **Fla**   Miami v South Miami Coach Lines (1952) 59 So2d 52.

Where a city, by ordinance, has granted a right to construct a street railway line over certain streets, it cannot by subsequent ordinance arbitrarily annul such license.

NC Boyce v Gastonia (1947) 227 NC 139, 41 SE2d 355.

A street railway franchise for use of the city streets, granted by ordinance, may be forfeited by a resolution of the city council, in the absence of any statutory or charter requirement that the forfeiture must be by ordinance, since a resolution ordinarily has the same effect as an ordinance except in matters of legislation.

Wash Sylvester v Superior Ct (1910) 60 Wash 279, 111 P 19.

The acceptance of an ordinance by one street railway to operate over the tracks of another creates a contract which the railway cannot revoke without consent of the city, and which the city can enforce.

Va Virginia Ry & Power v Richmond (1921) 129 Va 592, 106 SE 529.

Noncompliance with an ordinance granting a franchise to a street railroad is not a ground for revocation of the franchise, where the city has not previously objected to the noncompliance and the interruption of service was under order of a federal court.

Pa Dalton St Ry v Scranton (1937) 326 Pa 6, 191 A 133.

A bus franchise is property which, once granted, cannot be taken away except by the terms thereof or by due process of law.

NY Eighth Ave Coach v New York City (1939) 170 Misc 243, 10 NYS2d 170.

A municipality may by ordinance revoke a street railroad franchise for misuser or nonuser.

NY Bankers Tr v Yonkers (1938) 255 AD 173, 6 NYS2d 883.

Statutory authority to include in consents for operation of a street railroad conditions necessary in the public interest permits the city to control the use of tracks in the streets if the franchise is forfeited, purchase the equipment, operate the lines with statutory authority, convert the mode of transport, or entirely discontinue operation.

NY Bankers Trust v Yonkers (1938) 255 AD 173, 6 NYS2d 883.

A multi-privileged mass transportation franchise ordinance is not destroyed by nonuse of one of the several privileges conferred thereby.

Utah Salt Lake City Lines v Salt Lake City (1957) 6 Utah2d 428, 315 P2d 859.

An ordinance revoking an interurban railway franchise is ineffective where no notice of default is given pursuant to the original franchise ordinance and no opportunity given to correct the default.

Utah　Murray City v Utah Light & Traction (1920) 56 Utah 437, 191 P 421.

An ordinance revoking a franchise ordinance for an interurban railroad is ineffective if enacted because the original rates and fares established in the franchise ordinance are raised, where the revised rates and fares have been approved by the state public utilities commission.

Utah　Murray City v Utah Light & Traction (1920) 56 Utah 437, 191 P 421.

Where the privilege of using city streets is granted by ordinance to a street railway, and the ordinance is accepted and acted on by the railway in some substantial manner, it becomes a valid and binding contract and is not subject to revocation by the municipality.

Ill　Madison v Alton G & S L Traction (1908) 235 Ill 346, 85 NE 596.

The right reserved by a city in a street railway franchise ordinance to forfeit the franchise because of noncompliance with certain conditions may be waived by the city by its acts; or the city may be estopped by reason of its acts to enforce a forfeiture.

Ill　Wight v Chicago (1907) 137 IllAp 240.

A city council may not repeal an accepted street railroad franchise ordinance without the consent of the company, for the reason that to permit it to do so would sanction a violation of the federal Constitution prohibiting the impairment of the obligation of contract.

Iowa　Van Horn v Des Moines (1922) 195 Iowa 840, 191 NW 144.

While the general rule is that a court of equity will not issue an injunction to restrain a municipal corporation from exercising legislative or governmental power, though the contemplated action may be in disregard of constitutional restraints and may impair the obligation of a contract, the Federal Court properly issued a preliminary injunction restraining a municipality from passing any ordinances or resolutions for the purpose of effecting a forfeiture of a street railway's franchise where: (1) receivers had been appointed by the Federal Court; (2) the state court had ordered restoration of some of the company's services; and (3) the Federal Court ordered such restoration on condition that the council grant an increase in rates in order to prevent dissipation of the assets in the control of the receivers.

Iowa　Des Moines v Continental Ill Nat Bk & Tr (1953) 205 F2d 729.

Under statute granting power to a city council to authorize or forbid the location and laying down of tracks for street railroads, a council cannot by ordinance grant a perpetual franchise; and it may not do indirectly what it cannot do directly. Therefore, a perpetual franchise would not result from estoppel of the city to forfeit a franchise.

> **Iowa** State v Des Moines City Ry (1913) 159 Iowa 259, 140 NW 437.

Where a street railway company is unable to pave, in accordance with the terms of its franchise ordinance, due to financial difficulties, it is not relieved of the duty to pave, nor can it prevent a forfeiture of its franchise. He who fails to perform, from whatever cause, must suffer the consequences he has agreed to suffer.

> **Mich** Grandville v Grand Rapids H & C RR (1923) 225 Mich 587, 196 NW 351, 34 ALR 1408.

A village may enforce a forfeiture of a street railway company's franchise, according to its terms, to the detriment of other municipalities and communities along the railway line, and thereby interfere with the public duties of the railway as a common carrier.

> **Mich** Grandville v Grand Rapids H & C RR (1923) 225 Mich 587, 196 NW 351, 34 ALR 1408.

If the street railway franchise itself provides for forfeiture of the franchise on breach of certain stipulations, it is not necessary for a court to determine that the breach warrants a forfeiture.

> **Mich** Union St Ry v Snow (1897) 113 Mich 694, 71 NW 1073.

Where a street railway franchise provides that on the company's failure to pay the cost of paving between its tracks the city may forfeit the franchise, a forfeiture will not be enjoined merely because, from insufficiency of earnings, the company has become insolvent and unable to pay such costs.

> **Mich** Union St Ry v Snow (1897) 113 Mich 694, 71 NW 1073.

The carriage of unauthorized freight, by a corporation authorized by statute to construct its railroad on streets pursuant to the consent of the municipality, and possessing a franchise to operate a street railroad in the city pursuant to an ordinance imposing the conditions on which the railroad should be operated, and the charging of excessive fares and obstruction of the streets of the city, is not cause for forfeiture of the franchise, but calls for regulation of the business done by the corporation.

> **Mich** Monroe v Toledo & M Ry (1908) 151 Mich 473, 115 NW 422.

A municipality may not forfeit a grant of a franchise to a street railway company, where the company constructed its road after the time prescribed by the ordinance expired, but where such construction was carried on without interference from the municipality.

Mich Sandstone v Mich Ry (1917) 198 Mich 234, 164 NW 404.

A forfeiture clause in a street railway franchise which would be self-executing and would dispense with judicial proceedings for the intervention of the attorney general must be plain and unmistakable in its terms.

Mich Sandstone v Mich Ry (1917) 198 Mich 234, 164 NW 404.

§24. Amendment or Modification

An ordinance purporting to give the traffic and transportation board authority to change routes specified in licenses granted to operate bus companies is invalid because repugnant to a statute authorizing the licensing by a city of motor vehicles conveying passengers for hire so as to afford a means of transportation similar to that afforded by a railway company by indiscriminately receiving and discharging passengers along certain routes.

Mass Springfield v Springfield St Ry (1951) 327 Mass 4, 97 NE2d 196.

An ordinance granting a franchise for the operation of a street railroad over the streets of the city is subject to the right of the public. Therefore, a subsequent ordinance forbidding the railroad company to use a certain street, between certain termini, on the ground that such use would destroy the rights of the public, is valid.

Okla Piatt, Ex parte (1913) 38 Okla 572, 134 P 53.

An ordinance authorizing a transit franchise holder to discontinue giving passenger transfers is valid if it complies with the advertising requirements of the statute governing amendments of franchise ordinances which affect public benefits.

Va Commonwealth v Richmond & R R RR (1914) 115 Va 756, 80 SE 796.

Where a legislative charter grants a street railway company a franchise to operate its cars over specified streets and routes within the city, an ordinance purporting to give the company authority to use routes materially different from those provided in the charter is void.

Tenn Citizens' Ry v Africa (1897) 100 Tenn 26, 42 SW 485.

A franchise ordinance authorizing a transit utility to operate streetcar lines on the city's streets, and requiring that the utility pay to another utility a percentage of the maintenance costs, for use of viaducts constructed by the other utility, is construed, not technically, but from a consideration of all surrounding circumstances, to include the use thereof by motor buses and trolley buses resulting from modernization, improvement and expansion of the street railway system.

Mo Kansas City Term Ry v Kansas City Transit (1962) 359 SW2d 698.

Where an ordinance grants a franchise to a street railway company to use the city streets, and thereafter the territorial limits of the municipality are extended, the franchise immediately attaches, without any further action on the part of the municipality, to the newly acquired territory.

Mich Bay City v Saginaw-Bay Ry (1919) 207 Mich 419, 174 NW 193.

A declaration in an ordinance that it amends all franchises owned and held by a specified street railroad company is not vague or ambiguous, since it is not necessary to name, identify and reordain each section of every ordinance involved.

La Long v Shreveport (1921) 151 La 423, 91 So 825.

The obligation of a contract is unconstitutionally impaired when an ordinance granting a street railway the right to lay double tracks is partially repealed. The franchise was single and specific; it was accepted by the company and the franchise was an entirety. The company acquired land to lay double track and had actually put down some track.

Ind Grand Trunk Western Ry v South Bend (1912) 227 US 544, 57 LEd 633, 33 SCt 303.

Since the grant of a franchise to a street railway gives complete authority to operate and maintain its buses, an attempt to add any additional money burden, under a penal ordinance, is clearly violative of the company's contractual rights, and the persistent threat of prosecution justifies injunctive relief to prevent enforcement of the license ordinance.

Ohio Cincinnati v Cincinnati St Ry (1933) 45 OA 511, 15 Abs 347, 187 NE 312.

Where a city ordinance granted a street railway company a franchise, provided that it might operate in such streets as might be designated from time to time, and gave the company an exclusive privilege for five years, subsequent permission to the company to operate a track in a street did not amount to an extension of the time for the exclusive privilege.

Iowa Thurston v Huston (1904) 123 Iowa 157, 98 NW 637.

Where a franchise ordinance puts no limitations on the time within which a street railway's tracks must be laid over city streets, the railway has municipal authority to change the route over which its railway runs.

Ky Louisville & N RR v Bowling Green Ry (1901) 110 Ky 788, 63 SW 4.

Ordinances amending or modifying previously granted franchises to operate a street railway in the city are valid, since there is no rule of law that inhibits modification of contracts when all parties in interest consent.

> **Ky** Poggel v Louisville Ry (1928) 225 Ky 784, 10 SW2d 305.

Where ordinances modifying previous ordinances granting franchises to a street railway company go no further than to confer administrative duties on a board of public works, they are not invalid as conferring regulatory powers over the operations of the company or power to decide on legislative matters.

> **Ky** Poggel v Louisville Ry (1928) 225 Ky 784, 10 SW2d 305.

The purpose of granting a street railway franchise is to provide for the rapid and convenient transportation of the public; and where this basic right is already granted the motive power or method of propulsion of vehicles is subordinate or subsidiary and a change from electrically operated cars to motor buses may be authorized by resolution of the city council, so as to amend the franchise granted without granting a new franchise.

> **Ky** Russell v Ky Utilities (1929) 231 Ky 820, 22 SW2d 289.

Where the regulatory provisions of an ordinance providing for the adjustment of controversies between the city and a street railway change or alter the franchise granted to the street railway, this does not vitiate the ordinance, since the regulatory provisions may be changed or altered at any time by agreement of the parties.

> **Ky** Scott v Cincinnati N & C Ry (1937) 268 Ky 383, 105 SW2d 169.

Under an ordinance authorizing a street railway company operating under a franchise granted by the city, a change from streetcars to buses not requiring the use of fixed tracks is permissible to meet changed conditions.

> **Ky** Scott v Cincinnati N & C Ry (1937) 268 Ky 383, 105 SW2d 169.

An ordinance amending a contractual grant of a right to construct, maintain, and operate a street railway system within the municipality, and effecting changes within the scope of the provisions made in the original grant and recognition of need for future change, is valid and binding on the parties.

> **Minn** Minneapolis St Ry v Minneapolis (1949) 229 Minn 502, 40 NW2d 353, (1952) 236 Minn 109, 52 NW2d 120.

Where a franchise ordinance granting permission to a horse railway company to lay tracks in certain streets and requiring their completion within 18 months is amended to extend the time for completion to 10 years beyond the time first named, the amendatory ordinance must be construed as extending the time for completion for 10 years after expiration of the time fixed in the first ordinance.

> **Ill** McNeil v Chicago City Ry (1871) 61 Ill 150.

Where a franchise ordinance provides that the street railway shall allow transfers at its track intersections, the city may not by a subsequent ordinance require the company to allow transfers at points other than intersections.

Ill Chicago v Chicago City Ry (1916) 272 Ill 245, 111 NE 983.

Where a street railway franchise ordinance specifies the character and nature of improvements to be made by the railway in connection with its operation, the city cannot, by subsequent ordinance, change materially the nature of the improvements provided for in the original ordinance, as to grade, location, size or character.

Ill Lincoln v Harts (1911) 250 Ill 273, 95 NE 200.

A provision in an ordinance granting a street railway the right to use the streets for its wires and poles, that it shall be subject to all reasonable ordinances that may be thereafter passed concerning streets and street railways, does not reserve in the city the power to increase the compensation to be paid for the grant, but only reserves the power to make additional regulations under its governmental or police powers regarding the manner in which the use of the streets shall be exercised.

Ill Springfield v Springfield Consolidated Ry (1917) 208 IllAp 11.

Where a bus franchise enumerates two-way streets on which routes are to be operated in both directions but in conformance with police regulations, two-way traffic along such main routes may not be changed to one-way traffic by a regulation of the police commissioner if the value of the franchise and contract rights would be thereby destroyed. The consideration for the franchise is in part based on the permitted two-way operation on main route streets.

NY Eighth Ave Coach v New York City (1939) 170 Misc 243, 10 NYS2d 170.

A railroad that obtains a city's consent to use its streets, agreeing to conform to all regulations pertaining to the streets and to remove any obstructions or impediments it creates therein, may not thereafter in litigation with the city repudiate the existence of the street on the ground that it was not actually in use as a street when the grant was made.

NY People v Priest (1912) 206 NY 274, 99 NE 547.

An ordinance amending the city's consents to a street railroad corporation's operation of buses instead of streetcars on city streets by increasing bus license fees deprives one of his property without due process of law and impairs the obligation of contracts embodied in his franchises.

NY Tilton v Utica (1946) 60 NYS2d 249.

An ordinance provision that consents previously given to a bus company to operate buses in the city were subject to state laws or city ordinances then or thereafter enacted reserved to the city the right to enact police regulations for the public safety, such as speed limits and regulations of time and manner of operation, but the city could not enact an ordinance impairing or destroying a contract with the bus company, such as an ordinance increasing bus license fees fixed by a previous ordinance. Therefore the ordinance is unconstitutional.

NY   Tilton v Utica (1946) 60 NYS2d 249.

§25. Required Construction of New Facilities

The validity of a resolution prohibiting construction by a street railway of switches on a bridge and its approaches does not present a federal constitutional question, since a company operating under a franchise does not obtain property rights in matters relating to its regulation which may be the subject of constitutional guaranties.

Wis   Eastern Wis Ry & Light v Hackett (1908) 135 Wis 464, 115 NW 376.

The right of a street railroad company under its franchise to connect its road in a village with a branch line which it afterward built to the village boundary was not forfeited by its failure to construct the branch within the time fixed for constructing its road through the village.

Mich   Houghton County St Ry v Laurium V (1904) 135 Mich 614, 98 NW 393.

The requirements of an ordinance directing a street railway company to construct extensions of its lines are subject to review by the public utility commission, which is authorized, on hearing, to determine whether the requirements are reasonable.

Ohio   Cincinnati v Public Utilities Comm (1915) 91 OS 331, 110 NE 461.

A street railway company accepting a franchise to operate a streetcar system, subject to the right of the city at any time to designate other lines as demanded by public necessities, with the right of the city to grant to any other company an exclusive right to construct and operate a street railway in the streets so designated on the first company's failure to comply with the orders of the city, may be put to its election on the adoption of an extension ordinance as to whether it will build the line ordered to allow another company to build it. This does not deprive the company of its property without due process of law or impair the obligation of a contract.

Minn   Minneapolis St Ry v Minneapolis (1911) 189 F 445.

An ordinance directing a street railway to construct and equip tracks on designated streets and put them in operation does not deny equal protection of the laws to the company, which accepted a franchise giving the city the right to designate other lines or extensions of existing lines, as demanded by public necessity.

Minn   Minneapolis St Ry v Minneapolis (1911) 189 F 445.

Where street railway franchise reserves to the city the right to direct the construction of new lines and extensions of existing lines when demanded by public necessity, an ordinance directing the construction of lines nine miles in length cannot be adjudged invalid as arbitrary and unreasonable, on the ground that the public necessities do not demand the work, where the city council determined that public necessities did demand the work and the general manager of the company stated that 9.5 miles of extensions during the year would not be unreasonable.

Minn Minneapolis St Ry v Minneapolis (1911) 189 F 445.

A street railway franchise ordinance is construed to justify the common council in ordering construction of a new line only when public convenience and necessity will be promoted thereby.

Minn State v St Paul City Ry (1913) 122 Minn 163, 142 NW 136.

An ordinance requiring a street railway to construct a new car line, enacted under the terms of the franchise, does not violate any constitutional right of the street railway. And the city may direct whether the new line shall be a single or a double track line. The railway under its franchise has no vested right or option to determine the character of the line in this respect.

Minn State v St Paul City Ry (1914) 127 Minn 191, 149 NW 195.

A resolution providing for the construction of a 2,700 foot extension of a double streetcar track is arbitrary and unreasonable, where public convenience and necessity do not exist. Public necessity should be construed as meaning urgent public convenience.

Minn State v Duluth St Ry (1930) 179 Minn 548, 229 NW 883.

Where a previous franchise ordinance permitted the city to require the construction of additional streetcar lines on streets on which sewers had been constructed and where because of the topography of certain unsewered blocks along the contemplated carline and other existing conditions there is no necessity of having a sewer there, the construction of a sewer is not a condition precedent to the requiring of a new carline.

Minn State v St Paul City Ry (1930) 180 Minn 329, 230 NW 809.

An ordinance requiring the construction of additional streetcar lines is an exercise of the police power, and all questions of propriety and public necessity, being legislative in character, are committed to the city council.

Minn State v St Paul City Ry (1930) 180 Minn 329, 230 NW 809.

§ 26. Relocation or Removal of Facilities

A subway holding an irrevocable franchise to use the city's sidewalks for access may not be compelled to pay the costs of alteration and relocation of exits required by a street widening ordinance, where there is no special statutory delegation of the police power to compel such relocation.

> **NY**   New York City v Hudson & M R (1919) 188 AD 294, 177 NYS 4.

In the absence of special statutory authorization a street railroad authorized by ordinance to lay tracks in the street may not be compelled to remove the trackage after it has performed in compliance with the grant. General charter power to alter and improve streets will not be extended to imply the right to compel such relocation.

> **NY**   People v Western NY & Pa Traction (1915) 214 NY 526, 108 NE 847.

Under an ordinance requiring companies using poles and wires to remove the same temporarily to allow passage of buildings being moved along or across a street, an ordinance giving a franchise to a streetcar company and providing that the company shall so construct its tract "as to present the least possible obstruction to the ordinary and public use" of the street may be construed to include the moving of buildings along the street as a public use, and to require the company to remove its wires to allow the passage of buildings.

> **Neb**   State v Omaha & C B St Ry (1916) 100 Neb 716, 161 NW 170.

Where an ordinance grants a street railway franchise, requires the company at its own expense to remove its tracks when the city desires to make improvements on the streets, including the laying of sewers, and reserves power to the city to designate any other lines of railway as demanded by public necessity; and a subsequent ordinance accepted by the company provides that sewers should be built in the streets before new lines should be ordered or existing lines extended, a later amended ordinance omitting all reference to sewers is binding on the company though not accepted by it, because the amendment is an exercise of the power of the city to regulate the manner of carrying on the business of the road and the use of the streets. Hence, an ordinance directing the construction of a line over a street in which there are no sewers is not invalid as impairing the obligation of a contract.

> **Minn**   Minneapolis St Ry v Minneapolis (1911) 189 F 445.

Though under express provisions of a statute a municipality can grant the right to a street railway company to operate a line on the streets only by an ordinance regularly passed and accepted by the company, a city which has by ordinance granted to a company the right to operate a car line, subject to a provision that the location of poles, sidetracks, spurs and switches shall be under the control of the council, may by a mere motion adopted by the council authorize the company to change the location of a curve in the track connecting a street with a cross street.

Mich Mannel v Detroit Mt C & M C Ry (1905) 139 Mich 106, 102 NW 633.

A street railway corporation operating under a franchise granting it the use of streets if they are maintained in first class order between the tracks and two feet on each side of the tracks is not required by the covenant of the ordinance and franchise to reconstruct the entire surface of streets on either side of its tracks, nor may the covenant be used to oppose the elevating of the entire surface of the street on either side of the tracks to the height of the road bed.

La State v New Orleans Traction (1896) 48 LaAnn 567, 19 So 565.

The grant of a franchise by a city to a street railway company to lay its tracks in the streets is subject necessarily to the power of the city to make any reasonable regulation by ordinance of its use: and the city may require the company to relocate its track in a public street at its own expense.

Ga Atlantic Coast Line RR v Southern Ry (1958) 214 Ga 178, 104 SE2d 77.

Where the city council granted a street railway company the right to lay tracks on public alleys and streets on payment for injuries to abutting owners, and an abutting owner consented to the construction of a side-track by the company in a certain alley and waived all damages resulting therefrom, and the company agreed that if it became necessary to close the alley in question it would vacate its track, the subsequent passage of an ordinance, with the consent of the abutting owners, providing that the alley should be vacated and granted to the use of a certain railroad, made it incumbent on the street railway company to vacate the track.

Iowa Getchell & Martin Lumber & Mfg v Des Moines Union Ry (1901) 115 Iowa 734, 87 NW 670.

Where an ordinance ordered a street railway company to move its tracks, and six years later the city passed a repealing ordinance again ordering removal of the tracks, but also ordering the paving and lowering of the tracks to grade, the second ordinance was not invalid as a violation of a contract or vested right, since a city cannot be divested by ordinance or contract of its legislative power to make changes in its streets in the exercise of reasonable discretion.

Iowa Snouffer v Cedar Rapids & M C Ry (1902) 118 Iowa 287, 92 NW 79.

Building owner who constructed building at lower grade as designated by the city engineer in conformity with an invalid amending ordinance could not enjoin maintenance of street railway tracks at higher grade. Railway maintained its tracks on grade designated by city engineer in conformity with original ordinance. Building owner could not claim estoppel against the city to deny his grade; a similar but conflicting estoppel favored the railway.

    Iowa   Rocho v Boone Elec Co (1913) 160 Iowa 94, 140 NW 193.

A street railway is not an improvement on the streets of a city, within the legislative meaning of that term. Consequently, when a city enacts an ordinance to change the grade of a street traversed by the tracks of a street railway company, the city is not liable for the expense incurred by the company in conforming its tracks to the change in grade.

    Iowa   Des Moines City Ry v Des Moines (1927) 205 Iowa 495, 216 NW 284.

§ 27. Abandonment of Facilities

The privilege of operating an electric street railway, created by a municipal franchise ordinance, became inseparable from that of operating an electric power and light system, on merger of the two companies, and together they constituted a unified franchise that could not be abandoned in part and retained in part without the consent of the state. As long as the merged company retains and operates its electric power system it cannot be permitted to abandon its street railway system, notwithstanding that the railway may be showing a loss.

    SC   Broad River Power v State (1930) 281 US 537, 74 LEd 1023, 50 SCt 401.

An ordinance granting a 49-year franchise to a company to construct, operate and maintain over certain streets and alleys an electric railway is permissive as to the length of time of the grant, though obligatory, insofar as the law permits, as to rates and like matters during the time of operation; and spur lines installed under authority of the franchise may be removed on leave granted by the state public service commission on a showing of continued financial loss.

    Mo   State v Pub Service Comm (1924) 303 Mo 505, 260 SW 973.

A provision in an ordinance granting a franchise to a street railway company that it shall not be construed to require the grantee to continue the operation of the railway lines or any portion thereof at a loss does not authorize the abandonment of part of one unit, but only grants permission to abandon the entire system or any entire line in the system, under application of the rule that governmental grants to individuals are to be construed most strongly against the grantee.

    Mont   Helena v Helena Light & Ry (1922) 63 Mont 108, 207 P 337.

An ordinance authorizing a tramway corporation to eliminate rail lines and operate trolley coaches or motor buses on certain streets, and adjusting fares, constitutes an attempt to grant, extend, and enlarge franchise privileges and regulate charges for bus service by a public utility corporation, and is void as violating the Constitution and charter provisions that no franchise relating to a street may be granted without approval of the electors.

Colo Berman v Denver (1949) 120 Colo 218, 209 P2d 754.

The state corporation commission has power to order discontinuance of a street railway and permit abandonment of facilities, if the railway's continued maintenance and operation would constitute the taking of property without due process; and an ordinance granting to the railway the privilege to operate its car over the streets of the city is not such a contract as to render it inviolable.

Va Hampton v Newport News & Hampton Ry (1926) 144 Va 29, 131 SE 328.

An ordinance granting a competitive transit franchise, which is not illegal since the city is authorized to grant competitive transit franchises, may be enjoined on a prima facie showing that the ordinance and resulting competition would adversely affect the present non-exclusive franchise holder's financial condition and might require it to abandon the transit facilities now furnished, or to continue operations while in an unsound economic condition.

La Westside Transit Lines v New Orleans Pub Service (1961) 135 So2d 278.

Where a franchise ordinance imposes no contract obligation on a company to operate its street railway in the city for any specified time, and the company cannot continue its operations as a whole under good business management except at a loss, it may be permitted to remove all of its tracks and equipment and abandon the franchise, on restoring the streets to the condition of adjacent highways at the time the abandonment takes place.

Ky Potter Matlock Tr v Warren County (1919) 182 Ky 840, 207 SW 709.

A street railway company operating under a franchise cannot be required, in the absence of a contract obligation, to continue to render service contemplated by a merely permissive grant to use public ways if the operation cannot be continued under efficient management without a loss. To require otherwise would be to hold that private property might be taken for public use without compensation.

Ky Potter Matlock Tr v Warren County (1919) 182 Ky 840, 207 SW 709.

§28. Expiration

After an ordinance granting a franchise to a street railway company has expired, without renewal or extension, continued occupancy and use of the streets by the company constitutes the exercise of a power not conferred by law, within the statute providing for a civil action in the name of the state against any corporation exercising powers not conferred by law.

Iowa State v Des Moines City Ry (1906) 135 Iowa 694, 109 NW 867.

A street railway that has continued operations and making improvements for a number of years after expiration of its franchise, which the city did not contest, should have a reasonable time to negotiate an extension or renewal of its franchise, dispose of its property or remove its property.

Iowa State v Des Moines City Ry (1913) 159 Iowa 259, 140 NW 437.

The authority delegated to cities to grant franchises for street railways includes, by implication, the right to grant a temporary permit for continued operation of the railway after expiration of the original franchise.

Wash Neils v Seattle (1936) 185 Wash 269, 53 P2d 848.

Use of the streets for operation of a bus line after expiration of a short term franchise is illegal and may be enjoined by the city, but the city is not entitled to compensation for the use and occupation of the streets where no franchise or contract exists and it does not possess title to the streets.

NY New York City v Bee Line (1935) 246 AD 28, 284 NYS 452.

A street railway granted by ordinance the right to lay tracks in certain streets and to operate a railway for 30 years, during which period the time was extended by ordinance to 37 years, had during the enlarged term, an unexpired franchise that the courts could protect against wrongful impairment, with the remedy being the same whether its rights in the streets were perpetual or limited, though the two positions are inconsistent.

Ind Citizen's Street Ry v City Ry (1894) 64 F 647.

A city that extends the duration of a street railway franchise granted by ordinance, to enable the railway company to refund its bonded indebtedness at a lower rate of interest, is estopped, after the negotiation of new bonds on the faith thereof, to attack the validity of the extension for want of consideration. Continued operation is a sufficient consideration for the extension.

Ind City Ry v Citizen's St Ry (1897) 166 US 557, 41 LEd 1114, 17 SCt 653.

Acceptance by a street railway company of an amendatory ordinance extending the period of its franchise may be presumed from the fact that the amendment was beneficial to it, and that it issued bonds, and made them fall due at the expiration of the extended franchise.

Ind City Ry v Citizen's St Ry (1897) 166 US 557, 41 LEd 1114, 17 SCt 653.

Where municipal authorities have granted a franchise to a street railway company for a definite time, the company is not entitled to continue to occupy the streets indefinitely after expiration of that time on the theory that there is an implied obligation on the part of both the company and the municipality to continue the operation of the railroad for the benefit of the public, since the municipal authorities constitute the only governmental agency provided for protecting the interests of the public.

Mich   Detroit v Detroit United Ry (1912) 172 Mich 136, 137 NW 645.

A street railway company whose franchise to use the city streets has, by its terms, expired has no implied contract right to remain in the streets under such reasonable arrangements for public service as the situation may require, which would be impaired by requiring it to stop operating its cars and to remove its tracks and other property from the streets within a reasonable time.

Mich   Detroit United Ry v Detroit (1912) 229 US 39, 57 LEd 1056, 33 SCt 697.

A city cannot arbitrarily, without the consent of a street railway company whose franchise has expired, impose terms for the further use of the streets, where the company denies the expiration of the franchise and refuses to accept such terms.

Mich   Detroit v Detroit United Ry (1912) 172 Mich 136, 137 NW 645.

The occupancy of a street by a street railroad after its franchise has expired is a continuing trespass, for the restraint of which the municipality is entitled to a writ of injunction, as well as to its removal.

Mich   Detroit v Detroit United Ry (1912) 172 Mich 136, 137 NW 645.

A railway company's franchise ordinance provided it would remain in force for one year after expiration unless amended or repealed. The railway did not have rights in the streets after the franchise expired.

Mich   Detroit United Ry v Detroit (1921) 255 US 171, 65 LEd 561, 41 SCt 285.

A city council's direction to its city attorney to sue to oust a street railway from streets where its franchise has expired amounts to administrative rather than legislative action. It is not a permanent regulation requiring action by ordinance, but is an act of a temporary nature, properly effectuated by resolution.

Mich   Detroit v Detroit United Ry (1921) 215 Mich 401, 184 NW 516.

C. REGULATING OPERATIONS OF SYSTEM

§29. Authority of Municipality Generally

On failure of the city to enforce its air pollution control code, an individual may bring an action to abate the nuisance of bus exhaust in the terminal. The plaintiff's cause of action is not necessarily so clear and convincing as to entitle him to a permanent injunction, but does present a question of fact for determination of nuisance and proximate cause.

> **NY**   Stock v Ronan (1970) 63 Misc2d 735, 313 NYS2d 508.

A city by specific statutory authority is authorized to regulate, by ordinances, the operation and maintenance of a local railway company, since this is a matter concerning primarily the citizens of the city and it may be better regulated by local authorities who are cognizant of the local situation.

> **Ky**   South Covington & C St Ry v Covington (1912) 146 Ky 592, 143 SW 28.

Where the power to regulate, license and control motor vehicles for hire is vested by the legislature in the city council, there is a broad presumption in favor of the validity of an ordinance undertaking to exercise such power, and one attacking the ordinance must show affirmatively that it is not expressly authorized by statute or that it is, as applied to him, unreasonable and oppressive.

> **NC**   Suddreth v Charlotte (1943) 223 NC 630, 27 SE2d 650.

No one has the inherent right to carry on his private business along the public street. Such a right can be exercised only under terms and conditions imposed by the city authorities.

> **SC**   Huffman v Columbia (1928) 146 SC 436, 144 SE 157.

Under its police power, a city may regulate passenger buses operating as common carriers on its streets.

> **Cal**   People v Willert (1939) 37 CA2d 729, 93 P2d 872.

An ordinance prohibiting the use of certain streets by buses and trucks does not impose an unreasonable burden on interstate commerce though the street was improved by the state as a state highway.

> **Pa**   Commonwealth v Kennedy (1937) 129 PaS 149, 195 A 770.

In the absence of federal legislation to the contrary, the state and its municipalities may prescribe uniform regulations for public safety and order, with respect to the operation on their highways of all motor vehicles, those moving in interstate commerce as well as others.

> **NJ**   People Rapid Transit v Atlantic City (1929) 105 NJLaw 286, 144 A 630.

The public service commission cannot declare an ordinance invalid if it does not relate to the quality or character of the service required of a public utility or to the terms and conditions on which the utility is permitted to use a street.

> **Ind**   Stuck v Beech Grove (1928) 201 Ind 66, 163 NE 483.

Where an ordinance regulates bus service, fixes rates, requires certificates of convenience and necessity to operate buses on public streets, requires a licensee to operate and maintain a certain schedule of trips, and requires maintenance of insurance, the city's offer to permit operators of buses to furnish service under stated terms and conditions and the acceptance of the offer of the license and of all the terms of the ordinance or franchise, which bound bus operators to give a definite service, constitutes a furnishing of motor transportation "by color of a contract," which thus exempts the municipality from the power of the state public service commission.

Ind   Denny v Brady (1928) 201 Ind 59, 163 NE 489.

The power to grant certificates of convenience and necessity, to regulate service, to fix rates, and to prevent ruinous and unrestricted competition is a power granted to the public service commission to safeguard the public interest and promote public convenience and necessity; but municipalities retain their rights to regulate traffic, control streets and exercise police power generally by ordinances on subjects of municipal concern. Such regulatory ordinances are valid as long as they regulate within reasonable limits and do not prohibit or unreasonably impair or interfere with the right of operation of motor vehicle utilities which have received certificates of convenience and necessity from the public service commission.

Ind   Poparad v Indianapolis Rys (1942) 111 IndAp 314, 39 NE2d 781.

The Constitution reserves to municipalities reasonable control over their streets, and empowers them to enact ordinances regulating interurban and suburban buses operating therein.

Mich   Highway Motorbus v Lansing (1927) 238 Mich 146, 213 NW 79.

A municipality has a constitutional right to enact ordinances for the reasonable regulation of interurban motor buses, provided such regulation does not affect business outside the municipality.

Mich   North Star Line v Grand Rapids (1932) 259 Mich 654, 244 NW 192.

Under its delegated power, a city may regulate the use of its streets and fix the terms and conditions on which motor buses may be permitted to operate thereon.

Ill   Chicago Motor Coach v Chicago (1929) 337 Ill 200, 169 NE 22, 66 ALR 834.

A city in granting a street railway franchise by ordinance may regulate the service for the public convenience, safety, or health.

Minn   Minneapolis St Ry v Minneapolis (1911) 189 F 445.

223

An ordinance regulating the operation of motor vehicles carrying passengers for hire on streets where a double track of street railway exists is not void as discriminatory or as class legislation, since no one has a right, as a matter of course, to conduct a private business on public streets.

> **Minn** Schultz v Duluth (1925) 163 Minn 65, 203 NW 449.

An ordinance regulating the operation of vehicles transporting passengers for hire, but not the transportation of freight for hire, is not violative of the equal protection of the law guaranty. The classification is valid.

> **Tex** Reed v Waco (1949) 223 SW2d 247.

A city has power to regulate how and in what manner the streets may be used by vehicles to transport the public on the streets, and all persons engaged in the business of soliciting such public patronage must abide by the terms and conditions imposed by the city.

> **NY** People v May (1917) 98 Misc 561, 164 NYS 717.

A municipality does not by grant of a bus franchise part with the right to regulate the business conducted thereunder, where the right of regulation otherwise exists by law or is reserved by the terms of the contract.

> **NY** Eighth Ave Coach v New York City (1939) 170 Misc 243, 10 NYS2d 170.

In dealing with the problem of traffic control in a proper exercise of the police power, a city may adopt the expedient of prohibiting operations on its streets by additional carriers.

> **Neb** Council Bluffs Transit v Omaha (1951) 154 Neb 717, 49 NW2d 453.

An ordinance regulating the use of buses as common carriers of persons within the city is regulatory in character, and not of the class of ordinances properly described as "any ordinance or resolution granting, extending, changing or modifying the terms and conditions of a franchise;" permits granted in accordance with its terms are valid.

> **Neb** Omaha & C B St Ry v Omaha (1926) 114 Neb 483, 208 NW 123.

Where there is an uninterrupted transportation of passengers between states, on the same cars, under practically the same management, and for a single fare, this course of business constitutes interstate commerce. But it is of a class which a city may regulate by ordinance passed under the exercise of its police power in the interest of public health and safety, notwithstanding that it may incidentally or indirectly affect interstate commerce.

> **Ky** South Covington C St Ry v Covington (1915) 235 US 537, 59 LEd 350, 35 SCt 158.

ANNOTATIONS

Motorbus or truck terminal as nuisance, 2 ALR3d 1372.

Right of carrier to discontinue line or branch on ground that it is unprofitable where by ordinance it is obligated to continue service in its entirety, 10 ALR2d 1134.

§ 30. Limitations on Authority

An ordinance prohibiting the operation of motor vehicles for hire on certain streets, the effect of which is to interfere with the use of a state highway that approaches and passes through the city, is invalid as being extraterritorial in effect and beyond the power of local government.

Tex Arlington v Lillard (1927) 116 Tex 446, 294 SW 829.

The right to regulate a business operating under a bus franchise does not carry with it the right to destroy it, nor may the terms of the grant be substantially modified or changed under the guise of regulation.

NY Eighth Ave Coach v New York City (1939) 170 Misc 243, 10 NYS2d 170.

An ordinance regulating the operation of and licensing of motor vehicles carrying passengers for hire on city streets is unconstitutional where the public notice and hearing prescribed by statute were not given.

NY Tilton v Utica (1946) 60 NYS2d 249.

A city may not, by mere resolution, regulate the manner and method of operation of a street railway, since a resolution is not a law, and such a regulation can only be effectuated by an ordinance having the effect of a law.

Ill Aurora v Elgin A & S Traction (1906) 128 IllAp 77, rev on other grnds in 227 Ill 485, 81 NE 544.

The operation of motor buses under a certificate from the public utilities commission is not amenable to regulation by a municipality; and an ordinance impinging on their right of operation under such a certificate is invalid.

Ill Chicago Motor Coach v Chicago (1929) 337 Ill 200, 169 NE 22, 66 ALR 834.

An ordinance provision attempting to regulate street railway transfers outside the city limits and within another municipality is invalid, since municipal ordinances cannot have extraterritorial effect.

Ill People v Chicago Ry (1915) 270 Ill 87, 110 NE 386.

Enactment of statutes regulating motor vehicles for hire will withdraw from a city all authority over such vehicles, except such power as is strictly referable to reasonable control of the streets or is granted by the Constitution.

Mich   Detroit W & T Transit v Detroit (1932) 260 Mich 124, 244 NW 424.

§ 31. Jitney Buses

Where an ordinance forbids any person, firm or corporation operating a jitney to receive or discharge passengers on any street on which there are streetcar tracks, a certificate of convenience and necessity to operate motor vehicles as common carriers of passengers from one municipality to another does not authorize one to whom the certificate was issued, or a subsequent purchaser thereof, to receive and discharge passengers for intracity service in violation of the ordinance.

Ind   Poparad v Indianapolis Rys (1942) 111 IndAp 314, 39 NE2d 781.

The common council of a municipality is authorized to enact and enforce an ordinance prohibiting drivers of "jitney buses" to receive and discharge passengers on certain streets under penalty of a fine, under a statute giving municipalities exclusive power, by ordinance, to control and care for their streets and to regulate motor driven commercial vehicles used within the city limits for public hire.

Ind   Frick v Gary (1922) 192 Ind 76, 135 NE 346.

An ordinance prohibiting drivers of "jitney buses" from receiving and discharging passengers on certain streets of the city does not violate the state Constitution in that it excepts streetcars and taxicabs. "Taxicab" has a well known and definite meaning as a vehicle that operates from a fixed station in which drivers receive passengers or receive telephone calls directing them where passengers will be found, and drives to the destination of the passenger over any street available. Taxicabs should not be classified with vehicles that drive back and forth along one street on which traffic is heaviest, picking up passengers from the sidewalks. Thus, the ordinance does not grant special privileges and immunities in violation of the state Constitution.

Ind   Frick v Gary (1922) 192 Ind 76, 135 NE 346.

An ordinance regulating and licensing jitney buses does not violate the constitutional provision against the taking of property without just compensation, since the owner and operator of a jitney bus does not have any natural right to carry on his business on the street, so that no property is taken from him by the ordinance without just compensation.

Ind   Denny v Muncie (1925) 197 Ind 28, 149 NE 639.

Ordinance sections regulating jitney buses, but not prohibiting their operation over part of a street where there are no street railway tracks, even if streetcars are operated on another part of the same street, and not prohibiting buses on streets where there are street railway tracks when the buses are not being operated for hire, do not contravene the equal protection clauses of the federal and state Constitutions. The classification is reasonable, and city may adopt an ordinance regulating jitney buses, though it benefits a street railway company.

Ind Denny v Muncie (1925) 197 Ind 28, 149 NE 639.

An ordinance regulating the operation of jitney buses carrying passengers for a fare of 10 cents or less and requiring the driver of such a bus to have at least 30 days' experience in the operation of an automobile in the city reasonably distinguishes the low fare jitney from other conveyances and validly assumes that a driver should have practical knowledge of the streets and grades of a city such as San Francisco.

Cal Cardinal, In re (1915) 170 Cal 519, 150 P 348.

An ordinance regulating jitney buses does not involve a franchise so as to require its reading before the council at three regular meetings before final passage. A franchise imports a grant of an exclusive privilege to a named person, and the ordinance does not name any certain person or grantee, but permits the grant of a license to any person who is qualified to engage in the jitney business.

Tex Dallas v Gill (1918) 199 SW 1144.

If the enforcement of an ordinance restricting the operation of jitneys to specified streets will drive the jitney operators out of business, or at least render their business less profitable than under the former routing, this will not render the ordinance unreasonable or confiscatory, since the operators have no inherent or natural right to use the streets for their business. Such operation is a privilege granted by the city and one that can reasonably be controlled and limited by it.

Tex San Antonio v Fetzer (1922) 241 SW 1034.

An ordinance undertaking to regulate the jitney business but not containing any rules or conditions, and granting arbitrary power to the mayor and city commissioner to give or withhold a license and control routes of travel, is invalid.

Okla Tulsa v Thomas (1923) 89 Okla 188, 214 P 1070.

A statute giving municipalities power to enact ordinances relative to the city streets empowers the city to enact an ordinance regulating jitneys and prescribing routes for them.

> **SC**   Huffman v Columbia (1928) 146 SC 436, 144 SE 157.

An ordinance regulating the operation of jitney taxicabs, and providing that routes that may be used by nonresident operators shall be designated by the police department, does not discriminate against resident operators, since it prohibits all operators from using excepted streets.

> **Mich**   Red Star Motor Drivers Assn v Detroit (1928) 244 Mich 480, 221 NW 622.

The validity of an ordinance regulating jitney buses is a legal question of whether the regulation is unreasonable as a matter of law, rather than a question of policy resting in the legislative department of the city.

> **Mich**   Red Star Motor Drivers Assn v Detroit (1926) 234 Mich 398, 208 NW 602.

An ordinance prescribing the routes and hours of service of motor vehicles commonly called "jitney buses", and requiring indemnity against injury to persons and property occasioned by their operation, is valid.

> **W Va**   Dickey, Ex parte (1915) 76 W Va 576, 85 SE 781.

An ordinance regulating the operation of jitney buses over the city streets is within the police power of the city and is presumed to be valid, unless no state of facts could exist to warrant its passage.

> **Wash**   Schoenfeld v Seattle (1920) 265 F 726.

An ordinance regulating jitney buses and requiring them to operate on fixed schedules over designated routes, and regulating their stopping places, is not discriminatory for not including other types of vehicles carrying passengers for hire, since the business of jitney buses differs substantially from the operations of other vehicles.

> **Wash**   Allen v Bellingham (1917) 95 Wash 12, 163 P 18.

An ordinance prohibiting a jitney bus from receiving or discharging passengers within 700 feet of any street over which streetcar service is maintained is invalid in view of its manifest purpose to curtail use of jitneys where they will compete with streetcars. It unreasonably deprives the public of the use of jitneys in streets from which they are arbitrarily excluded, without any basis in matters affecting the public safety, health, or welfare.

> **Fla**   Curry v Osborne (1918) 76 Fla 39, 79 So 293, 6 ALR 108.

An ordinance granting an exclusive franchise to operate buses over designated streets to the exclusion of jitney service and taxicabs is valid, since there is a clear distinction between the two types of services, the purpose being to secure for the public an efficient and dependable service to require use of first class equipment, and to prevent ruinous competition.

> **Fla** Jarrell v Orlando Transit Co (1936) 123 Fla 776, 167 So 664.

§32. Definitions

The word "vehicle" in a traffic ordinance generally means any carriage or conveyance used or capable of being used as a means of transportation on land, but does not ordinarily include locomotives, cars, and streetcars, unless the context clearly indicates an intention to include them.

> **Ga** Ga Power v Clark (1943) 69 GaApp 273, 25 SE2d 91.

"Vehicles", as used in municipal traffic ordinances, is a general term having application to all kinds of contrivances fitted with wheels or runners for carrying something, and is broad enought to include streetcars on tracks.

> **Tex** Havins v Dallas Ry & Terminal (1939) 130 SW2d 878.

An ordinance defining "vehicle" as a device in, upon or by which any person or property is or may be transported or drawn on a public street, except devices used exclusively on stationary rails or tracks, excludes streetcars, unless the contrary is clearly stated.

> **Va** Burch v Va Pub Service (1938) 169 Va 460, 194 SE 698.

An ordinance regulating streetcars refers to cars operated on rails along and on the city streets, not to cars or trains operated on a private right-of-way that at intervals merely cross a street. And an electric car operated on a private right-of-way as part of an interurban rapid transit system between two cities is not subject to the ordinance regulating streetcars.

> **Cal** Dolton v Green (1945) 72 CA2d 427, 164 P2d 795.

"Conductor", in an ordinance regulating the operation of streetcars, signifies the chief official on the train who controls its movements and usually collects the fares.

> **Ill** Chicago West Div Ry v Hair (1894) 57 IllAp 587.

"Cabman", in an ordinance licensing and regulating the operation of public passenger vehicles, means a person engaged in business as a proprietor of one or more public passenger vehicles.

> **Ill** Jones v Chicago (1952) 348 IllAp 310, 108 NE2d 802.

"Livery vehicle", in an ordinance licensing and regulating the operation of public passenger vehicles, means a public passenger vehicle for hire, at a charge or fare for each passenger per trip, fixed by agreement in advance.

> **Ill**   Jones v Chicago (1952) 348 IllAp 310, 108 NE2d 802.

The term "street railway cars", in an ordinance regulating their use, is free from ambiguity and expresses a single, definite and sensible meaning. It is not susceptible of any construction or interpretation that will enlarge its meaning to extend to any other type of cars.

> **Ill**   Chicago v South Side Elevated RR (1913) 183 IllAp 181.

§33. Indemnity Bond or Liability Insurance Policy

An ordinance requiring a motor bus company to give a $50,000 bond for each bus was invalid as requiring a prohibitive bond, in view of a statute that provided that a motor bus company should give bond for at least $10,000.

> **Iowa**   Star Transportation v Mason City (1923) 195 Iowa 930, 192 NW 873.

Temporary injunction to prevent street railroad company from operating cars on certain street, as being unauthorized by ordinance, was unwarranted where it was not shown public would suffer if the cars were operated pending the hearing.

> **Mich**   Mich United Ry v Kalamazoo Circuit Judge (1909) 159 Mich 399, 123 NW 1100.

Where an ordinance requires public carriers, including street railway companies, to secure indemnity bonds for the protection of passengers, failure of a damage claimant to introduce the surety bond in evidence precludes recovery on the bond.

> **La**   Gardner v O'Keefe (1924) 155 La 447, 99 So 398.

Where an ordinance requires public carriers to supply an indemnity bond and gives persons damaged due to fault of the carriers a direct right of action against the surety, such provisions of the ordinance are incorporated in the bond agreement and affect the rights and obligations of the surety as well as the principal.

> **La**   Horsthemke v Nat Surety (1921) 151 La 55, 91 So 544.

Where an ordinance requires public carriers to secure indemnity bonds for the protection of passengers, the obligation of the surety company under the ordinance is discharged when an injured party secures judgment and payment from the principal in excess of the bonded indemnity. The bond is not an original indemnity contract, but merely a collateral undertaking. It is merely cumulative security, and gives no greater or additional rights to an injured party.

La Hopkins v Nat Surety (1924) 157 La 1035, 103 So 314.

An ordinance requiring each public passenger motor vehicle to be insured for $50,000 against liability for injury or death to one person, and $100,000 for injury to more than one person in more than one accident, is not invalid as in conflict with the statute provision that a policy of insurance for carriers of passengers shall insure the owner for $15,000.

Ill Jones v Chicago (1952) 348 IllAp 310, 108 NE2d 802.

An ordinance requiring bus operators to pay a license fee and obtain liability insurance from a company authorized to do business in the state is reasonable, as applied to one operating a bus between the city and an out of state city. It does not violate the equal protection clause of the Fourteenth Amendment by discriminating against companies not authorized to do business within the state.

Ind Sprout v South Bend (1928) 277 US 163, 72 LEd 833, 48 SCt 502, 62 ALR 45.

An ordinance providing that an intracity bus company shall carry public liability insurance on each of its buses, but that the insurer shall not be directly liable to a claimant, is valid.

Okla Missouri K & O Transit Lines v Baker (1964) 393 P2d 868.

An ordinance requiring operators of motor vehicles carrying passengers for hire to provide indemnity insurance of $5,000 on each car to cover liability to passengers is invalid as outside the charter provision authorizing the city to regulate the running of automobiles and the persons in charge of them, which refers only to traffic rules.

Tenn State v Bates (1930) 161 Tenn 211, 30 SW2d 248.

§34. Restrictions on Routes and Parking Areas

A city may be given authority to regulate the operation of a mass transit company within its boundaries and a prescribed distance outside. Ordinances establishing routes under such authority are not subject to review by the public utilities commission.

Ore Portland Stages v Portland (1969) 252 Ore 633, 450 P2d 764.

An ordinance prohibiting the operation of buses on a street occupied by lines of a street railway, and on the first two parallel streets on each side of any such street is valid.

> **Okla**   People Transit v Henshaw (1927) 20 F2d 87.

An ordinance establishing bus routes in a city is invalid where it is in conflict with an order of the state public service commission establishing different routes, regardless of a statute providing that common carriers must operate motor vehicles in a city in accordance with municipal regulations.

> **Wis**   Safe Way Motor Coach v Two Rivers (1949) 256 Wis 35, 39 NW2d 847.

A municipality may, by ordinance, prohibit the operation of motor buses in certain areas as a proper regulation of traffic and as a reasonable classification between types of vehicles allowed to operate in congested areas.

> **Fla**   State v Quigg (1927) 94 Fla 1056, 114 So 859.

An ordinance leaving all the streets of the municipality open to motor buses, except those whereon streetcars operate on double tracks, is not unreasonable or arbitrary as a matter of law.

> **Minn**   Schultz v Duluth (1925) 163 Minn 65, 203 NW 449.

A bus storage facility may be maintained in a zone in which any use, "not prohibited in the city," is expressly permitted, there being no zoning ordinance either expressly allowing or expressly prohibiting such a facility.

> **Cal**   People v Binzley (1956) 146 CA2d 889, 303 P2d 903.

An ordinance enacted in connection with an agreement with franchised transit companies, reserving to the city control over the routing of cars on all lines operated by the companies, is an expression of public policy not prohibited by Constitution or law, and though a change in routing may result in a loss to some property owners they have no right to perpetuation of fortuitous advantages enjoyed by them to the disadvantage of the public at large.

> **Mo**   Heidegger v Metro St Ry (1910) 142 MoApp 335, 126 SW 990.

A charter provision authorizing the police commissioner to make traffic regulations does not confer the power to completely deny access to a specific district to buses operated in interstate commerce and prohibit their use of terminal buildings otherwise lawfully constructed on private property. Complete denial to one class of vehicles of access to a district is not justified as an attempt to reduce congestion.

> **NY**   Bus Depot Holding v Valentine (1942) 288 NY 115, 41 NE2d 913.

An ordinance prohibiting the use of certain streets by buses and trucks, except buses whose principle routes are within the city limits and trucks using streets to receive or deliver shipments of goods, is reasonable and not unduly discriminatory or burdensome, where the streets in question contain steep grades and are in a residential district, and other routes are available.

Pa   Commonwealth v Kennedy (1937) 129 PaS 149, 195 A 770.

An ordinance prohibiting the use of a street included within a bus route is not invalidated by the state public service commission's certificate of public convenience authorizing the operation of buses on a designated route, where the certificate does not authorize transportation of local passengers between the municipality in which the street is located and intermediate points and reserves to municipal authorities the right to prescribe what streets may be used by buses.

Pa   Commonwealth v Kennedy (1937) 129 PaS 149, 195 A 770.

An ordinance prohibiting the operation of passenger buses on or across certain streets is not discriminatory merely because it does not regulate buses of another company using other streets and does not prohibit freight trucks from operating on or across the streets prohibited to passenger buses.

Tex   Waid v Fort Worth (1924) 258 SW 1114.

An ordinance prohibiting the operation of motor buses on certain streets is not invalid as in conflict with the statute providing that the fees and certificate registration of motor vehicles shall be in lieu of all other registration and that no "other like burdens" shall be required, since the statute is purely a revenue measure, while the ordinance is regulatory.

Tex   Waid v Fort Worth (1924) 258 SW 1114.

An ordinance prohibiting the operation of motor buses on certain streets on which the bus company had rented terminals is not an unlawful taking of property, where it has no direct relation to the terminal stations, and there is no showing that their market value is decreased by virtue of the ordinance.

Tex   Waid v Fort Worth (1924) 258 SW 1114.

An ordinance restricting the operation of motor buses to specified streets is not in conflict with state laws relating to vehicular traffic.

Tex   San Antonio v Fetzer (1922) 241 SW 1034.

§35. Loading and Unloading Passengers.

Requiring that buses only stop at prescribed bus stops and that in loading and unloading passengers the right front wheel shall be not more than 18 inches from the curb is within the city's right to regulate its streets.

> **Ill**   Watson v Chicago Transit Auth (1973) 12 IllAp3d 684, 299 NE2d 58.
> Perzovsky v Chicago Transit Auth (1974) 23 IllAp3d 896, 320 NE2d 433.

A municipality, under its authority to regulate vehicular traffic, may exercise reasonable discretion in limiting, by ordinance, the number of stops of commercial buses for the purpose of receiving and discharging passengers.

> **W Va**   Eastern Ohio Transport v Wheeling (1934) 115 W Va 293, 175 SE 219.

Where an ordinance regulates bus stops and penalizes violations of its provisions by fine or imprisonment, enforcement is not enjoinable as unconstitutional. No arrests were made.

> **Ga**   Hartwell v Old South Lines (1934) 179 Ga 820, 177 SE 340.

An ordinance requiring pedestrians to keep to the right on sidewalks and keep off roadways, except when crossing at street intersections or getting in and out of streetcars or vehicles, and to cross roadways at right angles is valid as a proper exercise of the power conferred on the city to regulate traffic and the use of its streets.

> **Ill**   Benison v Dembinsky (1926) 241 IllAp 530.

An ordinance requiring that when specified distances exist at a properly located loading zone a bus must stop so as to permit any passenger alighting or boarding to do so directly from the sidewalk or curb line without entering the public highway was clearly meant to provide adequate and unobstructed bus stops, to avoid delays in loading and prevent traffic hazards. Though it may have been passed to protect passengers, such purpose is not clear.

> **Wis**   Burke v Milwaukee & Suburban Transp (1968) 39 Wis2d 682, 159 NW2d 700.

An ordinance imposing a fine on motor buses when they take on or discharge passengers anywhere except at the stations to be established and maintained at their own expense is a valid exercise of the police power over the streets, and is not inconsistent with the power of the state railroad commission to regulate motor buses.

> **Ark**   Pine Bluff v Ark Traveler Bus (1926) 171 Ark 727, 285 SW 375.

An ordinance requiring streetcars to stop for the purpose of discharging and taking on passengers at the near side of any intersecting street before crossing it applies to electric trolley buses, and a person injured while alighting from a trolley bus operated in violation of the statute may look to the transit company for indemnity. The ordinance is a safety measure, as well as one fixing a regular place for buses to stop for the convenience of passengers.

Ark   Capitol Transit v Burris (1955) 224 Ark 755, 276 SW2d 56.

An ordinance prohibiting buses and other motor carriers from loading or unloading passengers on any public thoroughfare being for the prevention of congestion, is valid.

Tenn   Tennessee Coach v Lenoir City (1943) 179 Tenn 453, 167 SW2d 335, 144 ALR 1116.

An ordinance prohibiting any motor bus from stopping to discharge or receive passengers at other than designated points, unless the operator has a franchise from the city, is not discriminatory since all operators in the same class, those without franchises, are treated alike under like conditions.

Tex   Ascarate v Villalobos (1949) 148 Tex 254, 223 SW2d 945.

An ordinance authorizing the city marshal to designate stands at railroad depots and other points in the city where cabs, coaches, omnibuses or other vehicles shall stand while waiting for passengers, property or employment, construed to authorize the marshal to designate more favorable locations for the vehicles of one company than for others, is invalid as an unreasonable and oppressive manner of exercising the power to regulate the business, and as tending to create a monopoly.

Ill   Danville v Noone (1901) 103 IllAp 290.

An ordinance providing for a restricted parking area for buses is valid, since a well located bus terminal is a necessity in any city for the convenience of the traveling public and parking is generally considered a privilege of the public and is incidental to the use of a street for travel.

Ky   Gibson v Hardinsburg (1952) 247 SW2d 331.

The purpose of an ordinance requiring that a bus discharging passengers be stopped within a foot of the curb is to expedite traffic and prevent stopped buses from blocking the roadway. The slipping or falling of a passenger after alighting from a bus is not a risk which the ordinance was designed to protect against.

Ky   Louisville Transit v Jones (1956) 291 SW2d 49.

An ordinance prohibiting interstate buses from stopping except at certain places on a congested street is not discriminatory in permitting a street railway to operate its cars over the same street without limiting its right to stop, since cities have the right to classify buses separately from street railways.

Ohio   Eastern Ohio Transport v Bridgeport (1932) 44 OA 433, 15 Abs 257, 185 NE 891.

An ordinance allowing trucks to stop in front of businesses to load and unload and allowing parking of cars for a reasonable time but preventing interstate buses from stopping on congested street except at certain places is not discriminatory.

Ohio   Eastern Ohio Transport v Bridgeport (1932) 44 OA 433, 15 Abs 257, 185 NE 891.

An ordinance prohibiting interstate buses from stopping except at certain places on a congested street may cause the bus company to lose some passenger trade it would otherwise receive, but it does not take away or destroy any property rights and is not confiscatory.

Ohio   Eastern Ohio Transport v Bridgeport (1932) 44 OA 433, 15 Abs 257, 185 NE 891.

An ordinance denying to a motor bus company for hire the right to use a municipal street for the purpose of a bus stop to let off or take on passengers is within the constitutional grant of municipal power, and is valid.

Ohio   Perrysburg v Ridgway (1923) 108 OS 245, 140 NE 595.

Ordinance providing that motor buses carrying passengers for hire shall load, unload and park only at specified terminals, and prohibiting their use on certain streets of city, is a police regulation of local concern, devoted entirely to regulation of public traffic within municipality, and, since it only incidentally affects interstate commerce, is not constitutionally impermissible under the interstate commerce clause.

NJ   Peoples Rapid Transit v Atlantic City (1929) 105 NJLaw 286, 144 A 630.

Ordinance providing that all motor buses whether engaged in intrastate or interstate commerce shall park, unload and load only at specified terminals, and prohibiting their use of certain streets, is not invalid because exempting hotel and school buses, since the exempted class serve a vital public interest which forms an ample basis for a separate classification.

NJ   Peoples Rapid Transit v Atlantic City (1929) 105 NJLaw 286, 144 A 630.

An ordinance establishing a bus zone and loading area in a street fronting certain property, and prohibiting parking except to load or unload passengers, is invalid where there is no expressed or statutory authority to grant individuals the right to use streets for business purposes.

Iowa   Gates v Bloomfield (1951) 243 Iowa 1, 50 NW2d 578.

An ordinance establishing a bus zone and loading area in a street fronting certain business property and prohibiting parking except to load or unload passengers or freight is invalid as constituting an unlawful obstruction where ingress and egress to and from the building to the sidewalk and street is blocked by buses, passengers and baggage, the property is deprived of parking space and traffic on the street is halted when buses stop in the zone.

Iowa Gates v Bloomfield (1952) 243 Iowa 671, 53 NW2d 279.

An ordinance prohibiting the operation of motor buses on streets where a streetcar is in operation, and further prohibiting the taking on or discharging of passengers within one block of a streetcar line is not unreasonable.

Iowa Star Transport v Mason City (1923) 195 Iowa 930, 192 NW 873.

§36. Frequency of Scheduled Operations

A city council, in enacting an ordinance prescribing the frequency with which a street railway shall run its cars, will be presumed to have exercised reasonable discretion with regard to the facts, which determination will control unless it clearly appears arbitrary and unreasonable.

Mich People v Detroit Citizens St Ry (1898) 116 Mich 132, 74 NW 520.

Ordinance prohibiting a streetcar carrying passengers from digressing from its usual schedule as designated on the vehicle, unless in an emergency, is for the purpose of preventing arbitrary changes in the running of the streetcars whereby passengers may be compelled to abandon a car before it reaches its scheduled destination.

Wis Milwaukee v Becker (1921) 173 Wis 169, 180 NW 838.

An ordinance may validly require the driver or operator of a self-propelled vehicle carrying passengers for a fixed charge to operate on a regular schedule during prescribed hours.

Cal Lee, Matter of (1915) 28 CA 719, 153 P 992.

The court properly issued mandamus ordering a street railway company to operate its cars in both directions at 15 or 20 minute intervals, as required by the ordinance granting the franchise.

Iowa State v Ottumwa Ry & Light (1916) 178 Iowa 961, 160 NW 336.

A municipality has no power to enact legislation inconsistent with the public service commission orders, and may not by ordinance require a street railway to supply more frequent service along a particular line than that established by order of the commission.

NY   Troy v United Traction (1911) 202 NY 333, 95 NE 759.

An ordinance requiring a street railway to provide 5 and 10-minute streetcar service over certain routes during specified rush hours is a reasonable exercise of the city's police power, and does not impair the contract embodied in the franchise ordinance.

Wash   Tacoma v Boutelle (1911) 61 Wash 434, 112 P 661.

An ordinance requiring a street railway company to continuously provide and operate on each line a sufficient number of cars to receive and carry all persons desiring transportation, without admitting into the car more passengers than the carrying capacity thereof, does no more than declare obligations imposed on the company by franchise, and is not invalid as subjecting the company to a forfeiture of its franchise for failure to comply with the ordinance.

Minn   Minneapolis St Ry v Minneapolis (1911) 189 F 445.

§37. Licensing and Compensating Motormen and Drivers

An ordinance requiring a driver's license for operators of vehicles carrying passengers for hire within the city is invalid as an interference with interstate commerce, as applied to vehicles passing through the city while transporting passengers from one state to another.

Wash   Internat Motor Transit v Seattle (1926) 141 Wash 194, 251 P 120.

An ordinance requiring a motor bus chauffeur to obtain a city license to operate within the city does not vest judicial power in executive officers of the city, since the revocation of a license is not a judicial act.

Ohio   Klein v Cincinnati (1929) 33 OA 137, 168 NE 549.

A charter provision that the basic hours for platform men or bus operators shall be 8 hours, to be completed within 10 consecutive hours, that there shall be one day of rest in each week of 7 days, and that all labor performed in excess of 8 hours in any one day, or 6 days in any one week, shall be paid at the rate of time and one half does nothing more than specify the basis of compensation. The number of hours of work to which an employee may be entitled is outside its scope.

Cal   Gowanlock v Turner (1954) 42 C2d 296, 267 P2d 310.

§38. Duties and Responsibilities of Motormen and Drivers.

Where an ordinance regulates the speed of emergency vehicles, and the conduct of other persons, including operators of streetcars, with respect to emergency vehicles, streetcar operators are charged with knowledge of the ordinance and with the duty of exercising the highest degree of care in observing it, and operators of emergency vehicles have the right to rely on the ordinance and on the duties of operators of streetcars in observing it.

> **Mo**   McEntee v Kansas City Pub Service (1942) 159 SW2d 336.

An ordinance, known as the vigilant watch ordinance, which requires motormen on streetcars to keep vigilant watch for all vehicles and persons on foot, and, on the first appearance of danger, to stop the car in the shortest time and space possible, requires a higher degree of care than is required by common law, and is valid under the city's police power, to regulate the operation of its public utilities, and to prohibit acts detrimental to the health, safety and welfare of its people.

> **Mo**   Johnson v St Louis Pub Service (1953) 255 SW2d 815.
>   State v Reynolds (1922) 295 Mo 375, 244 SW 929.

The vigilant watch ordinance, requiring motormen to be prepared to stop their car at the first appearance of danger within the shortest time and space possible, demands a higher degree of care than is required of motormen at common law, which requires greater care at certain places than at others, since the ordinance calls for exercise of such care throughout all parts of the city.

> **Mo**   Rowe v United Rys (1923) 211 MoApp 526, 247 SW 443.

An ordinance requiring vigilant watch on the part of the motorman of a streetcar with respect to persons and vehicles, and that on the first appearance of danger he shall stop the car in the shortest time and space possible, requires only that he exercise ordinary care under the circumstances.

> **Mo**   Vogt v United Rys (1920) 226 SW 75.

A motorman's duty, under an ordinance requiring a motorman in charge of a streetcar to keep a vigilant watch for all vehicles and persons on foot, and on the first appearance of danger to a person or vehicle to stop the car in the shortest time and space possible, is not conditioned on negligence of the person in danger, but on the appearance of danger, though he is not required to stop the car every time he sees a person in or near the track ahead of the car.

> **Mo**   Blyston-Spencer v United Ry (1911) 152 MoApp 118, 132 SW 1175.

An ordinance requiring streetcar motormen to keep a vigilant watch for all vehicles and persons on foot, and at the first appearance of danger to stop the car in the shortest possible time, is a reasonable exercise of the city's power to control the streets.

> **Tex**   Dallas Ry & Terminal v Bankston (1930) 33 SW2d 500.

An ordinance requiring streetcar motormen to keep a vigilant watch for persons and other vehicles, and at the appearance of any possible dangerous situation to stop the car "in the shortest time and space possible", is not invalid as too indefinite to furnish a rule of civil conduct.

> **Tex**   Dallas Ry & Terminal v Bankston (1932) 51 SW2d 304.

An ordinance requiring the driver of a vehicle to look out for and give the right-of-way to vehicles approaching simultaneously from the right at street intersections does not negate the legal duty of a streetcar motorman to keep a proper lookout for persons or vehicles approaching from his left.

> **Tex**   El Paso Elec Ry v Benjamin (1918) 202 SW 996.

An ordinance providing that a bell or gong shall be sounded at least 100 feet from all street intersections is not pertinent in the case of a collision that occurred before the streetcar reached the intersection.

> **Ohio**   Youngstown Municipal Ry v Chismar (1935) 54 OA 481, 20 Abs 417, 8 Op 256, 8 NE2d 156.

An ordinance providing that a streetcar must approach a curve with the greatest care and shall be under the complete control of the person running the same does not require the operator to have the car under such control that it can be stopped instantly.

> **Ohio**   Youngstown Municipal Ry v Chismar (1935) 54 OA 481, 20 Abs 417, 8 Op 256, 8 NE2d 156.

An ordinance providing that on the first appearance of danger to vehicles moving toward a streetcar the latter shall be stopped within the shortest time and shortest distance possible is too vague and indefinite to constitute a rule of conduct for the operation of streetcars.

> **Ohio**   Youngstown Municipal Ry v Chismar (1935) 54 OA 481, 20 Abs 417, 8 Op 256, 8 NE2d 156.

An ordinance requiring a motorman or other person having charge of a streetcar to exercise all possible care and vigilance on approaching any other car that has stopped for the purpose of receiving or letting off passengers, and requiring that any car approaching another car that has stopped for any purpose, or approaching a curb, shall do so with the greatest care, and be under complete control of the person operating the same, is reasonable and valid.

> **Ohio**   Leis v Cleveland Ry (1920) 101 OS 162, 128 NE 73.

An ordinance giving a streetcar the right-of-way at an intersection does not relieve the motorman of the imperative duty, in the operation of the car, to exercise ordinary care to avoid injuring a pedestrian.

Ky   Louisville Ry v Breeden (1934) 257 Ky 95, 77 SW2d 368.

An ordinance requiring a street railway to provide stools for the drivers or motormen in control of street railway cars, being conducive to the comfort and safety of the citizens is not unreasonable.

Ky   Silva v Newport (1912) 150 Ky 781, 150 SW 1024.

Ordinances relating to the speed of cars within a city's corporate limits and at street crossings, the right-of-way of fire departments over its streets, and the duty of persons in charge of streetcars to stop them and remain stationary on the approach of any fire apparatus are clearly within the police power as conferred by state statute, and such power is a continuing power, and one of which the city cannot divest itself by contract or otherwise.

Ind   Union Traction of Ind v Muncie (1921) 80 IndAp 260, 133 NE 160.

The point at which one street merges with another is the same as a "street crossing", within the terms of an ordinance requiring all streetcars to sound a bell or gong when approaching any street crossing or other regular crossing.

Ark   Pankey v Little Rock RR & Elec (1915) 117 Ark 337, 174 SW 1170.

Ordinance requiring bus driver to wear in a prominent position on his clothing a number, the same as that issued for his motor bus, is a reasonable traffic regulation in exercise of police power.

NJ   Atlantic City v Freretti (1904) 70 NJLaw 489, 57 A 259.

§39. Two-Man Operation

Though a city is empowered by its charter to enact an ordinance requiring two-man operation of streetcars, such an ordinance will be superseded by an order of the state railroad commission providing for one-man streetcars.

Wis   Milwaukee v RR Comm (1924) 182 Wis 498, 196 NW 853.

An ordinance that requires two trainmen on every streetcar is void in view of the fact that the public utilities commission has, under authority of statute, exclusive jurisdiction of such matters.

Conn   Connecticut Co v New Haven (1925) 103 Conn 197, 130 A 169.

An ordinance requiring every street railway car to be operated by both a motorman and a conductor is not unconstitutional, though competing automotive gas driven buses are not subject to the same regulation.

> **Cal**   San Francisco v Market St Ry (1938) 98 F2d 628.

An ordinance requiring streetcars to have a motorman and conductor while passengers are aboard is void, where the city voted not to retain powers of control over public utilities, and such power is thus vested in the state.

> **Cal**   Key System Transit v Oakland (1932) 124 CA 733, 13 P2d 979.

In the exercise of its police power a municipality has the absolute right to regulate by ordinance whether streetcars shall be operated by one or two men.

> **Iowa**   Des Moines City Ry v Amalgamated Assn (1927) 204 Iowa 1195, 213 NW 264.

§ 40. Passenger Capacity

A municipality may in the exercise of its police regulations limit the number of passengers on commercial buses to their seating capacity.

> **W Va**   Eastern Ohio Transport v Wheeling (1934) 115 W Va 293, 175 SE 219.

An ordinance limiting the number of passengers on each streetcar to 75 is a valid exercise of the power of the municipality to regulate the service of a company having a franchise to operate a streetcar system. The company cannot restrain the enforcement of the ordinance on the ground that obedience to it will necessitate an enormous expense where the claim that such expense will be incurred results from an erroneous construction of the ordinance.

> **Minn**   Minneapolis St Ry v Minneapolis (1911) 189 F 445.

An ordinance prohibiting a street railway from admitting passengers on its cars in excess of the carrying capacity of the car as defined related only to the city, prohibits the company only while in the city from taking passengers after the prescribed number has been reached, and is not invalid insofar as it affects interurban business, so that the railway may come into the city carrying more passengers than the maximum.

> **Minn**   Minneapolis St Ry v Minneapolis (1911) 189 F 445.

A proviso, in an ordinance fixing the maximum number of streetcar passengers and imposing a penalty on the streetcar company for violation, that the company shall not be liable to the penalty in any case wherein another car on the same line proceeding on the same track and in the same direction and containing fewer passengers than the carrying capacity shall at the time be within 300 feet of the point where the excess passenger is admitted, does not impose any obligation on the company, and does not require it to run its cars 300 feet apart, but merely relieves it from the obligation imposed on it in another part of the ordinance; and the proviso is not violative of the federal Constitution.

> **Minn** Minneapolis St Ry v Minneapolis (1911) 189 F 445.

An ordinance regulating the number of passengers in proportion to the number of seats provided and the numbers of cars a street railway company is required to provide for public transportation is not unreasonable, arbitrary or impracticable, since it merely requires a sufficient number of cars to meet the transportation requirements of the city.

> **Ky** South Covington & C St Ry v Covington (1912) 146 Ky 592, 143 SW 28.

Where an ordinance in one city making it unlawful for a street railway company to permit more than a certain proportion of passengers to be transported over and above the number of seats would require more than half again the present numbers of cars, and where the same kind of legislation but of a different degree could be enacted by a city in a neighboring state in which such street railway runs, interstate commerce could be impeded by the conflicting and varying regulations and the ordinance is invalid.

> **Ky** South Covington & C St Ry v Covington (1914) 235 US 537, 59 LEd 350, 35 SCt 158.

Though a city enacts an ordinance limiting the number of passengers to be carried by a street railway in its cars, an indictment that charges that the railway company permitted a large and unreasonable number of people to assemble and gather on its car is insufficient, because there is no charge in the indictment that the public place of assemblage was unhealthy, unsafe or unsanitary, or that anything the company did was injurious to good morals or detrimental to the comfort or convenience of the public.

> **Ky** Commonwealth v South Covington & C St Ry (1918) 181 Ky 459, 205 SW 581.

§41. Refusal to Carry Certain Passengers; Segregated Seating

An ordinance requiring driver of motor bus, under all circumstances, to accept person tendering himself as a passenger, is not void in its entirety, but only so far as it operates to penalize a driver whose refusal to accept a person as a passenger, is justified by the circumstances and conditions under which the refusal occurs.

> **NJ** Atlantic City v Brown (1905) 72 NJLaw 207, 62 A 428.

A franchised transit company's rules requiring racially segregated seating on its buses, under authority of an ordinance granting it the right to do so and imposing criminal sanctions for violating such rules, are state acts and violative of a passenger's constitutional rights.

    Ala   Boman v Birmingham Transit (1960) 280 F2d 531.

An Administrative Code provision prohibiting discrimination in the discharge of carriers' public transportation obligations does not restrict a carrier in the exercise of its private proprietary rights that are consonant with its public obligations, and a bus company may exclude third persons from entering its buses to conduct business without its license.

    NY   Third Ave Transit Corp, In re (1956) 233 F2d 310.

ANNOTATION

Transportation, race discrimination 15 LEd2d 990, 21 LEd2d 915.

§42. Riding on Steps

There is a clear distinction between the conduct of one who over a period of time deliberately stands or "rides" on the steps of a moving streetcar in violation of an ordinance and the conduct of one who merely undertakes after a stop signal to use the steps in the course of a continuous route from his seat to the station platform.

    Cal   Connard v Pac Elec Ry (1939) 14 C2d 375, 94 P2d 567.

An ordinance providing that "no person shall ride upon any vehicle or railway except within the body thereof" is free from ambiguity and should be given effect according to its terms.

    Okla   Smith v Langston (1951) 204 Okla 444, 230 P2d 736.

An ordinance forbidding passengers to ride on the platforms of streetcars unless they are equipped as provided in an ordinance and requiring the company to clean and ventilate its cars at stated times comes within the class of regulations that local authorities may enact to safeguard the traveling public and promote their comfort and convenience. Where it only incidentally affects the interstate business it is valid.

    Ky   South Covington & C St Ry v Covington (1914) 235 US 537, 59 LEd 350, 35 SCt 158.

§43. Smoking

An ordinance prohibiting smoking in streetcars is a valid exercise of the police power delegated to the city under its charter and is not vague, indefinite or insufficient in its terms when it reasonably defines the acts prohibited. Prominent display of cards in a streetcar is a proper method of notifying passengers that smoking is prohibited in that particular car.

> **La** State v Heidenhain (1890) 42 LaAnn 483, 7 So 621.

While a city may prohibit smoking in certain public places, such as streetcars, theaters, and the like, where a large number of persons are crowded together in a small space, it may not prohibit smoking on the open streets and in the parks, where open air and space would counteract any harmful results.

> **Ill** Zion v Behrens (1914) 262 Ill 510, 104 NE 836.

The courts will not, on a claim of injury to one's health that is conjectural and speculative, enjoin a street railway from permitting smoking on streetcars in violation of an ordinance penalizing such smoking as a misdemeanor. Where the violation is a crime its commission will not be enjoined unless there is also some interference, actual or threatened, with property or rights of a pecuniary nature.

> **NY** Mellen v Brooklyn Heights RR (1914) 87 Misc 65, 150 NYS 222.

§44. Temperature on Vehicles

Where it appears impossible in the operation of streetcars to keep them uniformly up to a specified temperature owing to the opening and closing of doors and other interferences, an ordinance regulating the temperature of streetcars and providing that they shall not be permitted to fall below a designated temperature is invalid.

> **Ky** South Covington & C St Ry v Covington (1914) 235 US 537,
> 59 LEd 350, 35 SCt 158.

Since the term "street railway cars" has a definite meaning and is free of ambiguity, an ordinance requiring the maintenance of a minimum 50-degree Fahrenheit temperature on street railway cars will not be construed to include cars of an elevated railroad, despite another provision in the ordinance that such temperature shall be maintained on street railway cars operating "either on elevated, surface or subway lines".

> **Ill** Chicago v South Side Elevated RR (1913) 183 IllAp 181.

An ordinance requiring a street railroad company to provide a sufficient number of streetcars to prevent overcrowding, and requiring temperatures in the cars to be maintained at a minimum of 50 degrees Fahrenheit, is valid as a reasonable exercise of the police power in the interest of public health and welfare.

> Ill   Chicago v Chicago City Ry (1906) 222 Ill 560, 78 NE 890.

§45. Speed

An ordinance establishing a maximum speed for streetcars is not authority for such cars to be operated in all circumstances to the limit of the speed prescribed.

> Mo   Brandt v United Rys (1910) 153 MoApp 16, 132 SW 39.

An ordinance limiting the speed of streetcars to 12 miles per hour is not repealed by a later ordinance requiring that all cars at all times be run at a "reasonable rate" of speed under the particular circumstances. The two ordinances are entirely in harmony.

> Mo   Duffy v Kansas City Rys (1920) 217 SW 883.

An ordinance limiting the speed of streetcars to 15 miles per hour in a congested district and not more than 25 miles per hour in a noncongested district is not repealed by, and is not in irreconcilable conflict with, an ordinance subsequently enacted prohibiting streetcars from being operated at a greater speed than is reasonable in any residence or business district.

> Mo   Petty v Kansas City Pub Service (1946) 355 Mo 824, 198 SW2d 684.

An ordinance prohibiting streetcars from being run "at a greater average speed between terminals than 12 miles per hour" is construed to mean what it says, and not as limiting streetcars to a maximum speed of 12 miles per hour.

> Mo   Norton v East St Louis Ry (1918) 199 MoApp 550, 203 SW 1006.

Although a city has power to regulate the speed of streetcars and to enact other appropriate regulations with respect to their operation, it is not clothed with power to determine what manner or nature of their operations shall constitute negligence on which recovery for damages might be predicated.

> Ill   Rockford City Ry v Blake (1898) 173 Ill 354, 50 NE 1070.

A limitation by ordinance of the rate of speed at which streetcars may be operated does not constitute permission to run them up to the speed limit, regardless of circumstances and conditions.

> Ill   Quincy Horse Ry v Gnuse (1889) 38 IllAp 212, rev on other grnds (1891) 137 Ill 264, 27 NE 190.

Ordinances regulating the speed of trains and streetcars within city limits are proper police regulations.

> **Cal** Wright v Los Angeles Ry (1939) 14 C2d 168, 93 P2d 135.

Neither "railroad train" nor "interurban train" is synonymous with streetcar, and an ordinance regulating the speed of streetcars is not applicable to an interurban train.

> **Cal** Lund v Pac Elec Ry (1944) 25 C2d 287, 153 P2d 705.

An ordinance may, under the constitutional power given to cities to approve any street railroad built within the city, regulate and limit the speed that an interurban railroad may travel in the city streets.

> **Utah** Shortino v Salt Lake & U R Co (1918) 52 Utah 476, 174 P 860.

An ordinance making it unlawful for any locomotive railroad car or other vehicle to be propelled or drawn on such part of any railroad as shall be within the limits of the city at a rate faster than 6 miles per hour has no application to a street railroad operated in the city.

> **Del** Licznerski v Wilmington City Ry (1904) 21 Del 201, 62 A 1057.

Where the word "vehicle", as used in an ordinance prohibiting the driving of any vehicle at a speed greater than 25 miles per hour, does not include streetcar, the ordinance does not limit streetcars to such speed outside the municipality's inner fire limits.

> **Ga** Ga Power v Clark (1943) 69 GaApp 273, 25 SE2d 91.

An ordinance providing that no person shall ride or drive on any boulevard at a rate faster than 10 miles per hour is not applicable to streetcars that cross boulevards and parkways.

> **Ind** Krause v Indianapolis Traction & Terminal (1919) 76 IndAp 349, 124 NE 401.

An ordinance providing "that no automobile, locomobile or horseless vehicle propelled by electricity, gasoline, or steam shall be propelled along or over any public street at a speed exceeding a given limit" does not apply to streetcars, though they are amenable to the description of vehicles in the ordinance, because their mode of operation is entirely different than that of the other vehicles.

> **Ark** Pankey v Little Rock RR & Elec (1915) 117 Ark 337, 174 SW 1170.

§46. Overtaking and Passing Transit Vehicles

An ordinance requiring an automobile traveling behind a streetcar to stop 10 feet in the rear of the car when it stops to let off or take on passengers is not inconsistent with state law requiring the driver of an automobile in passing a streetcar to operate the vehicle with due care and caution and bring it to a full stop if reasonably necessary for the safety of passengers boarding or alighting.

    Cal Mann v Scott (1919) 180 Cal 550, 182 P 281.

A streetcar is not a "vehicle", within the meaning of a statute providing that a motor vehicle shall pass to the left of an overtaken vehicle so as to invalidate an ordinance requiring that streetcars be passed on the right, since the statute was intended to apply only to country roads or streets where there are no streetcars, and it would be unreasonable to construe "vehicles" to include streetcars running on rails.

    Ill Chicago v Keogh (1920) 291 Ill 188, 125 NE 881.

An ordinance prohibiting overtaking motor vehicles from passing or approaching within 8 feet of a streetcar that has stopped to receive or discharge passengers applies only to a passing vehicle which is proceeding in the same direction. The word "overtake" is not synonymous with "to catch up with in the course of motion", so as to include vehicles moving in the opposite direction.

    NY Burgujian v Ames Transfer (1932) 234 AD 303, 255 NYS 172.

An ordinance that prohibits overtaking motor vehicles from passing or approaching within 8 feet of a streetcar that has stopped to receive or discharge passengers extends to passing situations where the automobile is abreast of the rear exit, and even where it is abreast of the front platform of the streetcar.

    NY People v Merkert (1921) 198 AD 246, 190 NYS 474.

A statute requiring a vehicle overtaking a streetcar that is stopped to discharge or receive passengers to stop at least 10 feet to the rear of the streetcar repeals an ordinance providing that streetcars driven in the same direction should not approach each other nearer than a distance of 200 feet.

    Minn LeVasseur v Minneapolis St Ry (1946) 221 Minn 205, 21 NW2d 522.

An ordinance authorizing the director of public safety to establish safety zones along any streetcar line at any regularly designated streetcar stop, and requiring all vehicles, excepting streetcars, to pass only to the right of such zones, unless a police officer should direct otherwise, is not in conflict with Constitution or statutes.

    Ohio Cleveland v Gustafson (1932) 124 OS 607, 11 Abs 416, 180 NE 59.

An ordinance regulating the speed of one streetcar passing another at passenger pick-up point may be antiquated and an anachronism; it may be harsh, inconvenient, or inappropriate to the times; and it may be indefinite, uncertain and unintelligible; but unless it be shown to be unconstitutional or so defective as to be incomprehensible or wholly unintelligible it may not be set aside by the courts.

Mo   Marczuk v St Louis Pub Service (1946) 355 Mo 536, 196 SW2d 1000.

§47. Operation of Vehicles at Intersections

An ordinance regulating the operation of motor vehicles and streetcars at intersections is invalid, where it imposes a different penalty than does the statute covering the same subject.

Tex   El Paso Elec v Collins (1928) 10 SW2d 397.

An ordinance regulating the operation of streetcars and other vehicles at intersections, though invalid to the extent that it controls the operation of motor vehicles, because it conflicts with a statute providing a different penalty, is nevertheless valid with respect to the requirement that where vehicles and streetcars approach the intersection on different streets at the same time the one approaching from the right shall have the right-of-way.

Tex   El Paso Elec v Collins (1930) 23 SW2d 295.

An ordinance giving a streetcar that has started to cross an intersection the right-of-way over another vehicle in or approaching the intersection is a reasonable traffic regulation and clearly within the purview of municipal power.

Tex   Havins v Dallas Ry & Terminal (1939) 130 SW2d 878.

Where a statute governing the right-of-way at intersections by its terms does not apply to vehicles that travel exclusively on rails, a right-of-way ordinance that applies to all vehicles is controlling.

Ky   Louisville Ry v Everett (1923) 199 Ky 33, 250 SW 103.

An ordinance requiring every operator of a vehicle, streetcar or other conveyance to stop at stop signs on designated through streets is valid as to operators of interurban cars.

Utah   Thorpe v Bamberger RR (1944) 107 Utah 265, 153 P2d 541.

An ordinance requiring streetcars to stop at every intersection, when signaled, is not void as unreasonable.

Mich   People v Detroit United Ry (1919) 207 Mich 143, 173 NW 396.

An ordinance requiring that a streetcar be brought to a full stop before arriving at and within 10 feet of a streetcar intersection is invalid, as being a regulatory measure embraced within the power conferred by statute on the state commerce commission.

> Ill   Ewald v Chicago Ry (1927) 247 IllAp 77.

§48. Safety Devices

An ordinance requiring an electric railway to stretch and maintain suitable guard wires along and above its electric cables in the streets is a reasonable exercise of the city's power to regulate the use of its streets.

> Ill   Conrad v Springfield Consolidated Ry (1908) 145 IllAp 564.

§49. Fenders

Where an ordinance requires a street railway to use the "most approved life guard", the language contemplates a type of fender so practical and efficient in avoiding injury as to meet the greatest measure of general approval of those concerned in streetcar operation, and contemplates types changing with future inventions.

> Ind   Waters v Indianapolis Traction & Terminal (1916) 185 Ind 526, 113 NE 289.

A provision in an ordinance granting a license to operate a street railway, that the cars shall be of such style and class as are used on the best approved street railway in the United States, and that gates and guards shall be placed on the front platform, cannot be construed to require fenders.

> Ill   Englund v Miss Valley Traction (1908) 139 IllAp 572.

An ordinance requiring that street railway cars be equipped with fenders is a valid exercise of the police power in the interest of public safety, but a requirement that such fenders be placed not more than two inches above the ground is void as impracticable and unreasonable, and as resulting in interference with operation of the cars.

> Ill   Chicago & Joliet Elec Ry v Freeman (1906) 125 IllAp 318.

Where the power to regulate the use of streets was transferred by statute to the board of directors of the street and sewer commission, the city council had no power to pass an ordinance regulating safety appliances on street cars.

> Del   Bullock v Wilmington City Ry (1905) 21 Del 209, 64 A 242.

Where a statute empowers the mayor and common council, for safety purposes, to prescribe the type of fenders to be used on streetcars, an ordinance enacted thereunder is ultra vires to the extent that it unreasonably postpones the requirement of compliance with its terms.

Ore Rudolph v Portland Ry Light & Power (1914) 72 Ore 560, 144 P 93.

§50. Brakes

The discretion of a city council in enacting an ordinance requiring street railways to equip their cars with certain brakes for the greater safety of the public will not be interfered with if the regulation can fairly be said to tend toward a better and safer condition.

Mich People v Detroit United Ry (1903) 134 Mich 682, 97 NW 36.

An ordinance requiring a street railway to equip its cars with air or electric brakes is not invalid for requiring a large outlay of money on the part of the company.

Mich People v Detroit United Ry (1903) 134 Mich 682, 97 NW 36.

§51. Weight of Vehicles

An ordinance prohibiting the operation of street railway interurban and suburban cars in excess of a specified weight and with other than specified wheels exceeds the jurisdiction of the city, where the weight and character of wheels is a matter of operation solely within the jurisdiction of the state public service commission. The absence of an emergency or critical accident rate attributable to weight and wheels, thereby requiring exclusion of the cars from the city streets, precludes justifying the ordinance as an exercise of the police power for public safety.

NY NY State Rys v Rochester (1922) 119 Misc 128, 195 NYS 783.

§52. Color of Vehicles

An ordinance requiring the outside body of each livery vehicle to be of a uniform black, blue or blue-black color is not invalid as bearing no relation to the public welfare, but is a reasonable regulation of a class of motor vehicles known as liveries which may not solicit passengers for hire on the public ways, and is designed to keep the livery vehicle within its proper sphere by making it more difficult to solicit passengers while cruising the public streets.

Ill Jones v Chicago (1952) 348 IllAp 310, 108 NE2d 802.

§53. Advertising on Transit Facilities

A ban on advertising on benches at bus stops is constitutional. The owner of the benches, which has a year to year license, may be denied renewal without violating free speech and the intention behind the ordinance, claimed to be to secure federally paid benches, is immaterial to the constitutionality of the ordinance. Bus benches are a proper classification without requiring that all outdoor advertising be included.

> **Cal**   Coast—United Adv v Long Beach (1975) 51 CA3d 766, 124 CaR 487.

An ordinance prohibiting the installation or maintenance of advertising structures, including bus benches, on streets or highways within the county that are constructed with federal aid funds, is a valid regulation enforceable by removal of benches that violate the ordinance.

> **Fla**   Bus Benches v Homer (1966) 189 So2d 524.

An ordinance granting an exclusive permit for the placing of bus benches bearing advertisements is not void for uncertainty, and need not conform with the statutory requirements for sale of park or recreational facilities, where it provides that the permittee may place benches in "localities which serve the public convenience and necessity," because these "localities" can be interpreted only as sidewalk areas, and not public park property.

> **Ark**   Hood v Pine Bluff (1964) 238 Ark 826, 385 SW2d 1.

An ordinance granting a franchise to a stagecoach company to use the city streets confers no right to a use for advertising purposes or to carry or maintain exterior advertisements on stages. Display of advertisements is not a necessary or essential incident of the business, and in no way relates to transportation of passengers for hire.

> **NY**   Fifth Ave Coach v New York City (1909) 194 NY 19, 86 NE 824.

§54. Claims against Transit System

A charter provision directing the comptroller to settle and adjust all claims involving the city applies to settlements and adjustments or ordinary routine claims, but does not extend to claims arising under bus franchises.

> **NY**   Greenberg v New York City (1934) 152 Misc 488, 274 NYS 4.

D. FARES AND TRANSFERS

§55. Authority to Regulate

A resolution making it a punishable offense to refuse to pay the established bus transfer fare may be passed as an emergency ordinance, and the regulations authorizing adoption on one reading are effective.

DC Hobson v DC (1973) 304 A2d 637.

While the proof must be clear that the legislature has given municipalities authority to fix rates for a streetcar company by ordinance, such authority does not have to be proved by an express legislative enactment.

Iowa Ottumwa Ry & Light v Ottumwa (1919) 173 NW 270.

Under a street railway franchise ordinance, a reservation by the city of the right to make further rules or regulations as the council may deem proper, does not include the rights of the city to reduce rates of fares agreed on in the franchise ordinance.

Mich Detroit v Detroit Citizens' St Ry (1901) 184 US 368, 46 LEd 592, 22 SCt 410.

Where statutory authority exists, a city may by ordinance grant or amend a street railway franchise and provide increases and adjustments in fares charged for public transportation, and such an ordinance is not invalid for want of consideration if the public derives a benefit and the increase is granted to prevent operation at a loss.

La Long v Shreveport (1921) 151 La 423, 91 So 825.

Where, in an ordinance granting a franchise to a street railway, the city and the company agreed to be bound by fares for a specified period, and such are not agreed on as a maximum for any other part of the franchise term, the right of the company thereafter to charge fares producing a reasonable rate of return is not contracted away, nor is the city's power and duty thereafter to prescribe fares that are just and reasonable contracted away.

Ky Paducah v Paducah Ry (1923) 261 US 267, 67 LEd 647, 43 SCt 335.

A city commission has the primary duty to fix bus fares and the board of supervisors is concerned with fares only when it rejects the commission's proposals, where the city charter requires fares to be sufficient to pay, at least for the succeeding fiscal year, all operational expenses plus interest and sinking fund requirements for bonds and provides that the commission might propose a fair schedule that will not produce such revenue if the board approves, but that the board shall then provide by tax levy for amounts needed to meet the deficit.

Cal Hurst v San Francisco (1949) 33 C2d 298, 201 P2d 805.

An ordinance granting a bus company a franchise for bus service for fares not exceeding 10 cents over designated streets, to the exclusion of taxicabs and other carriers charging less than 15 cents, is not invalid for fixing rates for taxi and bus service, inasmuch as the ordinance has reference to the minimum charges that may be imposed, and this is within the regulatory power of the city.

> **Fla**   Jarrell v Orlando Transit Co (1936) 123 Fla 776, 167 So 664.

Where an ordinance granting a franchise to a city railroad company is accepted by the company, and the ordinance reserves the right to the city council after five years to fix just and reasonable rates provided they shall not be reduced below 5 cents per passenger on any continuous line; and provides for the use of animal or pneumatic power on the company's lines but permits it to connect with other lines using power "similar to that authorized to be used on street railways by the city council," subject to the restriction that it should not allow locomotive or ordinary railroad cars to be run over its tracks unless with the consent of the council, a change, after a number of years, to electricity, with the consent of the council, does not terminate the contract made by the ordinance so as to give the city the right to reduce fares below 5 cents.

> **Minn**   Minneapolis St Ry v Minneapolis (1907) 155 F 989.

The right of future control, reserved to a municipality in a street railway franchise, with respect to the "construction, maintenance, and operation" of the lines, does not include the power to reduce fares below the rate prescribed in an existing contract between the municipality and the company, but has reference only to the manner of carrying on the business of the road, the laying of its tracks, the use of streets, the keeping of equipment, the safety of passengers and public, and similar matters not involved in the right to charge fares.

> **Minn**   Minneapolis v Minneapolis St Ry (1910) 215 US 417, 54 LEd 259, 30 SCt 118.

A statute authorizing a city to regulate and prescribe the compensation of cabmen, omnibus drivers and "all others pursuing a like occupation" authorizes the city to enact an ordinance limiting the fares to be charged by a street railway, since the phrase, "others pursuing a like occupation", includes a street railway company.

> **Ill**   Chicago Union Traction v Chicago (1902) 199 Ill 484, 65 NE 451.

A city, under its delegated power to license, tax and regulate hackmen, draymen, omnibus drivers and others pursuing like occupations, and to prescribe their compensation, may enact an ordinance prescribing the fares to be charged by street railways.

> **Ill**   Dean v Chicago Gen Ry (1896) 64 IllApp 165.

A street railway rate ordinance that is invalid at the time of its adoption, by reason of its failure to provide a fair and adequate return, may later become valid, when by reason of a change in conditions it commences to yield a fair return.

> **Tex** Galveston Elec v Galveston (1922) 258 US 388, 66 LEd 678, 42 SCt 351.

Under the constitutional provision that no irrevocable or uncontrollable grant of special privilege or immunity shall be made, but that all privileges granted by the legislature, or created under its authority, shall be subject to its control, a city does not have power to enact an ordinance establishing an irrevocable contract fixing the fares in a franchise to a street railroad company. Such a provision is merely regulatory, and is subject to change by the city.

> **Tex** San Antonio Pub Service v San Antonio (1919) 257 F 467.

It is beyond the power of a home rule city to enact an ordinance providing that if utility rates fixed by the city return more than a reasonable profit reparation shall be made to the city, either in its proprietary capacity or in its capacity as trustee.

> **Tex** El Paso v El Paso City Lines (1949) 227 SW2d 278.

An ordinance that defines a common carrier as a "vehicle" and requires the vehicle (not the owner or operator) to file its tariff, schedule, etc. with the chief of police is wholly devoid of force or effect, since no inanimate object can perform an act and no legislative mandate can alter or change this positive law of physics.

> **Haw** Territory v Merseberg (1939) 35 Haw 248.

§56. Conflict with State Regulation

A county ordinance approving an omnibus franchise may not require the holder to submit applications for rate increases for the county's approval. Regulation of rates is under the exclusive control of the state public utilities commission.

> **NY** Beeline v Nickerson (1969) 60 Misc2d 931, 303 NYS2d 950.

A charter provision conferring power on the city and its aldermen to regulate issuance and use of street railway transfer tickets is void, since by statute the power to supervise rates, fares, or charges of a street railway corporation rests exclusively with the state public service commission.

> **Mo** Packman, Ex parte (1927) 317 Mo 732, 296 SW 366.

An authorization by the state public service commission for an increase in fares charged by a city railroad company is valid, though a city ordinance authorizes a lesser fare. The constitutional inhibition against any legislative grant of the right to construct and operate a street railroad within a city without the consent of local authorities does not authorize the city to fix rates.

Mo   St Louis v Pub Service Comm (1918) 276 Mo 509, 207 SW 799.

An ordinance granting a franchise to a city railway company, and establishing rates, does not prohibit the state public service commission from revising said rates in the exercise of delegated authority from the legislature.

Mo   Kansas City v Pub Service Comm (1919) 276 Mo 539, 210 SW 381.

Rate regulation of public service corporations is a governmental power vested in the state in its sovereign capacity, and any ordinance setting rates differently than set by a state commission vested by the legislature with such power is void. Thus, an ordinance setting a street railway rate lower than that set by the public utility commission is invalid.

Ore   Portland Ry Light & Power v Portland (1914) 210 F 667.

An ordinance fixing the rates that may be charged by a street railway within the city is superseded by a subsequent higher rate, fixed by the state public service commission.

Ore   Portland v Pub Service Comm (1918) 89 Ore 325, 173 P 1178.

Any contract ordinance passed by a city with statutory authority fixing, by agreement, streetcar fares, as an incident to the granting of a franchise to a street railroad, is subject to legislative control.

Fla   State v Burr (1920) 79 Fla 290, 84 So 61.

A street railroad franchise ordinance, which provides that the city does not thereby waive or abandon the right to make all needful police regulations concerning the operation and maintenance of the railroad, does not reserve to the city the right to prescribe rules and fares to be observed by the railroad company.

Okla   Oklahoma Ry v Powell (1912) 33 Okla 737, 127 P 1080.

A provision fixing passenger fares, in an ordinance granting a franchise to a street railway company is ineffective where a different rate of fare is established by the state acting through the corporation commission.

Okla   Swain v Okla Ry (1934) 168 Okla 133, 32 P2d 51.

Charter authority for a city to fix rates for the conveyance of passengers by street railway is insufficient to empower the city by contract to establish rates.

Cal   RR Comm of Cal v Los Angeles Ry (1929) 280 US 145, 74 LEd 234, 50 SCt 71.

An ordinance authorizing the use of city streets for a street railroad and purporting to fix train fares both inside and outside the city is void for want of power to enact it.

Cal South Pasadena v Terminal Ry (1895) 109 Cal 315, 41 P 1093.

A franchise ordinance fixing the rates of a street railway operating in the city is invalid as in conflict with the statute establishing a public service commission with power to fix the rates of common carriers, since a municipality cannot, by a franchise in the nature of a contract, foreclose the exercise of the police power of the state unless clearly authorized to do so by the legislature.

Wash Puget Sound Traction Light & Power v Reynolds (1916) 244 US 574, 61 LEd 1325, 37 SCt 705.

An ordinance requiring street railways to provide commutation tickets for sale on each of their cars at prescribed prices is invalid as having been superseded by the public service commission law, which vested in the commission power to regulate rates for the operation of street railways.

Wash Seattle Elect v Seattle (1913) 206 F 955.

Charter authority to fix fares by franchise agreement with a bus company may be superseded where by statute the state occupies the field of rate making and delegates such power to the public service commission. Franchises or consents executed subsequent to the statutory delegation of power are subject to the rate making authority of the commission.

NY Queens-Nassau Transit v Maltbie (1946) 186 Misc 424, 61 NYS2d 81.

The effect of the statute creating the board of public utilities commissioners is to pre-empt the field of regulation and control of motor carriers for hire, and to divest municipalities of power to fix and regulate by ordinance passenger fares. Consequently an ordinance fixing bus fares within town at a lower rate than fixed by state commission is invalid.

NJ Morrison v West New York (1927) 5 NJM 222, 136 A 175.

That rate fixing powers are conferred by a later statute on the state public service commission does not authorize a modification of the rates of a railroad fixed by a prior ordinance and contract consenting to use of the streets. In the absence of a specific grant of power the commission may not increase rates and nullify conditions attached to consents acted on by both parties.

NY Niagara Falls v Pub Service Comm (1920) 229 NY 333, 128 NE 247.

An ordinance granting supplemental franchises for extension of street railway lines, conditioned on the road's compliance with rates set by the railroad law, consents to exercise of the rate fixing power by the state public service commission, and fare restrictions of the original franchise are not enforceable.

NY   United Traction v Pub Service Comm (1927) 219 AD 95, 219 NYS 421.

The exercise of municipal powers to grant franchises and fix rates is subject to the paramount sovereignty of the state. When a rate limit set by ordinance is unreasonable and confiscatory, because it operates to destroy the value of the property of the franchise holder, it is unconstitutional as a taking of property without due process of law or just compensation.

NY   Westinghouse Elect v Binghamton RR (1919) 255 F 378.

Street railroad franchise holders, whose maximum fares for horse and mule drawn cars are restricted by ordinance, are not subject to such restrictions on fares after the railroads are electrified; and when a constitutional amendment places the regulation of fares with the legislature the rates may be set and increased by the public service commission.

NY   Evens v Phelps (1925) 214 AD 122, 211 NYS 650.

An ordinance limitation on the fares of a street railway franchise holder, is abrogated by consents subsequently given by the city for extension of the line, where one of the express conditions of the consents is compliance with a statute which reserves the right to the legislature to regulate fares.

NY   Evens v Pub Service Comm (1927) 246 NY 224, 158 NE 310.

Where by statute the state acts to absolutely and exclusively control the subject of rate making for street railroads, the rate making provisions of franchise contract ordinances of a city are abrogated, and the fixing of rates becomes the prerogative of the state public service commission. The commission cannot adjust rates, however, while a valid contract is still in force between the railway and the municipality.

NY   Westinghouse Elec v Binghamton RR (1919) 255 F 378.

The contract right of a street railway company to charge a designated fare permitted by ordinance vests in the company security against impairment by a subsequent ordinance, when ratified by a state act. A subsequent ordinance lowering the rate is void.

Minn   Minneapolis v Minneapolis St Ry (1910) 215 US 417,
             54 LEd 259, 30 SCt 118.

An order of the state railroad commission reducing streetcar rates fixed by city ordinance is valid as an exercise by the state through its administrative agents of its lawful power to fix utility rates.

Wis   Milwaukee Elec Ry & Light v RR Comm (1915) 238 US 174, 59 LEd 1254,
            35 SCt 820.

While an ordinance granting a street railway franchise, on acceptance, constitutes a contract authorizing a five cent fare, the legislature, acting directly or through the state railroad commission, may exercise its paramount authority to regulate rates.

Wis Duluth St Ry v RR Comm (1915) 161 Wis 245, 152 NW 887.

The issues in an action for an injunction against enforcement of a transit rate ordinance are rendered moot by state legislative action expressly conferring authority to regulate transit company rates on the public service commission.

Ala Birmingham Transit v Birmingham (1963) 275 Ala 321, 154 So2d 676.

The state corporation commission can regulate the rates of street railroads though railroad and city pursuant to ordinance have entered into a valid contract fixing rates; and such regulation by the commission does not constitute an unconstitutional impairment of contract rights.

Va Richmond v Va Ry & Power (1925) 141 Va 69, 126 SE 353.

Any provisions with respect to rates and services contained in a franchise ordinance contract between a utilities company and a municipal corporation, authorizing the company to transport passengers over the streets, are subject to the orders of the utilities commission with respect thereto.

NC Winston-Salem v Winston-Salem City Coach Lines (1956) 245 NC 179, 95 SE2d 510.

When a city enacts an ordinance granting a franchise to a street railway company and fixing its rates, a contention that the city is exercising delegated state powers, either of rate control or enforcement of the franchise conditions, is not so wholly lacking in merit as to afford no basis for jurisdiction of a federal court to determine whether the rates are confiscatory.

Ky Louisville v Louisville Ry (1930) 39 F2d 822.

The legislature has power to change a contract granted by a municipal franchise ordinance to a street railroad company where the statute negates franchise ordinance provision which required the company to sell half-fare tickets to certain passengers.

Iowa Dubuque Elec v Dubuque (1919) 260 F 353.

An ordinance relating to common carriers, and regulating service, fixing rates, and providing the common council with power to control competition is void where a statute grants such powers to the state public service commission, unless the city is within that class of cities to which the grant of power to the commission over buses was excluded.

Ind Denny v Brady (1928) 201 Ind 59, 163 NE 489.

A city may by ordinance grant franchises to street railways and regulate the use and operation of the railway facilities; but rate making is a sovereign power of the state and is regulated through a state commission, and when the city and the railway enter into a contract to fix rates, which are shown to be confiscatory and to deprive the corporation of a fair return and thus to take private property for public use without just compensation or due process, the court will enjoin enforcement of the rate provisions.

La O'Keefe v New Orleans (1921) 273 F 560.

Though a transportation franchise ordinance constitutes a binding contract between the granting city and the franchise holder, the municipality may not foreclose the state from compelling a change in rates and fares, including commutation tickets sold in advance.

Utah Salt Lake City v Utah Light & Traction (1918) 52 Utah 210, 173 P 556, 3 ALR 715.

§57. Basis for Rate Making

In fixing transit rates, the justification for a depreciation allowance on abandoned property depends on whether the transit's investors in the past have been compensated for assuming the risk that the property would have to be abandoned before the investment in the property was entirely recovered.

DC Bebchick v Pub Utilities Comm (1963) 318 F2d 187.

Under a streetcar franchise ordinance, the determination of what is a reasonable rate should be made on the net return which the railway receives on its invested capital, after expenses and depreciation.

Wis Duluth St Ry v RR Comm (1915) 161 Wis 245, 152 NW 887.

In assessing the reasonableness of the rate provided in a street railway franchise ordinance the court should consider the fact that a utility may reach financial success only in time or not at all, as a reason for allowing a liberal return on investment; but past losses are not to be considered in deciding what the base value is and whether the rate is confiscatory.

Tex Galveston Elec v Galveston (1922) 258 US 388, 66 LEd 678, 42 SCt 351.

In a charter requiring rates for the city's bus service to be sufficient to pay, for at least the succeeding fiscal year, all expenses of every kind and nature, the reference to the "succeeding fiscal year" means the next complete fiscal year after the date the schedule is fixed, rather than the rest of the fiscal year in which the rate is established.

Cal   Hurst v San Francisco (1949) 33 C2d 298, 201 P2d 805.

§58. Submission of Rate Change to Public Vote

The regulation and fixing of street railway fares by a city, is not subject to the referendum provision of the charter, where another provision thereof delegates to the board of commissioners the right to fix and regulate the charges of any persons enjoying a franchise or other public privilege.

Tex   Dallas Ry v Geller (1925) 114 Tex 484, 271 SW 1106.

Where the initiative and referendum provision of a charter is general as to the passage of ordinances, and does not mention the regulation of rates and service of public utilities, but another provision delegates this duty to the board of commissioners, an ordinance adopted at a popular election, purporting to regulate street railway fares, is invalid, since under the charter the board is the only tribunal to which the power to regulate utilities is delegated.

Tex   Dallas v Dallas Consolidated Elec St Ry (1913) 159 SW 76.

§59. Challenge of Rate by Transit System

It is a prerequisite to a challenge of the validity of a bus fare ordinance that the bus company first exhaust its legal remedies by seeking a fare increase from the city council.

Tex   San Antonio Transit v San Antonio (1959) 323 SW2d 272.

In an action to enjoin the enforcement of an ordinance reducing street railway fares, it is not incumbent on the railway company to show that the reduced fare is confiscatory, but it will suffice to show that the rate is unreasonable, unjust, and insufficient to pay a fair return on the value of the company's property.

Tex   Houston Elec v Houston (1919) 212 SW 198.

In assessing the reasonableness of a rate established in a street railway franchise ordinance, the court will take judicial notice of the existing condition of the economy as compared with the situation that prevailed at the time of enactment of the ordinance.

Tex   Galveston Elec v Galveston (1922) 258 US 388, 66 LEd 678, 42 SCt 351.

Where the maximum street railway fares fixed in an ordinance are shown to be too low under conditions then existing, the enforcement of the ordinance will be enjoined only until such times as conditions change, since they may change enough to justify the rates fixed or even lower rates.

Ky Paducah v Paducah Ry (1923) 261 US 267, 67 LEd 647, 43 SCt 335.

An ordinance reducing the allowable fares of a streetcar company, clearly within the city's delegated legislative authority, presents a federal constitutional question of impairment of contract.

Ore Portland Ry Light & Power v Portland (1912) 201 F 119.

A provision in a street railway franchise ordinance requiring the company to issue 25-ride commutation tickets for $1, without transfer privileges, was properly canceled by the state public service commission, in view of a showing that the company was not recieving any net returns, that there was a deficit in its operations, and that its revenue returns were less than two per cent of the actual cost of the railway system.

Wash Seattle v Pub Service Comm (1918) 103 Wash 72, 173 P 737.

An ordinance requiring a streetcar company which charges 5 cent fares, pursuant to its franchise, to sell 6 tickets for 25 cents, or 25 tickets for $1.00, is unreasonable, where the company is deriving only 3.3 to 4.5 per cent on its bona fide investment.

Wis Milwaukee Elec Ry & Light v Milwaukee (1898) 87 F 577.

An ordinance reducing street railway fares in annexed city territory from rates established in a prior franchise ordinance relating to the annexed territory is invalid as impairing the obligation of contract.

Mich Detroit United Ry v Mich (1916) 242 US 238, 61 LEd 268, 37 SCt 87.

Where a franchise ordinance provides that the company shall pay, from fares collected because there is no other source of income, (1) the cost of operation, (2) taxes, (3) five per cent on the company's indebtedness represented by bonds, (4) six per cent on the remainder of the indebtedness, (5) a depreciation fund, to be fixed each year, with reference to replacement, renewals, and maintenance of equipment, the company cannot raise fares above the level fixed by the ordinance. If it is receiving insufficient income, the quality of the service will decrease.

Iowa North Amer Constr v Des Moines City Ry (1919) 256 F 107.

An ordinance creating a contract between the city and a street railway company, and granting "the right to said company to obtain a reasonable profit on its investments," clearly shows that the intention of the parties is to establish and maintain rates that are not confiscatory. Consequently, the court has power to prevent irreparable injury to the company by raising its rates, on a showing that the rates have become confiscatory, until a final determination of the merits of the case, by issuing an interlocutory injunction restraining the city from compelling the company to carry passengers at the confiscatory rate level.

Iowa Council Bluffs v Omaha & C B St Ry (1925) 9 F2d 246.

§60. Challenge of Rate by Taxpayer or Passenger

A regular commuter on the transit system is entitled to intervene in proceedings to raise transit system fares.

DC Bebchick v Pub Utilities Comm (1961) 287 F2d 337.

A street railroad customer and taxpayer does not have such a vested interest in the ordinance granting a company's franchise and fixing its rates as will entitle him to bring a suit to enjoin the repeal of an existing franchise and prevent the enforcement of a new franchise empowering the company to charge higher fares.

Iowa Van Horn v Des Moines (1922) 195 Iowa 840, 191 NW 144.

A qualified elector may sue to contest the legality of an ordinance increasing fares of a street railroad if he alleges that the ordinance is illegal as being not in compliance with statutory directives and that he is injured by having to pay an illegal fare.

La Long v Shreveport (1921) 151 La 423, 91 So 825.

A cause of action under the federal constitutional prohibition against impairing the obligation of contracts is stated in a complaint by taxpayers seeking a preliminary and permanent injunction and damages based on increases in bus fares by a bus company that had been granted a franchise.

Colo Pudlik v Public Service of Colo (1958) 166 FSupp 921.

§61. Enforcement of Rate by Municipality

A city has a real interest in enforcement of its ordinances by injunctive procedure in the protection of the citizens and the public where it is alleged that a utility company is attempting to charge fares for streetcar transportation in excess of those authorized by the ordinance.

La Lake Charles v Lake Charles Ry Light & Water (1918) 144 La 217, 80 So 260.

The district court has jurisdiction over a suit by a city for an injunction against a utility company which is allegedly violating the provisions of an ordinance limiting streetcar fares. The injunction is justified on allegations showing that the company may work irreparable injury on the city and its citizens unless the ordinance is enforced. It is not necessary for the city to allege that money is due, nor is it necessary to pray for revocation of the railway franchise.

La   Lake Charles v Lake Charles Ry Light & Water (1918) 144 La 217, 80 So 260.

§62. Reduced Fares and Free Service for Specified Groups

An ordinance revoking a provision in a prior franchise ordinance, which allowed mail carriers to ride streetcars free, is not an abuse of the city's discretion because the franchise between the city and the streetcar company created no privity of contract between the city and the mail carriers.

Ark   Little Rock Ry & Elec v Dowell (1911) 101 Ark 223, 142 SW 165.

A street railroad may not invoke the objection that an ordinance fixing fares is discriminatory and denies to persons under 21 not attending school the equal protection of the law by lower fares for school children.

Cal   San Francisco-Oakland Term RR v Alameda (1914) 226 F 889.

An ordinance granting a franchise to a street railway company on condition that the company will transport school children at reduced rates, and firemen, policemen, mail carriers, and children under five years of age free, is valid and enforceable by mandamus.

Okla   Oklahoma City v Okla Ry (1907) 20 Okla 1, 93 P 48.

An ordinance requiring a street railway to sell half fare "tickets" to pupils presenting a certificate of enrollment in some school applies to students of a business college.

Va   Northrop v Richmond (1906) 105 Va 335, 53 SE 962.

City ordinance giving residents of the city the special privilege of obtaining transportation on a street railroad at a lesser rate than other residents of the state violates the state constitutional provision that all laws of a general nature shall have uniform operation.

Iowa   State v Omaha & C B Ry & Bridge (1901) 113 Iowa 30, 84 NW 983.

The life of street railway franchises granted respectively by a city and an adjoining township for a definite and fixed term was not extended to the date fixed by the township for termination of other street railway franchises, by the adoption of a municipal ordinance, after annexation of part of the township to the city, requiring the street railway company "for the full term of said township grants" to sell workmen's tickets at a reduced rate, the other provisions of the township grants to remain unchanged, since a fair construction of the ordinance required such services at the rates fixed only while the railway had a lawful right to use the street under its grant.

Mich Detroit United Ry v Detroit (1912) 229 US 39, 57 LEd 1056, 33 SCt 697.

§63. Transfers

An ordinance regulating the operation of street railroads and prohibiting the issuance or delivery of transfers to passengers except on or within the car from which the passenger is transferred is valid.

Cal Lorenzen, Ex parte (1900) 128 Cal 431, 61 P 68.

An ordinance making it unlawful for any person to sell, barter or exchange a transfer ticket issued by a street railway is void, being an encroachment on the statutory authority of the state public service commission to regulate rates charged by streetcar companies.

Mo Packman, Ex parte (1927) 317 Mo 732, 296 SW 366.

Where a transit company under a franchise operates streetcars on city streets, an ordinance requiring passengers thereon, in using transfers, to go by a reasonably direct route is valid, and one may not recover damages from the company for refusal to accept a transfer otherwise tendered.

Mo Duke v Metropolitan St Ry (1912) 166 MoApp 121, 148 SW 166.

The power of a city under its charter, to limit the fares to be charged by street railway companies includes, as necessarily incidental thereto, the power to require such companies to furnish transfer tickets to passengers, entitling them to ride on connecting lines of the company without payment of additional fare.

Ill Chicago Union Traction v Chicago (1902) 199 Ill 484, 65 NE 451.

The acceptance of an ordinance requiring a street railway company to issue transfers does not abrogate an existing contract right, secured against impairment by subsequent legislation, to charge a 5 cent fare for one continuous passage not exceeding three miles in length.

Minn Minneapolis v Minneapolis St Ry (1910) 215 US 417, 54 LEd 259, 30 SCt 118.

E. Construction, Repair and Upkeep of Facilities

§64. Paving and Repairing Roadbed Area

A street railroad franchise which requires the company to pay for track removal and repaving places the liability to do the work on the city.

> **DC**   Joseph v DC (1973) 366 F Supp 757.

Since an ordinance provision requiring a street railroad to use a certain type of material in repaving streets in its track zone is a regulatory measure rather than a contract, a practical construction placed on the provision by the city is not binding on it, and will not estop it to compel strict compliance with the provision. It is broad enough to require repaving with the same material of which the street is composed.

> **Wis**   State v Milwaukee Elec Ry & Light (1917) 165 Wis 230, 161 NW 745.

That an ordinance requiring a street railway to repave its track zone will reduce its earning capacity below a reasonable return on its investment will not affect the validity of the ordinance, since the company can at any time apply to the railroad commission for an increase.

> **Wis**   State v Milwaukee Elec Ry v Light (1917) 165 Wis 230, 161 NW 745.

A requirement in a street railway franchise that the company repave its track zone when it is defective does not violate due process or equal protection of the laws, since the condition is an integral part of the franchise as accepted by the company.

> **Wis**   State v Milwaukee Elec Ry & Light (1917) 165 Wis 230, 161 NW 745.

An ordinance requiring street railway company to pave or repave between its rails, and with like material, when city paves streets is a reasonable regulation.

> **Wis**   Superior v Duluth St Ry (1918) 166 Wis 487, 165 NW 1081.

Under a provision of a franchise ordinance requiring a street railway to keep its track zone in good repair, an order requiring repaving does not violate the obligation of contract or equal protection of the laws, in view of the contractual duty to repave arising from acceptance of the franchise. No constitutional guaranties are involved.

> **Wis**   Milwaukee Elec Ry & Light v State (1920) 252 US 100, 64 LEd 476, 40 SCt 306.

A municipality, in enacting an ordinance granting a street railway a franchise to occupy portions of the streets for operation of its cars, may require the company to pave the portions occupied by its tracks and may prescribe the material to be used and the method of paving.

Ill Madison v Alton G & S L Traction (1908) 235 Ill 346, 85 NE 596.

An ordinance requiring a street railroad to keep its tracks at street level and to keep in good repair the portion of streets used by its tracks does not require the railroad to keep in repair any other portion of a street.

Ill Brun v P Nacey Co (1915) 267 Ill 353, 108 NE 301.

Where ordinance granting a street railway franchise requires the railway to pave a portion of the street occupied by its tracks, the city is precluded from paving that portion by special assessment.

Ill Lincoln v Harts (1911) 250 Ill 273, 95 NE 200.

Under a street railway franchise ordinance requiring the company to pave portions of the streets used by its tracks, a provision that if the company fails to pave its right-of-way the city may remove the tracks and pave that part also is invalid, by reason of the uncertain and indefinite description of the improvement to be made by the city.

Ill Lincoln v Harts (1911) 250 Ill 273, 95 NE 200.

An ordinance authorizing a street railway to operate on certain streets and requiring the grading and paving of the portions of the streets occupied by it constitutes a contract, on acceptance by the railway, and the city may not thereafter, by ordinance, impose further obligations relating to the matters that were subjects of agreement in the ordinance.

Ill Chicago v Chicago Rys (1918) 282 Ill 383, 188 NE 728.

"Repair", in an ordinance requiring a street railway company to keep in repair portions of streets used by it, is synonymous with "restore".

Ill Chicago City Ry v Chicago (1925) 238 IllAp 402.

A city, having exclusive authority to grant or refuse permission to a railway company to operate on its streets, may impose such reasonable conditions as it sees fit, by requiring the company to fill, grade, pave and otherwise improve the portions of the streets occupied by its tracks.

Ill Chicago City Ry v Chicago (1925) 238 IllAp 402.

In a statute providing that all street railway companies shall be required to pave the streets between the rails of their tracks and one foot outside thereof at their own expense, unless it may be bound to pave other portions of the street as specified by ordinance, the words "other portions of said street" mean not something less, but something more, that the statute requires.

> **Iowa**   Des Moines City Ry v Des Moines (1911) 152 Iowa 18, 131 NW 43.

The fact that a street railway company constructed its track under an ordinance granting it a franchise does not exempt it from the power reserved to the legislature of imposing any conditions on the franchise of a corporation which it deems necessary for the public good. Therefore, though the original franchise granted by the city required the company to pave only the space inside the rails, the obligation of the contract is not impaired by a subsequent ordinance, passed pursuant to a statute requiring the company also to pave one foot outside each of the rails.

> **Iowa**   Sioux City St Ry v Sioux City (1891) 138 US 98, 34 LEd 898, 11 SCt 226.

Under an ordinance authorizing a corporation to operate a street railway over certain streets and requiring it to keep in repair the portion of the paved streets included between its tracks and one foot on either side, the company is not bound to refloor with oak plank any portion of a bridge over which its tracks pass.

> **Iowa**   Cedar Rapids v Cedar Rapids & M C Ry (1899) 108 Iowa
> 406, 79 NW 125.

A street railway company is obligated to improve the space between its tracks where the ordinance under which it was permitted to use a bridge for its tracks referred to prior ordinances placing this obligation upon the company.

> **Iowa**   Burlington Ry & Light v Burlington (1920) 188 Iowa 272, 176 NW 285.

Street railway was required by ordinance to plank unpaved crossings when ordered to do so by the city council and to maintain unpaved crossings in a reasonably safe condition.

> **Iowa**   McClosky v Iowa Ry & Light (1924) 198 Iowa 1146, 197 NW 989.

Mandamus will lie to compel a street railway company to pave the streets between its tracks, as required by the ordinance granting it a franchise to lay its tracks in the street.

> **Mich**   Lansing v Lansing City Elec Ry (1896) 109 Mich 123, 66 NW 949.

A franchise ordinance requiring a street railway to reimburse the city for paving between the rails of the tracks, and specifically granting the city a lien therefor on all of the property of the company, makes the lien prior to that of a trustee in favor of the bondholders.

> **Ohio**   Real Estate-Land Title & Tr v Springfield (1932) 125 OS 531,
> 182 NE 501.

Ambiguous language implying the duty by street railways to repair portions of the streets containing railroad tracks cannot prevail over clearly inconsistent statutes.

DC Fisher v Capital Transit (1957) 246 F2d 666.

Where a city by a contract made under an ordinance granting a franchise agrees to accept fixed yearly sums in lieu of streetcar licenses or bonus payments such contract may not be construed to require the street railway company to pay for street repairs as required under its prior franchise.

Ky Covington v South Covington & C St Ry (1912) 147 Ky 326, 144 SW 17.

A street railroad required by ordinance to maintain the paving between and adjacent to its trackage may be compelled at its own expense to relay such paving, though it is then in good repair, where the municipality decides to repair the street.

NY New York City v NY City Ry (1909) 132 AD 156, 116 NYS 939.

A charter provision that a railway is to keep that portion of the street occupied by its tracks well paved and in good repair without expense to the city is mandatory, and an ordinance which undertakes to repeal it, in whole or in part, is void.

Va Norfolk & P Traction v Norfolk (1913) 115 Va 169, 78 SE 545.

Where a street railway franchise ordinance provides that in the event a street is repaved the city is to furnish the material and the railway is to pay the cost of labor for the pavement between the tracks and two feet on each side, and further provides that the railway is to keep that part covered by its tracks in "thorough repair", the railway is liable for the cost of labor as well as material if it is necessary to construct a concrete base as a permanent bed on which the rails and ties rest. The base is not part of the "paving."

Va Va Ry & Power v Norfolk (1926) 147 Va 951, 133 SE 565.

If a street improvement ordinance directs that the streets be paved from curb to curb, as set out in plans and specifications adopted and on file, which plans and specifications confine the work to be done to that portion of the streets between the curbs and "granite block headed adjacent to the outside rails of the streetcar track," and there is an ordinance in effect requiring a streetcar company to do all paving between its rails and a space of two feet outside its rails, the ordinance will not be construed to mean that the traction company will be relieved of its obligation and the burden transferred to the property owners.

W Va Holswade v Huntington (1924) 96 W Va 124, 122 SE 449.

§65. Sprinkling, Snow Removal, Upkeep

An ordinance requiring the street railways to sprinkle the streets occupied by them is not repealed by a subsequent resolution authorizing the city council to determine whether streets should be sprinkled, and to charge the costs to abutting owners. Repeal of an ordinance by implication is not favored, and intent to repeal must be clearly evident.

Wis   State v Milwaukee Elec Ry & Light (1911) 144 Wis 386, 129 NW 623.

An ordinance requiring a street railway to sprinkle the streets it occupies by its tracks creates a public duty which is enforceable by mandamus.

Wis   State v Milwaukee Elec Ry & Light (1911) 144 Wis 386, 129 NW 623.

An ordinance requiring a streetcar company to remove snow and other substances from the part of a street where they have tracks does not shift the burden of keeping the streets reasonably safe from the city to the company.

Minn   Phelion v Duluth-Superior Transit (1938) 202 Minn 224, 277 NW 552.

An ordinance requiring a street railway to clean the portions of the streets between its rails is valid as a reasonable exercise of the police power.

Ill   Chicago v Chicago Union Traction (1902) 199 Ill 259, 65 NE 243.

Where a state statute provides that municipalities may require street railroad companies to keep gutters and street crossings clean along their right-of-way, may carry out objects of the corporation not specified, may exercise exclusive power over the streets, may declare what shall be a nuisance to prevent it, require its abatement, and authorize its removal, and where another statute provides the cost of sprinkling streets is to be assessed against the real estate abutting on the streets sprinkled, or paid out of the municipal treasury, a municipality is not authorized to adopt an ordinance requiring a street car company to sprinkle the space between its tracks so as to effectually lay dust.

Ind   South Bend v Chicago S B & N I Ry (1913) 179 Ind 455, 101 NE 628.

§66. Assessment of Abutting Owners for Paving

Where a prior ordinance required a street railway company to pave and keep in repair a portion of a certain street, a subsequent ordinance assessing the entire cost of improvement of that street against abutting owners is invalid.

Ill   Amer Hide & Leather v Chicago (1903) 203 Ill 451, 67 NE 979.

An ordinance requiring a street railway to pave and repair the portions of streets occupied by its tracks does not preclude the city from assessing abutting property owners for paving the portion of a street not occupied by the railway.

Ill   Chicago v Chicago Rys (1919) 290 Ill 607, 125 NE 327.

If, under a charter silent as to charges against street railway companies for the cost of paving between rails and along the sides thereof, the council, by ordinance, imposes such a charge, an abutting owner is not entitled to the benefit of any portion thereof by abatement from the amount with which he is chargeable.

W Va   Hager v Melton (1909) 66 W Va 62, 66 SE 13.

An ordinance providing for a rebate to property owners who have been assessed for the pavement of a street, occasioned by reason of a street railway company's paying the city the cost of paving the portion of the street between its tracks, refers to the owners at the time the assessment was made and not subsequent owners. "Rebate" means "to draw back", and one cannot draw back something he never put forward.

Wash   Savage Scofield v Tacoma (1909) 56 Wash 457, 105 P 1032.

The words, "property owners abutting," in an ordinance providing that where railway tracks are laid on a street already paved the company shall pay the property owners abutting for the paving between the rails, do not apply to the city, as owner of the streets, so as to require the company to pay for paving at street intersections.

Iowa   Council Bluffs v Omaha & C B St Ry & Bridge (1901) 114 Iowa 141, 86 NW 222.

Where a street railway company obtained the right to lay, and did lay, its track in alley before passage of ordinance vacating the alley, and the city later, without repealing the ordinance, ordered the paving of the alley, the city, in proceedings to confirm an assessment against abutting owners for the paving of the alley, could not urge that the vacating ordinance was void as affecting vested rights of the company, which was not in court, and had asserted no rights inconsistent with the ordinance.

Iowa   Bradley v Centerville (1908) 139 Iowa 599, 117 NW 968.

Within a statute providing that a street railway company laying its tracks on a paved street shall pay into the city treasurer the value of all paving between its tracks, and that the money shall be refunded to the abutting owners on said street in proportion to the amount originally assessed by ordinance against the property abutting thereon, neither another street railway company, which has

271

occupied the street but whose rights have been fully forfeited and extin-
guished, nor the city by reason of ownership of such pavement between the
tracks or ownership of the street, is an abutting owner.

Iowa Oskaloosa v Oskaloosa Traction & Light (1909) 141 Iowa 236, 119 NW 736.

§67. Assessment of Transit System for Municipal Paving

Where an ordinance authorizes the paving of a street, and assessment of the
costs by tax bills levied on abutting property, including property owned by a
street railway company which under its franchise has the use of a part of the
street which the railroad has previously paved, such bills are valid charges
against the railroad's entire abutting property in return for benefits, since the
previous paving was part of the consideration given for the use of the streets
and was unrelated to the paving done as a public improvement.

Mo Municipal Securities v Metro St Ry (1917) 196 MoApp 518, 196 SW 400.

Enforcement of an assessment ordinance cannot be enjoined merely because a
street railway was allowed to remove its rails from the street to be paved
instead of paving the space formerly occupied thereby as required by statute,
or because the contractor guaranteed the quality of the work and agreed to
make good any defect that appeared within five years, or because no formal
personal notice of the formation of the paving district and subsequent actions
of the council was given to it.

Neb Diederich v Red Cloud (1919) 103 Neb 688, 173 NW 698.

An ordinance assessing costs of a street improvement to a street railway
because of its right-of-way in and use of the street, enacted under a charter
provision for assessments "on the lots, parts of lots, and parcels of land
benefited thereby", is invalid. The railway right-of-way is merely an easement,
and is not thus assessable.

Ore Fay v Portland (1921) 99 Ore 490, 195 P 828.

Where a city, in conformity with legislative authority and its ordinances,
paved and incurred the expense of paving a street occupied by a street railway
company, and where the company, with knowledge that the city intended to
charge the company with part of the expense of the paving, stood by and saw
the paving done and the expense incurred, without instituting legal action to
prevent it, it is thereafter too late for the company to avoid payment on the
ground that enforcement of the assessment will deprive it of its property, in
violation of the due process clauses of state and federal Constitutions.

Ga Ga Power v Decatur (1935) 181 Ga 187, 182 SE 32.

Where a statute authorizes repaving assessments against companies operating
on public places, "public places" encompassing a bridge, the statute controls a

streetcar company's liability for repaving the bridge, notwithstanding that the franchise ordinance under which the company is operating provides that the company shall at its own expense pave each bridge crossed by its tracks.

Iowa Walnut Street Bridge in Des Moines, In re (1935) 220 Iowa 55, 261 NW 781.

An objection presented to a city council, that its proceedings in attempting to levy and assess taxes against a street railroad for paving are in many respects irregular, invalid, and without authority of law, is insufficient to raise the question of validity of the council's action in estimating the number of square feet of paving for which the railroad should pay, arising out of the fact that it included not only the space between the rails and the space of one foot outside the rails, but also the space occupied by the rails themselves.

Iowa Marshalltown Light Power & Ry v Marshalltown (1905) 127 Iowa 637, 103 NW 1005.

A street railway company operating under a franchise authorized by a statute and ordinance is subject to a paving assessment levied by another ordinance and is liable for the cost of paving its road beds and two feet on the outside of the rail on each side of the track, where the additional space is required for the operation of its tracks in the exercise of its franchise and right-of-way.

La Shreveport v Shreveport City Ry (1900) 104 La 260, 29 So 129.

Where a statute authorizes the levy by ordinance of paving assessments against a street railway company and establishes the area and basis on which its liability is to be ascertained, the city and the company may not, by convention, change the basis so as to reduce the company's liability to less than that set by statute.

La Shreveport v Shreveport City Ry (1900) 104 La 260, 29 So 129.

The mere silence and inaction of a street railway company, while streets traversed by its tracks are being paved under authority of an ordinance, does not estop it to plead lack of jurisdiction in the council to levy a special paving tax assessment against it, where it is shown that the contract was let on the basis of payment only by the city and the abutters, and no benefits are shown to accrue to the railroad.

La La Improvement v Baton Rouge Elec & Gas (1905) 114 La 534, 38 So 444.

An ordinance authorizing the assessment of costs of street improvements against a street railway company is not discriminatory for authorizing an assessment and a lien against all the property, assets and franchises of a street railway, and in the case of other property owners providing for an assessment only against property abutting the improvements, since street railway tracks alone abutting the improvement have little value and it is therefore proper that all property used by the company in exercising its franchise be regarded as one entire property and be assessed in its entirety.

Ky Newport v Silva (1911) 143 Ky 704, 137 SW 546.

Where a statute gives a city council discretion to determine the question of assessing street improvement costs against a street railway company, its action in refusing to make such an assessment does not constitute an exemption of the company from taxation, nor a donation of public funds to the company's benefit.

Ky Frankfort v Morris (1923) 200 Ky 59, 252 SW 142.

Where an interurban line is built along a street before it is opened for public travel by the city, ordinances take effect and become binding on the traction company as soon as the street becomes a public way, and the company is liable for its proportionate part of the costs of constructing the thoroughfare.

Ky Ky Traction v Carey-Reed (1920) 188 Ky 226, 221 SW 1078.

Under an ordinance authorizing a bond issue to finance a street improvement, a street railway company, having duly executed an agreement to pay the assessment made against it, is precluded from questioning the validity of the assessment after the bonds are issued.

Ky Evansville & O V Ry v La Plante (1934) 252 Ky 712, 68 SW2d 44.

Under an ordinance levying special assessments the oiling of streets is a permanent improvement, and thus a reasonable part of the cost may be assessed against a street railway company that enjoys the use of such streets.

Ky Henderson Traction v Henderson (1917) 178 Ky 124, 198 SW 730.

A statute requiring a city, granting a street railway franchise, to reserve the right to require the company to pay certain costs of street improvements is a part of the franchise contract though not written into it.

Ky Henderson v Henderson Traction (1923) 200 Ky 183, 254 SW 332.

In ascertaining whether a petition for an ordinance creating an improvement district was signed by a majority in value of the owners of real property, a street railway company, holding a franchise to use portions of the street within the improvement district, cannot be considered a property owner necessary to the determination of a majority, where it has no easement or freehold interest and all of its property is assessed as personalty for taxation.

Ark Lenon v Brodie (1906) 81 Ark 208, 98 SW 979.

§68. Lights

"Railroad", as used in a statute empowering a city to require the lighting of any railroad track or route within city, used by car propelled by steam or otherwise, does not, considering the context and intent of the statute as a whole, include street railways. Consequently, an ordinance requiring a street railway to light its tracks is outside the scope of municipal power.

Mont   Helena Light & Ry v Helena (1913) 47 Mont 18, 130 P 446.

Under an ordinance making it the duty of every street railway company to cause a red light to be placed at the crossings and intersections of other street railways and at all curves of their own roads, in such a manner as to give warning to motormen and citizens, it is necessary in order to support a conviction of violation of the ordinance to show that a crossing and intersection at which defendant was alleged to have failed to place a light was made by the lines of separate companies.

Mich   People v Detroit United Ry (1908) 152 Mich 359, 116 NW 186.

§69. Removal of Unsafe Facilities

Where a city has statutory authority to enact and enforce ordinances necessary for the protection of lives and property, for the preservation of health, and for the promotion of comfort, convenience and general welfare of its inhabitants, including, specifically, the power to regulate the use of its streets and maintain them in a safe condition it has the authority, in the exercise of the police power, to enact an ordinance requiring demolition of a viaduct found to be unsafe, and requiring the railroad franchise holder to reestablish two lines of tracks and a grade crossing at the same place.

La   New Orleans v New Orleans Pub Service (1929) 168 La 984, 123 So 648.

The enforcement, without coercion, of uncompensated obedience to an ordinance passed in the legitimate exercise of the police power is not a taking of property without due process of law, even where the ordinance directs demolition of a viaduct which is unsafe and the reconstruction of additional trackage at street grade level.

La   New Orleans Pub Service v New Orleans (1930) 281 US 682, 74 LEd 1115, 50 SCt 449.

III. TAXATION

A. LICENSE AND FRANCHISE TAXES AND FEES

§70. Authority and Limitations

The license fee for buses is a revenue tax rather than a license fee when no inspections or requirements are made for the operation of the buses. The tax may not be applied against the metropolitan transit authority or its agencies due to their governmental function.

Pa Philadelphia v Southeastern Pa Transit Auth (1973) 8 PaCmwlth 280, 303 A2d 247.

An ordinance authorizing the operation of motor buses, requiring license therefor, and imposing license taxes and gross receipts taxes on companies operating thereunder may not be attacked as unconstitutional by a utility which for many years has operated under and enjoyed its benefits.

Mo St Louis Pub Service v St Louis (1957) 302 SW2d 875.

Cities may tax businesses carried on within their boundaries and enforce such taxes by requiring licenses for revenue and by imposing criminal penalties. A state permit as an intercity charter bus operator does not render the operator immune to a city tax on the apportioned gross receipts of charter vehicles for hire.

Cal Willingham Bus Lines v Mun Ct (1967) 66 C2d 893, 59 CaR 618, 428 P2d 602.

Under charter authority to levy and collect a license tax on trades and businesses, the city could levy a license tax on a stagecoach company receiving and discharging passengers and making contracts for their conveyance in the city, though the larger portion of the work was transportation outside the city.

Cal Sacramento v Cal Stage (1859) 12 Cal 134.

City could require payment of actual compensation for wear and tear on the city's streets and bridges as a condition of the franchise to the street railway even though the city's power to tax or license for revenue had been removed by legislation.

Wis Oshkosh v Eastern Wis Elec (1920) 172 Wis 85, 178 NW 308.

An ordinance imposing a license fee on motor buses is not invalid merely because it provides for a full year's fee to be paid or because it makes no provision for a pro rata license, where the statute authorizing the imposition makes no such provision.

Ky Northern Ky Transportation v Bellevue (1926) 215 Ky 514, 285 SW 241.

An ordinance licensing a motor bus company in the use of city streets is not invalid as an unauthorized occupation tax, because, while a municipality has no inherent power to license any occupation or require payment of a tax for engaging in it, it does have power to impose such conditions for a grant of the use of the streets as it may deem for the best interests of the public, including the requirement of a reasonable contribution as a regulatory provision and for damages to the streets.

> **Ill** People v Chicago Motor Bus (1920) 295 Ill 486, 129 NE 114.

In an ordinance providing that a specified rate of annual payment to operate a street railway is to continue until readjusted, the term "rate" does not make the annual payment apportionable to the number of months that the franchise is exercised. "Rate" means "amount" or "charge".

> **Pa** Mechanicsburg v Valley Ry (1933) 109 PaS 48, 165 A 541.

Money due a city under a franchise ordinance for the use of the streets does not constitute a tax, nor is it a charge in the nature of a tax.

> **Md** Baltimore v Williams (1932) 61 F2d 374.

An ordinance imposing a franchise tax on those operating a street railway, including automobile buses for the transportation of freight or passengers for hire, does not apply to "for hire" passenger vehicles, though operated on a definite route, unless used in connection with or in substitution for a street railway.

> **NC** Safe Bus v Maxwell (1938) 214 NC 12, 197 SE 567.

An ordinance imposing an annual license tax against persons, firms, or corporations owning or operating motor vehicles or buses carrying passengers for hire over city streets is invalid, where it conflicts with a statute inhibiting a municipality from imposing such a tax on carriers holding permits from a state commission.

> **Ky** Russell v Fannin (1943) 296 Ky 236, 176 SW2d 384.

Exaction of a license fee under an ordinance requiring a fee of bus operators engaging in interstate commerce cannot be sustained as a police measure, when it does not appear that the fee was imposed as an incident of the scheme of regulation, that the proceeds are applied to defray the expenses of the regulation, or that the amount is no more than was reasonably required.

> **Ind** Sprout v South Bend (1928) 277 US 163, 72 LEd 833, 48 SCt 502, 62 ALR 45.

A license tax imposed by an ordinance on bus operators engaging in intrastate and interstate commerce cannot be sustained as an occupation tax on those engaging solely in interstate commerce, since the privilege of engaging in interstate commerce cannot be denied or conditioned by a municipality on payment of an occupation tax.

> **Ind** Sprout v South Bend (1928) 277 US 163, 72 LEd 833, 48 SCt 502, 62 ALR 45.

Since the rolling stock of an intrastate bus company operating buses within the state has a situs for tax purposes in the city of the company's domicile or principal place of business within the state, an ordinance enacted by another city levying a tax on such rolling stock is invalid.

> **Tex**   Fort Worth v Southland Greyhound Lines (1934) 123 Tex 13, 67 SW2d 354.

When there are two taxing ordinances, one taxing buses generally and one taxing buses operated by street railways specifically, the specific taxing ordinance covers the buses operated by a street railway and the general taxing ordinance does not apply to these buses.

> **Ga**   Savannah v Savannah Elec & Power (1949) 205 Ga 429, 54 SE2d 260.

An ordinance imposing a license tax on the owner of any public passenger vehicle except a railroad car, in addition to the tax imposed on the same vehicles as a part of the owner's whole property falls within the state law proscribing double taxation.

> **Cal**   Flynn v San Francisco (1941) 18 C2d 210, 115 P2d 3.

Where the Constitution and statute forbid a city to levy a license tax on street railways and limit the tax on a corporation furnishing water, heat or light to half of one per cent of the gross receipts from such business, a license tax on a railroad's use of streets pursuant to a franchise ordinance is void as claiming a right of taxation which the legislature has withdrawn.

> **Va**   Lynchburg v Lynchburg Traction & Light (1919) 124 Va 130, 97 SE 780.

An ordinance requiring a permit for the operation of a public passenger vehicle within the city, and charging a fee therefor, is invalid as in conflict with the statute permitting municipalities to license and regulate motor vehicles for hire, but withholding the power to levy and collect license fees therefor.

> **Tex**   El Paso v Look (1926) 288 SW 506.

§ 71. Gross Receipts

An ordinance imposing a franchise fee based on gross revenues as compensation for use by a motor bus company of the streets is sustainable as a valid exercise of the city's regulatory powers over its streets.

> **Ill**   Peoria v Peoria Transit Lines (1957) 11 Ill2d 520, 144 NE2d 609.

A transportation franchise ordinance imposing a license tax based on a percentage of gross revenues of the franchise holder is not invalid for being not uniform with respect to class, there being a valid distinction between a mass transportation system with fixed fares, routes and schedules, and sight seeing buses, taxicabs, and similar means of public transportation.

> **Utah**   Salt Lake City Lines v Salt Lake City (1957) 6 Utah2d 428, 315 P2d 859.

An ordinance providing for an annual charge based on a specified percentage of gross receipts of a street railway, in consideration of rights, privileges, and franchises granted, does not constitute a "license tax" within constitutional and statutory prohibitions, but is an agreement between the parties for the use of the streets of the city, within constitutional and statutory provisos.

> **Va**   Danville Traction & Power v Danville (1937) 168 Va 430, 191 SE 592.

An ordinance granting a franchise to a street railway company for the right to occupy streets, and fixing the compensation to the city at 55 per cent of net earnings, is not invalid as constituting the railroad and the city partners, since the city has nothing whatsoever to do with operation of the railroad, and only receives a percentage of net earnings as rental for use of the streets.

> **Ill**   Venner v Chicago City Ry (1908) 236 Ill 349, 86 NE 266.

In contesting the levying of a license tax based on gross revenues, a transportation franchise holder is estopped to assert the invalidity of the ordinance granting the franchise.

> **Utah**   Salt Lake City Lines v Salt Lake City (1957) 6 Utah2d 428, 315 P2d 859.

An ordinance imposing a rental charge of two per cent of the gross income received for transporting passengers for hire in motor buses over the city streets is not invalid as an attempt to tax fares collected on a military base within the city. It is not a tax measure, but purely one fixing a rental charge based on the gross income.

> **Tex**   Wichita Falls v Bowen (1944) 143 Tex 45, 182 SW2d 695.

An ordinance imposing a license tax on receipts from the transportation of passengers by common carriers, and an ordinance imposing a further tax on the storage of gasoline based on number of gallons stored, are not in violation of the city's charter authority restricted to the imposition of but one license tax on any business, since the passenger transportation tax is a tax on the business or occupation of the carrier, whereas the storage tax is an excise on a privilege.

> **Mo**   State v Blaine (1932) 332 Mo 582, 58 SW2d 975.

Street railway could cross bridge built after receiving its authority to operate in the city for 30 years for a percentage of gross receipts without having to pay the city a toll for the crossing.

> **Va**   Richmond v Va Ry & Power (1917) 120 Va 802, 92 SE 898.

An ordinance imposing a tax on the gross receipts of all utilities subject to the supervision of the department of public service is not unreasonable, and the inability of a utility to shift the tax to its customers because of a contract limitation on maximum fares does not render the ordinance unconstitutional.

> **NY**   Southern Boulevard Ry v New York City (1936) 86 F2d 633.

An ordinance imposing a tax on the gross receipts of utilities subject to supervision of the department of public service does not deny equal protection of the laws to a street railroad, though other corporations and persons are subjected to a lesser tax. It is not necessary to apportion taxes in exact proportion to the ability to pay, and discrimination against one class, in relation to other classes, is permissible if all therein are treated uniformly and a reasonable basis exists for the variation.

> **NY**   Southern Boulevard Ry v New York City (1936) 86 F2d 633.

An ordinance imposing a 3 per cent tax on the gross receipts of public utilities is not so heavy a tax burden as to amount to a taking of property without compensation in violation of due process.

> **NY**   NY Rapid Transit v New York City (1938) 303 US 573, 82 LEd 1024, 58 SCt 721.

§72. Number of Vehicles

A city license tax per car operated by a street railway was invalid, where the railway operated in the city by virtue of franchises granted under the constitutional provision for a tax measured by a percentage of gross receipts, such taxes to be in lieu of all other taxes and licenses, provided that nothing should be construed to release the railway from an amount agreed to be paid for any franchise granted by a city. The license tax was not an amount agreed to be paid.

> **Cal**   San Francisco v Market St Ry (1937) 9 C2d 743, 73 P2d 234.

An ordinance imposing a tax on transportation of people for hire, making the taxable event the doing of business in the city and measuring the tax by the number of individual buses carrying passengers in the city is discriminatory and void, as applied to the operator of bus lines between cities and a charter bus business in and from a city outside the taxing one. The measure of the tax has no reasonable connection with the taxable event or the quantity of business carried on in the city.

> **Cal**   Los Angeles v Drake (1961) 195 CA2d 744, 16 CaR 103.

A business license tax imposed on those operating charter buses into the city and measured by the number of buses used within a quarter is discriminatory and void as to those engaged not only in a charter service but also in a public transportation system on a regular schedule, since the measure of tax bears no reasonable connection to the taxable event or the quantum of business carried on in the city.

Cal Los Angeles v Carson (1960) 181 CA2d 540, 5 CaR 356.

An ordinance purporting to amend an earlier street railway franchise ordinance by increasing the annual license fee for each car from $25 to $100, is a valid exercise of the police power, provided the increases are necessary to defray the reasonable cost of regulation and the ordinance does not impair any obligation of contract or deprive the railway of property without due process.

Minn Minneapolis St Ry v Minneapolis (1949) 229 Minn 502, 40 NW2d 353, (1952) 236 Minn 109, 52 NW2d 120.

Where an ordinance adopted in 1890 imposed on a street railway company a license fee of $25 per year per car for the average number of cars operated during the preceding year, an amendatory ordinance adopted in 1946 raising the fee to $100 per year per car was invalid, because the fee was excessive.

Minn Minneapolis St Ry v Minneapolis (1949) 229 Minn 502, 40 NW2d 353 (1952) 236 Minn 109, 52 NW2d 120.

An ordinance imposing a license tax on omnibuses, carts, wagons and other vehicles used on the streets for hire at the rate of $25 per year was invalid where it conflicted with a statute.

Okla Phillips, Ex parte (1917) 64 Okla 276, 167 P 221.

An ordinance imposing a license tax on the business of transporting passengers for pay in automobiles or other motor vehicles at $25 per year for each vehicle, "for the purpose of raising revenue for said city," is not an exercise of the police power and therefore is invalid because in conflict with statutes.

Okla Mayes, Ex parte (1917) 64 Okla 260, 167 P 749.

Where a city is authorized by its charter to grant franchises for the use of its streets by street railway companies and to regulate such use, and is also authorized in return for such franchise to impose a per capita tax on passengers transported thereby, an ordinance imposing an annual license fee of $25 for each car used by the utility in transporting passengers for hire within the city is valid under the city's power to license, tax and regulate such utilities, and does not prevent the city from enacting another ordinance, as a revenue producing measure, imposing a tax for each pay passenger carried.

Mo St Louis v United Rys (1908) 210 US 266, 52 LEd 1054, 28 SCt 630.

An ordinance imposing a license tax of $25 on each car operated by a franchised transportation company within the city, and another imposing a tax on each pay passenger transported by the company, are both valid, and do not offend the constitutional requirement of uniformity of taxation.

> **Mo**   St Louis v United Rys (1916) 263 Mo 387, 174 SW 78.

A license fee may properly be exacted by city under a franchise permitting a street railroad company to operate its cars on the city streets, and where a company accepts a franchise providing for a license fee for each car in use, and operates thereunder, such acceptance will constitute a complete and valid contract with reference to the fee imposed.

> **Ill**   Byrne v Chicago Gen Ry (1896) 63 IllAp 438.

An ordinance imposing an annual license fee of $75 for a motor bus and $10 for a motor vehicle known as a "rent car" is not discriminatory, but is based on a reasonable classification.

> **Tex**   Booth v Dallas (1915) 179 SW 301.

An ordinance levying a $300 annual license fee for motor buses is not unreasonable, where such buses are exempt from ordinary property taxes.

> **Iowa**   Star Transp v Mason City (1923) 195 Iowa 930, 192 NW 873.

An ordinance imposing an annual license fee of $15 per streetcar constitutes a revenue rather than a regulatory measure, and is abrogated by a subsequent statute imposing an annual license fee on street railroads based on gross receipts, in lieu of all other taxes.

> **Wis**   Milwaukee v Milwaukee Elec Ry & Light (1911) 147 Wis 458, 133 NW 593.

An ordinance imposing a charge characterized as an "annual fee" on all buses and motor trucks operated within the city constitutes a privilege tax, and as such is invalid as in violation of the statute pursuant to which the legislature withdrew from municipalities the right to assess a privilege tax on motor vehicles.

> **Tenn**   Southeastern Greyhound Lines v Knoxville (1944) 181 Tenn 622, 184 SW2d 4.

An ordinance imposing license fees on buses, ranging from $15 to $40 per annum depending on seating capacity, is a revenue measure as applied to buses licensed by the state, and is unconstitutional.

> **Ariz**   Phoenix v Sun Valley Bus Lines (1946) 64 Ariz 319, 170 P2d 289.

Where under an ordinance regulating the use of a bus terminal and providing that a bus control committee should collect a fixed monthly charge from the owner for each bus operating from the terminal, a bus owner, formerly operating two buses on alternate days, was permitted to operate a single bus every day for double the amount of the single bus charge, under a regulation adopted by the committee, and where, after electing to come under the regulation and later seeking to recover half of the parking fees charged, contending that the plan was illegal and that the committee had no authority to charge more than the single bus rate for any one bus using the terminal, the bus owner, having voluntarily elected to come under the regulation, was precluded from recovery on the basis of estoppel.

Haw Godoy v Hawaii (1960) 44 Haw 312, 354 P2d 78.

§73. Passengers Carried or Seating Capacity

Requiring the owners of passenger vehicles for hire having a seating capacity of eight or more in addition to the driver to pay a license tax of $100 per year for each vehicle does not interfere with interstate operation.

DC DC v Monumental Motor Tours (1941) 122 F2d 195.

It is unnecessary that ordinances levying a seat mile tax or tax in lieu thereof, as authorized by statute, provide for the allocation and appropriation of the funds raised to street purposes.

W Va Charleston Transit v Condry (1955) 140 W Va 651, 86 SE2d 391.

In the absence of legislation regulating and licensing automobiles and automobile transportation companies by the Congress, a municipality may prescribe by ordinance regulations for the use of its streets and charge license fees graduated according to seating capacity of the vehicles. So long as such regulations and fees are reasonable they are valid, though they may incidentally affect interstate commerce.

Ky Northern Ky Transportation v Bellevue (1926) 215 Ky 514, 285 SW 241.

An ordinance providing for a graduated license fee on intercity motor buses, based on seating capacity, is not arbitrary or discriminatory.

Minn Jefferson Highway Transport v St Cloud (1923) 155 Minn 463, 193 NW 960.

An ordinance imposing a license tax on cars operated by a street railway in the amount of one mill for each passenger carried is not a property tax, but license tax on a privilege connected with property, and so does not violate the constitutional requirement that property be taxed in proportion to its value.

Mo St Louis v United Rys (1916) 263 Mo 387, 174 SW 78.

An ordinance imposing a license tax on cars operated by a street railway in the amount of one mill for each passenger carried is presumed to be reasonable and therefore valid, where it bears no onerous features on its face. If the ordinance is claimed to be oppressive, the remedy lies, not with the courts, but with the municipal legislature.

Mo   St Louis v United Rys (1916) 263 Mo 387, 174 SW 78.

§74. Miles of Track

An ordinance imposing an annual tax at the rate of $500 per mile of street railroad tracks, as a provision of the franchise rather than a general ordinance, is not violative of due process, since the enactment is a special franchise rather than a general ordinance, and the city's power to grant franchises being discretionary, it is not to be exercised by general ordinance applicable to all cases, but each case must be acted on with reference to its peculiar conditions and circumstances.

Ill   Chicago Gen Ry Co v Chicago (1898) 176 Ill 253, 52 NE 880.

B. Excise Taxes

§75. In General

An ordinance imposing an excise tax on the gross receipts of all public utilities under the supervision of the public service commission is not discriminatory as applied to a street railroad, and does not deprive it of equal protection of the law. The franchises granted to the classified businesses give them some protection against competition, and other advantages over the general business community, that justify the classification.

NY   NY Steam v New York City (1935) 268 NY 137, 197 NE 172, 99 ALR 1157.

An ordinance imposing an excise tax on all utilities holding franchises for unemployment relief purposes, does not deny equal protection of the laws to the utilities. Taxes may be imposed on any group or class without regard to responsibility for the creation or relief of the conditions to be remedied with the funds. No relation between the class of taxpayers and the purpose of the appropriation need exist.

NY   N Y Rapid Transit v New York City (1938) 303 US 573, 82 LEd 1024, 58 SCt 721.

As applied to a utility which by contract shares a portion of its gross receipts with the city, an ordinance imposing an excise tax on gross receipts does not impair the obligations of the contract, where the contract contains no express tax exemption. Surrender of the power to tax will not be implied.

NY   N Y Rapid Transit v New York City (1938) 303 US 573, 82 LEd 1024, 58 SCt 721.

A corporation operating buses on the streets, after expiration of a limited franchise and without a public service permit, is not subject to an excise tax imposed by ordinance on all public utilities, where a "utility" is defined as any person subject to the supervision of the department of public service.

NY Rosenthal v New York City (1938) 277 NY 488, 14 NE2d 803.

An ordinance imposing an excise tax on all utilities holding franchises is not discriminatory, though the fares of public transportation utilities are limited by contract while other utilities are not so restricted.

NY N Y Rapid Transit v New York City (1938) 303 US 573, 82 LEd 1024, 58 SCt 721.

C. TAX EXEMPTIONS

§76. In General

An ordinance authorizing a street railway company to substitute electrical for animal power and inducing the company to lower its fares, in return for which the city exempts the company from the payment of taxes, is ineffective to grant an exemption, where the charter as well as the constitution prohibits the city from exempting any person or corporation from taxes. Accordingly, the city has power to levy an ad valorem tax on the value of the company's franchise, as determined by a state board.

Ky South Covington & C St Ry v Bellevue (1899) 105 Ky 283, 49 SW 23.

Where an enactment, nominally an ordinance, is in effect simply a contract between a city and a street railway company to pay so much money annually in lieu of all other taxes and charges, including street assessments, the enactment is void, because the city is prohibited by the constitution from granting a tax exemption.

Ky South Covington & C St Ry v Henkel (1929) 228 Ky 271, 14 SW2d 1068.

Where a common carrier permits other carriers to use its terminal for compensation, and rents its facilities to others for restaurant and parcel locker purposes, but receipts from such sources are less than operation expense of terminal, operation of such terminal is "in connection with and incidental to" the company's business as a common carrier, and is not for profit. Accordingly, it is exempt from license tax under an ordinance imposing such tax for the privilege of operating or conducting terminals for use by common carriers of passengers by motor vehicle.

Va Atl Greyhound v Winchester (1953) 195 Va 302, 78 SE2d 666.

Where the enabling act places the impact of a use tax on city residents, using or consuming in the city goods purchased without, the tax may not be imposed on any portion of the rental price of bus tires used on buses traveling over city streets, where neither the local law nor the statute provides for allocation of the bus line's routes located within and without the city.

NY Bee Line v Joseph (1954) 284 AD 98, 130 NYS2d 437.

An ordinance imposing a three per cent gross receipts tax on street railway or traction companies, to be levied on gross receipts from traffic, does not include dividends paid to the company by a wholly owned subsidiary operating motor buses.

Pa Harrisburg v Harrisburg Rys (1935) 319 Pa 140, 179 A 442.

An ordinance imposing a tax on the gross receipts of all utilities subject to the supervision of the department of public service is not unconstitutional for exempting city owned subways and taxicabs that are in competition with street railroads. A tax may be validly imposed on utility companies as a class, without including other industries and businesses.

NY N Y Rapid Transit v New York City (1938) 303 US 573, 82 LEd 1024, 58 SCt 721.

The statutory exemption for a transit company from the District's tax on motor fuel unless the company earns a return of 6.5 per cent on its rate base or operating revenues does not limit the discretion of the rate fixing commission by guaranteeing a 6.5 per cent minimum revenue for a transit company.

DC DC Transit Sys v Washington Metro Area Trans Comm (1965) 350 F2d 753.

STREETS; SIDEWALKS; BRIDGES

EDITORIAL COMMENT. In this topic we have brought together nearly all of the cases dealing with the construction and maintenance of roadways of various kinds, and with some aspects of their use. Thus, we include here such matters as dedication, opening and vacating, construction and maintenance, and the various means of financing. Also treated here are private uses, vaults under streets and sidewalks, excavations, landscaping, and obstructions.

Of interest is the inclusion of one very old case, from Alexandria, Virginia, decided in 1820. The case makes a valid point, to the effect that a property owner who is liable for a street assessment cannot avoid payment on the ground that the work on the street was badly done (§ 275).

Many other topics contain material that is related to streets in one way or another. Thus, public utility companies are involved in franchises for the use of streets, and these are treated separately in Electric Light and Power; Gas, Natural; Railroads; Streetcars and Buses; Taxis; in Telephones; Telegraph; Alarm Systems; and in Water Systems; Water Supply. The erection of billboards along streets is covered in Billboards; Signs; Posters, and the use of streets for parades and demonstrations is covered in Demonstrations; Parades; Meetings. A different kind of use of streets is covered in Street Vendors.

The drainage of streets, by storm sewers, is part of the subject matter of Drainage; Flood Control, and excavation other than in streets themselves are treated in Excavations. The duty of a subdivider to dedicate and lay out streets is dealt with in Subdivisions. The moving of houses through the streets is one facet of the topic Moving Businesses; Trucking; Shipping. The use of the streets for the parking of vehicles is dealt with in Parking, and the regulation of the movement of vehicles on the streets is covered in Traffic.

I. IN GENERAL

I. IN GENERAL

§1. Construction of Ordinances

Though the title of an ordinance may be broad enough to embrace sidewalk construction, it will not be so construed in an ordinance for street improvements, unless the body of the ordinance by its terms includes sidewalk construction.

Ky Paris v Fuhrman (1928) 226 Ky 72, 10 SW2d 475.

Where an ordinance authorizes work and invites bids for paving a street, and a contract is entered into for the work, the contract and the ordinance will be construed together so as to uphold their validity.

Mo Boonville v Stephens (1911) 238 Mo 339, 141 SW 1111.

Where an ordinance authorizes the paving of a street and assessment of costs thereof by tax bills against benefited properties with interest at 15 per cent, "interest" is construed to mean "penalty", and so does not offend the general statute limiting interest to six per cent.

> **Mo**   Barber Asphalt Paving v Hayward (1912) 248 Mo 280, 154 SW 140.

§2. —Local Improvements

A local improvement ordinance must be construed with reference to the description of the proposed improvement, estimate of cost, and plat filed therewith, all of which must sufficiently describe the improvement without recourse to any parol testimony except to explain the meaning of the plat.

> **Ill**   Harvard v Roach (1924) 314 Ill 424, 145 NE 618.

In all matters dealing with ordinances and statutes, the court, if possible, must so construe the official map law as to sustain constitutionality of the ordinance and in such a manner as to prevent the erection of permanent buildings in the bed of proposed streets if such construction will operate to impede or destroy a comprehensive street development plan.

> **NY**   Rochester Business Inst v Rochester (1966) 25 AD2d 97, 267 NYS2d 274.

Where a city is authorized by charter to charge the cost of street improvements to abutting lots marked off in blocks, the word "block" is construed to mean, for uniformity and equality in taxing, blocks as ordinarily platted, and tax bills issued against lots within an improvement district are subject to adjustment for deduction therefrom of proportionate amounts chargeable to lots in blocks improperly excluded from the district.

> **Mo**   Commerce Tr v Keck (1920) 283 Mo 209, 223 SW 1057.

§3. —Strict Construction against Municipality

An ordinance requiring approval by the council before making any repairs, alterations or construction of any roads within the city may not be applied to a political subdivision. The rebuilding of a county maintained road is not subject to regulation by the city.

> **Ill**   Highland Park v Cook County (1975) 37 IllAp3d 15, 344 NE2d 665.

The legislative power delegated to a city of the first class to construct local improvements and levy assessments is to be strictly construed, and every reasonable doubt about the extent or limitation of such power should be resolved against the city and in favor of the taxpayer.

La Bell v Shreveport (1958) 234 La 607, 100 So2d 883.
Mo Bigelow v Springfield (1914) 178 MoApp 463, 162 SW 750.
Neb Danielson v Bellevue (1959) 167 Neb 809, 95 NW2d 57.
      Chicago & NW Ry v Omaha (1953) 156 Neb 705, 57 NW2d 753.

Special assessments are strictly construed in favor of the taxpayer and against the taxing authority.

Neb State v Thomas (1934) 127 Neb 891, 257 NW 265.

§4. —In Favor of General Public

So as to relieve congested traffic conditions in the city, an ordinance relating to participation by the city in state highway construction should be liberally construed in favor of the general public and not strictly so as to favor individual interests.

Fla Morrison v Farnell (1936) 126 Fla 385, 171 So 528.

§5. —In Favor of Validity

All portions of a public improvement ordinance are to be construed together, and the whole ordinance must be given a construction, if reasonably possible, that will support rather than defeat it.

Ill Highwood v Chicago & M Elec RR (1915) 268 Ill 482, 109 NE 270.

§6. —Sidewalks Included in Streets

In construing statutes and ordinances relating to the power of municipalities to regulate the use of their streets, sidewalks are considered a part of the streets, but are set apart for pedestrians.

Ill Heineck v Grosse (1902) 99 IllAp 441.

In construing ordinances and statutes relative to municipal authority over highways, unless the context indicates otherwise, a "street" is included in the term "highway", and a sidewalk is as much a part of the highway as the roadway.

Ill Chicago v Pittsburgh, CC & S L RR (1909) 146 IllAp 403.

§7. —Singular Includes Plural, and Vice Versa

In an ordinance authorizing construction of a tunnel "for public uses," the singular number includes the plural and the plural the singular. The tunnel is a public use if it is open to the general public for travel in the manner to which it is adapted, though it is not open to all modes of travel.

Cal Larsen v San Francisco (1920) 182 Cal 1, 186 P 757.

§8. —Related Ordinances Read Together

Where an ordinance provides for grading and paving a sidewalk, and another ordinance authorizes assessment of damages and benefits therefor, both being adopted at the same time and relating to the same subject should be read together with respect to a claimed ambiguity or uncertainty as to the change of grade proposed.

Mo Kirksville v Ferguson (1914) 262 Mo 661, 172 SW 4.

§9. Municipal Rights

An ordinance provision that concrete sidewalks may be required when a building permit is issued for a principal structure is invalid. The statutory authorization for townships to require sidewalks provides only for sidewalks on petition by owners or along public highways when necessary for public safety. Any other ordinance requires public notice and hearing.

Mich Damico v Shelby Township (1975) 64 MichAp 271, 236 NW2d 69.

On annexation of a portion of land to a city title to the streets vests in the city. The county may not subsequently vacate a portion of a street within the city limits since they lose all control except for such interests as they may own. The ordinance vacating a 15-foot strip on each side of a right-of-way is invalid and full authority and use of the street right-of-way is in the city.

Ohio Sparrow v Columbus (1974) 69 Op2d 405, 40 OA2d 453, 320 NE2d 297.

Primary control of public streets in cities or towns is vested in the state, and any municipal powers or control by resolution or ordinance over public streets are only such as are delegated by the legislature.

Ind Larson v Wynnedale (1962) 133 IndAp 337, 179 NE2d 578.

A city cannot by ordinance grant any greater rights in a road than it possesses, which is only a fee in trust for public uses, that is, for all uses as a street, subject always to the property rights in the street of abutting lot owners.

> **Ohio** Anthony Carlin v Halle Bros (1926) 23 OA 115, 155 NE 398.
> **Tex** Uvalde Constr v Dallas (1936) 99 SW2d 644.

§10. Acquisition

When the city appropriates land by possession and by the act of laying pavement thereon, the land automatically becomes part of the street, and the servitude of passage, or easement thereover, in favor of the city or the public, comes into existence as fully as if the land had been acquired by contract or condemnation.

> **La** Shreveport v Selber (1945) 21 So2d 738.

A municipality may extend its streets into and through an adjoining municipality in order to connect any street with a street in the first municipality, and may acquire the necessary land in the adjoining municipality by purchase or condemnation, but any such extension must conform to the applicable ordinances of the adjoining municipality.

> **NJ** Verona v Cedar Grove (1958) 49 NJS 293, 139 A2d 584.
> Ridgewood v Glen Rock (1936) 15 NJM 65, 188 A 698.

§11. Sale

An ordinance authorizing sale of the fee of city streets, subject to the condition that title will revert to the city in the event an elevator corporation ceases its operations, is illegal because the statutory authority to discontinue streets and sell them at public auction to the highest bidder does not permit incorporation of conditions that stifle or deter bidding.

> **NY** Deed Rlty v Yonkers (1955) 1 Misc2d 280, 147 NYS2d 136.

The sale of a street is within the sound discretion of the council, functioning as the executive officers of the city.

> **La** Schernbeck v New Orleans (1923) 154 La 676, 98 So 84.

ANNOTATION

Power of city to exchange a street or alley, 60 ALR2d 237.

§12. Public Rights

The titles of streets and parks have immemorially been held in trust for use of the public as a part of the privileges, immunities, rights and liberties of citizens, and may not constitutionally, be infringed by municipalities through the enactment of ordinances containing unreasonable regulatory or prohibitory measures.

> **NJ**   Hague v CIO (1939) 307 US 496, 83 LEd 1423, 59 SCt 954.

The paramount right of the public to use the streets is the right of all persons to pass over them freely and without impediment, but that right is not absolute. It is subject to such incidental, temporary or partial obstruction as manifest necessity may require.

> **Cal**   People v Amdur (1954) 123 CA2d 951, 267 P2d 445.
> **Ill**   Chicago v McKinley (1931) 344 Ill 297, 176 NE 261.
>   Chicago Motor Coach v Chicago (1929) 337 Ill 200, 169 NE 22, 66 ALR 834.
> **Mass**   McKenna v Andreassi (1935) 292 Mass 213, 197 NE 879.

Ordinances regulating the use of streets must be construed in the light of the doctrine that the right of the public to the use of the streets is not confined to the surface, but includes the earth below and the air and light above.

> **Ill**   Northwestern Elevated Ry v Chicago (1904) 1 Ill CC 480.

§13. Regulation

A municipality may, by appropriate ordinances, supervise and control all public highways within its limits, but such supervision and control must be exercised reasonably.

> **Cal**   Haggerty v Kings County (1953) 117 CA2d 470, 256 P2d 393.
>   San Jose v Lynch (1935) 4 C2d 760, 52 P2d 919.
> **Conn**   Cassidy v Waterbury (1943) 130 Conn 237, 33 A2d 142.
> **Ga**   Gardner v Brunswick (1943) 197 Ga 167, 28 SE2d 135.
> **Ill**   Good Humor Corp v Mundelein (1965) 33 Ill2d 252, 211 NE2d 269.
>   Wilmot v Chicago (1927) 328 Ill 552, 160 NE 206, 62 ALR 394.
> **Kan**   Burke & McCaffrey v Merriam (1967) 198 Kan 325, 424 P2d 483.
> **Ky**   Reuter v Meacham Contracting (1911) 143 Ky 557, 136 SW 1028.
> **La**   Scott v West Monroe (1957) 95 So2d 343.
> **Me**   State v Barbelais (1906) 101 Me 512, 64 A 881.
> **Neb**   Dell v Lincoln (1959) 168 Neb 174, 95 NW2d 336.
> **NJ**   Levin v Livingston (1960) 62 NJS 395, 163 A2d 221.
>   Verona v Cedar Grove (1958) 49 NJS 293, 139 A2d 584.
> **NY**   People v Patrick (1939) 171 Misc 705, 14 NYS2d 249.
>   People v Banks (1938) 168 Misc 515, 6 NYS2d 41.
> **Tenn**   Paris v Paris-Henry County Pub Utilities Dist (1960) 207 Tenn 388, 340 SW2d 885.
> **Tex**   San Antonio v United Gas Pipe Line (1965) 388 SW2d 231.
>   Waco v Archenhold Auto Supply (1965) 386 SW2d 174.
> **W Va**   Brouzas v Morgantown (1958) 144 W Va 1, 106 SE2d 244.

A city may, through a condemnation ordinance, exercise the right to select the location of its streets, regardless of the wishes of the property owners whose land is taken for that purpose.

Ariz McCune v Phoenix (1957) 83 Ariz 98, 317 P2d 537.
Tenn Georgia v Chattanooga (1927) 4 TennApp 674.

An ordinance empowering the city to issue certificates of indebtedness for the acquisition and installation of traffic control signals and signs does not include within its scope street signs and block number plates.

Md Pressman v Baltimore (1952) 200 Md 107, 88 A2d 471.

A city's express powers respecting the cleaning and regulation of streets and public places, and the promotion of health and suppression of disease, constitute authority for enactment of an ordinance for execution of a contract for the removal and disposition of condemned meats and dead animals.

Ill Avery v Chicago (1931) 345 Ill 640, 178 NE 351.

The test of the validity of an ordinance regulating use of streets and sidewalks is its reasonableness.

NY Karl's Mariner's Inn v Northport (1963) 39 Misc2d 951, 242 NYS2d 297.

LAW REVIEW

Lenamyra Saulson, Constitutional Law—Municipal Control of Public Streets and Parks as Affecting Freedom of Speech and Assembly, 49 Mich LR 1185.

ANNOTATION

Snow removal as governmental or proprietary function, 92 ALR2d 801.

§14. —Restriction

A municipality by valid ordinance may restrict the location of streets to not less than 250 feet apart, thereby allowing for back to back lots that meet the minimum depth restriction. This right does not depend on enactment or incorporation of the Municipal Planning Act or the Official Map and Building Permit Act.

NJ Kligman v Lautman (1969) 53 NJ 517, 251 A2d 745.

Though cities may regulate the use of their streets, they do not have absolute power to exclude vehicles from the streets.

> **NY** People v Francis (1967) 53 Misc2d 606, 279 NYS2d 483.

A statute authorizing joint maintenance and repair of highways by cities and counties cannot be construed to give a municipality extra-territorial regulatory authority over roads that extend into an adjoining village. Such regulatory ordinances may not be enforced beyond city boundaries.

> **NY** Buffalo v Int Bus Corp (1932) 144 Misc 662, 259 NYS 237.

Any regulation designed to carry out a city council's power to maintain streets and sidewalks for public use must have a just relation to the object in view and a reasonable tendency to preserve or protect the public safety or convenience.

> **Cal** Laura Vincent Co v Selma (1941) 43 CA2d 473, 111 P2d 17.
> **Conn** Stevens v Neligon (1933) 116 Conn 307, 164 A 661.
> **SC** Grady v Greenville (1924) 129 SC 89, 123 SE 494.

§15. —Removal of Soil

An ordinance prohibiting the removal of dirt or gravel from the streets is a proper exercise of regulatory authority over streets, and is applicable to the owner of the fee of a street from which dirt is removed.

> **Ill** Palatine v Krueger (1887) 121 Ill 72, 12 NE 75.

§16. Street Names

The naming of streets and public places, and the numbering of houses and buildings, are legislative matters, and, where the legislature has delegated such power to a municipality, the courts may not disturb its exercise on the ground that such exercise is unreasonable.

> **Ill** Hagerty v Chicago (1935) 360 Ill 97, 195 NE 652, 98 ALR 1210.
> **NJ** Darling v Jersey City (1910) 80 NJLaw 514, 78 A 10.

§17. —Right to Change

A requirement that any legislative act can be accomplished only by ordinance applies to the change of name for a city street. A motion changing the name of a street is invalid since it constitutes a legislative rather than an administrative act.

> **Tex** Austin v Findlay (1976) 538 SW2d 9.

Under a city's expressly delegated power to name and change the name of any street or other public place, an ordinance changing the name of a street is a legislative act, not subject to review by the courts.

> **Ill** Hagerty v Chicago (1934) 274 IllAp 39.
> **Kan** Brown v Topeka (1937) 146 Kan 974, 74 P2d 142.
> **NY** Belden v Niagara Falls (1930) 230 AD 601, 245 NYS 510.
> **Wash** Eldridge v Fawcett (1924) 128 Wash 615, 223 P 1040.

City may not change the designation of boulevards in annexed territory to streets, and thus render lot owners liable to special assessments for paving.

> **Mich** Oprisiu v Detroit (1929) 248 Mich 590, 227 NW 714.
> Miller v Detroit (1928) 244 Mich 38, 221 NW 292.

§18. —Property Rights

Owners of property abutting on a street have no property right in its name; and the city can change the name of a street without resorting to eminent domain or exercising its police power.

> **Ill** Hagerty v Chicago (1935) 360 Ill 97, 195 NE 652, 98 ALR 1210.
> **Kan** Brown v Topeka (1937) 146 Kan 974, 74 P2d 142.

§19. Numbering Buildings

Under a city charter, the board of aldermen is given power to enact ordinances regulating the numbering of houses.

> **NJ** Darling v Jersey City (1910) 80 NJLaw 514, 78 A 10.

II. DEFINITIONS

§20. Abut, Abutting

Land is abutting a street improvement if it touches against the street. The existence of an easement for screening from the property across the street is not an intervening area.

> **Tex** Clements v Corpus Christi (1971) 471 SW2d 83.

An irregular or triangular lot is subject to a paving assessment along the line abutting the improvement, since the word "abut" means that there intervenes no other land that may be put to private use between that assessed and the improvement.

> **La** Shreveport v Selber (1945) 21 So2d 738.

"Abutting", as used to indicate the location of property in a street improvement ordinance, means "joined to or adjoining," but does not necessarily require that the things spoken of be in contact with each other.

Ill People v Willison (1909) 237 Ill 584, 86 NE 1094.
La Alexandria v Chicago, R I & P RR (1961) 240 La 1025, 126 So2d 351, 97 ALR2d 1073.

§21. Adjoining

Property described in an ordinance as "adjoining" the locality to be affected by a street improvement district is any land connected to or near the improvement which is physically or commercially affected in excess of property in the city generally.

Ark Freeze v Improvement Dist 16 of Jonesboro (1916) 126 Ark 172, 189 SW 660.

§22. Avenue

Under a city's charter authorization to establish boulevards and assess the costs against abutting property, and to establish streets and assess the costs against both abutting and nonabutting property, an ordinance authorizing establishment of an avenue as a public highway is construed to refer to the establishment of a street, since an "avenue" is a wide street, and a public highway is merely a name given to a particular thoroughfare, and neither one is the designation of a boulevard.

Mo St Louis v Breuer (1920) 223 SW 108.

§23. Cement Sidewalk

An ordinance providing for construction of a sidewalk is not invalid as uncertain because of its provision for a "cement" sidewalk in one portion, and in another for a "cement-concrete-sand-and gravel" walk, since "cement sidewalk" is a generic expression, and the further description is merely a statement of the ingredients to be used.

Ill Gage v Chicago (1902) 196 Ill 512, 63 NE 1031.

§24. Contiguous

"Contiguous", in a statute authorizing municipalities to render a special assessment against property contiguous to a local improvement, means "in actual or close contact", "touching", "adjacent", or "near".

Ill Adams County v Quincy (1889) 130 Ill 566, 22 NE 624.

§25. Expedient

In an ordinance authorizing the director of public works to grant permission to work on any unaccepted public street if he determines after the investigation the public interest requires the proposed work and that it is expedient and will not be detrimental to the public safety or convenience, the word "expedient" means suited to the circumstances.

Cal Portman v Clementina (1957) 147 CA2d 651, 305 P2d 963.

§26. Fund

"Fund", in a tax levy ordinance providing for items of "sidewalk fund", will not render such itemizations vague and indefinite, since the meaning of "fund" is readily understood.

Ill People ex rel Wilson v Wabash Ry (1938) 368 Ill 497, 14 NE2d 650.

§27. May

"May" is not to be construed as "must" or "shall" but merely as permissive and discretionary, in an ordinance providing that the grade of alleys, not otherwise fixed, at the points of intersection with streets whose grades are established by the ordinance, shall be the same as said streets, and continuous from one street to the next, but between any two adjacent streets along the line of the alley vertical curves of grade "may" be used when necessary to facilitate drainage or afford better access to property.

Iowa Kelly v Cedar Falls (1904) 123 Iowa 660, 99 NW 556.

§28. Pavement

"Pavement", in a charter provision authorizing a city to pave and improve its streets, is not limited to uniformly arranged masses of solid material, such as blocks of wood, brick, or stone, but pavement may be formed of pebbles, gravel or other hard substance, which will make a compact, even, hard way or floor.

Ill Burnham v Chicago (1860) 24 Ill 496.

§29. Public Highway

Where a city by its charter has authority to cause to be established both boulevards and streets, and an ordinance is enacted establishing "Kingsbury boulevard" as a "public highway", the ordinance is not sufficient for the opening of a street and assessment of benefits against adjacent lands, since "public highway" may embrace either a boulevard or a street, and a doubt is thereby created, rendering the ordinance void for uncertainty.

> **Mo** St Louis v Breuer (1920) 223 SW 108.
> St Louis v Bell Place Rlty (1914) 259 Mo 126, 168 SW 721.

§30. Public Square

"Public square", in a street improvement ordinance, means certain property that has been dedicated to public use, and the public square of a county is of a public nature and is held for governmental purposes.

> **Ill** People v Willison (1909) 237 Ill 584, 86 NE 1094.

§31. Repave

Repave as used in a franchise ordinance means a replacing by similar or different material of the paving on a street. This is usually occasioned by a generally unfit condition of the old surface and is from curb to curb and all or part of a block.

> **Ohio** Cleveland Ry v Cleveland (1918) 97 OS 122, 119 NE 202.

§32. Road

"Road", as used in a public improvement ordinance, is now commonly used as denoting a public way in the country rather than the street of a town or city.

> **Ill** Mushbaugh v East Peoria (1913) 260 Ill 27, 102 NE 1027.

§33. Road Poll Tax

A "road poll tax" ordinance is in the nature of a police regulation, and does not impose a tax in the sense used when referring to general taxation under statutory and constitutional concepts.

> **Utah** Salt Lake City v Wilson (1915) 46 Utah 60, 148 P 1104.

§34. Separate Property Area

"Separate property area", in an ordinance setting up a special street assessment district means geographically separate or noncontiguous areas.

> **ND** Murphy v Bismarck (1961) 109 NW2d 635.

§35. Sidewalk

A grassy section between the paved portion of a sidewalk and the curbing is a sidewalk and not a parkway, within the meaning of an ordinance defining a sidewalk as any portion of a street between the curb line and the adjacent property line intended for pedestrian use, excluding parkways, which are broad thoroughfares beautified with trees and turf.

> **Ill** Elmhurst v Buettgen (1946) 394 Ill 248, 68 NE2d 278.
> **La** Labruzza v Boston Ins Co (1967) 198 So2d 436.

§36. Street

Street within an ordinance means the area within the right-of-way whether open for public travel or not. The distance for planting hedges or creating other obstructions at an intersection is determined from the edge of the right-of-way rather than the traveled portion of the street.

> **Ariz** Slavin v Tucson (1972) 17 ArizApp 16, 495 P2d 141.

Access roads to several apartment buildings constructed on the same lot and for the use of the inhabitants are not public thoroughfares subject to subdivision requirements.

> **Pa** Cassidy v Lawrence U Ginter (1972) 6 PaCmwlth 430, 296 A2d 293.

The word "street", in an ordinance ordering a street to be improved at the cost of abutting property, means the entire width of the public way, and includes the sidewalk. A narrower interpretation may be applied to a contractual relationship, but in general application the word does not exclude sidewalks and neutral grounds adjacent thereto.

> **Ill** Elmhurst v Buettgen (1946) 394 Ill 248, 68 NE2d 278.
> Mushbaugh v East Peoria (1913) 260 Ill 27, 102 NE 1027.
> **Ky** Morton v Sullivan (1906) 29 KLR 910, 96 SW 807.
> **La** Shreveport v Selber (1945) 21 So2d 738.5

§37. Streets and Alleys

In an ordinance regulating the use of streets and alleys and the space underneath sidewalks, the words "streets and alleys" are virtually synonymous, since there is no distinction in law between a public street and a public alley, and the only popular distinction is an indefinite difference in width.

> **Ill** J Burton Co v Chicago (1908) 236 Ill 383, 86 NE 93.

305

§ 38. Street Improvements

Street improvements do not fall within the term "public utilities", as used in the state constitutional provision authorizing municipal corporations to incur indebtedness, on the approving vote of a majority of qualified voters, for purchasing or constructing public utilities. Thus, an ordinance directing the issuance of bonds for the construction of public utilities did not authorize the financing of street improvements.

Okla   Coleman v Frame (1910) 26 Okla 193, 109 P 928.

§ 39. Way

An off street parking area designated as such by a city ordinance, but not established by statutory layout as a highway or parking area, and which has not been in use for 20 years, constitutes a "road which has been constructed for public travel" and is a "way" within the statutory definition of "public highway"; and travel thereon is subject to statutory regulations applicable to travel on public highways.

NH   State v Rosier (1963) 105 NH 6, 191 A2d 526.

III. DEDICATION

§ 40. Generally

A city's delay in using property to widen a street does not in law constitute an abandonment by the city when there is no evidence the city has renounced a planned widening of the street or has taken any action amounting to affirmative abandonment.

Fla   Miami v J C Vereen & Sons (1978) 359 So2d 533.

An ordinance placing a street dedicated by a subdivider on the city planning map, when it has not been used or opened within the statutory time limit, is invalid.

Pa   Bruce Ave, Matter of condemnation (1970) 438 Pa 498, 266 A2d 96.

A requirement that any person constructing or developing any industrial property along a major street shall dedicate a right-of-way equivalent to 50 feet from the center of the major street and shall pave the same requires a determination that the construction will increase the traffic. The paving requirements are invalid particularly where the construction will decrease the amount of traffic to be generated.

> **Okla** Associated Milk Producers v Midwest City (1978) 583 P2d 491.

Approval of a site plan may not be conditioned on granting a strip of land for eventual widening of the street. The site as a law office will have only nominal effect on the traffic and the county may not bank land for future use as a condition to approval.

> **NJ** 181 Inc v Salem County Planning Bd (1975) 133 NJS 350, 336 A2d 501.

Where in dedicating real property to a city for use as a public street no restriction is imposed on the city's right to extend, straighten, widen or close the street, the city may exercise those rights in the enactment of an ordinance.

> **Ky** Henderson Elevator v Henderson (1920) 187 Ky 453, 219 SW 809.
> **La** St James Parish v Borne (1941) 198 La 959, 5 So2d 301.
> **Okla** Dorris v Hawk (1956) 292 P2d 417.

Appropriation of long range city plans for proposed streets does not constitute inverse condemnation. The plans which are subject to change or modification on future conditions do not deprive the owner of his property without compensation.

> **Cal** Selby Rlty Co v San Buenaventura (1973) 10 C3d 110, 514 P2d 111,
> 109 CaR 799.

Where mode of dedicating municipal property for a public street is prescribed by the municipal charter, a dedication made without regard to the prescribed mode is unenforceable.

> **Cal** Oakland v Burns (1956) 46 C2d 401, 296 P2d 333.

Announcement and the passage of a resolution and ordinance providing for an express system of streets which will cross applicant's property does not constitute inverse condemnation due to the mere passage of time without any action. Any loss suffered due to the inability to sell the property or develop it is a personal rather than a property loss.

> **Okla** Empire Construction v Tulsa (1973) 512 P2d 119.

The dedication of a street to the use of the public is valid regardless of whether or not it is accepted by an ordinance.

> **Iowa** Louden v Starr (1915) 171 Iowa 528, 154 NW 331.

The law authorizing commissioners to open, extend, widen, or straighten alleys and minor streets, subject to certain conditions, does not apply to a voluntary dedication accepted by the commissioners under authority of law.

> **DC**   Barnard v Comm of DC (1957) 246 F2d 685.

Where a property owner dedicated a strip of ground in front of his lots to the public for the purpose of providing a street, but reserved a strip 12 feet wide for the purpose of courtyards (sidewalks), the city may not direct that such strip be converted into a roadway that would deprive the property owner of all use of the sidewalk.

> **Ill**   Carter v Chicago (1870) 57 Ill 283.

LAW REVIEW

Inverse Condemnation: Its Availability in Challenging the Validity of a Zoning Ordinance, 26 Stan LR 1439.

§41. What Constitutes

When a street has regularly been shelled and graded, and garbage collected, and has otherwise been maintained in a continuous and uninterrupted manner for at least seven years, it is undisputably a dedicated public right-of-way and presents no legal obstacles to paving.

> **Fla**   Johnson v Arcadia (1978) 450 F Supp 1363.

Where property owners request the extension of a street through land they own, and the city by ordinance directs that the street be graded and graveled, it amounts to a dedication of the land for street purposes.

> **Ky**   Bloomfield v Allen (1911) 146 Ky 34, 141 SW 400.
> Terrell v Hart (1906) 28 KLR 901, 90 SW 953.

Where a landowner by moving a fence and stating that he is giving the ground for the purpose of a sidewalk, thereby dedicates it to the city, and the city enacts an ordinance for its improvement, these acts of dedication and of acceptance perfect the title of the city.

> **Ky**   Harrison v Greenville (1912) 146 Ky 96, 142 SW 219.
> **Mo**   St Louis v Koch (1934) 335 Mo 991, 74 SW2d 622.

An ordinance directing the construction of a sidewalk is not subject to the objection that the sidewalk was not dedicated to the city, where its original use as a private sidewalk was only permissive, but a long continued public use thereafter serves as a sufficient dedication to the public use.

Ky Bloomfield v Allen (1911) 146 Ky 34, 141 SW 400.

§42. —By Implication

Regardless of the ownership of land on which a street improvement and paving assessment is lawfully laid in the absence of protest from the owner, an implied dedication results on acceptance of the work by the city and use by the public, and assessments levied by ordinance against the abutting property for costs of the improvement are proper and legal.

La Shreveport v Selber (1945) 21 So2d 738.

Where paving is laid under an ordinance and the street is used by the public generally, the owner of the fee is precluded from reclaiming the property if he fails to object to the appropriation, since the doctrine of implied dedication operates as an estoppel, on acceptance and use by the public with the tacit consent of the owner.

La Ford v Shreveport (1943) 204 La 618, 16 So2d 127.

§43. Estoppel to Deny

Where property owners bring suit to prevent the extending and opening of a street under an ordinance on the ground that the street was not dedicated by their predecessor in title, if the predecessor, on the basis of sales of land with reference to a subdivision map showing a dedication of the street, would have been estopped to assert as against his vendees or the general public that the strip of land was a street, his heirs are estopped to deny that the city, which has acquired the interest of the predecessor's grantee, can open the street to public use.

La Richard v New Orleans (1940) 195 La 898, 197 So 594.

§44. Effect

Dedication of a public street does not invest the municipality with a fee title to the land on which the roadway rests. The municipality acquires the right to use, maintain, regulate and control that land as a street or road for the benefit of the public. What the public obtains is a right of passage; the fee continues to be in the owner or owners of the land.

Pa Altoona, In re Appeal of (1978) 479 Pa 252, 388 A2d 313.

By accepting the dedication of a street the city has a duty to maintain the street in a reasonable condition or vacate it. In the event of vacating compensation must be paid to any homeowner who is denied access to his property. A refusal of the city to repair or vacate a street damaged by flood constitutes a breach of duty to the abutting land owners. A city must either restore the access or compensate abutting owners on vacating.

> **Cal**   Clay v Los Angeles (1971) 21 CA3d 577, 98 CaR 582.

Where a street has been dedicated by a common-law dedication, the fee remains in the abutting property owners, but its use is dedicated to the city in trust, for street purposes only.

> **Ill**   Greenlee Foundry v Borin Art Prod (1942) 379 Ill 494, 41 NE2d 532.

After a street is dedicated to public use, in the absence of proof showing its abandonment as a street, when it is incorporated or reincorporated into city limits it remains a public street, and may be improved under an ordinance authorizing street improvements.

> **Ky**   Henderson v Blackwell (1920) 189 Ky 746, 226 SW 370.

§45. Acceptance

Offering to dedicate a street or walk in a subdivision does not make them subject to the city's control until accepted. Where a walk was not accepted nor any overt action taken to constitute an acceptance, there is no liability on the city.

> **Cal**   Ackley v San Francisco (1970) 11 CA3d 110, 89 CaR 480.

To have a valid dedication of a street there must be an offer and acceptance. Failure of the city to accept by action, maintenance, or use as a public thoroughfare justifies a withdrawal of the offer.

> **Md**   Glenarden v Lewis (1971) 261 Md 1, 273 A2d 140.

A dedication of a street to public use by plats and deeds does not make the street a public highway. Such a deed does not become final and irrevocable until acceptance by the public authorities.

> **Cal**   Sacramento v Jensen (1956) 146 CA2d 114, 303 P2d 549.
>   Barber Asphalt Paving v Jurgens (1915) 170 Cal 273, 149 P 560, 9 ALR 597.
> **Md**   Hackerman v Baltimore (1957) 212 Md 618, 130 A2d 732.
>   Baltimore v Canton of Baltimore (1915) 124 Md 620, 93 A 144.

Though the dedication of a street is accepted by the city, until the city manifests some intent to use it or it is used as a street there is no public use, and no rights will accrue in such street as against the city.

Neb Aro Inv v Omaha (1966) 179 Neb 569, 139 NW2d 349.

A city is without power to accept dedication of any portion of a street outside its city limits, and approval of a subdivision map does not work such an acceptance.

Cal Miller v Fowle (1949) 92 CA2d 409, 206 P2d 1106.

Any presumption of acceptance of a dedication of streets and alleys to public use is rebutted by continued adverse possession of the original dedicator and his vendees who occupy the territory for the statutory period of limitations, and though the dedication be evidenced by the recording of a plat the later annexation of the territory by the city does not remove the bar of the statute so as to make lawful an attempt by the city to open up such streets by ordinance.

Ky Latonia v Latonia Agricultural Assn (1908) 139 Ky 732, 109 SW 356.

ANNOTATION

Acceptance of some of streets, alleys, and the like appearing on plat as acceptance of all, 32 ALR2d 953.

§46. —What Constitutes

The plat alone is an insufficient basis for determining whether a dedication has been accepted. A finding that the dedication of an alley has been accepted may be based on such factors as the city's graveling of an alley and construction of curbing to permit ingress and egress, use of land under the alley by public utilities, and refusal of the city to vacate.

SD Haley v Rapid City (1978) 269 NW2d 398.

Though a dedication has not been formally accepted by a municipality, the public's acceptance by public use of the street is effective, and prevents the person dedicating the land from closing the road or preventing further public use.

Mo Hoechst v Bangert (1969) 440 SW2d 476.

Expenditures to install water mains, fire hydrants, lights, and sewer system, together with maintenance and paving of a street, constitute acceptance of a dedication to public use.

Mich Sharkey v Petoskey (1971) 30 MichAp 640, 186 NW2d 744.

Annexation by ordinance of a platted addition is a sufficient acceptance of the streets in a dedication of land.

> **Ind**   Walmer v Bremen (1934) 99 IndAp 186, 191 NE 175.

Evidence of the acceptance of a street by a municipality is found in the affirmative act of taking possession for the purpose of placing sewers therein.

> **Conn**   Whippoorwill Crest v Stratford (1958) 145 Conn 268, 141 A2d 241.

Where a city enacts several ordinances recognizing existence of a dedicated street, such ordinances constitute an acceptance of the offer of dedication.

> **Cal**   Los Angeles v McCollum (1909) 156 Cal 148, 103 P 914.
>   London & San Francisco Bk v Oakland (1898) 90 F 691.
> **Iowa**   Burroughs v Cherokee (1906) 134 Iowa 429, 109 NW 876.
> **Ky**   Sullivan v Louisville (1942) 291 Ky 60, 163 SW2d 17.
>   Steinacker v Gast (1905) 28 KLR 573, 89 SW 481.
> **NY**   Feldman v Pulitzer (1957) 7 Misc2d 709, 162 NYS2d 449.

Where a strip of land forming a cul-de-sac at the end of a street was never improved as a street and was fenced with the adjoining land, an ordinance adopting an official grade map and including the strip in the street, and the adoption of assessment district maps, did not constitute a formal acceptance of a purported offer to dedicate the strip. Whether there was an implied acceptance by the passage of ordinances and the adoption of the maps was a question of fact.

> **Cal**   Santa Clara v Ivancovich (1941) 47 CA2d 502, 118 P2d 303.

A statute providing that no street dedicated to public use shall be deemed a public street unless accepted and confirmed by an ordinance or resolution specially passed for that purpose is for the protection of municipalities against liabilities that might otherwise be created by the dedication of streets without the consent or knowledge of the city, and the city may waive it and accept the street for the public without either an ordinance or a resolution.

> **Iowa**   Hunter v Des Moines (1909) 144 Iowa 541, 123 NW 215.

§47. —Necessity

An offer of dedication of a street for public use is incomplete without acceptance either by public use or by other action by public authorities.

> **Del**   Nolan v Eastern (1968) 241 A2d 885.

§48. —Effect

A municipality which accepts a dedicated street is not restricted in its use of the street to the public's right of passage, but is entitled to make any additional use of the property consistent with its character as a public street. Dedication does not impose on a municipality a duty to maintain the roadway in perpetuity, but only for as long as the designated use continues to serve the public interest.

Pa   Altoona, In re Appeal of (1978) 479 Pa 252, 388 A2d 313.

After its dedication and acceptance by an ordinance, a street becomes a public street of the city, and the manner of its improvement is wholly discretionary with city authorities.

Ky   Barnett v Figg (1915) 165 Ky 479, 177 SW 275.

§49. Revocation

By adopting an ordinance for public accommodation the county may bring an action against a subdeveloper who has dedicated a proposed street and then attempts to revoke the dedication. A subdivider filing a plat and selling lots off of it has made a formal irrevocable dedication.

Ga   Lee v Warren (1973) 230 Ga 165, 195 SE2d 909.

Where statutory authority exists, a municipality may revoke the dedication of roads, streets or alleyways by ordinance.

La   State v Shreveport (1957) 231 La 840, 93 So2d 187.
Metairie Park v Currie (1929) 168 La 588, 122 So 859.

A resolution revoking the dedication of a street was not an abuse of discretion, or arbitrary or capricious action, where the portion of the street affected had not been used for almost three years, there was no diminution in value of the properties affected, no serious inconvenience was caused by the compelled use of other nearby streets and the public had not recently made use of the street.

La   Torrance v Caddo Parish (1960) 119 So2d 617.
Caz-Perk Rlty v East Baton Rouge Parish (1945) 207 La 796, 22 So2d 121.

Where by ordinance a dedication of streets and alleys is rescinded the courts must assume, in the absence of contrary allegations, that the streets and alleys were abandoned and no longer necessary.

La   State v Hickman (1930) 13 LaApp 173, 127 So 659.

§50. —Effect

When under authority of a special statute a city enacts an ordinance revoking the dedication of an alley, the adjoining property owners at the time the ordinance is officially recorded acquire title to the alleyway.

> **La**　Martin v Fuller (1948) 214 La 404, 37 So2d 851.

An ordinance revoking the dedication of streets and alleys in a subdivision does not affect the rights of purchasers in good faith until recorded. A purchaser of land may rely on the public records in the absence of notice of irregularities or facts indicative of litigation.

> **La**　Arkansas Fuel v Weber (1963) 149 So2d 101.

ANNOTATION

Right of grantor of land for parkway in center of street to reversion, 81 ALR2d 1447.

IV. VACATION; CLOSING

§51. Generally

An ordinance vacating a portion of a street in order to permit construction of a large warehouse facility is reasonable on showing the betterment of the community and the lack of individual harm. A claim that property which touches at one corner is being denied its right of ingress and egress is insufficient to set aside the vacating when access to the property is still available. Likewise the sale to the one party is reasonable on showing that the price plus the improvements made by the purchaser in the utilities and their relocation was for the public benefit.

> **Neb**　Cather & Sons Const v Lincoln (1978) 200 Neb 510, 264 NW2d 413.

A private sale of streets and sidewalks to conform to the original plat, or because they no longer serve the particular purpose for which they were laid out and thus are obsolete, is valid. A finding in the ordinance that the exchange of property was made to implement a river front improvement plan satisfies the requirements, without the use of the special words from the statute.

> **Ga**　Save The Bay Committee v Savannah (1971) 227 Ga 436, 181 SE2d 351.

When the purposes for which the land was dedicated to a public street no longer exist or the public is no longer benefited by such use, the municipality has the power and sometimes a duty to vacate the road. Thereafter, the municipality may not legally reserve to itself an easement extending throughout the area of the road for the construction, maintenance and operation or reconstruction of utilities in, through, over or under the same.

> **Pa** Altoona, In re Appeal of (1978) 26 PaCmwlth 1, 361 A2d 458, affd 479 Pa 252, 388 A2d 313.

The right to vacate a street is to be exercised only when the municipal authorities, in the exercise of sound official discretion, determine that the street is no longer required for the public use or convenience.

> **Cal** People v San Rafael (1928) 95 CA 733, 273 P 138.
> **La** Torrance v Caddo Parish (1960) 119 So2d 617.
> **SC** Bethel Methodist Episcopal Church v Greenville (1947) 211 SC 442, 45 SE2d 841.

In selling the right-of-way of a vacated street the property must be valued at fair market value and sold to the abutting owners for at least 90 per cent of this value. The city may not allow an automatic 50 per cent reduction for rights of ingress and egress.

> **Cal** Harman v San Francisco (1972) 7 C3d 150, 496 P2d 1248, 101 CaR 880.

In establishing a value on a vacated street the city may properly consider the increase in value to an adjoining building due to the permitted size increase and the restricted amount of use by the general public. Benefits received by the city such as a parkway or pedestrian mall are properly deducted from the value in determining whether 90 per cent valuation bid has been made.

> **Cal** Meakin v Steveland (1977) 68 CA3d 490, 137 CaR 359.

While the city may properly close a street it may not dispose of the property by gift. The city may only dispose of its property in good faith and for an adequate consideration, thus a gift to the school board is improper.

> **Utah** Sears v Ogden City (1975) 533 P2d 118.

Adoption of an ordinance closing a street is a determination that the public interest or convenience requires the improvement.

> **Cal** Beals v Los Angeles (1943) 23 C2d 381, 144 P2d 839.
> People v Los Angeles (1923) 62 CA 781, 218 P 63.
> **Iowa** Walker v Des Moines (1913) 161 Iowa 215, 142 NW 51.
> **Kan** Kinney v Reno Community High Sch (1930) 130 Kan 610, 287 P 258.
> **Ky** Henderson Elevator v Henderson (1920) 187 Ky 453, 219 SW 809.
> **Miss** Puyper v Pure Oil (1952) 215 Miss 121, 60 So2d 569.

Under statutory authority, the vacation of streets and alleys by a municipality may be effectuated by ordinance only.

> **Ill**   Arlington Heights Nat Bk v Arlington Heights (1966) 33 Ill2d 557, 213 NE2d 264.
> **NJ**   Barnegat Light v Ocean County (1957) 44 NJS 316, 130 A2d 409.

A resolution was a proper instrument to handle the city's abandonment of a street, where the charter provided that ordinances and resolutions should become effective 30 days after their passage; and though an ordinance has to be introduced at a meeting prior to the one in which it is passed, the resolution may be introduced and passed at the same meeting.

> **Cal**   Oakland v Burns (1956) 46 C2d 401, 296 P2d 333.
> **Ga**   Campbell v Columbus (1968) 224 Ga 279, 161 SE2d 299.

Adoption of an ordinance approving a freeway construction plan that would result in a barricade of a street, preventing traffic on it, together with the actual physical closing of the street, constitutes a legal vacation, thereof, though the ordinance did not specifically declare the street vacated.

> **Pa**   Hasenflu v Commonwealth (1962) 406 Pa 631, 179 A2d 216.

Where an ordinance declares a vacation of a 10 foot strip of street and dedication to the abutting lot owners for the purpose of improving the appearance of the street, but provides that no buildings shall be erected on said strip, and no charter authority exists for street vacation, the ordinance is not a vacation, but merely a revocable permit to use a portion of the street for parking.

> **Ore**   Bernitt v Marshfield (1918) 89 Ore 556, 174 P 1153.

Where a city had previously declared a street to be a 70-foot right-of-way, a subsequent ordinance establishing it as a 50-foot right-of-way results in an abandonment of the remainder to the abutting property owners.

> **Fla**   Woodlawn Park Cemetery v Miami (1958) 104 So2d 851.

Adoption of an ordinance specifically declaring the vacation of a street is generally requisite to a legal vacation.

> **Pa**   Hasenflu v Commonwealth (1962) 406 Pa 631, 179 A2d 216.

The courts will not ordinarily interfere with an ordinance vacating a street or alley.

> **Iowa**   Pederson v Radcliffe (1939) 226 Iowa 166, 284 NW 145.

ANNOTATION

Effect of regulations as to subdivision maps or plats upon vacation of streets, 11 ALR2d 587.

§52. Power of Municipality

A city ordinance providing that the assent of the city council to the vacation of any street or public way shall not be given until the applicant pays the city an amount equal to the reasonable market value of the land is invalid as beyond the city's statutory authority where the statute only provides that the city council must give its assent to vacation of a street or alley, but there is not express or implied authority to require payment of fair market value of the land before the city gives assent.

> **Ala** E C Overton v Scott Co Inc (1978) 356 So2d 134.

While a city can take land for streets by eminent domain it must be for a public purpose, and evidence must be presented that a street to be taken and vacated is for the public benefit rather than the private gain of the developers of the shopping center proposed in the area.

> **Pa** Bruce Ave, Matter of condemnation (1970) 438 Pa 498, 266 A2d 96.

The power to vacate public streets is as necessary for the public good as the power to establish them, in order that the public may be relieved of the expense of maintaining useless streets and highways, and of liability for their nonrepair or defective condition, and in order that the space may be devoted to more pressing public needs.

> **Fla** Sun Oil v Gerstein (1968) 206 So2d 439.
>   Roney Inv v Miami Beach (1937) 127 Fla 773, 174 So 26.
> **Ga** Harbuck v Richland Box (1951) 207 Ga 537, 63 SE2d 333.
> **Ill** Ferguson Coal v Thompson (1931) 343 Ill 20, 174 NE 896.
>   Hill v Kimball (1915) 269 Ill 398, 110 NE 18.
> **Iowa** Walker v Des Moines (1913) 161 Iowa 215, 142 NW 51.
> **Kan** Eastborough Corp v Eastborough (1968) 201 Kan 491, 441 P2d 891.
> **Ky** Fulton v Penny (1938) 273 Ky 465, 116 SW2d 963.
> **Md** Baltimore v Baltimore Gas & Elec (1959) 221 Md 94, 156 A2d 447.
> **NY** Gillen Place, In re (1952) 304 NY 215, 106 NE2d 897.
> **Ohio** Zetzer v Lundgard (1953) 95 OA 51, 52 Op 407, 117 NE2d 445.
> **Okla** Blackwell v Gist (1907) 18 Okla 516, 90 P 889.
> **Tenn** Sweetwater Valley Memorial Park v Sweetwater (1963) 213 Tenn 1, 372 SW2d 168.
> **Tex** Johnson v Lancaster (1924) 266 SW 565.

Under a city's delegated power to vacate any street or alley or part thereof, a city may vacate that portion of an alley extending indefinitely upwards from an imaginary horizontal plane 16 feet above the elevation of the center line of the alley as presently graded.

Wash Taft v Wash Mutual Sav Bk (1923) 127 Wash 503, 221 P 604.

§53. —Motives; Wisdom; Expediency

A court is without right to inquire into the motives of a city council in vacating a street or alley, or into the wisdom of expediency of such action, the court's power being limited to a determination of whether the council's act is beyond the scope of its legislative power.

Ill People v Eakin (1943) 383 Ill 383, 50 NE2d 474.
People v Chicago (1926) 321 Ill 466, 152 NE 141.
Ky Henderson v Lexington (1908) 132 Ky 390, 111 SW 318.
Mich Tomaszewski v Palmer Bee (1923) 223 Mich 565, 194 NW 571.
Neb Dell v Lincoln (1960) 170 Neb 176, 102 NW2d 62.
NJ Con Rlty v Ellenstein (1940) 125 NJLaw 196, 14 A2d 544.
Ohio Smith v Wintersville (1962) 90 Abs 47, 26 Op2d 40, 187 NE2d 511.
Pa Cohen v Simpson Real Estate (1956) 385 Pa 352, 123 A2d 715.
Tenn Sweetwater Valley Memorial Park v Sweetwater (1963) 213 Tenn 1, 372 SW2d 168.
W Va Barker v Charleston (1950) 134 W Va 754, 61 SE2d 743.

Where the closing of an alley serves a public purpose it is immaterial that a private individual may receive some benefit. That the portion closed is in exchange for a tract of land to permit a further opening of the alley that will aid fire emergency vehicle travel is a sufficient public purpose.

Ky Barth v Louisville (1969) 449 SW2d 24.

That some parties may receive more direct benefits than the public at large from the enactment of an ordinance closing a particular street does not mean that such closing is a private rather than a public use.

Md Baltimore & O R Ry v Kane (1914) 124 Md 231, 92 A 532.

A city may properly close a portion of a city street which has been converted from a collection street within a residential area into a throughway by the actions of the adjoining city. The designation of a street as a collection street in the city's system may be changed on a showing that the general intent and character of the use and neighborhood is seriously affected by the increased traffic flow.

Cal Snyder v South Pasadena (1975) 53 CA3d 1051, 126 CaR 320.

Though the motives of the city council in enacting an ordinance vacating an alley are not a proper subject of judicial inquiry, the purpose of the ordinance and the object to be attained is a proper subject.

Ill People v Corn Products Refining (1919) 286 Ill 226, 121 NE 574.
People v Wieboldt (1907) 138 IllAp 200.

§54. —Limitations

On approval and recording of a subdivision plat all streets dedicated are both offered and accepted. They may not be subsequently vacated without a showing of no damage to the city or the public.

Mo Rockville v Geeraert (1971) 261 Md 709, 276 A2d 642.

A city cannot use its delegated power to close any of its streets in such a way as to foreclose it from exercising the power to open, extend and widen a street when the public convenience so requires.

Tex Bowers v Taylor (1929) 16 SW2d 520.

When no public purpose is perceived to be served, an owner may not be denied access to a public street, and a village may not close a street terminating at the village boundary line depriving abutting owners of their only means of ingress to or egress from their property.

NY Quaglia v Munsey Park (1978) 44 NY2d 772, 406 NYS2d 30.

Absent legislative authority to the contrary, a city may not restrict the right to travel on one of its streets to residents or other exempted dirvers since municipal streets belong to every citizen of the state. A section of the state vehicle code authorizing local authorities to close roads not needed for vehicular traffic must be strictly construed and does not impliedly empower a municipality to enact an ordinance which partially closes a road to all but certain exempt motorists. Any ordinance attempting to effect such a closure will be held void as not being within the scope of a city's police powers.

Cal Lafayette v Contra Costa County (1979) 154 CaR 374.

Although a home rule city has plenary power over its streets and alleys relative to their vacation, abandonment or closure, it exercises such power as a public trustee, and may not abandon or close a street solely for private benefit or use.

Ill People v Atchison T & S F Ry (1905) 217 Ill 594, 75 NE 573.
Iowa Kelroy v Clear Lake (1942) 232 Iowa 161, 5 NW2d 12.
NY Stahl Soap v New York City (1959) 5 NY2d 200, 182 NYS2d 808, 156 NE2d 443.
Tex Jacobs v Denison (1952) 251 SW2d 804.

Though a city council may not vacate an alley if the sole purpose and effect is to benefit a private use, the existence of some private benefit will not invalidate the ordinance, since that is always the case where a city has the fee, which reverts on vacation.

Ill People v Benson (1920) 294 Ill 236, 128 NE 387.

Where a town council acts arbitrarily and without regard for or against the interest of the public, its action in attempting to vacate a street or alley by ordinance will be declared invalid.

> **Iowa** Pederson v Radcliffe (1939) 226 Iowa 166, 284 NW 145.
>   Krueger v Ramsey (1919) 188 Iowa 861, 175 NW 1.
> **NJ**   Pyatt v Dunellen (1952) 9 NJ 548, 89 A2d 1.

A municipality cannot vacate a street or a park for the sole purpose of benefiting an abutting owner; and the power to vacate streets cannot be exercised in an arbitrary manner without regard to the interest and convenience of the public or individual rights.

> **SC**   Bethel Methodist Episcopal Church v Greenville (1947) 211 SC 442,
>   45 SE2d 841.

§55. Conditional Vacation

A decision to vacate and abandon a street and alley, based on general welfare and best interest, is valid though conditions were made with adjoining owners. Where the conditions are not connected or essential to the validity of the ordinance they may be eliminated and the valid portions continued independently. Failure of the property owner to comply with his expansion does not invalidate the vacation of the street.

> **Fla**   Naples v Miller (1971) 243 So2d 608.

Where an ordinance vacates a street to allow construction of a baseball park, on condition that the baseball club construct the park within a given time, the condition is valid, and on failure of the condition the city may reopen the street.

> **Ore**   Portland Baseball Club v Portland (1933) 142 Ore 13, 18 P2d 811.

§56. Consent and Rights of Abutting Owners

The fact that a property owner has access to his property does not make the closing of a street with consent of the city valid. In order to secure a unilateral closing of a street it is necessary that it be reasonably incidental to the public welfare.

> **Ala**   Gwin v Bristol Steel & Iron Works (1979) 366 So2d 692.

An ordinance to close and abandon both ends of an alley is void without the consent of the owners of all the property abutting the alley, because of a statute requiring "the written consent of the owners of all lots abutting on the street or alley, or the portion thereof, to be vacated."

> **Ark**   Roberts v Pace (1959) 230 Ark 280, 322 SW2d 75.

A municipal ordinance vacating and closing a street or alley for the benefit of abutting owners is valid. The city is not liable in damages to the complaining adjoining owner when access is provided though by a circuity of travel.

Tex   San Antonio v Olivares (1974) 505 SW2d 526.

Where the charter requires consent of not less than ¾ of the owners of abutting property for the city to vacate a street or alley, the mere passage of an ordinance improving the street with macadam to a width of 40 feet, though the street was originally dedicated to the city as 90 feet wide, does not have the effect of vacating the unimproved portion.

Ore   Eugene v Garrett (1918) 87 Ore 435, 169 P 649.

On an ordinance determination to vacate a street the owner of land who used the road for access to his property is entitled to be compensated for the loss.

Fla   Pinellas County v Austin (1975) 323 So2d 6.

The right of ingress and egress is ordinarily of substantial value, and a real property owner may not be deprived thereof without compensation, by an ordinance vacating a street or alley.

Ill   Tibbetts v West & South Town St Ry (1894) 54 IllAp 180.
Iowa   Hubbell v Des Moines (1918) 183 Iowa 715, 167 NW 619.
           Sutton v Mentzer (1912) 154 Iowa 1, 134 NW 108.
Neb   Jones v Aurora (1915) 97 Neb 825, 151 NW 958.

Where an ordinance vacates a street or alley, damages may be recovered where any particular lot or tract served by the street or alley has been made to suffer substantial injury of a kind other than that suffered in common with the neighborhood or public in general.

Iowa   Krueger v Ramsey (1919) 188 Iowa 861, 175 NW 1.
           Hubbell v Des Moines (1918) 183 Iowa 715, 167 NW 619.
Mo   Kings Highway Supply v Banner Iron Works (1915) 266 Mo 138, 181 SW 30.
Neb   Kraft & Sons v Lincoln (1967) 182 Neb 187, 153 NW2d 725.

§57. Effect

A city may properly vacate a dedicated street and the title reverts to the adjoining owners. The plat dedicating the streets is a matter of public record and a claim of adverse possession may not attach to the property until the property is vacated.

Tex   Miller v Cretien (1972) 488 SW2d 893.

Where an ordinance specifically vacates or abandons streets acquired by dedication, title to the property reverts to the owners of abutting realty.

Ark Hoxie v Gibson (1921) 150 Ark 432, 234 SW 490.
Mo Prewitt v Whittaker (1968) 432 SW2d 240.
Marks v Bettendorf's (1960) 337 SW2d 585.
NY Yonkers v Harlan (1965) 24 AD2d 633, 262 NYS2d 161.
Ohio Greenberg v L I Snodgrass (1953) 95 OA 307, 53 Op 230, 119 NE2d 114.
Okla Lindauer v Hill (1953) 262 P2d 697.
McPike v Avery (1926) 119 Okla 140, 249 P 273.

An ordinance vacating a street returns the title to the land to the adjoining property owners. They are then able to do with their property as they wish, but may not block pedestrian traffic where an easement to a park has vested.

Fla Hurt v Lenchuk (1969) 223 So2d 350.

The reversion of the title to a vacated street or alley, under the terms of the vacation ordinance, to the dedicator of adjoining owner, does not affect the validity of the ordinance.

Ill Lockwood & Strickland v Chicago (1919) 214 IllAp 25.
Hill v Kimball (1915) 269 Ill 398, 110 NE 18.
Okla Stillwater v Hamilton (1925) 112 Okla 10, 239 P 897.

Where a town, by resolution, officially abandons and closes to public travel a portion of a highway after a new highway is in operation, it is not liable for an accident caused by failure to barricade or place warning signs on the abandoned portion. The resolution is the formal step in the process of abandonment, and results in a reversion of the property to private ownership.

Wis Karle v Commonwealth (1941) 236 Wis 500, 295 NW 687.

On vacation of a street by an ordinance enacted under a statute, the title of the land formerly occupied by the street does not revest in the abutting owners but remains in the city, and may be disposed of for other purposes.

Iowa Krueger v Ramsey (1919) 188 Iowa 861, 175 NW 1.
Harrington v Iowa Cent Ry (1905) 126 Iowa 388, 102 NW 139.
Miss Puyper v Pure Oil (1952) 215 Miss 121, 60 So2d 569.
NY Gillen Place, In re (1949) 195 Misc 685, 90 NYS2d 641.

An ordinance authorizing the closing of parts of streets in a subdivision does not constitute a taking of the property of owners of lots abutting such streets, in the absence of actual physical invasion or appropriation of their property.

Ark Greer v Texarkana (1941) 201 Ark 1041, 147 SW2d 1004.
Mich Clayton & Lambert Mfg v Detroit (1929) 34 F2d 303.
Ore Lockwood v Portland (1923) 288 F 480.
Tex Gambrell v Chalk Hill Theatre (1947) 205 SW2d 126.

A street, when properly vacated by ordinance, ceases to be a street, the rights of the public therein are divested, and it becomes private property.

> **Iowa** Tomlin v Cedar Rapids & Iowa City Ry & Light (1909) 141 Iowa 599, 120 NW 93.

An ordinance vacating a platted street and alleyway is not effective to vacate more than the public easement or right in the vacated land.

> **Utah** Boskovich v Midvale (1952) 121 Utah 451, 243 P2d 435.

§58. Validity

Compliance with statutory provisions is essential to the valid enactment of an ordinance vacating a street or alley.

> **Neb** Hanson v Omaha (1951) 154 Neb 72, 46 NW2d 896.

A town council resolution closing a street to vehicular traffic is a proper exercise of the town council's home rule powers where there is evidence of a serious traffic problem in a residential area.

> **Conn** Pizzuto v Newington (1978) 174 Conn 282, 386 A2d 238.

A city ordinance closing a portion of the street is invalid and arbitrary where the developer incurs great expense in reliance upon continued access to the street. The right to ingress and egress is a property right of which the developer may not be deprived without payment of just compensation.

> **Ark** Sherwood v Dupree Co (1978) 565 SW2d 425.

An easement dedicated to the city, but not accepted, may not be vacated by ordinance. The abutting owners may not be deprived of their rights of access without payment of compensation.

> **Ark** Flake v Thompson (1970) 249 Ark 713, 460 SW2d 789.

An ordinance closing a street may be void for taking private property for public use without just compensation, and the abutting property owner may collect damages from the municipality.

> **SC** Houston v West Greenville (1922) 126 SC 484, 120 SE 236.

An ordinance vacating a roadway that was not the only means of access to the property of abutting landowners is not void as a taking of private property without just compensation. An injunction will not issue to restrain the city from vacating the roadway.

> **Colo** Colorado Springs v Crumb (1961) 148 Colo 32, 364 P2d 1053.
> **Ga** Jones v Decatur (1940) 189 Ga 732, 7 SE2d 730.
> **Ida** Canady v Coeur d'Alene Lumber (1911) 21 Ida 77, 120 P 830.
> **Miss** Puyper v Pure Oil (1952) 215 Miss 121, 60 So2d 569.

The test of the validity of an ordinance vacating a portion of an alley is whether any consideration of public interest could have actuated the council in its enactment, which is a question of law for the court to decide, from the terms of the ordinance and other circumstances disclosed by the record.

> **Ill** People v Chicago (1958) 13 Ill2d 157, 148 NE2d 481.
> People v Chicago B & Q RR (1924) 314 Ill 445, 145 NE 647.

Before an ordinance vacating a street will be declared void, it must clearly appear that no consideration of public interest could have led to its enactment.

> **Ill** Ray v Chicago (1960) 19 Ill2d 593, 169 NE2d 73.
> Wolbach v Rubens (1923) 307 Ill 186, 138 NE 521.

An ordinance vacating an alley is void where the alley serves as a thoroughfare, and sale is made to landowners for their private interests rather than for the public good.

> **Ark** Brooksher v Jones (1965) 238 Ark 1005, 386 SW2d 253.
> **Iowa** Lerch v Short (1921) 192 Iowa 576, 185 NW 129.
> **Md** Perellis v Baltimore (1948) 190 Md 86, 57 A2d 341.

A private benefit resulting from an ordinance vacating streets that were unused, unpaved and had buildings abutting thereon does not render the ordinance invalid as not being for a public purpose.

> **Ill** People v Elgin J & E Ry (1921) 298 Ill 574, 132 NE 204.

The vacation of a street at the instigation of an individual owner of abutting property, to enable him to use the vacated portion in his business, does not of itself invalidate the vacation or constitute such fraud or abuse of discretion as will authorize equity to interfere and declare the vacating ordinance void.

> **SC** Bethel Methodist Episcopal Church v Greenville (1947) 211 SC 442, 45 SE2d 841.

In determining whether a street vacating ordinance is for a public or a private benefit, the courts may hear oral testimony bearing on that issue.

> **Ill** People v Elgin J & E Ry (1921) 298 Ill 574, 132 NE 204.

A city claiming that a resolution closing a street is void for failure to comply with state law has the burden of proving the invalidity. All presumptions favor the validity of an ordinance passed with respect to matters over which a municipality has legislative power.

> **Cal**   National City v Dunlop (1948) 86 CA2d 380, 194 P2d 788.

A police jury does not abuse its discretion by enacting an ordinance requiring the closing of a street when a preponderance of the evidence shows that the street was for all intents and purposes abandoned and serving no useful public purpose.

> **La**   Caz-Perk Rlty v East Baton Rouge Parish (1948) 213 La 935, 35 So2d 860.

Where an ordinance vacates an alley but fails to describe its boundaries accurately, it is void.

> **Iowa**   Pederson v Radcliffe (1939) 226 Iowa 166, 284 NW 145.

§59. —Notice; Hearing

A resolution closing a portion of a street is invalid when notice to the non-petitioning owners is not sent by registered mail. It is not necessary that they have a special interest, but an opportunity must be offered to all interested parties in opposition to be heard.

> **NC**   Washington Closing a Portion of West Fourth St, In the Matter of (1972) 15 NCApp 505, 190 SE2d 309.

Replatting to close a six-foot alley is invalid when the notice requirements are not followed and the interested adjoining property owners do not have knowledge of the action.

> **Fla**   Little River Inv v Fowler (1972) 266 So2d 68.

An ordinance vacating a platted street and alleyway is ineffective, without reasonable notice, fair hearing and payment of just compensation, to extinguish any vested proprietary interests in the vacated land held by nearby property owners.

> **Neb**   Hanson v Omaha (1951) 154 Neb 72, 46 NW2d 896.
> **NC**   Blowing Rock v Gregorie (1956) 243 NC 364, 90 SE2d 898.
> **Utah**   Boskovich v Midvale (1952) 121 Utah 451, 243 P2d 435.

A resolution vacating a street is not invalid for failure to serve notice on an adjoining owner who may be affected by the closing when the party did not show any evidence of the effect on his business, and he had actual notice and attended and participated in the meeting at which the resolution was adopted.

> **NY**   Penney v Halstead (1973) 75 Misc2d 413, 347 NYS2d 786.

A municipality may enact an ordinance abandoning or closing an alley, without giving any advance notice to abutting owners.

Tex   Cobb v Dallas (1966) 408 SW2d 292.

§60. Estoppel

A resolution passed in 1935 to close the end of a street may not be acted on in 1975 to the detriment of adjoining property owners. The change in circumstances during the 40-year lapse makes the purpose of the resolution inappropriate and arbitrary as to the developers of the adjoining property even though they had knowledge of the intention to eventually erect the barricade at the end of the street.

NY   Quaglia v Munsey Park (1976) 54 AD2d 434, 389 NYS2d 616.

A city is not estopped to claim that an ordinance vacating part of a street was never legally adopted as against abutters, where the city has not misled them by anything done, to their prejudice or otherwise.

Iowa   Sutton v Mentzer (1912) 154 Iowa 1, 134 NW 108.
Mo   Laclede-Christy Clay v St Louis (1912) 246 Mo 446, 151 SW 460.

Where an alley runs through a city block which has never been platted into lots, and there is no showing of a prescriptive use of the alley, a city is not estopped to close it by ordinance so that the block may be used as a unit for a factory site.

Ark   Cernauskas v Fletcher (1947) 211 Ark 678, 201 SW2d 999.

§61. Attack

To entitle a property owner to certiorari to review a city council's action in enacting an ordinance vacating and closing a street, the petitioner must allege that his property abuts on that part of the street vacated, or that he will suffer special or peculiar damage or inconvenience not common to all.

Ark   Risser v Little Rock (1955) 225 Ark 318, 281 SW2d 949.
Mich   Tomaszewski v Palmer Bee (1923) 223 Mich 565, 194 NW 571.
Miss   Hattiesburg v Colson (1959) 236 Miss 237, 109 So2d 868.
Mo   Arcadia Rlty v St Louis (1930) 326 Mo 273, 30 SW2d 995.
NJ   Con Rlty v Ellenstein (1940) 125 NJLaw 196, 14 A2d 544.
NC   Shaw v Liggett & Myers Tobacco (1946) 226 NC 477, 38 SE2d 313.
W Va   Barker v Charleston (1950) 134 W Va 754, 61 SE2d 743.

To contest an ordinance vacating a street or alley the party must show that their right-of-way and easement to their property has been impaired. A person whose property does not abut on the portion vacated, but on a portion of the street affected, still has standing to prove impairment.

Mont   Kemmer v Bozeman (1971) 158 Mont 354, 492 P2d 211.

An ordinance vacating a portion of a street may not be attacked by one not an abutter or who does not otherwise suffer special or different damages than the general public.

Neb   Feldman v Omaha (1969) 184 Neb 226, 166 NW2d 421.

An ordinance vacating a street and determining that no damages are due to abutting owners is the subject matter of an appeal, not the denial of the remonstrance. An appeal from a second hearing when the remonstrance was filed does not confer jurisdiction on the circuit court.

Ore   Bitte v St Helens (1968) 251 Ore 548, 446 P2d 978.

Where an ordinance vacates a street and reroutes traffic to another street, thereby changing the latter from a quiet street to a busy highway, resulting in depreciation of property thereon, owners on the latter street have a special interest apart from the rest of the community that gives them sufficient standing to attack the ordinance.

NJ   Pyatt v Dunellen (1952) 9 NJ 548, 89 A2d 1.

To contest vacating a street an owner must show special damages. A landowner who has other access to his property and has incurred no inconvenience different than the general public may not contest the action.

Wash   Hoskins v Kirkland (1972) 7 WashAp 957, 503 P2d 1117.

In an action challenging the validity of an ordinance vacating a portion of an alley, parol evidence is inadmissible to show the motives of the council members, but is admissible to show whether the purpose is private or public.

Ill   Moskal v Catholic Bishop of Chicago (1942) 315 IllAp 461, 43 NE2d 206.
Amboy v Ill Cent RR (1908) 236 Ill 236, 86 NE 238.

An ordinance closing a street which contains a declaration of emergency is not subject to referendum. The declaration of emergency unless proscribed by statute is a legislative function and conclusive in judicial proceedings.

Okla   Ponca City, In re referendum petition (1974) 530 P2d 120.

Where a city is vested with power from the legislature to close streets, a resolution closing a street is equivalent to an act of the legislature, and abutting lot owners are not entitled to injunctive relief on the ground that the act of the council is invalid or their constitutional rights are invaded.

Va   Lynchburg v Peters (1926) 145 Va 1, 133 SE 674.

As long as the municipal council acted honestly, a mistake in its exercise of discretion in closing a street, or hasty and ill-advised action not for the best interest of the inhabitants, constitutes no ground for injunction; but in case of an abuse of discretion whereby property rights are or will be injuriously affected, the council's acts may be enjoined.

> **SC** Bethel Methodist Episcopal Church v Greenville (1947) 211 SC 442, 45 SE2d 841.

Where a street is laid out in a recorded plat, but never improved or used as a street, and the property is fenced in and a building constructed thereon, an ordinance vacating the street at the request of an adjoining property owner is valid regardless of the council's motives. Such ordinance may only be attacked in a direct proceeding in which the city is a party.

> **Mo** Windle v Lambert (1966) 400 SW2d 89.

Certiorari is the proper remedy to test the validity of an ordinance vacating an alley.

> **Iowa** Lerch v Short (1921) 192 Iowa 576, 185 NW 129.

Antitrust laws are not intended to apply to an agreement in good faith to test in the courts the validity of a municipal ordinance; and parties with probable cause to believe an ordinance invalid under which certain streets were vacated for a proposed shopping center did not violate antitrust laws though their attack was motivated by a desire to prevent a shopping center that would compete with downtown facilities.

> **Ill** Bracken's Shopping Center v Ruwe (1967) 273 F Supp 606.

§62. Repeal

The repeal of an ordinance vacating an alley cannot reestablish the alley, that being possible only by following the method prescribed by statute, or by prescription or dedication.

> **Iowa** Bradley v Centerville (1908) 139 Iowa 599, 117 NW 968.

V. ACCESS; INGRESS; EGRESS

§63. Generally

A city does not have unlimited ownership of the street area, and a lot owner has an easement in the street fronting his property that accords him the right of reasonable ingress and egress and to make any reasonable use of the street area that does not interfere with its use by the public.

> **Ky** Marshall v Louisville (1951) 244 SW2d 755.

The right of ingress and egress is ordinarily of substantial value, and a real property owner may not be deprived thereof without compensation, by an ordinance vacating a street or alley.

> **Ga** Gardner v Brunswick (1943) 197 Ga 167, 28 SE2d 135.
> **Iowa** Hubbell v Des Moines (1918) 183 Iowa 715, 617 NW 619.

Recitals in an ordinance that a certain tract of land is needed to open a street to afford access to 71 acres of land that have not become a part of the city does not authorize the court to interfere with the exercise of discretion by the mayor and council in opening the street, though the area reached by the street is outside the city.

> **Ga** Du Pre v Marietta (1957) 213 Ga 403, 99 SE2d 156.

ANNOTATIONS

Attracting people in such numbers as to obstruct access to neighboring premises, as nuisance, 2 ALR2d 437.

Validity of license tax on abutter's means of access to street, 73 ALR2d 677.

§64. Right—Nature of

An access road across residential property leading to a commercial area is illegal and may be ordered closed by barricades which are removable in nature so that the owner and users of the residential property have access. Residential classifications are limited to accessory uses of the same character which precludes the road.

> **Mass** Building Inspector of Dennis v Harney (1974) 317 NE2d 81.

While the provisions that permit existing ways to continue under a special permit has been declared invalid the establishment of new ways cannot be limited to access to similarly zoned property. A street or way dedicated to the public and providing access across residential zoning to an industrial track is valid and subject to general public use.

> **Mass** Harrison v Textron (1975) 328 NE2d 838.

The owner of property abutting a street has a right of ingress and egress that the city council cannot, by legislative enactment, either take away or unreasonably abridge.

> **NY**   Small v Moss (1938) 279 NY 288, 18 NE2d 281.
>   Small v Moss (1938) 255 AD 1, 5 NYS2d 432.
> **Tex**   Gulf Refining v Ft Worth (1931) 36 SW2d 285.

Where by ordinance abutting owners are granted a revocable privilege to use a portion of the sidewalk for courtyard purposes, the grant includes the right to fence off courtyards and build stoops or stairways for access to their homes.

> **NY**   New York City v Masten (1916) 174 AD 661, 161 NYS 196.

ANNOTATION

Power to condemn abutting owner's right of access to limited access highway or street, 43 ALR2d 1073.

§65. —Regulation

Where a county code provision banning reserve or spite strips which control access to streets was adopted after the approval of a subdivision plat, the subdivider's reservation of a two-foot strip between the south end of the road which he dedicated when he built the subdivision and the north end of the adjoining property to the south was held not to violate public policy.

> **Ill**   J C Penney Co v Andrews (1979) 68 IllApp3d 901, 386 NE2d 923.

An ordinance prohibiting vehicular ingress and egress from certain property onto a road is invalid as unlawful discrimination against one specific property within the municipality.

> **NJ**   Allendale Nursing Home v Allendale (1977) 149 NJS 286, 373 A2d 714.

Though access to a public way is a vested right and one of the incidents of ownership of land bounding thereon, this right of access may be regulated, for it is subservient to primary rights of the public to the free use of the streets for travel and incidental purposes.

> **Cal**   Stevenson v Downey (1962) 205 CA2d 585, 23 CaR 127.
> **Ida**   Johnston v Boise (1964) 87 Ida 44, 390 P2d 291.

ANNOTATIONS

Power to directly regulate or prohibit abutting owner's access to street or highway, 39 ALR2d 652.

Power to restrict or interfere with access of abutter by traffic regulation, 73 ALR2d 689.

§66. —Denial

A driveway to handle tractor trailers across residential property is a business use contrary to the residential zoning. The fact that other access to the property is not available by motor vehicle due to lack of a bridge does not justify an exception.

> **Md** Leimbach Const Co v Baltimore (1970) 257 Md 635, 264 A2d 109.

Refusal to grant a corporation, granted approval to use its property, located in a residential district, as a recreational park, the right of passage to the property is arbitrary and a denial of due process.

> **Mo** Twenty-third St Traffic Way, In re (1919) 279 Mo 249, 214 SW 109.
> **Pa** Young Men & Women's Hebrew Assn v Monroeville (1968)
> 429 Pa 283, 240 A2d 469.

ANNOTATION

Power to directly regulate or prohibit abutter's access to street or highway, 73 ALR2d 652.

§67. —Impairment

The right of ingress and egress to existing buildings may not be taken away by an ordinance zoning neighboring property passed subsequent to the motion approving the rezoning. When a rezoning has been allowed for multiple dwellings conditioned on no exit from the new buildings to a particular street the ordinance passed on discovery that the rezoning ordinance was improperly enacted may not close the access to the existing buildings on the adjoining plot owned by the applicant.

> **Wash** Selah v Waldbauer (1974) 11 WashAp 749, 525 P2d 262.

Where a bridge approach constructed by a private company, by authority of an ordinance, seriously impairs access to the abutting property, the ordinance constitutes a taking of property and requires compensation to its owners.

> **Ore** Ail v Portland (1931) 136 Ore 654, 299 P 306.
> Willamette Iron Works v Ore Ry & Navigation (1894) 26 Ore 224, 37 P 1016.

A property owner's right of access to the public street adjoining his property may be restricted by the city only to the extent that it is reasonable and consistent, and for the public good.

> **Ill**   Pure Oil v Northlake (1957) 10 Ill2d 241, 140 NE2d 289.

ANNOTATION

Closing street to facilitate traffic as unlawful interference with access of abutter, 73 ALR2d 701.

§68. —Enforcement

Mandamus will not lie to force the granting of access to a limited access road. The public policy is to protect the city in the interests of safety and preservation of the public investment in its streets, and this, coupled with a study of the street system, made the granting of access an administrative decision subject to discretion.

> **Wash**   State ex rel Ryder v Pasco (1970) 2 WashAp 928, 478 P2d 262.

A temporary injunction may not be issued to enforce an ordinance prohibiting the use of land locked property which does not have a 25-foot access easement. Where the property is served by all public utilities, is heated by oil, and is accessible to fire protection, there is no danger of irreparable damage to the public.

> **Ill**   Sycamore v Gauze (1970) 130 IllAp2d 606, 264 NE2d 597.

An abutting property owner, deprived by ordinance of his means of ingress and egress over his lot to a street, may sue in equity for relief, and may join in the same action a demand for damages.

> **NC**   Crawford v Marion (1910) 154 NC 73, 69 SE 763.

§69. Abandonment

A property owner abandoning his easement of access to a particular street places the matter of access entirely in the hands of the governing body controlling the street; and where a property owner seeking permission to build a shopping center adjacent to private residences abandons his easement of access to the street, the governing body may weigh the demands of commercial interest for easy access against the desires of neighbors for quiet streets, consider the convenience of the general public and the effect on the traffic flow on adjacent streets, and then place the emphasis as it thinks best, free from any claim of property right by the commercial owner.

Cal Stevenson v Downey (1962) 205 CA2d 585, 23 CaR 127.

VI. ENCROACHMENTS; OBSTRUCTIONS

§70. Generally

A violation of the set back requirements from a major arterial road is not shown when the center line of the right-of-way has not been established nor has the road been projected for construction.

Colo Bd of Comm of Boulder County v Stamp (1974) 530 P2d 994.

The violation of an ordinance regarding the placing of traffic barricades does not constitute actionable negligence. Since the barricades were interspersed over a distance of more than 300 feet the failure of one or more blinkers on the first barricades does not relieve driver of negligence in failing to observe them.

La Cobbs v Shreveport (1978) 365 So2d 1.

An ordinance authorizing construction of a building for a market place to be located in a dedicated street is not a valid exercise of the city's power to control the streets and to control and regulate market places, and being ultra vires, the city can and should plead its invalidity.

Mo Peters v St Louis (1910) 226 Mo 62, 125 SW 1134.

A city may by ordinance properly require that all mailboxes be located six inches inside of the sidewalk line, but it cannot order the postal service to make home delivery. Since the mailboxes are in violation of postal regulations for curb-side delivery the post office department is justified in refusing to make delivery, but its actions in no way interfere with the city's rights to enforce its ordinance.

Cal Grover City v US Postal Service (1975) 391 F Supp 982.

Violation of an ordinance forbidding the maintenance of an obstruction in the street is in its nature not peculiarly an offense against the city but rather against the public at large; and one accused of a violation is entitled to a jury trial.

Cal Taylor v Reynolds (1891) 92 Cal 573, 28 P 688.

An ordinance forbidding the obstruction of a street and prescribing a penalty for failure to remove the obstruction after notice does not conflict with a statute declaring the obstruction of a street to be a nuisance and a misdemeanor punishable by both fine and imprisonment, where the penalty for violation of the ordinance is of the same character as that prescribed by the general law but less in degree.

> **Cal**   Taylor, Ex parte (1890) 87 Cal 91, 25 P 258.

§71. Obstructions; Deposits in Streets

An ordinance making it unlawful for anyone to obstruct, restrict or prevent the use of any portion of a sidewalk or roadway except for specified exceptions and temporary uses at the locations and under the conditions authorized by resolution of the city council, though valid on its face, should not be construed as applying to First Amendment freedoms.

> **Cal**   People v Amdur (1954) 123 CA2d 951, 267 P2d 445.

An ordinance prohibiting obstructions and encumbrances in the streets is not applicable to an elevator shaft in the sidewalk but located within the building line and constructed in a reasonably safe manner.

> **NY**   Lessin v Bd of Educ (1928) 247 NY 503, 161 NE 160.

§72. —Prohibition

An ordinance prohibiting the deposit of any materials in the streets or obstructing them in any way is a reasonable exercise of the police power.

> **Ga**   Thompson v Rockmart (1936) 53 GaApp 275, 185 SE 363.
> **Wis**   Neenah v Krueger (1932) 206 Wis 473, 240 NW 402.

An ordinance prohibiting the placing of any building or obstruction on any street, alley, sidewalk or other public ground is limited in its application to such streets and alleys as have been opened to public use.

> **Ill**   Chicago v Gosselein (1879) 4 IllAp 570.

§73. —Regulation; Licensing

Obstructions incidental to the primarily intended use of a street are subject to reasonable regulation by the municipality, since its authorities, as trustees for the public, have the duty to keep their community's streets open and available for movement of people and property. Any obstruction not within the above category or not properly authorized by ordinance or otherwise constitutes a public nuisance per se.

> **Cal**   People v Amdur (1954) 123 CA2d 951, 267 P2d 445.

The provision of a building ordinance limiting the storage of material and equipment to the one third of the street that is nearest the curb in front of and adjoining the building site, and to adjacent alleys and sidewalks, provided passage space remains, is a reasonable exercise of the police power to further the safety and general welfare of the community.

Cal Benwell v Dean (1964) 227 CA2d 226, 38 CaR 542.
Kan Watson Inc v Topeka (1965) 194 Kan 585, 400 P2d 689.

In the application of an ordinance permitting the deposit of building materials in a street by an abutting owner who obtains a permit and complies with regulations, whether a deposit constitutes a reasonable use depends on the size of the building, and on street, traffic and other conditions affecting the situation.

Wis Trester & Trester v Kahn (1925) 189 Wis 60, 205 NW 826.

§74. Lighting

An ordinance providing that every person who makes an excavation in a street and leaves any portion thereof obstructed with building or other material during the nighttime shall cause the same to be enclosed with sufficient barriers and be lighted, and that anyone who shall in any manner cause any sidewalk to be dangerous shall place barriers and lights around such dangerous place, applies on a charge of negligence to the city, and also to a railway company which, with the city's consent, removes bricks from a street, in connection with the laying of tracks, and stacks them between the street and the sidewalk, where children develop a habit of playing with the bricks and scattering them on the walk.

Mo Sutter v Metro St Ry (1916) 188 SW 65.

An ordinance providing that every person who leaves any part of a street obstructed with material during the nighttime shall cause the same to be enclosed and lighted with a red light is not applicable to a property owner who has a load of coal delivered and dumped in the street in front of his house, or to the party making the delivery, since the property owner has an easement of access to the street, separate and distinct from the right of the public to the use of the street, and his temporary obstruction of the public easement is an incident thereto and not a limitation thereof.

Mo Searcy v Noll Welty Lumber (1922) 295 Mo 188, 243 SW 318, 23 ALR 813.

§75. Stairways

Ordinances granting permission to property owners to erect areaways and stairways in portions of streets, but reserving in the city the right to compel removal, do not violate the constitutional requirement that general laws have uniform operation.

Iowa   Mettler v Ottumwa (1924) 197 Iowa 187, 196 NW 1000.

§ 75.1. Malls

An ordinance creating a special service area and imposing a tax on properties within the area, but excepting from the tax properties used exclusively for residential purposes and three specific industrial properties, is valid where the special service to be provided is the creation of a "semi-mall" to improve the atmosphere for shopping and to generate revenue. The exclusion of residential and industrial property from the service area is reasonable because the commercial property which will be immediately and directly benefited is the area subject to the tax, and the irregular geographic area created by the ordinance is contiguous within the meaning of state statute.

Ill   Hiken Furniture v Belleville (1977) 53 IllAp3d 306, 368 NE2d 961.

A special services ordinance authorizing a real property tax to pay for construction of a shopping mall and to provide free parking therewith is invalid. The home rule authority of a city does not extend to revenue matters not specifically granted by the legislature.

Ill   Oak Park Federal Sav & Loan Assn v Oak Park (1973) 54 Ill2d 200, 296 NE2d 344.

A transportation administration having charge of the designing, construction, and repairing of public streets does not have the authority to require a mall be constructed and the basic characteristics of the street and sidewalk changed. Their power is limited to the charter grant, and the board of estimate which controls all other segments of street work including establishing uniform widths for streets and sidewalks is the proper party to make such a determination.

NY   Fifth Ave Assn v Lindsay (1973) 73 Misc2d 111, 341 NYS2d 473.

A city may properly designate a 100-foot wide right-of-way street into a transitway mall and a 28-foot street with limited usage. The city has the right to control both the street and the traffic thereon.

Pa   GC Murphy Co v Redevelopment Auth of Erie (1974) 458 Pa 219, 326 A2d 358.

§ 76. Curb Depositories

A municipality has, under its police power, authority to regulate movement and free flow of vehicular traffic within its territory, and employ as a medium the issuance of a permit for a curb depository in order to relieve traffic congestion, in the interest of the welfare of the community.

> **NJ**   Kirzenbaum v Paulus (1958) 51 NJS 186, 144 A2d 25.

§77. Sidewalk Obstructions

A prohibition against storage of personal property on the sidewalks, or occupying over four feet of the outer edge for receiving and delivering merchandise, is to facilitate the movement of traffic, and is not a public safety measure.

> **Ill**   Cecola v Ill Bell Tel Co (1970) 130 IllAp 446, 264 NE2d 809.

A littering conviction is proper when the property owner leaves furniture on the sidewalk in an area obstructing public passage. The exceptions for showcases and sale merchandise does not apply to defendant's furniture used in a "casual living arrangement".

> **NY**   People v Feldman (1973) 73 Misc2d 824, 342 NYS2d 956.

A statute empowering municipalities to prevent the encumbering of sidewalks with obstacles and materials carries with it the implied power to enact ordinances that will compel observance of the statutory purpose.

> **Mont**   Lazich v Butte (1944) 116 Mont 386, 154 P2d 260.

Whatever space in a public place in a city is set apart for the use of the public as a sidewalk, the public has the right to use it in its entirety, free from unauthorized obstructions, though the fee in the street may be in adjacent property owners and not in the public.

> **ND**   Kennedy v Fargo (1918) 40 ND 475, 169 NW 424.

§78. —Prohibition

A city is charged with the duty to exercise reasonable care to have and keep its sidewalks reasonably safe for normal pedestrian travel; and an ordinance prohibiting anyone from leaving any object on a public sidewalk so as to obstruct or interfere with the use of or pedestrian traffic on such sidewalk is a constitutional exercise of the police power.

> **Conn**   State v Fultz (1953) 18 Conn Supp 239.

An ordinance prohibiting the placing of merchandise on sidewalks or above a sidewalk, enacted for the protection of the public, is constitutional.

> **NY**   People v Lieberman (1961) 32 Misc2d 741, 228 NYS2d 878.

337

§79. —Regulation; Licensing

The power of a city to grant permission to erect and maintain structures on a public sidewalk or street is limited by its charter to a use that is not inconsistent with or does not unreasonably impair the public use to which the public sidewalk or street may be dedicated.

    Tex   L-M-S Inc v Blackwell (1950) 227 SW2d 593.

A charter prohibition against encroachment or obstruction of sidewalks except for booths, stands and displays under license requires that licenses for the use of sidewalks be obtained, and authorizes ordinances regulating any uses that partially obstruct free movement of pedestrians.

    NY   People v Rapkine (1956) 144 NYS2d 187.
          People v Berner (1939) 170 Misc 501, 10 NYS2d 339.

It is not uncommon for abutting owners to use part of a sidewalk for doorsteps, awnings, the display of goods, similar purposes, and a municipality to a reasonable extent may license such use by ordinance, provided the license does not interfere with public use of the sidewalks for passage or make them dangerous for that purpose.

    La   Cross v Baton Rouge (1926) 161 La 921, 109 So 742.

An ordinance requiring a license to place an obstruction on a sidewalk or to construct an underground area under a sidewalk does not prohibit, by implication, a property owner from maintaining an underground area constructed by a previous owner who did not obtain a license. There is a distinction between the erection and the maintenance of a structure.

    Mass   Turturro v Calder (1940) 307 Mass 159, 29 NE2d 744.

An ordinance permitting persons to place goods and merchandise on sidewalks, within specified limits, is invalid, as in violation of the right of the public to free access to and unobstructed travel on the sidewalks of the city.

    Ill   Chicago v Pooley (1904) 112 IllAp 343.
         Pagames v Chicago (1904) 111 IllAp 590.

§80. —Temporary; Christmas Week

A person who, as occasion requires, obstructs a sidewalk by a skid from his store door to a delivery wagon for purposes of moving merchandise between them is not within an ordinance imposing a penalty for constructing or placing any portico, porch, door, window, step, fence, or other projection which shall project into the street. That ordinance applies only to obstructions of a permanent character.

> **Va** Gates & Son v Richmond (1905) 103 Va 702, 49 SE 965.

An ordinance authorizing storekeepers and peddlers to display Christmas trees, holiday decorations and toys on sidewalks during December may not be interpreted as an amendment to a charter provision prohibiting encroachments or obstructions on sidewalks if it fails to meet the legislative requirements for sufficiency of an amendment.

> **NY** People v Berner (1939) 170 Misc 501, 10 NYS2d 339.

§81. —Awnings

An ordinance providing that canvas awnings of the folding or hinged class or metal awnings may be erected beyond the building line when they are not less than 8 feet above the sidewalk is valid under a statute authorizing enactment of ordinances concerning use of sidewalks and streets and regulating structures in, over, or under the sidewalks and streets.

> **Ind** Indianapolis v Cent Amusement (1918) 187 Ind 387, 119 NE 481.

In determining the scope and purpose of an ordinance requiring the removal of awnings with posts resting on the sidewalk, it is immaterial whether the posts are just inside or outside the edge of the sidewalk.

> **NC** Small v Edenton (1908) 146 NC 527, 60 SE 413.

ANNOTATIONS

Municipalities power to permit private owner to construct awnings or signs above public street or sidewalk, 76 ALR2d 898.

Awning in condition as to cause it to fall, as a nuisance, 34 ALR2d 489.

§82. —Construction Sheds

An ordinance requiring erection of a substantial shed over the sidewalks while buildings are being erected or demolished imposes liability on the city, where it has notice through its inspection agents that such a shed is being improperly used for the storage of building materials which use causes it to collapse.

> **NY** Metzroth v New York City (1926) 241 NY 470, 150 NE 519.

No individual has the legal right to conduct his business in the street or to obstruct any portion of the street on or above the ground, by sheds or other structures; and an ordinance prohibiting the erection of signs, sheds or other obstructions on the sidewalk or roadway of a specified street is valid.

> **La**   New Orleans v Kaufman (1916) 38 La 897, 70 So 874.

§ 83. Openings

An ordinance requiring the owner or occupant of a building using a trap door in a sidewalk or street to keep the door or covering in good repair and safe for passage of customary traffic requires the owner or occupant to keep the door in safe condition at all times, whether open or closed, for customary traffic.

> **Utah**   Clawson v Walgreen Drug (1945) 108 Utah 577, 162 P2d 759.

§ 84. Inconsequential Use

Inconsequential uses of a sidewalk, such as placing a carpet or mat during inclement weather in front of the owner's doorway, do not violate an ordinance prohibiting the encumbrance or obstruction of a public street with any article or thing whatsoever.

> **NY**   Cameron v Purdue Rlty (1930) 231 AD 149, 247 NYS 36.

§ 85. Building Erection; Materials

Municipalities may not authorize permanent obstruction of public streets, although by ordinance they may permit temporary use of part of a street by owners of abutting property while engaged in building or paving.

> **Ind**   House-wives League v Indianapolis (1933) 204 Ind 685, 185 NE 511.

Under an ordinance prohibiting a person erecting or repairing a building from using or occupying, for the placing of materials, more than one-third the width of a street or alley, without the consent of persons owning or controlling the adjoining premises, a person erecting a building has the right to use one-third of the width of the street in front of his own lots.

> **Ky**   Louisville Ry v Esselman (1906) 29 KLR 315, 93 SW 51.
> **Mo**   McWhorter v Dahl Chevrolet (1935) 229 MoApp 1090, 88 SW2d 240.
>   Shafir v Carroll (1925) 309 Mo 458, 274 SW 755.
> **Tex** American Constr v Seelig (1911) 104 Tex 16, 133 SW 429.

§86. Permanent

An ordinance authorizing a private company to construct a platform over a public sidewalk is invalid as outside the city's power, since a city is without authority to grant a permanent easement in a street for the benefit of private parties or for exclusively private purposes.

Tex J M Radford Groc v Abilene (1929) 20 SW2d 255.

Where an abutting owner seeks to appropriate part of the sidewalk, to erect a permanent obstruction thereon and to make an excavation therein, the city has the power to require a permit, or to refuse such an appropriation of the sidewalk and resulting limitation of the surface over which the public may travel.

ND Kennedy v Fargo (1918) 40 ND 475, 169 NW 424.

An ordinance permitting property owners to plant shade trees in the street abutting their property does not preclude the city from subsequently removing such trees, since though an owner has a property right to light, air and access to his property from the street, that does not include the right to maintain shade trees or other permanent obstruction in the street, which is always under the control of the city.

Wash Robinson v Spokane (1912) 66 Wash 527, 120 P 101.

§87. Intersections, Obstruction of View

Violating a prohibition against fences, hedges, and buildings obstructing visibility at a corner is negligence per se. An injured bicyclist is within the class of persons being protected.

Ariz Hall v Mertz (1971) 14 ArizApp 24, 480 P2d 361.

The validity of an ordinance limiting the height of a wall will be sustained under the exercise of the police power to prohibit obstructing the view of street crossings and intersections, except that where the ordinance exempts a retaining wall a property owner will be required to remove only such portion of a retaining wall as extends from the street line to a height above the natural level of the lot.

NC Parker, Appeal of (1938) 214 NC 51, 197 SE 706.

A resolution declaring certain ornamental stone columns standing at street intersections to be public nuisances per se, and directing their removal, is valid despite a provision in the subdivision plat dedicating the area by which the dedicator expressly reserved the right to erect and maintain ornamental columns at street entrances.

> **Tex** Ft Worth v Ryan Properties (1955) 284 SW2d 211.

A refusal to issue a building permit for store buildings cannot be justified on the grounds that the structures would obstruct the views of travelers at a road junction, for this objection would apply to any structure and would require the owner to leave the land vacant.

> **NJ** Eaton v Montclair (1926) 4 NJM 507, 133 A 400.

Provisions of zoning ordinance limiting the height of shrubbery, walls, and other obstructions on corner lots to three feet above curb level, to aid in traffic safety, are valid under the police power, and no compensation need be paid.

> **Md** Stevens v Salisbury (1965) 240 Md 556, 214 A2d 775.

§88. Unopened Streets

Storage of a pile driver in a street that has been dedicated but not yet open to traffic is not a violation of an ordinance prohibiting the obstructing of or trespassing on a public street by placing a dangerous object thereon.

> **La** O'Neill v Hemenway (1941) 3 So2d 210.

§89. Encroachment as Nuisance

Generally, with the exceptions of (1) the use of a street by the municipality itself for public purposes, such as sewers, drains, or water pipes, and (2) the use by franchise holding corporations, such as street railway and gas and electric companies, no person, whether an abutting property owner or not, can permanently encroach on a street for a private use, and all such encroachments are nuisances, at least until a permit has been granted where the municipality has power to permit the encroachment.

> **Md** Adams v Trappe (1954) 204 Md 165, 102 A2d 830.

Under a statute providing that incorporated towns are authorized to declare by ordinance what shall constitute a nuisance, and to abate it, an unauthorized obstruction in a street is a nuisance that may be abated.

> **Ind** Carlisle v Pirtle (1917) 63 IndAp 475, 114 NE 705.

An ordinance authorizing a cold storage company to construct a platform above the public sidewalk in front of its premises, which platform would compel pedestrians to climb steps at one end and walk down an incline at the other, is invalid as authorizing a nuisance, and as not for the benefit of the public generally.

> **Ill** People v Western Cold Storage (1919) 287 Ill 612, 123 NE 43.

An ordinance that makes every encroachment on a street beyond the street line a common nuisance applies to an overhead merchandise conveyor across a street.

> **Conn** Andrew B Hendryx v New Haven (1926) 104 Conn 632, 134 A 77.

LAW REVIEW

William L. Prosser, Private Action for Public Nuisance, 52 Va LR 997.

§90. Removal

A city may properly authorize removal of a barricade, which changes a dead end street into a throughway.

> **Mich** Sharkey v Petoskey (1971) 30 Mich Ap 640, 186 NW2d 744.

The city may properly regulate the air space above a street and require the removal of a canopy which extends beyond the curb line. Existing structures may be removed at the owner's expense when they extend beyond the permitted curb line.

> **La** Baton Rouge v State Nat Life Ins Co (1972) 271 So2d 571.

While the city may not restrict the right of free traffic by the public an ordinance based on settlement of a claim authorizing use for private purposes of a portion of a street dead ending on a railroad track is valid since there is no encroachment on the right of free traffic. Subsequent events which change the traffic pattern and constitute an encroachment justify revoking the grant; however, equitable estoppel may arise against the city and authorize damages by the property owner for the required removal or destruction of their buildings.

> **Wash** Seattle v P B Inv Co (1974) 11 WashAp 653, 524 P2d 419.

A city may by ordinance require the removal of houses or other structures encroaching on streets or alleys, but since an order to remove obstructions requires the exercise of discretion the city council must act on each particular case, and may not delegate its power to a street commissioner.

> **Del** Murden v Comm of Lewes (1919) 30 Del 428, 108 A 74.
> **La** Agurs v McKellar (1911) 129 La 186, 55 So 758.
> **ND** Jamestown v Miemietz (1959) 95 NW2d 897.

A private stucco wall encroaching on a public street constitutes a nuisance per se which the city, by resolution, may summarily remove without notice to the owner, both under its common-law power and under its home rule charter.

ND   Kennedy v Fargo (1918) 40 ND 475, 169 NW 424.
Tex   Joseph v Austin (1936) 101 SW2d 381.

§ 91. Enforcement

An ordinance making it unlawful for anyone to encumber or obstruct any street is susceptible of arbitrary enforcement, and the total prohibition rather than reasonable regulation renders it unconstitutional.

NY   People v Katz (1967) 21 NY2d 132, 286 NYS2d 839, 233 NE2d 845.

A petition alleging that the owner of a tract of land dedicated a public street by recording a plat of a subdivision showing the street, that the street was accepted as a public street by the municipality, and that the defendant maintained a continuing nuisance by appropriating the land to his exclusive use alleged a cause of action to enjoin obstruction of the street.

Ga   Young v Sweetbriar (1966) 222 Ga 262, 149 SE2d 474.

In a criminal proceeding for violating a city ordinance by obstructing a street, an information is the proper paper to be filed, both in the municipal court and on appeal.

Del   Pratesi v Wilmington (1903) 20 Del 258, 54 A 694.

§ 92. —Discrimination

A prosecution under an ordinance prohibiting obstruction of streets or sidewalks cannot stand if the arrest and removal from the street or sidewalk were based on an intent to discriminate against the arrested person on account of race.

Ky   Covington v Gausepohl (1933) 250 Ky 323, 62 SW2d 1040.
Miss   Calhoun v Meridian (1966) 355 F2d 209.

An ordinance giving the city council uncontrolled discretion to grant or deny permits to place an obstruction on a street does not permit the council to act arbitrarily or to discriminate among applicants. Implicit in the rule upholding ordinances of this character is a binding legal obligation for administrators to exercise reasonable discretion and refrain from discrimination.

Cal   People v Amdur (1954) 123 CA2d 951, 267 P2d 445.

§93. —Estoppel

A city is not estopped, by reason of its past failure to enforce its ordinances against obstruction of sidewalks, to subsequently remove obstructions therefrom.

ND Kennedy v Fargo (1918) 40 ND 475, 169 NW 424.

ANNOTATION

Estoppel of municipality as to encroachment upon public streets, 44 ALR3d 257.

§94. Validity

Before an ordinance regulating the storage of building materials in the street in front of a building site may be sustained as a legitimate exercise of the police power, it must bear a rational relationship to the rightful regulation of the use and management of city streets.

Kan Watson Inc v Topeka (1965) 194 Kan 585, 400 P2d 689.

A classification of street obstructions into temporary and permanent, with a provision that the ordinance shall operate only on temporary obstructions, is a real and reasonable classification, and does not violate any constitutional provision.

Ohio Xenia v Schmidt (1920) 101 OS 437, 130 NE 24.

An ordinance requiring property owners abutting on a street to move any dirt or rubbish that might fall on the street does not violate federal and state constitutional provisions on the ground that it imposes penalties and liabilities on property owners for damage caused by the forces of nature without fault or negligence on the part of the owner.

Pa Pittsburgh v Pa RR (1958) 394 Pa 58, 145 A2d 700.

In an action challenging the validity of an ordinance authorizing the obstruction of a public street, a recital in the preamble of supposed benefits to the city is not conclusive on the courts, with respect to the true nature of the transaction.

Ill Ginter-Wardein v Alton (1938) 370 Ill 101, 17 NE2d 976.

§95. —Tested by Mandamus

Mandamus will not lie against a municipal judge or city attorney to prosecute construction workers for violation of an ordinance by obstruction of a city street, where the purpose of the mandamus action is merely to test the validity of an ordinance.

    Ore   Collins v Grant (1911) 59 Ore 77, 116 P 334.

§96. Penalties

A provision authorizing a separate and cumulative penalty for each and every day that streets are obstructed by construction activities limits the number of violations to no more than one each day, but does not require that the violation exist for a full day.

    NY   New York City v Benenson (1963) 41 Misc2d 20, 244 NYS2d 653.

VII. CREATION OF IMPROVEMENT DISTRICTS

§97. Generally

The statutory sequence in providing for a special street improvement district is the creation of the district, the ordering, filing, and approval of plans and specifications, the passage and publication of the resolution of necessity, and the advertisement for proposals.

    Ida   McEwen v Coeur d'Alene (1913) 23 Ida 746, 132 P 308.
    ND   Boynton v Minot (1926) 54 ND 795, 211 NW 441.

A valid resolution establishing a paving district is a jurisdictional prerequisite to the paving.

    ND   Green v Beste (1956) 76 NW2d 165.

Where a municipality creates a special street improvement district for purposes specified by statute, any two or more of such purposes may be included in the special district if they constitute a single improvement.

    Ark   Meyer v Bd of Improvement Paving Dist 3 (1921) 148 Ark 623, 231 SW 12.
    ND   Rybnicek v Mandan (1958) 93 NW2d 650.

In fixing the limits of an assessment district for street improvements and the amount of expense to be borne by the city as a whole, the city council's acts are purely legislative. The passage of an ordinance ordering the performance of the work must be considered as being a finding of fact on all prerequisite issues.

> **Ark** Mullins v Little Rock (1917) 131 Ark 59, 198 SW 262.
> **Cal** Allen v Los Angeles (1930) 210 Cal 235, 291 P 393.

The legislature in enacting a city charter may make conclusive a finding of the city council that a petition for creation of an improvement district is regular, legal and sufficient, except on appeal.

> **Neb** Hoopes v Omaha (1916) 99 Neb 460, 156 NW 1047.

An ordinance creating a sidewalk improvement district cannot include more territory than that described in the original petition by property owners, and the Chancery Court has no jurisdiction to determine the question of inclusion, since the petition for the establishment of the district is jurisdictional.

> **Ark** Riddle v Ballew (1917) 130 Ark 161, 197 SW 27.

§98. Notice

Although the publication of city ordinances establishing street improvement districts is mandatory and notice of them must be given in the manner prescribed by statute, a typographical discrepancy between an original petition and an ordinance as enacted, which adds an immaterial amount of territory to a notice description, cannot mislead landowners within the improvement district and will not invalidate the ordinance.

> **Ark** Bennett v Kelley (1929) 179 Ark 530, 16 SW2d 992.
> Gibson v Hoxie (1913) 110 Ark 544, 162 SW 568.

§99. Procedure

Where the legislative grant of power to create special street assessment districts by ordinance is mandatory, the methods and procedure set forth in the grant must be strictly observed.

> **Mont** Hinzeman v Deer Lodge (1920) 58 Mont 369, 193 P 395.
> **ND** Murphy v Bismarck (1961) 109 NW2d 635.

In determining whether two-thirds in value of property owners had petitioned to create a street improvement district, the city council could properly consider the assessed value of a church and school in the district as tax exempt, where their value was added to the county assessment rolls after the time of the petition.

> **Ark** Brown v Headlee (1954) 224 Ark 156, 272 SW2d 56.
> Holt v Ring (1928) 177 Ark 762, 9 SW2d 43.

The council of a city of the second class is not required to establish by ordinance a grade on a street forming part of the paving district, as a condition precedent to the establishment of the district.

> **Neb** Schreifer v Auburn (1923) 110 Neb 179, 193 NW 350.

§100. —Referendum

A referendum petition on an ordinance extending a street and authorizing construction of a bridge is valid. The original resolution for extension of the street is not subject to referendum and the ordinance is the first opportunity of the voters to express their views.

> **Mo** State ex rel Ford v Brawley (1974) 514 SW2d 97.

An ordinance setting up an improvement district to pave streets and stating that an emergency exists for the preservation of the public health, peace and safety, is subject to referendum, since ordinances for the peace, health, and safety of citizens may not be enacted to the detriment of the rights of citizens to exercise the referendum.

> **Colo** Burks v Lafayette (1960) 142 Colo 61, 349 P2d 692.

§101. Specification of Improvements

An improvement district for street improvement must be established on blocks as platted rather than the creation of "fictional blocks". A charge for construction costs of intersections of a major traffic street is improper since the benefit received is minimal.

> **Kan** Bell v Topeka (1976) 220 Kan 405, 553 P2d 928.

An ordinance purporting to create a local improvement district pursuant to statute, which fails to declare the kind of improvement proposed, is invalid.

> **Neb** Danielson v Bellevue (1959) 167 Neb 809, 95 NW2d 57.

An ordinance establishing a paving improvement district was not invalid on the grounds that it failed to designate the streets to be paved, the kind of paving to be used, or the boundaries of the district. The use of specific names of streets to be paved and boundary lines according to street names and water courses was sufficient.

> **Ark** Ruddell v Monday (1929) 179 Ark 920, 18 SW2d 910.

An ordinance creating a street improvement district which describes the area therein as the public square and specific streets connecting thereto is void for want of particularity in description, and an act of the legislature properly defining the boundaries validates such ordinance as to the initiatory petition, but does not cure a lack of consent by a majority in value of the owners of real property in the district.

Ark   Bell v Phillips (1915) 116 Ark 167, 172 SW 864.

§102. —Discretion

Ordinance creating a paving improvement district and providing for curbing and guttering along specified streets is not void, and therefore unenforceable as to assessments against a property owner therein, on the grounds that curbing and guttering are not placed on the streets adjacent to his property, where the petition for the ordinance leaves the character of work to the sound discretion of the improvement district commissioners.

Ark   Laflin v Mena (1942) 205 Ark 24, 166 SW2d 653.

Where the petition for an improvement district asks that sidewalks be laid as needed and streets improved within a territory described, and the ordinance to create the district provides that sidewalks and streets shall be improved, the discretion of the city commissioners must determine the sidewalks to be improved, and this variance between the petition and the ordinance is fatal.

Ark   Less v Improvement Dist 1 of Hoxie (1917) 130 Ark 44, 196 SW 464.

§103. Effect

An ordinance creating a street paving district subjects the land therein to public improvement by legislative action, and the cost of the improvements may be imposed on the property only according to a percentage in value of the type of benefit received.

Ark   Kelley Tr v Paving Dist 46 of Fort Smith (1931) 184 Ark 408, 43 SW2d 71.

§104. Validity

A sidewalk improvement district to construct a proposed skeletal sidewalk system with an assessment on front footage against all property owners within the district is unreasonable. The skeletal system which only covers one side of certain streets could conceivably cost a property owner a great distance from the sidewalk more money than the abutting owner and does not confer any benefit on the distant property owner. The property owner for whom no sidewalk was constructed would still be obligated to pay the full cost of construction of his sidewalk at a later date with no charge against the parties securing sidewalk construction on the original improvement district.

Kan   Davies v Lawrence (1976) 218 Kan 551, 545 P2d 1115.

In determining the validity of a resolution of a county board in creating, defining and establishing a street improvement district such matters as whether a given district shall be improved, the nature of the improvement, whether the cost shall be assessed against the land benefited on a frontage or an area basis, etc., are questions within the jurisdiction of the board of supervisors, and its decision, except in case of fraud or mistake, is conclusive.

Haw   De Mello v Wilson (1925) 28 Haw 298.

An ordinance creating a street improvement district, including territory previously covered by prior improvement districts, is not rendered invalid where improvements are to be made only on portions of those streets.

Ark   Freeze v Improvement Dist 16 of Jonesboro (1916) 126 Ark 172, 189 SW 660.

An ordinance creating a street improvement district is not invalidated by failure of the city council to fix the street grade elevation by separate ordinance before the district is created and contracts let.

Ark   Williams v Sewer Improvement Dist 86 (1929) 180 Ark 510, 22 SW2d 405.

The omission from a municipal street improvement district of lots similarly situated to those assessed does not, of necessity, invalidate the ordinance creating the district. The discretion of the city council is controlling, in the absence of mistake or fraud.

Ark   Blytheville v Baker (1926) 171 Ark 692, 286 SW 945.

An ordinance that recreates a street improvement district to include property inadvertently omitted from the description in petitions for a prior ordinance, is valid when supported by new petitions of real property owners within the district, under the statutory authority of cities to organize municipal improvement districts, and is not an ordinance to pay for improvements made or commenced by a void district.

Ark   Christian v Forrest City (1938) 196 Ark 523, 118 SW2d 868.

An ordinance creating a street improvement district, and providing for attorneys' fees for its organization, is valid as expressly authorized by statute, and judicial notice will be taken that the services of an attorney are necessary in the proper formation of an improvement district.

Ark   Bourland v Coleman (1933) 187 Ark 392, 60 SW2d 1021.

Where a city commission, in attempting to set up a statutory special improvement district, approves the plans, specifications, and estimates of the city engineer, and passes and publishes a resolution of necessity, all before the creation of the district, such acts were without authority and void.

ND Boynton v Minot (1926) 54 ND 795, 211 NW 441.

§105. —Estoppel

A person is not estopped to challenge the validity of an ordinance creating a street improvement district merely because he is passive during construction of the improvement and pays all prior assessments levied against his property, for improvement districts cannot be created, nor liabilities for the improvements fixed, by estoppel.

Ark Harnwell v White (1914) 115 Ark 88, 171 SW 108.

§106. —Collateral Attack

An attack on the validity of an ordinance creating a street improvement district, brought after the statutory period for objection has passed, is a collateral attack on the validity of the city council's proceedings establishing the district, and cannot be sustained without a showing of fraud or demonstrable mistake by council members.

Ark Bd of Comm Paving Improvement Dist 13 v Freeman (1941) 201 Ark 1061, 148 SW2d 1076.
Carney v Walbe (1927) 175 Ark 746, 300 SW 413.

§107. Laches

Where a city enacts an ordinance creating a paving district, mere failure of the council to proceed with the paving for a period of years operates neither to repeal the ordinance creating the district nor to destroy the council's right subsequently to proceed with the paving.

Neb Hiddleson v Grand Island (1927) 115 Neb 287, 212 NW 619.

§108. Action to Enjoin

A suit to enjoin assessments under an ordinance creating a paving improvement district is a direct attack on the ordinance, and the test of validity is whether the improvements will increase the actual value of property, not whether they will present a benefit to the present owner.

> **Ark**   Kelley Tr v Paving Dist 46 of Fort Smith (1931) 184 Ark 408, 43 SW2d 71.

VIII. PRIVATE USE

§ 109. Regulation

Use of the public streets of a city for the conduct of private business is subject to regulation, and to prohibition if such use renders the streets dangerous to the general public, or impedes the free flow of traffic.

> **Fla**   Pittman v Nix (1943) 152 Fla 378, 11 So2d 791, 144 ALR 1341.

The right to use the streets for business purposes is a privilege which can be acquired only by permission which the municipality may grant or withhold, and in granting permission the city may prescribe such terms and conditions as it sees fit.

> **Ill**   Lombard v Ill Bell Tel (1950) 405 Ill 209, 90 NE2d 105.
> **Mich**   Fostini v Grand Rapids (1957) 348 Mich 36, 81 NW2d 393.
> **NY**   Poulos v Minetti (1949) 197 Misc 611, 92 NYS2d 869.
>   Green v Miller (1928) 249 NY 88, 162 NE 593.
> **Wash**   Baxter-Wyckoff v Seattle (1965) 67 Wash2d 555, 408 P2d 1012.

With express legislative authority, a municipality may permit encroachments on public streets for private purposes, provided the property rights of others are not invaded and the public use of the street is not unreasonably obstructed.

> **NC**   Clayton v Liggett & Myers Tobacco (1945) 225 NC 563, 35 SE2d 691.

ANNOTATION

Public regulation and prohibition of sound amplifiers or speaker broadcasts in streets, 10 ALR2d 627.

§ 110. —Market Stalls

Occupancy of streets by market stalls and stands is a right subject to such changes and modifications in the market, during its existence, as the public needs may require. Consequently, an ordinance changing the limits of the market is within the city's police power.

> **Md**   Liberto v Baltimore (1941) 180 Md 105, 23 A2d 43.

§111. —Sidewalk Stands

Charter authorization to establish, care for and supervise city streets allows the city to license newsstands adjacent thereto by resolution, where the use is not clearly detrimental to abutting owners.

> **NY** People v Friedman (1940) 16 NYS2d 925.
> Langley, In re (1928) 140 Misc 203, 250 NYS 124.

ANNOTATIONS

Authorization, prohibition or regulation by municipality of a sale of merchandise on streets or highways, 14 ALR3d 896.

Liability of abutter to one colliding with or falling over scale or other machine dispensing merchandise or services on the sidewalk, 65 ALR2d 965.

§112. —Loading; Unloading

An ordinance requirement that in the commercial use area they shall provide adequate offstreet loading and unloading space contains a negative pregnant which by implication prohibits onstreet loading.

> **Ida** State ex rel Moore v Bastian (1978) 575 P2d 486.

A provision expressly authorizing an abutting owner to use the sidewalk for purposes of loading and unloading in connection with business operated on such owner's property involves a reasonable use, both as to the extent of the obstruction and the time involved.

> **NY** Graceland v Consolidated Laundries (1958) 7 AD2d 89, 180 NYS2d 644.

§113. —Discrimination

The city is vested with control over its streets, and, save for the purpose of public passage and travel thereon, may prohibit their use altogether as places of business and may make reasonable regulations for their use, in whatever way it chooses, so long as the rules apply uniformly to all persons of the same class.

> **La** New Orleans v Badie (1920) 146 La 550, 83 So 826.
> **Neb** Pierce v Schramm (1927) 116 Neb 263, 216 NW 809.
> **NY** People v Friedman (1940) 16 NYS2d 925.

An ordinance regulating the use of streets for business enterprises, applicable only to a designated portion of the city, is not discriminatory where the exclusion is reasonably required.

> **Tenn**   Dooley v Cleveland (1940) 175 Tenn 439, 135 SW2d 649.

A city license commissioner is without authority to restrict certain areas by issuances of rules and regulations contrary to the municipal administrative code. Where the code provides for the display of articles on the sidewalk in front of buildings he can not override the special provisions of the code.

> **NY**   People v Gerand (1940) 21 NYS2d 428.

§114. Temporary Use

A municipality is without power to authorize use of its streets by private persons, from which neither the city nor the public derives any consideration or benefit, except where such use is temporary, or the power has been specifically delegated by legislature.

> **La**   New Orleans v Kaufman (1916) 38 La 897, 70 So 874.
> **NJ**   Kirzenbaum v Paulus (1958) 51 NJS 186, 144 A2d 25.

§115. Prohibition

An ordinance prohibiting the construction or maintenance of any mercantile business, or equipment pertaining thereto, on any public street, alley, boulevard, parkway, sidewalk or parking area, is a proper exercise of the police power.

> **Ill**   Greenlee Foundry v Borin Art Prod (1942) 379 Ill 494, 41 NE2d 532.
>   People v Wolper (1932) 350 Ill 461, 183 NE 451.
> **NY**   Acme Rlty v Schinasi (1913) 154 AD 397, 139 NYS 266.
> **Okla**   Stillwater v Lovell (1932) 159 Okla 214, 15 P2d 12.
>   Palace Garage v Oklahoma City (1928) 131 Okla 122, 268 P 240.

An ordinance that prohibits the use of streets for the sale of merchandise does not interfere with any essential incidents of transportation, such as would render it inimical to the principle that public streets exist to facilitate transportation, and that activities essential to that end must be permitted.

> **Ill**   Good Humor Corp v Mundelein (1965) 33 Ill2d 252, 211 NE2d 269.

Since sidewalks are considered part of the public streets, and cannot be devoted to private purposes, a city has no right to authorize the use of any portion of its sidewalks for private purposes.

> **Ill**   Heineck v Grosse (1902) 99 IllAp 441.

§116. Creation of Nuisance

Though a city may by ordinance authorize structures in public streets for private benefit, when incident to ordinary street uses and which do not unreasonably interfere with traffic, the power is limited and may not be extended to authorize occupations of a street which create a public nuisance resulting in injury to private rights.

NY   Green v Miller (1928) 249 NY 88, 162 NE 593.

§117. Validity

An ordinance granting a company the right to construct and maintain, on a public sidewalk, a structure for the private use and benefit of a company, which serves no public use but interferes with the use of the sidewalk by the public, is invalid as outside the scope of municipal power.

Ill   Chicago Cold Storage Warehouse v People (1906) 127 IllAp 179.

IX. CONSTRUCTION; OPENING

§118. Generally

A subdivision control ordinance applies only to streets in new subdivisions, and when a comprehensive zoning plan does not contain any requirements for minimum street width the opening of a street is a legislative determination which, in the absence of an abuse of discretion or unreasonableness, will not be interfered with by judicial determination.

Ill   Colville v Rochelle (1970) 130 IllAp2d 541, 268 NE2d 222.

The right of a city to construct and maintain its highways is one of the rights of local self-government deriving from the state Constitution.

Mich   Bird v Detroit (1907) 148 Mich 71, 111 NW 860.

An ordinance providing for the opening and improvement of a street that will furnish access to private buildings for a housing project is valid under the doctrine that municipalities have wide latitude with respect to public improvements, and the courts will not interfere with the legislative judgment in the absence of fraud or palpable abuse of discretion.

NJ   Hoglund v Summit (1959) 28 NJ 540, 147 A2d 521.

Where under an ordinance the jurisdiction of a city council to exercise the power of laying out and constructing streets and taxing any portion of the expense to the abutting owners is dependent on a petition bearing signatures of the requisite number of abutting owners, the existence of the petition is a condition precedent to the power of the council to exercise the authority, and an abutting owner is not estopped to question the sufficiency of the petition.

> **Alas**   Ketchikan Delinquent Tax Roll, In re (1922) 6 Alas 653.

Under municipal code provisions two general procedures are involved in the creation of a new street. First is the acquisition of the necessary realty, and second is the building of the roadway. The city is empowered to place the cost of both procedures on abutting properties in the proportion they benefit from the improvement.

> **NY**   Hunt v New York City (1958) 13 Misc2d 466, 176 NYS2d 11.

Where a city under ordinances for road construction gains control of certain funds granted to it by a railroad company and a federal agency, when the work is completed and the road constructed the city will not be permitted to repudiate a construction contract and refuse to pay the contractor on grounds that the city had no authority to construct a road extending beyond its corporate limits.

> **Ky**   Womack v Worthington (1936) 262 Ky 710, 91 SW2d 13.

§119. Authority

An ordinance establishing a mapped street which constitutes an encumbrance on title must follow due process notice requirements. On failure to do so the ordinance is invalid.

> **NH**   Burgess v Concord (1978) 391 A2d 896.

The appropriation of money for a freeway by the federal government does not abrogate the municipal requirements for public hearings on proposed highways.

> **DC**   DC Federation of Civil Assn's v Airis (1968) 391 F2d 478, 129 ADC 125.

A city's power to establish, lay out and open streets and crossings, and to regulate the construction and operation of railroads within the city, includes the power to open a street across an existing railroad and to regulate railroad operations at the crossing as well as elsewhere. The power to acquire land for that purpose applies to the land of the railroad as well as to that of any other person.

> **Cal**   Los Angeles v Cent Tr (1916) 173 Cal 323, 159 P 1169.
> **NJ**   Ridgewood v Glen Rock (1936) 15 NJM 65, 188 A 698.
> **NY**   Ely Ave in New York City, In re (1916) 217 NY 45, 111 NE 266.
> **Tex**   Dykes v Houston (1966) 406 SW2d 176.

Where it is imperative that a street be constructed connecting two portions of a town in order that the people may have opportunity to go from their homes to their places of business, and the only practicable route over which to construct the street is the route adopted by the council, the city council undoubtedly has the power, where it is granted the authority to make such improvement in the first instance, to make it efficacious by extending it as far as necessary beyond the incorporated limits of the town. The authority of a city or town to provide improvements beyond the city limits may be implied from the existence of a state of facts which renders it actually necessary or manifestly desirable.

Alas Ketchikan v Zimmerman (1911) 4 Alas 336.

The city council, in an ordinance providing for the opening up and laying out of new streets, has the right to determine, insofar as it can, the reasonable future needs of traffic at any given point.

Ill Jacksonville v Dorwart (1928) 333 Ill 143, 164 NE 129.

Requirements that any construction involving the opening of trenches or disturbance of streets or sidewalks within the city must be stamped and signed by a registered land surveyor or registered professional engineer and that in the case of location of installations in sidewalk areas a registered land surveyor will locate and refer to the boundary points prior to construction are invalid as applied to the telephone company. The regulation of public utilities is within the state, and the ordinance frustrates the statutory scheme of regulation.

Mass New England Tel & Tel v Lowell (1976) 369 Mass 831, 343 NE2d 405.

§120. Necessity

The question of the necessity of a local improvement is, by law, committed to the city council, and the courts have no right to interfere except where it clearly appears that discretion has been abused, and in such event, the basis of judicial interference is that the ordinance is so unreasonable as to render it void.

Cal Oakland v Burns (1956) 46 C2d 401, 296 P2d 333.
Ill Chicago v Van Schaack Bros Chemical Works (1928) 330 Ill 264, 161 NE 486.
Field v Western Springs (1899) 181 Ill 186, 54 NE 929.
ND Ashley v Minneapolis, St P & S S M Ry (1917) 37 ND 147, 163 NW 727.

The provision of the statute requiring the passage of a resolution of necessity by the governing body of a city is mandatory and an indispensable prerequisite to further proceedings in connection with the creation of the street improvement to be paid for in whole or in part by special assessments.

ND Mitchell v Parshall (1961) 108 NW2d 12.

§ 121. Notice

Where ordinances provide that a resolution laying out a street or altering street lines or establishing building lines should not be passed by the common council until it has caused the proposed resolution duly attested to be published, together with a notice to property owners to file objections, the publication of such notice is a condition precedent to jurisdiction to pass the resolution and to establish the improvement.

> **Conn** Hartford v Poindexter (1911) 84 Conn 121, 79 A 79.
> **Ill** Hoover v People (1898) 171 Ill 182, 49 NE 367.
> **Iowa** Burget v Greenfield (1903) 120 Iowa 432, 94 NW 933.

Where an ordinance relating to local improvements is properly published before final adoption, failure to mail a copy of proposed ordinance to persons whose lands may be affected will not invalidate ordinance, in view of statutory provision to effect that such failure to mail notice will not invalidate.

> **NJ** River Edge Homes v River Edge (1943) 130 NJLaw 376, 33 A2d 106.

An ordinance for the construction of sidewalks, allowing them to be built with brick, cement, concrete or plank at the option of the city council, and empowering the council to compel property owners to begin sidewalk construction within 30 days of written notice, is not void for failure to designate in the notice provision, the kind of materials and specifications for building walks.

> **Ark** Gregg v Stuttgart (1909) 88 Ark 597, 115 SW 394.

§ 122. Bidding

An advertisement for bids is untimely and ineffective, when at the time there is no ordinance passed authorizing the work described in the advertisement.

> **Ky** Hartford v King (1952) 249 SW2d 13.

A statute that uses the words "proper advertisement" and "due notice" clearly contemplates that a request for bids shall be published at such time as will allow prospective bidders a reasonable time to examine specifications, estimate costs, and present fair bids. An ordinance requiring that bids be submitted the morning of the day following the first publication of the ordinance fails to meet the requirement.

> **Ky** Hartford v King (1952) 249 SW2d 13.

Under a statute providing that sidewalk construction contracts exceeding $500 shall require advertising and bidding, an ordinance for the construction of a sidewalk costing more than $500, and providing for the letting of several contracts of less than $500 each for the aggregate improvement, but with no provision for advertising and bidding, is invalid as an evasion of and in conflict with statutory authority.

> **Ill** People v Lamon (1908) 232 Ill 587, 83 NE 1070.

A city council in the exercise of its discretion is not required to accept a bidder's proposal merely because it is for the least sum, since a better quality material for paving streets may be selected at a higher price. Judgments on these matters are peculiarly within the province of those vested by law with the power of determining the type of improvement.

> **Ky** Campbell v Southern Bitulithic (1908) 32 KLR 799, 106 SW 1189.

§123. Plans; Specifications

The requirement in a charter for "complete specifications" for street construction improvements is satisfied by an ordinance in substantial compliance therewith.

> **Tex** Scanlan v Gulf Bitulithic (1932) 44 SW2d 967, 80 ALR 852.

Under ordinances directing the construction of certain streets in accordance with the plans and specifications of the city engineer, where the ordinances do not in express terms provide for culverts but the plans and specifications do, the plans are not required to be incorporated into the ordinance or published therewith.

> **Ky** Hazard v Adams (1929) 229 Ky 598, 17 SW2d 703.

A resolution of intention authorizing and directing a readvertisement for sealed proposals for graveling certain streets in accordance with plans and specifications on file in the office of the city clerk was equivalent to the adoption of the survey, diagrams and specifications filed with the clerk and tantamount to a prior direction to the city surveyor to make the survey, diagram, estimates and specifications.

> **Cal** Stockton v Skinner (1878) 53 Cal 85.

§124. Description of Improvement

In a local improvement ordinance for the construction of combined curbs and sidewalks, the description of the improvement must be sufficiently definite to inform abutting property owners of its terms, i.e., what they are to get for their money.

> **Ark** Nelson v Nelson (1922) 154 Ark 36, 241 SW 370.
> **Ida** Coughanour v Payette (1914) 26 Ida 280, 142 P 1076.
> **Ill** Chicago v Russo (1930) 339 Ill 349, 171 NE 523.
> Danville v McAdams (1894) 153 Ill 216, 38 NE 632.
> **Ohio** Sun Oil v Euclid (1955) 164 OS 265, 58 Op 25, 130 NE2d 336.

An ordinance of intention to commence street improvements and a notice of public work are fatally defective where the description employed incorrectly designates the streets affected and fails to describe the opening of a proposed new street.

> **Cal** O T Johnson Corp v Los Angeles (1926) 198 Cal 308, 245 P 164.
> **Ill** Mansfield v People (1897) 164 Ill 611, 45 NE 976.

An ordinance providing for construction of a sidewalk is not invalid as uncertain because of its provision for a "cement" sidewalk in one portion, and in another for a "cement-concrete-sand-and gravel" walk, since "cement sidewalk" is a generic expression, and the further description is merely a statement of the ingredients to be used.

> **Ill** Gage v Chicago (1902) 196 Ill 512, 63 NE 1031.

An ordinance entitled, "An ordinance to condemn and open Gwynn's Falls Parkway," sufficiently describes the subject matter in the title.

> **Md** Bouis v Baltimore (1921) 138 Md 284, 113 A 852.

A patent inconsistency of description between the preamble and the enacting clause of an ordinance creating a paving improvement district will not render the ordinance invalid, if the error is so glaring that any property owner seeking to discover the through boundaries of the district could not be misled by the words of the enacting clause.

> **Ark** Bostick v Pernot (1924) 165 Ark 581, 265 SW 356.

Where an ordinance authorizes construction of a parkway and defines by metes and bounds property to be condemned therefor, and the description in the published notice is at variance with that in the ordinance, the ordinance controls.

> **Mo** State v Ellison (1916) 191 SW 49.

§ 125. Type of Material

Where a statute makes no provision for the kind of material out of which streets shall be constructed, the matter is left to the judgment of the city council in enacting an ordinance to pave streets. So long as the council does not abuse its discretion, the court has no control over its action.

> **Ky**   Campbell v Southern Bitulithic (1908) 32 KLR 799, 106 SW 1189.

Under an ordinance authorizing sidewalk construction the city council has power to specify that one of two materials specified shall be used.

> **Ky**   Olive Hill v Tabor (1911) 143 Ky 336, 136 SW 649.

Where a local improvement ordinance specifies asphaltic cement to be used in the construction of a street, parol evidence is admissible to show that the term "asphaltic cement" has a well defined meaning among paving contractors.

> **Ill**   Chicago Union Traction v Chicago (1906) 223 Ill 37, 79 NE 67.

§126. —Patented

An ordinance authorizing street construction whose specifications call for a type of patented pavement is invalid where but one company holds the patent and is therefore the only company eligible to bid on the improvement.

> **Ore**   Temple v Portland (1915) 77 Ore 559, 151 P 724.

A provision in a street construction ordinance prescribing the use of a creosote oil, which cannot be produced without infringing a patent, is invalid as restricting free competition among bidders.

> **Ill**   Schoelkopf v Chicago (1919) 216 IllAp 52.

§127. Grades

The only manner by which grades of streets can be established for the building of sidewalks or permanent improvements in a street is by ordinance, a resolution being ineffective for that purpose.

> **Ill**   McDowell v People (1903) 204 Ill 499, 68 NE 379.
> **Iowa**   Collins v Iowa Falls (1910) 146 Iowa 305, 125 NW 226.

An ordinance establishing the grade of two streets intersecting a third cannot be extended by implication to include the intersected street between the two intersections.

> **Iowa**   Morton v Burlington (1898) 106 Iowa 50, 75 NW 662.

An ordinance establishing a grade for the center of a street operates to establish a grade for that portion of the street occupied by sidewalks.

> **Iowa**   Beirness v Missouri Valley (1913) 162 Iowa 720, 144 NW 628.

§128. Liability of Municipality

The mere establishment of the grade of streets does not damage property. It is the change in the surface of the streets that creates damage, if any, and for which allowance of damages must first be provided. If no change is ever made or undertaken, there is no damage.

    Mo   Bray v Land Constr Co (1920) 203 MoAp 642, 221 SW 818.
    Neb   Hilger v Nebraska City (1914) 97 Neb 268, 149 NW 807.

A city may be liable for damages caused by the grading of a street, though done in accordance with the provisions of a grade ordinance, if thereby the natural drainage is destroyed, and no adequate means is provided for the escape of surface water.

    Iowa   Wilbur v Fort Dodge (1903) 120 Iowa 555, 95 NW 186.

Although a city is responsible for damage to private property resulting from street grading, the measure of damage is the resulting diminution of the market value.

    La   Shreveport v Curcio (1934) 157 So 317.

A property owner cannot recover damages for establishment of the grade of a street by ordinance, until actual grading is begun.

    Pa   Costello v Scranton (1933) 108 PaS 573, 165 A 670.

An ordinance establishing street grades, on land dedicated to the city for street construction, which cause a subsiding of the lateral support for the land of the dedicator, does not constitute a taking of property without compensation.

    Ore   Kropitzer v Portland (1964) 237 Ore 157, 390 P2d 356.

The fact that the work of bringing a street to the grade established by ordinance was begun without the adoption of a resolution ordering the work did not create a right of action in favor of a property owner for damages resulting from the raising of the street to grade.

    Iowa   Wilbur v Fort Dodge (1903) 120 Iowa 555, 95 NW 186.

§129. Validity

A decision to open a previously platted and dedicated street and eject the abutting owner using the land will only be set aside if it is arbitrary and capricious. A determination that a street improvement plan is necessary having in mind a school located near the junkyard as well as a park and the rerouting of traffic makes the question fairly debatable and not subject to judicial determination.

Minn Medford v Wilson (1975) 304 Minn 250, 230 NW2d 458.

An ordinance prohibiting the laying out or opening of a road, or the making of any other public improvement in the city, without consent of the council, is valid as a reasonable and necessary restraint on private rights in order to apprise the city of construction of potential public concern, of which it would otherwise be unaware.

Tex Dykes v Houston (1966) 406 SW2d 176.

An ordinance authorizing the opening and establishment of a street, and the condemnation of a right-of-way therefor over the right-of-way of a railroad, though adopted at the behest of a manufacturer wishing to move his facilities to a more convenient location, is not invalid as an appropriation of private property for private use where it is shown that the improvement would be of great public benefit.

Mo Kansas City v Mo Pac Ry (1921) 229 SW 771.

Ordinances authorizing road construction are valid, though the record thereof may not be recited in the choicest and most explicit English, where they are passed at meetings of the council attended by a sufficient number of councilmen to constitute a quorum and received the affirmative vote of the councilmen present.

Mo Carrollton v Thomas (1930) 24 SW2d 218.

Where at the time of adoption of an ordinance that purported to establish a street, the common council was not authorized to establish a street by ordinance, the ordinance is thus invalid and properly excluded by the trial court.

Ind Pa RR v Hemmer (1933) 206 Ind 311, 186 NE 285.

A resolution of a city council fixing the grade of a street is invalid, since such action is legislative in character and must be in the form of an ordinance that prescribes a permanent rule of conduct.

Ill Chicago & N P RR v Chicago (1898) 174 Ill 439, 51 NE 596.

An ordinance adopting a street plan that divides a single parcel into four separate parts, proposes a street to run through a residence thereon, and makes the property unsalable is unreasonable, where no provision is made to compensate the owner for the loss.

NY Caperton v Lawrence (1936) 161 Misc 23, 290 NYS 1016.

§130. Eminent Domain

A zoned right-of-way ordinance which prohibits construction in the proposed right-of-way rather than the existing street is the first step in the eminent domain proceedings. In enforcing this right the county is required to pay compensation for the property between the existing street right-of-way and the zoned right-of-way regardless of the length of time involved since its passage.

> **Fla**   Dade County v Bar-zac (1971) 35 Fla Supp 122.

A resolution to condemn property for street widening is invalid when no hearing has been held before the board of aldermen. A hearing before a committee of the board is insufficient to meet the requirements.

> **NH**   Nashua v Gaukstern (1977) 117 NJ 30, 369 A2d 211.

A municipality that enacts an ordinance in collaboration with a plan of the state department of highways to open a new street and relocate a state highway over it has power to condemn land needed and is liable for the damages.

> **Pa**   Adams v New Kensington (1953) 374 Pa 104, 97 A2d 354.

Under an ordinance authorizing the extension of a street the necessity for opening or extending streets, as well as the necessity for condemning rights-of-way for such purposes, is a matter for decision by the municipal authorities, and their judgment is conclusive unless it appears that the use is palpably private, or that the necessity for the taking is without any reasonable foundation.

> **Ky**   Louisville & N Ry v Louisville (1921) 190 Ky 214, 227 SW 160.

Property owned by a school district, and devoted to a public use, may not be condemned, under an ordinance authorizing condemnation proceedings for the establishment and opening of a street, since the right to condemn property for street purposes is limited to private property.

> **Mo**   St Louis v Moore (1916) 269 Mo 430, 190 SW 867.

X. SIDEWALKS; IMPROVEMENTS, MAINTENANCE

§131. Generally

A special county tax area or district established for road improvement purposes is not authorized to spend its road money for construction of sidewalks abutting a state highway. The funds must come from other sources.

> **Md**   Serota v Hoover (1969) 252 Md 248, 249 A2d 720.

A subdivision may not be denied or conditioned on installing sidewalks on each side of the streets, where the ordinance only requires them when the lots average 3½ lots per gross acre and the area is adjacent to other subdivisions with sidewalks. A plat with 2.93 lots per gross acre and not adjoining any other subdivision may not be denied platting until sidewalks are intalled.

> **Ind**   Suburban Homes v Anderson (1970) 147 IndAp 419, 261 NE2d 376.

A cul-de-sac serving five lots is a minor street and therefore exempt from sidewalk requirements. It does not constitute a secondary or collector street within the ordinance requirements.

> **Ill**   Clark v Oswego (1973) 10 IllAp3d 964, 295 NE2d 733.

When a street has been improved, a sidewalk requirement may be enforced against unimproved farmland.

> **Pa**   Sweigart v Ephrata (1975) 21 PaCmwlth 280, 344 A2d 766.

It is within the power and duty of municipalities to establish sidewalks within their limits, where necessary, and to establish their grade, location, character or construction, and material to be used.

> **Ill**   Ill Cent RR v Stewart (1907) 230 Ill 204, 82 NE 590.
> **Iowa** Kaynor v Dist Ct of Black Hawk County (1916) 178 Iowa 1055, 158 NW 557.
> Burget v Greenfield (1903) 120 Iowa 432, 94 NW 933.

A statute requiring sidewalks to be kept in reasonable repair and in a condition reasonably safe for travel requires only that a sidewalk be kept in such repair as to render it safe for ordinary uses, and does not mean that it shall be kept in a safe condition for bicycle riding, though an ordinance authorizes such use.

> **Mich**   Lee v Port Huron (1901) 128 Mich 533, 87 NW 637.

Ordinances for the building, maintenance, repair and rebuilding of sidewalks, with specifications of the type of material to be used, are within the police power of the city. This power includes the ability of cities to require original construction of sidewalks, as well as maintenance and repair.

> **Ark**   Malvern v Cooper (1913) 108 Ark 24, 156 SW 845.

Although a sidewalk is used for pedestrian rather than vehicular travel, it is as much a public highway as the street itself, and the difference in the manner of use does not render one any more public than the other.

> **Ill**   Chicago v O'Brien (1884) 111 Ill 532, 53 ALR 640.

A grassy section between the paved portion of a sidewalk and the curbing is a sidewalk and not a parkway, within the meaning of an ordinance defining a sidewalk as any portion of a street between the curb line and the adjacent property line intended for pedestrian use, excluding parkways, which are broad thoroughfares beautified with trees and turf.

> **La**   Labruzza v Boston Ins Co (1967) 198 So2d 436.

§132. Description; Specifications

The description of the location of a sidewalk in a street improvement ordinance is sufficient if a competent surveyor can, by the description, fix the locality of the improvement.

> **Ill**   People v Willison (1909) 237 Ill 584, 86 NE 1094.
> **Mo**   Huntsville v Eatherton (1916) 182 SW 767.

An ordinance for the improvement of sidewalks on both sides of a street fully enough describes the location of the parts of the sidewalks to be improved by giving the numbers of the lots or houses bordering on the proposed improvement.

> **Ky**   Dumesnil v Hexagon Tile (1900) 22 KLR 791, 58 SW 705.

A sidewalk construction ordinance provision that no stone shall be used less than 4½ feet in width and 10 inches in thickness is a sufficient description, as against a claim that the ordinance does not sufficiently describe the improvement.

> **Ill**   Hyman v Chicago (1900) 188 Ill 462, 59 NE 10.
> **Mo**   Platte City v Paxton (1910) 141 MoApp 175, 124 SW 531.

An ordinance is not void merely because it fails to specify the grade and width of a sidewalk, for such matters may properly be left to the authorities having charge of the improvements.

> **Ky**   Nell v Power (1908) 32 KLR 952, 107 SW 694.

A proposition submitted to electors "to pave and improve sidewalks" is sufficiently definite to sustain an ordinance and assessment, since the authority to pave includes the authority to grade, curb and drain.

> **La**   Judice v Scott (1929) 168 La 111, 121 So 592.

§133. Grades

In a local improvement ordinance, the grade for sidewalks must be established either directly or by reference to another ordinance. This is a legislative function to be exercised by the council which may not be delegated, and an ordinance not containing a specification of grade is fatally defective.

> Ill   Staunton v Bond (1917) 281 Ill 568, 118 NE 47.
> People v Meerts (1915) 267 Ill 210, 108 NE 57.

Where an ordinance does not prescribe the grade of a proposed sidewalk, and the sidewalk merely replaces a condemned one, the grade is by necessary inference left as it was.

> Ky   Augusta v McKibben (1901) 22 KLR 1224, 60 SW 291.

An objection to a sidewalk ordinance that no grade is established is not tenable, where the ordinance incorporates the "plan and profile" of the engineer attached to it as part of the ordinance, and such plan and profile clearly indicate the grade.

> Ill   People v Howell (1928) 330 Ill 527, 162 NE 189.

§134. Abutting Owners—Rights

A tract of land separated from a street right-of-way by a vacant strip owned by the city is not abutting for the purposes of a street assessment. The city land which is not part of the right-of-way and not contemplated in the street expansion and which varies from 25 to 52 feet in width between the street and the tract successfully separates the properties.

> Tex   Wichita Falls v Thomas (1975) 523 SW2d 312.

An ordinance giving an abutting owner an opportunity to construct sidewalks and curbing before the city contracts for the work is valid.

> Iowa   Zalesky v Cedar Rapids (1902) 118 Iowa 714, 92 NW 657.
> Ky   Frankfort v Murray (1896) 99 Ky 422, 36 SW 180.

The allowing of some owners to use a more expensive material than a sidewalk improvement ordinance requires, at their expense, does not affect the validity of the ordinance.

> Ky   Anderson v Bitzer (1899) 20 KLR 1450, 49 SW 442.

Since the title to a sidewalk is vested in the city in trust for the public, an abutting owner can have no vested right to continued maintenance of the sidewalk at any specified width, so as to invalidate an ordinance providing for narrowing the sidewalk for the purpose of widening the roadway.

> Ill   Campbell v Chicago (1941) 119 F2d 1014.

§135. —Duties and Liabilities

A proceeding to collect a fine imposed for conviction of failure to remove and replace a sidewalk cannot be maintained against the personal representatives of the deceased defendant by substitution.

> **Mo**   Clayton v Sigoloff (1970) 452 SW2d 315.

A city by ordinance may not remove its obligation to maintain sidewalks in such a condition to be reasonably safe for public travel.

> **Wis**   Kobelinski v Milwaukee & Suburban Transport Corp (1972) 56 Wis2d 504, 202 NW2d 415.

An ordinance requiring that the owner or occupant keep the abutting sidewalk in good and safe repairs is not for the benefit of any injured party nor does it impose any liability on the owner.

> **NY**   Sheridan v Hempstead (1973) 78 Misc2d 1000, 359 NYS2d 382.

Charter provisions dealing with sidewalks and providing that on failure to construct sidewalks when ordered the city may construct them and assess the cost against the adjoining owner do not provide for criminal penalties. The catch-all criminal ordinance may not be applied to a charter provision in the absence of amendment to the sidewalk provisions.

> **Mich**   Valenti Homes v Sterling Heights (1975) 61 Mich Ap 537, 233 NW2d 72.

An ordinance providing a penalty for failure to maintain sidewalks does not impose liability on the abutting owner. A municipality is liable for injury to a pedestrian and does not have a third party indemnity action against the abutting owner when the ordinance fails to impose liability.

> **Ill**   Summers v Springfield (1975) 33 IllAp3d 474, 337 NE2d 74.

A requirement that city sidewalks be maintained by the owner is valid. The provisions for notice and requirement that repair be made in a certain manner is not arbitrary and does not deprive the owner of any property rights.

> **Mo**   Mutual Auto Parks v Kansas City (1976) 537 SW2d 820.

A city ordinance requiring the abutting owner or occupant to maintain the sidewalk in proper repair does not render the owner or tenant liable for injuries sustained by a member of the public as a result of a defect in the sidewalk.

> **Tex**   Parra v FW Woolworth Co (1977) 545 SW 596.

Charter provisions authorizing a municipality to make and pass such resolutions, bylaws and ordinances as are necessary and proper, and to regulate and make improvements to streets and sidewalks, authorize the city to enact an ordinance requiring the owners of lots fronting on particular streets to construct and keep in repair sidewalks and curbings.

Cal	Calvert v Burnett Est (1916) 43 CA 456, 185 P 428.
	Heath v Manson (1905) 147 Cal 694, 82 P 331.
Ky	Vissman v Koby (1958) 309 SW2d 345.
	Ashland v Vansant Kitchen Lumber (1926) 213 Ky 518, 281 SW 503.
La	Mayor v Fontelieu (1902) 108 La 460, 32 So 369.
	Toppi v Arbour (1960) 119 So2d 621.
Mich	Walker v Detroit (1906) 143 Mich 427, 106 NW 1123.
Minn	Sternitzke v Donahue's Jewelers (1957) 249 Minn 514, 83 NW2d 96.
NY	People v Lathers (1910) 141 AD 16, 125 NYS 753.
	Konowalski v Buffalo (1909) 131 AD 465, 115 NYS 467.
NC	Marion v Pilot Mountain (1915) 170 NC 118, 87 SE 53.
Okla	King v Crosbie (1942) 191 Okla 525, 131 P2d 105.
Ore	Haner v Eugene (1920) 95 Ore 596, 187 P 841.
Tex	Tex Co v Grant (1944) 143 Tex 145, 182 SW2d 996.
W Va	Maxey v Bluefield (1966) 151 W Va 302, 151 SE2d 689.

An ordinance requiring owners and tenants to remove snow and ice from their sidewalks does not unfairly impose a duty on certain citizens that should fall on the municipality. Rather, it uniformly imposes a duty according to one's ownership, possession and enjoyment of abutting land.

NJ State v Giacchetto (1979) 399 A2d 1031.

A provision for removal of snow and ice from abutting sidewalks imposes on property owners the performance of a part of the municipality's duties and is for the benefit of the municipality, not of the public. A breach is remedied only by the action of the municipal government, and does not confer a right of action on the individual, even on those injured.

Neb Mackey v Midwest Supply Co (1971) 186 Neb 834, 186 NW2d 916.

An ordinance requiring removal of snow and ice from any building fronting on a sidewalk and further providing a duty to keep the pavement or sidewalk situated in the front, at the rear, or at the side free from snow and ice, applies to a sidewalk on the side of a building.

W Va Gillespie v Charleston (1970) 154 W Va 565, 177 SE2d 354.

Snow and ice removals from sidewalks required by ordinance is a delegation of the city's duty to adjoining owner. It carries a criminal penalty, but does not constitute the basis for a standard of care to third parties or of negligence per se by an injured third party.

Del Burns v Boudwin (1971) 282 A2d 620.
Ind Nyers v Gruber (1971) 275 NE2d 863.

A snow removal ordinance which does not contain a provision for civil liability does not make a violation negligence per se. Failure to include the penal provisions does not make the ordinance civil for the benefit of the pedestrian traffic.

> **Colo**   Winn v First Baptist Church of Englewood (1972) 500 P2d 160.
> **Ore**   Fitzwater v Sunset Empire (1972) 263 Ore 276, 502 P2d 214.
>   Anthis v Bordeaux (1975) 271 Ore 73, 530 P2d 836.
> **Wash**   Gardner v Kendrick (1972) 7 WashAp 852, 503 P2d 134.

A wall constructed by a state pursuant to a permanent easement, separating a sidewalk from the front of a landowner's premises, does not affect the owner's obligation under an ordinance to remove snow and ice from the sidewalk, since the owner retains all rights and benefits of ownership consistent with the easement.

> **NY**   People v Bronxville-Palmer Ltd (1978) 94 Misc2d 1067, 406 NYS2d 248.

A snow and ice removal ordinance cannot shift the city's responsibility to remove an accumulation which creates a dangerous condition on the city's sidewalk.

> **Colo**   Brame v Schroeder (1975) 532 P2d 763.
> **Ind**   Nyers v Gruber (1971) 150 IndAp 117, 275 NE2d 863.

An ordinance requiring the tenant or owner of property to remove all snow and ice which has accumulated is invalid. The authority given to a city to raise revenue to pay for street maintenance includes the care of sidewalks. A property owner cannot be required to pay both for the general maintenance and be under an obligation to remove all snow that may accumulate.

> **NH**   State v Jackman (1898) 69 NH 318, 41 A 347.

The purpose of an ordinance requiring the board of burgesses to repair a sidewalk, when the abutting owner neglects to repair it within the time and in the manner ordered by the board, and making the cost a lien in favor of the borough, is to cast on the abutting owner only the cost of repair, and in this manner to save the borough the expense that would otherwise fall on its treasury.

> **Conn**   Ryan v Beckwith (1940) 8 Conn Supp 512.

The power to compel the owners of property to construct sidewalks and keep them in repair and free from obstruction is not an exercise of the taxing power, but of the police power; and it may be exercised under more general grants of authority.

> **Iowa**   Bowman v Waverly (1910) 155 Iowa 745, 128 NW 950.
> **Ky**   Forester v Coombs Land Co (1939) 277 Ky 279, 126 SW2d 433.
>   Barret v Falls City Artificial Stone (1899) 21 KLR 669, 52 SW 947.

La   Mayor v Fontelieu (1902) 108 La 460, 32 So 369.
NJ   Whelan v Chatham (1950) 9 NJS 341, 74 A2d 429.
NC   Marion v Pilot Mountain (1915) 170 NC 118, 87 SE 53.
Tex   Lampasas v Huling (1919) 209 SW 213.
W Va   Sleeth v Elkins (1921) 87 W Va 750, 106 SE 73.

Requiring a property owner to have his basement set back to conform to a new curb constructed pursuant to an ordinance reducing the width of the sidewalk does not deprive him of private property without just compensation and without due process of law.

Cal   Fallon v San Francisco (1941) 44 CA2d 404, 112 P2d 718.

Under a statute authorizing cities or towns to order property owners to construct sidewalks in front of their property, and, on failure of the owners to do so, to construct such improvements and assess the costs to the owners on a frontage basis, an ordinance enacted and tax warrants issued pursuant thereto are valid and do not constitute the taking of private property without compensation.

Ill   Western Springs v Hill (1899) 177 Ill 634, 52 NE 959.
Iowa   Halley v Fort Dodge (1897) 103 Iowa 573, 72 NW 756.
Mo   Maret v Hough (1916) 185 SW 544.
Okla   Shultise v Taloga (1914) 42 Okla 65, 140 P 1190.
Tex   Lampasas v Huling (1919) 209 SW 213.
Wis   Griswold v Camp (1912) 149 Wis 399, 135 NW 754.

An ordinance making it unlawful to wash sidewalks between 8 AM and 6 PM was designed to protect people from inconvenience or the danger of wet and slippery sidewalks during the hours they are most used.

Cal   Della Mora v Favilla (1918) 37 CA 164, 173 P 770.

A regularly enacted ordinance which, without inequality or discrimination, imposes the duty on all persons subject to its provisions to remove, or cause to be removed, within a specified reasonable period of time, snow and ice from a public sidewalk fronting on a paved street of the municipality is valid.

Conn   State v McMahon (1903) 76 Conn 97, 55 A 591.
DC   Radinsky v Ellis (1948) 167 F2d 745.
Md   Weisner v Rockville (1967) 245 Md 225, 225 A2d 648.
Mo   Russell v Sincoe Rlty (1922) 293 Mo 428, 240 SW 147.
    Kansas City v Holmes (1918) 274 Mo 159, 202 SW 392.
NY   Van Slyke v N Y Cent RR (1964) 21 AD2d 147, 249 NYS2d 462.
    Nelson v Schultz (1939) 170 Misc 681, 11 NYS2d 184.
Va   Johnson v J S Bell & Co (1960) 202 Va 274, 117 SE2d 85, 82 ALR2d 995.
W Va   Rich v Rosenshine (1947) 131 W Va 30, 45 SE2d 499.
Wyo   Kalman v Western Union (1964) 390 P2d 724.

An ordinance requiring property owners to keep sidewalks and gutters free of ice and snow, or to sprinkle them with ashes or sand when the ice and snow cannot be removed without injury to the pavement, is outside the constitutional power of the legislature to authorize, in view of the doctrine that sidewalks are part of the public highway, which private property owners have no obligation to repair or maintain.

Ill   Chicago v O'Brien (1884) 111 Ill 532, 53 ALR 640.

An ordinance requiring an abutting owner to remove snow from public sidewalks and gutters is a police regulation, and does not go behind the building line.

NY   Green v Green (1925) 212 AD 381, 208 NYS 689.

An ordinance prohibiting any person or firm from discharging water from his residence or place of business on any street, alley or public place within the city forbids the permitting of waste water from sprinkling operations to flow onto the sidewalk.

Ariz   Cobb v Salt River Valley Water Users (1941) 57 Ariz 451, 114 P2d 904.

The duty to clean sidewalks imposed on an owner of real property, is enforceable only at the instance of the city.

NY   Spector v Puglisi (1957) 9 Misc2d 250, 172 NYS2d 524.

A local law imposing tort liability on abutting owners for personal injuries sustained due to defective sidewalks is a valid enactment pursuant to the authority granted to every city by the state constitution and by the statute.

Iowa   Case v Sioux City (1955) 246 Iowa 654, 69 NW2d 27.
NY   Karom v Altarac (1957) 3 AD2d 925, 162 NYS2d 968.
W Va   Barniak v Grossman (1956) 141 W Va 760, 93 SE2d 49.

The failure of the abutting owner to maintain a sidewalk in good repair in compliance with an ordinance, without more, does not give rise to a right of action on the part of a pedestrian who is injured by reason of the defect.

Kan   Dixon v Mo Pac Ry (1919) 104 Kan 787, 180 P 733.
Mich   Grooms v Union Guardian Tr (1944) 309 Mich 437, 15 NW2d 698.
NY   Holcomb v Wincuinas (1964) 22 AD2d 715, 253 NYS2d 190.
   Pryga v Will (1949) 275 AD 52, 87 NYS2d 162.
Ohio   Dennison v Buckeye Parking (1953) 94 OA 379, 52 Op 38, 115 NE2d 187.

An ordinance requiring designated property owners to repair sidewalks adjoining or abutting their property will not render the property owners liable to pedestrians allegedly injured by holes in the sidewalk due to failure to make the required repairs. The ordinance creates a duty on the property owner that is enforceable only by the municipality.

Ark   Epps v Remmel (1963) 237 Ark 391, 373 SW2d 141.

A municipal ordinance requiring adjoining owners to keep sidewalks in a state of repair does not create a cause of action, for injuries sustained in a fall, against the adjoining owner, since the city has the primary responsibility for maintenance and control of its sidewalks.

Mich Levendoski v Geisenhaver (1965) 375 Mich 225, 134 NW2d 228.

§136. Municipalities, Duties and Liabilities

When a village ordinance provides that individual property owners rather than the village have the responsibility of constructing sidewalks along public streets and where the village has not undertaken such construction, it has no duty to continue an existing sidewalk which ends about 125 feet from the end of the block. In the event a village undertakes a plan for constructing sidewalks under such an ordinance, it still cannot be held liable for the deaths of two pedestrians hit by a car while walking on the street after having reached the end of the sidewalk where the adopted plan has not been completed.

Ill Best v Richert (1979) 389 NE2d 894.

Damages against a city for failure to remove snow and ice that has accumulated over 48 hours and of which the city has notice may be sustained, even without a showing that the same snow and ice is present. A showing of notice to the city and that the condition is comparable to that existing at the time of notice, and that the condition was not rectified, constitutes sufficient evidence of the accumulation.

ND Haugen v Grand Forks (1971) 187 NW2d 68.

A home rule city's requirement of a 30-day notice of claim may not be used to deny recovery for injury in a sidewalk accident. The statutory authority for recovery on defective sidewalks may not be avoided by requiring a claim.

W Va Toler v Huntington (1969) 153 W Va 313, 168 SE2d 551.

An agreement between a city and county whereby the county is to construct a road and be liable for maintenance when it connects two county roads and extends into the existing road system into the city of Houston is valid and enforceable. The option to extend the agreement does not expire until the date of acceptance by the county rather than the date of passage of the resolution. The county by implication secures the right of eminent domain under the agreement.

Tex Piney Point Village v Harris County (1972) 479 SW2d 358.

An ordinance authorizing the sale of certain city property to private investors for a stated purchase sum does not authorize the contract purchaser to require the city to install sidewalks, The ordinance authorization for the city to install sidewalks at their expense is a legislative delegation and may not subsequently be delegated to the mayor and city attorney.

NY   Syrtel Building v Syracuse (1974) 78 Misc2d 780, 358 NYS2d 627.

The primary duty to maintain sidewalks and thoroughfares in a reasonably safe condition lies with the municipality which controls them.

Alas   Burke v Columbia Lumber (1952) 14 Alas 145, 108 F Supp 743.
Ky   Hale v Louisville (1938) 273 Ky 361, 116 SW2d 656.
Wis   Willmer v Goebel (1909) 137 Wis 419, 119 NW 115.

Municipalities are responsible in damages for accidents resulting from failure to repair or maintain defective sidewalks, and they may not by ordinance relieve themselves of this obligation by shifting the burden to abutting property owners.

La   Toppi v Arbour (1960) 119 So2d 621.

Under a resolution requiring the construction of a sidewalk and making a change in its grade, the city is liable for damages to the property of an abutting owner caused by the change in grade.

Ky   Cassell v Bd of Councilmen (1909) 134 Ky 103, 119 SW 788.
La   Brown v Baton Rouge (1961) 126 So2d 173.

§ 136.1. Soiling by Animals

Dogs are a valid classification in themselves. Due to the continual fight against pollution a municipality may properly regulate and prohibit dogs from soiling, defiling, defecating on or committing any nuisance on any common street or sidewalk. They may further require that the owner of any dog committing such an act immediately remove feces in a sanitary manner and dispose of the same. The restriction requiring a dog be curbed, walked in the street area along side the curb, is invalid as it subjects the owner, the dog, and the traffic to undue hazards.

NJ   Nutley v Forney (1971) 116 NJS 567, 283 A2d 142.

§ 137. Validity of Ordinance

A preliminary injunction against the mandatory installation of sidewalks will not prevail where there is no indication that the complainants would win the suit. Where the city council has made a uniform requirement for sidewalks and has shown an effort to preserve and prevent unnecessary destruction of shrubbery and trees, and construction was motivated by public interest, it undoubtedly will be sustained.

Del Arbour Park Civic Assn v Newark (1970) 267 A2d 904.

Although an abutting owner is seized with title to the center of the street, his estate is subject to the paramount right of the municipality to use the public way in any reasonable and proper public manner. A narrowing of the sidewalk to widen the street may cause damages recoverable in law, but it does not involve taking property without compensation.

Ill Campbell v Chicago (1941) 119 F2d 1014.
Glencoe v Stone (1921) 296 Ill 177, 129 NE 700.

An ordinance providing for construction of a cement sidewalk 20 feet wide, for a half mile on each side of a 100-foot wide curbed street, is not unreasonable, in view of the sidewalk's location in a business locality adjacent to the finest residential section of the city, and of the existing sidewalks' variations in width, materials, and state of repair.

Ill Chicago v Wilson (1902) 195 Ill 19, 62 NE 843.

An ordinance establishing a building line at a busy street corner so as to create a 10-foot rather than a 5-foot sidewalk is not unconstitutional as being arbitrary or unreasonable.

NY Gnecco v Great Neck Plaza (1942) 41 NYS2d 436.

An ordinance compelling a lot owner to construct a 1256-foot cement sidewalk along an unimproved street, to replace a wooden plank sidewalk constructed five months before in compliance with a prior ordinance, is void as unreasonable, oppressive and unjust.

Ill Hawes v Chicago (1895) 158 Ill 653, 42 NE 373.

Ordinances authorizing sidewalk improvements and the issuance of tax bills on assessments for payment of the costs, are not invalidated where the completed walk is uneven and not as sightly as might be, but nevertheless is substantial and durable and suited to sidewalk purposes as a valuable addition to abutting properties, and probably worth the actual costs charged.

Mo Glendale v Armstrong (1929) 17 SW2d 604.

A city ordinance granting a private corporation right to construct a sidewalk 3½ feet above street grade is invalid as constituting an unreasonable impediment to pedestrian traffic.

Ill People v Western Cold Storage (1919) 287 Ill 612, 123 NE 43.

As local improvement ordinance may provide for sidewalks on more than one street in the same city, if such streets are adjacent, without rendering the ordinance invalid as a double improvement.

> **Ill**   Staunton v Bond (1917) 281 Ill 568, 118 NE 47.

XI. STREETS; IMPROVEMENT, MAINTENANCE

§138. Improvements, Generally

A street assessment on property fronting a commercially zoned tract is valid even though a divider has been placed in the road since safe means of access are provided. The assessment against adjoining residential property is invalid when proof is offered that the value of the property has decreased. The fact that the property may subsequently be rezoned commercial and was purchased with that thought in mind does not confer any benefit since it is a contingent matter.

> **Wis**   Molbreak v Shorewood Hills (1975) 66 Wis2d 687, 225 NW2d 894.

A street improvement district may not be changed by the action of the assessor in determining benefits. The assessment based on a theory that no benefit is available to a lot with over a 135-foot depth is inappropriate and an attempt to shorten the area of the assessment district. When lots run up to 549 feet the assessment is void and must be remade.

> **Cal**   Costello v Los Angeles (1975) 54 CA3d 28, 126 CaR 462.

Street improvement bonds to facilitate relocation of railroad rights-of-way, bridges, and a freight depot, to alleviate traffic congestion, may be issued on vote of the people. The fact that the railroad will benefit does not make the project any less a street improvement, nor does it constitute the giving of public property for private use. The agreement between the railroad and the city is a valid exercise of the city's authority to secure rights-of-way or to correct street problems.

> **SC**   Sadler v Lyle (1970) 254 SC 535, 176 SE2d 290.

A city council is clothed with power to determine what street improvement is required, its nature and character, when it shall be made and the manner of construction, all of which are matters of discretion not subject to judicial review when honestly and reasonably exercised.

> **Ariz**   Mosher v Phoenix (1932) 39 Ariz 470, 7 P2d 622.
> **Ill**   Chicago v Wacker-Wabash (1940) 372 Ill 521, 25 NE2d 23.
> **Iowa**   Martin v Oskaloosa (1905) 126 Iowa 680, 102 NW 529.
> **ND**   Green v Beste (1956) 76 NW2d 165.

Where the legislature provides different or alternative methods for improvement of public streets the choice of method is optional with the governing city authorities in enacting an ordinance.

> **Ky** Coke v Dowell (1940) 281 Ky 362, 136 SW2d 3.

An ordinance enacted under charter authority to regrade and improve a street will not be declared unreasonable or void on a claim of ulterior motives on the part of the council, in the absence of a showing of an evil purpose or fraud in the passage thereof.

> **Mo** Goodson v Ferguson (1961) 345 SW2d 381.

The matter of improving streets, alleys, and highways within the corporate limits is a subject of strictly municipal concern.

> **Neb** Salsbury v Lincoln (1928) 117 Neb 465, 220 NW 827.

A city, in regulating the repair and improvement of its streets, exercises a legislative function, and in performing such work it exercises a governmental rather than a proprietary duty.

> **Wis** State v Milwaukee Elec Ry & Light (1914) 157 Wis 121, 147 NW 232.

A municipality has the power to protect itself against future expenditure of public money for the maintenance and repair of streets by enactment of an ordinance requiring that a better pavement be installed in newly constructed streets.

> **NJ** Levin v Livingston (1960) 62 NJS 395, 163 A2d 221.

The cost of traffic signals and fire alarms is not properly included within a local improvement district.

> **Wyo** Mealey v Laramie (1970) 472 P2d 787.

§139. Necessity

The necessity for the enactment of a street improvement ordinance is committed by the legislature to the judgment of the city council, and that judgment is conclusive, unless the evidence convinces the court that the council's action is so unreasonable and oppressive as to render it void.

> **Cal** People v Chevalier (1959) 52 C2d 299, 340 P2d 598.
> **Ill** Chicago v Thielans (1929) 334 Ill 231, 165 NE 615.
> **Tex** Massie v Fort Worth (1924) 262 SW 837.
> **W Va** Holswade v Huntington (1924) 96 W Va 124, 122 SE 449.

The necessity, expediency, and extent of an appropriation of property for public use are legislative, not judicial, questions, and the court may not inquire into the motives of the city in legislating to widen streets, thus requiring such appropriation.

> **Ky**   Hicks v Ashland (1933) 254 Ky 397, 71 SW2d 988.
> **Ore** Keane v Portland (1925) 115 Ore 1, 235 P 677.

Implementation of a policy of making deadend streets the lowest priority for street paving is inequitable when it discriminates against black citizens of the city.

> **Fla**   Johnson v Arcadia (1978) 450 F Supp 1363.

Where, in connection with the proposed improvement of a city street, the resolution of necessity is proposed by an initiative petition containing the requisite number of signers, is submitted to the voters for approval, and is approved, the law relative to initiative and referendum has no application to subsequent ordinances or other measures relating thereto.

> **Kan**   State v Kingman (1927) 123 Kan 207, 254 P 397.
> **Ohio** James v Ketterer (1932) 125 OS 165, 180 NE 704.

§ 140. Notice, Publication

The publication of a notice of the enactment of an ordinance of necessity for street improvements confers jurisdiction on the city to proceed with the improvements.

> **Ga**   Story v Macon (1949) 205 Ga 590, 54 SE2d 396.
> **Ill**   Holland v People (1901) 189 Ill 348, 59 NE 753.
> **Ky**   Maysville v Davis (1915) 166 Ky 555, 179 SW 463.
> **Mo**   Reinert Bros Const v Tootle (1918) 200 MoApp 284, 206 SW 422.
>   Springfield v Owen (1914) 262 Mo 92, 170 SW 1118.
> **Okla** McKnight v Oklahoma City (1933) 165 Okla 210, 25 P2d 638.
>   Mansell v New Cordell (1926) 120 Okla 187, 250 P 920.
> **Ore**   Bk of British Columbia v Portland (1902) 41 Ore 1, 67 P 1112.
>   Shannon v Portland (1900) 38 Ore 382, 62 P 50.

In exercising the power of eminent domain for the purpose of street improvement, the municipality must allege and prove compliance with procedural requirements. Failure to pass a resolution of purpose and intent, appointing a time and place for final determination, and causing notice of time and a brief description to be published, deprives the city of the right to condemn the property.

> **NC**   Charlotte v McNeely (1970) 9 NCApp 649, 175 SE2d 348.

An ordinance authorizing street improvements and allocating costs to the benefited district in accordance with a properly adopted state law is valid without publication or notice of such adoption, this being a different situation from the notice requirements embodied in the city's charter.

Ariz Collins v Phoenix (1931) 54 F2d 770.

Where an ordinance authorizes improvement of an avenue, charter requirements with respect thereto will be presumed to have been complied with unless controverted in a proceeding thereunder, and the proceeding being in rem, constructive notice by publication of a hearing before finally establishing the boundaries of the benefit district is sufficient.

Mo Wiget v St Louis (1935) 337 Mo 799, 85 SW2d 1038.

§141. Description

A street improvement ordinance which prescribes the nature, character, locality and description of the improvement and names the streets involved is in substantial compliance with a statute requiring description of the street improvement. The ordinance is not void for failing to establish the grade of streets and ditches where a cost estimate for grading is filed with the ordinance.

Ill Creve Coeur, Matter of (1977) 46 IllAp3d 772, 361 NE2d 290.

In a street improvement ordinance, the improvement must be specified in detail and described with such particularity that a contract can be intelligently let for its construction, and an assessment legally levied with which to obtain funds to construct it.

Cal Schwiesau v Mahon (1900) 128 Cal 114, 60 P 683.
Ill Mattoon v Stump (1953) 414 Ill 319, 111 NE2d 551.
Mo Bryant v Kansas City (1921) 209 MoApp 210, 232 SW 1080.

Where the amount of excavation necessary under a public street improvement ordinance can be readily ascertained from a profile attached to and made a part of the ordinance, it will not be declared invalid as not containing a sufficient description of the improvement.

Ill Hillsboro v Grassel (1911) 249 Ill 190, 94 NE 48.

When objection to a street paving ordinance for insufficient description with respect to sewers, manholes and catchbasins is filed the defect must be pointed out. Where it fails to specify wherein the description is insufficient the court will not search for the errors.

Ill Decatur v Barteau (1913) 260 Ill 612, 103 NE 601.

A local improvement ordinance that designates the elements of the improvement, by providing that they shall be of the same material and character as used in another local improvement, does not contain a sufficient description to render the ordinance valid.

Ill   Peoria v Cowen (1927) 326 Ill 616, 158 NE 414.

§142. —Alternative Specifications

A street paving ordinance providing three alternative specifications according to three different methods is invalid, as in conflict with the statute requiring such an ordinance to prescribe the nature, character and description of the improvement.

Ill   Rockford v Armour (1919) 290 Ill 425, 125 NE 356.

§143. —Approaches to Public Square

An ordinance providing that the "public square" shall be improved by grading, paving and curbing the square and that the approaches shall be graded is invalid as indefinite, since what is meant by "approaches" is not defined, nor is the height of the grade fixed expressly or by any mode of reference.

Ill   De Witt County v Clinton (1902) 194 Ill 521, 62 NE 780.

§144. —Real Estate

Where a petition for an ordinance erroneously describes the real property to be included in a street improvement district and this description is incorporated in the ordinance, a subsequent resolution and ordinance are void when neither before nor after the passage of the resolution or second ordinance a majority in value of the owners of real property within the district have submitted a petition accurately describing the boundaries.

Ark   Bell v Phillips (1915) 116 Ark 167, 172 SW 864.

§145. —Costs

For a local improvement ordinance to escape the fatal vice of insufficiency, the engineer's estimate of cost should be sufficiently itemized to inform the property owners of the probable cost of each of the substantial component elements of the improvement.

Ill   Dixon v Sinow & Weinman (1932) 350 Ill 634, 183 NE 570.
Harvard v Roach (1924) 314 Ill 424, 145 NE 618.

§146. —Location

A street paving ordinance must designate the location of the improvement with reasonable certainty, either in the ordinance itself, or in plats or profiles attached thereto.

> **Ark** McLeod v Purnell (1924) 164 Ark 596, 262 SW 682.
> Freeze v Improvement Dist 16 of Jonesboro (1916) 126 Ark 172, 189 SW 660.
> **Fla** Sabins v Daytona Beach (1937) 130 Fla 62, 177 So 229.
> **Ill** Springfield v Gillespie (1929) 335 Ill 388, 167 NE 61.
> Peoria v Cowen (1927) 326 Ill 616, 158 NE 414.
> **Ky** Meahl v Henderson (1956) 290 SW2d 593.

§147. —Drainage

An ordinance providing for the repaving of, and "otherwise improving," a street with provision for "drainage where necessary and ... doing any and all other work necessary and incidental to the said paving and draining," is not void as so broad in its description of improvements as to mislead property owners.

> **Ark** Kempner v Sanders (1922) 155 Ark 321, 244 SW 356.

§148. —Height; Depth; Curbs; Drains

Where an ordinance imposing a special assessment for the construction of curbing on a street fails to prescribe the height of the combined curb and gutter, or to state where the curb is to be placed, it is invalid as insufficient and indefinite.

> **Ill** Fehring v Chicago (1900) 187 Ill 416, 58 NE 303.
> Holden v Chicago (1898) 172 Ill 263, 50 NE 181.

A street paving ordinance that provides for construction of six catch basins to be connected by the most direct route to public sewers is invalid for indefiniteness, where the length and depth of the drains are not described and there is no reference to the sewers with which the catch basins are to be connected.

> **Ill** Geneseo v Brown (1911) 250 Ill 165, 95 NE 172.

§149. —Non-Arterial Streets

Ordinances authorizing paving of non-arterial streets are unsupported by charter authority and are therefore unenforceable, where the ordinances were adopted pursuant to a statute amending the municipality's charter but not defining what is meant by "non-arterial streets" and not giving the city's governing body any standard or guide, and since the term has no generally accepted meaning, it is too vague, indefinite, and uncertain and is therefore void.

> **Ga**   Atlanta v Southern Ry (1958) 213 Ga 736, 101 SE2d 707.

§ 150. —Street Numbers

Where the lots of property owners within a street improvement district are described in both of two plats filed with the petition for the ordinance to establish the district, and such descriptions are by identical lot, alley, and street numbers, the statutory requirement that the property to be included in an improvement district be described with such certainty as to notify owners that an assessment is to be made against their property is met.

> **Ark**   Jarrett v Baird (1923) 161 Ark 31, 255 SW 564.

§ 151. —Tiling

An ordinance providing for the improvement of a street by tiling it is invalid as insufficient, where there is no description of the type, quality or size of the tile and no specification of location or depth to which it is to be laid, number of lines of tile, or inlets, outlets or connections.

> **Ill**   Ill Cent RR v Effingham (1898) 172 Ill 607, 50 NE 103.

§ 152. —Type of Material

A resolution or intention for street improvements must describe the work. A description specifying granite or artificial stone curbing in a specified street suffices.

> **Cal**   San Jose Improvement v Auzerais (1895) 106 Cal 498, 39 P 859.

A street improvement ordinance providing for curbstones, to be bedded by flatstones, is invalid for insufficiency, where the size and quality of the flatstones are not specified.

> **Ill**   Nichols v Chicago (1901) 192 Ill 290, 61 NE 435.
> Kuester v Chicago (1900) 187 Ill 21, 58 NE 307.

A resolution of intention providing for the construction of "wooden bridges" over gutters from the crosswalk to the sidewalk at certain points was not fatally defective for failing to describe the kind of wood to be used.

> **Cal**   Remillard v Blake & Bilger (1915) 169 Cal 277, 146 P 634.

§153. —Width and Grade

It is not necessary to the validity of a street paving ordinance that it state the width of the street to be paved, where that is a matter of easy ascertainment.

> **Ill** Adams County v Quincy (1889) 130 Ill 566, 22 NE 624.
> **Ky** Barber Asphalt Paving v Gaar (1903) 24 KLR 2260, 73 SW 1106.
> **Okla** Wilson v Duncan (1928) 129 Okla 181, 264 P 203.

An ordinance authorizing street improvements, but not indicating whether specified grade differentials are above or below the directrix, is invalid for ambiguity, and is not validated by profile maps being on file in the office of the city clerk showing more particular data with reference to the grades.

> **Mo** McGuire v Wilson (1916) 187 SW 612.

§154. —Permanent Street Improvements

A city council's resolution appropriating money for "permanent street improvements" is not so indefinite as to amount to an invalid delegation of legislative power to executive officers.

> **NH** Hett v Portsmouth (1905) 73 NH 334, 61 A 596.

§155. Plans; Specifications

An ordinance providing for a public improvement should contain, either on its face or by reference to specifications, sufficient data for estimating its cost, to enable bidders to make intelligent bids, and thereby invite healthy competition.

> **Ill** Chicago v Russo (1930) 339 Ill 349, 171 NE 523.

Where a resolution adopted by a city council establishes the necessity for a street improvement, an ordinance authorizes such work, and both measures require the work to conform to specifications on file in the office of the board of public works, the specifications by reference become a part of the ordinance.

> **Mo** Parker-Washington Co v Field (1922) 239 SW 569.

Where an ordinance providing for a street improvement to be paid for by assessment against abutting property requires that the improvement conform to plans and specifications filed with the recorder, the assessment is invalid if the specifications were not observed by the city in soliciting bids for the improvement.

Mo Mayes v Adair County (1917) 194 SW 58.
Ore Montague-O'Rielly v Milwaukie (1920) 101 Ore 478, 193 P 824.

Where an ordinance is adopted for grading and paving a street in accordance with specifications declared to be on file with the city clerk, the reference to the specifications is equivalent to their incorporation.

Mo Rolla v Studley (1938) 120 SW2d 185.

Where an ordinance authorizing street improvements and assessing the costs against abutting property owners provided that the work should be done in accordance with plans and specifications then on file, but the plans were later revised and were not specifically approved by the board of commissioners, the validity of the ordinances was not affected, the city having determined, by resolution, before the making of the improvements, that the specifications should be changed.

Ky Meahl v Henderson (1956) 290 SW2d 593.

An ordinance authorizing street improvements is not invalid merely because the construction contract was not made in accordance with general specifications in existence when the ordinance was passed, since it is a uniform custom of a board of public works when an improvement is ordered to prepare the plans and specifications after passage of the ordinance and as the exigencies of the work demand.

Ky Barber Asphalt Paving v Gaar (1903) 24 KLR 2260, 73 SW 1106.

An ordinance requiring the city engineer to prepare plans and specifications for paving, to be approved by the street committee of the council, is not illegal as delegating to the city engineer legislative duties imposed on the mayor and council.

Ga Story v Macon (1949) 205 Ga 590, 54 SE2d 396.

§156. Bidding

Under an ordinance authorizing street improvements the city council is without power to let a contract for the construction work without competitive bidding; and this is a jurisdictional requirement necessary to charge the property owner with costs of the improvement.

Ky Hartford v King (1952) 249 SW2d 13.
Wait v Southern Oil & Tar (1925) 209 Ky 682, 273 SW 473.
Tex Bush v Denton (1926) 284 SW 251.

An ordinance that all curb and gutter work be on approval of the abutting owners and their agreement to pay the cost of the improvements does not exempt the city from meeting its mandatory bid requirements. The work and contract is still with the city and payment made by the city though on request of and with repayment by the abutting owners.

> **Cal** Martin v Corning (1972) 25 CA3d 165, 101 CaR 678.

In letting a contract under an ordinance for street improvements, though only one bid is submitted, the statutory requirements of competitive bidding are met where the bidding is open to competition; and a single bid is legally acceptable in the absence of collusion or fraud.

> **Ky** Blanton v Wallins (1927) 218 Ky 295, 291 SW 372.
> Denton v Carey-Reed (1916) 169 Ky 54, 183 SW 262.
> **Tex** Elmendorf v San Antonio (1922) 150 Tex 441, 242 SW 185.

That the bidding specifications of a paving improvement ordinance call for a patented Bitulithic pavement does not prevent competitive bidding where no statutory prohibition against inclusion of patented articles exists.

> **NY** Adams v Van Zandt (1923) 199 NYS 225.
> Whitmore v Edgerton (1914) 87 Misc 216, 149 NYS 508.

Where neither the statute nor the ordinance fixed the date for commencement of work an extension of the beginning date till after winter does not void the contract, it being for the benefit of all parties and having been awarded in fair and honest competition.

> **W Va** Holswade v Huntington (1924) 96 W Va 124, 122 SE 449.

A street paving tax is not void on the ground that bids were let for four paving districts under a single contract, where it is shown that the assessment is based on a percentage of the total improvements and the property in each district is charged with its pro rata share.

> **Neb** Schreifer v Auburn (1923) 110 Neb 179, 193 NW 350.

A requirement in a paving ordinance that bidders submit specimens of the paving material they intend to use is not invalid as an unreasonable restraint. Such a provision would not deter from bidding any contractor who intended to provide and use brick of the quality and kind demanded by the ordinance.

> **Ill** Chicago v Singer (1903) 202 Ill 75, 66 NE 874.

§ 157. Materials

A street improvement ordinance authorizing the macadamizing or graveling of streets, leaving the particular nature of the materials to be determined by the improvement district commissioners, is valid.

> **Ark**   Thacker v Paving Improvement Dist 5 (1930) 182 Ark 368, 31 SW2d 758.
> Baird v Paving Improvement Dist 1 (1921) 148 Ark 248, 229 SW 712.

A determination to remove paving and its sub-base is a question of fact to be determined from expert testimony. Summary judgment may not be granted the city on a complaint against an improvement district that includes this provision.

> **Wyo**   Mealey v Laramie (1970) 472 P2d 787.

An ordinance specifying a particular known material to be used in street improvements is not invalid as impairing competitive bidding, since there may be free and fair competitive bidding when a certain material is required.

> **Ill**   Quincy v Kemper (1922) 304 Ill 303, 136 NE 763.
> Oak Park v Galt (1907) 231 Ill 365, 83 NE 209.
> **Ky**   Springfield v Haydon (1926) 216 Ky 483, 288 SW 337.
> **Mo**   Barber Asphalt Paving v Kansas City Hydraulic Press Brick (1913) 170 MoAp 503, 156 SW 749.
> Miner's Bk v Clark (1913) 252 Mo 20, 158 SW 597.

Where a local improvement ordinance specifies asphaltic cement to be used in the improvement of a street, parol evidence is admissible to show that the term "asphaltic cement" has a well defined meaning among paving contractors.

> **Ill**   Chicago Union Traction v Chicago (1906) 223 Ill 37, 79 NE 67.

§ 158. —Patented

An ordinance setting up a paving improvement district and designating a certain patented pavement is not repugnant to a charter provision or an ordinance requiring competitive bidding, on the ground that specifying the pavement prevents competitive bidding.

> **Colo**   Sanborn v Boulder (1923) 74 Colo 358, 221 P 1077.
> **Mo**   Meek v Chillicothe (1914) 181 MoApp 218, 167 SW 1139.
> Rackliffe-Gibson Const v Walker (1913) 170 MoApp 69, 156 SW 65.
> **Ore**   Grimes v Seaside (1918) 87 Ore 256, 170 P 310.

An ordinance specifying patented pavement for a street improvement, which patent is held by only one company, is invalid, since public contracts that tend to prevent competition are void.

> **Ill**   Rossville v Smith (1912) 256 Ill 302, 100 NE 292.
> Siegel v Chicago (1906) 223 Ill 428, 79 NE 280.
> **Ore**   Terwilliger Land v Portland (1912) 62 Ore 101, 123 P 57.

A charter requirement that the owner of patent rights for pavement shall transfer to the city all right to the use of the patented paving material within the city before any pavement protected by letters patent is ordered by the city does not require the transfer to the city of the right to manufacture the patented article.

Cal Braun, Bryant & Austin v McGuire (1927) 201 Cal 134, 255 P 808.

An ordinance setting up a paving improvement district and specifying "Warrenite Bitulithic" pavement does not violate a general ordinance prohibiting a patented or copyrighted brand or material, since this pavement is not a material at all, but is a completed or finished product.

Colo Sanborn v Boulder (1923) 74 Colo 358, 221 P 1077.

§159. Grade

Where in making street improvements it is necessary that the original grade be fixed by ordinance, and the grades are fixed in the ordinance by reference to existing plans and specifications, they are sufficiently identified.

Ill Highwood v Chicago & M Elec RR (1915) 268 Ill 482, 109 NE 270.
Claflin v Chicago (1899) 178 Ill 549, 53 NE 339.
Ky Peters v Morehead (1936) 266 Ky 99, 98 SW2d 41.
Mo City Tr v Crockett (1925) 309 Mo 683, 274 SW 802.
Albers v Acme Paving & Crusher (1917) 196 MoApp 265, 194 SW 61.

An ordinance providing that the grade of a certain street shall be a fall of one-tenth of a foot for every 287 feet of length is not invalid merely because the angle of grade fails to conform to the best engineering practice.

Wis Van Hecke v Stevens Point (1924) 183 Wis 654, 198 NW 732.

An ordinance providing that the "public square" shall be improved by grading, paving and curbing the square, with the approaches to be graded to such grade as the engineer may direct, is invalid, since the matter of grading cannot be left to the discretion of the engineer, but must be specified in the ordinance.

Ill De Witt County v Clinton (1902) 194 Ill 521, 62 NE 780.
Gross v People (1898) 172 Ill 571, 50 NE 334.

A local improvement ordinance providing for the paving of a street is not invalid merely because it establishes for the first time, or changes, the grade of a street or the width of a roadway.

Ill Chicago v Hulbert (1908) 234 Ill 321, 84 NE 922.

An ordinance of intention to grade a street must inform the property owner that a project to improve the street is planned and, where an official grade has previously been established, that a new grade is to be used. But a notice sufficed though it did not specify a different grade where the property owner was put on inquiry and the grade actually used was less damaging than the grade of which notice had been given.

> **Cal**   Gianni v San Diego (1961) 194 CA2d 56, 14 CaR 783.

Where the amendment to an ordinance setting grade was defective, but the council passed a new ordinance prior to assessment this action was proper and valid.

> **Iowa**   Audubon & 9th St, In re (1924) 198 Iowa 1103, 199 NW 983.

In the absence of an ordinance changing the legally established grade so as to establish it at the level actually adopted in a street improvement plan, the city council is not empowered to assess plaintiff's property for the improvement.

> **Iowa**   Landis v Marion (1916) 176 Iowa 240, 157 NW 841.

Where the grade of the streets of a city has been established and the level of a street reduced in part to the grade, and only a limited expense would be incurred in finishing the grade, the work may be completed by city authorities without the formality of requiring an estimate to be made by the city engineer, bids advertised, assessments of damages made, and special taxes levied. The work may be done by the city under the direction of the proper officer, and payment made from the proper revenues of the city.

> **Neb**   Hilger v Nebraska City (1914) 97 Neb 268, 149 NW 807.

An ordinance authorizing the grading and paving of a street is not subject to the statutory limitation of 60 cents per foot on assessments for repairing and resurfacing streets, it being common knowledge that no street can be graded and paved with concrete the first time at a cost of 60 cents per front foot.

> **Mo**   Miners Bk of Carterville v Clark (1924) 216 MoApp 130, 257 SW 139.

§ 160. —Change

A lowering of street grades, pursuant to a resolution of the city council, does not constitute a taking of abutting property without due process.

> **Mich**   Detroit v Grigg Hanna Lumber & Box (1941) 296 Mich 415, 296 NW 310.

Since private property may not be taken or damaged for public use without just compensation, a homeowner is entitled to damages if the grade of the street is changed so as to make it impractical for him to use his driveway. That the ordinance provided for damages only for changing an established grade is not a defense under a claim that no grade had ever been established. A common-law right of action exists for changing an established street grade.

Mo   Lange v Jackson (1969) 440 SW2d 758.

Where statutory authority for a city to change the grade of streets provides that when such a grade shall have been established by ordinance it shall not be lawful to change it thereafter without compensating owners damaged thereby, one standing to suffer damages from proceedings for such a change of grade may enjoin the proceedings.

Iowa   Richardson v Sioux City (1907) 136 Iowa 436, 113 NW 928.
       Morton v Burlington (1898) 106 Iowa 50, 75 NW 662.
Mo   Heidorn v Kirkwood (1912) 169 MoApp 156, 152 SW 374.
      Shackleford v Jefferson City (1912) 167 MoApp 59, 150 SW 1123.

After the passage of an ordinance fixing the grade of a street a city council's consent by resolution to a change of the grade so fixed to lessen the cost of the improvement does not affect the validity of the assessments made, since the change does not add to the burden of the abutting owners.

Ky   Lindenberger Land v R B Park Co (1905) 27 KLR 437, 85 SW 213.
NC   Thompson v Seaboard Air Line RR (1958) 248 NC 577, 104 SE2d 181.

Where an ordinance provides for the grading of the entire width of a street, and the plan filed with the board of viewers shows the contemplated complete grading for the entire width, though only part of the grade is changed and there is no alteration in the grade of a foot walk, property owners are entitled to damages for the change of grade of the street in front of their property, for the entire width of the street.

Pa   Strausz v McKeesport (1934) 316 PaS 277, 175 A 404.

When a highway is annexed by a city and under an ordinance is improved, an abutting lot owner is not entitled to recover consequential damages resulting from the establishment of the original grade of the street.

Ky   Lewis v Whitesburg (1934) 253 Ky 480, 69 SW2d 989.

In an action against a subdivider for lowering the street grade, defendant met at least by prima facie evidence the burden placed on him by introducing into evidence a duly certified copy of the ordinance establishing the grade and setting forth the fact of its adoption and effective date, together with a certified copy of the resolution showing that they were, on the date specified, adopted by the city council.

Cal   Hollander v Denton (1945) 69 CA2d 348, 159 P2d 86.

The constitutional provision that private property shall not be taken or damaged for public use without just compensation having first been paid to the owner is not applicable to an ordinance authorizing a street improvement by raising the grade, in which case the abutting owner's claim is for consequential damages only, which cannot be ascertained until after the work is done.

Mo   McGrew v Granite Bituminous Paving (1912) 247 Mo 549, 155 SW 411.

§ 161. Intersections

In an ordinance apportioning assessments among abutting owners for street construction, an assessment for catch-basins constructed wholly within intersections cannot be made against the abutting owners, where the ordinances under which the improvements are made provide that the city shall pay the cost of improving intersections.

Ky   Frankfort v Jillson (1928) 225 Ky 61, 7 SW2d 859.

After elimination of a statutory requirement that cities must pay the cost of improving street intersections, it is optional with a city council to provide by ordinance that such cost be assessed as part of the cost of the street improvement to be borne by abutting owners, or that the city shall pay such intersection costs.

Ky   Shaver v Rice (1925) 209 Ky 467, 273 SW 48.

Where an ordinance authorizes the paving of a street, the costs to be assessed against abutting properties, the paving of intersections is to be included in prorated costs against pieces of ground abutting on the street improved, and not against other properties abutting on the intersecting streets.

Mo   Rolla v Schuman (1915) 189 MoApp 252, 175 SW 241.

Since the city has the undoubted right to provide for construction of a sidewalk as an entirety, including intersections, the question whether the city or the landowners shall pay for the intersection will not affect the validity of the ordinance.

Ill   Hyman v Chicago (1900) 188 Ill 462, 59 NE 10.

§ 162. Boulevards

Under a city's charter authorization to establish boulevards and assess the costs against abutting property, and to establish streets and assess the costs against both abutting and nonabutting property, an ordinance authorizing establishment of an avenue as a public highway is construed to refer to the establishment of a street, since an avenue is a wide street, and a public highway is merely a name given to a particular thoroughfare, and neither one is the designation of a boulevard.

> **Mo** St Louis v Breuer (1920) 223 SW 108.
> St Louis v Christian Bros College (1914) 257 Mo 541, 165 SW 1057.

Where property is conveyed to a municipal corporation in fee, determinable on a condition subsequent, namely, failure to use the land for boulevard purposes, there is no reversion to the grantor merely because the roadway is not declared to be a boulevard by ordinance.

> **Okla** Putnam v Oklahoma City (1956) 296 P2d 797.

§163. Alleys

An alley is not to be regarded as a principal street under an ordinance defining the territory of a street improvement district, unless it appears that either necessarily or within the immediate contemplation of the city it will be converted into or become itself a principal street.

> **Ky** Vernon v George M Eady Co (1933) 247 Ky 48, 56 SW2d 552.

The establishment of a public way, such as an alley, calls for the exercise of the legislative power of the city, by ordinance or resolution.

> **Iowa** Bradley v Centerville (1908) 139 Iowa 599, 117 NW 968.

An ordinance providing for the opening of a new alley running east and west, and the widening of an alley running north and south in same block, is invalid as constituting separate and distinct improvements in one proceeding.

> **Ill** Weckler v Chicago (1871) 61 Ill 142.

§164. —Opening; Improvement

An easement for a 30-foot alley may be a condition imposed for rezoning an area to commercial. The ordinance authorizing the rezoning passed for the public health, welfare, and safety may require the alley be set aside for loading and unloading trucks and for utility and garbage service.

> **Okla** Kammerlocher v Norman (1973) 509 P2d 470.

In order to open, extend, widen or straighten an alley there must be a petition by over ½ of the abutting owners, a commission decision that it is necessary in the public interest or certificate of necessity from public health officer. It is not necessary to fulfill all three requirements as any one will justify action.

> **DC**   Bailey v Young (1945) 149 F2d 15.

§ 165. —Closing; Abandonment

A municipality may enact an ordinance abandoning or closing an alley, without giving any advance notice to abutting owners.

> **Tex**   Cobb v Dallas (1966) 408 SW2d 292.

Use of portions of public alleys by the public for parking and by vehicles traversing the area constitutes, as a matter of law, such a use as to negative abandonment by the public and to render ineffectual an ordinance declaring that the area had been abandoned as an alley.

> **Ga**   Dunlap v Tift (1952) 209 Ga 201, 71 SE2d 237.

§ 166. Lighting

A charter provision authorizing the city council to provide for lighting the streets will, by implication, warrant the enactment of an ordinance providing for the construction, or acquisition by purchase, of a lighting plant.

> **Tenn**   Keenan & Wade v Trenton (1914) 130 Tenn 71, 168 SW 1053.

An ordinance authorizing construction of a municipal overhead electric street lighting system and the procurement of bids therefor is a ministerial, not a legislative act.

> **Pa**   Morganstern Elec v Coraopolis (1937) 326 Pa 154, 191 A 603.

Though an ordinance requires headlights on automobiles, which shall produce sufficient light to reveal objects 150 feet ahead, the city is not relieved of its duty to passengers or guests in automobiles to keep its streets in reasonably safe condition for traveling, and to light dangerous places.

> **Mo**   Boyd v Kansas City (1922) 291 Mo 622, 237 SW 1001.

Where a municipality failed to perform an alleged contract provided by ordinance for the construction of a municipal electric street lighting system, and the company did not furnish performance bonds as required by state law, notwithstanding that the municipal solicitor may have told the company that it need not furnish bonds until notified to do so, the company could not maintain an action for loss of profits resulting from the municipality's failure.

> **Pa**   Morganstern Elec v Coraopolis (1937) 326 Pa 154, 191 A 603.

XII. DRIVEWAYS; CURB CUTS

§167. Generally

Though municipalities are granted no express power of regulation of driveways, nevertheless, in order to discharge its responsibilities regarding the grading of sidewalks, control of traffic, and regulation of drainage, a city will be deemed to have a necessarily implied power over driveways.

> **Ill**   Pure Oil v Northlake (1957) 10 Ill2d 241, 140 NE2d 289.

A "curb cut ordinance", which provides in substance that a person owning land abutting on a public street and who desires an entrance or driveway over a sidewalk must make application to the commissioner of public works and file a plat showing the particulars, does not conflict with the zoning ordinance and is valid.

> **RI**   Newman v Newport (1948) 73 RI 385, 57 A2d 173.

§168. Regulation

A requirement that two driveways into the same property be at least ten feet apart is not vague and indefinite when read in conjunction with the entire ordinance and the illustrations attached thereto. An application for two 35-foot driveways to be approximately two feet apart constitutes an attempt to turn the entrance into one continuous entry and parking in the commercial establishment contrary to the requirements.

> **La**   Fleming v Maturin (1975) 314 So2d 356.

The city ordinances regarding obstructing or injuring a street and requiring excavation permits for work done on public streets may not be used as a basis to deny a curb cut. While the city may properly regulate access a denial of a curb cut is invalid when there are no rules or regulations pertaining thereto and the state has issued a permit for access to a state highway.

> **Ind**   Richmond v SMO (1975) 333 NE2d 797.

An ordinance providing that no permit shall be issued for the construction of any curb cut or driveway leading onto specified portions of certain streets is within the council's police power, though it operates to place a restriction on the right of a property owner to construct a driveway across the sidewalk in front of his property.

> **La**   State v Gruber (1942) 201 La 1068, 10 So2d 899.
> **Tex**   San Antonio v Pigeonhole Parking of Tex (1958) 158 Tex 318, 311 SW2d 218.

§169. —Unreasonable

An ordinance requiring abutting property owners to construct or repair their driveways with cement, in replacement of existing blacktop, which according to expert testimony is just as durable as cement, is arbitrary, unreasonable, and represents a clear and palpable abuse of power.

Ohio   Stueve v Cincinnati (1960) 15 Op2d 424, 168 NE2d 574.

§170. License or Permit

Denying a driveway cut permit providing access to a lot is not unreasonable or arbitrary where the owner has other access to the property, and where the facts are debatable the court will not substitute its opinion for that of the legislative body.

Cal   Delta Rent-A-Car Systems v Beverly Hills (1969) 1 CA3d 781, 82 CaR 318.

An ordinance requiring a property owner to obtain a permit from the council for the construction of a driveway that changes the grade of a sidewalk is not unreasonable or discriminatory, since it applies uniformly to all owners similarly situated. Since permit must be by resolution changing a legally established grade it must be by action of the council, not just one councilman.

Ill   Jacobs v Chicago (1927) 244 IllAp 132.
      Wilmont v Chicago (1927) 328 Ill 552, 160 NE 206, 62 ALR 394.
Ky   Dayton v Thompson (1963) 372 SW2d 407.
NY   Cauldwell-Wingate v New York City (1954) 205 Misc 625, 129 NYS2d 188.

Where an owner has a private right-of-way connecting his premises with a public street, he may be considered an abutter on the public street by means of his private right of way, and under a city ordinance, as "an owner of abutting property", is entitled to a permit authorizing the construction of a driveway connecting with the public street.

Haw   Paterson v Rush (1939) 34 Haw 881.

§171. —Standards for Issuance

An ordinance prohibiting a property owner from constructing a driveway across any public walk or curb without a permit from the city council, but not containing any reasonable standard the owner must meet as a condition for the permit, and purporting to authorize outright denial thereof depending on the will of the council, is invalid as vesting unlimited discretion in the council, and as a denial of due process.

Ill   Salem Nat Bk v Salem (1964) 47 IllAp2d 279, 198 NE2d 137.
      Pure Oil v Northlake (1957) 10 Ill2d 241, 140 NE2d 289.
NY   Singer-Kaufman Rlty, In re (1922) 196 NYS 480.
Ohio Northern Boiler v David (1951) 61 Abs 529, 105 NE2d 451, affd (1952) 157 OS 564, 47 Op 416, 106 NE2d 620.

§172. —Invalid

An ordinance requiring a property owner with a curb cut to pay an annual fee, labeled a regulatory measure, but the regulation or restraint being almost negligible, is not a license, but a revenue raising measure based on the right of ingress and egress to private property, which is illegal.

Colo Heckendorf v Littleton (1955) 132 Colo 108, 286 P2d 615.
Ohio Northern Boiler v David (1952) 157 OS 564, 47 Op 416, 106 NE2d 620.
Okla Shawnee v Robbins Bros Tire (1928) 134 Okla 142, 272 P 457, 66 ALR 1047.

§173. Enforcement; Enjoining

The quasi-legislative action of an administrative agency in denying a driveway permit is subject to judicial review, but limited to an examination of the proceedings to determine whether the refusal was arbitrary, capricious, or entirely lacking in evidentiary support, or whether the agency failed to follow the required notice provisions.

Cal   Delta Rent-A-Car Systems v Beverly Hills (1969) 1 CA3d 781, 82 CaR 318.

An injunction will not be issued to prevent constuction of a driveway where there is no knowledge of the proposed use of the land. Expenditures are at the landowner's risk if the ultimate use is not permitted.

Pa   Erie v Metropolitan (1970) 440 Pa 528, 269 A2d 464.

Evidence that a driveway at a particular place would not interfere with the full use of the sidewalk by pedestrians supported an injunction against interference by the city with construction of the driveway, and it was not necessary for plaintiff to assail the validity of an ordinance prescribing minimum width of sidewalks.

Ohio Stueve v Cincinnati (1959) 81 Abs 11, 160 NE2d 725.
Okla Norman v Safeway Stores (1944) 193 Okla 534, 145 P2d 765.

When the city council grants a property owner a permit for a curb cut, it may not after the cut is made, rescind the permit; and such property owner may enjoin enforcement of an ordinance prohibiting curb cuts.

Wis   Russell Dairy Stores v Chippewa Falls (1956) 272 Wis 138, 74 NW2d 759.

§174. Prohibition

A city does not have an absolute right to prohibit a property owner from constructing a driveway across a sidewalk, but may only reasonably restrict, and an ordinance must spell out reasonable standards for owners to meet as a condition precedent to acquiring a driveway permit.

> **Ill**   Salem Nat Bk v Salem (1964) 47 IllAp2d 279, 198 NE2d 137.

Where city purchases land for "park and boulevard" purposes, it may locate and construct thereon at its own expense a divided highway with a park space between the outside curb and the line of adjoining property, and by ordinance prohibit the owners of the property from crossing the park space and cutting the curb of the pavement to give them vehicular access to the highway from their properties.

> **Ohio**   Copland v Toledo (1944) 75 OA 378, 31 Op 144, 62 NE2d 256.

§175. —Confiscatory

Where an oil company is deprived of access it formerly had to a street in the use of a driveway on adjacent property, the industrial use of the company's property antedated the enactment of the zoning ordinance, and its continued industrial use would be impossible without access to the street, denial by a board of adjustment of the use by the company of its own land for a right-of-way to the street amounts to confiscation.

> **NJ**   Home Fuel Oil v Glen Rock (1949) 5 NJS 63, 68 A2d 412.

XIII. VAULTS

§176. Generally

The city owes a duty to the traveling public and to those lawfully in occupation of any part of the subsurface of a street to exercise reasonable care to maintain the street in a safe condition, which duty requires supervision of construction of vaults, their inspection and safe maintenance, and justifies an ordinance requiring permits and the collection of a reasonable fee to cover expenses of supervision and inspection.

> **Ill**   Chicago v Lord (1917) 277 Ill 397, 115 NE 543.
> **NY**   Oltarsh v Levy (1934) 152 Misc 674, 274 NYS 650.
> Appleton v New York City (1914) 163 AD 680, 148 NYS 870.

ANNOTATION

Effect of ordinance on liability of owner or occupant for condition of a covering over opening or vault in sidewalk, 31 ALR2d 1347.

§177. Private Use

A city has the right, by ordinance, to authorize the use of space underneath sidewalks for private use, provided it does not infringe the full, free and safe use of the street in all its parts by the public.

> **Ill** Heineck v Grosse (1902) 99 IllAp 441.

§178. Regulation

An ordinance regulating the use of space under streets or public grounds, providing for permits for such use, and prohibiting use of any space under the surface of any street or public ground is not invalid as discriminatory or for lack of uniformity, since it operates alike on all persons similarly situated, except in cases of contract rights acquired prior to adoption of ordinance.

> **Ill** J Burton Co v Chicago (1908) 236 Ill 383, 86 NE 93.
> **NY** Bauman v Be-Jel Rlty (1939) 171 Misc 845, 12 NYS2d 485.
> Kowalchick v Reshin (1933) 146 Misc 770, 262 NYS 808.

§179. —Lighting; Safeguards

An ordinance requiring that gates and chains at entrances to cellars be closed during the night unless a burning light is maintained over the steps, places a duty of constant vigilance and adherence to the requirements during the entire night.

> **NY** Swartzman v Socol Rlty (1931) 233 AD 374, 253 NYS 332.
> Silverman v Konig (1918) 170 NYS 368.

§180. Permits; License Fees

Where the fee title to streets is in the city, it may enact an ordinance requiring persons who use subways beneath the sidewalks adjoining their property to pay for the use of such space.

> **Ill** Tacoma Safety Deposit v Chicago (1910) 247 Ill 192, 93 NE 153.

The right to control vaults under a street or sidewalk regardless of the ownership of the fee is an element in the authorized regulation and supervision of the streets.

> **NY** New York City v Gerry (1917) 100 Misc 297, 165 NYS 659.
> Mahoney v New York City (1911) 145 AD 884, 130 NYS 602.

XIV. TUNNELS

§ 181. Generally

A charter power to construct tunnels must include the power to do things necessary to fit the tunnels for use. Paving of a tunnel and the laying of sidewalks are necessary to enable the public to use the tunnel; such paving and sidewalking are, therefore, proper incidents of the constuction power.

    Cal   Mardis v McCarthy (1912) 162 Cal 94, 121 P 389.

The factual findings of a city council, set forth in an ordinance, that the construction of a proposed tunnel facility will be to the best interest of the residents of the municipality, and that the estimated net earnings from the proposed project, over and above the necessary cost of operating and maintaining the same, will be sufficient to pay principal and interest of the bonds, are legislative in their nature and not subject to judicial inquiry.

    W Va   State v Dailer (1955) 140 W Va 513, 85 SE2d 656.

ANNOTATION

New or additional compensation for use by municipality of subsurface of streets or highway, 11 ALR2d 180.

§ 182. Expense, Apportionment

A charter authorization to construct tunnels does not authorize the selection of any limited area of property within the city and county on which the cost of construction may be imposed. In the absence of a grant of power to assess the cost of an authorized work on a special assessment district, the expense must be borne by the city as a whole, either from current revenues or by a bond issue.

    Cal   Gassner v McCarthy (1911) 160 Cal 82, 116 P 73.

The failure of a charter to mention the power granted by state law to levy an assessment for tunnel construction does not constitute a denial of that power to the city or a limitation on its rights to do anything authorized by state law. A subsequent amendment of the charter to confer on the city the power conferred previously only by state law does not prove that the city was limited to the express terms of its charter.

    Cal   Barber v Los Angeles (1923) 191 Cal 253, 215 P 897.

§183. License; Permit

Recital that enactment is a contract does not make it so and a store secured only a conditional permit or license to construct a street tunnel and building over the street when it agreed to city's terms.

Ohio   Kraus v Halle Bros (1950) 60 Abs 418, 45 Op 115, 100 NE2d 103.

XV. BRIDGES; VIADUCTS

§184. Bridges, Generally

A city may properly amend its comprehensive zoning plan to provide for construction of new or replacement bridges with funds from the permanent improvement funds used for land acquisition. Where there is a dispute as to the location and type of bridge to be constructed the legislative determination will be upheld unless arbitrary and unreasonable.

Minn   Lerner v Minneapolis (1969) 284 Minn 46, 169 NW2d 380.

A city has authority to grant a license to a private developer to erect a bridge or passageway over a street, so long as it does not interfere with the reasonable and ordinary use of the street. A requirement that the passageway be no closer than 20 feet vertically from the surface is within the discretion of the municipal authorities.

Ga   Save The Bay Committee v Savannah (1971) 227 Ga 436, 181 SE2d 351.

Under authority expressly delegated to a municipality to build bridges over rivers and streams in the city, the power to regulate them and to prescribe the time and manner for vessels to pass through them is a necessary incident.

Ill   Chicago v McGinn (1869) 51 Ill 266.

A land owner is not entitled to damages for change in grade caused by construction of a duly authorized bridge. No property was confiscated and owner holds no right against public welfare in a continuing grade.

Md   Baltimore & O Ry v Kahl (1914) 124 Md 299, 92 A 770.

Where a bridge approach constructed by a private company, by authority of an ordinance, seriously impairs access to the abutting property, the ordinance constitutes a taking of property and requires compensation to its owners.

Ore   Willamette Iron Works v Ore Ry & Navigation (1894) 26 Ore 224, 37 P 1016.

An ordinance recognizing and acquiescing in the construction of a bridge by a state board does not make the city liable for negligent acts of the state while the control of the bridge construction was under the supervision and control of state officers.

La   Harrison v La Highway Comm (1939) 191 La 839, 186 So 354.

ANNOTATION

Municipalities power to permit private owner to construct bridge or passway above public street or sidewalk, 76 ALR2d 898.

§185. Construction—Authority

Where a bridge necessary for the use of the public generally is constructed by a county under a town ordinance granting that privilege, it is not the grant of a franchise requiring advertisement and call for bids, since the county without asking the consent of the town might have erected the bridge for the convenience of the citizens of the county.

Ky   Jackson v Breathitt County (1907) 32 KLR 199, 105 SW2d 376.

The factual findings of a city council, set forth in an ordinance, that the construction of a proposed bridge facility will be to the best interest of the residents of the municipality, and that the estimated net earnings from the proposed project, over and above the necessary cost of operating and maintaining the same, will be sufficient to pay principal and interest of the bonds, are legislative in their nature and not subject to judicial inquiry.

W Va   State v Dailer (1955) 140 W Va 513, 85 SE2d 656.

Where a municipality is without authority to provide for the construction of a bridge over a public street solely for private use, a mere recital in the preamble that it is deemed to be for the benefit of the public lends no weight to a claim of validity, where the ordinance itself shows that it is for a private use.

Ill   People v Corn Products Refining (1919) 286 Ill 226, 121 NE 574.

§186. —Financing

When the power to purchase or construct a bridge is given by statute the right to raise money by bond issue is implied. Mandamus will not lie to force a call of election on a bond issue, however, when the ordinances do not meet statutory requirements.

W Va   State v Steen (1928) 106 W Va 325, 145 SE 602.

A resolution to indemnify the United States for any damages resulting from the construction of a bridge, and providing for a tax to pay the interest and sinking fund requirements on any debt incurred thereby, is in compliance with the constitutional provision that a municipality shall not incur any debt unless provision be made at the time of its creation for levying and collecting sufficient taxes therefor, and is not objectionable on the ground that the amount of potential damages is not determinable.

Tex Brown v Jefferson County (1966) 406 SW2d 185.

A county bridge project is self-liquidating and bonds may be issued where an ordinance so determines. Agreement to pay the operating expense out of general funds not from ad valorem tax if the income is insufficient does not obligate the county in violation of statute.

Fla Sanibel-Captiva Taxpayers Assn v Lee County (1961) 132 So2d 334.

The provision in an ordinance relating to the construction of bridge approaches, that the cost of the improvement shall be paid by the state, the city, and by assessments on property within the local improvement district, is not invalidated or affected by the fact that the state is a party to the contract and agrees to pay a portion of the cost.

Wash Holton v Seattle (1932) 168 Wash 478, 12 P2d 754.

A contract whereby a city agrees to pay for the construction of a bridge creates a debt, and, in the absence of any revenue provision to defray the cost, is invalid as violative of the constitutional debt limitation provisions.

Tex Berlin Iron Bridge v San Antonio (1894) 62 F 882.

§187. —Special Assessment

An overhead railroad-highway separation structure, commonly called an overpass, is a portion of a municipality's street system, and may be the subject of a special assessment in a street improvement district.

ND Parker Hotel Co v Grand Forks (1970) 177 NW2d 764.

The construction of a bridge within a city may be treated as a local, rather than a public improvement, and subject to special assessment of property owners benefited.

Ark Mullins v Comm of Bridge Improv Dist 2 (1914) 114 Ark 324, 170 SW 65.
Ky Downing v Chinnville (1931) 237 Ky 121, 34 SW2d 961.

§188. —Attack on Validity

Individual persons suing on behalf of themselves and all qualified voters of a city, lack the requisite justiciable interest to challenge the validity of an ordinance authorizing the construction of a private vehicular bridge across a river, since the right sought to be enforced is one shared in common with the public in general, and any damage is sustained in common with the general public. Only lawfully constituted guardians of the public interest may maintain actions for the redress of injuries of such character.

> **Tex**   San Antonio Conservation Society v San Antonio (1952) 250 SW2d 259.

§ 189. Public Improvement

An ordinance providing for the construction of a bridge in the city is not for "local improvement," within the statute authorizing cities to levy special assessments for local improvements, since the bridge is in the nature of a public improvement, benefiting all the inhabitants of the city.

> **Ill**   Chicago Heights v Walls (1926) 319 Ill 411, 150 NE 241.
>   Waukegan v De Wolf (1913) 258 Ill 374, 101 NE 532.
> **Ky**   Downing v Chinnville (1931) 237 Ky 121, 34 SW2d 961.
>   Springfield v Haydon (1926) 216 Ky 483, 288 SW 337.
> **NC**   Warsaw v Malone (1912) 159 NC 573, 75 SE 1011.

§ 190. Eminent Domain

An ordinance authorizing condemnation of property for an approach to a bridge in a state on the other side of the river, in carrying out the intent of an act of Congress, is legislative in character, and is, therefore, subject to referendum.

> **Mo**   Chicago B & Q RR v Olin (1924) 218 MoApp 578, 266 SW 130.
>   State v Edwards (1924) 305 Mo 431, 266 SW 127.

An ordinance that condemns property and easements for construction of a viaduct obligates the city to pay only such damages as the owners are by law entitled to receive.

> **Mo**   Kansas City v Berkshire Lumber (1965) 393 SW2d 470.
> **Pa**   Commonwealth v Larkin & Co (1952) 371 Pa 594, 92 A2d 419.

§ 191. Toll Bridges

An ordinance authorizing the issuance of revenue bonds for the construction of a bridge within the city, and providing that they shall be payable out of tolls, is not invalid as repugnant to the federal act authorizing construction of the bridge, where that act placed no restrictions on the imposition of tolls.

> **Wash**   Driscoll v Bremerton (1955) 48 Wash2d 95, 291 P2d 642.

The toll for bridge use authorized by a bridge authority is not a charge or fee from which the metropolitan transit authority is exempt. The exemption authorized the MTA refers to tax and assessment type charges and fees.

> **Md**   Mass Transit Adm v Baltimore County Revenue Auth (1973) 267 Md 687, 298 A2d 413.

Where a toll bridge constructed by a municipal corporation becomes subject to the jurisdiction of the state and free to the public by operation of law, the finding of fact on the part of the common council as to the wisdom and advisability of making the bridge free, and its enactment of an ordinance so declaring and transferring the bridge to the state road commission, is immaterial.

> **W Va**   Baier v St Albans (1946) 128 W Va 630, 39 SE2d 145.

Where ordinances authorize construction of a bridge and its approaches, and bond issues are authorized for defraying the costs, and the ordinance authorizing the bond issue provides that the bridge and approaches shall be forever free, and many years later an ordinance is adopted imposing a toll charge for the use of the bridge, the toll charge ordinance is valid. The board of aldermen may not pass an irrevocable ordinance that no tolls shall ever be collected on a proposed bridge; and the fact of free operation for many years is immaterial on the question of charging tolls in the future.

> **Mo**   St Louis v Cavanaugh (1947) 357 Mo 204, 207 SW2d 449.

Under a federal enabling act authorizing a city to operate a toll bridge, conditioned on use of the receipts for maintenance of the bridge and amortization of indebtedness, an ordinance authorizing the use of such receipts for general corporate purposes of the city is invalid.

> **Ill**   US v Rock Island Centennial Bridge Comm (1964) 230 F Supp 654.

A bond issue for purchase of a toll bridge, authorized by an ordinance stipulating that the bond is neither payable from nor a charge on any funds other than the revenues of the bridge, does not create a general obligation on behalf of the city, and thus does not fall within the constitutional debt limitation.

> **Mo**   State v Smith (1934) 335 Mo 825, 74 SW2d 367.
> **SD**   Mettet v Yankton (1946) 71 SD 435, 25 NW2d 460.

In an ordinance providing for a license tax of $100 per month as well as two per cent of toll bridge revenues, the 2 per cent revenue was neither a license tax nor an ad valorem tax but in the nature of compensation for the franchise privilege granted, and thus not in violation of state law placing a limit of $100 per month on any license tax to be required of the holder of a toll bridge franchise.

> **Cal**   Contra Costa County v Amer Toll Bridge (1937) 10 C2d 359, 74 P2d 749.

§192. Franchises

A city, under its charter and pursuant to its police power, may grant a franchise to construct and operate a bridge, and it is immaterial that the bridge may cross an international border on the limits of the city.

> **Tex**   Malott v Brownsville (1927) 292 SW 606.

The grant by a city of an exclusive privilege for the use of a portion of its streets as a means of ingress and egress from an international bridge does not, of itself, constitute a monopoly within the constitutional provision that perpetuities and monopolies are contrary to the genius of a free government, and shall never be allowed.

> **Tex**   Laredo v International Bridge & Tram (1895) 66 F 246.

An ordinance granting permission to construct and operate a bridge, containing no time limit, is not invalid as granting a franchise or license beyond the constitutional limit of 30 years, and will be treated as effecting a valid license until repealed or revoked.

> **Mich**   Detroit International Bridge v Amer Seed (1930) 249 Mich 289, 228 NW 791.

Where a city council had charter authority to authorize the construction of a bridge across a certain river in consideration of a division of the toll proceeds, and an ordinance was passed granting the franchise for construction of the bridge, the grantee's assignee had a taxable estate in the bridge, and a tax thereon was valid.

> **Cal**   Fall v Marysville (1861) 19 Cal 391.

§193. Navigable Waters; Interstate Commerce

An ordinance regulating drawbridges in the city is invalid when in conflict with the federal statute regulating drawbridges on navigable waters, in view of paramount federal jurisdiction.

> **Wis**   Milwaukee v Amer Steamship (1935) 76 F2d 343.

A city has both express and implied power to construct bridges and causeways over navigable intrastate waters when reasonably necessary in constructing a highway improvement, provided approval of the proper state and federal authorities is first secured to insure that the proposed structure will not unduly interfere with navigation and commerce.

> **Cal**   Southlands v San Diego (1931) 211 Cal 646, 297 P 521.

§194. —Opening; Closing

An ordinance regulating the opening and closing of bridges over navigable rivers within the city is not invalid as obstructing navigation, or imposing a burden on interstate commerce, where it is a reasonable exercise of the police power in the interest of traffic regulation, and only incidentally affects interstate commerce.

> **Ill** Escanaba & Lake Mich Transportation v Chicago (1882) 12 F 777.
> Chicago v McGinn (1869) 51 Ill 266.

§195. Bridge Tenders

An ordinance providing that bridge tenders should be under the supervision and control of the bridge committee, which is empowered to prescribe rules and fix hours of duty, is not invalid as a delegation of legislative authority, since the council may properly authorize others to do those things which it might properly but cannot understandingly or advantageously do.

> **Ill** Pekin v Industrial Comm (1930) 341 Ill 312, 173 NE 339.

§196. Viaducts

An injunction will not be granted to prohibit the mere passage of an ordinance assertedly within the scope of delegated powers, which grants to private persons the right to construct a viaduct or overpass across a city street, where its passage will not cause irreparable damage, since refusal of injunction does not affect the rights of private parties to contest the ordinance after its passage if its enforcement will cause them damage.

> **La** Durrett v Monroe (1942) 199 La 329, 5 So2d 911, 140 ALR 433.

Where an ordinance and contract by the terms of which a viaduct was to be constructed by the state department of roads and irrigation, the city to pay the damages to abutting property owners, was excluded from evidence because it was at variance with plaintiff's petition, the exclusion was proper because it was a complete departure from the theory originally set out in plaintiff's petition.

> **Neb** Casford v McCook (1937) 133 Neb 191, 274 NW 464.

XVI. TOLLROADS

§197. Generally

Under a code section providing that a board of supervisors "may make ordinances and bylaws and prescribe fines and other punishment for violations thereof", a board has power to establish and maintain toll gates, and authority to penalize those who fail or refuse to pay prescribed tolls.

    Va Hamilton v Commonwealth (1925) 143 Va 572, 130 SE 383.

A county board of supervisors has no authority to grant a franchise to collect tolls on a free public highway.

    Cal Blood v Woods (1892) 95 Cal 78, 30 P 129.

XVII. PRIVATE ROADS

§198. Generally

Due to the unique nature of a religious camp community, it may be established with political rights as a body politic. These rights are subject to general construction and the ordinances to constitutional restrictions. An ordinance prohibiting motor vehicles on the street from midnight Sunday to midnight Monday and prohibiting the distribution of newspapers during that time interval is invalid for the portion of time necessary to make home deliveries of the newspaper. Since the papers are unavailable for distribution prior to midnight, the prohibition constitutes a restriction on freedom of the press and may not be applied during the time necessary to deliver the papers.

    NJ Schaad v Ocean Grove Camp Meeting Assn (1977) 72 NJ 237, 370 A2d 449.

A statute authorizing municipalities to enter into contracts to build and improve private roads and driveways, and an ordinance or resolution enacted pursuant thereto, is invalid as resulting in the appropriation and expenditure of public funds for a private purpose without any direct advantage accruing to the public.

    Wis Heimerl v Ozaukee County (1949) 256 Wis 151, 40 NW2d 564.

A prohibition against the laying out of private roads for "access to more than one dwelling house," or the use of such roads for that purpose unless they meet the requirements of the ordinance, is valid legislation in the interest of the health, morals, safety and welfare of the community.

    Ohio Huber v Richmond Heights (1954) 68 Abs 470, 121 NE2d 457.

XVIII. EXCAVATIONS

§199. Generally

An ordinance providing for tamping and backfilling street excavations is for the protection of vehicles and pedestrian traffic. Violation of the ordinance is not negligence per se as to persons not within the class protected, such as other utilities and adjoining homeowners. However, it is evidence of negligence which a jury may consider.

Wis Schroeder v Northern States Power Co (1970) 46 Wis2d 637, 176 NW2d 336.

In the absence of an ordinance prescribing rules or regulations governing the conduct of citizens in making excavations in the street, it is not unlawful for the owner of the fee to dig a ditch and lay a gas line thereunder, provided he leaves the surface in as good condition as he found it and does not materially interrupt travel.

W Va Lynch v Northview (1914) 73 W Va 609, 81 SE 833.

An ordinance providing that a landowner maintaining an excavation under a street adjacent to his land could not hold the city liable for damages from water leaking into the excavation does not relieve the city of liability for escape of water into a basement from a broken city water main, where the basement was not illegal and did not interfere with the use of the way, and there was no causal connection between the location of the basement and the break in the main.

Mass Iver Johnson Sport Goods v Boston (1956) 334 Mass 401, 135 NE2d 658.

§200. License; Permit

An ordinance prohibiting the excavation of public streets and highways without a permit is valid.

NJ Bayonne v North Arlington (1911) 78 NJEq 283, 79 A 357.
NY Tabor v Buffalo (1910) 136 AD 258, 120 NYS 1089.
Tenn Paris v Paris-Henry County Pub Utilities Dist (1960) 207 Tenn 388, 340 SW2d 885.

An ordinance forbidding the excavation of "any hole or pit extending below the established grade of the adjacent road, street or alley, or to enlarge or extend such hole or pit now excavated, for the purpose of removing sand, gravel, or other materials, without first obtaining from the city council a permit," is sweeping and arbitrary in its terms, and is void as an unreasonable exercise of legislative powers.

Iowa Hawarden v Betz (1917) 182 Iowa 808, 164 NW 775.

§201. —Security Deposit

An ordinance requiring from a public utility desiring to make a street excavation a deposit to cover the cost of restoring the streets and the expense of inspection is sustained under the constitutional grant of power to make regulations and require indemnity for damages.

Cal   Keppelman, Ex parte (1914) 166 Cal 770, 138 P 346.
NJ   Cook v North Bergen (1905) 72 NJLaw 119, 59 A 1035.

An ordinance requiring a lineal foot deposit for a permit to lay water pipes may not be waived or the rules changed by a city administrative authority or the court. A bond in a lesser amount, accepted on the theory that the trench would be dug and refilled on numerous occasions, is not sufficient compliance to authorize a permit, and the city is justified in requiring suspension of work until a deposit for the entire amount required by the ordinance is made.

Ore   Bankus v Brookings (1969) 252 Ore 257, 449 P2d 646.

An ordinance prohibiting excavation in city streets without a deposit of money as indemnity for possible damages, and assessing a high percentage of the deposit for repairs to be made thereunder, but offering the alternative of filing a bond to secure restoration of the streets to their original condition, is void for lack of uniformity in application.

Cal   Wilcox, Ex parte (1910) 14 CA 164, 111 P 374.

§202. Indemnification

An ordinance requiring a landowner maintaining an excavation under part of the street to keep the structure in repair and to indemnify the city, if claims are made against it by persons injured because the structure is in disrepair, extends the duty of repair and indemnification to the owner as distinguished from a person in control. Construed otherwise, the ordinance would be superfluous as being affirmative of existing law.

Mass   Boston v A W Perry Inc (1939) 304 Mass 18, 22 NE2d 627.

§203. Regulation; Warning Signs; Barricades; Lighting

An established use or custom among men engaged in the same line of work cannot avail as against the positive provision of an ordinance that excavators or others creating a dangerous condition on or near a street without giving sufficient warning to the public are guilty of actionable negligence.

NC   Stultz v Thomas (1921) 182 NC 470, 109 SE 361.

An ordinance requiring fences around excavations is to protect travelers on the highway, and creates no duty to protect trespassers.

> **Ariz**   Welch & Son Contr v Gardner (1964) 96 Ariz 95, 392 P2d 567.
> **NY**   Hockstein v Congregation Talmud (1932) 144 Misc 207, 258 NYS 479.

A city may properly require by ordinance that every person who makes any excavation in a street and leaves any part thereof obstructed during the nighttime shall cause the same to be enclosed with substantial barriers and lighted.

> **Mo**   Von der Haat v St Louis (1950) 226 SW2d 376.
> Robson v Kansas City (1915) 181 SW 1004.

§204. Prohibition

An owner of property cannot relieve himself of the duty of complying with an ordinance forbidding the maintenance of an excavation in a sidewalk by having the excavation made by an independent contractor.

> **Cal**   Spence v Schultz (1894) 103 Cal 208, 37 P 220.

§205. Closing; Removal

If one makes excavations in a street without permission, and erects structures thereover, the governing body of the city may in its discretion order removal of the obstruction or the closing up of the excavation.

> **Iowa**   Callahan v Nevada (1915) 170 Iowa 719, 153 NW 188.

XIX. TREES; SHRUBS

§206. Municipal Control

Where a sidewalk cannot be constructed in conformity with an ordinance, without cutting down trees in the public streets, the city has the implied power to remove them, since trees in the public streets are the property of the municipality, and it has complete control over them.

> **Ga**   Albany v Lippitt (1941) 191 Ga 756, 13 SE2d 807.
> **Ill**   Dixon v Sinow & Weinman (1932) 350 Ill 634, 183 NE 570.
> Mt Carmel v Shaw (1895) 155 Ill 37, 39 NE 584.
> **Ky**   Franklin v Lacey (1914) 157 Ky 261, 162 SW 1126.

A limitation of three feet for the height of shrubbery and obstructions on corner lots is valid under police powers. It applies equally to all parties and is not a taking of property without compensation.

> **Md** Stevens v Salisbury (1965) 240 Md 556, 214 A2d 775.

§207. —Limitations

The courts will not order the enforcement of an ordinance authorizing a street improvement so as to injure or destroy shade and ornamental trees where that would be an arbitrary and unnecessary destruction of private property, and will enjoin the city from injuring or destroying such trees along the street to be improved.

> **Mo** Webb v Strobach (1910) 143 MoApp 459, 127 SW 680.

§208. Removal

An ordinance requiring that trees be trimmed at least eight feet above the street does not place the duty and liabilities solely on the abutting owner. The city may not legislate away its liability and is jointly liable with the landowner for injuries caused by a violation of the ordinance.

> **Pa** Green v Freeport (1971) 218 PaS 334, 280 A2d 412.

A right-of-way for a city street is an easement, and an abutting lot owner owns the fee to the half of the street contiguous to his property. However, the city has certain powers and privileges incident to the right-of-way, and may enact legislation to remove or trim trees planted or maintained by an abutting lot owner, when reasonably necessary for improvement of the street.

> **NJ** Sproul v Stockton (1905) 73 NJLaw 158, 62 A 275.
> **ND** Murphy v Bismarck (1961) 109 NW2d 635.
> **Wash** Robinson v Spokane (1912) 66 Wash 527, 120 P 101.

Where a lot owner's title extends to the center of the street, the fee is in the owner of the lot, and the right of the village is paramount only for street purposes. Such an owner who cuts a decayed tree in the sidewalk area which has become a menace to public travel is not subject to an ordinance prohibiting destruction of shade trees.

> **NY** Cattaraugus v Johnson (1931) 139 Misc 368, 249 NYS 327.

§209. Liability to Abutting Owners

Ordinances regulating the planting and care of shrubs and trees in the public streets do not relieve defendant of liability for maintenance of a nuisance. They gave city the right to remove a dead tree, but in no way limited the power or duty of defendant to remove the tree on his property.

> **Wis** Plesko v Allied Inv (1961) 12 Wis2d 168, 107 NW2d 201.
> Brown v Milwaukee Terminal Ry (1929) 199 Wis 575, 227 NW 385.

XX. AIR; SUBSURFACE RIGHTS

§210. Air

A city may by ordinance provide for the regulation of air rights above its streets.

> **Ill** People v Chicago (1953) 415 Ill 165, 112 NE2d 616.
> Kane v Chicago (1943) 384 Ill 361, 51 NE2d 523.

An ordinance that makes every encroachment on a street beyond the street line a common nuisance applies to an overhead merchandise conveyor across a street.

> **Conn** Andrew B Hendryx v New Haven (1926) 104 Conn 632, 134 A 77.

Under a city's delegated power to vacate any street or alley or part thereof, a city may vacate that portion of an alley extending indefinitely upwards from an imaginary horizontal plane 16 feet above the elevation of the center line of the alley as presently graded.

> **Wash** Taft v Wash Mutual Sav Bk (1923) 127 Wash 503, 221 P 604.

ANNOTATION

Municipalities power to permit private owner to construct building or structure overhanging or crossing the air space above public street or sidewalk, 76 ALR2d 896.

§211. Subsurface

Ordinances regulating the use of streets must be construed in the light of the doctrine that the right of the public to the use of the streets is not confined to the surface, but includes the earth below.

> **Ill** Kane v Chicago (1943) 384 Ill 361, 51 NE2d 523.
> Northwestern Elevated Ry v Chicago (1904) 1 IllCC 480.

ANNOTATIONS

Right of municipality or public to use of subsurface of street or highway for purposes of other than sewers, pipes, conduits for wires and the like, as affected by ownership of fee as between public and abutting owner, 11 ALR2d 186.

Relative rights, as between municipality and abutting landowners, to minerals underlying streets or alleys, 62 ALR2d 1311.

XXI. COMPULSORY ROAD LABOR

§212. Generally

A man suffering from a pulmonary disease that produced hemorrhage and shortness of breath, accompanied by coughing and expectoration of blood, is not an able-bodied man within the meaning of an ordinance requiring every able-bodied male between 21 and 50 to labor on the streets of the village at least two days each year, or to pay, in lieu thereof, $1.50.

Ill Harvel v McGlothlin (1912) 176 IllAp 512.

In an ordinance levying a poll tax on all able-bodied males between 21 and 50, a requirement that the collector give notice of the tax list by posting in public places "without delay" is directory only, and failure to give such notice does not invalidate the levy.

Mo Berger v La Boube (1953) 260 SW2d 527.

§213. Nature

A road poll tax ordinance is in the nature of a police regulation, and does not impose a tax in the sense used when referring to general taxation under statutory and constitutional concepts, but is subject to the limitation that it be applied and enforced within reasonable bounds.

Ill Macomb v Twaddle (1879) 4 IllAp 254.
Utah Salt Lake City v Wilson (1915) 46 Utah 60, 148 P 1104.

§214. Validity

Where a statute grants power to villages to levy a road poll tax on able-bodied males between 21 and 50, an ordinance levying such a tax is valid.

Ill Wahl v Nauvoo (1895) 64 IllAp 17.
Mo Nixa v Wilson (1918) 199 MoApp 33, 200 SW 703.
Wash McMannis v Superior Ct (1916) 92 Wash 360, 159 P 383.

Where a statute authorizes a city by ordinance to require of able-bodied males three days of work each year on streets and alleys, or in lieu thereof to pay not to exceed $4, and authorizes the city to levy a poll tax of not to exceed $4, an ordinance imposing a $3 poll tax on such persons without the option of working is valid, since the election whether to require money or work rests with the city, and not with the taxpayer.

    Mo   Berger v La Boube (1953) 260 SW2d 527.

§215. —Discriminatory

An ordinance authorizing a road poll tax on all males between 21 and 50 who are physically not incapacitated to work and not exempt is not in violation of the constitutional provision that male and female citizens shall enjoy equal civil, political and religious rights and privileges.

    Utah   Salt Lake City v Wilson (1915) 46 Utah 60, 148 P 1104.
    Wash   Tekoa v Reilly (1907) 47 Wash 202, 91 P 769.

An ordinance requiring every able-bodied male inhabitant between the ages of 21 and 50 except certain persons exempt by law, and the officers and attorneys of the village, to labor on the streets or public places two days each year, is invalid, in its provision for exemption of the officers and attorneys, as discriminating between persons of the same class, and its failure to bear equally on all the inhabitants of the village.

    Ill   Kilbourne v Blakely (1913) 184 IllAp 370.

§216. —Express Authority

An ordinance requiring all males between 21 and 50 who have resided in the city for 30 days to perform road duties for four days or pay a tax in lieu thereof is invalid in the absence of statutory authorization.

    Ind   Newburgh v House (1922) 191 Ind 609, 134 NE 292.
    La   Winnfield v Long (1909) 122 La 697, 48 So 155.
        Farmerville v Mathews (1907) 120 La 102, 44 So 999.
    Okla   Lankford, In re (1919) 72 Okla 40, 178 P 673.

§217. Enforcement

Lack of uniform enforcement of an ordinance that levies a tax on residents or subjects them to road duty is not a valid defense to a prosecution for failure to pay money or perform a duty under the ordinance.

    Ga   Grier v Waycross (1934) 49 GaApp 111, 174 SE 221.
        Miller v Waycross (1934) 50 GaApp 1, 176 SE 826.

Where an ordinance requiring residents to perform street duty or pay a tax is in effect a revenue measure, collection of the tax may be enforced by a criminal proceeding.

> **Ga** Miller v Waycross (1934) 50 GaApp 1, 176 SE 826.

XXII. STREET OR ROAD COMMISSIONERS

§218. Generally

A charter provision transferring the duties of road commissioners from members of the board of supervisors to the county engineer is a valid charter enactment, and determines the official of the county who shall exercise those duties.

> **Cal** Reuter v San Mateo County (1934) 220 Cal 314, 30 P2d 417.
> **Okla** Johnson v Vinita (1935) 172 Okla 376, 45 P2d 1089.

An ordinance may reduce the salary of a deputy street commissioner, fixed by the board of public works, where a statute revising a city charter gives the board power to hire subordinate officers and provides that the city council may alter the powers of the board by ordinance.

> **Mass** Faulkner v Sisson (1903) 183 Mass 524, 67 NE 669.

Where a municipal superintendent of streets and drains is designated as an employee by an ordinance authorizing his employment, prescribing a three year term of office, and entitling him to a trial by the council for dereliction of duty, disobedience of orders, or misconduct in office in order to discharge him before expiration of his term, such a superintendent cannot be removed except in the manner provided.

> **Ga** Elliott v Augusta (1934) 49 GaApp 568, 176 SE 548.

Where an ordinance establishes the office and salary of a street commissioner, and one is appointed to such office by contract for a term of one year or until his successor is appointed and qualified, and the appointee is informed by letter from the mayor at year's end that the city council has terminated the office, the termination is invalid since suspension of the ordinance may be only by an ordinance of equal dignity and not by a mere resolution. However, when such employee accedes to such termination of his office and accepts other city employment he thereby abandons his right to the office and is estopped to claim remuneration thereof.

> **Mo**   Stratton v Warrensburg (1942) 237 MoApp 280, 167 SW2d 392.

XXIII. CONTRACTS; CONTRACTORS

§219. Contractors—Duties, Liabilities

Where an ordinance authorizing public improvements imposes a duty of care on prime contractors constructing the improvement, the prime contractor may not shift liability for the breach of this duty by subcontracting the work, and is liable to a subcontractors' employees, or to members of the public generally for injury caused by breach of this duty.

> **Ore**   Larson v Heintz Constr (1959) 219 Ore 25, 345 P2d 835.

A provision in a street improvement contract requiring the contractor to use all necessary precautions to prevent accidents and to be responsible for all loss, damage or injury to persons, property or the work due to the nature of the work or the action of the elements means that the contractor is liable for all injuries to persons, property, or the pavement to be constructed by reason of his negligence in constructing the pavement. So construed such provision does not violate the law or invalidate the contract.

> **Cal**   McQuiddy v Worswick St Paving (1911) 160 Cal 9, 116 P 67.

A charter requirement that a contractor for a street improvement make and file an affidavit, to the effect that he has not privately agreed with anyone liable to be assessed to accept a price less than that named in the street improvement contract nor agreed on any rebate, refers only to a private agreement with relation to a contemplated street improvement by the city under the street law, and has no reference to a private contract between a contractor and property owners for doing street work directly for them.

> **Cal**   Ransome-Crummey v Coulter (1918) 177 Cal 574, 171 P 308.

Where the terms of a franchise obligate a utility to pave streets on demand of the city, that the utility does not sign a paving contract authorized by ordinance does not insulate it from liability on the ground that no privity of contract exists between the paving contractor and the utility company.

> **La**   Bond v New Orleans (1936) 186 La 60, 171 So 572.

§220. —Penalties for Delay

A provision, in a contract let under an ordinance providing for a local improvement, that damages shall be $10 for each day's delay of the contractor in completing the improvement, is enforceable.

> **Ore**   Star Sand v Portland (1920) 96 Ore 323, 189 P 217.

§221. —Rights

Where an ordinance creates a contract for a city improvement, to be paid for from a special assessment fund, and the city through negligence fails to enact valid ordinances making the assessment and funding the project, the contractor-obligee has a right of action for damages in the amount due under the contract with interest.

> **Ore**   O'Neil v Portland (1911) 59 Ore 84, 113 P 655.

A contractor who paves city streets and receives paving certificates which he is unable to enforce against the abutting property owners because the city did not give them the special notice required by the paving ordinance may bring an action against the city for the value of the certificates.

> **La**   Bruning v New Orleans (1908) 122 La 316, 47 So 624.

§222. Contracts

An administrative ruling by the department of transportation that bids for asphalt to be delivered during the nighttime may only be by plants that are located in a particular area is outside the department's authority. The rulemaking power given the department applies to departmental operations and may not be used to restrict competitive bidding or to satisfy complaints of neighbors against a plant which is a permissive use within its area.

> **NY**   Edenwald Contracting Co v New York City (1974) 86 Misc2d 711, 384 NYS2d 338; affd (1975) 47 AD2d 610, 366 NYS2d 363.

Where there is uncertainty and ambiguity in the plans and specifications drafted by the city engineer under an ordinance authorizing the paving of sidewalks in a street buffer area, such plans, specifications and paving contract must be construed in favor of the paving contractor and against the city.

> **La**   Bond v New Orleans (1936) 186 La 60, 171 So 572.

A city cannot make a valid contract for extensive street paving without an estimate, as required by statute. If the city engineer is not competent to make the estimate, and a proper estimate is made by competent engineers employed by the city for that purpose, owners of adjoining property cannot, after the paving is completed, enjoin an assessment of benefits against their property on the ground that the estimate was not made by the city engineer.

Neb Diederich v Red Cloud (1919) 103 Neb 688, 173 NW 698.

An ordinance providing for the paving of streets, building of sidewalks and construction of storm sewers is valid, under statutes authorizing general law cities to make contracts for construction and building of such improvements.

Ida Byrns v Moscow (1912) 21 Ida 398, 121 P 1034.

The mere enactment of an ordinance acceptng the bid of a particular person to perform street paving work does not constitute a contract, especially where the advertisement for bids and the specifications state that the successful bidder must enter into a written contract.

Okla McCormick v Oklahoma City (1915) 236 US 657, 59 LEd 771, 35 SCt 455.

Where a street improvement is to be paid for by special assessment against benefited property, a municipal contract providing that the contractor shall be paid from such assessments does not create an "indebtedness," within the meaning of constitutional and statutory limitations.

Ill Randolph-Perkins v Highland Park (1941) 311 IllAp 308, 35 NE2d 826.

An ordinance assessing the costs of a local improvement, where the contract for it provides that for five years the contractor will, at his own expense, repair defects in the work arising from faulty materials or workmanship, is not invalid as a contract for repairs.

Ore Gamma Alpha Bldg v Eugene (1919) 94 Ore 80, 184 P 973.

§223. —Subletting

Where an ordinance creates a paving district and adopts plans and specifications for grading, rolling and oiling designated streets, contracts let thereunder may be sublet if such procedure is not proscribed by the contract or by the ordinance.

Mo Schreck v Parker (1965) 388 SW2d 538.

§224. —Completion of Improvement

Where an ordinance authorizes the grading, curbing and paving of a street, to be completed within 60 days of award of contract, but the work is not completed within an extension of time granted, time is of the essence, and it is for the courts to determine whether completion was accomplished within a reasonable time. If not, tax bills levied on benefited property are void.

Cal Flinn v Shafter Rlty (1923) 190 Cal 316, 212 P 194.
Mo Casteel v Dearmont (1927) 221 MoApp 1217, 299 SW 816.
Maplewood v Martha Inv (1924) 267 SW 63.

Where an ordinance authorizes a street improvement on which a contract is executed, and the ordinance and the contract provide for completion on or before a certain date unless the time be extended by the board of aldermen, the completion date is uncertain, and is construed as being within a reasonable time.

Mo Webster Groves v Reber (1920) 226 SW 77.

Where an ordinance provides that the city may declare a forfeiture of any contract for a local improvement under which work is delayed beyond the contract completion date, the city is not required to declare a forfeiture where delays were at the request of a city official for good cause.

Ore Irelan v Portland (1919) 91 Ore 471, 179 P 286.

§225. —Union Labor

An ordinance requiring that in all contracts by the city relating to public works the contractor shall agree to hire only members of labor unions is unconstitutional as discriminating between different classes of citizens, restricting competition and increasing the cost of public works.

Ill Fiske v People (1900) 188 Ill 206, 58 NE 985.

§226. —Obtained by Fraud

Where a municipal street paving contract is obtained through fraud, no recovery against the property owners assessed can be had on a quantum meruit, and they would also be entitled to defeat the levy of any tax to pay the contract price.

Iowa Swan v Indianola (1909) 142 Iowa 731, 121 NW 547.

§227. Rights and Liabilities of Municipality

A township whose commissioners by approving plans enable developers to record plans showing proposed public improvements and to sell lots cannot thereafter tell purchasers of lots that the public improvements for which the township was required to obtain the developers' guarantees will not in fact be supplied because of the township's failure to comply with the law and its own regulations. Since subdivision plans should not be approved by the municipality without the developers' guarantees for the completion of streets and storm sewers, on failure of a developer to make such improvements a township is required to complete the construction necessary for the protection and maintenance of the streets.

Pa   Safford v Bd of Comm Annville Township (1978) 35 PaCmwlth 631, 387 A2d 177.

Under a charter requiring an engineer's estimate of the cost of a paving project and limiting the contract price thereto, the city council may reject a bid, in excess of the estimate, advertise for new bids and subsequently let the paving contract to the original bidder under a new bid, if the latter is within a revised estimate made in good faith by the engineer and approved by the council in the meantime.

Neb   Superior v Simpson (1926) 114 Neb 698, 209 NW 505.

Where a city under an ordinance for street improvements fails to take the necessary steps to hold property owners liable for the cost, and the statutory period of limitations has run, the city is liable to the contractor for the work done.

Ky   Mayfield v Carey-Reed Co (1935) 260 Ky 43, 88 SW2d 891.

A city is not liable for interest on a contractor's claim for construction costs of street improvements though the delay in payment is occasioned by the fault of the city making a wrong apportionment against an abutting property owner.

Ky   Orth v B B Park Co (1904) 117 Ky 779, 79 SW 206.

An ordinance provision requiring a street improvement contractor to file a bond conditioned on his satisfactory maintenance and repair of the street for five years after construction may not be enforced, for the city has no statutory power to enter into a contract for future repairs of streets.

Ore   Portland v Bituminous Paving & Improvement (1898) 33 Ore 307, 52 P 28.

Where a contract made pursuant to an ordinance authorizing street improvements contains a guaranty that does not include repairs made necessary by any cause other than defective work or materials used in the original construction, the abutting property owners, and not the city, are properly made liable for the costs of the guaranty.

Ky   Louisville v Mehler (1900) 108 Ky 436, 56 SW 712.

XXIV. ASSESSMENT FOR LOCAL IMPROVEMENTS

§228. Generally

An attempt to amend a new city charter immediately prior to its effective date to authorize collection of special assessments is invalid. The provision in the new charter which eliminated all special assessments and became effective one year prior to total enactment of the charter prevails and special assessments are automatically nullified.

> **NY**   Acca v Bureau of Assessors (1972) 73 Misc2d 50, 340 NYS2d 476;
> affd (1974) 45 AD2d 1005, 358 NYS2d 213.

A special service district and tax to construct a shopping mall is valid even though the entire city may benefit and the property owners' tax exceed the benefits.

> **Ill**   Coryn v Moline (1978) 71 Ill2d 194, 374 NE2d 211.

The cost of construction plus interest may be added in computing the costs assessed against abutting owners for street improvement.

> **Ore**   Sisters of St Mary v Beaverton (1970) 4 OreAp 297, 478 P2d 412.

A municipality has power to enact an ordinance levying an assessment for street paving under the constitutional grant.

> **Alas**   Kissane v Anchorage (1958) 17 Alas 514, 159 F Supp 733.
> Ketchikan Delinquent Tax Roll, In re (1922) 6 Alas 653.
> **Ga**   Ga Power v Decatur (1935) 181 Ga 187, 182 SE 32.
> **Ill**   Burnham v Chicago (1860) 24 Ill 496.
> **Ky**   Elder v Richmond (1920) 186 Ky 706, 218 SW 239.
> Creekmore v Cent Const (1914) 157 Ky 336, 163 SW 194.
> **Neb**   Superior v Simpson (1926) 114 Neb 698, 209 NW 505.
> **Okla**   St Louis-San Francisco Ry v Tulsa (1935) 170 Okla 398, 41 P2d 116.
> **SC**   Blake v Spartanburg (1937) 185 SC 398, 194 SE 124, 114 ALR 395.
> Farrow v Charleston (1933) 169 SC 373, 168 SE 852, 87 ALR 981.

Special assessments for local street improvements, authorized by ordinance, will be sustained under the municipal power to tax.

> **La**   Kelly v Chadwick (1901) 104 La 719, 29 So 295.
> **ND**   Murphy v Bismarck (1961) 109 NW2d 635.

Where a street improvement is to be paid for by special assessments against benefited property, a municipal contract providing that the contractor shall be paid from such assessments does not create an "indebtedness", within the meaning of constitutional and statutory limitations.

> **Ill**   Randolph-Perkins v Highland Park (1941) 311 IllAp 308, 35 NE2d 826.

In the absence of a statute requiring that paving contracts in all municipalities be estimated at the same unit cost, a variance in cost in localities of close proximity is not unreasonable if there is no proof of fraud or collusion since costs necessarily depend on local conditions.

> **La** Palmer v Ponchatoula (1940) 195 La 997, 197 So 697.

§229. —Source of Power

The power of a municipality to make public improvements does not of itself confer power to levy assessments to pay for them, and such power must be conferred by Constitution, statute or charter.

> **Neb** State v Cunningham (1954) 158 Neb 708, 64 NW2d 465.
> **NJ** Gabriel v Paramus (1965) 45 NJ 381, 212 A2d 550.

§230. Construction of Ordinances

Special assessments are strictly construed in favor of the taxpayer and against the taxing authority.

> **Neb** Cullingham v Omaha (1943) 143 Neb 744, 10 NW2d 615.
> State v Thomas (1934) 127 Neb 891, 257 NW 265.

§231. Nature of Proceeding

Where owners of property abutting street improvements were afforded a hearing on the question of benefits and given an opportunity to contest the amount of the proposed assessment but did not complain in any manner, the property owners were afforded a proper and adequate hearing prior to the time the assessment actually became irrevocably fixed and were not deprived of due process of law under the United States Constitution.

> **Tex** Tramel v Dallas (1977) 560 SW2d 426.

A curb and gutter assessment ordinance passed without a public hearing after its introduction is invalid. The charter requires that a public hearing be had after a special assessment order is introduced and before its final passage.

> **Colo** Englewood v Weist (1974) 184 Colo 325, 520 P2d 120.

A street improvement assessment for a main county road running through the city is proper even though the city determines the cost prior to establishing the assessment and construction was begun prior to approval of the sale of bonds.

Interior lot owners may be assessed for beneficial interest since their access has been substantially improved.

> **Mich**   Johnson v Inkster (1974) 224 NW2d 664.

A local street improvement ordinance is one under which the improvement enhances the value of adjacent property, as distinguished from benefits diffused throughout the municipality.

> **Ill**   Marissa v Jones (1927) 327 Ill 180, 158 NE 389.
> **Mich**   Sawicki v Harper Woods (1965) 1 Mich Ap 352, 136 NW2d 691.

A judgment on a paving assessment is not personal against the property owner but is an in rem proceeding restricted to the value of the property against which the lien was assessed.

> **La**   Hinkle v McGuire (1938) 190 La 397, 182 So 551.
>   Ruston v Adams (1928) 9 LaApp 618, 121 So 661.
> **SC**   Orangeburg v Southern Ry (1944) 55 F Supp 171.
> **Tex**   Dallas v Atkins (1917) 197 SW 593.
> **W Va**   Moundsville v Brown (1943) 125 W Va 779, 25 SE2d 900.

An ordinance assessing the cost of street improvements against abutting owners personally is valid.

> **Tex**   Dallas v Atkins (1920) 110 Tex 627, 223 SW 170.

Special assessments levied for the purpose of improving streets in front of the property of a municipality are not taxes in the sense intended by the constitutional provision for exemption of school property from taxation.

> **Colo**   Bradfield v Pueblo (1960) 143 Colo 559, 354 P2d 612.
> **Ill**   Randolph-Perkins v Highland Park (1941) 311 IllAp 308, 35 NE2d 826.
>   Troutman v Zeigler (1927) 327 Ill 251, 158 NE 355.
> **Ky**   Wickliffe v Greenville (1916) 170 Ky 528, 186 SW 476.
> **La**   Alcus v New Orleans (1939) 187 So 557.
>   Hagmann v New Orleans (1938) 190 La 796, 182 So 753.
> **Ore**   Sproul v State Tax Comm (1962) 234 Ore 579, 383 P2d 754.
> **SC**   Sutton v Fort Mill (1933) 171 SC 291, 172 SE 119.
> **Tenn**   South Fulton v Parker (1930) 160 Tenn 634, 28 SW2d 639.
> **Tex**   West Tex Constr v Doss (1932) 59 SW2d 866.
> **Wash**   Austin v Seattle (1891) 2 Wash 667, 27 P 557.

Although a special assessment is not a pure tax, an ordinance imposing such an assessment is an exercise of a branch of the taxing power, and the fundamental doctrine of special assessments is not based on contract principles.

> **Mo**   St Louis v Senter Comm Co (1935) 336 Mo 1209, 84 SW2d 133.
> **Ore**   Brown v Silverton (1920) 97 Ore 441, 190 P 971.

Where a local assessment or charge is levied on property for street improvements under an ordinance, a case of "tax" is presented in the sense in which the word is used in the article of the Constitution conferring jurisdiction on the Supreme Court.

> **La** Judice v Scott (1929) 168 La 111, 121 So 592.
> Kelly v Chadwick (1901) 104 La 719, 29 So 295.
> **Tex** Evans v Whicker (1936) 126 Tex 621, 90 SW2d 554.

An ordinance levying special assessments for street improvements does not involve a taking of private property for which compensation must be paid.

> **Tex** Special Assessment Securities v Brown (1937) 106 SW2d 340.

§232. Right to Assess

A county levy for roads assessed against residents of the municipality is valid. The road improvement is for the benefit of all the residents of the area rather than exclusively for the benefit of property in the unincorporated area.

> **Fla** Burke v Charlotte County (1973) 286 So2d 199.

A local improvement assessment to separate storm sewers and sanitary sewers with repaving and the installation of curbs and gutters is a local improvement. The fact that separation of the two systems is required by the environmental protection act does not nullify the local benefit in the affected area and thus require that a general assessment be attached.

> **Ill** Hinsdale v Lowenstine (1974) 23 IllAp3d 357, 319 NE2d 83.

An ordinance levying taxes on property owners for paving a street constitutes a valid exercise of councilmanic power, and therefore is constitutional.

> **Neb** Sandell v Omaha (1927) 115 Neb 861, 215 NW 135.

Paving of a boulevard is not a local improvement for which a city may by ordinance impose special assessments on property owners.

> **Mich** Oprisiu v Detroit (1929) 248 Mich 590, 227 NW 714.

It is no objection to an ordinance levying an assessment for street improvement that the land assessed is used for railroad purposes, and, while so used, is not benefited by the improvement. The property must be viewed in the light of its general relations, apart from the particular use to which it is being put at the time.

> **SC** Carolina & N W Ry v Clover (1931) 46 F2d 395.

Where no statutory limitation exists, a street improvement assessment authorized by ordinance may validly be imposed 3½ years after completion of the work.

> **NY**　People v Marvin (1936) 249 AD 293, 292 NYS 93.

Where an existing highway has never been improved at the cost of the abutting owners, a city under an ordinance may impose the costs for its improvement on abutting owners, since there is no original construction at the expense of the abutting owners.

> **Ky**　Ludlow v Ludlow (1918) 252 F 559.

§233. Property Subject to

A 99-year lease of railroad property to the city for street purposes and other public purposes does not exempt the railroad from an assessment for paving. The assessment against the property abutting the street confers a benefit on the lessor in the absence of evidence to the contrary or evidence that the lease will last longer than the paving.

> **La**　New Orleans Great Northern Ry Co v New Orleans (1974) 299 So2d 426.

A street improvement ordinance assessing the properties benefited is unenforceable as to properties that do not come within either a specific or a general description of the properties covered as set forth in the published notice, which is jurisdictional.

> **Utah**　Jones v Foulger (1915) 46 Utah 419, 150 P 933.

Under its charter, a city has authority to create a paving district more extensive than the boundary of the lots on the street to be paved, to order the paving on a petition representing a majority of the foot frontage on such street, and to make assessments for benefits against all lots in the improvement district if benefited.

> **Neb**　Gall v Beckett (1927) 115 Neb 347, 213 NW 370.

City may not after annexation change the designation of boulevards to streets, and thus render lot owners liable to special assessments for paving.

> **Mich**　Oprisiu v Detroit (1929) 248 Mich 590, 227 NW 714.

§234. —Abutting

Where a city enacts an ordinance authorizing the paving of a street, and the statutory authority therefor authorizes assessment of benefits against property abutting on the street paved, assessments levied against lots in blocks fronting on intersecting streets but not abutting on the paved street are invalid, though the authorizing statute, as amended subsequent to adoption of the ordinance, permits such assessments.

> **Mo** Prescott Wright Snider Co v Mellody-McGilley Funeral Home (1938) 233 MoApp 332, 118 SW2d 499.
> State v Chillicothe (1911) 237 Mo 486, 141 SW 602.
> **NY** Martin, In re (1931) 140 Misc 327, 249 NYS 549.
> **Ohio** Mrusek v Reading (1935) 51 OA 198, 19 Abs 700, 4 Op 575, 200 NE 136.
> **W Va** Sturm v St Albans (1953) 138 W Va 911, 78 SE2d 462.

Although "abutting" means adjoining, it is not necessary that the actual pavement touch the line of the owner's property in order for it to be abutting for purposes of assessment under a paving ordinance.

> **La** Alexandria v Chicago R I & P RR (1961) 240 La 1025, 126 So2d 351, 97 ALR2d 1073.

A statute providing that the cost of permanent sidewalks may be assessed by ordinance against "the lots or parcels of land in front of which the same shall be constructed" means properties lying contiguous to the street improved, whether specifically outlined on a plat or not.

> **Iowa** Northern Light Lodge 156 I O O F v Monona (1917) 180 Iowa 62, 161 NW 78.

An ordinance imposing a street improvement assessment on land three feet removed from the original street line is valid where the city, by a dedication, appropriates the buffer strip for street purposes and uses it in the street improvement.

> **NY** Martin, In re (1931) 140 Misc 327, 249 NYS 549.

ANNOTATION

What property abuts on improvements so as to be subject to assessment, 97 ALR2d 1079.

§235. —Non-Abutting

A special assessment ordinance may impose a charge on property that is not abutting or contiguous to the improvement, the only requirement being that the property be benefited by the improvement.

> **Mo** Thompson v St Louis (1923) 253 SW 969.
> **Ore** Raz v Portland (1955) 203 Ore 285, 280 P2d 394.

§236. Agricultural or Vacant Land

Use of land within the city limits for an agricultural purpose does not exempt it from local assessments under an ordinance for street improvement, since it benefits from the improvement of the district.

> **Ky**   Barber Asphalt Paving v Gaar (1903) 24 KLR 2260, 73 SW 1106.
> Duker v Barber Asphalt Paving (1903) 25 KLR 135, 74 SW 744.

Tax bills issued pursuant to an ordinance authorizing construction of a sidewalk will not be held invalid on the ground that the land on both sides of the street is vacant.

> **Mo**   Maret v Hough (1916) 185 SW 544.

§237. Municipal Project

A city ordinance authorizing the levy of a special assessment for street improvement purposes is invalid as applied to lots owned by a park district (a municipal corporation) and used for park purposes.

> **Ill**   Chicago v Ridge Park Dist (1925) 317 Ill 123, 147 NE 803.
> **Mo**   Thogmartin v Nevada Sch Dist (1915) 189 MoApp 10, 176 SW 473.

Since special assessments for local improvements are not taxes, in the strict sense of that term, and property held for a public use is not exempt from such assessments, a statute exempting from taxation public buildings belonging to a county will not prevent enactment of a city ordinance levying an assessment on the county courthouse to defray the cost of paving the street in front of the courthouse.

> **Ill**   Adams County v Quincy (1889) 130 Ill 566, 22 NE 624.

§238. Incorporeal Rights

An ordinance providing for the improvement of a street, with special benefits to be recouped by special assessment against property that abuts on the street, does not apply to a property owner possessing an easement to the street, for an easement is incorporeal and cannot abut anything.

> **Ohio**   Menefee v Cincinnati (1959) 109 OA 97, 10 Op2d 261, 159 NE2d 917.

An ordinance authorizing imposition of a paving assessment on owners or occupants of all houses and lots benefited does not authorize an assessment against the incorporeal rights of wharfage and cranage attendant on a dock area.

> **NY**   Knickerbocker Ice v New York City (1924) 209 AD 434, 204 NYS 632.

§239. Corner Lots

Under a street improvement ordinance, a corner lot abutting on two improved streets is chargeable with its portion of the costs of the improvements on each street.

> Ga   Holland v College Park (1962) 105 GaApp 427, 124 SE2d 693.
> Ky   Louisville v Colby (1936) 262 Ky 578, 90 SW2d 1036.
>   Vogt v Oakdale (1915) 166 Ky 810, 179 SW 1037.
>   Anderson v Bitzer (1899) 20 KLR 1450, 49 SW 442.

Under a street improvement ordinance a corner lot may be assessed on either street on which it abuts, and such assessments may be made up to the permissible maximum percentage value of the property assessed.

> Ky   Williamsburg v Perkins (1931) 240 Ky 160, 41 SW2d 915.

An ordinance assessing the cost of street improvements on the abutting real estate in proportion to the frontage of the several lots is not invalid as discriminatory for favoring outside corner lots with additional frontage on other streets, since such corner lots may be liable to further assessment.

> Ill   Wilbur v Springfield (1888) 123 Ill 395, 14 NE 871.

§240. Apportionment

Where abutting owners are benefited by street improvements, in the absence of fraud or collusion between the council and the contractor the acceptance of the work by the council is conclusive on the abutting owners so as to require them to bear the cost in the proportion in which their property is benefited.

> Ky   Hazard v Duff (1943) 295 Ky 628, 175 SW2d 146.
>   Maysville v Davis (1915) 166 Ky 555, 179 SW 463.
> SC   Cheves v Charleston (1927) 140 SC 423, 138 SE 867.
> W Va   Avis v Allen (1919) 83 W Va 789, 99 SE 188.

Where a city by statute is vested with discretion over the manner in which an assessment for street improvements shall be apportioned, an ordinance in which the city agrees to pay for costs of improving intersections is valid.

> Ky   Shaver v Rice (1925) 209 Ky 467, 273 SW 48.

An ordinance levying a special assessment for road improvement is invalid as violative of due process of law where it fails to contain any provision for notice to the taxpayers of the apportionment of the assessment against their real estate, or any opportunity to object.

> Kan   Johnston v Coffeyville (1953) 175 Kan 357, 264 P2d 474.

§241. —Reapportionment Where Erroneous

Where an owner of property abutting a street improvement can show that the burden is increased on his property because of the way the ordinance apportions the cost, he may avail himself of a reapportionment and thus lessen his burden.

    Ky   Louisville & N RR v Garrard (1934) 255 Ky 127, 72 SW2d 1024.
            Louisville v Amer Standard Asphalt (1907) 125 Ky 497, 102 SW 806.

§242. —Arbitrary

A special assessment ordinance for the purpose of street widening, creating a benefit district that omits from the assessment approximately half of the property benefited, is invalid as arbitrary and unreasonable for failure to distribute the cost equitably.

    Kan   Bowers v Gardner (1961) 187 Kan 720, 360 P2d 17.
    Mo   Wetterau v Farmers' & Merchants' Tr (1920) 285 Mo 555, 226 SW 941.
            Municipal Securities v Moriarty (1917) 195 MoApp 579, 193 SW 892.
    NJ   Sarty v Millburn (1953) 28 NJS 199, 100 A2d 309.
    Okla   Paine v Guymon (1947) 199 Okla 336, 185 P2d 941.

§243. —Joint Owners

An ordinance levying a special assessment against persons owning property jointly must, to be valid, separate the amount of the liability of each owner.

    Tex   Dallas v Atkins (1920) 110 Tex 627, 223 SW 170.

§244. Method of Assessment

Where the city and county cooperated in improving streets and assessments were limited by the amount of benefit conferred, the fact that assessments were made against abutting property owners along the street where improvements were made by the city but no assessment was made of property owners abutting the street where improvements were made by the county did not constitute a "statutory scheme" under which paving charges were assessed in denial of equal protection of the law.

    Tex   Tramel v Dallas (1977) 560 SW2d 426.

An apportionment of the costs of improving or constructing a street or alley will not be disturbed on complaint of an abutting owner unless it affirmatively appears that under a different and proper method he would be charged materially less, and that the apportionment as made by the city would be prejudicial to his interests.

> **Ky** Button v Gast (1903) 24 KLR 2284, 73 SW 1014.

Where lots are consolidated into one ownership and treated as one piece of property by the owners, they may be assessed as one piece of property for the purpose of making public improvements, though but one of the lots abuts on the street improved.

> **Ky** Pursiful v Harlan (1928) 222 Ky 658, 1 SW2d 1043.

A municipality may adopt any of the methods authorized by statute to assess street paving costs, and it is presumed that the ordinance is enacted and assessment classifications of property are made after investigation and consideration, and that the ordinance reflects a reasonable exercise of discretion.

> **NY** Bath v Stocum (1923) 206 AD 179, 200 NYS 520.

Where due to the irregular lines of a street a heavier burden will be imposed on certain lots than on others the unequal burdens that follow are unavoidable, and an ordinance for street improvements will not on that account be declared invalid.

> **Ky** Engelhard v Ky & Ind Const Co (1915) 162 Ky 774, 173 SW 131.

§245. —Erroneous

Where an erroneous method of assessment is used, under an ordinance authorizing street improvements, the court is empowered by statute to make all corrections and orders that are necessary to do justice among the parties.

> **Ky** Specht v Barber Asphalt Paving (1904) 26 KLR 193, 80 SW 1106.

An ordinance levying a special assessment for street improvements, and assessing property owners on one side of the street at greater amounts than their awards of damages for property taken, while assessing owners on the other side of the street, having the same frontage, at only 10 or 12 per cent as much, is invalid as being unreasonable and arbitrary on its face.

> **Wash** Spokane v Kraft (1914) 82 Wash 238, 144 P 286.

Where it is not shown that an assessment, under an ordinance apportioning the costs of street improvements against abutting owners, in any way prejudices such owners, the method of apportionment adopted under the ordinance does not render it invalid.

> **Ky** Barber Asphalt Paving v Gaar (1903) 24 KLR 2260, 73 SW 1106.

Under an ordinance assessing the costs of street improvements the city may not combine separate and entirely different lots not used as one lot and assess them as a unit.

> **Ky**   Mt Sterling v Bishop (1929) 228 Ky 529, 15 SW2d 416.

If an ordinance levying an assessment for street improvements is plainly arbitrary or unreasonably discriminatory, whether by the front foot rule or not, it violates the due process and equal protection clauses of the Fourteenth Amendment, and will not be upheld.

> **SC**   Carolina & N W Ry v Clover (1931) 46 F2d 395.

§246. —Square Foot

A special assessment for curbs, streets, and storm sewers based on front foot, square foot assessment is valid. By affording the property owners notice of hearing and time to file objections the due process requirements have been met.

> **Colo**   Orchard Court Devel Co v Boulder (1973) 182 Colo 361, 513 P2d 199.
> Satter v Littleton (1974) 185 Colo 90, 522 P2d 95.

Since the legislature may authorize assessments for public improvements to be made according to the frontage of the lots benefited, and may also at the time of creation of taxing districts authorize assessments for local improvements based on valuation, superficial area or frontage, an ordinance of paving district apportioning costs by the square foot rule is valid.

> **Ky**   German Protestant Orphan Asylum v Barber Asphalt Paving (1904) 26 KLR 805, 82 SW 632.
> **La**   Hagmann v New Orleans (1938) 190 La 796, 182 So 753.

§247. —Front Foot

Front foot assessment for new paving is a valid method of apportioning cost. A determination that special benefits are greater to the owners further down the street is invalid and an unrealistic method of apportionment. The special benefits conferred are not for the amount of paved street traveled, but the lessening of dirt, noise, and mud.

> **Mich**   Carmichael v Beverly Hills (1971) 30 Mich Ap 176, 186 NW2d 29.

A charge per front foot against each improved lot, for street improvements, is reasonable, and is not an arbitrary or unreasonable classification. Occupied lots receive the benefit of the maintenance and improvements, and the tax is spread equally between all interested parties, whether owners or renters.

W Va   Moundsville v Steele (1968) 152 W Va 465, 164 SE2d 430.

A charter requirement that assessments shall not exceed the benefits received from the improvement is not violated by a front footage assessment. Exceptions for irregular shaped lots and corner lots do not constitute discrimination nullifying the assessment.

Mich   Davis v Westland (1973) 45 Mich Ap 497, 206 NW2d 750.

A special assessment for curbs, streets, and storm sewers based on front foot, square foot assessment is valid. By affording the property owners notice of hearing and time to file objections the due process requirements have been met.

Colo   Orchard Court Devel Co v Boulder (1973) 182 Colo 361, 513 P2d 199.
Satter v Littleton (1974) 185 Colo 90, 522 P2d 95.

Ordinarily, without authorizing an inquiry into the extent of the benefit received by particular property, a municipality may direct, by ordinance, that the cost of improvement of a street be assessed against abutting property by the front foot rule. It is manifestly impossible to apportion the cost in exact accord with benefits received, and this rule as nearly approximates just apportionment as any that could be devised.

Ill   Ryder's Est v Alton (1898) 175 Ill 94, 51 NE 821.
Ky   Louisville & Nashville v Garrard (1934) 255 Ky 127, 72 SW2d 1024.
Louisville & N RR v Southern Roads (1927) 217 Ky 575, 290 SW 320.
La   Hinkle v McGuire (1938) 190 La 397, 182 So 551.
Minden v Glass (1913) 132 La 927, 61 So 874.
Mo   Rackliffe-Gibson Const v Zeilda Forsee Inv (1914) 179 MoApp 229, 166 SW 849.
Ohio   Rice v Danville (1930) 36 OA 503, 8 Abs 574, 173 NE 621.
Ore   King v Portland (1902) 184 US 61, 46 LEd 431, 22 SCt 290.
SC   Carolina & N W Ry v Clover (1931) 46 F2d 395.
W Va   La Follette v Fairmont (1953) 138 W Va 157, 76 SE2d 572.

Assessments for street paving, following the front foot method, which are levied on the basis of the actual cost of paving each individual street, are in violation of the statute authorizing adoption of ordinances levying local or special assessments. If a single contract is let for the paving of several streets, the fact that the contract itemizes the cost per street is not sufficient to allow assessment on a street-by-street basis. Under the enabling statute, the front foot apportionment must be determined from the total contract price. While street-by-street assessment may be fairer to property owners, the language of the statute is clear and specific.

La   Pierson v East Baton Rouge Parish (1977) 353 So2d 726.

A street and curb assessment based strictly on the costs per front foot is invalid. The assessment must be based on the benefits conferred on the individual pieces of property and the assessment may not exceed the benefits received.

> **NJ**   McNally v Teaneck Township (1975) 132 NJS 442, 334 A2d 67.

An ordinance authorizing the paving of a street and providing for levying the costs by special assessment against property fronting thereon according to front footage without regard to benefits is unconstitutional as a taking of private property for public use without compensation, and as a deprivation of property without due process, the property owner not having been accorded his day in court.

> **Ky**   Zehnder v Barber Asphalt Paving (1901) 106 F 103.
> **Mo**   Fay v Springfield (1899) 94 F 409.

§ 248. —Proximity to Improvement

A street improvement assessment based on a larger percentage of benefit to adjoining owners and decreasing percentage at a distance from the project is valid. The engineer may be authorized to furnish costs and breakdown of expenses to the assessor for his determination of percentages.

> **NY**   So Ferry Street Project v Schenectady (1972) 72 Misc2d 134, 338 NYS2d 730.

Where the city council, as a board of equalization, adopted a zoning ordinance for the apportionment of assessments, so that property within the zone nearer to the paving was assessed with a higher per cent of the tax, the zone next farther removed with a median per cent, and so on, reducing the amount until the property in the farther zone was required to pay the least proportion, and where no evidence was introduced by the complaining property owners to show that the resulting assessment was not in accordance with or was in excess of benefits, the court should presume that the plan adopted was proper.

> **Neb**   Broghamer v Chadron (1922) 107 Neb 532, 186 NW 362.

§ 249. —Frontage Cost

A street paving ordinance that imposes a special assessment, on the principle of assessing each lot with the cost of improving that portion of the street in front of the lot, is void as imposing the burden unequally, and not in proportion to the overall benefits conferred.

> **Ill**   Davis v Litchfield (1893) 145 Ill 313, 33 NE 888.

An ordinance providing for the construction of a street improvement and assessing the cost to the frontage property is not void for failing to provide that the assessment must be in proportion to the special benefits conferred and not in excess thereof, or of 25 per cent of the value of the lot, as provided by statute.

Iowa Brush v Liscomb (1927) 202 Iowa 1155, 211 NW 856.

§250. —Street as Unit

An ordinance providing that apportionment of the costs of street improvements shall be made on a basis that treats each street as a separate unit or improvement, instead of adopting each block as a unit, is permissible.

Ky Elder v Richmond (1920) 186 Ky 706, 218 SW 239.

§251. —Width of Street

Where under an ordinance apportioning the costs of street improvements the city council makes assessments less against a narrow street than against a wide street, its action is fair and just since it may not be denied that it costs more to build a broad than it does a narrow street.

Ky Chesapeake & O Ry v Olive Hill (1929) 231 Ky 65, 21 SW2d 127.

§252. —Assessed Value

A determination to base a street construction assessment on appraised value requires that the property be viewed and appraised without its improvements. An assessment based on the tax roll appraisal of property with no valuation for exempted property is a violation of the statutory requirement. Likewise an assessment for ½ of the cost of a "T" intersection is improper since intersections are a city's expense.

Kan Dodson v Ulysses (1976) 219 Kan 418, 549 P2d 430.

A city, in fixing and determining the assessment of special benefits to be imposed against property owners in the enactment of a local improvement ordinance, is not required to take into consideration the assessed valuation of those properties for ad valorem tax purposes.

Wyo Marion v Lander (1964) 394 P2d 910.

Where the municipality provides that assessments in a condemnation proceeding shall be distributed in proportion to benefits received from removal of an elevated railway structure, an assessment in proportion to the assessed values of lands benefited is void.

> NY   6th Ave Elec RR, In re (1943) 181 Misc 1028, 50 NYS2d 363.

§ 253. Limitations

An assessment under an ordinance authorizing street improvements though it is in excess of the benefits received by the property is not a spoliation, since spoliation exists only in cases where the assessment exceeds the value of the property when improved.

> Ky   Duker v Barber Asphalt Paving (1903) 25 KLR 135, 74 SW 744.
> Pfaffinger v Kremer (1903) 24 KLR 2381, 74 SW 238.

Under a charter and ordinance providing for installment payments for an assessment exceeding half the value of the improved property, the right to impose an assessment exceeding half the actual value depends on the provision for installment payments. An owner not accepting the installment benefit reserves the right to discharge the debt at once; but if he refuses to pay, a judgment for foreclosure of the lien must be for the whole amount.

> Cal   Eaton v Hanlon (1924) 193 Cal 715, 227 P 484.

Where a statute limits assessments for local improvements to $33\,^1/_3$ per cent of the actual value of the property assessed after completion of the improvement, and the village council pursuant thereto, by ordinance, fixes the mode of payment, either in cash within 20 days or in 10 annual installments, and the owner elects to pay in installments, the interest charges on the installments are not in violation of the code, so long as he is given the option of paying it all in one payment, within the $33\,^1/_3$ per cent.

> Ohio   Wilcox v Edgerton (1921) 103 OS 267, 133 NE 78.

A paving assessment imposed by ordinance that includes as part of the assessment benefit a contract for street maintenance is void, where the charter limits the assessment on abutting owners to the cost of original construction. The city at large must bear the expenses of keeping pavement in repair. It is not necessary to prove what portion of the contract price represents the maintenance cost.

> NY   Segfried Const v New York City (1925) 124 Misc 622, 209 NYS 429.

An ordinance assessing a lot for street improvements is unenforceable to the extent that the assessment exceeds half of the value of such lot.

> Ky   Harris v Hummel (1922) 195 Ky 359, 242 SW 356.

§254. Costs Subject to

The reasonable costs of engineering, inspection and administrative services performed by city employees in connection with an ordinance levying a special street paving assessment are actual costs of the improvement, and, are includable in the assessments.

La Thalheim v Gretna (1937) 171 So 591.
Mich Sawicki v Harper Woods (1965) 1 Mich Ap 352, 136 NW2d 691.

In the absence of ordinance or charter authority, extras or incidentals incurred in making a public improvement, such as supervisory charges of an unsalaried city engineer, the cost of an abstract showing the names of the owners of the affected property, and clerical costs in making up the assessment, may not be assessed against property benefited.

Ore Giles v Roseburg (1916) 82 Ore 67, 160 P 543.

A city has authority to authorize street improvements and assess the costs on its own abutting owners for an improvement that goes only to the middle of the street, where the street is the boundary line between it and another city.

Ky Central Covington v Busse (1904) 25 KLR 2179, 80 SW 210.

§255. —Bridge

An ordinance providing for the construction of a bridge in the city is not for a "local improvement", within the statute authorizing cities to levy special assessments for local improvements, since the bridge is in the nature of a public improvement, benefiting all the inhabitants of the city.

Ill Chicago Heights v Walls (1926) 319 Ill 411, 150 NE 241.

§256. —County Road

An ordinance providing for a street improvement and payment of a part of the cost from taxes on assessable property in the city is invalid where the street is a county road. A city cannot lay out money raised by taxation for improving a county road within its borders.

Ore Cooper v Fox (1918) 87 Ore 657, 171 P 408.
Cole v Seaside (1916) 80 Ore 73, 156 P 569.

§257. —Curbing

Under an ordinance assessing abutting owners for street improvements on an installment plan, curbing may be properly included as part of the construction costs of the street, rather than the sidewalk.

> **Ky**   Hoerth v Sturgis (1927) 221 Ky 835, 299 SW 1074.

§258. —Driveway

A property owner subjected to a paving assessment under an ordinance is not estopped to contest an extra charge resulting from construction of a driveway into the premises of an adjoining owner, though such construction was part of the paving contract and made with his acquiescence.

> **La**   DeRidder v Lewis (1916) 139 La 903, 72 So 447.

§259. —Engineering Fees

Where a statute mandatorily requires a city to employ a competent engineer, it is improper under an ordinance apportioning street improvement assessments among property owners to include engineers' fees.

> **Ky**   Frankfort v Jillson (1928) 225 Ky 61, 7 SW2d 859.

An ordinance assessing the cost of street improvements against abutting property owners, including the five per cent charged for engineering services and the actual cost of publishing notices, is valid.

> **Okla**   Tulsa v Weston (1924) 102 Okla 222, 229 P 108.
> **Ore**   Gamma Alpha Bldg v Eugene (1919) 94 Ore 80, 184 P 973.

§260. —Intersections

A statute empowering a city to levy a special assessment against property for an amount not exceeding the actual value of the improvement is sufficiently broad to authorize the city to include the cost of improving intersecting streets and alleys in the charge against the property benefited; and that is a matter within the discretion of the city council that the courts will not review.

> **Mo**   Blackwell v Lee's Summit (1930) 326 Mo 491, 32 SW2d 63.
> **Wash**   Lewis v Seattle (1902) 28 Wash 639, 69 P 393.

§261. —Light Poles

An ordinance assessing the cost of ornamental electric light poles to the abutting property owners is valid as for a street improvement.

> **Ore** Fisher v Astoria (1928) 126 Ore 268, 269 P 853, 60 ALR 260.

§262. —Oiling

An ordinance authorizing the oiling of streets, the cost to be assessed by special tax bills against abutting property, is valid, though not for a permanent improvement.

> **Ky** Sebree v Powell (1927) 221 Ky 478, 298 SW 1103.
> **Mo** Scales v Butler (1959) 323 SW2d 25.
> Laclede v Libby (1926) 221 MoApp 703, 285 SW 178.

§263. —Repairs

Where an assessment under a street improvement ordinance is increased on account of a requirement of an ordinance that the contractor guarantee to keep the pavement in repair the increased cost is properly chargeable against the city and not against abutting owners, because abutting owners may be charged with original construction but the city must pay the costs of repairs.

> **Ark** Searcy Federal Sav & Loan Assn v Searcy (1952) 221 Ark 360, 253 SW2d 211.
> **Ky** Covington v Bullock (1907) 126 Ky 236, 103 SW 276.
> Louisville v Selvage (1899) 106 Ky 730, 51 SW 447.
> **Mo** Cushing v Fleming (1910) 151 MoApp 471, 132 SW 52.

ANNOTATION

What constitutes reconstruction or the like, as distinguished from repair, of pavement, 41 ALR2d 613.

§264. —Sodding

A city has power to enact an ordinance assessing the cost of placing sod on each side of a cement sidewalk and is not limited to merely assessing the costs of the cement walkway itself, where a muddy and slippery and unsafe condition would otherwise result.

> **Ky** Holmes v Heeter & Son (1912) 146 Ky 52, 142 SW 210.

§ 265. —Sprinkling

An ordinance providing for the sprinkling of streets and assessing the cost against abutting property owners does not violate the owners' constitutional right to due process of law, where it also provides for the assessment of the cost according to frontage of the lots bordering on the streets within the district. Accordingly, a lien placed on property for nonpayment of assessments may be foreclosed.

> **NM**   Roswell v Bateman (1915) 20 NM 77, 146 P 950.

A statute authorizing a municipal corporation to assess by ordinance the cost of street sprinkling on abutting land in proportion to frontage, without reference to benefits, is invalid.

> **Ky**   McCormack v Henderson (1908) 33 KLR 854, 111 SW 368.
> **Mich**   Stevens v Port Huron (1907) 149 Mich 536, 113 NW 291.

§ 266. Benefits, Property Owners

Street improvements have been held to provide special benefits to abutting owners, and there is no need for the city to make an express showing of the special benefit received by the individual. The assessment can only be overturned if it is an arbitrary and unwarranted exercise or a denial of equal protection. Where the largest proportion of the assessment was borne by the city it will be assumed that the landowner received benefits for his portion.

> **Fla**   Bodner v Coral Gables (1971) 245 So2d 250.

The foundation of the power to enact an ordinance imposing a special assessment or special tax for a local improvement of any character is the benefit which the object of the assessment or tax confers on owners of abutting properties or owners in the assessment or special district, which differs from the general benefits which such owners enjoy in common with other inhabitants of the municipality.

> **Cal**   Donovan v Los Angeles (1930) 209 CA 552, 288 P 1083.
> **La**   Alexandria v Chicago, R I & P RR (1961) 240 La 1025, 126 So2d 351, 97 ALR2d 1073.
> **Mo**   Oak St, In re (1925) 308 Mo 494, 273 SW 105.
> **NJ**   Appeal of Pub Service Elec & Gas (1952) 18 NJS 357, 87 A2d 344.
> **Ohio**   Pickering Hardware v Cincinnati (1948) 149 OS 275, 36 Op 577, 78 NE2d 563.

The assessment for widening a street from a poorly maintained and repaired 18-foot street to a 40-foot street contains both special and general benefits. The abutting owners are not liable for the general benefits to the public particularly when the improvement was made to facilitate overall transportation and expansion of the city, but only for special benefits particular to their tract.

> **Iowa** Goodell v Clinton (1971) 193 NW2d 91.

A change of grade for a dead end street into a four laned heavy traffic thoroughfare does not confer a benefit on the adjoining owners. There is no liability to pay a special assessment as they receive no benefit and actually suffer a detriment to their property.

> **Mo** DeFraties v Kansas City (1975) 521 SW2d 385.

Where an ordinance authorizes a street improvement, whether a parcel of land would or would not be benefited is a legislative, not a judicial, question.

> **Mo** West v Burke (1921) 286 Mo 358, 228 SW 775.

The city council is not required to insert in the resolution containing assessments for paving, a finding that the benefits are equal and uniform.

> **Neb** Superior v Simpson (1926) 114 Neb 698, 209 NW 505.

Where an ordinance authorizes the opening and establishment of a street, assessment of the costs therefor may not be limited as to lots in the benefit district, to actual benefits, but must be assessed as a single improvement made up of various united elements.

> **Mo** Twenty-Third St Traffic Way, In re (1919) 279 Mo 249, 214 SW 109.

§267. —Presumptions

The usual presumption is that a local improvement is for the special benefit of the property assessed.

> **Md** Silver Spring Memorial Post v Montgomery County (1955) 207 Md 442, 115 A2d 249.
> Maryland & P Ry v Nice (1945) 185 Md 429, 45 A2d 109.

To overcome the presumption of validity of a special assessment for street, sidewalk, sewer, and gutter the property owner must show by substantial competent evidence that no benefit was received.

> **Colo** Cline v Boulder (1975) 35 ColoAp 349, 532 P2d 770.

A determination that property benefits from street construction will only be set aside when it is arbitrary and unreasonable. The fact that the street does not directly connect to a through street and is required because of an adjacent subdivision does not make the determination invalid.

> **Ore** Western Amusement Co v Springfield (1975) 21 OreAp 7, 533 P2d 825.

An ordinance imposing a special assessment for street paving is not discriminatory for failure to assess certain property on the street, since the mere fact that certain real estate is contiguous to an improvement is not conclusive evidence that it is specially benefited.

> **Ill**   Holdom v Chicago (1897) 169 Ill 109, 48 NE 164.

§268. —Necessity

In a street improvement district there must be a finding of special benefit to the abutting owners, but the fact that other facilities serve the parcels and that the street will be a public improvement do not preclude a finding of special benefit.

> **Haw**   Brock v Lemke (1969) 51 Haw 175, 455 P2d 1.

An improvement district assessment that confers no special benefits on the property owners is invalid; but where benefits are conferred the owners should bear their fair proportion of costs.

> **Neb**   Gilliam v Lincoln (1969) 183 Neb 847, 164 NW2d 658.

A special assessment for pavement widening, which changes a quiet residential street into a thoroughfare to reach a recreation area, is not a benefit to the residential owners. No special assessment is justified against them, though special assessments may be shown to the commercial ventures on the street.

> **Mich**   Cusumano v Detroit (1971) 30 Mich Ap 603, 186 NE2d 740.

The cost of improving a railroad crossing may not be included in a paving assessment. There is no special benefit to the abutting owners over and above that received by the general residents of the city.

> **Ore**   Sisters of St Mary v Beaverton (1970) 4 OreAp 297, 478 P2d 412.

Where a city enacts an ordinance levying special taxes, the only foundation is the special benefits conferred by the improvement, and a local assessment beyond the special benefits is a taking of private property for public use without compensation.

> **Neb**   Hayman v Grand Island (1939) 135 Neb 873, 284 NW 733.

To justify a special assessment for a local improvement such as the paving of a street, there must be both a public purpose and a special benefit to the properties assessed, over and above that accruing to the public.

> **Ariz**   Collins v Phoenix (1931) 54 F2d 770.
> **Cal**   Taylor v Palmer (1866) 31 Cal 240.
> **Md**   Silver Spring Memorial Post v Montgomery County (1955) 207 Md 442, 115 A2d 249.
>   Maryland & P Ry v Nice (1945) 185 Md 429, 45 A2d 109.

The constitutional provisions against the taking of private property for private or public use are applicable when a city attempts to impose a special assessment against properties that will not be benefited by the improvement.

> **Md** Maryland & P Ry v Nice (1945) 185 Md 429, 45 A2d 109.
> **Okla** Lawton v Akers (1958) 333 P2d 520.

§269. —Exceptions

A lot owner may be compelled to pay his portion of the cost of a street improvement under an ordinance though his property is not benefited thereby unless he can show that the cost of the improvement is equal to or greater than the value of the property improved.

> **Ariz** Collins v Phoenix (1931) 54 F2d 770.
> **Ky** Otter v Barber Asphalt Paving (1906) 29 KLR 1157, 96 SW 862.

§270. —Determination

Where land is taken by eminent domain the award may not be offset by the special benefits against the particular land. The separate procedures for special benefits must be followed as applied to all of the persons at the one hearing. If the award in condemnation could be offset a particular owner might be paying a greater proportion of the special benefits than the balance of the people benefited.

> **Minn** St Louis Park v Engell (1969) 283 Minn 309, 168 NW2d 3.

An ordinance establishing a front footage assessment for curb and gutter is invalid when the city fails to produce any evidence as to the benefit to the property owner. A remand was ordered in order to enable the city to furnish proof of the benefit to the adjoining owners.

> **Tex** Garcia v Alice (1974) 505 SW2d 611.

Costs of an improvement district established for sidewalks and bicycle paths may be assessed against the adjoining owners on showing of benefit to the property. The fact that residents within the district, which is residential and commercial, would receive more benefits due to the distance involved than parties outside of the district constitutes a sufficient benefit.

> **Ore** Chrysler Corp v Beaverton (1976) 25 OreAp 361, 549 P2d 678.

A paving assessment for an improvement consisting of replacing a two-lane asphalt road with four-lane concrete, construction of driveover type curbs and elimination of roadside drainage ditches confers a benefit on the property owners. The improvements alone with the esthetic improvement constitute a benefit sufficient for a front foot assessment.

> **La** Butaud v Lake Charles (1976) 338 So2d 358.

The determination by the city council that abutting property is benefited by a local improvement is a legislative matter that is not subject to review by the court, in the absence of fraud or arbitrary action.

> **Fla** Lots 1685 v DeFuniak Springs (1937) 127 Fla 348, 174 So 29.
> **Ill** Mushbaugh v East Peoria (1913) 260 Ill 27, 102 NE 1027.
> **NY** Baldwin Street in Rochester, In re (1915) 169 AD 128, 154 NYS 728.
> **Ore** Wagoner v La Grande (1918) 89 Ore 192, 173 P 305.
> **Wash** Northern Pac Ry v Seattle (1907) 46 Wash 674, 91 P 244.

An ordinance assessing costs of a street improvement may be valid notwithstanding a claim that the assessment charge exceeds actual benefit. A city council's determination of benefit is conclusive, in the absence of fraud or demonstrable mistake of fact.

> **Ore** Reiff v Portland (1914) 71 Ore 421, 142 P 827.

Whether property charged by a special assessment ordinance is benefited by the improvement is a judicial question, but the scope of review is limited. In the absence of fraud or mistake, the determination of the proper administrative body is conclusive.

> **Ore** East 3rd St Improvement Dist v Bend (1963) 234 Ore 91, 380 P2d 625.

§271. —Validity

Special assessments imposed in local improvement ordinances, to be valid, must be levied in the ratio of benefits, and must be imposed equally on all property equally benefited.

> **Ill** Springfield v Gillespie (1929) 335 Ill 388, 167 NE 61.

A statement that garbage collection would be made from the rear of the complainant's residence, made at the time of protesting a paving assessment, does not affect the validity of the assessment. It does not affect the question of the existence or amount of special benefit resulting from the improvement.

> **Tex** Armstrong v Dallas (1970) 461 SW2d 226.

A street paving ordinance will be declared invalid where the special assessment imposed exceeds the amount of benefits to the property sought to be charged.

> **Tex** Beatty v Panhandle Const (1925) 275 SW 716.
> **W Va** N Y Cent RR v Glasgow (1956) 142 W Va 291, 95 SE2d 420.

A street improvement ordinance directing a special assessment of a certain amount to be assessed on the real estate deemed benefited, without reference to whether the property is actually benefited to that amount, is invalid as being in disregard of the principle of equality between burden and benefit in the levy of special assessments.

> **Ill** Greeley v People (1871) 60 Ill 19.
> **Ore** Morgan v Portland (1909) 53 Ore 368, 100 P 657.

Where the physical facts are such that the property is not and could not have been specially benefited in any amount, or could not have benefited to any extent approaching the assessment the levy of assessment is arbitrary and constructively fraudulent, and therefore void and subject to collateral attack.

> **Ky** Zehnder v Barber Asphalt Paving (1901) 106 F 103.
> **Mich** Dix-Ferndale Taxpayers v Detroit (1932) 258 Mich 390, 242 NW 732.
> **Neb** Chicago & NW Ry v Omaha (1953) 156 Neb 705, 57 NW2d 753.
> **Okla** Lawton v Akers (1958) 333 P2d 520.
> Tulsa v McCormick (1917) 63 Okla 238, 164 P 985.

An ordinance levying paving assessments according to frontage and without inquiry into the benefits to be derived by the property owner does not automatically or solely for that reason constitute a taking of property without due process of law.

> **La** Alexandria v Chicago, R I & P RR (1961) 240 La 1025, 126 So2d 351, 97 ALR2d 1073.

That as part of a street improvement program the city assumed a portion of the costs, but by ordinance imposed an assessment on property owners specially benefited by the extension of the improvement into a less traveled area, does not deny the assessed abutting owners of equal protection of the laws, since the point at which traffic conditions will not warrant imposition of the entire cost on the city as a whole is a matter of legislative discretion, subject to review only if the action is arbitrary or capricious.

> **NY** People v Marvin (1936) 249 AD 293, 292 NYS 93.

Ordinances placing real estate in more than one improvement district are valid if the land receives benefits from the improvements being constructed in each district.

> **Ark** Harrison v Abington (1919) 140 Ark 115, 215 SW 255.

Where an ordinance levying an assessment for the cost of paving a street is attacked on the ground that no special benefits have accrued to the abutting properties, the burden rests on the contestants to establish that fact, and a finding by the trial court on conflicting evidence will not be disturbed on review unless plainly wrong.

    W Va   Bowling v Bluefield (1927) 104 W Va 589, 140 SE 685.

The validity of a street improvement assessment may not be impeached by evidence that part of the assessed costs of the improvement exceeded the benefits.

    Cal   Duncan v Ramish (1904) 142 Cal 686, 76 P 661.

§272. —Description of Improvement

In order to supply a basis for local assessment for improvements, an ordinance should be reasonably certain and definite as to character, location, and description of the improvements, so that from it an intelligent estimate can be made of the nature and extent of the improvements.

    Cal   Bay Rock v Bell (1901) 133 Cal 150, 65 P 299.
    Pa   Weatherly v Warner (1942) 148 PaS 557, 25 A2d 831.

§273. —Sufficient

A street improvement ordinance must be of such specificity as reasonably will inform the assessed owners as to the nature of the improvement, its cost, and the property to be assessed.

    Ill   People ex rel Wilson v Wabash Ry (1938) 368 Ill 497, 14 NE2d 650.
        Springfield v Gillespie (1929) 335 Ill 388, 167 NE 61.
    Mo   Blair v Glenn (1915) 187 MoApp 392, 172 SW 1195.
        Cushing v Fleming (1910) 151 MoApp 471, 132 SW 52.
    Neb   Chittenden v Kibler (1917) 100 Neb 756, 161 NW 272.
    NY   Ransom, Appeal of (1914) 87 Misc 1, 149 NYS 1056.
    Ore   Klovdahl v Springfield (1916) 81 Ore 168, 158 P 668.
        Rubin v Salem (1911) 58 Ore 91, 112 P 713.

§274. —Insufficient

A street improvement ordinance is invalid as insufficient and indefinite where it fails reasonably to apprise the assessed owners of the nature of the improvement, its cost, and the owners to be assessed.

    Cal   Peck v Stassforth (1909) 156 Cal 201, 103 P 918.
    Ill   People ex rel Franklin v Wabash RR (1944) 387 Ill 450, 56 NE2d 820.
        Chicago v Cummings (1911) 250 Ill 423, 95 NE 478.
    Ore   Dyer v Bandon (1913) 68 Ore 406, 136 P 652.
    Tex   Uvalde Rock Asphalt v Lacy (1939) 131 SW2d 698.

§275. Challenge by Property Owners

An ordinance approving a street improvement district consisting of two or more streets is valid when less than 2/3 of the property owners object to the project. The fact that over 2/3 on a particular block remonstrance against the project does not require that it be removed from the district when the feasibility of the project depends on including all of the property.

> **Ore**   Aldahl v Corvallis (1977) 28 OreAp 683, 560 P2d 678.

Where a property owner is liable for a paving assessment levied under an ordinance, the court will not receive evidence that the paving was badly done. The only proper defense to the assessment would be that the contract was fraudulent, or was not made in good faith.

> **Va**   Alexandria v Mandeville (1820) 1 FC 393.

In attacking the validity of an assessment ordinance for street improvements an owner must point out in what particular the assessment is unequal, illegal, erroneous, or void.

> **Ky**   Jones v Carey Const (1949) 311 Ky 704, 225 SW2d 301.

An objection to a street paving ordinance, that provision for a new curb when the present curb is in good condition is unreasonable, presents a legislative matter for determination by council, and the provision will not be held invalid unless the council's determination is manifestly unreasonable and arbitrary.

> **Ill**   Chicago Union Traction v Chicago (1906) 223 Ill 37, 79 NE 67.

§276. —Notice

Landowners are not exempt from paying assessments due and owing for street improvements because the city failed to publish the improvement resolution or because there were discrepancies in the dates stated in the apportionment ordinance.

> **Ky**   Thomas v Berea (1977) 557 SW2d 214.

Though the city has actual knowledge of the names of affected owners, it is not necessary that personal notice of the creation of an improvement district be sent to them by mail. The following of publication and posting requirements is sufficient, since the determination to institute a public improvement district is legislative.

> **Ore**   Brown v Salem (1968) 251 Ore 150, 444 P2d 936.

Notice requirements for imposition of an assessment are mandatory, and where the ordinance does not make any provision the statutory requirements prevail.

> **Ore**   Brown v Salem (1968) 251 Ore 150, 444 P2d 936.

A special assessment ordinance providing only for notice and opportunity to protest concerning assessment amount after completion of the local improvement not also providing for notice and opportunity to protest construction and assessment district boundaries prior to actual construction of the local improvement, is invalid, in that both notice provisions are required by statute, unless the ordinance provides equivalent substitute procedures.

> **Md**   Mylander v Baltimore (1934) 166 Md 658, 172 A 234.
> **Ore**   Bennet v Oceanlake (1967) 247 Ore 539, 430 P2d 1004.
> **W Va**   Herbert Heller & Co v Charleston-Dunbar Traction (1932) 112
>   W Va 299, 164 SE 853.

§277. —Presumptions

An ordinance ordering street improvements and levying assessments is presumed to be regular, and the burden is on the party attacking the legality of the proceedings to show that they were irregular.

> **Neb**   Chicago St P M & O Ry v Randolph (1957) 163 Neb 687, 81 NW2d 159.
>   Chicago & NW Ry v Omaha (1953) 156 Neb 705, 57 NW2d 753.
> **NY**   Pinkus v Hempstead (1962) 225 NYS2d 959.
> **Okla**   Rawlins v Warner-Quinlan Asphalt Co (1918) 70 Okla 309, 174 P 526.

In the case of objection by one joint tenant to a street improvement district created by ordinance, in which the other joint tenant has not joined, a presumption arises that the one objecting represents the entire property and his joint tenant, which presumption obtains unless the contrary is made to appear.

> **Neb**   Bonner v Imperial (1948) 149 Neb 721, 32 NW2d 267.

§278. —Fraud

In attacking the validity of an assessment ordinance for street improvements on the ground of fraud on the part of the city's legislative body it is essential to specify the acts or conduct constituting the alleged fraud, since public officials are presumed to have acted lawfully in the performance of their duties to the public.

> **Ky**   Jones v Carey Const (1949) 311 Ky 704, 225 SW2d 301.

Where fraud exists in the acceptance of bids for a street paving contract, property owners subject to the ordinance levying an assessment have an adequate remedy at law in their right to defend a proceeding to foreclose assessments against their property.

Iowa Swan v Indianola (1909) 142 Iowa 731, 121 NW 547.

§279. —Right to Challenge

A special assessment imposed by ordinance may be protested even by those who petitioned for the improvement.

Ore Temple v Portland (1915) 77 Ore 559, 151 P 724.

Where the charter requires that property assessed by ordinance for a street improvement abut on the improvement, only nonabutting assessed property owners may challenge the ordinance, for an assessment on nonabutting property.

Ore Birnie v La Grande (1915) 78 Ore 531, 153 P 415.

An ordinance allowing property owners 10 days after a hearing on street improvements within which to bring suit to contest the validity of any proceeding with respect thereto is valid, and will preclude the maintenance of any action not relating to jurisdictional matters after the 10-day period.

Ky Raceland v McCoy (1934) 254 Ky 827, 72 SW2d 454.
La Amen v Pineville (1964) 247 La 89, 170 So2d 1.
NY Del Lackawanna & W RR v Assessors (1961) 12 AD2d 852, 209 NYS2d 942.
Okla Wright v El Reno (1934) 168 Okla 594, 35 P2d 473.
Tex Vilbig Bros v Dallas (1935) 80 SW2d 784.

ANNOTATION

Cotenancy as factor in determining representation of property owners in petition for or remonstrance against a public improvement, 3 ALR2d 127.

§280. —Procedure; Remedies

Where an entire assessment made against certain property, by ordinance, for a street improvement, is illegal or substantially in excess of benefits, it is not necessary for the owner to tender, as a condition of relief in equity, any sum as representing what he supposes or is willing to concede is the excess of cost over the benefit.

Iowa Iowa Pipe & Tile v Callanan (1904) 125 Iowa 358, 101 NW 141.

447

Where a city council improperly placed a person's property in a special assessment district and thereafter denied his protest, he may renew his protest in a court of equity.

> **Mich**   Dix-Ferndale Taxpayers v Detroit (1932) 258 Mich 390, 242 NW 732.

Where property owners are aggrieved by the disposition of a sum paid to the village in connection with improvement assessments, their remedies lie elsewhere than in a proceeding to review the assessments.

> **NY**   Eckhart v Zion (1958) 12 Misc2d 344, 172 NYS2d 363.

An ordinance, providing for the levy of a street paving assessment and for the contesting of assessments by affidavits of illegality does not violate due process.

> **Ga**   Lewis v Augusta (1959) 215 Ga 427, 110 SE2d 665.

§ 281. —Injunction

A court of equity may grant an injunction to prevent the collection of void assessments against private property to pay for special benefits resulting from the paving of streets.

> **Neb**   Sioux City Bridge v South Sioux City (1924) 112 Neb 271, 199 NW 528.
> Rooney v South Sioux City (1923) 111 Neb 1, 195 NW 474.
> **Okla**   St Louis & S F RR v Ada (1917) 66 Okla 80, 167 P 619.

§ 282. Estoppel; Laches

A landowner having notice of a special assessment for street improvements and paying one installment and part of another is precluded from contesting the validity of the assessment. Laches and estoppel arise from the three-year-delay in contesting.

> **Mich**   Romisch v Feder (1974) 222 NW2d 782.

A property owner cannot stand by and permit a contractor to improve the streets abutting his property under a contract authorized by an ordinance, and then after the work is accepted by the city attack the proceedings under which the work was done for minor irregularities that do not render the proceedings void.

> **Colo**   Trinidad v Madrid (1926) 80 Colo 210, 250 P 158.
> **Haw**   McCandless v Honolulu (1918) 24 Haw 524.
> **Iowa**   Marshalltown Light Power & Ry v Marshalltown (1905) 127 Iowa 637, 103 NW 1005.

Ky   Bradshaw v Yager (1953) 265 SW2d 486.
        Rlty Sav Co v Southern Asphaltoilene Co (1918) 180 Ky 242, 202 SW 679.
Neb   Wookey v Alma (1929) 118 Neb 158, 223 NW 953.
        Kister v Hastings (1922) 108 Neb 476, 187 NW 909.
Okla Wey v Hobart (1917) 66 Okla 175, 168 P 433.
        Kerker v Bocher (1908) 20 Okla 729, 95 P 981.
Ore   Paget v Pendleton (1959) 219 Ore 253, 346 P2d 1111.
        Wingate v Astoria (1901) 39 Ore 603, 65 P 982.
SC   Cleveland v Spartanburg (1937) 185 SC 373, 194 SE 128.
        Ballentine v Columbia (1924) 129 SC 410, 124 SE 643.
W Va La Follette v Fairmont (1953) 138 W Va 517, 76 SE2d 572.

§283. —Payment, Effect

Protesting landowners against whom a special assessment is imposed by ordinance may not contest the validity of the ordinance after making payment under it, even under protest.

Ore Bechtell v Salem (1960) 226 Ore 1, 358 P2d 563.

§284. —Laches

Where a property owner made no objection on the enactment of an ordinance for the erection of a concrete pavement and curb, and no objection to the ordinance assessing the costs, and did not appeal to the Circuit Court for the purpose of objecting to the improvements, but applied for certiorari five months after confirmation of the assessment, he is barred by laches from contesting the proceedings.

NJ Pico v North Arlington (1928) 7 NJM 22, 143 A 861.

§285. —When No Estoppel

A property owner is not estopped to assert irregularity of a special assessment ordinance, where the irregularity is of such a character as to defeat the jurisdiction of the city to act.

Ky   Henderson v Lieber Exr (1917) 175 Ky 15, 192 SW 830.
La   State v Shreveport (1932) 142 So 641.
Neb   Cullingham v Omaha (1943) 143 Neb 744, 10 NW2d 615.
Mich Forest Hill Cemetery v Ann Arbor (1942) 303 Mich 56, 5 NW2d 564.
Ore   Baker City Mutual Irr v Baker City (1911) 58 Ore 306, 113 P 9.
        Strout v Portland (1894) 26 Ore 294, 38 P 126.

Where a property owner has notice that his property is to be assessed for benefits by reason of a public improvement, and a law affords him an opportunity to appear and protest, and, if aggrieved to appeal to the courts, but he neglects to avail himself of such provisions, he may not thereafter, in a collateral proceeding, attack the validity of the assessment, except for fraud, actual or constructive, a fundamental defect, or entire want of jurisdiction.

> **Neb**　Wead v Omaha (1933) 124 Neb 474, 247 NW 24.

§286. Exemptions

In the absence of express authorization, a municipality has no power to exempt land or other property from special assessments.

> **Md**　Church Home & Infirmary v Baltimore (1940) 176 Md 326, 13 A2d 596.

A street improvement ordinance providing that no error in the proceedings shall exempt any property from the lien of the assessments after the work has been done and accepted, and permitting a court to make corrections to do justice to all parties, is valid.

> **Ky**　Newport v Silva (1911) 143 Ky 704, 137 SW 546.

An ordinance assessing street improvement costs is not invalid merely because the affected property owners had formerly paid for an elevated roadway on the street under a charter provision that their property would thereafter be exempt from special taxes for future street maintenance, where such charter provision was subsequently amended. The amendment was not a violation of any contract with the property holders.

> **Ore**　Hochfeld v Portland (1914) 72 Ore 190, 142 P 824.

ANNOTATION

Exemption from special assessment, of property of agricultural fair society or association, 89 ALR2d 1113.

§287. —Cemeteries

See **CEMETERIES; MAUSOLEUMS; CREMATORIES,** Volume 1B

§288. —Public Property

Since special assessments for local improvements are not taxes in the strict sense of that term, property held for a public use is not exempt from such assessments. A statute exempting from taxation public buildings belonging to a county will not prevent enactment of a city ordinance levying an assessment on the county courthouse to defray the cost of paving the street in front of the courthouse.

Ill Adams County v Quincy (1889) 130 Ill 566, 22 NE 624.
Ky Mt Sterling v Montgomery County (1913) 152 Ky 637, 153 SW 952.
Mo State v Sch Dist Of Kansas City (1933) 333 Mo 288, 62 SW2d 813.
Okla Blythe v Tulsa (1935) 172 Okla 586, 46 P2d 310.

An assessment for street improvements may not exclude public property abutting the street.

La Williams v Shreveport (1970) 241 So2d 598.

A school district is not subject to an assessment for street improvement in the absence of authorization for expenditure of the funds. It is not necessary that they contest the ordinance within 15 days since the assessment is void, not voidable.

Tex Garland v Garland Indep Sch Dist (1971) 468 SW2d 110.

§289. Notice

An ordinance assessing costs of a local improvement is valid where the notice given is sufficient to apprise a man of ordinary intelligence that the improvement is contemplated. No particular form of notice is essential.

La Selber v Lake Charles (1960) 122 So2d 661.
Mo St Louis v Bell Place Rlty (1914) 259 Mo 126, 168 SW 721.
Ore Manley v Marshfield (1918) 88 Ore 482, 172 P 488.
   Paulsen v Portland (1893) 149 US 30, 37 LEd 637, 13 SCt 750.

§290. —Constructive

A paving assessment is valid against a subsequent purchaser. The owner at the time of determination being afforded due process the subsequent purchaser prior to completion of the project has been adequately protected.

Md Murphy v Montgomery County (1972) 267 Md 224, 297 A2d 249.

Notwithstanding that a property owner does not have actual knowledge of an ordinance levying an assessment for street paving, he will be held to have constructive knowledge after a period of eight years and after having received the benefits of the paving.

SC Blake v Spartanburg (1937) 185 SC 398, 194 SE 124, 114 ALR 395.

§291. Referendum

An ordinance authorizing street improvements and the issuance of bonds chargeable to the district to be benefited is not a matter required by the Constitution to be submitted to the taxpayers.

Ariz   Collins v Phoenix (1931) 54 F2d 770.

Street improvements are not public utilities, within the constitutional provision requiring approval by the voters of any ordinance incurring an indebtedness larger than a specified amount for the purchase, construction, or repair of public utilities to be owned exclusively by the city.

Okla   Dingman v Sapulpa (1910) 27 Okla 116, 111 P 319.

A street improvement ordinance and levy of special taxes will stand where, under a statute providing for defeat of the ordinance if the owners of two thirds of the abutting property file objections, two thirds of the owners do file objections, but prior to the time set for final filing enough of the owners withdraw their objections to reduce the objecting total to less than two thirds of the owners in interest.

Utah   Salt Lake & Utah Ry v Payson (1926) 66 Utah 251, 244 P 138.

§292. Reassessment

A special street improvement district may not be extended to include recently annexed land. When the land was outside the city limits at the time of initiating the improvement district and the work has been virtually completed and the improvement bond sold a new district including the recently acquired land may not be established covering the costs of the initial district.

ND   Dakota Land Co v Fargo (1974) 224 NW2d 810.

A special assessment for paving which is rendered void due to the failure to pass a resolution of necessity does not preclude reassessment by the city. The reassessment may be on the city's own authority or on order of the court holding the original assessment void.

SD   LeRoy v Rapid City (1972) 86 SD 201, 193 NW2d 598.

On reassessment by ordinance of property within a special assessment district, statutory notice and hearing requirements must be complied with as on original assessment, whether the charge on the reassessed property be increased or decreased.

Ore   Wing v Eugene (1968) 249 Ore 367, 437 P2d 836.

An ordinance may **reassess street** improvement costs where the resolution supporting it recites **that an earlier** assessment was set aside by the Circuit Court.

Ore   Hochfeld v Portland (1914) 72 Ore 190, 142 P 824.

A special assessment **ordinance reassessing** improved property because the original assessment **was procedurally** invalid cannot be reviewed by a Federal Court for an alleged **violation of the** Fourteenth Amendment, where such allegation is merely **a legal conclusion.**

Ore   Lord v Salem (1922) 282 F 720.

§293. —Authority

Reassessments for **highway purposes** are not to be made except where there has been an original **assessment which** has been set aside by appropriate action.

NM   Assessment Paving Dist 5, In re (1958) 65 NM 25, 331 P2d 526.
Okla   Norman v Allen (1915) 47 Okla 74, 147 P 1002.
Ore   Brown v Portland (1920) 97 Ore 600, 190 P 722.

A city cannot make **a reassessment for** street improvements, against abutting property and its owner, **after collection** of the original assessment has become barred by the statute **of limitations that** was pleaded in a suit thereon.

Okla   Oklahoma City v Eastland (1929) 135 Okla 155, 274 P 651.
Tex   Big Spring v Tate (1942) 162 SW2d 1066.

The power of a city **to enact** an ordinance reassessing costs of a local improvement is not **inherent in the** city, and can be exercised only in a manner prescribed by statute.

Ore   Brown v Portland (1920) 97 Ore 600, 190 P 722.

§294. —Enforcement

An ordinance reassessing **costs of a** local improvement against protesting property owners is **enforceable against** them after an appeal to the Circuit Court, as provided **by the charter, has** been decided against them.

Ore   West v Scott-McClure Land (1917) 84 Ore 296, 164 P 554.
     Portland v Nottingham & Co (1911) 58 Ore 1, 113 P 28.

§295. —Mandamus

Where a city council determines, from an accountant's report, that a sidewalk improvement district is not indebted to the extent that prompted passage of a reassessment ordinance, the council is without power, on objection by property owners in the district, to repeal the ordinance passed pursuant to statute, where no property owner appealed the ordinance within the time provided by law. A bank holding notes of the city for the improvements is thus entitled to mandamus to compel reassessment of the property in accordance with the ordinance, and to judgment in the amount of the notes with interest.

Ark Camden v Merchants & Planters Bk (1936) 191 Ark 1139, 89 SW2d 739.

§296. —Validity

Where a charter allows reassessment by ordinance following a defect in special assessment proceedings, such an ordinance is valid if there was a good faith attempt at assessment by the city, the assessment was set aside by a competent court, the improvement contract was substantially complied with, and affected property owners have an opportunity to appear and object to the reassessment.

Mo Kansas City v St Louis & Kansas City Land (1914) 260 Mo 395, 169 SW 62.
Ore Reiff v Portland (1914) 71 Ore 421, 142 P 827.
Gardner v Portland (1920) 95 Ore 378, 187 P 306.

Although a street improvement causes large amounts of earth to encroach and trespass on abutting property, rendering the city liable in damages, that does not affect the validity of an ordinance reassessing the cost of the improvement.

Ore Reiff v Portland (1914) 71 Ore 421, 142 P 827.

Where the owners of a majority of property in a street improvement district file written protests against a paving project, and the assessment ordinance is voided, a reassessment ordinance is invalid.

Okla New Cordell v Mansell (1934) 169 Okla 166, 36 P2d 508.
Norman v McGinley (1930) 142 Okla 216, 286 P 3.
Ore Cook v Portland (1914) 73 Ore 299, 144 P 120.
Hughes v Portland (1909) 53 Ore 370, 100 P 942.

§297. Liens

The expense of a municipal public works project, consisting of the paving or repaving of a street, may be prorated against the land abutting thereon, and the pro rata part of such expense may be made a lien on the abutting land and a personal obligation of the owner.

W Va Moundsville v Brown (1945) 127 W Va 602, 34 SE2d 321.

Though no personal liability may be constitutionally imposed on a property owner for street improvements under a public contract, a charter city has authority by ordinance to impose a lien on the property benefited.

Cal Flinn v Zerbe (1919) 40 CA 294, 180 P 650.

Under an ordinance providing that whenever the owner abutting a street neglects to make a gutter within the time ordered by the common council the city may make the same at his expense and have a lien therefor on the property, a lien does not exist until the owner has failed in his duty, the city has constructed the gutter, and the cost has been ascertained.

Conn Hamlin v McCormick (1912) 85 Conn 647, 84 A 106.

§298. —Creation

It is necessary to comply with all literal requirements of statutes authorizing paving assessments in order to bring into existence a lien or privilege under an ordinance, since the liens are in derogation of common-law rights.

Ky Hartford v King (1952) 249 SW2d 13.
La State v Shreveport (1932) 142 So 641.
Tenn South Fulton v Edwards (1923) 148 Tenn 130, 251 SW 892.

Where statutory authority exists, a paving assessment imposed by ordinance may become a lien at the time of enactment, though no improvement has yet been made.

La Palmer v Ponchatoula (1940) 195 La 997, 197 So 697.
Okla Runnels v Oklahoma City (1931) 150 Okla 292, 1 P2d 740.

The evidence of the existence of a paving lien is the timely recordation of the assessment ordinance in the mortgage records of the parish where the property lies.

La Winnfield v Jackson (1942) 10 So2d 655.

§299. —Status

A paving assessment ordinance recorded within the statutory period creates a first privilege on the property and outranks all other charges except taxes; but when recorded after lapse of the statutory period the assessment is superior only to claims arising after the recordation date.

Conn   Hartford v Mechanic's Sav Bk (1906) 79 Conn 38, 63 A 658.
La   Carr v Eby (1937) 177 So 455.
SC   Cheraw v Turnage (1937) 184 SC 76, 191 SE 831.
Tex   Marriott v Corder (1927) 4 SW2d 213.
        Wooten v Tex Bitulithic (1919) 212 SW 248.

An ordinance levying an assessment for street paving creates a lien superior to every private interest in the land; and the procedure by which it becomes a charge on the land is a proceeding in rem. Like taxes it is collectible without a summons to court.

La   Cook v Lemoine (1934) 178 La 1014, 152 So 689.
SC   Beatty v Wittekamp (1933) 171 SC 326, 172 SE 122.

Two separate pavement assessment liens, created by ordinances, are of equal rank and are subordinate to general tax liens. Neither is inferior to the other on the ground that one is recorded first, since there can be no conflict of liens within the same class.

La   Cent Sav Bk v Tucker (1935) 161 So 780.

Where a paving assessment is duly authorized and recorded as required the city becomes in effect the mortgagee and has all of those rights. A suit to enforce the lien is under the same time limitation as a mortgage.

W Va   Horn v Charleston (1922) 91 W Va 73, 112 SE 239.

§ 300. —Extent

Under an ordinance assessing the costs of street improvements against abutting owners, the lien of the city is limited to the lot itself, and the value of the buildings or other improvements is excluded.

Ky   Thompson v Williamsburg (1929) 229 Ky 81, 16 SW2d 772.

§ 301. —Change in Ownership

Where an ordinance authorizes a street improvement and assessment of costs against abutting property, a change in ownership of such property, which takes place after the contract has been let out before the tax bills are issued, does not affect the lien created by the tax bills.

Mo   Union Nat Bk of Springfield v Mobley (1935) 228 MoApp 1235, 78 SW2d 512.

§302. —Homestead Rights

A special assessment ordinance, to the extent that it imposes a lien against resident homesteads abutting the improvement, is invalid as violative of the constitutional provision forbidding the creation of any lien on homestead property for improvement purposes.

> **Tex** Continental Inv v Bodenheimer (1937) 102 SW2d 304.
> Dallas v Atkins (1920) 110 Tex 627, 223 SW 170.

§303. —Late Recordation or Filing

Failure to file the lien created by a paving assessment ordinance within the period directed by statute creates a lien from the time of filing, but does not give it priority over an existing recorded mortgage.

> **La** Cook v Lemoine (1933) 149 So 263.
> Dixie Inv v Player (1933) 149 So 269.

The only effect the late recordation of a paving assessment ordinance has on the lien is that it then becomes prior only to those liens filed thereafter. Late filing precludes the advancement in rank granted by statute, but does not affect the validity of the lien from the time of actual filing.

> **La** Lemoine v Wheless Inv (1935) 159 So 434.

§304. —Validity

A charter provision that a lien for street improvement assessments shall relate back and become effective as of the date of the original resolution ordering the improvement is not unconstitutional as a local or special law.

> **Tex** Anderson v Brandon (1932) 121 Tex 188, 47 SW2d 261.

An innocent purchaser at a forfeited land sale is not estopped to contest the validity of a claimed lien for public improvement assessments, where no notice of the assessing ordinance was filed with the county recorder as required by the statute then in effect.

> **Ohio** Gundersen v South Euclid (1952) 157 OS 437, 47 Op 326, 105 NE2d 863.

A paving ordinance creating assessment liens that exceed the value of the property is not unconstitutional on the ground that it constitutes a taking of private property for public use without compensation or deprives a person of his property without due process of law. That the city has the right to cause a sale that might not satisfy the liens does not amount to a taking for public purposes without due process, since a city may apportion the entire cost of a street paving project on the abutting lots according to frontage without making any inquiry into benefits to the property owners.

La State v New Orleans (1937) 186 La 705, 173 So 179.

XXV. ASSESSMENT BONDS

§305. Generally

Under a charter authorizing a city to construct paved streets, an ordinance providing for the paving of streets is valid, as are paving bonds issued by the city.

Fla Venice v State (1928) 96 Fla 527, 118 So 308.

Failure of an ordinance providing for the issuance of bonds for street improvements to state definitely the proportion of the cost of the proposed improvements to be assessed against abutting property is not a violation of due process.

NC Leak v Wadesboro (1923) 186 NC 683, 121 SE 12.

An ordinance providing for payment from the city street fund of one-fifth of the maturing bonds and interest for each year to any street improvement district subsequently formed within the city is valid under the statutory proscription that no county or city shall "obtain or appropriate money for, or loan its credit to, any corporation, association, institution or individual." A street improvement district is not a company, association or corporation, but rather the municipality acting through an agency of its own creation.

Ark Paris v St Improvement Dist of Paris (1943) 206 Ark 926, 175 SW2d 199.

§306. Nature

An ordinance authorizing street improvements and issuance of bonds, payment thereof to be assessed to the benefited district, does not constitute a tax, within the meaning of the constitutional requirement that every law that imposes a tax state the facts and object for which it is to be applied.

Ariz Collins v Phoenix (1931) 54 F2d 770.

An ordinance authorizing a bond issue to finance street improvements, which merely levies assessments against abutting owners, does not create an indebtedness of the municipality within the meaning of constitutional debt limitations.

Ky Prestonsburg v People's State Bk (1934) 255 Ky 252, 72 SW2d 1043.

§307. Validity

Where an ordinance authorizing a bond issue to finance street improvements is not published as required by statute, it is invalid.

Ky   Newport v Newport Nat Bk (1912) 148 Ky 213, 146 SW 377.

Statutory authorization empowering municipalities by ordinance to incur debt and issue bonds for paving and improving sidewalks does not conflict with a constitutional authorization for public improvements that does not mention sidewalks, since sidewalks are included as works of public improvement.

La   Judice v Scott (1929) 168 La 111, 121 So 592.

Bonds issued by a city, and sold for full value, to obtain money with which to pay in the first instance for street improvements, where the improvements have been made, are not void merely because the method provided by ordinance for assessing the cost against abutting property is illegal.

Iowa   Burlington Sav Bk v Clinton (1901) 106 F 269.

That four of the five commissioners who passed an ordinance for paving streets and issuance of bonds were officers of a private company that was already bound to the purchasers of lots by contracts to make the identical improvements provided for by the bond proceeds will not negate the validity of the bonds, where there is no showing that the commission did not issue the bonds in good faith and for the good of the whole community.

Fla   Coral Gables v Hayes (1935) 74 F2d 989.

§308. Authority

Where the charter authorizes the issuance of sidewalk improvement bonds and the freeholders approve the amount and purpose, other requirements, such as denomination, maturities and series, are within the discretion of the issuing authority, so long as constitutional and statutory limitations are not violated.

Fla   State v Miami (1949) 41 So2d 888.

Although a city is authorized by its charter to defray the cost of sidewalk improvements by levying assessments on abutting owners, and to issue bonds limited to a specific purpose—not including sidewalk improvements, that authority will not include, by implication, the power to issue negotiable bonds.

Tex   Hitchcock v Galveston (1874) 96 US 341, 24 LEd 659.

§309. Allocation of Proceeds

Where part of an issue of general obligation bonds is for the widening and improving of certain streets this money is for the expenses of the city such as condemnation, damages, and retaining wall and does not apply to paving costs. This is a charge that can only be made on assessment of abutting owners.

    W Va   Bowling v Bluefield (1927) 104 W Va 589, 140 SE 685.

§310. Interest

Where a paving ordinance authorizes the collection of one per cent interest on principal, and interest on overdue paving certificate installments, but the collection is not authorized by statute, property owners are entitled to set off penalties and interest paid under protest, in equity proceedings.

    NM   Roswell v Levers (1934) 38 NM 419, 34 P2d 865.

A special paving improvement ordinance stating that the interest on the warrants issued thereunder shall be due and payable on the whole sum unpaid at the time each installment is due does not permit the issuing city, where prepayment of one or more installments is made, to withhold interest on any unpaid portion of a warrant until the next installment is payable. The interest is payable when due.

    Utah   R M Stinson & Co v Godbe (1918) 51 Utah 343, 170 P 782.

§311. Right of Bondholders

Where the city, under an ordinance authorizing street improvements to be financed by a bond issue, negligently fails to collect assessments or prosecute suits for the enforcement of liens, the resulting deficiencies may be recovered from the city in a suit by unpaid bondholders.

    Ky   Knepfle v Morehead (1946) 301 Ky 417, 192 SW2d 189.
            Henderson v Winstead (1919) 185 Ky 693, 215 SW 527.
    NM   Altman v Kilburn (1941) 45 NM 453, 116 P2d 812, 136 ALR 554.

Where an ordinance that authorizes highway improvement bonds payable from a proportion of the motor vehicle fuel tax to be allotted to the city contains a promise to the bond purchaser that no decrease in the proportion of the tax payable to the city may be made while any of the bonds are outstanding, such promise is ultra vires, and cannot prevent the legislature from decreasing the proportions.

    Ariz   Switzer v Phoenix (1959) 86 Ariz 121, 341 P2d 427.

§312. —Mandamus

A holder of paving bonds may resort to mandamus to compel the city to enact an ordinance assessing or reassessing properties benefited by completed street improvements that were made in accordance with statutes and ordinances, but cannot maintain an action for a money judgment against the city either ex contractu or ex delicto.

> **Okla** Severns Paving v Oklahoma City (1932) 158 Okla 182, 13 P2d 94.

§313. Refunding

An ordinance authorizing the substitution of new paving certificates for an old issue under a prior ordinance in order to save the taxpayers money is not invalid on the ground that some certificates to be reissued and called would be paid double interest charges during an overlap period. That is a normal incident of a refunding operation, and the cost is negligible compared to the savings.

> **La** State v Cave (1939) 193 La 419, 190 So 631.

Under an ordinance to refund street improvement bonds, whether the second issue of bonds wherein the credit and property of the city are pledged is valid may be questioned, but nevertheless, if the bonds are not valid, the obligation of the original bonds continues.

> **Ky** Catlettsburg v Self (1903) 115 Ky 669, 74 SW 1064.

§314. Payment

An ordinance authorizing the issuance of street improvement bonds, providing that the bonds shall be paid and discharged in numerical order, is not invalid merely because the title gives no notice of the payment in numerical order.

> **NM** State ex rel Ackerman v Carlsbad (1935) 39 NM 352, 47 P2d 865.

A resolution of town trustees attempting to amend state statutes and outstanding street improvement bonds by providing for remittance of penalties on unpaid assessments is a nullity. There is no authority to deprive bond holder of his security.

> **Okla** Brown-Crummer Inv v Paulter (1934) 70 F2d 184.

§315. Liabilities

The liability on street improvement bonds issued under a municipal ordinance, payable from special assessments against the properties benefited, is a liability in rem against the properties, not a liability of the city.

> **Ky**   Irvine v Wallace (1934) 254 Ky 564, 71 SW2d 974.
>   Catlettsburg v Self (1903) 115 Ky 669, 74 SW 1064.
> **Okla**   Chickasha v Foster (1935) 173 Okla 217, 48 P2d 289.
>   State v Armstrong (1932) 158 Okla 290, 13 P2d 198.

Where an ordinance authorizes the issuance of revenue bonds for sidewalk and sewer construction, the cost to be assessed against contiguous property, it does not obligate the municipality for the amount of the bonds, but only to collect the assessments and place them in a separate fund set aside for payment of principal and interest. Also, the issuance of the bonds does not create a general lien on the lands and, except for the assessment, no special lien.

> **Ida**   Mullen Benevolent v U S (1933) 290 US 89, 78 LEd 192, 54 SCt 38.
> **Ky**   Castle v Louisa (1920) 187 Ky 397, 219 SW 439.

Where an ordinance authorizing a bond issue to finance street improvements is invalid because enacted under an unconstitutional statute, the city is liable to the purchaser of a bond who in purchasing it directly from the city pays the purchase price into the city treasury.

> **Ky**   Henderson v Redmond (1919) 185 Ky 146, 214 SW 809.
> **Neb**   Refunding Bonds Red Cloud, In re (1922) 108 Neb 717, 189 NW 365.

§316. Referendum

An ordinance for the issuance of bonds for paving by a city of the second class does not involve work of internal improvement requiring submission of the proposition to the electors.

> **Ariz**   Collins v Phoenix (1931) 54 F2d 770.
> **Colo**   Sanborn v Boulder (1923) 74 Colo 358, 221 P 1077.
> **Ida**   Byrns v Moscow (1912) 21 Ida 398, 121 P 1034.
> **Neb**   Wookey v Alma (1929) 118 Neb 158, 223 NW 953.

The constitutional requirement of a two-thirds vote of the electorate for issuance of bonds for the construction, maintenance and operation of roads and turnpikes is not applicable to cities and towns, and hence a home rule city may issue bonds for such purposes when authorized by a majority of property taxpaying voters.

> **Tex**   Lucchese v Mauermann (1946) 195 SW2d 422.

462

XXVI. LIABILITY OF MUNICIPALITY

§317. Notice as Prerequisite

Notice provisions are enacted to insure that a municipality has a reasonable opportunity to cure defective conditions the existence of which it could not be expected to know absent some sort of positive apprisal. Almost daily inspection of an area by a city makes requirement for written notice unnecessary since there is no need in such case for apprisal when the city has constructive notice of a dangerous condition in an area which is has a nondelegable duty to maintain in a safe condition for the travelling public.

> **NY** Blake v Albany (1978) 63 AD2d 1075, 405 NYS2d 832.

Use by city vehicular traffic along with other traffic is not a sufficient cause of damage to a boardwalk to relieve an injured party of the requirement that notice of damage to a sidewalk be filed 48 hours before the accident.

> **NY** Kotler v Long Beach (1974) 44 AD2d 679, 353 NYS2d 800.

A local law providing that notice of a dangerous condition of a sidewalk or street must be given to the city as a condition precedent to action against the city for injuries is a valid exercise of the police power, and compliance with the law must be alleged or proved in an action falling within the statutory area.

> **Minn** Fuller v Mankato (1956) 248 Minn 342, 80 NW2d 9.
> Adler v Saranac Lake (1961) 14 AD2d 975, 221 NYS2d 284.
> **NY** Snyder v Delmin Rlty (1954) 207 Misc 218, 137 NYS2d 137.

In suing for injuries caused by the slipping of a manhole cover over a vault, there must be evidence of a defect which proximately caused the slippage. Manholes are annually inspected; and if there is no evidence of the cause, there is no notice or constructive notice to the municipality of the likelihood of slipping.

> **DC** DC v Jones (1970) 265 A2d 594.

Where a city by ordinance required notice of defective condition prior to bringing of an action for injuries, a defective curb is within the provision.

> **NY** Skelly v Port Chester (1958) 6 AD2d 717, 174 NYS2d 562.

A charter provision exempting a city from liability for damage or injury to persons or property caused by any defect in any public street, grounds or public work, unless the city commissioners had at least 24 hours' notice thereof, is violative of due process.

> **Tex** Hanks v Port Arthur (1932) 121 Tex 202, 48 SW2d 944.

§318. Improper Assessment

Where by paving ordinance a city has made assessments contrary to law, and it is necessary for the contractor to defend suits in attempts to cure the city's errors in failure to establish the liens properly, the city is liable for the cost of the litigation because of its failure to make the proper assessments and in order to protect the contractor and furnish him with enforceable notes and liens.

La   Hinkle v West Monroe (1941) 196 La 1078, 200 So 468.

§319. Expense of Repaving

Where an ordinance requires property owners to comply with the regulations and specifications of city engineers in paving a street, the city will be liable to the property owner for any expense of repaving resulting from faulty specifications provided by a city engineer.

Tex   Chapman v Houston (1937) 101 SW2d 348.

ANNOTATION

Right of owners of property abutting street to compensation for establishing or paving over parkway in center of street, or paving roadway adjacent to parkway, 81 ALR2d 1451.

§320. Deprivation of Access

Where an ordinance authorizes the opening and establishment of a street which, when completed, leaves an owner's property isolated, street access thereto having been to all essential purposes vacated, an owner of a lot thereby deprived of access is entitled to recover damages from the city.

Mo   Twenty-Third Street Traffic Way, In re (1919) 279 Mo 249, 214 SW 109.

LAW REVIEWS

Frank M. Covey, Jr., Frontage Roads: To Compensate or Not to Compensate, 56 NW LR 587.

Gardner Cromwell, Loss of Access to Highways: Different Approaches to the Problem of Compensation, 48 Va LR 538.

ANNOTATIONS

Right to damages where access of abutter is interfered with by municipal or public use of subsurface of street or highway for tunnel purposes, 11 ALR2d 206.

Abutting owner's right to damages or other relief for loss of access because of limited access to highway or street, 43 ALR2d 1072.

Regulation or prohibition of abutter's access to street or highway without compensation, 73 ALR2d 652.

Restriction or interference with access of abutter by traffic regulation without making compensation, 73 ALR2d 689.

§321. Defective Sidewalks

An ordinance requiring abutting property owners to reimburse the city for any judgment secured due to injury on a defective sidewalk is invalid. The city lacks statutory authorization to enact such an ordinance.

> **W Va**   Miller v Morgantown (1974) 208 SE2d 780.

A home rule city's ordinance requiring a 30-day notice of claim may not deny recovery for injury in a sidewalk accident. The statutory authority for recovery against the city on defective sidewalks may not be avoided by the requirement of a claim.

> **W Va**   Toler v Huntington (1969) 153 W Va 313, 168 SE2d 551.

A requirement that an adequate and effective barricade be provided during work on the sidewalk does not require provision of a safe alternate route for pedestrians.

> **Ga**   Hardin v Barrett (1970) 122 GaApp 156, 176 SE2d 455.

An ordinance vests the city with continuing and exclusive control of sidewalks within the radius of three feet of a monument, and the city, not an abutting owner, is liable for damages sustained in a fall from a break in the cement adjacent to the monument.

> **DC**   Curtis v DC (1966) 363 F2d 973.
> **Iowa**   Shumway v Burlington (1899) 108 Iowa 424, 79 NW 123.
> **NY**   Weiser v New York City (1957) 5 AD2d 702, 169 NYS2d 609.

Where the municipal administrative code provides that a property owner must maintain sidewalks in good repair, and that on failure to do so the city shall make repairs and assess the cost against the property benefited, a violation resulting in defective sidewalks does not release city from liability for injury resulting therefrom on the theory of assumption of risk.

> **Ky** Equitable Life v McClellan (1941) 286 Ky 17, 149 SW2d 730.
> **Mo** Barker v Jefferson City (1911) 155 MoApp 390, 137 SW 10.
> **NY** McEvoy v New York City (1943) 266 AD 445, 42 NYS2d 746.

In an action against a municipality for personal injuries resulting from a fall on an icy sidewalk, the court properly excluded an ordinance requiring the city to remove snow from sidewalks within 12 hours, where plaintiff failed to establish a causal relationship between the city's failure to remove and his injury.

> **Iowa** Beirness v Missouri Valley (1913) 162 Iowa 720, 144 NW 628.

§321.1. Trap Doors

A city may seek indemnity from an abutting property owner who has a steel trap door placed in the sidewalk for his exclusive use and benefit. An ordinance requiring cellar doors be of strong material and be uniform and flush with pavement is not an attempt to delegate the city's responsibility for repair of the sidewalk, but places primary liability for their installation on the persons receiving the major benefit.

> **Tenn** Continental Ins Co v Knoxville (1972) 488 SW2d 50.

§322. Defective Streets

A city cannot by ordinance shift to a property owner the burden of keeping city streets reasonably safe for public travel, and it is answerable to a person injured by reason of an unsafe condition of the street.

> **Cal** Wilkes v San Francisco (1941) 44 CA2d 393, 112 P2d 759.
> Douglass v Los Angeles (1935) 5 C2d 123, 53 P2d 353.
> **DC** Smith v D C (1951) 189 F2d 671.
> **Ky** Carlisle v Campbell (1912) 151 Ky 279, 151 SW 673.
> **La** Bond v Baton Rouge (1961) 129 So2d 887.
> **Minn** Nelson v Duluth (1927) 172 Minn 76, 214 NW 774.
> **Va** Newport News v Scott Adm (1905) 103 Va 794, 50 SE 266.

§323. Street Improvements

Where the grade of a street is originally established under an ordinance authorizing street improvements, the city is not liable for injuries or damages to abutting property resulting from such original establishment of the grade.

> **Ky** Prestonsburg v Hubbard (1928) 224 Ky 326, 6 SW2d 277.
> Pursiful v Harlan (1928) 222 Ky 658, 1 SW2d 1043.

§324. Vacated Streets

Where a town, by resolution, officially abandons and closes to public travel a portion of a highway after a new highway is in operation, it is not liable for an accident caused by failure to barricade or place warning signs on the abandoned portion. The resolution is the formal step in the process of abandonment, and results in a reversion of the property to private ownership.

Wis   Karle v Commonwealth (1941) 236 Wis 500, 295 NW 687.

Where the police power of a municipality is validly and reasonably exercised in rerouting, relocating, improving or vacating its streets, any damage resulting to abutting property is noncompensable and does not fall within the constitutional prohibition against the taking of property without compensation.

Tex   Waco v Archenhold Auto Supply (1965) 386 SW2d 174.

§325. Street Grades

Where an owner builds without regard to grade lines, he cannot recover for injury to his property when the actual grading established by ordinance, is done.

Iowa   Reilly v Fort Dodge (1902) 118 Iowa 633, 92 NW 887.
Pa   Costello v Scranton (1933) 108 PaS 573, 165 A 670.

Where an ordinance authorizes the opening of a street and the work incident thereto is directed by the city engineer, the city may be liable for consequential damages resulting to abutting property by an improper grading that diverts the natural flow of water so as to cause flood damage.

Ky   Pikeville v Riddle (1923) 200 Ky 395, 255 SW 63.
Pa   Adams v New Kensington (1953) 374 Pa 104, 97 A2d 354.

§326. —Change of Grade

To entitle an abutting owner to recover damages for change of grade of a street five elements are essential: (1) a grade must have been established by ordinance; (2) the owner must have improved his lot with reference to the grade so established; (3) a new and different grade must have been subsequently established by ordinance; (4) the municipality must have changed the physical grade to conform to the new paper grade; and (5) in consequence thereof, the owner's property must have been damaged or diminished in value.

Iowa   Ayer v Perry (1922) 193 Iowa 181, 186 NW 840.

467

The mere passage of an ordinance providing for a change in grade of a street does not give rise to an immediate cause of action on the part of an abutting owner. Such an action accrues only on the physical bringing of the street up to grade.

> **Iowa** Vilas v Chicago M & St P Ry (1917) 179 Iowa 1244, 162 NW 795.
> **Wis**   McDonald v De Pere (1959) 8 Wis2d 16, 98 NW2d 407.

Where a municipality approves a plan for construction of a highway on a municipal street and authorizes a change of grade according to the plan, the municipality makes itself liable for damage caused to abutting property by the change.

> **Ark**   Fayetteville v Stone (1912) 104 Ark 136, 148 SW 524.
> **Iowa** Witwer Bros v Cedar Rapids (1906) 107 NW 604.
> **Ky**   Erlanger v Cody (1914) 158 Ky 625, 166 SW 202.
>   Henderson v McClain (1897) 102 Ky 402, 43 SW 700.
> **Minn** Maguire v Crosby (1929) 178 Minn 144, 226 NW 398.
>   Sather v Duluth (1913) 123 Minn 300, 143 NW 906.
> **NY**   Leonard of Mechanicville, In re (1916) 176 AD 25, 162 NYS 285.
> **Pa**   Costello v Scranton (1933) 108 PaS 573, 165 A 670.

In an action for damages against a city for regrading a street, under an ordinance, testimony by the city to show the level of the street where the grade was established and the depth of the proposed cut was admissible to show the immediate surroundings of plaintiff's property and the effect of the grade, for if there was any benefit it should be considered in fixing the amount of recovery.

> **Iowa** Morton v Burlington (1898) 106 Iowa 50, 75 NW 662.
> **W Va** White v Charleston (1925) 98 W Va 143, 126 SE 705.

Where an ordinance authorizes a street improvement by changing its grade, the owner of property abutting on the improvement may not claim damages for a change in grade on an intersecting street a block away, on which his property does not abut.

> **Mo**   Kansas City v Brown (1920) 286 Mo 1, 227 SW 89.

Where a street grade is established by ordinance and an abutting owner improves her property without reference to the grade before the street was actually lowered to the established grade, she is not entitled to damages to her property by the subsequent lowering of the street to the established grade.

> **Iowa** Collins v Iowa Falls (1910) 146 Iowa 305, 125 NW 226.

LAW REVIEW

Eminent Domain in Virginia—Compensation for Damages and Nonphysical Takings, 43 Va LR 597.

ANNOTATION

Change in highway grade entitling owner to compensation, 2 ALR3d 985.

§327. —Requirement of Negligence

Though a city by ordinance changes the natural grade of a street in making street improvements, an abutting owner may not recover from the city consequential damages to his property if the work is not done negligently.

> **Ky**   Owensboro v Hope (1908) 128 Ky 524, 33 KLR 375, 108 SW 873.

§328. —Measure of Damages

Where real property suffers a diminution in value as the result of a lowering of the grade of the street as authorized by ordinance, the city is liable for the difference between fair market value of the property before and after the grading.

> **Ky**   Covington v Taffee (1902) 24 KLR 373, 68 SW 629.

The liability of a city to an abutting owner for making a change in the grade of a street by ordinance is the same in extent or character as for injuriously grading in the absence of an ordinance.

> **Iowa**   Richardson v Sioux City (1907) 136 Iowa 436, 113 NW 928.

In measuring damage to property from an ordinance changing the grade of a street, the cost of putting the property in the same condition with respect to the new grade as it was before is admissible.

> **Iowa**   Richardson v Sioux City (1907) 136 Iowa 436, 113 NW 928.

§329. Trespass

When in grading a street under an ordinance, the town trespasses and enters on the premises of an owner, the town is liable for the resulting damages, though it may have been engaged in the original improvement of the street.

> **Iowa**   Cooper v Cedar Rapids (1900) 112 Iowa 367, 83 NW 1050.
> **Ky**   Goodloe v Richmond (1938) 272 Ky 100, 113 SW2d 834.
>   West Covington v Schultz (1895) 16 KLR 831, 30 SW 410.

§330. Exemptions

When a city street becomes part of the state highway system, the board of transportation assumes responsibility for its maintenance which includes control of all signs and structures within the right-of-way. Consequently, in this type of situation, a municipality cannot be held liable for failing to post warning signs or for placing a telephone pole on a dangerous curve.

> **NC** Shapiro v Toyota Motor Co Ltd (1978) 38 NCApp 658, 248 SE2d 868.

A charter provision exempting the city from liability for injuries caused by defective streets is invalid as violative of the constitutional provision that every person shall have a remedy by due course of law for any injury done to him.

> **Ariz** Phoenix v Williams (1961) 89 Ariz 299, 361 P2d 651.
> **Tex** Lebohm v Galveston (1955) 154 Tex 192, 275 SW2d 951.

XXVII. VALIDITY OF IMPROVEMENT ORDINANCES

§331. Generally

An improvement and parking district which excludes part of the business area separated by major streets, railroad right-of-way, and railroad tracks complies with the statutory requirement of including the established business area. The occupational tax based on square footage of the business and graded according to nearness to the main thoroughfare is uniform and reasonable.

> **Neb** Blackledge v Richards (1975) 194 Neb 188, 231 NW2d 319.

Widening a street from two to four lanes within a home rule municipality is still a local improvement regardless of its state status. The fact that the street is a portion of a state highway does not make it less a matter of public interest, and the abutting owners may be assessed for the value of improvements.

> **Okla** Moore Funeral Homes v Tulsa (1976) 552 P2d 702.

The provisions for paving on petition of $2/3$ of the frontage owners is substantially complied with by including the project within the unified street improvement plan. Presenting the petition to the city engineer and not the city manager as designated by ordinance is a minor irregularity, not fundamental to the petition.

> **SC** Lathem v Greenville (1971) 256 SC 586, 183 SE2d 455.

Ordinances authorizing street improvements and issuance of tax bills against property within the improvement district are not invalid as a taking of property for public use without compensation, or as violating due process.

> **Mo** St Louis v Nicolai (1928) 321 Mo 830, 13 SW2d 36.

The constitutionality of an ordinance levying an assessment for street improvements is to be judged, not by a consideration of its language in vacuo, but by consideration of its effect in the situation to which it is actually applied.

SC Carolina & N W Ry v Clover (1931) 46 F2d 395.

Where a street improvement ordinance is declared void, all proceedings stemming from it are likewise void, and will be so treated whether attacked directly or collaterally.

Ill Bellwood v Galt (1927) 326 Ill 55, 156 NE 774.
Neb Chicago S P M & O Ry v Randolph (1957) 163 Neb 687, 81 NW2d 159.
Cullingham v Omaha (1943) 143 Neb 744, 10 NW2d 615.

§332. When Determined

The validity of an assessment for street improvements made by an ordinance passed on a particular date is determined by the law in force on that date, although the assessment is made after that date.

Ky Thompson v Williamsburg (1929) 229 Ky 81, 16 SW2d 772.

§333. Enactment

An ordinance establishing a paving assessment lien does not constitute violation of the Fourteenth Amendment depriving owners of property without due process of law. The ordinance which was passed and published authorizing the improvement with assessment against the property owners constitutes notice.

Pa Sager v Burgess (1972) 350 F Supp 1310.

Failure of the city clerk to record the engineer's report or roll as part of an improvement ordinance does not render the ordinance void.

Tex Tyler v Wynne (1968) 434 SW2d 938.

A special assessment ordinance enacted without compliance with jurisdictional requirements is void, as distinguished from irregular.

Neb Chicago S P M & O Ry v Randolph (1957) 163 Neb 687, 81 NW2d 159.

§334. —Burden on Contestant

In determining whether an ordinance for construction of a highway was properly enacted and was an emergency measure, the burden is on the one who denies its validity to show irregularity in its enactment.

> **Fla**   Morrison v Farnell (1936) 126 Fla 385, 171 So 528.

§335. —Publication

Notice to the property owner and an opportunity to perform sidewalk construction or repairs is a prerequisite to the city doing the work and assessing a lien. On failure to serve notice the lien is invalid.

> **NY**   Fread v New York City (1972) 72 Misc2d 61, 338 NYS2d 129.

A street extension ordinance that incorporated by reference a plat identifying the property it required is not invalid where the plat was not published, since the statute requiring that ordinances be published is inapplicable to those that do not impose any fine, penalty, imprisonment, or forfeiture, or make any appropriation.

> **Ill**   Hallstrom v Rockford (1959) 16 Ill2d 297, 157 NE2d 23.

Where an ordinance or resolution of necessity for paving streets was duly enacted but never published in accordance with statute, all proceedings based thereon, including the assessment and reassessment of abutting properties, are void.

> **Okla**   Enid v Gensman (1919) 76 Okla 90, 181 P 308.

§336. —Public Inspection

Under the statute requiring an ordinance for a street improvement to remain on file with the city clerk for public inspection for at least one week before final passage, an ordinance that is not left on file as provided is invalid, and the assessment provided for therein will not be confirmed.

> **Ill**   Ottawa v Hulse (1925) 317 Ill 276, 148 NE 1.

§337. Presumption of Validity

The burden of overcoming the presumption of the validity of an ordinance providing for special assessments and local improvements is cast on the property owner, and the presumption may be overcome only by clear and cogent proof.

Ill   Chicago v Thielans (1929) 334 Ill 231, 165 NE 615.
Ky   Weatherhead v Cody (1905) 27 KLR 631, 85 SW 1099.
Mo   Wabash Ry v St Louis (1933) 64 F2d 921.
Neb   Superior v Simpson (1926) 114 Neb 698, 209 NW 505.
NJ   Pub Service Elec & Gas, Appeal of (1952) 18 NJS 357, 87 A2d 344.

§338. Partial Invalidity

In an ordinance containing, in its first section, a provision for construction of a street improvement, which improvement is described in a second section, and providing for a special assessment in the third section, the invalidity of the third section will not invalidate the remainder of the ordinance, since the first two sections may be treated as distinct and independent of section three, and may stand alone.

Ill   Johnson v People (1903) 202 Ill 306, 66 NE 1081.
      Freeport St Ry v Freeport (1894) 151 Ill 451, 38 NE 137.
Md   Jarvis v Berlin (1927) 153 Md 156, 138 A 7.

§339. Conflict of Interest

A paving ordinance is not void merely because it provides for the paving of a street on which a council member who voted for the ordinance owns property.

Ga   Story v Macon (1949) 205 Ga 590, 54 SE2d 396.

§340. Taking of Property

If the impact of a comprehensive street planning ordinance produces such substantial damage as to render the property useless for any reasonable purpose, an unconstitutional taking occurs.

NY   Rochester Business Inst v Rochester (1966) 25 AD2d 97, 267 NYS2d 274.

§341. Extraterritorial Assessment

An ordinance providing for the paving of a street, part of which extends into another municipality, and imposing a special tax on adjacent property to pay for the improvement, is invalid, since one municipality cannot levy a tax for an improvement to be made within the limits of another.

Ill   Mushbaugh v East Peoria (1913) 260 Ill 27, 102 NE 1027.

§342. Duplicity

An ordinance providing for condemnation of several disconnected strips of land, to be improved into several streets, is not void for duplicity in containing more than one subject, where it appears from maps in the record that the purpose of the ordinance is to create a connected way under a general plan to create a continuous though sinuous course between two termini.

Wash   South Shilshole Place, In re (1910) 61 Wash 246, 112 P 228.

§343. Single or Double Improvement

An ordinance authorizing the opening and establishment of a street is for a single improvement, though work to be done at several intersections is separately specified; and the validity of the ordinance may not be attacked on the immaterial issue of whether property abutting on the improvement is damaged by one part of the improvement or another, and not by the improvement as a whole.

Ill   Peoria v Cowen (1927) 326 Ill 616, 158 NE 414.
      Greenville v Miller (1925) 315 Ill 565, 146 NE 463.
Mo   Twenty-third St Traffic Way, In re (1919) 279 Mo 249, 214 SW 109.

An item of "street and alley fund, $200," in a tax levy ordinance, is not objectionable as containing several purposes covered by one amount, since levies for streets and alleys are treated as being for a single purpose.

Ill   People v Ill Cent RR (1937) 366 Ill 408, 9 NE2d 310.

§344. Description of Improvement

A local improvement ordinance, to be valid, must prescribe the nature, character, locality and description of the proposed improvement, with such particularity as will secure to the property owners the exact improvement decided on.

Ill   Hairgrove v Jacksonville (1937) 366 Ill 163, 8 NE2d 187.
      Gray v W A Black Co (1930) 338 Ill 488, 170 NE 713.
Wash   Shryock v Hannenen (1910) 61 Wash 296, 112 P 377.

ANNOTATION

Description with reference to highway as carrying title to center or side of highway, 49 ALR2d 982.

§345. —Insufficient, Effect

Where a street improvement ordinance is not void, but is merely insufficient because of a defective description, that defect can be questioned only by a direct attack. It cannot be questioned collaterally, when application is made for judgment of sale against delinquent lots.

Ill Steenberg v People (1897) 164 Ill 478, 45 NE 970.

A mere insufficient description or other irregularity in the enactment of an ordinance assessing property for street improvements does not entitle an abutting owner to have the ordinance declared void. His right is, at most, limited to having a reassessment made conforming to the statute.

Okla Harper v Oklahoma City (1953) 208 Okla 307, 255 P2d 933.

Failure of a street paving ordinance of a city of the third class to describe the general character of the improvement and its probable cost does not render it invalid, since under the enabling statute those facts need not be contained in the ordinance.

Kan Horejsi v Holyrood (1951) 171 Kan 190, 231 P2d 215.

§346. —Plans; Specifications

It is not essential to the validity of an ordinance authorizing street improvements that it set out in full the plans or specifications for the work, or that they be published as part of the ordinance.

Ky Elder v Richmond (1920) 186 Ky 706, 218 SW 239.

§347. Estimated Cost

It is not essential to the validity of a street improvement ordinance that the estimate of cost contain a detailed statement of the amount and character of the necessary material, since the estimate is sufficiently itemized, so far as property owners are concerned, if it is specific enough to give them a general idea of the estimated cost of the component elements of the improvement.

Ill Dixon v Sinow & Weinman (1932) 350 Ill 634, 183 NE 570.
East St Louis v Vogel (1917) 276 Ill 490, 114 NE 941.
W Va La Follette v Fairmont (1953) 138 W Va 517, 76 SE2d 572.

§ 348. Reasonableness

An assessment ordinance for sidewalk construction substantially complies with statutory requirements where it shows total costs of the construction. Failure to itemize the expenses does not invalidate it. However, the taxpayer may properly show that the amount was unreasonable.

> **Mo** Eureka v Hunter (1971) 464 SW2d 518.

The reasonableness of a street improvement ordinance should be determined by judicial consideration of the object to be accomplished, the means for its accomplishment, and existing conditions and circumstances.

> **Ill** Chicago v McCluer (1930) 339 Ill 610, 171 NE 737.
> Carbondale v Reith (1925) 316 Ill 538, 147 NE 422.

An ordinance requiring that a macadam pavement less than four years old and in good condition be torn up and replaced by an asphalt pavement is void, as unreasonable and oppressive, where no reason for the replacement appears.

> **Ill** Chicago v Brown (1903) 205 Ill 568, 69 NE 65.

§ 349. Fraud

An objection to an ordinance providing for the paving of a street in connection with a railroad's franchise for the use of the street, that it is so inequitable and unjust as to be fraudulent, is not tenable, since an ordinance is not fraudulent merely because it may turn out to be improvident or inequitable, as long as the public authorities act from proper motives.

> **Ill** Lincoln v Chicago & A RR (1914) 262 Ill 11, 104 NE 277.

An ordinance assessing the costs of a local improvement is valid if the price for the work done is not so grossly excessive as to imply fraud. What constitutes a reasonable price is within the discretion of the city council.

> **Ore** Wagoner v La Grande (1918) 89 Ore 192, 173 P 305.

Where an ordinance authorizes the paving of a street, and a contract is let and the work completed, tax bills against benefited property are voided by fraud of the contractor in entering into agreements with some property owners for rebates in return for support of his bid for the work.

> **Mo** Rider v Parker-Washington Co (1910) 144 MoAp 67, 128 SW 226.

§350. Delegation of Legislative Discretion

A street improvement ordinance authorizing the board of public works to construct curb walls on a street where curb walls are not already built is not invalid as delegating legislative power, since it provides a precise standard of action and does not vest the board with any discretion.

> **Ill** Page v Chicago (1871) 60 Ill 441.

A street paving ordinance providing that improvements shall be made in the street, except for such portions as have already been done in a suitable manner, and providing that work shall be done under the superintendence of the board of public works, is invalid as a delegation of legislative discretion to the board.

> **Ill** Andrews v Chicago (1870) 57 Ill 239.

§351. Patented Material

A street paving ordinance that provides for the use of a patented pavement material is void under the local improvement act, because it prevents competitive bidding.

> **Ill** Rockford v Armour (1919) 290 Ill 425, 125 NE 356.

§352. Assessment—Before Completion

A contention that the assessment against abutting owners for the cost of street improvements under an assessment ordinance, is not enforceable because it was made before completion of the contract for the improvements may be rejected, where the work was substantially complete at the time and was conditionally accepted by the city council.

> **Ky** Bradshaw v Yager (1953) 265 SW2d 486.

§353. —After Completion

A valid paving lien may be established on petition of the abutting landowners. A subsequent owner with knowledge of the lien is estopped to deny its validity. Filing of the lien on a card in the register of deeds office is adequate notice and waives the requirement of filing in the assessment book.

> **NC** Jones v Asheville (1972) 15 NCApp 714, 190 SE2d 643.

A street improvement ordinance enacted after completion of the improvement is void, being in violation of the statute requiring every such ordinance to specify an estimate of the cost of the improvement, as a protection to property owners and as a restraint on the municipality.

> **Ill**   Conn Mutual Life Ins v Chicago (1900) 185 Ill 148, 56 NE 1071.

§354. Double Assessment

An ordinance declaring a necessity for street improvements at the cost of abutting owners is valid though the properties have previously been assessed for prior street improvements.

> **Ill**   Halsey v Lake View (1900) 188 Ill 540, 59 NE 234.
> **Mo**   Collins v A Jaicks Co (1919) 279 Mo 404, 214 SW 391.
> **Okla**   Wright v El Reno (1934) 168 Okla 594, 35 P2d 473.

An ordinance providing for an assessment for construction of pavements actually provides for reconstruction of an existing facility and is invalid, as applied to abutting owners who had sidewalks in front of their property originally constructed from public and private funds.

> **Pa**   Hinaman v Vandergrift (1962) 197 PaS 140, 177 A2d 174.

§355. Faulty Construction

An ordinance levying assessments for the cost of street improvements may not be declared invalid merely because the work may have been unskillfully done and the contractor who performed the work failed to comply with his contract since in the absence of fraud acceptance of the work done imports a finding that it was substantially done in accordance with the contract and precludes the property owners from questioning the validity of the assessments.

> **Haw**   Taylor v Honolulu (1919) 25 Haw 58.

§356. Non-Abutting Property

A street paving ordinance that attempts to levy a special assessment against property that does not abut on the streets to be improved is invalid.

> **Kan**   Sports Center v Wichita (1952) 176 Kan 84, 269 P2d 399.
>   Atchison T & SF Ry v Hutchinson (1930) 130 Kan 625, 287 P 587.

A local street improvement district assessment against abutting property owners may not include property one-half mile from the road and serviced by a private road. By singling out a particular tract and ignoring all other property similarly situated an arbitrary classification is reached.

> **Kan**   Snyder Rlty Co v Overland Park (1971) 208 Kan 273, 492 P2d 187.

§357. Change of Original Grade

An ordinance levying an assessment for street improvements is not invalidated by the decision of council to vary the original grade.

> **Iowa**   F M Hubbell Son & Co v Des Moines (1915) 168 Iowa 418, 150 NW 701.

§358. Failure to Complete

Tax bills issued on uncompleted street improvements are void, where the failure to complete constitutes a substantial nonperformance.

> **Mo**   Wills v Burbank (1914) 182 MoApp 68, 167 SW 608.

§359. Annexation, Effect

Where an ordinance authorizes the paving of a street and a contract is awarded to the successful bidder, and after work is begun, but before completion, the city merges with another city, tax bills for the work issued by the annexing city are valid.

> **Mo**   Barber Asphalt Paving v Hayward (1912) 248 Mo 280, 154 SW 140.

§360. Lack of Assessment District

An ordinance providing for a street improvement and for the institution of proceedings in circuit court for assessment of costs against benefited property is not invalid for failure to create or authorize the creation of a benefit district.

> **Mo**   Wabash Ry v St Louis (1933) 64 F2d 921.
> **Ore**   Wagoner v La Grande (1918) 89 Ore 192, 173 P 305.

§361. Suffrage, Right at Referendum

A parish bond election for local rural roads may be restricted to property holders. The improvements received and the payments are directly charged to the adjoining property owners, rather than to the general public as an ad valorem tax, and therefore within the exceptions to the requirement of vote by all electors.

> **La**   Hebert v Vermilion Parish (1971) 258 La 41, 245 So2d 349.

An assessment imposed and collected annually, for payment of principal and interest of bonded indebtedness incurred for paving improvements, is not unconstitutional on the ground that corporate property owners are discriminated against, since they are not permitted to vote at special bond elections. Conceding that corporations are citizens for certain legal purposes, the right of suffrage is not a privilege or immunity that a citizen of one state may require of any state to which he may remove, and it is not a right of property or persons.

> **La**   Judice v Scott (1929) 168 La 111, 121 So 592.

The constitutional prohibition prohibits the state only from discriminating on account of race, color, or previous condition of servitude, but does not affect the power of the state to confer or withhold suffrage rights for other reasons, conditions or qualifications.

> **La**   Judice v Scott (1929) 168 La 111, 121 So 592.

An ordinance establishing a road to a planned community is legislative, and subject to referendum.

> **Cal**   Wheelright v Marin County (1970) 2 C3d 448, 467 P2d 537, 85 CaR 809.

§362. Laches—Municipality

A lapse of 10 months after enactment of an ordinance of necessity for street improvements before further proceedings were taken by the city does not invalidate the ordinance or cause the city to lose jurisdiction.

> **Okla**   Berry v Drumright (1925) 110 Okla 223, 237 P 102.

§363. —Property Owner

The doctrine of laches applies to cases involving assessments for public improvements. Thus, where a property owner unreasonably delays bringing an action attacking the validity of street improvement ordinances, the action is barred though the circumstances were such that relief would have been granted had application been made promptly.

> **Okla**   Bartlesville v Holm (1914) 40 Okla 467, 139 P 273, 9 ALR 627.

§364. Repeal of Assessment

Where an ordinance levying property assessments for street improvements has been enacted and published, and improvement bonds have been issued and delivered to the contractor, an ordinance undertaking to repeal the assessment ordinance is void.

> **Okla** El Reno v Cleveland-Trinidad Paving (1910) 25 Okla 648, 107 P 163.

§365. Right to Hearing

Where an ordinance levying an assessment for street improvements fails to give an opportunity to the owner of the property to be heard with regard to any tax or assessment levied on his property, it is invalid.

> **Md** Johns Hopkins Club Building v Baltimore (1917) 130 Md 282, 100 A 298.

XXVIII. ENFORCEMENT OF ASSESSMENTS

§366. Collection, Generally

Where a city under an ordinance chooses to have the work done by assessments at the expense of abutting owners, it does not assume the payment of the obligations or the bonds issued to finance the improvements, but it is committed to use all legal measures to enforce collection of the assessments.

> **Ky** Knepfle v Morehead (1946) 301 Ky 417, 192 SW2d 189.

A charge imposed by a special assessment ordinance, enacted after the required legal notice and opportunity to be heard were given, may be enforced against protesting landowners who did not avail themselves of the notice and hearing opportunities within the specified time.

> **Ore** Bechtell v Salem (1960) 226 Ore 1, 358 P2d 563.

Provisions in paving assessment statutes and a paving ordinance that payment of assessments "may" be enforced in the same manner as city taxes do not require enforcement in the same manner as city taxes.

> **SC** Mason v Williams (1940) 194 SC 290, 9 SE2d 537.

Though public authority seeking to enforce an ordinance levying sidewalk assessments, like those undertaking to enforce payment of taxes, must proceed in strict accordance with the law in all essential matters affecting the rights of the persons concerned, they should not be deprived of any efficacious means of enforcement by a strained construction of the law.

> **SC** Cheraw v Turnage (1937) 184 SC 76, 191 SE 831.

§367. Prescribed Method Exclusive

Where adequate for enforcement, the procedure set out in an ordinance for the collection of special street improvement assessments, and the sale of property for delinquencies is exclusive.

Utah　Petterson v Ogden (1947) 111 Utah 125, 176 P2d 599.

§368. Action in Rem

A proceeding to enforce an assessment, levied by ordinance is in rem and not in personam.

SC　Cheraw v Turnage (1937) 184 SC 76, 191 SE 831.

§369. In Name of Municipality

Assessments made by a municipality against the owner of land abutting on a street paved or repaved as a municipal public works project may be collected by action in the name of the municipality.

W Va　Moundsville v Brown (1945) 127 W Va 602, 34 SE2d 321.

§370. Personal Action

Under an ordinance providing for the levy of special assessments for street improvements, and the collection thereof by suit before a competent court, the city may bring a personal action therefor against the property owner, before a justice of the peace, if the amount is within his jurisdiction.

W Va　St Marys v Locke (1914) 73 W Va 30, 80 SE 841.

§371. By Sale of Property

In an ordinance authorizing the sale of property on default in payment of any installment of street improvement bonds, a provision for issuance of a certificate for each sale required a separate sale of each parcel.

Cal　Sterling Rlty v Relfe (1942) 21 CA2d 164, 130 P2d 410.

§372. —To Municipality

A street improvement ordinance requiring property sold to satisfy a lien for the assessments to be sold to the city is not unconstitutional as imposing a burden on all taxpayers for the benefit of the bondholder who holds the same in private ownership, thus constituting a gift to the bondholder in contravention of the Constitution. The street improvement is for a public purpose and the city may expend its general funds for that purpose.

Cal Stege v Richmond (1924) 194 Cal 305, 228 P 461.

§373. Foreclosure

Since the constitutional provision that gives municipalities the power to impose, by ordinance, paving assessments contains no provision for enforcement of the liens thereby created, the assessments levied are enforceable in equity by way of foreclosure, as the only effectual remedy.

SC Cheraw v Turnage (1937) 184 SC 76, 191 SE 831.

§374. Prima Facie Case

A prima facie case is made in a suit to enforce a paving lien where the town offers in evidence, the abutting owners' petition for paving, newspapers in which the notice was published, all the ordinances, and a certified statement of the clerk of court showing that the ordinance accepting the paving is duly recorded.

La Ruston v Adams (1928) 9 LaApp 618, 121 So 661.

§375. Defenses

A statute providing that in an action to enforce an ordinance providing for a special assessment the landowner may deny the amount claimed, and plead irregularities in the assessment, or any fact destroying its legality, affords sufficient notice and opportunity to establish every defense available, and one cannot complain that a judgment against him in such an action is a taking of property without due process of law.

NC Kingston v Wooten (1909) 150 NC 295, 63 SE 1061.

In an action to enforce a street assessment, it is a valid defense that the assessment includes a charge for work not authorized by the resolution of intention and not included in the invitation for bids.

Cal Donnelly v Howard (1882) 60 Cal 291.

§376. Statute of Limitations

Where a city's levy of a special assessment for street improvements was more than two years past due, and the statute of limitations was pleaded against the enforcement of the levy, the city had no power to enact a new ordinance levying a new special assessment against the same property for the same improvement.

> **Tex**   Big Spring v Tate (1942) 162 SW2d 1066.

Where an ordinance levying paving assessments provides that they shall be collected in the same manner as taxes on real estate, and authorizes use of the same remedies, it does not bring the paving assessment within the four-year statute of limitations applicable to taxes.

> **Md**   St Paul Bldg v Baltimore (1926) 149 Md 685, 132 A 51.

§377. Failure to Enforce; Municipal Liability

Where an ordinance authorizing a bond issue to finance street improvements provides for the levy of special assessments against abutting property, and the city negligently fails to enforce collection of the assessments, it is liable to a bondholder who brings suit within the applicable period of limitations.

> **Ky**   Catlettsburg v Trapp (1935) 261 Ky 347, 87 SW2d 621.

XXIX. ENJOINING ENFORCEMENT

§378. Enjoining Collection

An action to enjoin the collection of street improvement assessments and cancel street improvement bonds is barred after 60 days from the date of enactment of the final assessment ordinance.

> **Okla**   Warner-Quinlan Asphalt v Smith (1918) 68 Okla 263, 173 P 516.
> Chickasha v O'Brien (1916) 58 Okla 46, 159 P 282.

§379. —Invalid Annexation

The collection of street paving assessments against property annexed to a city will not be enjoined at the instance of a landowner on the ground that the ordinance of annexation was void. The validity of the annexation ordinance is not open to such a collateral attack.

> **Okla**   Moore v Perry (1927) 126 Okla 153, 259 P 133.

Where certain property has not been validly annexed, an action to enjoin the levying and collection of assessments for street improvement purposes is not barred for failure to protest the ordinance of necessity which created the improvement district.

Okla Maud v Tulsa Rig Reel & Mfg (1933) 165 Okla 181, 25 P2d 792.

§380. Issuance of Injunction

Where a city adopts an ordinance accepting the responsibility and liability for furnishing all required right-of-way to the state for construction of a highway, an injunction by the property owners to be affected in the city, restraining the state highway commission from awarding a contract for that portion of the road, is proper, on a showing that the city is without funds to pay the landowners' damages.

Ark Keith v Ark State Highway Comm (1955) 225 Ark 86, 279 SW2d 292.

Equity will enjoin the enforcement of an ordinance that condemns a sidewalk newly constructed on property adjoining a new building, where it appears that members of the council were cognizant of the installation of the sidewalk while it was being constructed, but said nothing and did nothing to inform the owner that the sidewalk would not be accepted as conforming to ordinance requirements.

Mo Rubinstein v Salem (1948) 210 SW2d 382.

§381. —Invalid Ordinance

Unless an ordinance authorizing the opening of a street over private property has been legally enacted, municipal officers have no authority to open it, and they may be enjoined from doing so.

Pa Sollak v North Belle Vernon (1938) 131 PaS 459, 200 A 707.

§382. Denial of Injunction

Where all acts necessary to be done in connection with street improvements have been performed, including the enactment of an assessment ordinance and the certification of the assessments to the county clerk who has placed them on the tax rolls, an injunction will not lie against the county clerk and county treasurer to enjoin collection of the assessments.

Okla Harn v Oklahoma City (1915) 47 Okla 639, 149 P 868.

An action by property owners to enjoin a village from further permitting a certain sidewalk to be constructed contrary to established grade and in violation of an ordinance governing construction of sidewalks was properly dismissed, in the absence of evidence that the village had either authorized the construction or had taken any part therein.

Neb   Shanner Bros v Page (1921) 106 Neb 470, 184 NW 131.

§383. —Legislative Discretion

It is error to enjoin payment of costs of making street improvement, if paid out of bond issue money approved by the voters. An ordinance for the purpose of resurfacing, improving, and widening an existing street is within the sound discretion of the legislative and administrative officers.

Ohio   Kellogg v Sherrill (1927) 24 OA 169, 5 Abs 306, 156 NE 418.

§384. —Improbability of Injury

If there is no substantial probability of injury from irregularities in an ordinance and plan for a street widening project, the court may deny interference by injunction.

Md   Browne v Baltimore (1932) 163 Md 212, 161 A 24.

§385. —Fraud

Fraud of members of a city council, justifying an injunction against a street paving contract, is not shown by proof that the members took a junket on the invitation of the successful bidder, where such bidder had no monopoly of the materials or supplies and was the lowest bidder for the work among several other concerns, who were given equal opportunity to obtain the contract.

Iowa   Swan v Indianola (1909) 142 Iowa 731, 121 NW 547.

§386. —Improper Estimate

An ordinance levying special assessments for street improvement purposes will not, in the absence of fraud or collusion, be set aside or enjoined on the ground that the city engineer improperly included certain items in his estimate of cost.

Okla   Beggs v Kelly (1925) 110 Okla 274, 238 P 466.

§387. Status of Property Owner

Proof of ownership of property in a proposed street improvement district is essential to an action by persons seeking to enjoin the operation of an ordinance creating the improvement district.

Okla Rudnicki v Valley Brook (1967) 424 P2d 973.

A property owner is without standing to enjoin the city commissioners from proceeding under an ordinance to widen a street where the commission has not first paid him compensation for the taking of his property, since this rule of compensation applies only to individual property being taken by a private corporation.

Ark Cannon v Felsenthal (1930) 180 Ark 1075, 24 SW2d 856.

§388. Statute of Limitations as Bar

The statutory period of limitation within which an action may be brought to set aside an ordinance assessing property for street improvements does not bar an action to enjoin collection of an assessment when the proceedings on which it is based are void.

Okla Enid v Gensman (1919) 76 Okla 90, 181 P 308.

§389. Estoppel

In a suit for an injunction to prevent a city from collecting void assessments for special benefits accruing to plaintiff's land by municipal paving, estoppel by knowledge of the improvement and by failure to object thereto or to the assessments is not available as a defense.

Neb Rooney v South Sioux City (1923) 111 Neb 1, 195 NW 474.

If property owners who have appeared before the city council and urged their objections to a proposed special assessment for a public improvement fail to appeal from the council's action, they are thereafter estopped to question the assessment or to maintain an action to enjoin its enforcement, unless the council was wholly without jurisdiction.

Neb Burkley v Omaha (1918) 102 Neb 308, 167 NW 72.

§390. Laches

An action to enjoin collection of street improvements assessments, under an ordinance, is barred by laches after a long delay in commencing the action and acceptance of benefits of the improvements.

> **Okla**   Ardmore v Appollos (1916) 62 Okla 232, 162 P 211.

XXX. JUDICIAL INTERVENTION

§391. Judicial Abstention

It is not within the province of the judiciary to set up its judgment on the necessity and propriety of an ordinance regulating the use of streets and public places, so long as the enactment cannot be said to be clearly unreasonable.

> **Ill**   Chicago v Rhine (1936) 363 Ill 619, 2 NE2d 905, 105 ALR 1045.

Review by writ of certiorari of an action of the board of supervisors is only available as to judicial action by the board. The board's decision regarding the location of a highway overpass is not subject to review, when the board had no jurisdiction to determine the location of the overpass and the purported determination therefore could not possibly constitute judicial action.

> **Iowa**   Curtis v Bd of Supervisors of Clinton County (1978) 270 NW2d 447.

§392. —Legislative Discretion

Where legislative power is conferred on the governing body of a city to determine the size, form and boundaries of a street improvement district, the judiciary will not interfere with the governing board's legislative determination thereof, in the absence of jurisdictional defects, fraud, or arbitrary action.

> **Ill**   Batavia v Wiley (1930) 342 Ill 384, 174 NE 553.
> **Md**   Baltimore v Williams (1916) 129 Md 290, 99 A 362.
> **NC**   Crowell v Monroe (1910) 152 NC 399, 67 SE 989.
> **ND**   Murphy v Bismarck (1961) 109 NW2d 635.

§393. —Legislative Motives

Where a city purchases land for widening a street and thereafter under an ordinance assesses abutting owners for costs of the improvements, the purchase of the land is for a municipal purpose, and in the absence of bad faith the court will not inquire into the motives or control the city's discretion in order to relieve an abutting owner of assessments for costs of widening the street.

Ky Bosshammer v South Fort Mitchell (1934) 252 Ky 785, 68 SW2d 413.

§394. —Faulty Legislative Reasoning

That the city council proceeded on a fundamentally wrong basis and used wrong methods of reasoning in enacting a local improvement ordinance will not affect its validity, where the council decided that the property was benefited and properly included in the assessment roll, in view of the rule that the courts cannot inquire into the motive impelling the passage of an ordinance regular on its face.

Wash Twentieth Ave NE, In re (1917) 95 Wash 5, 163 P 12.

§395. Subjects of Judicial Inquiry—Standards

Where the legislature has not specified the precise manner in which a city shall regulate its streets, the reasonableness of the exercise of such power is open to judicial inquiry.

Ill Haggenjos v Chicago (1929) 336 Ill 573, 168 NE 661.

§396. —Exercise for Private Purpose

The courts will not interfere with the discretion manifested by the city council in exercising its legislative power to vacate an alley, unless that power is exercised solely for private purposes.

Ill Moskal v Catholic Bishop of Chicago (1942) 315 IllAp 461, 43 NE2d 206.

§397. —Fraud, Abuse of Power

Unless the enactment of an ordinance vacating a street is tainted with fraud, or is palpably not in the public interest, or is a clear perversion of power, there is no occasion for judicial intervention.

Mich Tomaszewski v Palmer Bee (1923) 223 Mich 565, 194 NW 571.
NJ Pyatt v Dunellen (1952) 9 NJ 548, 89 A2d 1.
SC Bethel Methodist Episcopal Church v Greenville (1947) 211 SC 442, 45 SE2d 841.

§398. —Apparent on Face of Ordinance

In order to justify judicial interference with the determination of a city council as to the reasonableness of a local improvement ordinance, an abuse of power must appear on the face of the ordinance itself.

Ill   Ottawa v Colwell (1913) 260 Ill 548, 103 NE 573.

§399. Mandamus

Mandamus will not lie against a municipal judge or city attorney to prosecute construction workers for violation of an ordinance by obstruction of a city street, where the purpose of the mandamus action is merely to test the validity of an ordinance.

Ore   Collins v Grant (1911) 59 Ore 77, 116 P 334.

STREET VENDORS

EDITORIAL COMMENT. This is where most of the Good Humor Man cases are classified. Many ordinances attempting to regulate or prohibit his activities have found their way into the courts. A city may not, under the guise of a high fee for revenue, prohibit rather than license the business (§27). In §28, we find that an Ohio case in 1946 held that an ordinance prohibiting the street vending of ice cream had no substantial relation to the public welfare, was destructive of a lawful business, and was invalid. The court refused to follow a contrary Ohio case decided in 1939.

Other forms of street vending are also covered herein, such as pushcarts (§15) and food vendors (§16). Several other topics contain closely related subjects. These include BAKERIES; CHARITABLE ACTIVITIES AND SOLICITATIONS; FOOD BUSINESS; HANDBILLS AND PAMPHLETS; NOISE; PEDDLERS AND SOLICITORS; PHOTOGRAPHY; RELIGION; and MILK; DAIRIES; DAIRY PRODUCTS; as well as NEWSPAPERS; MAGAZINES; BOOKS.

I. IN GENERAL

§1. Use of Streets for Business

Persons have no vested right to make marts of the streets, alleys, and public places in an incorporated town. Such use of the public ways is a privilege subject to reasonable regulation by the municipality.

>   **Haw**   Hawaii v Scruggs (1958) 43 Haw 71.
>   **Tex**   Bradshaw, Ex parte (1913) 70 TexCr 166, 159 SW 259.

The general rule is that a municipality, unless expressly authorized, has no power to permit, by lease, permit or otherwise, the use of part of a sidewalk for fruit, newsstands or the like. Consequently, an ordinance granting a license to operate a newsstand on a public sidewalk is void.

>   **Iowa**   Cowin v Waterloo (1946) 237 Iowa 202, 21 NW2d 705.

§2. —Prohibition; Regulation; Licensing

A ban on the sale of food from motor vehicles in which a customer is induced to approach the vehicle is an unreasonable restriction on a commercial activity. While protection of the public, especially children, is a justified police power, there must be a showing of a special hazard potentially raised by the business.

>   **Pa**   Simco Sales Service v Lower Mervin Township (1978) 394 A2d 642.

An ordinance against sidewalk sales which does not designate the areas contained within the prohibition or make any reference to sales of farm products may not be a basis for prosecution. A separate ordinance establishing areas opened for sale including a street market but not restricting sales to the designated areas may not be used in conjunction with the prohibition ordinance to limit the areas to only those enumerated.

>   **Ill**   Chicago v Witvoet (1975) 30 IllAp3d 386, 332 NE2d 767.

A ban on packing, unpacking, soliciting and selling farm products on any street except those designated is a valid police power exercise by the city. The obstruction of city sidewalks and the dangers of spoilage and rodents involved in selling farm products on the street is subject to control. The statutory exemption of farm products does not apply to a home rule city when the statute precedes the Constitution.

>   **Ill**   Witvoet v Quinlan (1976) 41 IllAp3d 724, 354 NE2d 524.

A ban against street vendors of all products except flowers and ice cream is a reasonable restriction on the use of sidewalks to prevent obstruction of pedestrian traffic. The ordinance relating to itinerant merchants referring to sales from trucks or rental of store space with a required license may not be applied to a sale of jewelry on sidewalks in a downtown area.

> **Tex** Hixon v State (1975) 523 SW2d 711.

While a city may regulate the sale of commercial objects on the public streets and parkways they may not infringe on First Amendment rights to sell newsworthy articles. A map showing the location of movie star's homes is a First Amendment protected right. The ordinance may validly prohibit the sale of any produce including news items in the roadway as a protection for the general public. An injunction issued on the basis of the ordinance is invalid where it prohibits the sale of the maps on all sidewalks, streets, and parkways in any residential area.

> **Cal** Welton v Los Angeles (1976) 18 C3d 497, 556 P2d 1119, 134 CaR 668.

A city has authority to prohibit a private business on a street, or to grant a franchise or privilege to use the streets in the conduct of a business.

> **Tex** Greene v San Antonio (1915) 178 SW 6.

§3. Definitions

The sale of ice cream and confections from automobiles is "peddling" within the well known and generally accepted meaning of that term, and as denounced in an ordinance prohibiting peddling.

> **NJ** NJ Good Humor v Bradley Beach (1939) 123 NJLaw 21, 7 A2d 824.

II. CONDUCT OF BUSINESS

§4. Generally

A municipal corporation has the implied power to adopt an ordinance providing for reasonable regulation, but not prohibition, of the sale of merchandise on the streets from mobile units.

> **NC** State v Byrd (1963) 259 NC 141, 130 SE2d 55.

An ordinance prohibiting peddlers from crying their wares in the streets is merely regulative, and does not deprive a peddler of the right to engage in his business on a street, or deprive him of property without due process of law.

> **Ill** Goodrich v Busse (1910) 247 Ill 366, 93 NE 292.

§5. Hours of Operation

An ordinance imposing a license tax on peddlers and hawkers on the city streets, and restricting their business to certain hours, does not violate equal protection as applied to those selling popcorn and fruits, though it specifically exempts distributors of newspapers, Bibles, political literature, and producers of farm products, for the use of the streets may be prohibited or regulated, as the city deems best for the public good.

> **Ore** Rosa v Portland (1917) 86 Ore 438, 168 P 936.

§6. Sound Devices

In an ordinance regulating peddlers and street vendors, a prohibition against the use of a gong bell or other sound device is a proper exercise of the police power, where the means adopted are reasonably necessary for accomplishment of the purpose and are not unduly oppressive of individuals.

> **NJ** Mr Softee v Hoboken (1962) 77 NJS 354, 186 A2d 513.

In an ordinance prohibiting street vendors from producing annoying sounds and using a gong bell or other instrument or sound device, the doctrine of ejusdem generis will be applied to limit the scope of the prohibition to sound devices similar in nature to a gong bell.

> **NJ** Mr Softee v Hoboken (1962) 77 NJS 354, 186 A2d 513.

§7. Crying Wares; Other Noises

Under a statute authorizing municipalities to regulate sales in streets and public places, and to regulate hawkers and peddlers, a city may enact an ordinance prohibiting persons from crying or making other noises in connection with their sale of goods, except in amusement grounds, parks, halls and other public places.

> **Ill** Goodrich v Busse (1910) 247 Ill 366, 93 NE 292.

§8. Solicitation in Street

An ordinance prohibiting the manager or employee of a store or other place of business selling refreshments to solicit or to serve refreshments from or to any person on the further side from his storeroom of that portion of a street used for vehicular travel does not apply to an ice cream vending truck. The ordinance was not designed to apply to a mobile vending vehicle from which merchandise is usually dispensed to customers on both sides of the street.

Va   Vought v Jones (1965) 205 Va 719, 139 SE2d 810.

§9. Peddling from Vehicle

Where the possessor of a veterans state peddlers' license intentionally disregards an ordinance prohibiting peddling from a vehicle in the street, in order to test its validity, the court, considering the novelty of the ordinance and that defendant had no intent to flagrantly violate the same will suspend the fine and sentence.

NJ   Harrington Park v Hogenbirk (1958) 52 NJS 223, 145 A2d 161.

§10. Ice Cream Vendors

Street peddlers may be reasonably regulated, but their absolute prohibition is arbitrary and unreasonable. Where vehicles used for dispensing ice cream are not themselves dangerous instruments total prohibition is unreasonable. But since children frequently play in streets both the time and manner of sales from such vehicles may be controlled.

Kan   Delight Wholesale Co v Overland Park (1969) 203 Kan 99, 453 P2d 82.

A prohibition against selling any merchandise from vehicles stopped or parked at the curb in the absence of evidence showing a danger to health, traffic, or welfare is invalid. An uncontradicted showing that the vehicles are operated safely and with adequate precautions for the protection of all customers makes the ordinance arbitrary and nonreasonable.

Kan   Delight Wholesale Co v Prairie Village (1971) 208 Kan 246, 491 P2d 910.

A municipality may not entirely prohibit the business of vending ice cream or ice cream products on its public streets. A city, however, in the exercise of its police power, may regulate it by reasonable measures.

NY   Trio Distributor v Albany (1956) 2 Misc2d 627, 156 NYS2d 906.

§11. —Vehicles with Bells or Chimes

An ordinance restricting the activities of street vendors of ice cream from motor vehicles equipped with bells and chimes does not arbitrarily discriminate against them as compared with other forms of merchandising, for as long as a rational basis exists for classification among merchants, supported by pertinent facts, the classification is valid and non-discriminatory.

NJ   Mr Softee v Hoboken (1962) 77 NJS 354, 186 A2d 513.

The "tinkle" of Good Humor and the melodious chimes of Mister Softee are not within the prohibition of an ordinance prohibiting street vendors from producing annoying sounds or noises by use of a gong bell or other instrument or sound device, since they are not in the same category as a "gong bell".

NJ   Mister Softee v Hoboken (1962) 77 NJS 354, 186 A2d 513.

§12. Newspaper Vendors

A newspaper vendor authorized by ordinance to peddle on the streets without a license need not obtain a permit to sell in a street area adjacent to a park though the charter confers jurisdiction over and management of streets and avenues immediate to parks on a park commissioner, and by another ordinance sales in any park or parkway may be made only with a permit from the commissioner.

NY   People v Parelli (1916) 93 Misc 692, 158 NYS 644.

III. LICENSING

§13. Police Regulation

The law forbidding the sale on public streets of anything without a license except newspapers, requiring the licensee to wear a numbered badge, and imposing a fee of $1 a month is a police or regulatory measure, not for revenue purposes; and the fee is commensurate with cost of inspection, supervision or regulation.

DC   Busey v DC (1943) 138 F2d 592.

An ordinance regulating and licensing the use of public streets and sidewalks by tradesmen, so as to prevent them from becoming a nuisance and insure they will not remain in one place for extended periods, is a proper exercise of a municipality's police power.

Mass   Commonwealth v Pascone (1941) 308 Mass 591, 33 NE2d 522.

§14. Validity

Denial of a street vendor's license may not be made on a determination that rehabilitation was not accomplished some years prior. The applicant who had a criminal record, but indicated by qualified testimony his rehabilitation, is entitled to a license. The court further criticized failure of the ordinance to set standards for issuing and denying licenses.

DC   Miller v DC Bd of Appeals & Review (1972) 294 A2d 365.

An ordinance requiring a licensee to sell fresh produce, dairy products, fish, game, merchandise, tickets, coupons or receipts redeemable in service, photographs, works of art, magazine subscriptions or merchandise, in or along city streets, is valid.

Utah   Slater v Salt Lake City (1949) 115 Utah 476, 206 P2d 153.

§15. Pushcarts

Where an ordinance authorizes the licensing of itinerant peddlers, the commissioner of public markets, weights, and measures may not refuse to accept license applications from peanut vendors selling from pushcarts solely because he believes licenses should no longer be issued to itinerant peddlers but should be limited to persons having definite and fixed places of business.

NY   Katis v Morgan (1938) 168 Misc 552, 6 NYS2d 315.

§16. Food Vendors

A prohibition against peddling fresh or frozen meat or seafood by itinerant vendors within the city may properly be imposed against selling fish by members of a religious organization. The commercial aspect of their sales takes them out of their religious field and therefore subject to legitimate regulation. Since the fish had been headed, gutted, and frozen they are not within the exemption of products in their natural state.

La   Muhammad Temple of Islam-Shreveport v Shreveport (1974) 387 F Supp 1129.

Since officers are authorized to make arrests without warrants only in cases of felony and breaches of the peace, the president of a village is not justified in ordering the arrest without a warrant, which could have been procured, of an ordinary vendor of popcorn and peanuts, for violating an ordinance by the exercise of his vocation on the street without a license.

Mich   Tillman v Beard (1899) 121 Mich 475, 80 NW 248.

An ordinance authorizing the licensing of specified vending stands within stoop lines does not authorize a permit for the sale of vegetables, where it is not one of the listed businesses authorized to be licensed.

NY   Topoozian v Geraghty (1933) 239 AD 485, 267 NYS 598.

§17. —Exempting Farm Products

Where a statute exempts peddlers of perishable farm products from a license fee levied by the state or any of its subdivisions, an ordinance prohibiting the selling of fruits or vegetables in the streets without registration, bond, and license conflicts with the statute, both in letter and in spirit.

> **Ga**   Martin v Dublin (1934) 50 GaApp 151, 177 SE 279.

§18. Interstate Commerce

An ordinance requiring a license and imposing a license tax on vendors of tea sold at retail from wagons or other vehicles imposes an unconstitutional burden on interstate commerce, as applied to a corporation resident of another state which sells and delivers merchandise through an agent in the city.

> **Mo**   Jewel Tea v Lee's Summit (1912) 198 F 532, 217 F 965.

§19. Fees

A license fee of $300 for each bicycle used in connection with an ice cream peddling business that equals 30 per cent of a person's gross sales is clearly unreasonable, oppressive, and confiscatory in comparison with other license fees imposed on like legitimate businesses and, therefore, unconstitutional.

> **NJ**   Gurland v Kearny (1942) 128 NJLaw 22, 24 A2d 210.

Where a peanut and popcorn seller paid excessive license fees under an ordinance pursuant to the declaration of the commissioner of public safety that his business would be closed if he failed to pay the fees, the payment was involuntary, and consequently the trial court improperly sustained the city's demurrer to the seller's petition to recover the excessive fees paid.

> **Iowa**   Harbeck v Sioux City (1925) 199 Iowa 763, 202 NW 507.

§20. Revocation

An ordinance providing for the revocation of licenses of street food vendors when an abutting property owner or lessee objects to the licensee takes away no rights of abutting owners, but grants an additional remedy for the enforcement of rights they already possess.

> **Pa**   Hindin v Samuel (1946) 158 PaS 539, 45 A2d 370.

IV. PROHIBITION

§21. Generally

The power delegated to municipalities to regulate sales of merchandise on streets, sidewalks, and public places carries with it the authority, not only to impose reasonable restrictions and regulations, but also to suppress sales thereon.

> **Ill** Good Humor v Mundelein (1965) 33 Ill2d 252, 211 NE2d 269.

In the exercise of its broad authority over its streets, a municipality may prohibit the sale on its streets of foodstuffs and other articles of merchandise, in the interest of the public health, and to relieve congestion and promote safety.

> **NY** Carollo v Smithtown (1959) 20 Misc2d 435, 190 NYS2d 36.
> **Tenn** Dooley v Cleveland (1940) 175 Tenn 439, 135 SW2d 649.
> **Tex** Largent, Ex parte (1942) 144 TexCr 592, 162 SW2d 419.
> **Wis** Stevens Point v Bocksenbaum (1937) 225 Wis 373, 274 NW 505.

§22. Validity

An ordinance that prohibits certain street vendors from certain high traffic areas is a proper exercise of police power delegated to the town by the legislature.

> **NH** Paine v Conway (1978) 395 A2d 517.

An ordinance prohibiting the sale of any article except daily newspapers on any street or public place within two specified sections of the city is a valid exercise of the police power, since the right of a municipality to regulate sales on its streets, sidewalks and public places carries with it the authority, not just to impose reasonable regulations and restrictions, but to suppress sales entirely.

> **Ill** Chicago v Rhine (1936) 363 Ill 619, 2 NE2d 905, 105 ALR 1045.

An ordinance prohibiting peddling and hawking on the streets is not authorized by a statutory provision granting a city the power to regulate and license businesses, since hawking and peddling, though subject to regulation, is recognized as a legitimate business.

> **NY** Good Humor v New York City (1942) 264 AD 620, 36 NYS2d 85.

§ 23. —Discrimination

An ordinance prohibiting peddling and street vending in a summer resort town is invalid, where it appears that the motive for its enactment is to abolish any competition with local merchants.

> **NJ**   NJ Good Humor v Bradley Beach (1940) 124 NJLaw 162, 11 A2d 113.

A traffic regulation prohibiting one from standing in the traveled part of a street to talk with or sell or offer to sell anything to an occupant of a vehicle is not discriminatory because its application might have more impact on some trades than on others.

> **NY**   People v Murillo (1956) 148 NYS2d 572.

A provision prohibiting peddling in the city streets except for a limited enumerated class of persons and businesses is invalid where it has no reasonable relation to the public health, is not intended to protect food articles from contamination, and has no reasonable relation to the licensing of peddlers.

> **NY**   Good Humor v New York City (1943) 290 NY 312, 49 NE2d 153.

A provision prohibiting peddling in the city streets and specifically excepting pushcart peddlers with a market license, war veterans and their widows, adult blind persons, newspaper peddlers, and peddlers of home grown farm products is unreasonable, because the discrimination between what is purportedly harmful and harmless is impractical. Generally, the business of peddling is lawful where conducted in a manner that does not injure or annoy the public or impede street traffic.

> **NY**   Good Humor v New York City (1943) 290 NY 312, 49 NE2d 153.
> **Ohio**   Frecker v Dayton (1950) 153 OS 14, 41 Op 109, 90 NE2d 851.

§ 24. —Sales to Persons Under 18

An ordinance prohibiting any ice cream vendor from attempting to sell to a minor child when the minor is situated so that a street separates the vendor from the prospective minor purchaser is valid. The heavy duty placed upon the vendor is a matter of legislative policy and the operation of a vehicle which strikes the child is not an independent intervening cause precluding liability for the attempt to attract a customer.

> **Conn**   Neal v Shiels (1974) 166 Conn 3, 347 A2d 102.

Prohibiting a vendor from selling anything to a minor when the minor has crossed the street requires actual knowledge. Since the ordinance is a penal ordinance it must be specifically construed and constructive knowledge may not be implied.

> **Conn**   Duplin v Shiels (1973) 165 Conn 396, 334 A2d 896.

An ordinance is an unreasonable exercise of the police power if it prohibits the sale of any merchandise to a person under 18 on the street or on public grounds of the city and prohibits the sale of any merchandise that might attract a person under 18 onto the streets or public grounds of the city.

> **Ohio**   Frost Bar v Shaker Heights (1956) 75 Abs 358, 141 NE2d 245.

§25.   —Uniformity of Application

A ban on vendors in the Vieux Carre section based on its economic attraction and to preserve it's uniqueness is valid. A grandfather exemption for vendors in existence for over 8 years is likewise valid.

> **La**   New Orleans v Dukes (1976) 427 US 297, 49 LE2d 511, 96 SCt 2513.

An ordinance prohibiting the sale of any goods, except newspapers, on streets or public places within two especially congested sections of the city is not invalid as unreasonable because not applicable uniformly to all parts of the city, since uniformity of a police regulation is not required if it is based on a reasonable classification bearing a substantial relation to the ordinance.

> **Ill**   Chicago v Rhine (1936) 363 Ill 619, 2 NE2d 905, 105 ALR 1045.

An ordinance prohibiting peddlers from crying their wares in the streets, but permitting such practice in certain licensed amusement grounds and in parks, is not invalid as discriminatory, since the conditions with regard to sale of goods in parks and places of amusement are different from those obtaining in the public streets.

> **Ill**   Goodrich v Busse (1910) 247 Ill 366, 93 NE 292.

§26. Interstate Commerce

An ordinance provision prohibiting the sale of magazine subscriptions or merchandise on selected streets in the business district does not materially interfere with interstate commerce or abridge freedom of speech, but does constitute an unreasonable discrimination and unequal protection of the laws where another provision of the ordinance permits the street sale in the business district of coupons redeemable in photographs, works of art, magazine subscriptions or merchandise.

> **Utah**   Slater v Salt Lake City (1949) 115 Utah 476, 206 P2d 153.

§27. Ice Cream Vendors

A municipality may not, under the guise of a high fee for revenue, prohibit rather than license and regulate a legitimate business of peddling ice cream and ice cream products.

> NJ   Gurland v Kearny (1942) 128 NJLaw 22, 24 A2d 210.
>   Kohr Bros v Atlantic City (1928) 104 NJLaw 468, 142 A 34.
> NC   State v Byrd (1963) 259 NC 141, 130 SE2d 55.

§28. —Sale from Vehicles

Street peddlers may be reasonably regulated, but their absolute prohibition is arbitrary and unreasonable. Where vehicles used for dispensing ice cream are not themselves dangerous instruments total prohibition is unreasonable. But since children frequently play in streets both the time and manner of sales from such vehicles may be controlled.

> Kan   Delight Wholesale Co v Overland Park (1969) 203 Kan 99, 453 P2d 82.

A prohibition against selling any merchandise from vehicles stopped or parked at the curb in the absence of evidence showing a danger to health, traffic, or welfare is invalid. An uncontradicted showing that the vehicles are operated safely and with adequate precautions for the protection of all customers makes the ordinance arbitrary and unreasonable.

> Kan   Delight Wholesale Co v Prairie Village (1971) 208 Kan 246, 491 P2d 910.

An ordinance making it unlawful to sell within the city ice cream from any wagon, push cart, or other vehicle has no real or substantial relation to the safety, health or general welfare of the public, is completely destructive of a lawful business, and is not a valid exercise of the police power.

> Ohio   Schul v King (1946) 35 Op 238, 70 NE2d 378.

An ordinance prohibiting the sale of ice cream from any vehicles in the streets, but allowing the sale of other articles, does not amount to an unjust and unreasonably discriminatory classification, where the purpose of the city council in enacting the ordinance, was to eliminate traffic hazards incident to children rushing into the streets to purchase ice cream.

> Ohio   X-Cel Dairy v Akron (1939) 63 OA 147, 16 Op 422, 25 NE2d 700.

The sale of ice cream and confections from automobiles is "peddling" within the well known and generally accepted meaning of that term, and as denounced in an ordinance prohibiting peddling.

> NJ   NJ Good Humor v Bradley Beach (1939) 123 NJLaw 21, 7 A2d 824.

§29. Christmas Week as Exception

A provision of the Administrative Code allowing storekeepers and peddlers to sell Christmas trees, holiday decorations, and toys on the sidewalk during December, if they obtain permission of the abutting owner and keep clear a pedestrian passageway, is invalid, where the charter prohibits enactment of local laws allowing encroachments or obstructions of sidewalks.

NY People v Berner (1939) 170 Misc 501, 10 NYS2d 339.

In an ordinance prohibiting the sale of merchandise in public places and on streets in designated congested districts, a provision authorizing the mayor to issue temporary permits to street vendors to sell toys and novelties from December 15-25, may not be challenged by a person whose business is not within that exempted class and whose alleged offense was not committed during the designated period.

Ill Chicago v Rhine (1936) 363 Ill 619, 2 NE2d 905, 105 ALR 1045.

V. RESTRAINING ENFORCEMENT

§30. Generally

An injunction will not issue to restrain a criminal prosecution of an ice cream peddler for violating an allegedly unconstitutional ordinance prohibiting the peddling of ice cream and frozen confections.

Ga Hornsby v Bristow (1938) 185 Ga 577, 196 SE 25.

SUBDIVISIONS

EDITORIAL COMMENT. In these days of rapid urban growth, subdivisions are everywhere. They raise an abundance of municipal problems, bringing in, as they do, concentrations of population. In an attempt to insure some sort of orderly development, cities and counties have enacted ordinances setting out certain minimum standards that subdividers must meet. These have to do with such things as providing for streets, sewers, drainage, water, schools, and parks and recreation areas. Zoning, taxation, and annexation also get involved. These matters, and others, are discussed in the cases digested below. The local authorities are given very broad powers in the field.

As indicated above, many other subjects are involved in subdivisions. For research into those fields, other topics should be consulted. These include ZONING; SEWERS; TAXATION; PARKS; and STREETS; SIDEWALKS; BRIDGES. Also, for annexation questions, see ANNEXATION; CHANGE OF BOUNDARIES; for storm and other drainage generally see DRAINAGE; FLOOD CONTROL; and for problems relating to water supply, see WATER SYSTEMS; WATER SUPPLY.

I. FILING PLATS

A. Authority to Regulate

§1. Constitutional and Statutory

A municipality may require that a new subdivision plat tie in with the outside area as far as streets and alleys are concerned and for the streets and alleys to correspond in width, direction and connected to existing streets and alleys.

Wyo   Prudential Tr Co v Laramie (1972) 492 P2d 971.

The regulation of dividing or subdividing land is subject to statutory grant. A county prohibition against dividing land into sections larger than thirty-six acres, which is described as not a subdivision, is improper. The statutory authorization only granted the power to regulate subdivisions in tracts of less than thirty-six acres.

> **Ariz** Transamerica Title Ins Co v Cochise County (1976) 26 ArizApp 323, 548 P2d 416.

Approval of a subdivision plat by the planning commission does not make the city council's approval an automatic administrative action. The ordinance provision that approval of the final plat by the planning commission is revocable and does not constitute final approval or acceptance by the city council prevails. On withdrawal of a plat there is no automatic approval since there is nothing on file to be approved.

> **SD** Lohman v Aberdeen (1976) 246 NW2d 781.

Under a statute authorizing municipalities to create municipal planning boards, a city may enact an ordinance providing for such a board with power to supervise the orderly development of the city through regulation of land subdivision.

> **NH** Blevens v Manchester (1961) 103 NH 284, 170 A2d 121.
> **NJ** Highpoint v Bloomfield (1963) 80 NJS 570, 194 A2d 378.

Denial of a permit to subdivide a lot or tract is unreasonable where there is a showing of economic hardship on the owner, and no showing of public safety, health, and welfare by the city.

> **NY** Young v Great Neck Est (1970) 62 Misc2d 147, 307 NYS2d 895.

LAW REVIEW

Democracy in New Towns: The Limits of Private Government (1969) 36 UChiLR 379.

ANNOTATION

Validity under due process clause of regulations as to subdivision maps or plats or of conditions imposed to approval thereof, 11 ALR2d 532.

§2. Conflict with Statute

Under a statute providing for the platting of additions to incorporated towns, and explicitly declaring what are necessary as conditions precedent to the recording of such plats, a town has no power to pass an ordinance imposing the additional requirement that the plat of a new addition shall not be effective unless approved by resolution of the town council.

Ida   State v Clark (1965) 88 Ida 365, 399 P2d 955.
Iowa   Burroughs v Cherokee (1906) 134 Iowa 429, 109 NW 876.

LAW REVIEW

Uncle Tom's Multi-Cabin Subdivision Constitutional Restrictions on Racial Discrimination by the Developers, 53 Corn LR 314.

ANNOTATIONS

Construction of regulations as to subdivision maps or plats with respect to question of dedication of portions of lands to public use, 11 ALR2d 546.

Validity of conditions imposed for approval of subdivision maps or plat, 11 ALR2d 532.

Designation of public lands on maps or plats vesting title under statute, 11 ALR2d 567.

§3. Administrative Boards

A council passing on a subdivision application is acting in an administrative capacity and is controlled by regulations relating thereto. They have no discretion or choice in approving a plat if it meets the regulations. Therefore, that an attempted amendment of the plat was denied by the planning commission is not a ground for the council's denial of approval, where the plat complies in all respects with the ordinance requirements.

Conn   Bossert Corp v Norwalk (1968) 157 Conn 279, 253 A2d 39.

The town board may grant limited power to the planning board to approve or change subdivision plats within specific limits and conditions.

NY   Orrell v Planning Bd of Pound Ridge (1971) 66 Misc2d 843, 322 NYS2d 444.

A master plan which requires approval by the department of planning makes the decision subject to judicial review. The subdivision provisions which likewise provide for approval by the department of planning with an appeal to the planning board does not apply when the decision regards conformity to the master plan rather than the subdivision requirements.

Del   New Castle County v Richeson (1975) 347 A2d 135.

A requirement that if the board approves plans for rezoning, the plans together with the recommendation shall be submitted to the council for consideration and approval does not prohibit the council from considering plans disapproved. A separate ordinance authorizing approval by three-fourths vote of the council without the planning board approval may be applied.

Mich   Szyszkoski v Lansing (1975) 64 Mich Ap 94, 235 NW2d 72.

Pursuant to statute, a municipality may, by ordinance, require subdivision approval by its planning board, in lieu of the governing body, in accordance with regulations, requirements and standards established by the governing body.

NJ   Noble v Committee of Mendham (1966) 91 NJS 111, 219 A2d 335.

A county zoning resolution cannot prevent the board of county commissioners from reconsidering the filing of a subdivision plat under the resolution since the board, not the planning commission, is ultimately charged with such a decision by statute.

ND   Berger v Morton County (1979) 275 NW2d 315.

Zoning boards of review are not vested with jurisdiction to subdivide land, nor can they derive such jurisdiction by virtue of ordinances adopted by municipal legislatures.

RI   Slawson v Barrington (1966) 100 RI 485, 217 A2d 92.

A subdivision plat may not be denied recording for failure to comply with zoning ordinances. The planning commission itself must adopt plans or rules or regulations for their acceptance.

Ohio   Pelham Devel v Orange (1971) 25 OS2d 280, 54 Op2d 390, 268 NE2d 278.

The rules governing subdivisions in a village having a planning commission must be made by the commission, not by ordinance. On failure of the planning commission to adopt regulations governing plats and subdivisions, denial of recording is arbitrary and unlawful.

Ohio   Gates Mills Inv Co v Parks (1971) 25 OS2d 16, 266 NE2d 552.

A zoning ordinance regulating the subdivision of lands within the unincorporated area of a county, and specifying that the commission shall secure the approval and signatures of such officials as are prescribed by law before filing the final plat for recording, is not unconstitutional for leaving the approval of the property owner's plans to unidentified officials, since the modifying clause "as prescribed by law" makes it clear that the approval of only those officials whose duty it is to examine a plan or plat before it is recorded is required.

Ida State v Clark (1965) 88 Ida 365, 399 P2d 955.

A determination that a proposed subdivision would create a serious fire hazard is sufficient grounds for denial of subdividing. The requirements that the proposed subdivision be submitted to various agencies including the state forestry service requires that their report and recommendation be considered in determining whether the subdivision plan meets requirements of public health, safety and welfare.

Colo Shoptaugh v Bd of Comm of El Paso County (1975) 37 ColoAp 39, 543 P2d 524.

§3.1. Definition

Dividing a tract of rural agricultural land into five and six acre tracts with access on a state highway does not come within the statutory exemption of dividing farm land for agricultural uses. As such the property is subject to the subdivision ordinances of a county including the use and density requirements.

Ky McCord v Pineway Farms (1978) 569 SW2d 690.

The creation of a campground does not violate a local subdivision ordinance where the enabling statute defines subdivision as "the division of a tract or parcel of land into three or more lots within any five-year period whether accomplished by sale, lease, development, building or otherwise."

Me Arundel v Swain (1977) 374 A2d 317.

An ordinance defining a subdivision as a single lot divided into two or more lots with streets as public rights-of-way does not apply to development of a tract by constructing several apartment buildings. The streets to be laid out for the use of inhabitants are not public thoroughfares and the property is not being subdivided into two or more tracts.

Pa Cassidy v Lawrence U Ginter (1972) 6 PaCmwlth 430, 296 A2d 293.

A subdivision may be properly defined as the division of any parcel of land into two or more parcels, lots, or sites. Requirement of recording and submission to the planning board for approval before a building permit may be issued is a valid means of enforcing an ordinance.

NY Delaware Midland Corp v Westhampton Beach (1974) 79 Misc2d 438, 359 NYS2d 944.

A classification of subdivision as any division of a lot, tract or parcel into two or more lots, plots, sites or any other division of land is valid and enforceable.

> **NY**   Suffolk County Builders Assn v Islip (1975) 48 AD2d 692, 369 NYS2d 456.

Dividing a tract of land between co-owners for purely personal reasons does not constitute a subdivision.

> **Ill**   Armour v Mueller (1976) 36 IllAp3d 23, 343 NE2d 251.

B. FEES AND BONDS

§4. Authority to Require Bonds

A provision for a subdivision bond may not require a 10 per cent cash deposit along with a surety company bond.

> **NY**   Levine v Carmel (1970) 34 AD2d 796, 311 NYS2d 691.

Under the statute authorizing municipalities to require of subdivision developers adequate performance guarantees for purpose of insuring improvements, municipality, by ordinance, may require a performance bond calling for completion of improvements and for continued liability, surviving acceptance of subdivision plat, and also has implied authority to require a maintenance bond to insure against defects of material or workmanship which may develop in the future.

> **NJ**   Legion Manor v Wayne (1967) 49 NJ 420, 231 A2d 201.
> Savonick v Lawrence (1966) 91 NJS 288, 219 A2d 902.

§5. Protecting Contractors and Adjoining Property Owners

One of the main purposes for requiring a construction bond of a subdivider is so that he may lay out and construct streets and other improvements in accordance with state and county standards before maintenance is taken over by a public agency and to relieve the public of the burden that would otherwise exist. The bond is not intended as a punishment for nonperformance, but is intended to provide funds sufficient to pay construction costs on failure of completion of the public improvements by the subdivider. In light of the other language found within the ordinance, the use of the word "penal" does not make the bond of a penal or forfeiture nature.

> **Va**   Bd of Supervisors of Fairfax County v Ecology One Inc (1978) 245 SE2d 425.

A bond posted under an ordinance is to secure faithful performance to the city and does not inure to the benefit of contractors dealing with the subdivider.

> **Cal**   Weber v Pacific Indemnity Co (1962) 204 CA2d 334, 22 CaR 366.

Where an ordinance authorizes a subdivider, in lieu of completion of certain improvements in a planned subdivision, to post a bond for completion thereof, the bond so posted is a contract bond and does not protect third persons or adjoining owners against damages to their property resulting from failure of the subdivider to accomplish the required improvements.

> **Cal**   Evola v Wendt Const Co (1959) 170 CA2d 21, 338 P2d 498.
> **Mo**   University City v Frank Miceli & Sons (1961) 347 SW2d 131.

§6. Proving a Bonding Contract

A subdivider's express contract to develop streets and give security for his performance by a surety bond was established by evidence that his subdivision map was accepted prior to improvement of the streets, that a surety bond was then filed with the county, that a county ordinance required subdividers to provide for streets and to improve all land so dedicated as a condition precedent to acceptance and approval of the map, that the subdivider could agree to complete the work if it was uncompleted prior to acceptance of the map, and that his contract of completion should be secured by a surety bond.

> **Cal**   Fireman's Fund Indemnity Co v Sacramento County (1960) 179 CA2d 319, 3 CaR 607.

§7. Fees for Plat Examination

A city can establish an inspection fee schedule to reimburse it for fees paid an engineer for inspection of subdivision developments. However, an ordinance requiring a stated deposit is unconstitutional where billing of the fees is entrusted to the engineer. The city may not act as a pure trustee to collect fees for, and solely determined by, the engineer.

> **NJ**   Economy Enterprises v Manalapan (1969) 104 NJS 373, 250 A2d 139.

A requirement that subdividers pay a fee of $50, to be used in a public facilities purchase fund, is invalid. The ordinance does not specify or give assurance that the fees collected will be used to solve the problems peculiar to the subdivision, and there is no general authority for taxing.

> **NM**   Sanchez v Santa Fe (1971) 82 NM 322, 481 P2d 401.

Fees paid for inspecting and reviewing subdivision plats, paid without protest, cannot be recovered when the ordinance is held unconstitutional.

> **Va**   Crestwood Construction Co v Fairfax County (1971) 212 Va 6, 181 SE2d 635.

A municipality may not use the subdivision map act for general revenue producing purposes; and an ordinance requiring payment of a fee as a condition precedent to approval of a final map and issuance of building permits is contrary to the terms of the act.

> **Cal** Santa Clara County Contr v Santa Clara (1965) 232 CA2d 564, 43 CaR 86.
> Newport Building Corp v Santa Ana (1962) 210 CA2d 771, 26 CaR 797.
> **Ohio** Prudential Co-op Rlty Co v Youngstown (1928) 118 OS 204, 160 NE 695.
> **Va** Nat Rlty v Virginia Beach (1968) 209 Va 172, 163 SE2d 154.

C. COMPLIANCE WITH SUBDIVISION SPECIFICATIONS

§8. Consistent with Statutes and Ordinances

Subdevelopment improvement based on a series of points issued on availability of facilities, schools, and fire stations is a valid manner of determining priority. The city, being financially limited, may regulate the expansion of essential services and facilities.

> **NY** Golden v Ramapo (1972) 30 NY2d 359, 285 NE2d 291, 334 NYS2d 138, app dism 409 US 1003, 34 LEd2d 294, 93 SCt 440.
> Rockland County Builders Assn v McAlevey (1972) 30 NY2d 359, 285 NE2d 291, 334 NYS2d 138.

A limitation that no owner of land shall subdivide his land into more than five building lots in any one calendar year is an impermissible amendment to the subdivision ordinance.

> **NH** Stoney-Brook Devel Corp v Pembroke (1978) 394 A2d 853.

A subdivision of 20 or more acre plots is proper on a finding that the property in an agricultural and forestry district is not economically feasible to operate for farming. The special classification for agricultural and farming land which deletes the words "management" and "harvesting" and which attempts to provide for orderly development through development of both public and private recreational areas complies with comprehensive zoning map and the ordinance. It is necessary that the subdivision comply with the state land use provision as well as the county's classification.

> **Ore** 1000 Friends of Ore v Bd of Comm of Benton County (1978) 32 OreAp 413, 575 P2d 651.

A subdivision plan may not be rejected under a township's subdivision ordinance provision relating to the health, safety, morals and general welfare of a community where the plan violates no specific standards of the ordinance.

> **Pa** Scluffer v Plymouth Township (1977) 32 PaCmwlth 394, 379 A2d 1060.

Failure to submit a preliminary plat for approval under the town's subdivision regulations makes the persons ineligible for judicial review. The town may properly require preliminary plats and conditional approval before a sub-division is authorized.

NY   Greene v Brach (1970) 63 Misc2d 699, 313 NYS2d 230.

Where parcels or footage may be transferred from one adjoining subdivision to another to comply with density restrictions, the existence of streets does not destroy the adjoining status. An entire development may be completed on a piecemeal basis if where all joined together it comprises the entire subdivision as shown on the preliminary plans.

Md   Gruver-Cooley Jade Corp v Perlis (1969) 252 Md 684, 251 A2d 589.

A subdivision plan approved under the existing zoning ordinances of a town is exempt from the operation of the zoning ordinances of a village created from an area within the town, where the approval was secured prior to enactment of the village ordinance and the area is specifically excepted from its application by the terms of the village ordinance.

NY   Wesley Chapel v Van Den Hende (1969) 32 AD2d 565, 300 NYS2d 803.

A subdivision does not need approval by the town if it meets the statutory requirements that each lot abut on a public way. A subdivision on which all lots abut on a public street and contain the frontage and square foot requirements of the town's zoning does not require approval by the planning board.

Mass   Waldor Rlty Corp v Westborough (1968) 354 Mass 639, 241 NE2d 843.

A subdivision which has been approved though in violation of the zoning bylaws may not be revoked without the consent of a subsequent mortgage holder.

Mass   Bigham v Planning Bd of North Reading (1972) 362 Mass 860, 285 NE2d 408.

The provisions that a final subdivision map shall be accepted when all conditions are met is mandatory. On meeting the state and local subdivision and building requirements a map may not be denied acceptance on the claim the right is a discretionary matter.

Cal   Great Western Sav & Loan Assn v Los Angeles (1973) 31 CA3d 403, 107 CaR 359.

A moratorium on filing site plans and preliminary subdivision plats is invalid.

Va   Bd of Supervisors of Fairfax County v Horne (1975) 216 Va 113, 215 SE2d 453.

The commission has no discretion in granting approval of a subdivision plat when it needs the technical requirements of the ordinance. Denial of a proposed subdivision on the basis that the land will be used for public housing detrimental to the value of surrounding property is improper and outside the commission's authority.

> **Ind**　Dosmann v Area Plan Comm of St Joseph County (1974) 160 IndAp 605, 312 NE2d 880.

Approval of a tentative subdivision plat does not secure a vested right for the developer when zoning changes are required. The county still has jurisdiction over approval of the plan and therefore since no action has been taken at the time that environmental impact statements became a necessity a statement must be secured and approved.

> **Cal**　People v Kern County (1974) 39 CA3d 830, 115 CaR 67.

A subdivision of 80 acres divided into lots of varying sizes and then grouped in 16 clusters of five acres each does not meet the ordinance requirement of five-acre lots in an agricultural zone. Denial is not arbitrary when a purchaser would be misled into believing that he had a lot upon which he could construct a building.

> **Minn**　Nat Capital Corp v Inver Grove Heights (1974) 301 Minn 335, 222 NW2d 550.

Approval of a subdivision without making a finding that the plan is consistent with the area or district concept is invalid. A proposal to grade the top 90 feet from a ridge and fill the adjacent valley thereby creating a mesa with a density of three lots per acre is inconsistent with the district plan calling for minimum density and the retaining of natural physical features of the area.

> **Cal**　Woodland Hills Residence Assn v Los Angeles (1975) 44 CA3d 825, 118 CaR 856.

Subdivision requirements for approval by the planning commission and review de novo by the city council are limited to statutory and ordinance requirements. The subdivision ordinance which provides for approval on compliance with statute, ordinance, and regulation, makes approval regulatory. On compliance with the requirements there is no discretion in an approval.

> **Mich**　Hessee Rlty v Ann Arbor (1975) 61 Mich Ap 319, 232 NW2d 695.

A subdivision which follows the ordinance requirements must be approved. A letter of denial which fails to specify evidence of deficiencies or refer to any zoning violation is insufficient notice of disapproval.

> **Pa**　Swinehart v Upper Pottsgrove Township (1976) 23 PaCmwlth 282, 351 A2d 702.

A temporary interim zoning regulation prohibiting any subdivisions in a described area is invalid when notice and hearing have not been provided. Despite the emergency situation involved a moratorium may not be imposed without following procedural requirements.

> **Mont**　State ex rel Christian, Spring et al v Miller (1976) 169 Mont 242, 545 P2d 660.

A limitation on the length of blocks in a subdivision does not apply when the property is not being divided into blocks. The proposed subdivision which is bordered on only three sides by streets and on the fourth side by property not owned or controlled by the developer is not being divided into blocks.

Conn Westport v Norwalk (1974) 167 Conn 151, 355 A2d 25.

A decision to approve a subdivision plat without requiring an environmental impact study is subject to review under the clearly erroneous test. The decision after receiving reports from various agencies dealing with wildlife and recreation showing the potential for harm is clearly in error. Approval of the subdivision must be conditioned on an adequate showing of environmental impact.

Wash Swift v Island County (1976) 87 Wash2d 348, 552 P2d 175.

A resolution approving a subdivision is invalid when the environmental impact report does not answer the specific objections raised nor contain data upon which to base conclusions of the environmental impact. Prior practices of the political subdivision and the expenditure of money by the subdivider are insufficient basis on which to justify approving the subdivision without complying with the EIR requirements.

Cal People v Kern County (1976) 62 CA3d 761, 133 CaR 389.

A subdivision ordinance may require that the property have a certain frontage on an improved road. A variance by the planning board for lots facing a private road is not sufficient to justify approval of the plan.

NJ Holjes v Planning Bd of Alexandria Township (1976) 143 NJS 295, 362 A2d 1289.

A certificate of occupancy for model homes built in a subdivision which had been approved on posting of bond for completion of the outside facilities may not be denied on the subsequent invalidity of the subdivision ordinance. Good faith expenditures of money based on legal and valid building permits at the time of issuance are subject to equitable consideration and vested rights.

NY Northport v Guardian Fed Sav & Loan Assn (1976) 384 NYS2d 923.

Conditions imposed by a city for approval of a subdivision map are lawful where they are not inconsistent with the map act and ordinances of the city and are reasonably required by the subdivision type and use as related to the character of local and neighborhood planning and traffic conditions.

Cal Ayres v Los Angeles (1949) 34 C2d 31, 207 P2d 1.

The authority to adopt local ordinances containing requirements supplementary to the subdivision map act is limited by the terms of the act.

> **Cal** Newport Building Corp v Santa Ana (1962) 210 CA2d 771, 26 CaR 797.
> Longridge Est v Los Angeles (1960) 183 CA2d 533, 6 CaR 900.

ANNOTATION

Validity of zoning ordinance defining residential development until establishment of public services in area, 63 ALR3d 1184.

LAW REVIEWS

Roger A. Cunningham, Public Control of Land Subdivision in Michigan: Description and Critique, 66 Mich LR 3.

Ronald A. Zumbrum and Thomas E. Hookano, No-Growth and Related Land-use Legal Problems, an Overview, 9 Urban 122.

Robert C. Elleckson, Suburban Growth Controls: Economic and Legal Analysis, 86 Yale LR 385.

Zoning Program for Phased Growth: Ramapo Township's Time Controls on Residential Development, 47 NYU LR 723.

Golden v Town of Ramapo: Establishing a New Dimension in American Planning Law, 4 Urban IX.

Phased Zoning: Regulation of the Tempo and Sequence of Land Development, (1974) 26 Stan LR 585.

Freilich and Ragsdale, Timing and Sequential Control-Essential Basis for Effective Regional Planning, 58 Minn LR 1011.

§8.1. Name Restriction

Subdividing may be disallowed under an ordinance provision that the name of a subdivision must not duplicate or resemble the name of any other subdivision in the county. The subdivision name "Oswego Green" is improper when it is not developed by the same parties who developed the other "Oswego" subdivisions and it is not contiguous to the similarly named subdivisions.

> **Ore** Home Owners' Preservation League, Lower Tualatin Valley Chapter v Clackamas County Planning Comm (1975) 21 OreAp 27, 533 P2d 838.

§9. Zoning Restrictions

Both the statements in the master plan which calls for the preservation of land having exceptionally productive soils and those which were partially incorporated in the zoning ordinance referring to cluster development, transfer of development rights and maintenance of certain agricultural soil are both precatory in nature. A subdivision plan may be approved without regard to the statements.

> **NY**   Barton v Halsey (1979) 412 NYS2d 659.

A planning commission's impression at the time of approving a subdivision that single family dwellings would be built is immaterial where the zoning classification at that time permitted construction of any type residential dwelling, and a building permit for an apartment house must issue.

> **Mass**   McCarthy v Ashland (1968) 354 Mass 660, 241 NE2d 840.

An ordinance entitled agricultural districts in which the title indicates an intention to maintain the agricultural use but which in its text provides for single and multiple detached dwellings plus numerous uses that are not of an agricultural, but are of an urban use, may not be the basis for denying subdivision for single family development. The action of the board in approving the subdivision does not constitute rezoning which would require a hearing prior to approval.

> **Md**   Clarke v Comm of Carroll County (1973) 270 Md 343, 311 A2d 417.

Approval of a subdivision by the county when the township has no subdivision ordinance constitutes the time for the three-year right to construct regardless of zoning changes. The subsequent action of the township in overruling county zoning and installing their own does not affect the owner's right to follow the zoning in existence at the time the county approved the subdivision.

> **Pa**   Gable v Springfield Township Zoning Hearing Bd (1975) 18 PaCmwlth 381, 335 A2d 886.

A zoning ordinance which provides no more than one dwelling designed or available for dwelling purposes may be erected or placed on any lot in a subdivision does not preclude construction of multiple dwellings on each lot. There is no restriction that the dwelling be single family, and the prior approval of the subdivision has validly established the lots.

> **Mass**   Selectmen of Ayer v Planning Bd of Ayer (1975) 336 NE2d 388.

An application for subdivision of a tract of land may not be denied on suspicion of an intended violation of a zoning ordinance. The subdivision application which meets the requirements is authorized though a special exception for a gasoline service station has been approved on condition that the rear of the property be left in grass and shrubbery.

> **Pa**   Gulf Oil Corp v Warminster Township Bd of Supervisors (1975) 22 PaCmwlth 63, 348 A2d 485.

A subdivision request may not be denied on the basis that the trustees do not want the property used as contemplated. Once the application has been submitted in proper form, approval of a subdivision is a routine administrative procedure which may be enforced by mandamus.

> **Ill** People ex rel JC Penney Properties v Oak Lawn (1976) 38 IllAp3d 1016, 349 NE2d 637.

A city planning commission, by way of final approval of a plat that violates a zoning resolution adopted after the preliminary approval is given, cannot repeal or nullify the resolution. No preliminary approval of a proposed plat that the subdivider is not yet ready to record and develop can preclude the adoption of zoning resolutions.

> **Ohio** State v Kiefaber (1960) 113 OA 523, 18 Op2d 169, 179 NE2d 360.

LAW REVIEW

John W. Reps, Control of Land Subdivision by Municipal Planning Boards, 40 Corn LR 258.

§10. Defective Application

Under an enabling act municipal legislatures are authorized to create planning commissions, which may be vested with jurisdiction over the subdivision of land, by ordinance which shall also provide for a board of review for appeals from the commission. Where because of the statute, and rules adopted by ordinance, the planning board has jurisdiction to subdivide land only when the division of a single parcel into two lots requires provision for a street, an application for such a division of land without provision for a street is not properly before the planning board.

> **RI** Slawson v Barrington (1966) 100 RI 485, 217 A2d 92.

§11. Prerequisite to Building Permit

A building permit may be denied to an individual owner who purchases from an owner of a large tract. Failure to secure the subdividing required by ordinance may be enforced against the subsequent purchaser to prevent the owner of a large tract circumventing the requirements by individual sales.

> **NY** Adams v Westhampton Beach (1972) 71 Misc2d 579, 336 NYS2d 662.

A building permit may not be denied on the basis that a 20-acre lot is being subdivided into three building sites. The subdivision ordinance applies only to division into four or more lots and the three lots to be secured are all above the minimum requirements for the area.

> **Ariz** Wilkerson v Marks (1975) 24 ArizApp 316, 538 P2d 403.

The issuance of building permits on applications that do not comply with the requirements of a land subdivision ordinance is improper and must be set aside, where the subdivision has never been approved or declared to be exempt as required by the ordinance.

> **NJ** Stoker v Irvington (1961) 71 NJS 370, 177 A2d 61.

An ordinance requiring an owner of unplatted land to file a plat before a building permit will be issued is valid. However, a requirement that the owner donate a sufficient strip of land for half of a street easement is invalid. Though ordinances authorize the city to refuse subdivision applications, where the parcel is not being subdivided and there is no intention to do so, the city can only require filing of the plat and must then issue the building permit.

> **Tex** Corpus Christi v Unitarian Church (1969) 436 SW2d 923.

Denial of building permits for residences is invalid when the subdivision requirements have been complied with. The fact that the agreements for completion of public streets, sidewalks and utilities have not been completed does not give the city the right to refuse building permits since the ordinance provides for a bond and a time for completion of the improvements. The city has adequate means of forcing completion or collecting a fine from the builder or filing a claim in bankruptcy court for the cost of the completion.

> **Ill** Phillips Constr Co, In the Matter of (1978) 583 F2d 290.

Certificates of occupancy may not be denied pending completion of all subdivision requirements. Thus, a requirement for a cash and indemnity bond to guarantee completion would make it inequitable to deny a certificate of occupancy prior to completion of all improvements. However, standards may be set for their issuance.

> **NJ** J D Land Corp v Allen (1971) 114 NJS 503, 277 A2d 404.

Where an ordinance is adopted approving the plat of an area for a real estate subdivision, and a lot therein is purchased, an application for a building permit for the lot may not be refused by the building commissioner and board of adjustment on the ground that the subdivision is "out of order" for failure to comply with certain rules of ordinances relating to subdivisions. Denial of the permit will be set aside by the court as arbitrary and capricious where the applicant has fulfilled all legal requirements.

> **Mo** Phillips v Bellefontaine Neighbors (1958) 308 SW2d 765.
> **Pa** Deane v Edgeworth (1953) 172 PaS 502, 94 A2d 112.

A county ordinance prohibiting a building permit for a plot in a subdivision created in violation of its requirements cannot be enforced against an innocent purchaser. Though the county may have difficulty in keeping track of a subdivider's sales, the grantee has just as great a difficulty and less ready access to the files than the county.

> **Cal** Keizer v Adams (1969) 1 CA3d 86, 81 CaR 484.

§ 12. Amendment or Repeal

Approval of a subdivision does not give the subdivider a vested interest in the size of the lots. A subsequently enacted zoning ordinance increasing lot size is controlling, in the absence of previously issued building permits and substantial expenditures.

> **Pa**   Friendship Builders v West Brandywine (1970) 1 PaCmwlth 25, 271 A2d 511.

The continuation of a vested right to subdivide into quarter-acre tracts as opposed to a subsequent ordinance calling for half-acre tracts may be lost by the subdivider's action. The continuation of a vested right is subject to abandonment, recoupment, and the extent to which public safety considerations have manifested themselves over the intervening years. A trial to determine the fact situation involved in the three considerations is necessary.

> **NY**   Putnam Armonk v Southeast (1976) 52 AD2d 10, 382 NYS2d 538.

A town board can amend or repeal a subdivision control ordinance so as to eliminate its requirements; but as long as those requirements are in force, the board is bound thereby, and the citizens have a right to assume that their elected representatives will respect and follow the conditions precedent as contained in the ordinance.

> **Ind**   Dyer v Monaldi (1964) 245 Ind 585, 201 NE2d 268.

Where the operation of a statute giving a municipality power to regulate subdivisions is prospective only, an ordinance purporting to regulate a subdivision already in existence at the time of passage of the statute can rise no higher in its application than the legislative authorization, and thus does not apply to an existing subdivision.

> **NJ**   Lake Intervale Homes v Parsippany Troy Hills (1957) 47 NJS 334, 136 A2d 57.

An ordinance banning multiple dwellings in certain districts, which amends a previous ordinance permitting such uses, is invalid and unenforceable by the city, on the ground of equitable estoppel, against a developer who prior to the amendment submitted his plans to the board of aldermen and got them to zone the property in accordance with his request, and who in good faith expended and committed himself to the expenditure of huge sums of money.

> **Mo**   Murrell v Wolff (1966) 408 SW2d 842.
> **NJ**   Levin v Livingston (1961) 35 NJ 500, 173 A2d 391.

§ 13. Exceptions; Variances

A variance may be granted where the developer undertakes construction in good faith reliance on the prior approval of the subdivision plan and issuance of building permits, and where streets, utilities and ten houses have been already constructed when the city's subdivision ordinance is invalidated by the court. This does not constitute self-imposed hardship.

Ore Bienz v Dayton (1977) 29 OreAp 761, 566 P2d 904.

A grant of a variance to landowners is proper where traditional grounds for a variance have not been met but the variance is "de minimus" because the primary objection to the subdivision has been cured by the express conditions attached to the grant of the variance, and where the expressed purpose of the variance will further public health, safety and welfare.

Pa West Bradford Township v Evans (1978) 35 PaCmwlth 167, 384 A2d 1382.

A planning board may only approve a subdivision plan that meets the zoning requirements. It has no discretion to approve a plan on the basis of economic hardship, which was conditionally approved prior to the zoning ordinance, but became substandard after adoption of the ordinance and before final approval.

NY McEnroe v Planning Bd (1969) 61 Misc2d 937, 307 NYS2d 302.

That two previous subdivisions had been approved does not deprive the commission of the right to deny approval of the third, where the subdivision did not meet the street width requirements and no showing of hardship requiring a variance was made. There is no vested right to approval.

Wash Breuer v Fourre (1969) 76 Wash2d 582, 458 P2d 168.

An ordinance section regulating the design of a subdivision is not unconstitutional as unlawfully delegating legislative power by the city to a plan commission in authorizing it to grant a variance from the requirements of the ordinance that sets forth no standards or guides to aid the commission in determining whether or not to grant a variance, since another section requires that, after approval of a variance by the commission, the city council must give final approval; thus, the action of the plan commission in recommending a variance is advisory only, with the final determination made by the proper legislative authority.

Ill Petterson v Naperville (1956) 9 Ill2d 233, 137 NE2d 371.

A town is without power, in enacting a subdivision ordinance, to adopt its own definition of a subdivision by adding to the exceptions contained in the statute.

NJ Stoker v Irvington (1961) 71 NJS 370, 177 A2d 61.

Pursuant to statute a municipality may exempt, by zoning ordinance, from the requirement of local municipal approval, subdivisions wherein the number of new lots is less than a designated number, of plats that do not involve new streets, or such other classes of subdivisions as the ordinance shall designate.

> **NJ**   Noble v Committee of Mendham (1966) 91 NJS 111, 219 A2d 335.

§14. —Property Condemned by State

A subdivision resulting from an acquisition of land for highway purposes, whether title passes to the state by judgment in condemnation or by voluntary conveyance, is entirely exempt from regulation by municipal subdivision legislation.

> **NJ**   Union Building & Constr Corp v Totowa (1968) 98 NJS 446, 237 A2d 637.

D. Compliance with Resubdivision Specifications

§15. Not Appearing on Plat

Ordinance prohibiting a change of use of land without following required procedure for resubdivision does not apply to the continued use as a roadway of a strip of land between two lots which were sold and deeded to prospective buyers with a reservation of the roadway between them, which roadway did not appear on the recorded plat of subdivision.

> **Mo**   Vinyard v St Louis County (1966) 399 SW2d 99.

§16. Prerequisite to Building Permit

A building permit may be denied on the basis that the landowner resubdivided prior to the installation of the public sewer system in violation of a condition on the subdivision map. The condition is enforceable against the landowner even though it has not been inserted in the deed.

> **Cal**   Scrogings v Kovatch (1976) 64 CA3d 54, 134 CaR 217.

Under a statute requiring approval of resubdivisions by a planning board, refusal of a building inspector to issue a permit for a dwelling is proper, where lots previously singly platted were combined to make one single resubdivision without such approval.

> **NJ**   Clauss v Postma (1954) 32 NJS 147, 108 A2d 34.

§17. Conflict with Zoning

A subdivision ordinance is not by implication repealed by a zoning ordinance. The zoning ordinance provision that it does not repeal any ordinance other than those expressly repealed saves the subdivision ordinance.

W Va Fairlawns Homes v Morgantown (1971) 155 W Va 172, 182 SE2d 48.

Where an owner of lots obtains approval by a planning board to subdivide his lots into a minor subdivision, but his plans conflict with the zoning ordinance, the subdivision becomes a major subdivision, requiring recourse to a zoning board of adjustment for a variance.

NJ Smilow v Orange (1959) 58 NJS 108, 155 A2d 560.

§18. Lot Division Effecting Street Change

A division of a lot, which effects no street changes but is simply a division within lot boundaries of a previously approved subdivision, does not constitute a violation of an ordinance relating to prior approval by a commission of the subdivision, since the land was already subdivided.

Haw Akai v Lewis (1946) 37 Haw 374.

E. REJECTION AND APPROVAL

§19. Procedure

An ordinance is not void for failure to provide sufficient standards of compliance when it requires that plats shall be signed "as prescribed by law" and when the appropriate signatures are defined in other legislation.

Ida State v Clark (1965) 88 Ida 365, 399 P2d 955.

Where a statute grants to a municipality the right to delegate to a planning board the power to waive a hearing in the approval of plats for minor subdivisions, provided such authority is specifically granted under the terms of a municipal ordinance, but a municipality fails to make such a specific grant of authority, action taken by a planning board without such a hearing in approval of plats for minor subdivisions is ineffectual.

NJ Donovan v New Brunswick (1958) 50 NJS 102, 141 A2d 134.

Where, at the time a plat of a town addition was filed, the place was an incorporated town, and not a city, acceptance of the dedication by ordinance was not essential to the validity of the dedication, under a statute declaring that the plat of an addition to a "city" should be ineffective until confirmed by an ordinance of the city.

> **Iowa**   Burroughs v Cherokee (1906) 134 Iowa 429, 109 NW 876.

A procedure providing for tentative approval of a subdivision plan is proper and for the benefit of both the political subdivision and the subdivider. It is necessary, however, that a denial contain sufficient reasons to inform the subdivider of the actions necessary to receive subsequent approval. A fact that the comprehensive plan for the county is broadly worded does not require that a tentative plan be approved, but the subdivider is entitled to know the rules and regulations under which his plan is being considered.

> **Ore**   Commonwealth Properties v Washington County (1978) 35 OreAp 387, 582 P2d 1384.

A contract between a subdivider and a city, properly passed by the city council, is valid when signed by the city manager. His actions are as administrative officer for the enforcement of ordinances, and since the contract had prior approval, it is an act within his authority.

> **Del**   Hearn Bros v Newark (1969) 261 A2d 532.

An ordinance approving a subdivision, enacted without compliance with the required statutory notice of hearing, is invalid.

> **Vt**   Flanders Lumber & Building Supply Co v Milton (1969) 128 Vt 38, 258 A2d 804.

Denial of a two-lot subdivision is improper where there is no finding that the subdivision will affect the health, welfare, safety, or morals of the community, or that it violates any of the statutes or zoning ordinances.

> **Pa**   Brauns v Swarthmore (1972) 4 PaCmwlth 627, 288 A2d 830.

A preliminary plat of a subdivision does not need to meet all the requirements for a final plat. In the absence of action by the city council within 40 days of its submission the plat is approved though it may violate an official map or city ordinances.

> **Wis**   State ex rel Lozoff v Bd of Trustees of Hartland (1972) 55 Wis2d 64, 197 NW2d 798.

A requirement for action and approval on a subdivision within 40 days after filing applies to a mobile home plan.

> **Pa**   Dillsburg Borough Council v Gettys (1973) 7 PaCmwlth 519, 300 A2d 805.

Denial of a preliminary plat for the general layout of a subdivision is required when it indicates elements that would prohibit final approval. A plat showing heights of buildings in excess of the maximum permitted and which indicates an attempt to secure a planned unit development, a use not permitted in the area, must be denied since the board cannot modify the preliminary plat or disapprove a final plat conforming to the initial one.

Wash Loveless v Yantis (1973) 82 Wash2d 754, 513 P2d 1023.

When an ordinance provides that the county planning commission only makes recommendations to the board of supervisors on a subdivision their action must be within 50 days after filing the tentative map and the board must act within ten days. The ten-day limitation may be extended by mutual agreement of the parties, and when done the map is not automatically approved.

Cal Lenney v Bd of Supervisors of Riverside County (1974) 41 CA3d 902, 116 CaR 500.

A subdivision plat which meets all of the ordinance requirements may not be arbitrarily denied approval on the personal feelings of the commissioners. Their desire to prevent single-family development in an area isolated from other urban development is not a valid basis for denial.

Colo Interladco v Billings (1975) 538 P2d 496.

A refusal to consider a subdivision plat until the question of an undersized lot had been resolved constitutes disapproval. The subdivider has been advised of the disapproval and the reason therefore, and cannot complain that the zoning board took no action which constitutes approval.

NH Allard v Thalheimer (1976) 116 NH 299, 358 A2d 395.

§20. Rejection—When Future Condemnation Revealed

A moratorium on the development of nonresidential tracts may not be implemented in order to consider proposed changes in and widening of abutting streets. Developments must be considered in relation to the official map showing existing streets.

NH Leda Lanes Rlty v Nashua (1972) 112 NH 244, 293 A2d 320.

Inverse condemnation is not involved in a subdivision in which the highway department requests denial of a portion of the land due to contemplated highway construction. The landowner by failing to appeal or contest the highway department's request has acquiesced in it. He has not lost either value or rental by noninclusion in the subdivision and subsequent rezoning.

Mo Marvin E Nieberg Real Estate Co v St Louis County (1973) 488 SW2d 626.

A planned residential development may not be denied on the basis that the comprehensive zoning map shows part of the area as a proposed school site.

Private development of land may not be denied on the basis of a future public need.

Pa Doran Inv v Muhlenberg Township (1973) 10 PaCmwlth 143, 309 A2d 450.

An attempt to prevent any work from being done in an approved subdivision in order to keep down the cost of acquiring the land for a dam site based on a cooperation agreement between a river authority and a city is the basis for damages for temporary taking of property without compensation. The action of the department heads in refusing permits for sewer and water installation and street construction based on the policy of the council to prohibit further development seeking to keep the cost down are chargeable against the city since the acts were not ultra vires but within their apparent authority.

Tex San Antonio River Auth v Garrett Bros (1975) 528 SW2d 266.

Refusal of a planning board to grant approval of a subdivision is arbitrary and capricious, where the builder has complied with all the rules and regulations of the board and the refusal is based on possible future condemnation by the highway department of part of the area.

NJ Florham Park Inv Assn v Madison (1966) 92 NJS 598, 224 A2d 352.

LAW REVIEW

Inverse Condemnation: Its Availability in Challenging the Validity of a Zoning Ordinance, 26 Stan LR 1439.

§ 21. — When Traffic Increase Revealed

A subdivision regulation requiring paving of interior streets and streets abutting lots in the subdivision is reasonable where evidence shows that the proposed development will increase traffic within and abutting the subdivision.

Ariz Pima County v Ariz Title Ins & Tr Co (1977) 115 Ariz 344, 565 P2d 524.

Under the authorization to deny a subdivision when the premises are scattered or premature and involve a danger to the public, a denial based on the insufficient capacity of an off-site road is reasonable. The subdivision which would seriously overcrowd the road and create additional traffic problems in the area makes the proposal premature despite the fact houses have been constructed in the area. In determining whether a subdivision is premature the commission may properly consider the fact that existing housing has not overburdened the facilities, but that additional housing will do so.

NH Garipay v Hanover (1976) 116 NH 34, 351 A2d 64.

A planning board may not base its refusal to approve a residential subdivision plan on the ground that increased traffic hazards would result from the development, since an increase in the volume of traffic and the creation of a need for additional police supervision are mere incidents of a municipality's growth.

> **NJ** Mansfield & Swett v West Orange (1938) 120 NJLaw 145, 198 A 225.

LAW REVIEW

William C. Smith, Municipal Economy and Land Use Restrictions, 20 L&CP 481.

§22. Compelling Approval by Mandamus

A court order authorizing filing of a subdivision plan without the highway superintendent's approval, which has been arbitrarily refused, is complete. On failure of the town to take action within the 45 days of submission the plan is approved by operation of law.

> **NY** Pekar v Veteran Planning Bd (1977) 58 AD2d 703, 396 NYS2d 102.

A subdivision map which meets all requirements must be approved and submitted for recordation. The county is not authorized to hold the matter in abeyance in order to change the existing zoning requirements.

> **Ariz** Maricopa County v Anzwool (1973) 19 ArizApp 242, 506 P2d 282.

A writ of mandate may be employed to compel a city council to approve a resubdivision where the council, under the enabling ordinance, is not authorized to determine whether a subdivision shall be permitted, but is authorized only to pass on the map submitted.

> **Cal** Kling v Newport Beach (1957) 155 CA2d 309, 317 P2d 708.

§22.1. —Schools Insufficient

Denial of subdivision on lack of adequate schools is invalid when the schools within a reasonable distance have sufficient capacity to handle the proposed load. A distance of one or one and a half miles is a reasonable distance, and the boundaries of school service areas may be changed making the denial unreasonable.

> **Md** Md–Nat Capital Park & Planning Comm v Rosenberg (1973) 269 Md 520, 307 A2d 704.

A subdivision plan may not be denied on the basis that it will adversely affect public school enrollment. Neither the statutory authority nor the rules and regulations of the planning commission authorize consideration of school district problems in approving a subdivision.

> **Md**   Baltimore v Victor Devel Co (1971) 261 Md 387, 275 A2d 478.

A restriction on zoning or rezoning for residential use for a two-year period if the area is an impacted school district is valid. The prohibition is not invalid though passed by initiative and the alternatives of the developer assisting in supplying temporary school structures or solutions is valid.

> **Cal**   Builders Assn of Santa Clara-Santa Cruz Counties v Sup Ct of Santa Clara County (1974) 13 C3d 225, 529 P2d 582, 118 CaR 158.

II. CONDITION OF PROPERTY TO BE SUBDIVIDED

A. DEDICATING STREETS AND PUBLIC GROUNDS

§23. Authority to Require

Subdivision regulations which require a subdivider to dedicate .018 acres per dwelling unit for recreational purposes, or where such dedication is deemed impractical, to donate a sum equal to the fair market value of the land that would otherwise have been dedicated is an unconstitutional deprivation of property without just compensation. Without specific legislative authorization, the city has no power to require the payment of a fee in lieu of dedication of land for public parks.

> **Ala**   Montgomery v Crossroads Land Co (1978) 335 So2d 363.

A city plan commission may not require that, in order to obtain plat approval, the developer must dedicate a 100-foot wide right-of-way through the proposed subdivision for a major thoroughfare in addition to the dedication of interior residential streets. This requirement constitutes a confiscation of private property where the total area required to be dedicated equals 32 per cent of the subdivision and the thoroughfare would be for the benefit of the general public rather than of the subdivision.

> **Ohio**   R G Dunbar, Inc v Toledo Planning Comm (1976) 52 OA2d 45, 367 NE2d 1193.

A town planning board may not require the dedication of a strip of shore front property as a condition for the approval of a residential subdivision where the taking of the beach front would be confiscatory because of the strip's disproportionately high value in relation to the rest of the property.

> **NY**   East Neck Est v Luchsinger (1969) 61 Misc2d 619, 305 NYS2d 922.

Requiring a developer to set aside open areas in a planned community subdivision is common. Parks, lakes, and other recreation facilities are sometimes constructed in open areas, and goft courses are ideally adaptable to this concept. It is clearly established that the existence of open areas enhances the value of the surrounding land.

> **Ore** Tualatin Devel Co v Dept of Revenue (1970) 3 Ore Tax Ct 499; affd (1970) 256 Ore 323, 473 P2d 660.

While a municipality may properly require a subdivider to donate part of the land for recreational purposes, a definite percentage would create inequities. The amount to be donated must be determined on the specific and uniquely attributable formula of use of recreational facilities particular to the subdivision.

> **RI** Ansuini v Cranston (1970) 107 RI 63, 264 A2d 910.

A contract to pave a portion of an adjoining street may be enforced. The city by ordinance may regulate the nature of a subdivision, including zoning and connecting with street development plans.

> **Mo** Bellefontaine Neighbors v J J Kelley Rlty & Building Co (1970) 460 SW2d 298.

While the city has the right to adopt master street plans, it may not make a subdivision contingent on dedicating a tract for the proposective future extension of a street for the general benefit of the community. Private property may not be taken for a public purpose without compensation.

> **La** Schwing v Baton Rouge (1971) 249 So2d 304.

A requirement that a subdivision will be approved on dedication of additional land to meet the width requirements of abutting streets is invalid. The municipality may not require existing streets to be widened at the subdivider's expense, but may only require that newly constructed streets meet standards.

> **NJ** Princeton Research Lands v Planning Bd of Princeton (1970) 112 NJS 467, 271 A2d 719.

Designation of a minor subdivision, which is a subdivision containing two or less lots, may not be on condition that rights-of-way be increased. The conditional grant is void, and may be withdrawn by the planning commission.

> **NJ** Princeton Research Lands v Planning Bd of Princeton (1970) 112 NJS 467, 271 A2d 719.

A subdivision may be disapproved on failure to dedicate the 50-foot right-of-way required. An unsigned deed, requiring the signature of disinterested parties, does not satisfy the requirement.

> **Pa** County Builders v Lower Providence Township (1972) 5 PaCmwlth 1, 287 A2d 849.

An increase in the size requirements for a cartway may not be effected by resolution. The ordinance may only be amended on public notice and hearing.

> **Pa**   County Builders v Lower Providence Township (1972) 5 PaCmwlth 1, 287 A2d 849.

A subdivision requirement that plats be approved and that the streets be provided does not authorize a private corporation to compel another private corporation to open a street. Failure of the owning corporation to subdivide or make any use of the property does not authorize extension of the street across their private property except by city condemnation.

> **W Va**   Fairlawns Homes v Morgantown (1971) 155 W Va 172, 182 SE2d 48.

A subdivision may properly be denied approval when the plan does not call for an extension of the existing city streets through the subdivision. A private way which dead ends is not sufficient since the requirements are for travel through the city rather than through the individual subdivisions.

> **Mass**   McDavitt v Planning Bd of Winchester (1974) 308 NE2d 786.

Ordinances for location and alignment of subdivision streets and protection of natural features are not valid when no standards are provided. The ordinances which direct that streets be so located to make property attractive and with maximum livability and amenity and the natural features requirement of preserving large trees, water courses, scenic points and other similar community assets are incapable of any degree of control when no standards are provided.

> **Mass**   Chira v Planning Bd of Tisbury (1975) 333 NE2d 204.

A municipal ordinance requiring dedication of park property or a cash equivalent based on ten per cent valuation at the time of subdivision is reasonable. The statutory authorization and the ordinance provide for a reasonable amount of compensation or land in proportion to the amount to be developed and the needs to be generated which is only a prima facie showing and subject to judicial review. Basing the value on the time of platting constitutes a reliable criteria since it indicates the number of lots and the amount of use to be generated by the subdivision.

> **Minn**   Collis v Bloomington (1976) 310 Minn 5, 246 NW2d 19.

A city may properly require the dedication of land or payment of a cash in lieu fee on subdividing property. The use of the land by independent school districts and park districts does not make the requirement invalid. The schedule of value and of projected usage depending on the type subdivision involved is reasonable particularly where the subdivider has the right to set forth his own projections of population density and projected uses. A credit for private recreational facilities provided reasonably compensates the developer for facilities provided for the residents of the particular district.

> **Ill** Krughoff v Naperville (1976) 41 IllAp3d 334, 354 NE2d 489.

An ordinance provision requiring dedication of land when practicable for school, park, and recreational sites to get approval for a subdivision plat, is constitutional as a proper exercise of the police power.

> **Wis** Jordan v Menomonee Falls (1965) 28 Wis2d 608, 137 NW2d 442.

A subdivision ordinance requiring the subdivider to pay for all street grading and surfacing, curbing, sidewalk, water mains, and sewers on lots subject to the ordinance is not arbitrary and unreasonable, though these improvements benefit other lots not subject to the subdivision ordinance.

> **Ill** Petterson v Naperville (1956) 9 Ill2d 233, 137 NE2d 371.
> **NH** Blevens v Manchester (1961) 103 NH 284, 170 A2d 121.

LAW REVIEWS

Roger A. Cunningham, Public Control of Land Subdivision in Michigan: Description and Critique, 66 Mich LR 3.

Subdivision Land Dedication: Objective and Objections 27 Stan LR 419.

§24. When Required

An application to change an existing apartment building to a condominium may be made subject to the donation of park land or payment in lieu thereof. The fact that the apartment house was in existence prior to the enactment of the ordinance does not prohibit the payment when a change which involves a subdividing of the property occurs subsequently. Valuation for the "in lieu payment" must be on the basis of the land value rather than the improved value.

> **Cal** Norsco Enterprises v Fremont (1976) 54 CA3d 488, 126 CaR 659.

An ordinance requiring a subdivider to dedicate a portion of his land for recreational and educational facilities imposes an unreasonable condition precedent for the approval of a plat of a subdivision and purports to take private property for public use without compensation, where the need for the facilities is not specifically and uniquely attributable to the addition of the subdivision and should not be made the sole financial burden of the subdivider.

> **Ill** Pioneer Tr & Sav Bk v Mt Prospect (1961) 22 Ill2d 375, 176 NE2d 799.

It is no defense to conditions imposed in a subdivision map proceeding that their fulfillment will incidentally also benefit the city as a whole. Nor is it a valid objection that conditions contemplate future as well as more immediate needs. Potential as well as present population factors affecting a subdivision in the neighborhood generally are appropriate for consideration.

Cal Ayres v Los Angeles (1949) 34 C2d 31, 207 P2d 1.

§25. Apportioning Off-Site Costs

The failure of a township land subdivision ordinance to establish procedures for apportioning to the subdivider the cost of off-site improvements is fatal to the planning board's attempt to require the developer to pave an off-site right-of-way.

NJ Longridge Builders v Princeton (1968) 52 NJ 348, 245 A2d 336.

§26. Zoning after Acceptance

An ordinance requiring an agreement by the owners in a proposed subdivision to pave the subdivision streets before acceptance of the subdivision map merely prescribed requirements to be met before the city council accepted the map and did not purport to affect title to the lots therein plotted.

Cal Hocking v Title Ins & Tr Co (1951) 37 C2d 644, 234 P2d 625, 40 ALR2d 1238.

§27. Paving and Surfacing Roads

An ordinance prohibiting the selling of subdivided property not already fronting public streets without the construction and development of roads as to such subdivided parcels in conformity with the city's minimum requirements for new streets is within the general police powers granted to the city by its charter and is designed to promote the convenience, safety or public welfare of the citizens of the city. Such ordinance must be construed consistently with relevant provisions of the general state law.

Tenn Draper v Haynes (1978) 567 SW2d 462.

Conditioning acceptance of a subdivision on the granting of a right-of-way for continuation of a street envisioned on the master plan is a valid exercise of the city's authority. Moreover, where lots would be inaccessible without the proposed right-of-way the developer may be required, not only to grant the easement, but also to improve and pave the street.

NJ Brazer v Mountainside (1969) 55 NJ 456, 262 A2d 857; modifying 102 NJS 497, 246 A2d 170.

The filing of a subdivision map showing certain streets does not make them city streets subject to repair and maintenance, where the subdivision regulations relating to grade and improvement were not complied with.

> **Conn**   Thompson v Portland (1970) 159 Conn 107, 266 A2d 893.

A requirement that the creation of a street or way for the purpose of partitioning parcels of land be approved applies to private ways or roads as well as public. Failure to secure approval by the planning commission justifies an action to enjoin sales of land until the road meets county standards.

> **Ore**   Columbia County v O'Black (1974) 16 OreAp 147, 517 P2d 688.

A requirement that the road fronting a proposed subdivision be developed by the subdivider is reasonable. Under the ordinance authorization for subdivision regulations including existing unpaved streets the fronting property is included and since the subdivision is the only area which presently uses the street the area directly in front of the subdivision may be required to be improved by the developer with subsequent upkeep by the municipality.

> **NH**   KBW, Inc v Bennington (1975) 115 NH 392, 342 A2d 653.

A planning board is without authority to require a developer, as a condition of approval of a subdivision, to pave a road beyond his own subdivision, because neither the municipal planning act nor the land subdivision ordinance contemplates such a requirement.

> **NJ**   Longridge Builders v Princeton (1966) 92 NJS 402, 223 A2d 640.

A subdivision ordinance requiring the subdivider to pay for all street grading and surfacing, curbing, sidewalk, water mains, and sewers on lots subject to the ordinance is not arbitrary and unreasonable, though these improvements benefit other lots not subject to the subdivision ordinance.

> **NH**   Blevens v Manchester (1961) 103 NH 284, 170 A2d 121.
> **NJ**   Levin v Livingston (1961) 35 NJ 500, 173 A2d 391.

§28. Cul-de-Sacs

A subdivision may not be denied by requiring a cul-de-sac at a dead end street when the ordinance contains no such provisions. Approval may not be given or withheld on the whim of the board.

> **Pa**   County Builders v Lower Providence Township (1972) 5 PaCmwlth 1, 287 A2d 849.

Under the doctrine that reasonable limitation of length of dead end streets in residential areas is within the regulatory power of a city, a resolution rejecting

a proposed plat of a subdivision in the form of a cul-de-sac 1,000 feet in length
is not unreasonable.

> **Kan**   Burke & McCaffrey v Merriam (1967) 198 Kan 325, 424 P2d 483.

§29. Access to Properties

Where a subdivider of land fails to provide each lot, by means of either a public
street or an easement in a width required by ordinance, with satisfactory
access, and the result is that there is imposed on an existing right-of-way a
burden in excess of that contemplated by the ordinance, such failure to comply
with the ordinance constitutes a misuse of the easement, and the easement
owner has a right to equitable relief.

> **Haw**   Guard v Shimamura (1945) 37 Haw 270.

In establishing an easement over a servient estate, the subdivision ordinances
may be considered in determining that a 50-foot right-of-way is necessary.
Since both properties are eligible for subdivision, future problems of roadway
and access may be considered.

> **Mo**   O'Brien v Richter (1970) 455 SW2d 473.

A private road built across public property does not constitute the necessary
access to a public street required in a subdivision ordinance.

> **Miss**   Lancaster v Columbus (1971) 333 F Supp 1012.

Subdividing one lot into two which would be below the minimum lot
requirements and would create a lot which did not front on a public street may
properly be denied. The subdivision would adversely affect public health and
safety due to the increased density and the possible fire danger of the
nonaccessible lot.

> **NH**   Isabelle v Newbury (1974) 11 NH 453, 321 A2d 570.

A requirement that a subdivision provide access with a distance between the
center lines of the access roads of eight hundred feet to the fullest extent
possible is not mandatory. It allows specific deviations particularly where the
tract to be subdivided has a frontage of less than eight hundred feet. The final
approval of the subdivision should be conditioned on approval of the state
highway department rather than denied on the access road requirements.

> **Pa**   Harrisburg Fore Assn v Bd of Supervisors of Lower Paxton Township (1975)
> 21 PaCmwlth 137, 344 A2d 277.

A city ordinance requiring that subdivisions have connecting streets to the
existing city system is reasonable. Conditioning approval of a proposed

subdivision on its being connected to city streets is reasonable and affording the necessary facilities for the area. When the only access to the property is through a neighboring town and streets are nonexistent at the present time the condition may be attached though it effectively prohibits the subdivider from taking any action.

> **Conn**   Nicoli v Planning & Zoning Comm of Easton (1976) 171 Conn 89, 368 A2d 24.

§30. Schools

A county board may condition the grant of special use permits for construction of a sewage treatment plant, well sites, and a water tower for a subdivision on the contribution of land and money for school facilities where the need for such facilities is specifically and uniquely attributable to the subdivider's activities.

> **Ill**   Bd of Education of Sch Dist No 68, DuPage County v Surety Developers (1976) 63 Ill2d 193, 347 NE2d 149.

A school district has standing to enforce an ordinance requiring the donation of school property and/or money as a condition for final approval of a PUD. Since final approval of the plat is conditioned on the donation, the fact that the city has refused to fulfill the requirements gives the school district a vested right.

> **Ill**   Morris Community High School Dist v Morris Devel Co (1974) 24 IllAp3d 208, 320 NE2d 37.

A city may enact an ordinance requiring the developer of a subdivision to assume those costs in the development which are specifically and uniquely attributable to his activity, and which would otherwise be cast upon the public, but not costs of additional school facilities necessitated by the growth of the entire community.

> **Ill**   Pioneer Tr & Sav Bk v Mt Prospect (1961) 22 Ill2d 375, 176 NE2d 799.

§31. Playgrounds

A subdivision ordinance which provides for mandatory dedications for recreational purposes is valid if the requirement is within the statutory grant of power to municipality and if the burden cast upon the subdivider is reasonably attributable to his activity; if not, the ordinance is invalid as a confiscation of private property. In as far as the subdivision increases the recreational needs of the city, then to that extent, the cost of meeting the increase in needs may reasonably be required of the subdivider.

> **Mo**   Home Builders Assn v Kansas City (1977) 555 SW2d 832.

A requirement that subdividers either donate land for park and recreation purposes determined on a per capita acreage basis, or donate cash to the park and recreation districts, is a valid attempt by state and city to preserve open spaces for public recreation. Making the determination contingent on a master plan of the city's park purposes is reasonable, and gives the city an opportunity to determine the overall needs for the area.

> **Cal** Associated Home Builders of the Greater East Bay v Walnut Creek (1971) 4 C3d 633, 484 P2d 606, 94 CaR 630.

An agreement deferring payment on a subdivider's in-lieu payment for parks and schools may be conditioned on a determination of its legality. A note given for the in-lieu payment to the school is canceled when the ordinance is repealed and rewritten without provisions for school payment, but the same repeal and reenactment does not destroy the relationship with the town. The agreement provisions that the payment shall be due if the ordinance is legal and not repealed are not affected by a simultaneous repeal and reenactment.

> **Wis** Mequon v Lake Est Co (1971) 52 Wis2d 765, 190 NW2d 912.

Approval of the subdivision plan of a city planning board, conditioned on the donation of a community playground area, confers a vested right on the owner to develop the land in accordance with the plan when the conveyance of the playground area is made, and a zoning amendment upgrading the land and increasing the minimum area requirements in the district is illegal as to such owner.

> **NY** Ward v New rochelle (1959) 20 Misc2d 122, 197 NYS2d 64.

A requirement that a percentage of subdivided land be donated for park purposes is beyond the authority in the city's charter. While the right may be granted it is presently lacking in the charter making the ordinance invalid.

> **Fla** Admiral Devel Corp v Maitland (1972) 267 So2d 860.

Common land which is set aside for recreational use in a subdivision in order to permit smaller lot sizes may only be used for those purposes within the trust deed. The trustees do not have the authority to issue an easement for access to property when the easement is not within the scope of the trustee's duties and is not a way of necessity.

> **Mo** Cozart v Green Trails Management Corp (1973) 501 SW2d 184.

A requirement that land be dedicated for park and recreation purposes or a fee paid in lieu thereof is within a charter city's right. The city may require payment when a five-acre lot zone for 107 apartments is to be split and the fee may be based on the number of apartments.

> **Cal** Codding Enterprises v Merced (1974) 43 CA3d 375, 116 CaR 730.

LAW REVIEW

Jon A. Kusler, Open Space Zoning: Valid Regulation or Invalid Taking, 57 Minn LR 1.

ANNOTATION

Validity and construction of ordinance requiring land developer to dedicate portion of land for recreational or make payment in lieu thereof, 43 ALR3d 862.

B. FEES IN LIEU OF DEDICATION

§32. Authorization by Statute

Subdivision regulations providing that a petitioner for approval of a subdivision plat may be required both to dedicate land and to pay a fee are invalid as inconsistent with the enabling statute which authorizes payment of money "in lieu of" such dedication.

> **Colo** Cimarron Corp v Bd of County Comm (1977) 563 P2d 946.

A charter city, which derives its authority from the state constitution rather than from the legislature, may properly require by ordinance the payment of a park and recreation fee as condition for approval of a subdivision map of less than five parcels despite a state statute authorizing a city or county to require payment of such fees for a subdivision containing five or more parcels.

> **Cal** Hirsch v Mountain View (1976) 64 CA3d 425, 134 CaR 519.

A provision in a zoning ordinance requiring payment to the city by the subdivider of an amount equal to 10 per cent of the appraised value of the platted area, to be used for public parks and playgrounds in the event the subdivision does not contain public open spaces as required by law, is invalid as being a material departure from the statutory authorization, and outside the scope of the enabling act.

> **Cal** Kelber v Upland (1957) 155 CA2d 631, 318 P2d 561.
> **Ill** Rosen v Downers Grove (1960) 19 Ill2d 448, 167 NE2d 230.
> **Kan** Coronado Devel v McPherson (1962) 189 Kan 174, 368 P2d 51.

An agreement deferring payment on a subdivider's in lieu payment for parks and schools may be conditioned on a determination of its legality. A note given for the in lieu payment to the school is canceled when the ordinance is repealed and rewritten without provisions for school payment, but the same repeal and reenactment does not destroy the relationship to the town. The agreement provisions that the payment shall be due if the ordinance is legal and not repealed are not effected by a simultaneous repeal and reenactment.

> **Wis** Mequon v Lake Est Co (1971) 52 Wis2d 765, 190 NW2d 912.

§33. Police Power

An ordinance providing that a subdivider must pay $200 per lot in lieu of dedicating land of that value for school, park, or recreational needs, where the planning commission finds that a dedication of land for such purposes is not feasible, is a reasonable exercise of the police power.

Wis　Jordan v Menomonee Falls (1965) 28 Wis2d 608, 137 NW2d 442.

An ordinance requiring subdividers, as a condition precedent to approval of plats, to pay the village a fee in lieu of an allotment of land for parks is not unconstitutional on the ground of vagueness, where it directs that the money collected is to be put into a separate fund to be used for park, playground, and recreational purposes.

NY　Jenad Inc v Scarsdale (1966) 18 NY2d 78, 271 NYS2d 955, 218 NE2d 673.

LAW REVIEWS

Ira Michael Heyman & Thomas K. Gilhool, The Constitutionality of Imposing Increased Community Costs on New Suburban Residents through Subdivision Exactions, 73 Yale LJ 1119.

John D. Johnston, Jr, Constitutionality of Subdivision Control Exactions: The Quest for a Rationale, 52 Corn LR 871.

§34. As Tax

An ordinance requiring subdividers, as a condition precedent to approval of plats, to pay a fee in lieu of allotment of lands within the subdivision for park purposes is not unconstitutional on the ground that it is an unauthorized tax on subdividers in that the payments are for general governmental purposes. It is not a tax at all.

NY　Jenad Inc v Scarsdale (1966) 18 NY2d 78, 271 NYS2d 955, 218 NE2d 673.

A county planning regulation requiring as a condition of approval of a subdivision the dedication of land for park purposes or, at the county's option, a money payment in lieu of the land dedication is unconstitutional as applied to the county's exercise of the money option of the regulation, because it is an exercise of a taxing power which the county does not have without legislative grant from statutes relating to subdividing.

Ore　Haugen v Gleason (1961) 226 Ore 99, 359 P2d 108.

C. FRONTAGE AND ABUTMENT SPECIFICATIONS

§35. Charter Authortity

A charter provision requiring an owner, in platting his property within the city into blocks and lots, to conform to abutting streets and lots, and to the existing frontage on any street, is a reasonable exercise of the police power.

Tex Halsell v Ferguson (1918) 109 Tex 144, 202 SW 317.

§36. Enforcement

Where the town board of survey approves a subdivision which permits construction of a street in closer proximity to an existing dwelling than permitted by the zoning ordinance, and the owner has made substantial expenditures in reliance on the board's decision, the court will enjoin enforcement of the setback requirement.

Mass Marblehead v Deery (1969) 356 Mass 532, 254 NE2d 234.

That the developer was permitted to proceed without strict compliance with the frontage requirements for building lots provided for in an ordinance is not a satisfactory reason for permitting further exceptions that would effectively nullify the ordinance.

NJ Greenway Homes v River Edge (1948) 137 NJLaw 453, 60 A2d 811.

Anticipated profits loss by a home developer is not a controlling factor in deciding if the developer is entitled to any relief because of the governing body's refusal to approve the recommendation of the planning board, since the developer readily can change his plans to comply with the ordinance without hardship other than loss of some anticipated profits.

NJ Greenway Homes v River Edge (1948) 137 NJLaw 453, 60 A2d 811.

D. LOT SIZES

§37. Conflict with Zoning Restrictions

In computing the number of lots in a planned area development, the private streets, not dedicated, may be included in computing square footage. Since a planned area development allows for greater flexibility in planning and does not require dedicated streets, they may be figured in the total square footage to find the maximum number of lots.

Ariz Peabody v Phoenix (1971) 14 ArizApp 576, 485 P2d 565.

The lot size of a proposed subdivision may be increased above the zoning requirements for the benefit of the public as a whole. Reducing the number of lots in order to prevent pollution to a unique salt pond is a reasonable requirement.

> **NY** Landing Estates v Jones (1971) 67 Misc2d 354, 324 NYS2d 255.

The zoning board cannot deny landowners the right to subdivide their property into smaller lots that are compatible with the area and within the requirements of the existing zoning law just because there are pre-existing lots both bigger and smaller than those required by the law within the perimeters of the subdivision.

> **Fla** Dade County v Murphy (1975) 322 So2d 616.
> Dade County v Williams (1973) 278 So2d 634.

The approval of a preliminary subdivision plan may be conditioned on compliance with zoning regulations presently being considered. When the subdivider agrees to these conditions he is not automatically entitled to approval of a final plan which follows the preliminary plan when the ordinances have been amended to provide for different lot sizes.

> **Pa** Devonshire Rlty Corp v Maxatawny Township (1976) 22 PaCmwlth 555, 349 A2d 802.

Under the enabling act, standards in a subdivision regulatory ordinance with respect to minimum lot sizes and lot area requirements must be identical with those in a zoning ordinance covering the same territory.

> **NJ** Levin v Livingston (1961) 35 NJ 500, 173 A2d 391.

§38. Zoning Change after Plat Recordation

A variance may not be granted by the planning board to allow smaller lots than the area classification. The fact that the subdivision was approved before the reclassification does not constitute an unusual hardship or practical difficulty.

> **NY** Van Deusen v Jackson (1970) 35 AD2d 58, 312 NYS2d 853.

The size requirements for a lot may be increased though the subdivision has been approved. A subdivider does not secure a vested right when he owns adjoining property though the owner of one subsidized lot may be granted a vested right to build.

> **NH** R A Vachon & Son v Concord (1972) 112 NH 107, 289 A2d 646.

Up-zoning the size of lots in a new subdivision is valid when it is not confiscatory. On a showing of the threat of pollution of local wells and the water basin due to inability to put in a public water and sewer system a municipality may require 1½ acre lots.

NY   Salamar Builders Corp v Tuttle (1971) 29 NY2d 221, 325 NYS2d 933.

Subdivision of a tract within a residential area may be denied when the lots will not meet the minimum building requirements. A second proposal to build a duplex in the residential area without subdividing, but on a substandard size tract, may also be denied without being arbitrary and unreasonable.

Miss   Jackson v Ridgway (1972) 258 So2d 439.

An ordinance restricting a subdivision to one-acre lots and rescinding an agreement previously made with the subdivider to approve his plat on condition that multiple dwellings construction be ceased is invalid. The subdivider has secured a vested right by his action in desisting in the construction of the permitted multiple dwellings and by carrying forward the subdivision as approved.

NY   Greene v Brach (1972) 40 AD2d 1048, 338 NYS2d 677.

The five-year zoning freeze on a new subdivision is tolled by denial of an earth removal permit. The subdivision as approved may not subsequently be changed on a claim that the five-year limitation has expired when the municipal authorities are the parties causing the delay in construction.

Mass   M DeMatteo Construction Co v Bd of Appeals of Hingham (1975) 334 NE2d 51.

A subdivision plan approved prior to an amendment of the zoning ordinance retains its original zoning for a period of seven years, and a building permit issued may not be revoked on the basis of an agreement with the prior building examiner which was not made a part of the plat or record and was unknown to the present property owners.

Mass   Green v Bd of Appeals of Norwood (1970) 358 Mass 253, 263 NE2d 423.

A subdivider of property who has secured approval of his plan is entitled to the existing zoning classification. However, the statute setting a time limitation for continuance depends on the time of filing. Purchasers of adjacent property are entitled to rely on the zoning existing at the time of their purchase, in determining what use they will make of their property.

Mass   Vazza v Brockton (1971) 359 Mass 256, 269 NE2d 270.

Tentative approval of a subdivision plan may not be extended by a planning board beyond the period prescribed by statute so as to render subdivision plans immune from a change in lot size made by amendment to a zoning ordinance.

NJ Hilton Acres v Klein (1960) 64 NJS 281, 165 A2d 819.

Approval of a small subdivision does not prevent the municipality from upgrading lot sizes. While there is a statutory protection for a larger subdivision with a substantial expenditure for streets and improvements, a small subdivision combining three lots into two does not enjoy such protection, in the absence of substantial expenditures.

NJ Sandler v Bd of Adjustment of Springfield (1970) 113 NJS 333, 273 A2d 775.

A board of supervisors has no legislative authority to approve or disapprove a recorded plat since the plat becomes "legally established" when recorded in accordance with the provisions of the applicable ordinance. The board's refusal to approve a plat on the ground that there had been a change in the zoning regulation increasing minimum lot sizes was not authorized where the zoning change was made after the plat was recorded.

Ariz Robinson v Lintz (1966) 101 Ariz 448, 420 P2d 923.

A tract of land not divided into lots during subdivision does not justify an industrial classification due to its proximity to a railroad. By omitting the property at the time of subdividing the owners created the problem and are not entitled to relief.

Md Randolph Hills v Montgomery County (1972) 264 Md 78, 285 A2d 620.

§39. Development on Substandard Parcel

Variances for substandard size lots may not be granted when the developer has subdivided into lots which he knows are smaller than those permitted.

Tenn Union Tr Co v Williamson County Bd of Zoning Appeals (1973) 500 SW2d 608.

An exception to the lot size ordinance for lots not contiguous to other lots of the same owner may not be applied to a subdivision which became substandard prior to final approval. The lots had a common owner and were all contiguous making the exception inapplicable.

Ore Drain v Clackamas County (1975) 22 OreAp 332, 539 P2d 673.

The development of a subdivision will be enjoined where the size of the building lots fails to meet the requirements fixed by a zoning ordinance. In calculating the size of the lots, easements for access must be excluded.

NJ Loveladies Property Owners Assn v Barnegat Serv Co (1960) 60 NJS 491, 159 A2d 417.

E. SEWAGE AND WATER SYSTEMS

§40. Authority to Require Drainage

Refusing to record a subdivision plat that does not provide for adequate sewerage disposal, and a suggestion that lots be set aside for a holding pond for runoff water as a condition of approval, is not a form of illegal condemnation, though the right to file the plat is not conditioned on setting aside the lots.

> **Ill** Brown v Joliet (1969) 108 IllAp2d 230, 247 NE2d 47.

A subdivider may be required to pay a proportion of off-site improvements for drainage required by his subdivision to the extent that the work is necessary. The subdivider is liable for the costs of the improvement fairly allocable to him.

> **NJ** Divan Builders v Planning Bd of Wayne Township (1975) 66 NJ 582, 334 A2d 30.

A subdivision ordinance may not change the state law on runoff water. Approval of a subdivision plan which causes an increase in the flooding of lower property is invalid and does not confer a right on the subdivider to continue the practice.

> **Del** Glassman v Weldin Farms (1976) 359 A2d 669.

An ordinance requiring a property owner who seeks approval of a subdivision plat to dedicate land for drainage is a valid exercise of police powers.

> **Fla** Wald Corp v Dade County (1975) 43 Fla Supp 95.

Denial of a subdivision on the basis that the land is subject to flooding and the provisions for disposition of surface water and other drainage calls for ponding contrary to the ordinances is justified. Approval by the planning commission is insufficient when the board has retained power to approve all subdivisions.

> **Pa** Szeles-Naale v Bd of Comm of Swatara Township (1976) 28 PaCmwlth 563, 368 A2d 1336.

A city may properly require the developers of a subdivision to execute an undertaking to be expended for construction of a drainage facility, as a condition of approval of a final subdivision map.

> **Cal** Buena Park v Boyar (1960) 186 CA2d 61, 8 CaR 674.
> Mefford v Tulare (1951) 102 CA2d 919, 228 P2d 847.

A plat office may not withhold approval of a subdivision plat for drainage deficiencies where the county board has not adopted regulations concerning drainage requirements for plat approval.

> **Ill** Urban Inv & Devel Co v Graham (1977) 49 IllAp3d 661, 364 NE2d 628.

A city council may not impose on the developer as a condition of approving a subdivision plat the entire cost of construction of a drainage channel which will serve a greater area than the subdivision.

Colo Wood Brothers Homes v Colorado Springs (1977) 568 P2d 487.

Though an ordinance requires the road commissioner to approve or disapprove a subdivider's plan for a drainage system within 10 days after he receives it, this requirement does not exonerate the subdivider from the duty to provide an effective system.

Cal Eichler Homes v Marin County (1962) 208 CA2d 653, 25 CaR 394.

§41. Water Mains

Installation of water mains may be a valid requirement for approval of a subdivision. The manner of allocating the cost becomes a question of fact based on conditions of the utility company, the existing ordinances and precedent. Costs may be entirely paid by the city, installation by the city with assessment against adjoining owners, or installation required by the subdivider with or without reimbursement depending on the facts.

NJ Deerfield Est v East Brunswick (1972) 60 NJ 115, 286 A2d 498.

An ordinance requirement that the developers of any addition or subdivision within a city install all waterlines for household distribution up to eight inch size without expense to the city and that a prorata reimbursement of the costs of lines over eight inches will be paid by the city does not constitute inverse condemnation. The requirement is a legitimate regulation by the city and there is no condemnation since there is no requirement that the property be developed.

Okla MidContinent Builders v Midwest City (1975) 539 P2d 1377.

Subdivision requirements may be extended into the extraterritorial jurisdiction allowed. A subdivider, who filed plans showing compliance with the individual well and septic system requirements, may not install a central water system without approval by the city water board. His agreement to follow the exempting procedure does not permit him to change his plan and disregard the requirements for city approval of the central water system.

Tex Swinney v San Antonio (1972) 483 SW2d 556.

An ordinance requiring a developer of lands to extend water mains to the lands at his own expense is invalid for lack of statutory authority to impose the costs in the manner ordained.

NJ Reid Devel Co v Parsippany-Troy Hills (1954) 31 NJS 459, 107 A2d 20.

§42. Utility Contract Approval

An ordinance requiring utility contracts with subdivision developers to be submitted and approved by the county board will be enforced by requiring refund of any sum the board finds to be in excess of a reasonable charge for furnishing the service.

Fla Carol City Utilities v Miami Gardens Shopping Plaza (1964) 165 So2d 199.

§43. Sewer Installation

A city may by ordinance assess an owner for both a proportion of the cost of constructing a sewer in front of his lot and the initial expense of building the sewer. A subdivider installing his own sewer lines remains liable for his proportion of the initial expenses.

Mass Exeter Rlty v Bedford (1969) 356 Mass 399, 252 NE2d 885.

A city may by ordinance charge a subdivider a sewer entrance fee based on front footage, though the subdivider had installed sewers within the subdivision, where such entrance fee is lower than if the city had constructed the lines within the subdivision.

Mass Exeter Rlty v Bedford (1969) 356 Mass 399, 252 NE2d 885.

A difference in connecting fees between homes built by a developer in a new subdivision and those built by an individual on his separately owned property is invalid. A reasonable classification may be made to insure that the newer additions to the sewer system pay a fair proportion of the cost; however basing the difference on whether built by a developer who is required to install his own laterals without reimbursement or individuals is unreasonable.

NJ S S & O Corp v Bernards Township (1973) 62 NJ 369, 301 A2d 738.

The developer of a mobile home park qualifies as a subdivider or developer of a commercial center. As such he is bound by the requirements to provide extensions to the sewer system rather than lateral connections.

Ill Stoeber v Stookey (1974) 20 IllAp3d 252, 313 NE2d 627.

The expense incurred by a plat development firm beyond that usually involved in platting lots of sewer installation, that was voluntarily done after the adoption of a zoning resolution and that will be useful and valuable to the remaining land, though the zoning resolution is complied with, does not justify the granting of a variance to the zoning resolution as a pre-existing non-conforming use.

Ohio State v Kiefaber (1960) 113 OA 523, 18 Op2d 169, 179 NE2d 360.

§44. Reimbursement for Installations

An agreement whereby the city waived the assessment for installing sewer and waterlines is not an ultra vires act, under a subdivision ordinance stating that a developer may be required to pay where his subdivision is a considerable distance from the nearest city. A contract between the city and the developer to waive payment is valid.

> **Del**　Hearn Bros v Newark (1969) 261 A2d 532.

An agreement and subsequent ordinance to install sewer and waterlines in a new subdivision may not charge more than the actual cost of installation. The fact that the agreement provided for a per foot per dollar price does not authorize the city to collect more than the actual expenses involved.

> **Wis**　Atkins v Glendale (1975) 67 Wis2d 43, 226 NW2d 190.

An ordinance accepting a contract to construct streets, sewer and waterlines in a subdivision which provides that the money has been set aside is an insufficient basis for damages on failure of the city to comply with the requirements. The prohibition against debts which are not levied for may not be circumvented by a statement that "the money has been allocated" when in effect the allocation has not been made and the amount of the indebtedness is uncertain and extended over a considerable period of time.

> **Tex**　Brodhead v Forney (1976) 538 SW2d 873.

An ordinance providing for a subdivider's payment to the city on a footage basis of the expense of extending water mains and for periodic repayments to the subdivider of a percentage of the gross water revenues derived within a fixed period, but not exceeding the amount paid by the subdivider and without any charge for interest, is valid within a charter provision permitting the city, under its regular powers, to enlarge any water system and pay cash therefor.

> **Cal**　Long v Fresno (1964) 225 CA2d 59, 36 CaR 886.

§45. Future Additions

An agreement and a resolution incorporated therein by reference requiring a developer to advance the full cost of installing improvements, such as sanitary sewers and water lines, and providing for reimbursement to be made to the developer for the costs of the improvements and for payment of the cost of installing storm sewers, where the mayor and aldermen, in adopting the resolution, did not anticipate the necessity of having to install additions in the future to the existing water and sanitary and storm sewer systems, are not rendered ultra vires, since the city is authorized to agree to expand the needed utilities without the issuance of bonds.

Md Frederick v Brosius Homes Corp (1967) 247 Md 88, 230 A2d 306.

§45.1. Denial for Insufficient Capacity

Rezoning from multiple-dwelling to single-family residential on the basis of insufficient water and sewage service is invalid. Rezoning which singles out a particular developer in a situation which is uniform within the town amounts to confiscation without compensation.

NY Nattin Rlty v Ludewig (1972) 40 AD2d 535, 334 NYS2d 483; affirming (1971) 67 Misc2d 828, 324 NYS2d 668.

A requirement that a subdivision show what water utility mains, piping, and other facilities will be installed does not authorize an inquiry into the availability of water. The county's denial of a subdivision on a requirement of showing present and future availability of water is outside of the scope of subdivision requirements.

Ariz Owens v Glenarm Land Co (1975) 24 ArizApp 430, 539 P2d 544.

Denial of a condominium subdivision based on the board's opinion that existing power, light, water and fire protection are inadequate to meet needs and the fact that the high-density, high-rise development does not meet the concept of what is best for the area is invalid. The plans which meet ordinance requirements must be approved or the defects in the plans specified.

Pa Horst v Derry Township Bd of Supervisors (1975) 21 PaCmwlth 556, 347 A2d 507.

III. SALES OF LAND

§46. When Unlawful

A warrant charging a person with selling land not properly subdivided is deficient where the complaint does not state that the accused is the owner or agent of land platted and within the jurisdiction of the commissioners in charge of plats.

NC State v McBane (1969) 276 NC 60, 170 SE2d 913.

Requiring that a subdivision plat be recorded before a sign may be erected showing the property for sale is valid. Neither the recording requirement nor the sign restriction affect the owner's right to sell or dispose of his property as he sees fit, but applies only to the standards to determine whether or not the public health, safety, and welfare will be protected.

Fla Prescott v Charlotte County (1972) 263 So2d 623.

A prohibition against the sale of land in a subdivision before it has been approved and recorded does not make the contract void per se. A buyer may enforce the contract after the administrative actions which make the subdivision legal have been complied with. The ordinance, which makes the seller liable at every stage of the transaction whereas a buyer does not violate the act unless he either accepts the transfer or is knowingly a party thereto, may not be used by the seller to prevent the purchaser from completing an otherwise valid contract.

Md Montagna v Marston (1975) 24 MdApp 354, 330 A2d 502.

A subdivision ordinance does not constitute an undue interference with the owner's right to use or sell his land, but only provides adequate safeguards. Preparation of a plat and surveying of two tracts out of a large area which are sold and reconveyed to the owner constitute a violation of the subdivision ordinance when no recording or approval of the plat has been secured.

Pa Commonwealth v Fisher (1976) 23 PaCmwlth 25, 350 A2d 428.

A subdivision ordinance may only be applied against an owner or agent selling property by reference to a subdivision plat. An attempt to include a person selling a tract of property by metes and bounds is improper since no reference is made to any subdivision plat.

Fla Escambia County v Herring (1977) 343 So2d 63.

Under a city ordinance regulating the subdividing of land for the purpose of selling lots, and requiring prior approval as a condition precedent to the disposition or sale of lots in any proposed subdivision, failure to obtain approval is not an unlawful act until the lots are actually disposed of or offered for sale.

Haw Marques, Application of (1945) 37 Haw 260.

An ordinance forbidding an owner to agree to sell land until subdivision plans are approved and filed with the commission is not violated by an agreement to sell a parcel of land for the purpose of being subdivided where the agreement is placed in escrow, the contract for sale not to become effective until the subdivision plans are approved.

Haw Whitlow v Jennings & Kaneshiro (1954) 40 Haw 523.

ANNOTATION

Failure of vendor to comply with statute or ordinance requiring approval or recording of plat prior to conveyance of property as rendering sale void or voidable, 77 ALR3d 1058.

§47. Standards for Penalty Enforcement

An ordinance that makes it unlawful for an owner to sell lots in any subdivision without complying with certain provisions of an ordinance, and that fails to provide any rule of action for the guidance of the people of the municipality or any rule for enforcement by the executive officers of the municipality, does not sufficiently inform the members of the community of what they may or may not do and is invalid.

> **Haw** Territory v Achi (1926) 29 Haw 62.

§48. Penalties for Unapproved Sales

A subdivision ordinance imposing penalties on the sale of lots in unapproved subdivisions that applies to all lots shown on recorded maps that are conveyed after approval of the ordinance is not a retrospective law.

> **NH** Blevens v Manchester (1961) 103 NH 284, 170 A2d 121.

An ordinance imposing a penalty on the sale of land within municipality by reference to a plat plan, without prior approval of the plan by the municipality, is ultra vires and void.

> **NH** Blevens v Manchester (1961) 103 NH 284, 170 A2d 121.
> **NJ** Magnolia Devel Co v Coles (1952) 10 NJ 223, 89 A2d 664.

§49. Standing to Challenge

A party protesting subdivision of property is not required to exhaust administrative remedies since the statute only authorizes appeal by a subdivider. An ordinance requiring appeal by any aggrieved party is outside the statutory authority of the municipal corporation.

> **Cal** Friends of Lake Arrowhead v San Bernardino County (1974) 38 CA3d 497, 113 CaR 539.

An ordinance making it illegal to sell property by reference to a plat which has not been recorded does not justify rescission of a contract for sale made on mistake of the subdivision. The penal provisions completely encompass the transaction and are not a good basis for rescinding the contract.

> **NC** Marriott Financial Services v Capital Funds (1975) 288 NC 122, 217 SE2d 551.

The owners of a subdivided parcel of land in a village are proper parties to seek, by declaratory judgment, a decision on the validity of an ordinance prohibiting the sale of land on private roads not conforming to specifications set forth in the ordinance.

Ohio Huber v Richmond Heights (1954) 68 Abs 470, 121 NE2d 457.

IV. TAXATION

§50. Assessment of Unapproved Lots

Approval of a subdivision may not be conditioned on payment of taxes due and owing.

NJ Sussex Woodlands v West Milford (1970) 109 NJS 432, 263 A2d 502.

An ordinance authorizing the city to enter into contracts with developers of swamp and low lands to assess unimproved lots as acreage property until 60 per cent have been sold, or for 10 years, violates the constitutional provision relating to uniform and equal taxation.

Fla Naples v Conboy (1965) 182 So2d 412.

LAW REVIEW

Gerald E. Mullen, The Use of Special Assessment Districts and Independent Special Districts as Aids in Financing Private Land Development, 53 Cal LR 364.

SUBVERSIVE ACTIVITIES

EDITORIAL COMMENT. This is one of those topics that is regulated mainly by federal and state governments. However, there are, or have been, a few local regulations, and the cases arising therefrom are digested below. Los Angeles County enacted an ordinance requiring registration of certain subversives (held invalid, §1); Akron, Ohio, prohibited the possession of firearms by members of subversive organizations (held invalid, §2); and Columbus, Ohio, required licenses for the sale of merchandise from Communist countries (held invalid, §3, §4). No case has been found upholding any such local ordinance.

The related subject of loyalty oaths is covered under Oaths. And to some degree the subject of Civil Rights is related.

I. MEMBERS OF SUBVERSIVE ORGANIZATIONS

§1. Registration Requirements

An ordinance requiring under penal sanctions that any person belonging to an organization proposing to substitute communism for our system of industrial ownership and control and to overthrow the government by terrorism and sabotage must file an affidavit giving his name and the name of the organization is invalid.

    Cal   People v McCormick (1951) 102 CA2d 954, 228 P2d 349.

§2. Possession of Firearms

An ordinance providing that no person who is a member of a subversive organization shall possess a firearm within the city is so indefinite that the ordinance is invalid.

    Ohio   Akron v Williams (1960) 84 Abs 499, 172 NE2d 28.

II. COMMUNIST MANUFACTURED GOODS

§3. Licensing and Labeling

An ordinance requiring persons who offer for sale merchandise from Communist countries to post a license conspicuously authorizing the proprietor to sell Communist manufactured or processed goods, and to post a sign or to label the merchandise Communist manufactured goods violates the commerce clause by attempting to regulate commerce with foreign nations.

> **Ohio**   Columbus v McGuire (1963) 25 Op2d 331, 195 NE2d 916.

An ordinance requiring a person who offers for sale merchandise from Communist countries to post a license authorizing him to sell Communist manufactured or processed goods jeopardizes the work of the State Department, and is an undue interference with the direction of foreign affairs by the federal government.

> **Ohio**   Columbus v Miqdadi (1963) 25 Op2d 337, 195 NE2d 923.

§4. Book Distributions

An ordinance requiring a person who offers for sale merchandise from Communist countries to post a license authorizing him to sell Communist manufactured or processed goods is an unconstitutional suppression of freedom of the press, where it operates to prevent a proprietor from distributing any books printed in any of the 13 countries named in the ordinance.

> **Ohio**   Columbus v Miqdadi (1963) 25 Op2d 337, 195 NE2d 923.

SUNDAY LAWS

EDITORIAL COMMENT. Local ordinances prohibiting certain commercial activities on the Sabbath were once fairly common. They are not nearly so common in modern times; but many still exist. In fact, North Carolina as recently as 1964, and Nebraska in 1965, held that a city's police power embraced the power to prohibit or limit the operation of certain businesses on Sunday (§ 3). The object of Sunday legislation, it was said by a New Jersey court in 1961, is to insure a day of quiet, rest and relaxation in the community at large.

The cases are not at all in harmony, with regard to what Sunday laws can and cannot do. Thus, in § 52 we find that a number of states hold that an ordinance may validly limit or prohibit the operation of theaters or movies on Sunday; but in § 54 we find that Indiana and Kentucky deny that power to cities, while New York places limitations on it. A similar situation prevails with respect to the selling of automobiles on Sunday (§§ 61, 62). Missouri holds such a prohibition invalid, but Colorado, Nebraska, and Illinois permit it. And so it goes, with respect also to groceries and meat markets (§§ 78, 79) and household furnishings (§§ 84, 85).

Most of the Sunday law cases are included in the present topic. However, the limitations on sale of alcoholic beverages on Sunday are treated in ALCOHOLIC BEVERAGES.

I. APPLICATION TO BUSINESSES GENERALLY

A. IN GENERAL

§1. Types of Sunday Closing Ordinances

There are three principal types of Sunday closing ordinances: (1) prohibition of particular businesses, with others permitted to open; (2) general closing, but exemption of certain businesses and permitting them to sell the same products sold by prohibited businesses; (3) prohibition of all business activity, but exemption of the sale of certain commodities.

> **Ill**　Humphrey Chevrolet v Evanston (1956) 7 Ill2d 402, 131 NE2d 70.

§2. Purpose of Sunday Closing

The object of Sunday legislation is to ensure a day of quiet, rest and relaxation in the community at large.

> **NJ**　State v Patrignani (1961) 65 NJS 303, 167 A2d 671.
> Auto-Rite Supply v Woodbridge (1957) 25 NJ 188, 135 A2d 515.

§3. Police Power

A county wide Sunday closing ordinance may properly be enacted under the police power and the general statutory authority.

> **NC**　Whitney Store v Clark (1970) 277 NC 322, 177 SE2d 418.

A Sunday closing ordinance substantially similar to other city ordinances upheld will be sustained on demurrer.

> **NC**　S S Kresge Co v Davis (1970) 8 NCApp 595, 174 SE2d 629.

The police power delegated to a city embraces the power to enact laws prohibiting or limiting the operation of certain businesses on Sunday.

> **Ill**　Humphrey Chevrolet v Evanston (1956) 7 Ill2d 402, 131 NE2d 70.
> **NC**　Clark's Charlotte v Hunter (1964) 261 NC 222, 134 SE2d 364.
> High Point Surplus v Pleasants (1965) 264 NC 650, 142 SE2d 697.
> State v Davis (1916) 171 NC 809, 89 SE 40.
> **Neb**　Arrigo v Lincoln (1951) 154 Neb 537, 48 NW2d 643.
> Skag-Way Department Stores v Grand Island (1964) 176 Neb 169, 125 NW2d 529.
> **NJ**　Hertz Washmobile Sys v South Orange (1956) 41 NJS 110, 124 A2d 68.
> Masters-Jersey Inc v Paramus (1960) 32 NJ 296, 160 A2d 841.

B. Validity Factors

§4. Reasonableness

A Sunday closing ordinance which follows the statutory provisions but specifically exempts 26 different types of businesses including recreation facilities, amusement centers, fairs, and trade shows constitutes an arbitrary classification. There is no showing that these are a public necessity, or that the items offered for sale in them differ from those offered for sale in closed establishments.

> **Okla** Spartan's Industries v Oklahoma City (1972) 498 P2d 399.

A municipal corporation may legislate reasonably with respect to Sunday observance within its corporate area.

> **Neb** Skag-Way Department Stores v Grand Island (1964) 176 Neb 169, 125 NW2d 529.
> Arrigo v Lincoln (1951) 154 Neb 537, 48 NW2d 643.

A Sunday observance ordinance which is reasonable and does not discriminate against any class of competitors similarly situated is a valid exercise of the police power.

> **NC** State v Smith (1965) 265 NC 173, 143 SE2d 293.

To withstand the test of reasonableness in a Sunday closing ordinance, there must be moderation and proportionateness of means to ends.

> **Wyo** Nation v Giant Drug (1964) 396 P2d 431.

§5. Basis of Classification

A city's classification of business to be subjected to Sunday closing laws must rest on a reasonable basis.

> **Ill** Courtesy Motor Sales v Ward (1962) 24 Ill2d 82, 179 NE2d 692.
> Pacesetter Homes v South Holland (1960) 18 Ill2d 247, 163 NE2d 464.
> **NC** Clark's Charlotte v Hunter (1964) 261 NC 222, 134 SE2d 364.
> State v Towery (1954) 239 NC 274, 79 SE2d 513.
> **NJ** West Orange v Carrs Stores (1958) 53 NJS 237, 147 A2d 97.

A prohibition against any sale of food or food products or garden and lawn supplies on Sunday except by stores with less than 2400 square feet of sale space and having no more than three employees at any one time is valid. The fact that larger stores are prohibited from sales while smaller stores may be open is a reasonable classification. The restriction decreases the number of persons involved in selling food and garden supplies and limits the number engaged in handling traffic and performing police duties in general.

> **Miss**   Jackson v Luckett (1976) 336 So2d 776.

§6. Certainty

Where a Sunday closing ordinance expresses the conduct prohibited clearly enough that a reasonably intelligent person will know what is forbidden, the ordinance is not void on the ground of uncertainty and vagueness.

> **NC**   Clark's Charlotte v Hunter (1964) 261 NC 222, 134 SE2d 364.

ANNOTATION

Validity of Sunday law or ordinance as affected by vagueness or uncertainty in matters covered or excepted, 91 ALR2d 763.

§7. —Need to Define Hours

An ordinance requiring certain places of business to be kept closed and not to transact business during all of the daytime of either Saturday or Sunday is indefinite and uncertain in failing to limit the hours included within the expression "daytime."

> **Cal**   Deese v Lodi (1937) 21 CA2d 631, 69 P2d 1005.

§8. Severability of Invalid Closing Provision

Where an ordinance prohibiting the conduct of the business of selling household electrical equipment on Sundays is independent of and separable from a provision prohibiting such activities on legal holidays, the invalidity of the prohibition of holiday business will not serve to invalidate the prohibition with respect to business on Sunday.

> **NJ**   Elizabeth v Windsor-Fifth Ave (1954) 31 NJS 187, 106 A2d 9.

§9. Effect of State Law

A Sunday closing ordinance is invalid where the field has been pre-empted by a state statute. An attempt to clarify or interpret the statute by enumerating exemptions applicable to the phrase "works of necessity" in the statute is not within the permissible limits of the city's authority.

> **Ky** Boyle v Campbell (1970) 450 SW2d 265.

The power of municipalities to enact Sunday closing ordinances derives from statute empowering municipalities to regulate their police and to pass and enforce all necessary police ordinances.

> **Ill** Clinton v Wilson (1913) 257 Ill 580, 101 NE 192.

A Sunday ordinance, that does not contain terms irreconcilable with a statute and does not permit what the statute forbids or forbid what the statute permits, will not be found to be invalid as conflicting with the statute if it merely fails to make certain acts that are violations of the statute also violations of the ordinance.

> **Minn** Mangold Midwest Co v Richfield (1966) 274 Minn 347, 143 NW2d 813.

Where, under state law, the general ban on Sunday activities may be modified by ordinance, pursuant to referendum, to permit operations of certain businesses, fact that there is no municipal enactment in existence to be modified will not nullify result of referendum in favor of a municipal modification of state law, since the modification would have come into being even in the absence of a general prohibitory ordinance.

> **NJ** Williamson v Paramus (1962) 36 NJ 328, 177 A2d 537.

The power of a municipality to regulate Sunday activity stems from the statute enabling municipalities to enact ordinances for preservation of the public health, safety and welfare.

> **NJ** State v Patrignani (1961) 65 NJS 303, 167 A2d 671.

To interpret ordinance exemptions modeled after statute the court will have to look to legislative intent in the statute.

> **NJ** Collingswood v Boyer (1960) 59 NJS 561, 158 A2d 227.

If an ordinance authorizing Sunday activities is in conflict with state law, by authorizing activities prohibited by statute, it will be declared invalid.

> **NJ** Collingswood v Boyer (1960) 59 NJS 561, 158 A2d 227.

The provisions of a statute relating to Sunday closing will affect municipal power to the extent of limiting the municipality to the enactment of ordinances that do not conflict with the state law.

> **NJ** Masters-Jersey Inc v Paramus (1960) 32 NJ 296, 160 A2d 841.

A statute prohibiting worldly business on Sunday, except affairs of necessity or charity, stands as a declaration of state policy, within which framework municipalities may regulate and control Sunday activities.

NJ Auto-Rite Supply v Woodbridge (1957) 25 NJ 188, 135 A2d 515.

An ordinance authorizing Sunday activities that are prohibited by state law is invalid, as being palpably in conflict with the paramount legislative authority.

NJ Hertz Washmobile Systems v South Orange (1956) 41 NJS 110, 124 A2d 68.

A Sunday closing ordinance is not invalid for lack of power in the city to enact it, since a statute specifically delegates to municipalities the power to enact ordinances requiring the observance of Sunday.

NC State v McGee (1953) 237 NC 633, 75 SE2d 783.

A city council, so long as it stays within the state law, has wide discretion in enacting a Sunday closing ordinance, to determine what shall come within the class of permitted activities and what shall be excluded.

Tenn Kirk v Olgiati (1957) 203 Tenn 1, 308 SW2d 471.

An ordinance prohibiting places of amusement from being open between midnight Saturday and 2 PM Sunday, thereby tacitly permitting them to operate after 2 PM on Sunday, is invalid as in direct conflict with the statute prohibiting places of amusement from being open on Sunday.

Tex Zucarro v State (1917) 82 TexCr 1, 197 SW 982.

§10. Uniformity of Application

A Sunday closing order is constitutional. However, its enforcement may deprive the operators of their constitutional rights. A concerted effort to enforce the ordinance against one store to its detriment, with no enforcement against its competitors, constitutes a defense in a criminal prosecution. The ordinance retains its validity, but its enforcement must be on an equal, unbiased basis.

NC S S Kresge Co v Davis (1971) 277 NC 654, 178 SE2d 382; rev in part 8 NCApp 595, 174 SE2d 629.

A Sunday closing ordinance that is based on a reasonable classification and applies uniformly to all members or businesses of the same class is not unconstitutional on the ground of granting special privileges and immunities, or denying equal protection of the law.

Ill River Forest v Vignola (1961) 30 Ill App2d 52, 173 NE2d 515, rev on other grnds (1961) 23 Ill2d 411, 178 NE2d 364.

Sunday closing ordinances must be based on reasonable classifications, and an ordinance prohibiting the sale of a commodity is not discriminatory against particular dealers who are accorded the same treatment as all other dealers in that commodity.

Ill Humphrey Chevrolet v Evanston (1956) 7 Ill2d 402, 131 NE2d 70.

The fact that some localities permit the sale of commodities on Sunday while others do not, and that those who permit such sales may differ as to the type of articles permitted to be sold, does not of itself constitute improper classification or unjust discrimination.

NH State v Rogers (1964) 105 NH 366, 200 A2d 740.

LAW REVIEW

Similarly Situated Under the Sunday Closing Law, 119 Pa LR 190.

§11. Relation of Law to Religious Observance

A Sunday closing ordinance prohibiting all nonessential services, but excepting grocery stores during hours other than 10 AM to noon and sales of Christmas greeneries during December, is valid. The exceptions are not primarily for support of the Christian religion, and where the opponents are not affected by the grocery operation they have no grounds to contest it.

NC S S Kresge Co v Tomlinson (1969) 275 NC 1, 165 SE2d 236.

Since the object of a Sunday closing ordinance is the maintenance of quiet and order, and the evil to be remedied is the disturbance of others in their religious worship, the conduct of any business that can reasonably be said to entail such disturbance may be prohibited under the police power.

Ill Pacesetter Homes v South Holland (1960) 18 Ill2d 247, 163 NE2d 464.

A Sunday closing ordinance that has as its object the promotion of religion or worship is beyond the scope of governmental power, but one that seeks merely to protect those desiring to worship from disturbance and distraction by others is valid.

Ill Pacesetter Homes v South Holland (1960) 18 Ill2d 247, 163 NE2d 464.

An ordinance prohibiting any type of real estate business on Sunday, without exception, is invalid because in conflict with the state Sunday closing law, which exempts from its operations persons who conscientiously believe that Saturday should be observed as the Sabbath.

> **Mich**   Builders Assn v Detroit (1940) 295 Mich 272, 294 NW 677.

An ordinance having for its sole purpose the closing of a legitimate business on Sunday and other Sabbatical days, to promote religious observance, does not promote the health, safety, peace, and good order of the city's inhabitants and is void.

> **Neb**   Skag-Way Department Stores v Omaha (1966) 179 Neb 707, 140 NW2d 28.

The governing body of a city has power to enact and enforce ordinances for the observance of Sunday.

> **NC**   Clark's Charlotte v Hunter (1964) 261 NC 222, 134 SE2d 364.

LAW REVIEW

A Braunfeld v Brown Test for Indirect Burdens on the Free Exercise of Religion, 48 Minn LR 1165.

ANNOTATION

Sunday Laws, freedom of religion 21 LEd2d 928.

C. VALID SUNDAY CLOSING

§12. Prohibiting Certain Sales

A Sunday closing ordinance is valid and the classifications reasonable though neighboring counties have different classifications or ordinances. The ordinance which exempts incorporated territories is for the public health and welfare.

> **NC**   State v Atlas (1973) 283 NC 165, 195 SE2d 496.

A Sunday sales ordinance, prohibiting the sale of all but certain specified items is not unreasonable and arbitrary because of the classification and is not a prohibition of sales. It is a regulation of sales.

> **Ark**   Green Star Super Market v Stacy (1967) 242 Ark 54, 411 SW2d 871.

An ordinance providing for Sunday closing of any store, workshop, bank, place of business, or place of amusement, with exceptions for hotels, lodging houses, restaurants, bakeries, stables, drugstores, confectioneries, ice cream parlors, garages, railroad, telephone, telegraph and express offices, fruit packing houses, newspapers, and periodical agencies, is valid.

Cal Sumida, In re (1918) 177 Cal 388, 170 P 823.

A Sunday ordinance was not invalid notwithstanding discrimination between activities to be permitted and those not to be permitted. The mere fact of inequality is not enough to invalidate an ordinance, and the legislative body must be allowed a wide field of choice in determining what shall come within the class of permitted activities and what shall be excluded.

Md Ness v Ennis (1932) 162 Md 529, 160 A 8.

An ordinance prohibiting certain business activities on Sunday is not invalid as conflicting with and being pre-empted by state laws, and does not violate federal constitutional inhibitions.

Minn GEM of St Louis v Bloomington (1956) 274 Minn 471, 144 NW2d 552.

An ordinance prohibiting persons from engaging in certain kinds of businesses on Sunday, is not void as discriminatory, where the prohibited business is not one of public necessity.

Neb State v Somberg (1925) 113 Neb 761, 204 NW 788.

An ordinance prohibiting the conduct of the business of selling household electrical appliances on Sunday is not invalid as in conflict with the statute forbidding, in general, all worldly activity on Sunday, and the singling out of one activity for prohibition constitutes no violation of constitutional guaranties.

NJ Elizabeth v Windsor-Fifth Ave (1954) 31 NJS 187, 106 A2d 9.

Enactment by a city council of an ordinance prohibiting shops, stores, and similar business establishments from opening on Sunday is clearly within the city's legislative authority.

NC State v Trantham (1949) 230 NC 641, 55 SE2d 198.

A statute forbidding work in ordinary callings on Sunday does not make the keeping of a shop open and the selling of goods on Sunday an indictable offense, since the statute's operation is confined to manual, visible, or noisy labor, such as is calculated to disturb other people. Therefore, an ordinance prohibiting the keeping of stores open on Sunday, other than drugstores, is not invalid as being in conflict with the statute.

NC State v Medlin (1915) 170 NC 682, 86 SE 597.

An ordinance requiring the Sunday closing of certain listed businesses is not invalid as in conflict with the state law prohibiting the exercise of any of the common vocations of life on Sunday. It merely restricts certain named vocations, and does not attempt to single out some of one vocation and some of another, but lists a group of vocations and bans all within that category from Sunday business.

> **Tenn**　Kirk v Olgiati (1957) 203 Tenn 1, 308 SW2d 471.

An ordinance prohibiting any labor in any trade or manufacture on Sunday, except livery stables, garages, and works of necessity or charity, is not unreasonable, discriminatory or arbitrary, but is a reasonable exercise of the city's police power.

> **Wash**　Seattle v Gervasi (1927) 144 Wash 429, 258 P 328.

§ 13. Closing Exceeding Statutory Prohibition

That a Sunday closing statute merely prohibits the sale of certain articles on Sunday does not invalidate an ordinance prohibiting any business on Sunday, with certain exceptions. The statute does not prevent the municipality from proscribing activities outside the scope of the statute, if there is any evil justifying the exercise of municipal police power.

> **NJ**　State v Patrignani (1961) 65 NJS 303, 167 A2d 671.

That an ordinance prohibiting Sunday activities is wider in scope than the related statute will not render it invalid, for, while a municipality may not authorize what the statute prohibits, that does not prevent it from proscribing other activities where there is an evil justifying the exercise of its delegated police power.

> **NJ**　Masters-Jersey Inc v Paramus (1960) 32 NJ 296, 160 A2d 841.

§ 14. Prohibiting Work or Business

An ordinance that prohibits work or business on the Sabbath is valid.

> **Ky**　Marshall v Herndon (1914) 161 Ky 232, 170 SW 623.

An ordinance prohibiting persons from transacting business or allowing others than themselves or their clerks to enter their places of business on Sunday is neither unreasonable nor oppressive; nor is it in derogation of the common right. And since it is against public policy for one to pursue his ordinary business calling on Sunday, not only may an ordinance regulate ordinary business pursuits, but it may altogether prohibit them, on Sunday.

> **NC**　State v Burbage (1916) 172 NC 876, 89 SE 795.

§15. Prohibiting All of a Certain Activity

If an ordinance prohibits all of a certain type of activity on Sunday, it does not conflict with the Constitution, for its regulation of trade is merely incidental.

NC   State v Smith (1965) 265 NC 173, 143 SE2d 293.

§16. Prohibiting Most Businesses

A Sunday closing ordinance prohibiting most businesses from operating on Sunday is not unconstitutional as violating any provision of the First Amendment of the U S Constitution, or as impinging on freedom of conscience or compelling or denying the observance of any religious duty.

NC   State v McGee (1953) 237 NC 633, 75 SE2d 783.

D. Invalid Sunday Closing

§17. When Enabling Statute Void

An ordinance restricting or regulating the carrying on of business on Sunday, which derives its legislative grant from an invalid statute, is itself void.

NC   High Point Surplus v Pleasants (1965) 264 NC 650, 142 SE2d 697.

§18. Discriminatory Closing

An ordinance making it unlawful to carry on certain businesses on Sunday is invalid where it prohibits the exercise of businesses or occupations legitimate and lawful within themselves, which do not carry inherent reasons for special discrimination, while allowing general privileges to similar occupations.

Ariz   Elliott v State (1926) 29 Ariz 389, 242 P 340, 46 ALR 284.

An ordinance may prohibit the conducting of businesses or occupations on Sunday, except those of necessity or charity, on the ground that the peace, good order, good government, and welfare of the inhabitants will be promoted. But if such an ordinance is discriminatory or amounts to class or special legislation, it is not authorized.

Colo   Allen v Colorado Springs (1937) 101 Colo 498, 75 P2d 141.

An ordinance prohibiting the operation of any business on Sunday, but excepting motels, restaurants, eating places, drug, tobacco and confectionery stores, news dealers, ice dealers, shoe shine parlors, garages, gasoline filling stations, telephone exchanges, telegraph offices, and moving picture theaters, is invalid as arbitrary and discriminatory, since the distinctions are entirely arbitrary and have no relation to the public health, morals or welfare.

> **Ill** Mt Vernon v Julian (1938) 369 Ill 447, 17 NE2d 52, 119 ALR 747.

Where an ordinance prohibited certain stores from selling items which were permissible in other stores and did not prohibit manufacturing, warehousing, transportation or construction of these items, the ordinance was unreasonable and invalid.

> **Neb** Skag-Way Department Stores v Grand Island (1964) 176 Neb 169, 125 NW2d 529.

Under a statute prohibiting engagement in worldly affairs on Sunday, except works of necessity or charity, an ordinance forbidding listed business activities is invalid, for attempting to single out particular business enterprises for sanction.

> **NJ** Auto-Rite Supply v Woodbridge (1957) 25 NJ 188, 135 A2d 515.

A Sunday closing ordinance prohibiting the sale of all commodities, except a small selected list, not based on reasonable distinctions and not being a general Sunday closing law designed to accomplish the purposes it purports to effect, and there being no fair reason that requires with equal force its extension to other commodities which it leaves untouched, is arbitrary and discriminatory.

> **Utah** Gronlund v Salt Lake City (1948) 113 Utah 284, 194 P2d 464.

ANNOTATION

Validity of discrimination by Sunday law between different kinds of stores or commodities, 57 ALR2d 975.

§19. Activities Not Affecting Sunday Devotions

The ordinary activity of businesses such as those selling food, lodging and gasoline, and those exhibiting model homes, not being of such a nature as to disturb others in their Sunday devotions or to affect injuriously the peace and good order of the community, a Sunday closing ordinance prohibiting such activities will be declared invalid.

> **Ill** Pacesetter Homes v South Holland (1960) 18 Ill2d 247, 163 NE2d 464.

§20. Harmless Activities

An ordinance providing for Sunday closing cannot prohibit that which is harmless in itself, or require that to be done which does not tend to promote the health, comfort, safety or welfare of society.

> **Neb** Skag-Way Department Stores v Grand Island (1964) 176 Neb 169, 125 NW2d 529.

§21. Activities Unrelated to Regulation

Where a Sunday closing ordinance is so broad as to include businesses whose operation has no relation to the object of the regulation, the existence of other businesses that may validly be prohibited cannot save the ordinance.

> **Ill** Pacesetter Homes v South Holland (1960) 18 Ill2d 247, 163 NE2d 464.

E. Exemptions

§22. Valid Exemptions

An exemption to a Sunday closing law, of grocery store owner-managers who regularly employ not more than three persons, is not an unconstitutional discrimination. The council may properly designate classifications, and a limited number of persons who would be required to work on Sunday may form a valid basis for exemption.

> **ND** Bismarck v Materi (1970) 177 NW2d 530.

A Sunday closing ordinance, which applies to some lines of business but exempts others, is not necessarily invalid as discriminatory, or as a denial of equal rights and privileges.

> **Ill** Springfield v Richter (1913) 257 Ill 578, 101 NE 192.

A Sunday closing ordinance excepting certain businesses from its provisions is not unconstitutional as violating the equal protection or due process clause of the Fourteenth Amendment, or the synonymous law-of-the-land provision of the state Constitution.

> **NC** Charles Stores v Tucker (1965) 263 NC 710, 140 SE2d 370.

A Sunday closing ordinance need not be perfectly symmetrical in its pattern of exclusions and inclusions, for equal protection of the laws does not require the legislative body to achieve abstract symmetry.

> **NC** Clark's Charlotte v Hunter (1964) 261 NC 222, 134 SE2d 364.

An ordinance prohibiting business on Sunday, with certain exemptions, did
not deny department stores, which were not excepted, equal protection of the
law or deprive them of property without due process.

> **NC**   Clark's Charlotte v Hunter (1964) 261 NC 222, 134 SE2d 364.

§23. —Relation to Public Welfare

Exceptions to a general Sunday closing ordinance must, if the ordinance is to
be valid, bear some relation to the public health, safety, morals, or general
welfare.

> **Neb**   Skag-Way Department Stores v Grand Island (1964) 176 Neb 169, 125 NW2d
> 529.

§24. —Competition with Prohibited Business

A Sunday closing ordinance prohibiting sale of mobile homes, but permitting
sale of conventional homes, establishes a valid classification. That one housing
competitor may secure an advantage over the other does not make the
classification arbitrary.

> **NC**   Raleigh Mobile Home Sales v Tomlinson (1970) 7 NCApp 289, 172 SE2d
> 276; affd (1970) 276 NC 661, 174 SE2d 542.

Under an ordinance providing that only certain businesses can stay open on
Sunday, the fact that such businesses sell goods which other closed businesses
also sell does not make the ordinance unconstitutional.

> **NC**   State v Towery (1954) 239 NC 274, 79 SE2d 513.

§25. Invalid Exemption for Business Not within Statutory Limits of Necessity or Charity

A village ordinance prohibiting certain occupations on Sunday, and containing enumerated commercial activities allowed, is invalid as in conflict with
the policy of the state with respect to Sunday closing, as indicated by a statute
that requires a general prohibition of all business activities, with exceptions
accorded only to works of necessity and charity.

> **NJ**   Hertz Washmobile System v South Orange (1957) 25 NJ 207, 135 A2d 524.

§26. Invalid Exemptions for Non-Sunday Sabbath Observers

An ordinance that permitted persons who observed a day other than Sunday
as the Sabbath to operate their usual business on Sunday was in conflict with a

statute making it unlawful for any person to perform any worldly labor, business, or work of his ordinary calling on Sunday except work of necessity or charity and was void.

SC   State v Solomon (1965) 245 SC 550, 141 SE2d 818.

§27. Invalid Conditions for Exemption

An ordinance prohibiting businesses where personal property is sold from keeping open on Sunday, but excepting certain businesses with respect to the sale of listed items, providing a partition completely separates the portion of the store in which the permitted items are kept is invalid as arbitrary.

Wyo   Nation v Giant Drug (1964) 396 P2d 431.

§28. Work of Necessity—What Constitutes

"Necessity", within meaning of ordinance prohibiting worldly employment on Sunday, but exempting "works of necessity", signifies something indispensable, a requisite, a condition imperatively demanding relief or assistance, urgent need.

NJ   Collingswood v Boyer (1960) 59 NJS 561, 158 A2d 227.

§29. —As Jury Question

What constitutes "works of necessity" within the meaning of an ordinance excepting such works from Sunday closing is a question of fact for the jury.

NJ   Collingswood v Boyer (1960) 59 NJS 561, 158 A2d 227.
West Orange v Jordan (1958) 52 NJS 533, 146 A2d 134.

F. PROCEEDINGS GENERALLY

§30. Right to Challenge Validity of Sunday Law

Failure to indicate in the trial court record the ordinance and statute contested precludes their review on appeal. When a defendant contesting the validity of a Sunday closing fails to specify the ordinance challenged or the statute supposedly pre-empting the field, their constitutionality will not be considered by the Supreme Court.

Ga   Freeman v Valdosta (1969) 119 GaApp 345, 167 SE2d 170.

A merchant is in no position to attack a Sunday closing law as unconstitutional, where a state law already prohibited the carrying on of regular business on Sunday and the city ordinance thus inflicts no injury.

> **Ga**   Clark's Valdosta v Valdosta (1968) 224 Ga 331, 161 SE2d 867.

A person prosecuted for violation of a Sunday closing ordinance has no standing to claim that the ordinance violates the First Amendment guaranteeing freedom of religion, where he does not claim to be a member of the religious group discriminated against.

> **Ill**   River Forest v Vignola (1961) 30 IllAp2d 52, 173 NE2d 515
>   revd on other grnds (1961) 23 Ill2d 411, 178 NE2d 364.

A plaintiff who is allowed to sell nothing on Sunday has no standing to challenge the constitutionality of that portion of a Sunday closing ordinance listing items of merchandise that may not be sold on Sunday by businesses allowed to remain open.

> **NC**   Charles Stores v Tucker (1965) 263 NC 710, 140 SE2d 370.

Although evidence tending to show that the conditions of a Sunday closing ordinance are not enforced may serve to indict the police officers of the municipality, it forms no basis for an attack on the constitutionality of the ordinance itself.

> **NC**   State v Trantham (1949) 230 NC 641, 55 SE2d 198.

Where the defendant's business is not one of the classes affected by a Sunday closing ordinance, he is not injuriously affected by it. Hence he cannot challenge its constitutionality.

> **NC**   State v Trantham (1949) 230 NC 641, 55 SE2d 198.

A store has no justiciable interest sufficient to enable it to maintain a suit to prohibit the enforcement of an ordinance allowing businesses to remain open on Sundays as an accommodation to persons wishing to make emergency purchases, and making it unlawful for a purchaser to fraudulently sign a certificate of emergency as a condition of purchase, since the ordinance restricts only purchasers and does not prohibit stores from remaining open.

> **Tex**   Shoppers Fair of No Houston v Houston (1966) 406 SW2d 86.

§31. —On Religious Basis

Plaintiffs, most of whom are corporations, who do not allege that they are members of any religious group that would be affected have no status to challenge a Sunday closing ordinance on the ground that it violates the constitutional guaranty of freedom of religion.

> **Ill** Humphrey Chevrolet v Evanston (1956) 7 Ill2d 402, 131 NE2d 70.

§32. Validity of Sunday Closing—As Question of Law

The function of a court, in an attack on the validity of a Sunday closing ordinance, is to ascertain from the language of the law itself whether constitutional restraints have been exceeded, which question is one of law, not of fact.

> **Ill** Pacesetter Homes v South Holland (1960) 18 Ill2d 247, 163 NE2d 464.

In order to sustain the validity of a Sunday closing ordinance it is not necessary to offer proof that it protects the health and welfare of a particular class or group of employees. It will suffice if the governing body believes the enactment necessary for protection of the public health, safety and welfare of all its citizens.

> **NJ** West Orange v Carr's Store (1958) 53 NJS 237, 147 A2d 97.

§33. —Construction Favoring

In considering the validity of an ordinance providing that no worldly employment or business except works of necessity and charity shall be performed on Sunday, such enactment will be so construed as to sustain its validity if possible, and the term "necessity" will receive an interpretation that will avoid a fatal weakness if there be one.

> **NJ** Masters-Jersey Inc v Paramus (1960) 32 NJ 296, 160 A2d 841.

§34. —Burden of Proving

Where a person charged with violation of a Sunday closing ordinance asserts that the ordinance is so unreasonable as to be void, he has the onus of proof, and, if he is to succeed, his proof must be clear and perhaps even demonstrate that the ordinance is palpably unreasonable.

> **NJ** Elizabeth v Windsor-Fifth Ave (1954) 31 NJS 187, 106 A2d 9.

§35. Evidence—Presumption of Validity

The necessity and advisability of a Sunday closing ordinance is for the legislative power of the city to determine, and the presumption is that the ordinance is constitutional.

> **Tenn**   Kirk v Olgiati (1957) 203 Tenn 1, 308 SW2d 471.

§36. —Sunday Delivery of Saturday Sale as Violation

An ordinance prohibiting the keeping open of any business, or the sale of goods, on Sunday is violated by a person who sold goods to a customer on Saturday night, segregated them from the rest of the stock and wrapped them up but did not deliver them until Sunday morning.

> **Tenn**   McDowell v Murfreesboro (1900) 103 Tenn 726, 54 SW 976.

§37. —Judicial Notice

Courts, in assessing the validity of a Sunday closing ordinance, will judicially notice the public policy of the state against all worldly employment on Sunday, except works of charity and necessity.

> **NJ**   West Orange v Carr's Store (1958) 53 NJS 237, 147 A2d 97.

§38. Sunday Service of Process

The law forbidding anyone on the Lord's day to serve or execute any writ, process, warrant, order or decree except in cases of treason, felony or breach of the peace does not prohibit service or execution of writs and processes on Sunday in criminal cases.

> **DC**   Edwards v D C (1949) 68 A2d 286.

§39. Right of Appeal

In a prosecution for violation of a Sunday closing ordinance, where the question of constitutionality is not fairly debatable, in view of a decision involving a similar ordinance, the appeal is properly taken to the appellate rather than to the Supreme Court.

> **Ill**   River Forest v Vignola (1961) 30 IllAp 62, 173 NE2d 515 revd on other grnds (1961) 23 Ill2d 411, 178 NE2d 364.

§47. Valid Sunday Sale of Commodities for Recreation

A Sunday closing ordinance exception permitting the sale of commodities in connection with recreation has nothing to do with the private recreation of citizens, but exempts a person, firm or corporation from its operation while he is engaged in a business having to do with recreation.

Ohio   Euclid v MacGillis (1962) 117 OA 281, 19 Op2d 480, 179 NE2d 131.

D. Theaters and Movies

§48. Definitions—Sunday

The designation "Sunday", in an ordinance prohibiting the opening or operation of public amusements on that day, is the natural day between midnight at the end of Saturday and midnight at the beginning of Monday.

Fla   Gillooley v Vaughn (1926) 92 Fla 943, 110 So 653.

§49. —Operation of Theater as Labor

The operation and management of a theater and sale of tickets therein on Sunday constitutes "labor," within the ambit of an ordinance prohibiting the pursuit of "daily labor" on Sunday.

Ill   Clinton v Wilson (1913) 257 Ill 580, 101 NE 192.

§50. —Place of Business as Including Movie

The words, "or place of business," in a Sunday observance ordinance, providing that no person, firm or corporation may sell, barter or trade, or offer to sell, barter or trade, any goods, wares or merchandise or keep open any store, shop or place of business, is construed to include moving picture shows.

Neb   Dillard v State (1920) 104 Neb 209, 175 NW 668.

§51. —Place of Amusement as Excluding Movie

In an ordinance prohibiting the operation on Sunday of any billiard room, ball or pin alley, baseball grounds or other place of amusement, the phrase "other places of amusement" will not be deemed to relate to amusements in theaters, such as motion picture exhibitions.

Ill   Clinton v Wilson (1913) 257 Ill 580, 101 NE 192.

§52. Valid Sunday Closing

An ordinance may validly limit or prohibit the operation of theaters or movies on Sunday.

Cal	West Coast Theatres v Pomona (1924) 68 CA 763, 230 P 225.
Ga	Hicks v Dublin (1937) 56 GaApp 63, 191 SE 659.
Iowa	Ames v Gerbracht (1922) 194 Iowa 267, 189 NW 729.
	G W Mart & Son v Grinnell (1922) 194 Iowa 499, 187 NW 471.
La	West Monroe v Newell (1927) 163 La 409, 111 So 889.
Minn	Power v Nordstrom (1921) 150 Minn 228, 184 NW 967.
NJ	General Theatrical v Vineland (1934) 12 NJM 155, 170 A 241.
NY	New York City v Alhambra Theater (1910) 136 AD 509, 121 NYS 3.
Okla	Blackledge v Jones (1935) 170 Okla 563, 41 P2d 649.
	Johnson, Ex parte (1921) 20 Okla 66, 201 P 533.
Wash	Ferguson, In re (1914) 80 Wash 102, 141 P 322.

Classification of moving picture shows with cabarets and dance halls, in an ordinance prohibiting their operation on Sunday, is reasonable, in relation to the prohibitory purpose of the ordinance.

Fla	Gillooley v Vaughn (1926) 92 Fla 943, 110 So 653.

If the charter of a city authorizes the closing of "theaters" on Sundays, it includes the power to close moving picture shows by ordinance.

La	West Monroe v Newell (1927) 163 La 409, 111 So 889.

§53. —Drive-ins

A Sunday closing ordinance prohibiting the operation of all but specified businesses, and restricting in particular the hours of a drive-in theater, is not invalid as arbitrary or unreasonable.

NC	State v McGee (1953) 237 NC 633, 75 SE2d 783.

§54. Invalid Sunday Closing

A city has no power to prohibit the operation of theaters or movies on Sunday.

Ind	Crawfordsville v Jackson (1930) 201 Ind 619, 170 NE 850.
Ky	Harlan v Scott (1942) 290 Ky 585, 162 SW2d 8.

An ordinance clothing an officer with discretionary licensing power does not permit him to require Sunday closing of a moving picture theater as a condition of a license, where no law prohibits such exhibitions.

NY	People v Rand (1915) 91 Misc 276, 154 NYS 293.

Charter power to regulate amusements and common shows authorizes a licensing ordinance restricting operation of moving picture theaters to reasonable hours, but does not authorize Sunday closing where the legislature does not require it.

NY   People v Lent (1915) 166 AD 550, 152 NYS 18.

§55. Tax on Sunday Admission

An ordinance providing for tax upon admissions to motion picture theaters on Sunday, but not imposed on week days, is an invalid classification, as there is no reasonable basis for imposing a tax on admissions paid for Sunday performances, and exempting from the tax, admissions paid for performances given on other days of the week.

NJ   General Theatrical v Vineland (1934) 12 NJM 155, 170 A 241.

§56. Licensing for Sunday Operations

An ordinance requiring a license to hold public entertainment on Sunday is not unconstitutional. While there are no standards for granting or denial of a license there is a presumption that the agency will act reasonably.

Mass   Mosey Cafe v Boston (1958) 338 Mass 199, 154 NE2d 585.

§57. Use of Annual License for Sunday Operation

Under an ordinance providing that no person should operate a moving picture show without a license and that no permit should be given to play, show or exhibit on Sunday, a proprietor of a moving picture house, holding a yearly license, who opened his establishment on Sunday, was not guilty of operating his show without permission or license granted contrary to the terms of the ordinance.

Mich   People v Brown (1912) 172 Mich 50, 137 NW 535.

§58. Signature Requirements for Election Option

Theaters must be closed on Sunday, unless an ordinance authorizing their opening is enacted pursuant to a petition containing the signatures required by statute. If insufficient signatures are obtained the ordinance is valid only if accepted by referendum vote of the electorate.

Ida   Perrault v Robinson (1916) 29 Ida 267, 158 P 1074.

§59. Each Ticket Sale as Separate Offense

Provision of an ordinance that each sale of a ticket or tickets to any theater or moving picture show on Sunday constitutes a separate offense may not be attacked if the person convicted was not prosecuted under that provision.

La West Monroe v Newell (1927) 163 La 409, 111 So 889.

§60. Enjoining Prosecution

Prohibition is an appropriate remedy to prevent vexatious prosecution under an invalid ordinance prohibiting Sunday picture shows.

Miss New Albany v Benya (1956) 228 Miss 419, 87 So2d 889.

III. AUTOMOBILE SALES

§61. Invalid Sunday Closing

An ordinance prohibiting any dealer from keeping his place of business open on Sunday for the purpose of selling or trading automobiles is invalid as in contravention of the constitutional prohibition against enactment of a special law where a general law can be made applicable, since in singling out automobile dealers it excludes dealers in other commodities.

Mo McKaig v Kansas City (1953) 363 Mo 1033, 256 SW2d 815.

§62. Valid Sunday Closing

An ordinance prohibiting the sale of automobiles on Sunday, applicable to all automobile dealers, is not unconstitutional as class or special legislation.

Colo Rosenbaum v Denver (1938) 102 Colo 530, 81 P2d 760.

An ordinance prohibiting the selling or exchanging of motor vehicles and the keeping open of places of business on Sunday for such purposes is a valid exercise of the police power.

Neb Stewart Motor v Omaha (1931) 120 Neb 776, 235 NW 332.

Where the exempted items are necessities or for emergencies, their exclusion does not render a Sunday closing law invalid as applied to car dealers.

Ill Humphrey Chevrolet v Evanston (1956) 7 Ill2d 402, 131 NE2d 70.

§63. Enjoining Violations

The court will not enjoin a person from selling automobiles on Sunday, in violation of a Sunday closing ordinance, whereby the alleged violator would be deprived of the right of trial by jury, in the absence of any special injury to the person seeking the injunction that would warrant the intervention of a court of equity.

> **Wash** Motor Car Dealers Assn v Fred S Haines Co (1924) 128 Wash 267, 222 P 611, 36 ALR 267.

IV. FOOD AND DRUG SALES

A. GENERALLY

§64. Definitions—Prepared Food

A municipality, in enacting an ordinance prohibiting commercial activities on Sunday but exempting sale of ". . . meals, prepared food," intended those terms to be separate and distinct from each other, and accorded different meanings, and consequently "prepared food" will be taken to mean food fit for immediate consumption either on or off the premises where sale is made.

> **NJ** Collingswood v Boyer (1960) 59 NJS 561, 158 A2d 227.

§65. —Meal

In an ordinance prohibiting commercial activities on Sunday but exempting sale of meals, a "meal" is defined as a portion of food taken at one time to satisfy appetite.

> **NJ** Collingswood v Boyer (1960) 59 NJS 561, 158 A2d 227.

§66. —Food Sales as Excluded from Works of Necessity

In application of a Sunday closing ordinance, indiscriminate and general sales of food or food products to purchasers, regardless of need, are not generally considered "works of necessity" within the exception to the application of such ordinance.

> **NJ** Collingswood v Boyer (1960) 59 NJS 561, 158 A2d 227.

§67. —Food as Article of Immediate Necessity

A Sunday closing ordinance limiting its prohibition to the sale of food products is in direct conflict with the related Sunday closing statute prohibiting the sale of goods, wares or merchandise except drugs, medicines, or other articles of immediate necessity, and is void.

> **Kan**   House v Topeka (1955) 178 Kan 284, 286 P2d 180.

§68. Closing of Restaurant

A Sunday closing ordinance is unreasonable, insofar as it prohibits the keeping of a restaurant open at stated hours reasonably adapted to the sale and service of regular meals.

> **NC**   State v Blackwelder (1923) 186 NC 561, 120 SE 196.

§69. Invalid Enactment of Ordinance

An ordinance amendment prohibiting the sale of certain foods on Sunday, adopted by the selectmen at a special meeting, was not validly enacted where not approved at the next "regular election", as required by statute.

> **NH**   Mason v Salem (1961) 103 NH 166, 167 A2d 433.

§70. Sunday Licensing Requirements for Soft Drinks

The sale of a soft drink in a restaurant legally open on Sunday violates an ordinance that prohibits "laboring at any trade on Sunday", if a special soft drink license is required. The fact that it was served with meals is no defense.

> **Va**   Ellis v Covington (1917) 122 Va 821, 94 SE 154.

B. BAKERIES

§71. Definitions—Doughnuts as Prepared Food

The sale of doughnuts will fall within meaning of term "prepared food" in ordinance prohibiting commercial activity on Sunday but exempting certain activities, including sale of prepared food.

> **NJ**   Collingswood v Boyer (1960) 59 NJS 561, 158 A2d 227.

§72. —Doughnuts as Excluded from Work of Necessity

In a prosecution for violation of an ordinance prohibiting any worldly employment or business on Sunday except works of necessity and charity, the sale of 6 doughnuts will not be considered a "work of necessity" within exemption clause of ordinance.

NJ Collingswood v Boyer (1960) 59 NJS 561, 158 A2d 227.

§73. Restriction of Sales

An ordinance prohibiting bakers and bakeshops from selling bakery products on Sunday is valid under the city's charter authority to regulate business and other activities detrimental, or liable to be detrimental, to health, morals, comfort, safety, convenience or welfare.

Mo Komen v St Louis (1926) 316 Mo 9, 289 SW 838.

An ordinance regulating the sale on Sunday of bakery products is an industrial regulation, and is not unconstitutional as an interference with liberty of conscience or freedom of worship.

Mo Komen v St Louis (1926) 316 Mo 9, 289 SW 838.

§74. Delivery Restriction

An ordinance making it unlawful to deliver within the city any bakery goods on Sundays or holidays or on other days between 6 PM and 6 AM is an unwarranted and unreasonable interference with a lawful business.

Cal Skaggs v Oakland (1936) 6 C2d 222, 57 P2d 478.

C. DRUGSTORES

§75. Definitions—Work of Necessity as Including Drug Sales

A Sunday closing ordinance exception relating to "work of necessity" includes the sale of drugs, medicines or items of pharmaceutical value, but drug stores, as such, are not excepted, and the sale of other merchandise stocked by drug stores is not permitted.

Ohio State v Bunin (1963) 91 Abs 150, 187 NE2d 630.

§76. Valid Exemption for Prescriptions

An ordinance prohibiting a drug store from selling any merchandise on Sunday, except prescriptions and articles for the relief of the sick, and another ordinance prohibiting a restaurant or lunch stand from selling anything on Sunday, excepting an establishment conducted wholly as a restaurant or lunch stand, but not excepting a restaurant carried on in connection with a grocery store, do not unlawfully discriminate between persons engaged in the same business, but deal with distinct and severable occupations.

> **NC**   State v Davis (1916) 171 NC 809, 89 SE 40.

§77. Exemptions for Drugstores as Discriminatory

An ordinance prohibiting the operation of stores on Sunday, except drugstores, is unconstitutional as discriminating against grocery stores, since drugstores sell certain staple products usually carried by grocery stores.

> **Colo**   Allen v Colorado Springs (1937) 101 Colo 498, 75 P2d 141.

An ordinance prohibiting the keeping of stores open on Sunday, with the exception of drug stores, which are permitted to be open as a matter of public necessity, is not invalid as discriminatory.

> **NC**   State v Medlin (1915) 170 NC 682, 86 SE 597.

D. GROCERY AND MEAT MARKETS

§78. Valid Sunday Closing

A Sunday closing order allowing grocery stores to be open between 1 PM and 6 PM is not arbitrary. The fact that certain items of the grocery store sales are available in places allowed to remain open all day does not invalidate the classifications.

> **NC**   State v Underwood (1973) 283 NC 154, 195 SE2d 489.

Although a city cannot declare something to be a nuisance which is not a nuisance in fact, an ordinance declaring the sale of specified items on Sunday to be a public nuisance is valid, under statutes that likewise makes illegal sales on Sunday a public nuisance.

> **Ark**   Green Star Super Market v Stacy (1967) 242 Ark 54, 411 SW2d 871.

Evidence that certain business establishments other than grocery stores, which sell the same items as groceries, are permitted to remain open on Sunday does not establish purposeful discrimination by the city council passing an ordinance to prevent the operation of grocery stores on Sunday.

Ark Hickinbotham v Little Rock (1957) 228 Ark 67, 305 SW2d 844.

An ordinance prohibiting the operation of grocery stores and meat markets on Sunday is valid in the absence of proof indicating no reasonable basis for closing this class of stores. Grocery stores and meat markets represent a reasonable legislative classification.

Ark Hickinbotham v Williams (1957) 227 Ark 126, 296 SW2d 897.

A municipality has power to regulate meat markets, and an ordinance requiring the closing of places selling uncured and uncooked meats between 6 PM and 7 AM and on Sundays and certain holidays is constitutional.

Cal Lynch Meats of Oakland v Oakland (1961) 196 CA2d 104, 16 CaR 302.

An ordinance closing grocery stores and fruit stands on Sunday and leaving open, without limitation, places of amusement is discriminatory, and cannot logically be held to promote cleanliness, orderliness or public health.

Cal Deese v Lodi (1937) 21 CA2d 631, 69 P2d 1005.

An ordinance forbidding the sale of uncured or uncooked meat at night and on Sunday is not unreasonable or discriminatory in selecting some meat products to the exclusion of others.

Cal Lowenthal, In re (1928) 92 CA 200, 267 P 886.

The fact that a statutory Sunday law does not forbid the selling of vegetables and produce is not a guaranty of the right to do so, since the statute does not grant privileges but merely prohibits and sets penalties. Accordingly, a city may by ordinance prohibit such Sunday sales.

La Shreveport v Harris (1934) 178 La 685, 152 So 330.

Charter power to prohibit and suppress "desecration" of the Sabbath authorizes an ordinance prohibiting the sale of vegetables and produce on Sunday. "Desecrate" means "to violate the sanctity of, to profane, to put to an unworthy use". Sunday law regulations depend wholly on local public sentiment, since acts harmless in one community may be highly obnoxious and reprehensible in another due to local conditions and situations.

La Shreveport v Harris (1934) 178 La 685, 152 So 330.

An ordinance prohibiting the sale of groceries and meats on Sunday is valid, notwithstanding that it does not apply to all commodities.

Mich People v Krotkiewicz (1938) 286 Mich 644, 282 NW 852.

Under home rule, a municipality has power to enact an ordinance making it unlawful for any person to offer for sale any groceries or meats, or to keep open any grocery stores, meat market or other place in which groceries or meats are sold, on Sunday.

> **Mich**   People v Derose (1925) 230 Mich 180, 203 NW 95.

An ordinance prohibiting the keeping open of a grocery store on Sunday is not in conflict with a statute prohibiting the sale of goods, wares and merchandise on Sunday except drugs, medicines, provisions or other articles of immediate necessity, since the ordinance merely takes up where the statute left off.

> **Mo**   St Louis v Bernard (1913) 249 Mo 51, 155 SW 394.

An ordinance prohibiting grocery stores from remaining open after 9 AM on Sunday and prescribing a penalty for violation is not in conflict with a statute prohibiting the sale of all "goods, wares and merchandise" on Sunday, except "drugs, medicines, provisions, or other articles of immediate necessity," since the statute does not prohibit the sale of groceries on Sunday and the city is free to legislate with respect thereto.

> **Mo**   St Louis v Bernard (1913) 249 Mo 51, 155 SW 394.

General sales of meat, bread, milk, fruit and other foods from a market or store to customers on Sunday, merely because as a matter of convenience, they prefer to make purchases on Sunday rather than on a week day, cannot be justified as "works of necessity" within intent of exception in ordinance prohibiting Sunday commercial activities.

> **NJ**   Collingswood v Boyer (1960) 59 NJS 561, 158 A2d 227.

Though sales by hobby shops are not prohibited under the closing ordinance, a store handling groceries, hardware, prepared food and drink, and a multitude of other items is a variety store rather than a hobby shop, and its sale of groceries is illegal.

> **Tenn**   Bookout v Chattanooga (1969) 59 TennApp 576, 442 SW2d 658.

An ordinance requiring the Sunday closing of groceries, meat markets, supermarts, general merchandise, department, hardware, jewelry and furniture stores and other similar establishments is not discriminatory for permitting drugstores, curb markets, filling stations and places of that kind to remain open and sell some of the same goods as grocery stores sell, since the council may determine what are the proper occasions and subjects for the exercise of its police power.

> **Tenn**   Kirk v Olgiati (1957) 203 Tenn 1, 308 SW2d 471.

§79. Invalid Sunday Closing

A Sunday closing law which does not contain the exemption for private markets, grocery stores, is invalid. The state statute is paramount, and the city may not further restrict the statutory provisions.

> **La** Nat Food Stores of La v Cefalu (1972) 264 So2d 289; modified in nonaffecting manner (1973) 280 So2d 903.

An ordinance providing for food inspection and forbidding the sale of uncured or uncooked meats or other foods on any holiday or on Sunday, but excepting hotels, boardinghouses, lodging houses, restaurants, drugstores, confectionery stores, dispensers of beverages and milk distributors is a discriminatory closing law.

> **Cal** Justesen's Food Stores v Tulare (1938) 12 C2d 324, 84 P2d 140.

A legislative body has wide latitude in classifying commodities and businesses in Sunday closing ordinances, but such an ordinance cannot invidiously discriminate between those in the same business who properly belong in the same class. Thus, a grocer was entitled to an injunction against the enforcement of an ordinance prohibiting the sale of food on Sundays in retail groceries having more than 1,600 square feet of enclosed space, and further restricting the operation of groceries on Sunday to those that were owner-operated and that employed no more than one employee.

> **La** West v Winnsboro (1968) 252 La 605, 211 So2d 665.

An ordinance prohibiting the operation of businesses on Sunday except drugstores, hotels, restaurants, ice cream parlors, fruit stands, livery stables, service stations, paper plants, theaters and places of amusement is invalid as applied to a grocery store, because it is in violation of the Constitution and inconsistent with general law. The legislative branch of government may impose on the public the civil duty of observing one day out of seven in rest, but it cannot impose the observance of Sunday as a religious duty.

> **Okla** Hodges, Ex parte (1938) 65 Okla Cr 69, 83 P2d 201.

An ordinance prohibiting the sale of groceries or meats by business houses on Sunday is invalid as discriminating against certain business and as contrary to the general laws of the state. Provisions of a homerule charter, claimed to authorize the ordinance, cannot run counter or be repugnant to the general laws of the state.

> **Okla** Ferguson, Ex parte (1937) 62 Okla Cr 145, 70 P2d 1094.

§80. Application of Closing Law to Small Stores

An ordinance which provides that it is illegal to sell food or garden supplies on a Sunday except in stores with not more than 24,000 square feet of sales space and not more than three employees does not constitute a denial of equal protection because the limitation on the size of stores selling food and garden supply necessarily limits commerce in such items on Sunday.

Miss   Jackson v Luckett (1976) 336 So2d 776.

A Sunday closing ordinance adopting the state statute which exempts grocery stores employing four or less persons at any one time and located in a county of 500,000 or more on issuance of a license is a reasonable classification, based on legislative determination of necessity.

Ala   Southway Discount Cent v Moore (1970) 315 F Supp 617.

Classification of grocery stores for Sunday closing law violations may be based on the number of employees. Permitting stores with four or less employees to remain open is reasonable since it separates the supermarket from the convenience type store.

Ala   Caiola v Birmingham (1972) 288 Ala 486, 262 So2d 602.

An ordinance prohibiting the operation of a grocery store requiring more than two employees on Sunday is void, under a statute prohibiting the operation of any store, dramshop, or grocery on Sunday.

Ark   Hot Springs v Gray (1949) 215 Ark 243, 219 SW2d 930.

An ordinance provision that a statutory prohibition against the sale of groceries on Sunday should not apply to stores where not more than four persons are regularly employed is not as broad as the statute, but this does not invalidate the ordinance.

Minn   Mangold Midwest v Richfield (1966) 274 Minn 347, 143 NW2d 813.

An Administrative Code provision operating to exempt from the Sabbath Law small family operated stores does not extend to or include employees of multiple or chain store operations.

NY   People v Korman (1965) 47 Misc2d 945, 263 NYS2d 511.

§81. Enjoining or Prosecuting Violations

An injunction will issue to prevent a grocery store from operating in violation of a city ordinance prohibiting sales on Sunday, where the action is initiated by grocers adversely affected by the store's illegal sales and a fine would not substantially impair profits made on sales in violation of the ordinance.

Ark Hickinbotham v Corder (1957) 227 Ark 713, 301 SW2d 30.

A municipality may file an action to restrain desecration of the Sabbath; but this remedy does not apply to a small series of violations that can more properly be handled by prosecution under criminal laws. It must be shown that defendant engaged in an obstinate, continuing and extended series of violations with intent to continue them, that the city's traditional remedy in the criminal courts is inadequate to stop them, and that a multiplicity of such prosecutions is ineffective against a husband and wife continuing to operate grocery on Sunday despite 50 convictions.

Miss Walton v Tupelo (1961) 241 Miss 894, 133 So2d 531.
Tupelo v Walton (1960) 237 Miss 892, 116 So2d 808, 76 ALR2d 870.

§82. Evidence of Violation

When a police department has a policy of not enforcing the "blue laws" of the city except on complaint, enforcement by an officer on his own initiative without complaint is discriminatory and cannot stand. While the ordinance is valid on its face the four-employee restriction is vague and unenforceable when the arrest is made at the time of changing shifts and two of the employees are an uncle working voluntarily and a son of the owner.

Ala Simonetti v Birmingham (1975) 55 AlaAp 163, 314 So2d 83; cert den (1975) 294 Ala 192, 314 So2d 99.

A person may be convicted of violation of an ordinance prohibiting unnecessary labor on Sunday, on a showing that he was seen in his butcher shop and grocery in a white apron on Sunday waiting on customers, and that one customer bought merchandise from him in his place of business on Sunday.

Mo La Plata v Butler (1920) 225 SW 114.

V. HOUSEHOLD FURNISHINGS

§83. Sunday Closing Not Embracing Open House for Browsing

A Sunday closing ordinance that prohibits selling on Sunday, and carries a penalty clause, will not be expanded by construction to include the act of furniture store in having an "open house" on Sunday for "just browsing", where no sales are made or services rendered.

Ill River Forest v Vignola (1961) 23 Ill2d 411, 178 NE2d 364.

§84. Valid Sunday Closing

An ordinance making it unlawful to conduct or engage in the business of selling, renting, leasing or exchanging furniture on Sunday is not in conflict with the state Sunday law even though no other business was included. The commissioners in adopting it acted in a reasonable and nondiscriminatory manner and it does not constitute local legislation.

Mich   People's Appliance & Furniture v Flint (1959) 358 Mich 34, 99 NW2d 522.

§85. Sunday Closing without Restriction on Other Merchants

An ordinance prohibiting the sale on Sunday of major household appliances, furniture and specified household equipment, but placing no restriction on the sale of other articles of common use by the same or other merchants, is invalid as discriminatory.

Wash   Spokane County v Valu-Mart (1966) 69 Wash2d 712, 419 P2d 993.

§86. Evidence of Violation

The sole owner of three furniture and appliance stores is in violation of a municipal ordinance closing furniture and appliance stores on Sunday, but excepting those who conscientiously believe Saturday should be observed as the Sabbath, where one of his stores is closed on Saturday and open on Sunday while his other two stores are closed on Sunday and open on Saturday, notwithstanding that the stores open on Saturday are operated by persons who are not conscientious believers in Saturday as the Sabbath.

Mich   Berman's Petition, In re (1956) 344 Mich 598, 75 NW2d 8.

VI. JEWELRY AND FURS

§87. Exemptions for Saturday Observers of Sabbath

An ordinance prohibiting the sale of furs on Sunday, with a proviso excepting those who conscientiously observe Saturday as the Sabbath, is not invalid as failing to set up a clear definition of elements of the offense charged, nor is it unconstitutional as violating the state Constitution or the First or Fourteenth Amendments of the federal Constitution.

Mich   Marks Furs v Detroit (1961) 365 Mich 108, 112 NW2d 66.

§88. Valid Sunday Closing

An ordinance prohibiting the sale of jewelry on Sunday, and not discriminating between persons or corporations so engaged did not violate the guaranties of due process and equal protection of the laws, notwithstanding that other businesses were allowed to operate on Sunday, since the city presumably acted on facts that would make the classification reasonable.

Mich Watnick v Detroit (1962) 365 Mich 600, 113 NW2d 876.

An ordinance prohibiting the sale of jewelry on Sunday is not pre-empted by a statute forbidding in general language the carrying on of labor and business on Sunday other than works of charity and necessity.

Mich Watnick v Detroit (1962) 365 Mich 600, 113 NW2d 876.

A Sunday closing ordinance forbidding the sale of new or used clothing, shoes, jewelry, ready-to-wear items, hardware, groceries, and meat products is invalid, as not related to the health, safety, peace, and good order of society, and as discriminatory.

Neb Skag-Way Department Stores v Omaha (1966) 179 Neb 707, 140 NW2d 28.

VII. SERVICES

A. Barbershops

See **BARBERS,** Volume 1B

B. Cemeteries

§91. Distinction between Cemeteries and Monument Yards

An ordinance forbidding a stone cutting works or monument yard to be open for business on Sunday, but permitting other businesses, including cemetery offices and flower stands, to remain open, is arbitrary in classifying cemeteries differently from monument yards. Lacking some natural, intrinsic or constitutional distinction, the ordinance is unconstitutional.

Cal Gaetano Bocci & Sons v Lawndale (1930) 208 Cal 720, 284 P 654.

C. Laundries

§92. Laundromat Not Exempt Necessity

It is not feasible to consider it a necessity for an automatic laundromat to keep open on Sunday, and consequently such business will not be exempted from application of ordinance prohibiting operation of commercial businesses on Sunday.

NJ   State v Patrignani (1961) 65 NJS 303, 167 A2d 671.

§93. Invalid Sunday Closing

An ordinance making it unlawful to carry on laundry operations or to pick up or deliver laundry on Sundays and specified holidays, or on any other day between 6 PM and 7 AM, is an unreasonable exercise of the city's police power and violates state and federal constitutions.

Cal   Mark, In re (1936) 6 C2d 516, 58 P2d 913.

An ordinance forbidding the owner of or an employee in a public laundry to wash, mangle, starch, iron or do any other work on clothes between 6 PM and 7 AM or at any time on Sunday is void as an unreasonable interference with a citizen's occupation and as having no real or substantial relation to the purpose of preventing fires.

Cal   Yee Gee v San Francisco (1916) 235 F 757.

An ordinance making it unlawful for laundries to operate business between midnight Saturday and 6 AM the following Monday is void, because it bears no substantial relation to the public welfare.

Md   Spann v Gaither (1927) 152 Md 1, 136 A 41.

An ordinance requiring coin operated laundries to close on Sunday is invalid as in conflict with state pre-emption of the field of Sunday legislation.

NY   Schacht v New York City (1963) 40 Misc2d 303, 243 NYS2d 272.
Schacht v New York City (1961) 30 Misc2d 77, 219 NYS2d 53.

§94. Lack of Similar Ordinance in Other Municipalities

If a village's enactment of an ordinance prohibiting the operation of wash-mobiles and certain other businesses on Sunday is otherwise valid, that no other municipality in the state has prohibited such Sunday operations is immaterial, since the inaction of other municipalities neither curtails the village's authority nor evidences a purpose to discriminate invidiously.

NJ   Hertz Washmobile System v South Orange (1956) 41 NJS 110, 124 A2d 68.